Handbook of Research on Technical, Privacy, and Security Challenges in a Modern World

Amit Kumar Tyagi
Vellore Institute of Technology, Chennai, India

IGI Global
PUBLISHER of TIMELY KNOWLEDGE

A volume in the Advances in Information Security, Privacy, and Ethics (AISPE) Book Series

Published in the United States of America by
IGI Global
Information Science Reference (an imprint of IGI Global)
701 E. Chocolate Avenue
Hershey PA, USA 17033
Tel: 717-533-8845
Fax: 717-533-8661
E-mail: cust@igi-global.com
Web site: http://www.igi-global.com

Library of Congress Cataloging-in-Publication Data

Names: Tyagi, Amit, editor.
Title: Handbook of research on technical, privacy, and security challenges in a modern world / Amit Tyagi, editor.
Description: Hershey PA : Information Science Reference, [2023] | Includes bibliographical references and index. | Summary: "This book presents contributions that anticipate, assess risk and mitigate privacy and security threats as we deal with challenges in this post-COVID-19 world of working from home (home working), learning online (home schooling), shopping online, all acceptable practices but reminds us to revisit online security"-- Provided by publisher.
Identifiers: LCCN 2022018650 (print) | LCCN 2022018651 (ebook) | ISBN 9781668452509 (h/c) | ISBN 9781668452523 (ebook)
Subjects: LCSH: Technology--Social aspects. | Computer networks--Security measures. | Data privacy. | Artificial intelligence--Industrial applications.
Classification: LCC T14.5 .P4683 2023 (print) | LCC T14.5 (ebook) | DDC 303.48/3--dc23/eng/20220705
LC record available at https://lccn.loc.gov/2022018650
LC ebook record available at https://lccn.loc.gov/2022018651

This book is published in the IGI Global book series Advances in Information Security, Privacy, and Ethics (AISPE) (ISSN: 1948-9730; eISSN: 1948-9749)

British Cataloguing in Publication Data
A Cataloguing in Publication record for this book is available from the British Library.

Advances in Information Security, Privacy, and Ethics (AISPE) Book Series

Manish Gupta
State University of New York, USA

ISSN:1948-9730
EISSN:1948-9749

MISSION

As digital technologies become more pervasive in everyday life and the Internet is utilized in ever increasing ways by both private and public entities, concern over digital threats becomes more prevalent.

The **Advances in Information Security, Privacy, & Ethics (AISPE) Book Series** provides cutting-edge research on the protection and misuse of information and technology across various industries and settings. Comprised of scholarly research on topics such as identity management, cryptography, system security, authentication, and data protection, this book series is ideal for reference by IT professionals, academicians, and upper-level students.

COVERAGE

- Cyberethics
- Telecommunications Regulations
- Access Control
- Electronic Mail Security
- Network Security Services
- Device Fingerprinting
- Information Security Standards
- Internet Governance
- Risk Management
- Security Classifications

IGI Global is currently accepting manuscripts for publication within this series. To submit a proposal for a volume in this series, please contact our Acquisition Editors at Acquisitions@igi-global.com or visit: http://www.igi-global.com/publish/.

The Advances in Information Security, Privacy, and Ethics (AISPE) Book Series (ISSN 1948-9730) is published by IGI Global, 701 E. Chocolate Avenue, Hershey, PA 17033-1240, USA, www.igi-global.com. This series is composed of titles available for purchase individually; each title is edited to be contextually exclusive from any other title within the series. For pricing and ordering information please visit http://www.igi-global.com/book-series/advances-information-security-privacy-ethics/37157. Postmaster: Send all address changes to above address.

Titles in this Series

For a list of additional titles in this series, please visit: www.igi-global.com/book-series/advances-information-security-privacy-ethics/37157

Fraud Prevention, Confidentiality, and Data Security for Modern Businesses
Arshi Naim (King Kalid University, Saudi Arabia) Praveen Kumar Malik (Lovely Professional University, India) and Firasat Ali Zaidi (Tawuniya Insurance, Saudi Arabia)
Business Science Reference • © 2022 • 300pp • H/C (ISBN: 9781668465813) • US $250.00

Applications of Machine Learning and Deep Learning for Privacy and Cybersecurity
Victor Lobo (NOVA Information Management School (NOVA-IMS), NOVA University Lisbon, Portugal & Portuguese Naval Academy, Portugal) and Anacleto Correia (CINAV, Portuguese Naval Academy, Portugal)
Information Science Reference • © 2022 • 271pp • H/C (ISBN: 9781799894308) • US $250.00

Cross-Industry Applications of Cyber Security Frameworks
Sukanta Kumar Baral (Indira Gandhi National Tribal University, India) Richa Goel (Amity University, Noida, India) Md Mashiur Rahman (Bank Asia Ltd., Bangladesh) Jahangir Sultan (Bentley University, USA) and Sarkar Jahan (Royal Bank of Canada, Canada)
Information Science Reference • © 2022 • 244pp • H/C (ISBN: 9781668434482) • US $250.00

Cybersecurity Issues and Challenges for Business and FinTech Applications
Saqib Saeed (Imam Abdulrahman Bin Faisal University, Saudi Arabia) Abdullah M. Almuhaideb (Imam Abdulrahman Bin Faisal University, Saudi Arabia) Neeraj Kumar (Thapar Institute of Engineering and Technology, India) Noor Zaman (Taylor's University, Malaysia) and Yousaf Bin Zikria (Yeungnam University, Republic of Korea)
Business Science Reference • © 2022 • 300pp • H/C (ISBN: 9781668452844) • US $270.00

Methods, Implementation, and Application of Cyber Security Intelligence and Analytics
Jena Om Prakash (Ravenshaw University, India) H.L. Gururaj (Vidyavardhaka College of Engineering, India) M.R. Pooja (Vidyavardhaka College of Engineering, India) and S.P. Pavan Kumar (Vidyavardhaka College of Engineering, India)
Information Science Reference • © 2022 • 269pp • H/C (ISBN: 9781668439913) • US $240.00

Information Security Practices for the Internet of Things, 5G, and Next-Generation Wireless Networks
Biswa Mohan Sahoo (Manipal University, Jaipur, India) and Suman Avdhesh Yadav (Amity University, India)
Information Science Reference • © 2022 • 313pp • H/C (ISBN: 9781668439210) • US $250.00

IGI Global
PUBLISHER of TIMELY KNOWLEDGE

701 East Chocolate Avenue, Hershey, PA 17033, USA
Tel: 717-533-8845 x100 • Fax: 717-533-8661
E-Mail: cust@igi-global.com • www.igi-global.com

Editorial Advisory Board

List of Contributors

Table of Contents

Detailed Table of Contents

Preface xx

Acknowledgment xxviii

Chapter 1
Privacy Preserving in the Modern Era: A Review of the State of the Art 1
Rihab Boussada, National School of Computer Science (ENSI), Tunisia & Sesame University, Tunisia
Mohamed Elhoucine Elhdhili, National School of Computer Science (ENSI), Tunisia
Balkis Hamdane, Supcom, Tunisia & Iset'Com, Tunisia
Leila Azouz Saidane, National School of Computer Science (ENSI), Tunisia

The development of data communication technologies promotes large-scale sensitive data collection and transmission in various application areas. The sensitivity and criticism of the exchanged data raise several privacy issues. A lack of privacy may cause moral and emotional damage and discrimination. It can even create an unequal society. To fill this gap, a better understanding of privacy concept and its requirements is required. This chapter presents a comprehensive survey of privacy-preserving in the modern era. It deals with this concept of privacy-preserving from all perspectives, classifying its requirements into content-oriented and context-oriented ones. Based on the taxonomy, privacy attacks are described, and approaches and mechanisms for privacy protection are reviewed. A future research direction about privacy preserving in various fields is finally exposed.

Chapter 2
Industry 4.0: Design Principles,Technologies, and Applications 25
Sheetal Zalte, Shivaji University, India
Smita Deshmukh, Vishwakarma College of Arts, Commerce, and Science, Pune, India
Prajkta Patil, Vishwakarma College of Arts, Commerce, and Science, Pune, India
Minal Patil, Vishwakarma College of Arts, Commerce, and Science, Pune, India
Rajanish K. Kamat, Shivaji University, India

The fourth technological revolution, which is widely called Industry 4.0, works by incorporating the critical features like physical (object in existence), digital, and biological worlds. The attributes related to Industry 4.0 are more important as they change from producing a large amount of standardized products by using manual assembly, semi-automated assembly, or fully automated assembly with customization based on different product manufacturing. The fourth technological revolution is not progressing to modification; however, "it can modify us" and revolutionize societal life. The chapter elucidates the essential technologies behind Industry 4.0 and how they are shaping smart manufacturing and digital supply chain management. It also throws light on the policy frameworks required to be adopted to inculcate Industry 4.0 in the walks of societal life and reviews the upcoming trends.

Chapter 3
The Role of the Trucking Industry in the Pre-/Post-COVID-19 Environment for Modern Industries.. 46
Alan D. Smith, Robert Morris University, USA

Various economic, social, and environmental developments are converging to create an uncertain future for the U.S. trucking industry. These include, but are not limited to, the continuing truck driver shortage, an increased concern about environmental sustainability, and the industry volatility brought on partly by the effects of the COVID-19 pandemic, which includes consumers pivoting to online shopping in never previously seen before numbers. On the horizon, technologies, such as IoT and autonomous vehicle technologies, have the potential to provide supply chain managers with information and services needed to enact positive change and solve existing logistics problems. This chapter is an examination of the issues currently surrounding the trucking industry in the U.S., with a particular focus on the two compelling topics of the truck driver shortage and autonomous vehicle technology. For the purpose of context, two Pittsburgh-area trucking companies were examined to gain a better understanding of how small- to medium-sized trucking-based logistics companies are currently operating in this space.

Chapter 4
Unmasking the Masked: Face Recognition and Its Challenges Using the Periocular Region – A Review.. 62
Sheela R., Department of BCA, School of CS&IT, Jain University, India
Suchithra R., School of CS&IT, Jain University, India

Today, COVID-19 is one of the most severe issues that people are grappling with. Half of the faces are hidden by the mask in this instance. The region around the eyes is usually the sole apparent attribute that can be used as a biometric in these circumstances. In the event of a pandemic, the three primary biometric modalities (facial, fingerprint, and iris), which commonly enable these tasks, confront particular obstacles. One option that can improve accuracy, ease-of-use, and safety is periocular recognition. Several periocular biometric detection methods have been developed previously. As a result, periocular recognition remains a difficult task. To overcome the problem, several algorithms based on CNN have been implemented. This chapter investigated the periocular region recognitions algorithms, datasets, and texture descriptors. This chapter also discuss the current COVID-19 situation to unmask the masked faces in particular.

Chapter 5
The Impact of the COVID-19 Pandemic on Manpower (Labor) and the Supply Chain 82
Alan D. Smith, Robert Morris University, USA

The COVID-19 pandemic of 2020 has changed everything on a global scale. The lockdowns and general fear of the unknown caused a dramatic increase in ecommerce as buyers turned to the internet to get the goods and products they wanted. Many businesses had to close during this time due to lack of customers, lack of workers, and due to staffing issues due to the virus. As things started opening back up the demand for goods and services has been overwhelming to many industries. Ships are waiting off the coast for months to be unloaded, shelves are empty, the next day deliveries are taking days and weeks as the transportation system is overwhelmed. High demand and a lack of workers in every industry has led to a major global supply chain disruption that has not been experienced before. These disruptions affect every part of the supply chain from manufactures, warehouses, shipping, rail, truck, down to the retail level. This chapter will look at two companies in the Pittsburgh area (i.e., FedEx Ground and Ensinger, Inc.).

Chapter 6
The Role of Wireless Sensor Networks in Detecting and Predicting COVID-19 Using ML Algorithms 95
Sujatha Kesavan, Dr. M. G. R. Educational and Research Institute, India
Bhavani N. P. G., Saveetha School of Engineering, India
Kirubakaran D., St. Joseph's Institute of Technology, India
Janaki N., Vels Institute of Science, Technology, and Advanced Studies, India
Kavitha T., Dr. M. G. R. Educational and Research Institute, India
Su-Qun Cao, Huaiyin Institute of Technology, China

An embedded system is a specialized computer that is resource constrained to sense and controls its environment. Embedded systems usually consist of hardware and software. The most used hardware materials are processors, peripheral communication devices, actuators, sensors, power supplies, and memory storage. The application-specific algorithms, device drivers, and operating systems are typically used in software section. Normally there is a standard protocol to communicate the particular type of embedded system; for example, nodes in sensor networks are the specialized embedded systems for detecting COVID-19. Sensor nodes with wireless communication capabilities can form wireless sensor networks (WSN).

Chapter 7
The Role and Impact of Federal Learning in Digital Healthcare: A Useful Survey 127
Rajasree R. S., New Horizon College of Engineering, India
Gopika G. S., Sathyabama Institute of Science and Technology, India
Sree Krishna M., Sathyabama Institute of Science and Technology, India
Carlos Andrés Tavera Romero, Universidad Santiago de Cali, Colombia

During the COVID-19 pandemic, IoT and machine learning played a very important role in assisting doctors by remote patient monitoring. Machine learning and deep learning algorithms are used to process the data that are generated by IoT devices. However, there was major concern about the privacy of the patient data that is generated. The data that has been generated by the devices was sent to central servers which may cause data privacy issues. FL (federated learning), a type of machine learning, was created to address this problem. It provides a solution for data governance and privacy by processing the data rather than transferring the data to another location. The performance of FL models is better when compared to the models that are trained on datasets maintained centrally. In this work, certain insights are given on some of the challenges faced by the healthcare industry while employing digital healthcare techniques and how FL (federated learning) can improve the digital healthcare as well as how patient data can be preserved.

Chapter 8
Obstacles in Female School Education: The Importance of Online Learning During the COVID-19 Pandemic 148
Divya Budhia, Lovely Professional University, India
Tushinder Preet Kaur, Lovely Professional University, India

The importance of female education is gaining popularity among individuals, societies, and nations. They are getting full support from their families and society members as well. Government has also initiated many schemes to encourage female education, but still girls face many obstacles in their attainment of school education. The present study aims to bring to the fore the problems faced by girls while pursuing school education. A survey was conducted in which data were collected from 20 students and 10 parents with the help of interview schedules, and a qualitative study was undertaken. The results show that the main challenges faced by girls relate to adverse financial condition of their families, anomalies in school infrastructure, and lack of awareness of various government schemes. Moreover, online learning due to COVID-19 has added to these troubles. These results offer useful policy implications and can go a long way in removing the constraints in the way of female education.

Chapter 9
Industry 4.0 Revolution and Its Impact on Society 167
Sheetal Zalte, Shivaji University, India
Smita Deshmukh, Vishwakarma College of Arts, Commerce, and Science, Pune, India
Prajkta Patil, Vishwakarma College of Arts, Commerce, and Science, Pune, India
Minal Patil, Vishwakarma College of Arts, Commerce, and Science, Pune, India
Rajanish Kamat, Shivaji University, India

The term "fourth industrial revolution" is used as a framework for analyzing the influence of coming technologies on the full range of societal impact on the current generation, evolving cultural laws, governmental view, economical growth, and foreign affairs. The fourth industrial revolution idea confirms that technological change is the engine of change in relevant sectors and elements of society. It underscores the theme that many technologies have emerged at some point in history that has been combined in ways that have had an impact on incremental efficiency gains. This chapter introduces how this new revolution has brought great opportunities; the core potential of this industrial revolution is to increase manufacturing output globally to meet social needs and to enhance the capacity across all the different current systems. The chapter focuses on various novel techniques that sustain this ultra-modern era and delineates the influence, prospects, desires, and acclimation of Industry 4.0 from the social viewpoint.

Chapter 10
Preserving Privacy of Social Media Data Using Artificial Intelligence Techniques 186
Dhriti Rajani, Vellore Institute of Technology, Chennai, India
Sanjana Chelat Menon, PSG Institute of Technology and Applied Research, India
Shruti Kute, Vellore Institute of Technology, Chennai, India
Amit Kumar Tyagi, Vellore Institute of Technology, Chennai, India

Social media has a huge volume and variety of big data, which has enabled machine learning (ML) procedures and artificial intelligence (AI) frameworks. A few types of research have featured the dangers of revealing large amounts of information at various stages. The main aim is to connect the exploration and normalisation edge to build the consistency and proficiency of AI framework advancements ensuring user loyalty and moving towards a serious level of reliability. User security insight and the standards of its administrative assurance decide how the tech field works. It also introduces ways to deal with AI while demonstrating distinctions that are a result of comprehension of security, increasing user data privacy concerns and guidelines identified with information protection. The effect of AI systems on the relationship between clients and organisations has been stressed and examined concerning guidelines and client impression of security. With the rise of big data and AI, this issue of privacy of data has become significantly important.

Chapter 11
Privacy and Security Concerns During the COVID-19 Pandemic: A Mixed-Method Study............ 205
Poonam Sahoo, National Institute of Technology, Karnataka, India
Pavan Kumar Saraf, National Institute of Technology, Karnataka, India
Rashmi Uchil, National Institute of Technology, Karnataka, India

The study's objective is to ascertain healthcare personnel's perspectives and experiences on information privacy and security during the COVID-19 pandemic. Despite the abundance of research on privacy and security issues, this study focuses on the elements that influence privacy concerns in volatile, unpredictable, complicated, and ambiguous situations, which in the current scenario might include the COVID-19 pandemic. Three levels of coding were applied to all interview transcripts using the qualitative technique. The pandemic of COVID-19 has raised various concerns about technology, data privacy, and protection. The study's objective is to find, extract, summarize, and evaluate trends in a list of privacy threats associated with the COVID-19 pandemic. Participants were healthcare practitioners who worked closely with COVID-19 cases during the COVID-19 pandemic.

Chapter 12
A Visualization Dashboard for COVID-19 Tweets Sentiment Analysis 223
Devang Pathak, Vellore Institute of Technology, Chennai, India
Ishita Kumar, Vellore Institute of Technology, Chennai, India
Maheswari Raja, Centre for Smart Grid Technologies, Vellore Institute of Technology, Chennai, India
Carol Anne Hargreaves, National University of Singapore, Singapore

The COVID-19 pandemic has compelled the world to come to a standstill. Everyone including governments, researchers, organizations were caught off-guard. Social scientists and psychologists all try to understand the sentiment of the public so that they can help social organizations and governments to avert situations that ought to become worse if a negative sentiment persists among the commonality. With government-issued lockdowns in place during the pandemic, the public was mostly confined to their homes. So, the public started to share their status updates, discussions, photos, and videos over social media. Social media became the go-to place to obtain the public's sentiments and insights on the COVID-19 pandemic. This chapter introduces the utilization of the Twitter API to obtain tweets in real-time based on hashtags relating to the COVID-19 pandemic in order to gain insights on the sentiments of people at specific times. Each tweet received will be analyzed for emotional tone and sentiment. All data is stored in a Cloudant database.

Chapter 13
A Comparative Analysis of Urban Transport Using K-Means Clustering and Multi-Class Classification.. 243
Aswani Kumar Cherukuri, Vellore Institute of Technology, Vellore, India
Karan Bhowmick, Vellore Institute of Technology, Vellore, India
Firuz Kamalov, Candian University, Dubai, UAE
Chee Ling Thong, UCSI University, Malaysia

The transportation planning process requires a comprehensive study of the regions that need development. This study is an extension of the methodology of transportation planning. The authors use real-time data from Foursquare API to map out the number of transportation facilities and infrastructure available for each

city. This study will shed light on areas that need the most development in terms of intra-neighbourhood and inter-neighbourhood transportation. We use k-means clustering to organize and visualize clusters based on a calculated metric called "Availability Factor" that they have defined, and the number of transportation facilities available in each neighbourhood. Finally, they use the data at hand to create a model for multiclass classification to segregate new data into the predefined classes produced by the unsupervised learning model. The information procured in this work can be used to assess the quality of transportation available in the neighbourhoods of a location and help identify key areas for development.

The deep learning mechanism has indicated power in numerous applications and is recognized as a superior technique by an ever growing number of people than the conventional models of machine learning. In particular, the use of deep learning algorithms, particularly convolutional neural networks (CNN), brings immense benefits to the clinical sector, where an immense amount of images must be prepared and analyzed. A CNN-based framework is generated to automatically classify the images of blood cells into subtypes of cells. This chapter suggested the deep learning models, which are the convolutional neural network, the deep convolutional neural network, and a CNN-based model built in combination with the recurrent neural network (RNN), which is called RCNN, to identify the monocytes, lymphocytes, and types of WBCs. These are monocytes, eosinophils, lymphocytes, basophils, and neutrophils.

The previous proposal gains prognostic and regulatory examination. It uses boundary-based AI procedures to accomplish its task. It analyzes its received transmission utilizing a set of amenities. It verifies the data packets and detects the inconsistency in them. It also encompasses choosing the appropriate procedure to evaluate the data stored in the cloud. Kubernetes cases plan handles Docker similes vigorously. The dominant point has a trustable and stable credential supply. The system aims to manage the information of various groups. The leading device has a control component that aims to supervise the well-being of the other instruments. Replica set maintains anticipated mock-up count. The endpoints component seeks to spot and watch the modifications to the approaches in the service. The proposal suggests increasing the reliability by 4.37%, availability by 2.74%, and speed by 3.28%.

The world suffering from COVID-19. In this situation, people are focusing on virtual or online modes of working, which can be done from home or anywhere. Cybersecurity has become the priority for all of us to protect data. This chapter mentions the most used cyber-attack techniques for stolen money and data from different sectors.

Chapter 17
Computational Intelligence and Blockchain-Based Security for Wireless Sensor Networks............ 324
Renu Mishra, Department of CSE, Sharda School of Engineering and Technology, Sharda University, Greater Noida,India
Inderpreet Kaur, Galgotia College of Engineering and Technology, India
Vishnu Sharma, Galgotia College of Engineering and Technology, India
Ajeet Bharti, Galgotia College of Engineering and Technology, India

A wireless sensor network (WSN) provides the base architecture to all popular technologies like internet of things (IoT), unmanned arial vehicle (UAV), etc. Recently, a push came to make the information available to humans from the real-time environmental data collected through small sensing devices. WSN is self-organized wireless ad hoc networks to facilitate the interaction between the human and physical worlds. Rapid growth in sensing devices connected to the internet with intelligence and capabilities also opens the door because more devices connected devices means more chances of security vulnerabilities. Blockchain (BC) technology is introduced to address authentication and other security-related challanges by eliminating the role of central authority. This chapter starts with unique characteristics and security challenges in WSN and further identified different ways to apply blockchain with its potential benefits. The chapter presented the integration of blockchain in CI-enabled WSN with respect to focused sectors.

Chapter 18
Retrieval of Information Through Botnet Attacks: The Importance of Botnet Detection in the Modern Era 337
Zahian Ismail, Universiti Malaysia Pahang, Malaysia
Aman Jantan, Universiti Sains Malaysia, Malaysia
Mohd. Najwadi Yusoff, Universiti Sains Malaysia, Malaysia
Muhammad Ubale Kiru, Universiti Sains Malaysia, Malaysia

Services and applications online involve information transmitted across the network, and therefore, the issue of security during data transmission has become crucial. Botnet is one of the prominent methods used by cybercriminals to retrieve information from internet users because of the massive impact cause by the bot armies. Thus, this chapter provides a study of Botnet and the impact of Botnet attacks especially on the security of information. In order to survive, Botnet implemented various evasion techniques, and one of the notorious ones is by manipulating an encrypted channel to perform their C&C communication. Therefore, the authors also review the state of the art for Botnet detection and focus on machine learning-based Botnet detection systems and look into the capabilities of machine learning approaches to detect this particular Botnet. Eventually, they also outline the limitations of the existing Botnet detection approach and propose an autonomous Botnet detection system.

Chapter 19
A Review on Different Encryption and Decryption Approaches for Securing Data.......................... 357
Udochukwu Iheanacho Erondu, Landmark University, Omu-aran, Nigeria
Nehemiah Adebayo, Landmark University, Omu-aran, Nigeria
Micheal Olaolu Arowolo, Landmark University, Omu-aran, Nigeria
Moses Kazeem Abiodun, Landmark University, Omu-aran, Nigeria

With the advancement of network and multimedia technologies in recent years, multimedia data, particularly picture, audio, and video data, has become increasingly frequently used in human civilization.

Some multimedia data, such as entertainment, politics, economics, militaries, industries, and education, requires secrecy, integrity, and ownership or identity protection. Cryptology, which looks to be a viable method for information security, has been used in many practical applications to safeguard multimedia data in this regard. Traditional ciphers based on number theory or algebraic ideas, such as data encryption standard (DES), advanced encryption standard (AES), and other similar algorithms, which are most commonly employed for text or binary data, do not appear to be appropriate for multimedia applications. As a result, this research examines effective algorithms for data security.

We are currently at the beginning of a great technological transformation of our electrical power grids. These new grids will be "smart" as a result of improved communication and control systems but will also have new vulnerabilities. A smart grid will be better able to incorporate new forms of energy generations as well as be self-healing and more reliable. This chapter investigates a threat to wireless communication networks from a fully realized quantum computer and provides a means to avoid this problem in smart grid domains. This chapter examines the security, complexities and performance of device authentication in wireless mesh networks (WMN) using public-key encryption and then using Merkle trees. As a result, the authors argue for the use of Merkle trees as opposed to public-key encryption for authentication of devices in WMN used in smart grid applications.

Today the world is facing many cyber-crimes irrespective of the geographical boundaries, and privacy is being compromised all across the globe. According to some assessments, the extent and frequency of data breaches are increasing alarmingly, prompting organizations throughout the world to take action to address what appears to be a worsening situation. In today's world we cannot live without technology and cyber security is vital for keeping our personal information safe. This chapter would improve the awareness about technical, privacy, and security infringements and help in protecting data by prioritizing the most assailed sectors. It will help the key audience to learn about data leaks and other ways our privacy and security gets compromised due various challenges, diverse up-to-date prevention and detection policies, fresh challenges, favourable answers, and exciting opportunities.

Preface

COVID-19 has forced many of us to work from home (home working), learn online (home schooling), shop online and many more. It is envisaged that these trends (new normal) will remain post COVID-19 as well. This new normal will come at a price, especially with respect to privacy and security challenges. At one point during the pandemic, the WHO called the situation as an Infodemic due to the increased look for information. For instance, it is well documented that cyber-criminal exploited the opportunity to attack governments, organizations (e.g., healthcare facilities) and public in general due to the increased Internet presence with COVID-19. There were reported cyber-attacks (e.g., Phishing) targeting Coronavirus vaccine research, development and distributions. The local and nation-wide contact tracing efforts also came under heavy criticism due to privacy and security concerns. Even though these efforts were necessary to control the spread of the virus, the individuals' rights for their personal information have come under more scrutiny than ever before. Some even suggest to revisit the data protection laws and regulations (e.g., GDPR) in the wake of COVID-19. While it is necessary to address privacy and security concerns during COVID-19, it is also required to proactively address the threat landscape post-COVID-19. These new approaches need new paradigm shifts since we couldn't expect the world to behave in the same manner in comparison to pre-COVID-19. Therefore, it is necessary to anticipate, risk assess and mitigate privacy and security threats of new normal in post-COVID-19. This book covers almost all topics related to privacy and security beyond COVID 19 pandemic or in this modern era.

We assure that this book will be helpful to medical professionals, students, researchers who are working towards privacy and security components in this modern era. Now the description/the importance of each of the chapter (mentioned in this book) is provided:

Chapter 1: Privacy Preserving in the Modern Era – A Review on the State of the Art

The development of data communication technologies promotes large-scale of sensitive data collection and transmission in various application areas. The sensitivity and criticism of the exchanged data raise several privacy issues. A lack of privacy may cause moral and emotional damage, discrimination. It can even create an unequal society. To fill this gap, a better understanding of privacy concept and its requirements is required. This paper presents a comprehensive survey of privacy-preserving in the modern era. It deals with this concept of privacy-preserving from all perspectives, classifying its requirements into content-oriented and context-oriented ones. Based on our taxonomy, privacy attacks are described, approaches and mechanisms for privacy protection are reviewed. A future research direction about privacy preserving in various fields is finally exposed.

Chapter 2: Industry 4.0 – Design Principles, Technologies, and Applications

The fourth technological revolution (Industry 4.0) which is widely called Industry 4.0 works on by incorporating the critical features like physical (object in existence), digital, and biological worlds. The attributes related to industry 4.0 is more important as they change from producing a large number of standardized products by using manual assembly, semi-automated assemble or fully automated assembly with customization based on different product manufacturing. The fourth technological revolution is not progressing to modification; the means we tend to prepare the things solely; however, "it can modify us" and revolutionize societal life. The present chapter elucidates the essential technologies behind Industry 4.0 and how they are shaping smart manufacturing and digital supply chain management. It also throws light on the policy frameworks required to be adopted to inculcate Industry 4.0 in the walks of societal life and reviews the upcoming trends.

Chapter 3: The Role of Trucking Industry in the Pre-/Post-COVID-19 Environment for Modern Industries

Summary: Trucking is a global industry and a necessary component of almost all supply chains. While sea, rail, and air can move items to specified locations such as ports, stations, and airports, trucks have the flexibility to move items over both long and short distances to a wide variety of locations, including last-mile delivery directly to the customer. Trucks can also move different quantities of goods ranging from a full truckload (FT) or truckload (TL) and less-than-truckload (LTL). Currently, the U.S. trucking industry comprises approximately 75,000 companies which includes smaller single location and larger multi-location entities. A new post-Covid-19 world of supply chain shortages, uneven demand, and a general failure to attract enough qualified drivers have created a new set of constraints on management. Five significant trucking/logistics firms were analyzed in a brief qualitative business case study. While supply chain goals of efficiency and sustainability are lofty, new and potential disruptive technologies are emerging that can assist managers in reshaping their operations to thrive in this new environment. Current connected truck IoT and future autonomous vehicle technologies will allow managers to better assess the current supply chain, use data analytics to make efficiency improvements, and operate in ways that decrease dependence upon human labor and fossil fuels.

Chapter 4: Unmasking the Masked Face Recognition and Its Challenges Using Periocular Region – A Review

Summary: Today, COVID-19 is one of the most severe issues that people are grappling with. Half of the faces are hidden by the mask in this instance. The region around the eyes is usually the sole apparent attribute that can be used as a biometric in these circumstances. In the event of a pandemic, the three primary biometric modalities (facial, fingerprint, and iris), which commonly enable these tasks, confront particular obstacles. One option that can improve accuracy, ease-of-use, and safety is periocular recognition. Several periocular biometric detection methods have been developed previously. As a result, periocular recognition remains a difficult task. To overcome the problem, several algorithms based on CNN have been implemented. This Chapter investigated the periocular region recognitions algorithms, datasets and texture descriptors. This chapter also discuss the current COVID-19 situation to unmask the masked faces in particular.

Chapter 5: The Impact of COVID-19 Pandemic on Manpower (Labor) and Supply Chain

Since waiting for the labor shortage to improve itself organically is not a sustainable solution for businesses, companies are getting creative in their solutions. Companies are investigating methods for hiring, onboarding, and retaining both direct and indirect labor. Most of which is centered around benefit packages, total compensation, and work-life balance to motivate and incentivize either joining or staying with an organization. In addition to addressing the labor problem directly, companies are also pursuing options to improve internal processes and continue operations at near or greater capacities compared to before the labor shortage. Large companies are FedEx Ground, a global provider of logistics services and manufacturer, and Ensinger Group, a large region-based manufacturer. Through a closer examination of these two companies this chapter will look at how the labor shortages, pandemic, and supply chain disruptions have impacted their operations and what these companies are doing to overcome the challenges. A qualitative business case study approach was used in research supply chains and their responses to the current labor shortages. The basic structure was company description of both companies, followed by supply chain operations, supply chain problems, then potential supply chain solutions.

Chapter 6: The Role of Wireless Sensor Network for Detecting and Predicting COVID-19 Using ML Algorithms

An embedded system is a specialized computer that is resource constrained to sense and controls its environment. Embedded systems usually consist of hardware and software. The mostly used hardware materials are processors, peripheral communication devices, actuators, sensors, power supplies and memory storage. The application specific algorithms, devices drivers and operating systems are the typically used in software section. Normally need a standard protocol to communicate the particular type of embedded system, for example nodes in sensor networks are the specialized embedded systems for detecting COVID-19. Sensor nodes with wireless communication capabilities can form Wireless Sensor Networks (WSN).

Chapter 7: The Role and Impact of Federal Learning in Digital Healthcare – A Useful Survey

Machine Learning and Deep Learning algorithms are used to process these data that are generated by IoT devices. However, there was major concern about the privacy of the patient data that is generated. The data that has been generated by the devices was sent to central servers which may cause data privacy issues. FL (Federated Learning), a type of Machine learning was created to address this problem. It provides solution for data governance and privacy by processing the data rather than transferring the data to another location. The performance of FL models is better when compared to the models that are trained on datasets maintained centrally. In this work, certain insights are given on some of the challenges faced by health care industry while employing digital healthcare techniques and how FL (Federated Learning) can improve the digital healthcare as well as how patient data can be preserved.

Chapter 8: Obstacles in Female School Education – The Importance of Online Learning During the COVID-19 Pandemic

Importance of girl education is gaining popularity among individuals, societies and nations. They are getting full support from their families and society members as well. Government has also initiated many schemes to encourage female education, but still girls face many obstacles in their attainment of school education. Present study aims to bring to the fore the problems faced by girl child while pursuing school education. A survey was conducted in which data was collected from 20 students and 10 parents with the help of interview schedules and a qualitative study was undertaken. The results show that the main challenges faced by girls relate to adverse financial condition of their families, anomalies in school infrastructure and lack of awareness of various government schemes. Moreover, online learning due to COVID-19 has added to these troubles. These results offer useful policy implications and can go a long way in removing the constraints in the way of female education.

Chapter 9: Industry 4.0 Revolution and Its Impact on Society

The term Fourth Industrial Revolution is used as a framework for analyzing the influence of coming up technologies on the full range of societal impact on the current generation, evolving cultural laws, governmental view, economic growth, and foreign affairs. The fourth industrial revolution idea confirms that technological change is the engine of change in relevant sectors and elements of society. It underscores the theme that many technologies have emerged at some point in history that has been combined in ways that have had an impact on incremental efficiency gains. This chapter introduces how this new revolution has brought great opportunities; the core potential of this industrial revolution is to increase manufacturing output globally to meet social needs and to enhance the capacity across all different current systems. The chapter focuses on various novel techniques that sustain this ultra-modern era and delineates the influence, prospects, desires, and acclimation of Industry 4.0 from the social viewpoint.

Chapter 10: Preserving Privacy of Social Media Data Using Artificial Intelligence Techniques

Social media has a huge volume and variety of big data which has enabled Machine Learning (ML) procedures and Artificial Intelligence (AI) frameworks. A few types of research have featured the dangers of revealing large amounts of information at various stages. The main aim is to connect the exploration and normalisation edge to build the consistency and proficiency of AI framework advancements ensuring user loyalty and moving towards a serious level of reliability. User security insight and the standards of its administrative assurance decide how the tech field works. It also introduces ways to deal with AI while demonstrating distinctions that are a result of comprehension of security, increasing user data privacy concerns and guidelines identified with information protection. The effect of AI systems on the relationship between clients and organisations has been stressed and examined concerning guidelines and client impression of security. With the rise of "Big Data" and "AI" this issue of privacy of data has become significantly important.

Chapter 11: Privacy and Security Concerns During the COVID-19 Pandemic – A Mixed-Method Study

The study's objective is to ascertain healthcare personnel's perspectives and experiences on information privacy and security during the COVID-19 pandemic. Despite the abundance of research on privacy and security issues, this study focuses on the elements that influence privacy concerns in volatile, unpredictable, complicated, and ambiguous situations, which in the current scenario might include the COVID-19 pandemic. Three levels of coding were applied to all interview transcripts using the qualitative technique. The pandemic of COVID-19 has raised various concerns about technology, data privacy, and protection. The study's objective is to find, extract, summarize, and evaluate trends in a list of privacy threats associated with the Covid-19 epidemic. Participants were healthcare practitioners who worked closely with COVID-19 cases during the COVID-19 pandemic.

Chapter 12: A Visualization Dashboard for COVID-19 Tweets Sentiment Analysis

The COVID-19 pandemic has compelled the world to come to a standstill. Everyone including governments, researchers, organizations were caught off-guard. Social scientists and psychologists all try to understand the sentiment of the public so that they can help social organizations and governments to avert situations that ought to become worse if a negative sentiment persists among the commonality. With government issued lockdowns in place during the pandemic, the public was mostly confined to their home. So, the public started to share their status updates, discussions, photos, and videos over social media. Social media became the go-to place to obtain the public's sentiments and insights on the COVID-19 pandemic. This chapter introduces the utilization of the Twitter API to obtain tweets in real-time based on hashtags relating to the COVID-19 pandemic in order to gain insights on the sentiments of people at specific times. Each tweet received will be analyzed for emotional tone and sentiment, all data is stored in a Cloudant database.

Chapter 13: A Comparative Analysis of Urban Transport Using K-Means Clustering and Multi-Class Classification

The transportation planning process requires a comprehensive study of the regions that need development. This study is an extension of the methodology of transportation planning. We use real-time data from Foursquare API to map out the number of transportation facilities and infrastructure available for each city. This study will shed light on areas that need the most development in terms of intra-neighbourhood and inter-neighbourhood transportation. We use K-Means clustering to organize and visualize clusters based on a calculated metric called "Availability Factor" that we have defined, and the number of transportation facilities available in each neighbourhood. Finally, we use the data at hand to create a model for multiclass classification to segregate new data into the predefined classes produced by the unsupervised learning model. The information procured in this work can be used to assess the quality of transportation available in the neighbourhoods of a location and help identify key areas for development.

Chapter 14: Identification of Subtype Blood Cells Using Deep Learning Techniques

The Deep Learning mechanism has indicated power in numerous Applications and is recognized as a superior technique by an ever-growing number of people than the conventional models of machine learning. Current approaches that are used based on conventional models of machine learning. In particular, the use of deep learning algorithms, particularly Convolutional Neural Networks (CNN), brings immense benefits to the clinical sector, where an immense number of images must be prepared and analyzed. A CNN-based framework is generated to automatically classify the images of blood cells into subtypes of cells. This paper suggested the deep learning models, which are the Convolutional Neural Network, the Deep Convolutional Neural Network, and a CNN-based model built in combination with the Recurrent Neural Network (RNN), which is called RCNN, to identify the Monocytes, Lymphocytes, and types of WBCs, these are Monocytes, Eosinophils, Lymphocytes, Basophils, and Neutrophils.

Chapter 15: An Augmented Edge Architecture for AI-IoT Services Deployment in the Modern Era

The previous proposal gains prognostic and regulatory examination. It uses boundary-based AI procedures to accomplish its task. It analyzes its received transmission utilizing a set of amenities. It verifies the data packets and detects the inconsistency in them. It also encompasses choosing the appropriate procedure to evaluate the data stored in the cloud. Kubernetes cases plan handles Docker similes vigorously. The dominant point has a trustable and stable credential supply. The system aims to manage the information of various groups. The leading device has a control component that aims to supervise the well-being of the other instruments. Replica set maintains anticipated mock-up count. The endpoints component seeks to spot and watch the modifications to the approaches in the service. The proposal suggests increasing the reliability by 4.37%, availability by 2.74%, and speed by 3.28%.

Chapter 16: Emerging Cyber Security Threats During the COVID-19 Pandemic and Possible Countermeasures

Now a day's whole world suffering from Covid19 flue, in this situation people are focusing on virtual or online mode of working which can be done from home or anywhere. Also, use the maximum online platform for various tasks. Now a day's cybersecurity becomes the priority for all of us to protect the data. So many threats are raised during the covid19 pandemic. In this article mention mostly used different cyber-attack technique for stolen money and data from different sector. Information related to new threats added this time in a large amount.

Chapter 17: Computational Intelligence and Blockchain-Based Security for Wireless Sensor Networks

A Wireless Sensor Network (WSN) provides the base architecture to all popular technologies like Internet of Things (IoT), Unmanned Arial Vehicle (UAV) etc. Recently a push is coming to make the information available to humans from the real-time environmental data collected through small sensing devices. WSN is self-organized wireless ad hoc networks to facilitates the interaction between human and physical world. Rapid growth in sensing devices connected to the Internet with intelligence and capabilities also opens the door for because more devices are connected means more chances of security vulnerabilities. Blockchain (BC) technology is introduced to address authentication and other security related challenges by eliminating the role of central authority. This chapter starts with unique characteristics and security challenges in WSN and further identified different ways to apply blockchain with its potential benefits. The chapter presented the integration of blockchain in CI enabled WSN with respect to focused sectors.

Chapter 18: Retrieval of Information Through Botnet Attacks – The Importance of Botnet Detection in Modern Era

Services and applications online involve information transmitted across the network and therefore the issue of security during data transmission has become crucial. Botnet is one of the prominent methods used by cybercriminals to retrieve information from Internet users because of the massive impact cause by the bot armies. Thus, this chapter provides a study of Botnet and the impact of Botnet attacks especially on the security of information. In order to survive, Botnet implemented various evasion techniques, and one of the notorious ones is by manipulating an encrypted channel to perform their C&C communication. Therefore, we also review the state of the art for Botnet detection and focus on machine learning-based Botnet detection systems and look into the capabilities of machine learning approaches to detect this particular Botnet. Eventually, we also outline the limitations of the existing Botnet detection approach and propose an autonomous Botnet detection system.

Chapter 19: A Review on Different Encryption and Decryption Approaches for Securing Data

With the advancement of network and multimedia technologies in recent years, multimedia data, particularly picture, audio, and video data, has become increasingly frequently used in human civilization. Some multimedia data, such as entertainment, politics, economics, militaries, industries, and education, requires secrecy, integrity, and ownership or identity protection. Cryptology, which looks to be a viable method for information security, has been used in many practical applications to safeguard multimedia data in this regard. Traditional ciphers based on number theory or algebraic ideas, such as Data Encryption Standard (DES), Advanced Encryption Standard (AES), and other similar algorithms, which are most commonly employed for text or binary data, do not appear to be appropriate for multimedia applications. As a result, this research examines effective algorithms for data security.

Chapter 20: Quantum-Resistant Authentication for Smart Grid – The Case for Using Merkle Trees

Summary: We are currently at the beginning of a great technological transformation of our electrical power grids. These new grids will be "smart" as a result of improved communication and control systems but will also have new vulnerabilities. A smart grid will be better able to incorporate new forms of energy generations as well as be self-healing and more reliable. This chapter investigates a threat to wireless communication networks from a fully realized quantum computer and provides a means to avoid this problem in smart grid domains. This chapter examines the security, complexities and performance of device authentication in wireless mesh networks (WMN) using public-key encryption and then using

Merkle trees. As a result, the authors argue for the use of Merkle trees as opposed to public-key encryption for authentication of devices in WMN used in smart grid applications.

Chapter 21: A Close Glimpse on the Security Challenges in the Smart Era

Summary: Today the world is facing many cyber-crimes irrespective of the geographical boundaries and privacy is being compromised all across the globe. According to some assessments, the extent and frequency of data breaches are increasing alarmingly, prompting organizations throughout the world to take action to address what appears to be a worsening situation. In today's world we cannot live without technology and cyber security is vital for keeping our personal information safe. This chapter would improve the awareness about technical, privacy and security infringements and help in protecting data by prioritizing the most assailed sectors. It will help the key audience to learn about data leaks and other ways how our privacy and security gets compromised due various challenges, diverse up-to-date prevention and detection policies, fresh challenges, favourable answers, and exciting opportunities.

In the last, as conclusion of our book, this impacts the field of privacy, security which is a primary concern of many domain/ applications in today's smart era.

Amit Kumar Tyagi
Vellore Institute of Technology, Chennai, India

Acknowledgment

First of all, I want to extend our gratitude to my Family Members, Friends, and Supervisors, which stood with me as an advisor in completing this book. Also, I would like to thank my almighty "God" who makes me to write this book. I also thank IGI Global Publishers (who has provided their continuous support during this COVID-19 Pandemic) and my friends/ colleagues with whom we have work together inside the college/university and others outside of the college/ university who have provided their continuous support towards completing this book on Privacy Preserving Technologies beyond COVID 19 Pandemic/ Modern era.

Also, I would like to thank our Respected Madam, Prof. G Aghila, Prof. Siva Sathya, my Respected Sir Prof. N Sreenath and Prof. Aswani Kumar Cherukuri, for giving their valuable inputs and helping me in completing this book.

Chapter 1
Privacy Preserving in the Modern Era: A Review of the State of the Art

Rihab Boussada
National School of Computer Science (ENSI), Tunisia & Sesame University, Tunisia

Mohamed Elhoucine Elhdhili
National School of Computer Science (ENSI), Tunisia

Balkis Hamdane
Supcom, Tunisia & Iset'Com, Tunisia

Leila Azouz Saidane
National School of Computer Science (ENSI), Tunisia

ABSTRACT

The development of data communication technologies promotes large-scale sensitive data collection and transmission in various application areas. The sensitivity and criticism of the exchanged data raise several privacy issues. A lack of privacy may cause moral and emotional damage and discrimination. It can even create an unequal society. To fill this gap, a better understanding of privacy concept and its requirements is required. This chapter presents a comprehensive survey of privacy-preserving in the modern era. It deals with this concept of privacy-preserving from all perspectives, classifying its requirements into content-oriented and context-oriented ones. Based on the taxonomy, privacy attacks are described, and approaches and mechanisms for privacy protection are reviewed. A future research direction about privacy preserving in various fields is finally exposed.

DOI: 10.4018/978-1-6684-5250-9.ch001

INTRODUCTION

The common denominator of the emergent technologies and applications is col- lection, aggregation and transfer of personal data. While affirming the important role played by these applications to improve daily life, there are limits that could hinder their adoption. These limits are intrinsically linked to the sensitivity of the personal data exchanged and the risks of their disclosure.

Despite the ethical, legal and social vacuum that surrounds this concept, the privacy preserving is essential for promoting the adoption of each new system in a real environment Eckhoff and Wagner (2017). It is considered as a fundamental and individual right. Indeed, the disclosure of personal data, without the consent and the knowledge of its possessor, may have consequences often tragic. It is therefore necessary to protect the content by using, for example, cryptographic primitives. However, despite the protection of data, the extraction of personal information remains possible. Certainly, the meta-data, contained in the exchanges, are essential to ensure routing, but it is easily accessible by attackers. Indeed, based on these collected meta-data, an attacker can deduce information about his target which may make him subject to discrimination and cause him moral, physical and emotional distress. This observation is under- scored by the quote from Michael Hayden, "We kill people based on meta-data" Cole (2014).

However, privacy issue is relatively little covered in the literature. Indeed, most of the existing proposals do not meet all the privacy requirements. This is probably due to the fact that privacy protection is a complex task for a variety of reasons. Indeed, the privacy concept itself is a notion that is neither formalized nor clearly defined. In this context, it is imperative to circumscribe this issue and precisely define its requirements. A second source of complexity is the absence of a compromise between privacy preserving and performance.

In this article, we explore privacy issues in detail and take an in-depth look at existing protocols and mechanisms. We aim to present the privacy-preserving concept in modern era from the communication perspective. Particularly, this paper:

- gives a detailed explanation of privacy-preserving concept and its fundamental requirements from the communication perspective;
- presents the privacy-preserving message transmission approaches;
- reviews and classifies attacks that compromise privacy
- explores mechanisms and approaches and classifies them according to the privacy preserving properties.

The rest of this article is organized as follows. In Section 2, we present the concept of privacy and present the privacy properties. In Section 3, The privacy attacks and models are exposed. The fundamental message transmission approaches ensuring privacy are explored in Section 4, while exiting protocols and mechanisms are presented in Section 5. The open issues are identified in Section 6. Conclusions are presented in Section 7.

PRIVACY CONCEPT

Privacy is a vague notion and difficult to define Solove (2007). In the literature, there are several definitions of this notion Nair and Tyagi (2021).

By adopting a psychological perspective, Maslow defined the privacy as an essential element to satisfy the "need for self-fulfillment" which is considered as the pinnacle of human aspirations Maslow (1950). Schwartz believes that the privacy is a required condition to the establishment of stable social relations. Indeed, it can represent a solidarity index Schwartz (1968).

From a legal point of view, it was initially introduced by Warren and Brandeis as "the right to be left alone". Since this definition, many interpretations have emerged. It has been defined as the right to keep certain private information for oneself Martin (2009). It was considered a fundamental human right which guarantees each person respect for their personal and professional life Guarda and Zannone (2009). It has also been formalized as the right of individuals, institutions or groups to specify when, how and for what purpose their own data are collected Westin (1968). Indeed, it guarantees that only a legitimate person can access specific information. Kamat et al. (2005). Thus, it guaran- tees the absence of intrusion, surveillance and control of personal information Bhaduri (2003). Privacy is a basic human right representing the rational expectation of everyone Moreham (2008). Thus, any violation of this right represents a violation of human dignity Bloustein (1964).

In a contemporary context, this right has been formalized in the majority of international legal texts. It is challenged as technology evolves and increasingly invades the privacy of individuals. Thus, this right is continually reformulated to cope with a growing number of threats. Globally, more than 130 countries have adopted a set of laws to protect private information managed by government and private companies Banisar (2019). The European Union (EU), for example, adopted the "General Data Protection Regulation" (GDPR) which standardizes laws across European countries. The GDPR is one of the most rigorous data protection laws Regulation (2018). Indeed, its ambition is to popularize the data protection rights of individuals Wolford (2019). The GDPR outlines the conditions for personal data processing which made it harder than before. It also sets out the conditions of personal data collection, access, transfer, rectification and erasure Tikkinen-Piri et al. (2018).

The United States (US) does not have a specific data protection legislation but has adopted a number of privacy laws. The two most popular US federal laws that focus on the protection of privacy are the FTC Act("Federal Trade Commission Act") and the HIPAA ("Health Insurance Portability and Accountability Act"). However, these laws do not provide the perfect protection of individuals' data rules as desired Jamison (2019). The FTC Act is a federal law that ensures the protection of consumers data. It aims to improve security policies whether offline or online relating to privacy. The HIPAA focus on the collection and use of health data. It announces that the private part of medical information must be protected from any data leaks Hassanalieragh et al. (2015). Since the African Union (AU) adopted a Convention on Cyber-security and Personal Data Protection, the prevalence of data protection laws in Africa is increasing. Indeed, around 16 African countries have adopted data protection laws, five have instantiated data protection bills and nine are expected to instantiate such a bill. However, this process was not completed and some of them face implementation challenges Botha et al. (2017).

Privacy Taxonomy

To better understand the privacy concept variant, taxonomies was introduced Solove (2005), Pfitzmann and Hansen (2010), Finn et al. (2013),Eckhoff and Wagner (2017). For example, based on technology advances, Finn et al. introduced seven types of privacy: (1) privacy of person, (2) thoughts, (3) behavior, (4) communication, (5) association, (6) data and image and (7) location. In Eckhoff and Wagner (2017), authors admit that this taxonomy is confusing. Thus, they rearranged them by admitting that privacy forms five types namely (1) privacy of location, (2) privacy of state of body & mind, (3) privacy of social life, (4) privacy of behavior & action, and (5) privacy of media.

However, we argue that these categories include unnecessary distinctions and does not consider the exponential growth of the use of electronic data. Virtual social life has invaded our lives, and gave birth to the concept of "self-disclosure" Taddicken (2014). Despite this, this aspect was ignored. Thus, we cannot distinguish the privacy of media from the privacy of social life. Accordingly, we consider them to be part of the privacy of virtual life. So, our four types of privacy can be presented as follows:

- **Privacy of spatio-temporal information**: it represents the protection of spatio temporal information. Its infringement can uncover a person's location. It permits to conclude different sorts of individual data, for example, shopping habits.
- **Privacy of body and mind status:** it encompasses a person's body characteristics including health, biometrics, mental states, opinions, emotions and thoughts. Its violation can lead to discrimination and causes emotional, physical and moral damages.
- **Privacy of action:** it includes the habits, hobbies and actions of a person. This information often leads to deductions about the user's private life.
- **Privacy of virtual life:** it focuses on social interactions and action done online including images, audio, video and other private data uploaded or downloaded online. It also covers the meta-data about interactions, such as the duration of these interactions, with whom a person interacts and when. Its violation will have repercussions for other types of privacy. For example, interactions with specialized hospitals or research done about a specific disease may disclose information about a person's health state.

Privacy Preserving Classification

Privacy preserving can be envisaged at different levels Lin et al. (2017); Kumar and Patel (2014). Based on the life cycle of data, we propose the following classification:

- **Data collection:** during collection, sensitive data can be disclosed. For example, in the context of IoT, an intruder can reprogram an IoT object in such a way that the latter sends data not only to the legitimate entity, but also to the intruder.
- **Data aggregation:** when formulating complete information from a data- set, a leak of sensitive data can occur. Since this procedure can be carried out in different places, it is difficult to ensure the protection of privacy.
- **Data transmission**: when transmitting data, personal information may be revealed.
- **Data storage**: when stored at the database, personal data, such as identity, can be revealed. Only access to statistical data must be allowed.
- **Data processing and analysis**: when analyzing information, sensitive data can be revealed and retained by third parties.

Privacy Preserving Properties

Privacy preserving can be divided into two categories Ozturk et al. (2004); Lin et al. (2009): (1) content privacy and (2) context-oriented privacy (see figure 1). We dedicate this section to present of these two categories:

Content Privacy

Content privacy, or data protection, is the ability of an attacker to disclose user data by eavesdropping or altering data transmitted over communication networks. Although this property is essential, it is not difficult to ensure thanks to many cryptographic primitives Ozturk et al. (2004).

Context-oriented Privacy

It focuses on the item of interest (IOI). The IOI can represent actors, actions, or objects. It includes two properties: (1) anonymity and (2) pseudonymity Pfitzmann and Waidner (1987), Pfitzmann and Hansen (2008).

- **Anonymity** includes three sub-properties:
    - **Anonymity of the sender/ receiver**: requires to be unidentifiable in a set of subjects, called the set of anonymity.
    - **Unlinkability**: imposes the inability to establish a link between a person and his actions and/ or identify the sender and receiver as two communicating entities.
    - **Unobservability**: consists in not being able to admit that an action has taken place.

Figure 1. Privacy preserving properties

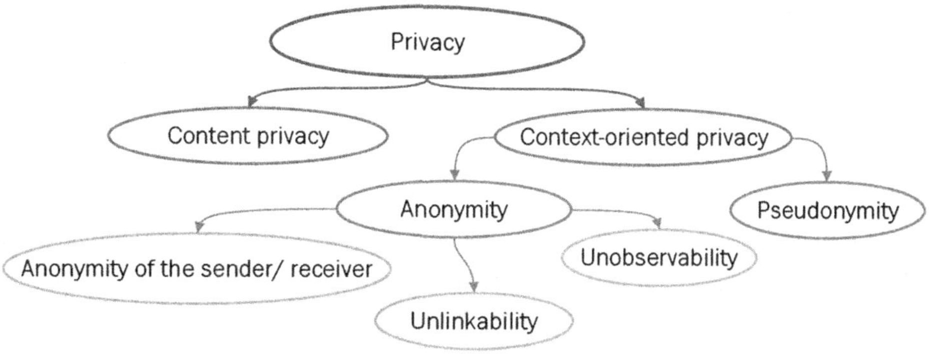

- **Pseudonymity** requires the use of pseudonym instead of true identities. Indeed, a pseudonym represents an identifier of a subject other than its true identity. It can be classified into three categories Pfitzmann and Hansen (2008):

- According to the possibility of transfer to other subjects:
  § A transferable pseudonym: is transferred from one owner to another entity.
  § A group pseudonym: assigned to an entity set.
  § A transferable group pseudonym: combines the features of group pseudonym and transferable pseudonym.
- According to the link between the pseudonym and its owner:
  § A public pseudonym: the link between the pseudonym and its owner is publicly known.
  § A pseudonym initially non-public: the link between the pseudonym and its owner can only be known by a trusted third party.
  § An initially non-associated pseudonym: the link between the pseudonym and its owner is known to anyone except the owner.
- According to the context of use:
  § A person's pseudonym implies the use of a pseudonym instead of the user-name.
  § A role pseudonym involves the specification of a well-defined role such as a client pseudonym.
  § A relationship pseudonym implies the use of a different pseudonym for each communication partner.
  § A role-relationship pseudonym combines the role and relation- ship pseudonym.
  § A transaction pseudonym implies the use of a new pseudonym for each transaction.

In general, a pseudonym held by several subjects offers a higher level of anonymity than a pseudonym belonging to a single subject. This degree reaches the maximum with transaction nicknames.

Privacy by Design

Privacy Enhancing Technologies (PETs), which have been developed over the last decades, are deployed to ensure certain properties of privacy preserving in a specific context. On the other hand, the privacy preserving is independent of the context Eckhoff and Wagner (2017). For this, the Privacy by Design *PbD* is often considered a necessary strategy to be adopted in order to solve the invasion of privacy Roman et al. (2011, 2013); Eckhoff and Wagner (2017). This strategy requires consideration of privacy requirements early in the development of any communication system. It encompasses the following seven principles Cavoukian (2009):

1. Proactive non-Reactive / Preventive non-corrective: the invasion of privacy must be anticipated and prevented before it occurs;
2. Privacy preserving as a default setting: no action is required from an individual to protect their privacy. This is natively integrated into the system; item Privacy preserving integrated during design: a system integrates privacy as an essential element of its core functionality;
3. Full functionality with full privacy protection;
4. Protection of privacy throughout the data life-cycle;
5. Visibility and transparency;
6. Respect for the privacy of the user.

PRIVACY ATTACKS

Figure 2. Attack classification

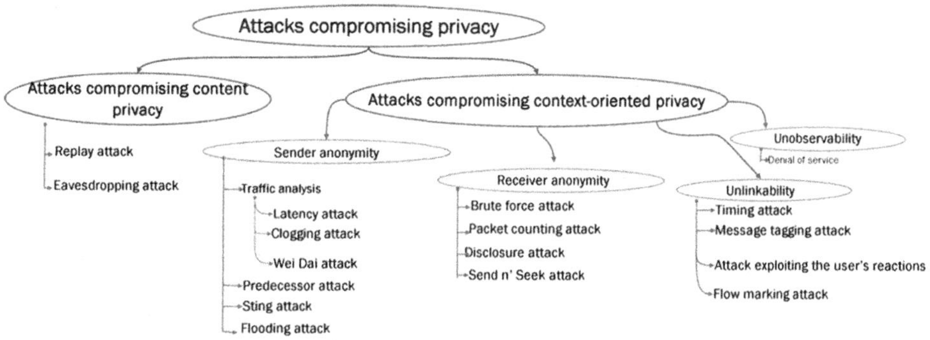

Attacker Model

An attacker (an adversary) is a malicious entity that deliberately attempts to compromise the privacy of one or more users communicating in a network. Thus, its purpose is to determine the identity of communicating entities. For that, it is based on the collection of several information, such as pseudonyms, the correlation of the packets, etc. In general, it results in identifying the source and the destination with a high probability. The attackers' capabilities could be classified into five categories Diaz (2006):

- Passive versus Active: a passive attacker only observes network traffic without having any information on encryption keys, exchanged data, paths... Indeed, he can simply derive information relying on his observations. If he is an active attacker, he represents a passive attacker with the ability to inject, modify or delete packets on a network.
- Internal versus External: an internal adversary monitors one or more system entities (for example: nodes, sender, recipient). The external adversary can only control the communication links.
- Local versus Global: a global attacker can observe the entire communication path. Nonetheless, a local attacker can only access a small set of nodes in a network.
- Static versus Adaptive: a static attacker controls a predefined set of re- sources throughout the execution of an action. An adaptive attacker can take control of new resources depending on the intermediate results of the attack.
- Temporary versus Permanent: contrary to permanent attackers, temporary attackers do not know the full history of the system since it was triggered. They begin to observe or attack at a moment *t*.

Attack Classification

In the literature, attacks are generally classified as passive or active. However, this classification does not suit our context. Therefore, we classify attacks according to the compromised privacy preservation properties. The new classification presents the problem more clearly. Note that we assume that all transferred traffic is encrypted. As shown in figure 2, attacks are categorized into two categories as follows: **(1) attacks that compromise the content privacy** and **(2) attacks that compromise the context-oriented privacy**.

Among the attacks compromising content privacy we present:

- Replay attack: an attacker can launch a replay attack by re-injecting the old sent messages.
- Eavesdropping attack: an adversary takes advantage of network communications to access data exchanged by others without their consent.

Among the attacks compromising context-oriented privacy, we define four sub-categories:

- **Attacks compromising the sender anonymity**: the main attacks that affect the anonymity of the sender are:
    - *Traffic analysis*: The purpose of this attack is to determine the location or identity of a specific node based on data collected by eavesdropping. It can come in many forms. One of these forms is latency attack Back et al. (2001). This attack is based on the calculation of the latency of the different paths. Indeed, the attacker tries to trace the path traveled by the packet to identify the source. Suppose that the communication between a specific node and an end node (server S) goes through nodes A and B. The adversary establishes a path through A and B to S. He determines the latency of the entire path. Then, he subtracts the latency of the path between him and the first visited node. Once a set of latency values are formed, the attacker can easily identify which path is used by a node to reach the server. Thus, he determines the sender, which compromises his anonymity.
    - The clogging attack Back et al. (2001) is another form of traffic analysis. According to this attack, an attacker observes the flow sent from a particular node C to a destination D. Then, it establishes a path including C and reaching D. Then, he overwhelms this path with many packets. If the flow from C to D decreases, the attacker can conclude that one of the nodes of the established route belongs to a potential path containing C. Thus, the path leading to D is known and the source is identified, which compromises his anonymity.
    - Wei Dai attacks Back et al. (2001): This attack affects systems that allocate bandwidth when making connections and set a threshold for traffic between nodes. According to this attack, the opponent establishes an anonymous path including nodes suspected of belonging to a potential path. Then, it increases the traffic until reaching the fixed bandwidth threshold. Thus, the exchange of packets is no longer possible and the real traffic passing through can be determined by omitting the attacker's traffic from the bandwidth limit.
    - Predecessor attack Figueiredo et al. (2004): according to this at- tack, we assume that a subset of uncompromising nodes, named *I*, communicates continuously with a destination D. The attacker controls a fixed number of nodes and seeks to discover the members of *I*. For this, all the malicious nodes maintain a counter shared between them and specific non-compromised node. These counters calculate the number of times a node was the predecessor of a malicious node that belongs to a path leading to D. When a malicious node is chosen to be part of a new anonymous path leading to the destination D, it increments the shared counter of its predecessor (see figure 3). Thus, the attacker will rely on the value of the counter to identify all the initiators.

- *Sting attack Raymond (2001)*: according to this attack, the at- tacker is the involved destination in a communication. The lat- ter can compromise the anonymity of the sender by trying to identify it. For example, he can create a fake site.
- *Flooding attack Raymond (2001)*: Suppose a node waits for receiving n messages before transmitting them. An attacker sends him n 1 messages. Then, he retrieves the message from the potential sender by associating the incoming messages with the outgoing messages. Hence, the anonymity of the source is com- promised.

Figure 3. Predecessor attack

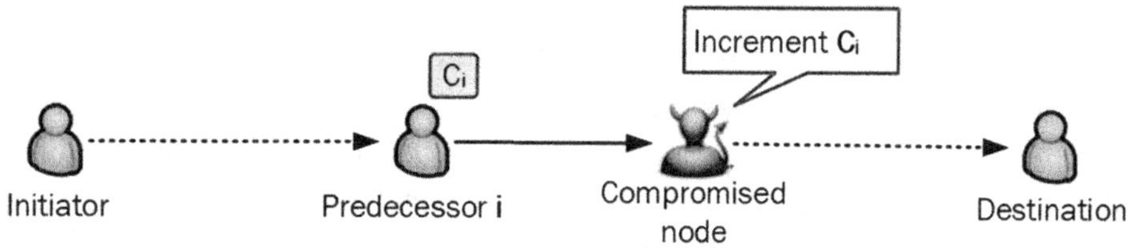

- **Attacks compromising the receiver anonymity:** The main attacks that identify the receiver are:
  - *Brute force attack Raymond (2001)*: an attacker follows the message hop-by-hop from the source until it reaches the destination. Thus, it identifies the destination and establishes the link with the receiver. Therefore, the anonymity of the latter is compromised.
  - *Packet counting attack:* In order to discover the receiving entity, an attacker must determine the path traversed. For this, he counts the number of incoming packets in a first node and coming from the potential source. He also focus on the number of outgoing packets. He repeats this procedure until reaching the destination Back et al. (2001).
  - *Disclosure attack:* this attack allows an attacker to identify the set of potential destinations based on multiple traffic observations. Nevertheless, this attack is very difficult to launch since it requires the resolution of the constraint satisfaction problem (CSP) which is considered to be NP-complete Danezis (2003).
  - *The Send n'Seek attack*: dissimilar from the sting attack, it is the sender who tries to determine the identity of the destination Raymond (2001).
- **Attacks compromising the unlinkability**: the main attacks that compromise the unlinkability are:
  - *Timing attack Raymond (2001)*: it is a serious problem of low latency anonymous communication systems. Based on the temporal correlation between the set of incoming and outgoing messages, the attacker can establish a link between the source and the recipient. For example, suppose that he can observe the source and the recipient, and that there are two paths, taking 1 second and 4 seconds, respectively (see figure 4). Suppose there are two messages injected respectively at 0:01, 0:03 and two mes sages arriving at the receiver at 0:04, 0:05. Thus, by correlation of the injected messages with those arriving at the recipient, the link between the communicating entities is established.
  - *Message tagging attack Raymond (2001)*: according to this at- tack, the adversary observes the packets exchanged between N entities, but does not know the relation between the com-

municating entities. For this, at the first node, he adds to the message a tag that will be removed just before reaching the receiver. Thus, it establishes the relation between the source and the receiver which compromises the unlinkability.
    - *Attack exploiting the user's reactions Raymond (2001)*: when the messages are received, the user performs an appropriate action. Thus, an attacker can exploit this fact to obtain information about the sender and the recipient. For example, he can intercept a message M and transmit it to a set of possible recipients. Indeed, the reactions of the entities probably differ between those who expect to receive this message or not.
    - *Flow marking attack Fu et al. (2007)*: the aim of this attack is to ensure that a source communicates with a destination. For this, an attacker implements a series of marks in the traffic generated by the source. Another attacker examines incoming traffic at the destination. By finding these marks, the attackers establish the link between these two entities.
- **Attack compromising the unobservability**: we identify the denial-of-service attack as an attack on unobservability. According to this attack, an attacker can obtain information about the sender and discover the paths used by making certain nodes inaccessible. This is possible because a node, which detects that the path which established is destroyed, will act in a different way from the others.

Figure 4. Timing attack

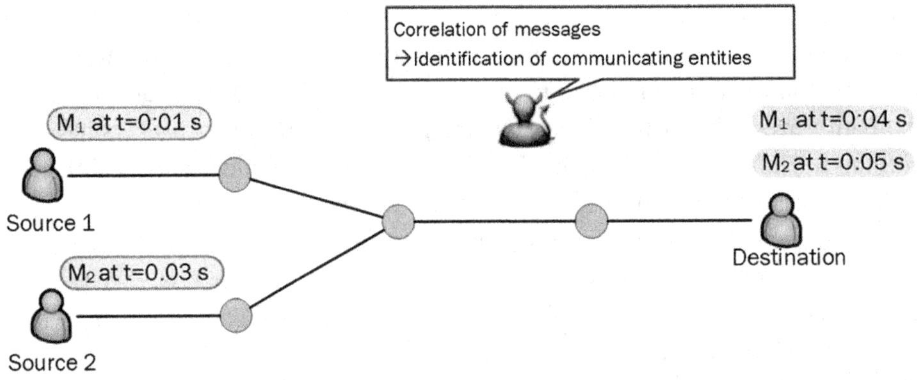

MESSAGE TRANSMISSION APPROACHES ENSURING PRIVACY-PRESERVING

To ensure privacy preserving, it is necessary that the sender does not communicate directly with the receiver. Thus, one or more intermediate nodes must appear within the communication path. The way in which messages are exchanged also has an impact on the privacy preservation. Indeed, we distinguish three types of transmission of messages guaranteeing the privacy Tao et al. (2015): Unimessage, message splitting and message replication.

Unimessage

The messages exchanged are sent in broadcast. Indeed, there are three types: (1) approaches based on the fundamental paths guaranteeing anonymity, (2) approaches based on random walk ensuring unlinkability and (3) approaches based on fake messages reinforcing unobservability.

Approaches Based on Fundamental Paths

Messages are encrypted and transmitted via a predefined path. This approach decreases the overhead of path establishment. Nonetheless, this type of path is not reliable. It is also hard to maintain in a dynamic environment, since the path nodes can disconnect during the transmission of the messages.

Approaches Based on Random Walking

According to these methods, there are two categories (1) probabilistic approaches and (2) the "rumor ridding" approach.

- Probabilistic approaches are used to define the routing path based on a probabilistic value. Indeed, each node of the path randomly generates a probabilistic value. Depending on this value, the node chooses either to transmit the message to the destination or to another intermediate node. This procedure is repeated until reaching the intended destination. Since the destination is known, only the anonymity of the sender is guaranteed.
- The "rumor ridding" approach is specific to peer-to-peer systems. Indeed, the initiator transmits the protected message and the secret key in two separate packets. These packets pass randomly through several nodes. The node that receives the two packets retrieves the original message and transmits it to a subset of its neighbors according to a probability p. Those who receive the message transmit it, in turn, to each of their neighbors according to a probability p. This procedure is repeated until the TTL field reaches 0. Thus, the anonymity of the destination is guaranteed Liu et al. (2011).

Approaches Based on Fake Messages

Contrary to the above, these approaches ensure unobservability by introducing fake messages. Each node periodically exchanges messages with its neighbors. Indeed, these messages may be useful or fake traffic. As a result, an attacker cannot differentiate between real and fake traffic. Thus, it cannot determine whether a node communicates or not, which ensures unobservability. However, these systems inevitably produce a significant overhead due to the number of the injected false messages. This can induce bandwidth saturation.

Message Splitting

Message splitting methods do not use the primitives of asymmetric cryptography. They divide the messages into a set of blocks by using a secret and a splitting function. These blocks are sent in unicast.

We can cite some examples of algorithms such as: information dispersion, Shamir's secret sharing and information splitting.

Information Dispersion Algorithms

The information dispersion algorithm (IDA) was originally introduced by Rabin in 1989 Rabin (1989). It is basically used to split a file F of L length in n fragments. The two key parameters of this algorithm are n and m. Indeed, n represents the total number of fragments resulting from IDA, of which only m fragments are sufficient to reconstruct the original file. Note that the F file is usually encrypted, and each fragment is sent to a neighbor.

Shamir's Secret Sharing

This algorithm Shamir (1979) allows the cutting a secret into n fragments and share it using a polynomial. It defines a threshold value t which represents the number of fragments needed for the reconstruction of the secret. Indeed, the coalition of $t - 1$ fragments among n does not allow the recovery of the secret.

Information Splitting

This technique, as described in Katabi (2007), randomly divides the message into n pieces and sends them across disjoint paths. These pieces meet only at the destination. Therefore, an attacker who gets n 1 parts of the message cannot retrieve the original message. To create an anonymous path, the routing information is sent to each intermediate node within a confidential message cut and sent in several disjointed paths. Made naively, this requires an exponential number of disjoint paths, and therefore an exponential number of nodes. To avoid these explosions, the source builds efficient transfer graphs that reuse nodes without information leakage. This technique also provides protection against node failures by using the same codes to send confidential messages and to prevent failure and loss. Network coding is also deployed to minimize redundancy and avoid overloading.

Message Replication

Message replication approach is based either on multicast or on broadcast strategy. According to the multicast strategy, the encrypted and replicated messages are addressed to a restricted set of nodes forming a multicast group. Thus, the anonymity of the receiver is guaranteed, since the latter is hidden in the multicast group. The broadcast strategy ensures the transmission of messages to all nodes of the network. This ensures a high level of receiver anonymity, but is only used in local networks. The major disadvantage of these two strategies is the saturation of the network since the large number of redundant messages. In addition, the nodes must attempt to decipher each received message, which induces a calculation overhead.

EXISTING PROTOCOLS AND MECHANISMS ENSURING PRIVACY PRESERVATION

The need to deploy effective protocols and mechanisms for privacy preservation is essential. In the following we present the main protocols and existing mechanisms guaranteeing privacy. These can be categorized into two broad categories: those that focus on content privacy and those that focus on the context privacy.

Protocols and Mechanisms Ensuring Content Privacy

Content-oriented privacy can be divided into two categories: **(1) Data storage and access**, and **(2) Data routing**. We focus on these two categories by presenting the different mechanisms existing in the literature.

Data Storage and Access

When storing and accessing data in databases, content privacy can be provided by several approaches.

- Data minimization: it aims to limit collection, processing, and storage of personal data Pfitzmann and Hansen (2010). By ensuring that there is no personal data collection, the potential impact of a system on privacy is limited
- Private Information Recovery (PIR) protocols: Introduced in 1995 in Chor et al. (1995), PIRs provide anonymous access to items stored in a dis- tributed database. Indeed, they allow users to query database servers without disclosing the query or the corresponding results, even to the owners of the database. The naivest method to ensure this is the recovery of the entire database disregarding of the query. The disadvantage is the cost of recovery that increases linearly with the number of records stored. For this, several protocols have been proposed to minimize this cost Chan et al. (2015), Freij-Hollanti et al. (2017);
- K-anonymity: it is a very well-known technique to preserve the privacy of persons when querying databases. The main idea is the elimination of columns including identification information and the grouping of rows into equivalence classes. Indeed, each equivalence class includes at least k rows with all the same values for each quasi-identifier, such as all indi- viduals with the same postal code, the same date of birth and the same sex. Quasi-identifiers do not recognize users but can do so when they are correlated with other data. For instance, the combination of three quasi-postal code identifiers, date of birth and gender identifies 87% of the AmericansEckhoff and Wagner (2017). Several approaches have been introduced to make a database k-anonymous, by applying for example a generalization and a deletion of data Samarati (2001). However, it has been shown that k-anonymity has limitations that allow re-identification of individuals and/or their critical data. Thus, many variations have been introduced, such as *l-diversity* which ensures the good representation of the sensitive attributes in each equivalence class Machanavajjhala et al. (2006), *t - closeness* which restricts the distribution of critical attributes Li et al. (2007), *m - invariance* which deals with cases of data republications Xiao and Tao (2007).
- Differential Privacy: It represents an approach that ensures the content privacy. Initially, it was introduced to handle requests for statistical databases. It represents an efficient way that maximizes the accuracy of these queries while minimizing the chances of determining its records Dwork et

al. (2014). For example, regardless of whether an individual's record is in a database or not, the result of a query should be roughly the same. Generally, this is ensured by adding random noise to the query results. Nevertheless, it is likely that a data disclosure occurs Dwork (2011).

Data Transmission

To ensure the content privacy during data routing, several approaches exist. These approaches can be divided into two broad categories: (1) non-cryptographic approaches and (2) Cryptographic approaches.

The first category represents approaches that do not use cryptographic operations such as:

- Steganography: it ensures the unobservability of messages, since the existence of the message itself is hidden. Indeed, the message is hidden in another multimedia file such as text, sound, video or image Dhamija and Dhaka (2015). Steganography through text can be applied by changing the layout of the text, using a code consisting of characters, lines and page numbers, etc. Hiding information in audio files can be made through inaudible frequencies. Regarding video files, since it is a mobile stream of images and sounds, any minor distortion may be invisible. The im- age is the most used file format used for steganography because it has a high degree of redundancy Subhedar and Mankar (2014). However, this technique lacks security.
- Network coding: it represents a technique that allows nodes to not only transmit but also process incoming information flows Fragouli et al. (2007). Indeed, it ensures the sending of a linear combination of packets instead of several separate packets. In other words, the packets to be sent are combined in the same packet that will be addressed to the next relay node. It has been theoretically proven that this technique maximizes network throughput Jaggi et al. (2007).

The second category includes approaches representing themselves cryptographic primitives as follows:

- Homomorphic encryption: this scheme allows arbitrary calculations on encrypted data without disclosing either the data in clear or the corresponding secret key Gentry (2009). The generated result is itself provided encrypted and can only be decrypted by the owner of the secret key.
- Broadcast encryption: it can broadcast a message to a subset of recipients T in a system S Fiat and Naor (1993). This subsystem can dynamically change. While all S entities can get the encrypted message, only privileged entities can decrypt it using the secret key. The system is said to be resistant to collusion if no entity beyond T can learn information about plain text.
- Symmetric / Asymmetric encryption: encryption ensures the confidentiality of messages. Traditionally, symmetric encryption requires a secret key shared between two parties to encrypt data. The public key encryption protects messages using a public key. Only the respective private key can decrypt the ciphertext.
- Identity Based Cryptography (IBC): It was introduced in 1984 by Shamir Shamir (1984). It represents a public key cryptosystem that eliminates the use of certificates. In the IBC, the public key is a unique and arbitrary character string which can be for example a user's name or email address. This allows to encrypt messages even if the destination has not yet generated his private key. The latter is generated by a trusted entity, named PKG (Public Key Generator), based on its secret key, the public parameters, and the public key of the user.

- Attribute-Based Encryption (ABE): Representing a public-key encryption scheme, it was introduced to provide access control Sahai and Waters (2005). In ABE, encrypted messages are not necessarily addressed to a specific user as in the case of traditional public-key cryptography. Unlike that, private keys and encrypted messages will be associated with a set of attributes, or a policy applied to the attributes. Thus, a user can decipher a message if the set of attributes of his key corresponds to the set of attributes of the encrypted message. Thus, access control over the data is achieved Bethencourt et al. (2007).

Protocols and Mechanisms Ensuring Context Privacy

In the literature, a panoply of solutions dealing with the issue of context-oriented privacy has been developed. At this level, we describe a set of these solutions.

Introduced in 1981 by Chaum, the networks of Mix Chaum (1981) represent a solution to guarantee the anonymity of communication. A MIX is a relay node that ensures the non-correlation of the incoming and outgoing flows. Indeed, it accepts messages of fixed length, encrypted by its public key (Pub_{Mix}), and come from multiple sources. The MIX decrypts them using his private key. After having waited for the reception of a number of messages, he reorders and transmits them. The use of a cascading topology is conceivable. It causes the generation of several layers of encryption that they will be removed at a rate of one each time a MIX. Mix networks provide source anonymity and unlinkability since an attacker cannot match the input and output messages Pfitzmann and Hansen (2010). Only one MIX is able to maintain anonymity even in the presence of corrupted MIX. Nevertheless, the use of public key cryptographic operations at each relay can induce a high cost. A prior knowledge of MIX nodes is also required to establish a path.

Inspired from MIX networks, onion routing Reed et al. (1998) was defined in 1997. This approach introduces the notion of onion routers (ORs). These ORs represent MIX relays that re-order the incoming stream and add the encrypted stuffing. Onion routing encompasses three phases: (1) establishing the connection, (2) exchanging data, and (3) releasing the connection Goldschlag et al. (1999). During the connection establishment phase, the first relay, called onion proxy (OP), freely selects n ORs. It then retrieves the n public keys specific to these ORs and generates the onion to be sent. An onion is formed by adding n encryption layers that specify the routing information, the different symmetric encryption algorithms, and the keys to be used during the data recovery phase. The presence of multiple nested encryption layers in a message is the origin of the onion designation. Each OR receiving a message takes off an encryption layer using its own private key, adjusts the size of the message, and transmits it to the next specified jump. This process will be redone until the message reaches the final onion router. Once the connection is established, the messages exchanged between the source and the destination pass through this channel, encrypted according to the algorithms and keys specified in the onion. The release of the connection may be affected by one of the ends or by one of the intermediate ORs if necessary.

In onion routing, each selected OR knows only its predecessor and successor. In addition, the onion changes appearance with each OR crossed. Thus, the anonymity of the source and the unlinkability are assured. However, the extra cost of the public key cryptography used during the establishment of the connection is very expensive. Indeed, the more the path contains OR, the higher the cost is important.

Tor Dingledine et al. (2004) represents a second generation of onion routing. It brings several improvements. It has abandoned the use of relays MIX, which is based on the re-ordering of messages, as well as encrypted stuffing. The OP is also redefined as a program launched by the initiator. It consults the directory servers that indicate the current state of the network and the list of ORs. It establishes a route by extending jump by hop and shares symmetric keys with each intermediate node. Not like onion routing which establishes a path for each flow, TOR shares a path for multiple flows. It guarantees not only the anonymity of the source but also the anonymity of the destination thanks to a mechanism for defining *rendezvous points*.

The Dining Cryptographers network, introduced by Chaum in 1988, is the first point-to-point approach Chaum (1988). The metaphor presented to de- scribe this protocol is a dinner of three cryptographers during which they want to know if anyone of them pay the bill without disclosing his identity. For this, a coin is shared between adjacent peers indicating the shared secret bit. The sum (XOR) of the two bits observed by a participant is broadcast to the entire group of participants. If one of the cryptographers is the payer, he says the opposite of what he sees. The sum (XOR) of the three public announcements reveals the answer to their question. If the result is 0, then none of them paid. Otherwise, it's one of them, but its identity remains unknown to other cryptographers. Thus, this protocol ensures the anonymity of the source and the destination as well as the unlinkability. Since a secret key must be shared between each adjacent participants, this protocol becomes complex when the number of participants increases. As at each stage, only one participant broadcasts a message, so collisions can be caused intentionally. The dissemination strategy itself generates a significant additional cost Angel and Setty (2016). This protocol also excludes the possibility of false message injection by malicious participants.

Crowds are another approach that ensures the anonymity of web connections Reiter and Rubin (1998). This approach introduces the notion of "merging into a crowd". Its main idea is to form groups so that the identification of a member of the group who is at the origin of an action is impossible. Indeed, the initiator has a process called "jondo". When launching this process, it contacts a server named "Blender" to gain access to the group. Then, he sets a path to the destination. For this, he randomly chooses a member of the group and sends him an encrypted message. Then, this message will be transmitted based on a probabilistic scheme: a random probabilistic value is generated to specify the next jump which can be either another member of the crowd or the final destination. The constructed path will be used for a limited period of time. Thus, the crowd ensures the anonymity of the source. Indeed, the sender cannot be differentiated from the other intermediate members. The communication between the members is protected by a shared secret key, which guarantees the content privacy. However, Crowds does not guarantee the anonymity of the receiver. In addition, the negotiation and distribution of keys entails a significant additional cost.

Hordes Levine and Shields (2002) represents an improvement of the Crowds. Similar to Crowds, Hordes relies on a probabilistic routing to establish paths. On the other hand, the multicast strategy is adopted instead of the reverse path when routing responses. Indeed, a multicast address is used for return responses, thus ensuring the anonymity of the source. However, just like crowds, the anonymity of the receiver is not assured because the latter is always contacted directly by the jondo.

Free Haven Dingledine et al. (2001) is a distributed storage system that pro- vides anonymous data release. It relies on the information dispersion algorithm (IDA). It encompasses a set of servers called "servnets," which have pseudonyms and exchange fragments between them. To store a file at the servnets, the editor cuts it into n pieces, generates a pair of asymmetric keys, encrypts each block and marks them with a unique identifier. As for the readers, they must specify the ID of the published file. This system ensures the anonymity of the source and the destination. Unlinkability between a document and the user is also guaranteed. However, the storage and the recovery of the fragments can generate a significant additional cost.

Tarzan Freedman and Morris (2002) is a peer-to-peer, decentralized solution dedicated to web browsing. It uses onion encryption as well as multi-hop routing. Indeed, the sender preselects randomly a set of relay nodes forming a path to the destination. Then, it creates static tunnels through these nodes and injects a fake traffic to ensure unobservability. The anonymity of the source is also guaranteed. However, a tunnel failure causes both a large computation time and a delay Kelly et al. (2012). If a node fails, entire connections must be restored.

Another strategy ensuring anonymity is to add a third party (a proxy) be- tween the source and the destination. In order to ensure confidentiality, proxy services eliminate personal information to protect the identity of the sender. One of these examples is the Anonymizer Boyan web proxy, which strips the credentials of a user from the HTTP data stream. Thus, instead of identifying the real user, a web server only learns the identity of the Anonymizer. Nonetheless, the message exchanged between the browser and the Anonymizer are not encrypted, which makes it sensitive to eavesdropping attacks.

Regarding the anonymity of a message signer, different solutions exist in the literature. The blind signature Chaum (1983), introduced by Chaum, is applied in the case where the editor of the message and the the signatory are dissociated. Indeed, it represents a variant of the digital signature. According to this solution, the editor masks the message, transmits it to the signatory who signs it and sends it back to him. Thus, the signatory knows nothing of the messages he signs. Then, the editor extracts the signature of the message. Chaum has also presented the concept of group signature, which ensures the anonymity of the source Chaum and Van Heyst (1991). In this context, a member of a group, who can't be individually identified, digitally signs a document. The group is set in advance by a group manager or created when needed. The ring signature Rivest et al. (2001) is considered a simplified group signature that includes only users without a manager. It protects the anonymity of the signatory, since the verifier knows that the signature comes from a member of a ring but cannot identify it.

A numeric pseudonym has been defined as a public key which is signed by a trusted authority without knowing the identity of the holder Chaum (1981). However, this authority is responsible for the generation of these pseudonyms. Thus, it can establish a correspondence between the pseudonym and its owner, which represents a violation of anonymity.

FUTURE RESEARCH DIRECTIONS

In this section, we expose the most relevant research directions and open research concerns that should be the focus of privacy-preserving Tyagi et al. (2020).

IoT

Although the Internet of Things (IoT) paradigm has been around for more than a decade, its popularization among the general public as well as the attention from researchers and manufacturers are recent. The IoT makes it possible to connect, on a large scale, uniquely identifiable, intelligent and heterogeneous objects. These objects can interact with each other without any human intervention Perera et al. (2014). The IoT thus creates a new environment that merges the physical world and the digital world. In this regard, interconnected and cooperative networks are being set up and a lot of new applications are available. The fields of application are varied and the examples as well. The sensitivity and cruciality of the data exchanged raises several privacy issues Camp et al. (2020). Despite concerns about privacy-preserving, this issue is relatively little covered in the literature. Most existing proposals do not meet all preservation requirements of privacy while respecting the heterogeneity of the IoT environment Hernandez-Ramos et al. (2020).

Intelligent Transportation System

The Intelligent Transportation System (ITS) improves drivers' safeties and traffic efficiency on road by exchanging traffic-related information among vehicles and infrastructures. Indeed, each vehicle broadcasts a traffic safety message every 100-300 ms, which keeps the other vehicles informed of the vehicle's driving related information, such as location, speed, turning intention, and driving status. With the collected information, other drivers can predict critical situations such as accidents. However, along with the benefits intelligent vehicles also face some serious challenges and issues related to privacy Campanile et al. (2020). Indeed, the communications are carried out in open environment via an open wireless channel. Thus, an attacker could capture, intercept, alter, replay and delete the traffic-related information and could compromise the security of such systems. Therefore, security and privacy of the traffic-related information have to be well addressed before putting these application scenarios into practice Ali et al. (2019).

Machine Learning

Machine learning (ML) is shaping the fourth industrial revolution. It is based on a set of algorithms and statistical models that computer systems use to perform or predict a particular task without being programmed beforehand. These algorithms have remarkable performance that can even surpass that of humans in some cases Molnar (2020). These performances depend directly on the volume of the data collected. This data may contain sensitive information such as travel history, medical records, images, etc. So, once again, privacy- preserving represent a critical issue. Many attacks compromising privacy and relayed to sensitive data disclosure could be launched De Cristofaro (2021). Despite this, the existing solutions are still naive and do not treat this problem deeply Riazi et al. (2019).

CONCLUSION

Various advanced technologies and applications (e.g. smart cities, Internet of Things, big data applications) interact to encompass and improve all aspects of our life. However, the growing need for privacy preservation may be a hindrance to emerging applications. Indeed, the collection of sensitive data severely threatens personal privacy. Privacy-preserving mechanisms allow individuals to communicate only needed information, while preventing the leakage of sensitive information throughout the data life cycle.

In this context, this survey studies the privacy concept in depth. We introduced taxonomies to privacy requirements, potential attacks and attackers, exiting message transmission approaches, and different protocols and mechanisms. These taxonomies allowed us to better understand the privacy-preserving concept and to present a deep analysis of privacy issues and solutions in terms of both content and context-oriented privacy. We also identified the most relevant research directions and open research concerns that should be the focus of privacy-preserving.

ACKNOWLEDGEMENT

The authors would like to thank Prof. Khalil El Khatib (Professor in information security and Director of the Institute for Cybersecurity and Resilient Systems, Faculty of Business and Information Technology, Ontario Tech, Canada) for his help and support during the writing of this manuscript.

REFERENCES

Ali, I., Hassan, A., & Li, F. (2019). Authentication and privacy schemes for vehicular ad hoc networks (vanets): A survey. *Vehicular Communications, 16*, 45–61. doi:10.1016/j.vehcom.2019.02.002

Angel, S., & Setty, S. T. (2016). Unobservable communication over fully un- trusted infrastructure. OSDI, 551–569.

Back, A., M¨oller, U., & Stiglic, A. (2001). Traffic analysis attacks and trade- offs in anonymity providing systems. In *International Workshop on Information Hiding*. Springer. 10.1007/3-540-45496-9_18

Banisar, D. (2019). *National comprehensive data protection/privacy laws and bills 2019*. Privacy Laws and Bills.

Bethencourt, J., Sahai, A., & Waters, B. (2007). Ciphertext-policy attribute- based encryption. In *Security and Privacy, 2007. SP'07. IEEE Symposium on*. IEEE.

Bhaduri, A. (2003). *User controlled privacy protection in location-based services*. Academic Press.

Bloustein, E. J. (1964). Privacy as an aspect of human dignity: An answer to dean prosser. *NYUL Rev., 39*, 962.

Botha, J., Grobler, M., Hahn, J., & Eloff, M. (2017). A high-level comparison between the south african protection of personal information act and inter- national data protection laws. *ICMLG2017 5th International Conference on Management Leadership and Governance*.

Camp, J., Henry, R., Kohno, T., Mare, S., Myers, S., Patel, S., & Streiff, J. (2020). Toward a secure internet of things: Directions for research. *IEEE Security and Privacy, 18*(4), 28–37. doi:10.1109/MSEC.2020.2970155

Campanile, L., Iacono, M., Levis, A. H., Marulli, F., & Mastroianni, M. (2020). Privacy regulations, smart roads, blockchain, and liability insurance: Putting technologies to work. *IEEE Security and Privacy, 19*(1), 34–43. doi:10.1109/MSEC.2020.3012059

Cavoukian, A. (2009). Privacy by design. Take the challenge. Information and privacy commissioner of Ontario, Canada.

Chan, T. H., Ho, S.-W., & Yamamoto, H. (2015). Private information retrieval for coded storage. In *Information Theory (ISIT), 2015 IEEE International Symposium on*. IEEE. 10.1109/ISIT.2015.7282975

Chaum, D. (1983). Blind signatures for untraceable payments. In *Advances in cryptology* (pp. 199–203). Springer. doi:10.1007/978-1-4757-0602-4_18

Chaum, D. (1988). The dining cryptographers problem: Unconditional sender and recipient untraceability. *Journal of Cryptology*, *1*(1), 65–75. doi:10.1007/BF00206326

Chaum, D., & Van Heyst, E. (1991). Group signatures. In *Workshop on the Theory and Application of of Cryptographic Techniques*. Springer.

Chaum, D. L. (1981). Untraceable electronic mail, return addresses, and digital pseudonyms. *Communications of the ACM*, *24*(2), 84–90. doi:10.1145/358549.358563

Chor, B., Goldreich, O., Kushilevitz, E., & Sudan, M. (1995). Private information retrieval. In *Foundations of Computer Science, 1995. Proceedings., 36th Annual Symposium on*. IEEE. 10.1109/SFCS.1995.492461

Cole, D. (2014). We kill people based on metadata. *The New York Review of Books*, *10*, 2014.

Danezis, G. (2003). Statistical disclosure attacks. In *IFIP International Information Security Conference*. Springer.

De Cristofaro, E. (2021). A critical overview of privacy in machine learning. *IEEE Security and Privacy*, *19*(4), 19–27. doi:10.1109/MSEC.2021.3076443

Dhamija, A., & Dhaka, V. (2015). A novel cryptographic and steganographic approach for secure cloud data migration. In *Green Computing and Internet of Things (ICGCIoT), 2015 International Conference on*. IEEE. 10.1109/ICGCIoT.2015.7380486

Diaz, C. (2006). Anonymity metrics revisited. In *Dagstuhl Seminar Proceedings*. Schloss Dagstuhl-Leibniz-Zentrum fu¨r Informatik.

Dingledine, R., Freedman, M. J., & Molnar, D. (2001). The free haven project: Distributed anonymous storage service. In *Designing Privacy Enhancing Technologies* (pp. 67–95). Springer. doi:10.1007/3-540-44702-4_5

Dingledine, R., Mathewson, N., & Syverson, P. (2004). *Tor: The second- generation onion router. Technical report*. Naval Research Lab Washington DC. doi:10.21236/ADA465464

Dwork, C. (2011). Differential privacy. In *Encyclopedia of Cryptography and Security* (pp. 338–340). Springer. doi:10.1007/978-1-4419-5906-5_752

Dwork, C., & Roth, A. (2014). The algorithmic foundations of differential privacy. *Foundations and Trends in Theoretical Computer Science*, *9*(3–4), 211–407.

Eckhoff, D., & Wagner, I. (2017). Privacy in the smart city–applications, technologies, challenges and solutions. *IEEE Communications Surveys and Tutorials*.

Fiat, A., & Naor, M. (1993). Broadcast encryption. In *Annual International Cryptology Conference*. Springer.

Figueiredo, D. R., Nain, P., & Towsley, D. (2004). On the analysis of the predecessor attack on anonymity systems. Computer Science Technical Report.

Finn, R. L., Wright, D., & Friedewald, M. (2013). Seven types of privacy. In *European data protection: coming of age* (pp. 3–32). Springer. doi:10.1007/978-94-007-5170-5_1

Fragouli, C., & Soljanin, E. (2007). Network coding fundamentals. *Foundations and Trends in Networking*, *2*(1), 1–133. doi:10.1561/1300000003

Freedman, M. J., & Morris, R. (2002). Tarzan: A peer-to-peer anonymizing network layer. In *Proceedings of the 9th ACM conference on Computer and communications security*. ACM. 10.1145/586110.586137

Freij-Hollanti, R., Gnilke, O. W., Hollanti, C., & Karpuk, D. A. (2017). Private information retrieval from coded databases with colluding servers. *SIAM Journal on Applied Algebra and Geometry*, *1*(1), 647–664. doi:10.1137/16M1102562

Fu, X., Zhu, Y., Graham, B., Bettati, R., & Zhao, W. (2007). On flow marking attacks in wireless anonymous communication networks. *Journal of Ubiquitous Computing and Intelligence*, *1*(1), 42–53. doi:10.1166/juci.2007.005

Gentry, C. (2009). *A fully homomorphic encryption scheme*. Stanford University.

Goldschlag, D., Reed, M., & Syverson, P. (1999). Onion routing. *Communications of the ACM*, *42*(2), 39–41. doi:10.1145/293411.293443

Guarda, P., & Zannone, N. (2009). Towards the development of privacy-aware systems. *Information and Software Technology*, *51*(2), 337–350. doi:10.1016/j.infsof.2008.04.004

Hassanalieragh, M., Page, A., Soyata, T., Sharma, G., Aktas, M., Mateos, G., Kantarci, B., & Andreescu, S. (2015). Health monitoring and management using internet-of-things (iot) sensing with cloud-based processing: Opportunities and challenges. In *2015 IEEE International Conference on Services Computing*. IEEE. 10.1109/SCC.2015.47

Hernandez-Ramos, J. L., Martinez, J. A., Savarino, V., Angelini, M., Napolitano, V., Skarmeta, A. F., & Baldini, G. (2020). Security and privacy in internet of things-enabled smart cities: Challenges and future directions. *IEEE Security and Privacy*, *19*(1), 12–23. doi:10.1109/MSEC.2020.3012353

Jaggi, S., Langberg, M., Katti, S., Ho, T., Katabi, D., & M'edard, M. (2007). Resilient network coding in the presence of byzantine adversaries. In *IN- FOCOM 2007. 26th IEEE International Conference on Computer Communications*. IEEE. 10.1109/INFCOM.2007.78

Jamison, S. G. (2019). Creating a national data privacy law for the united states. *Cybaris Intell. Prop. L. Rev.*, *10*, 1.

Kamat, P., Zhang, Y., Trappe, W., & Ozturk, C. (2005). Enhancing source- location privacy in sensor network routing. In *Distributed Computing Systems, 2005. ICDCS 2005. Proceedings. 25th IEEE International Conference on*. IEEE.

Katabi, S. K. J. C. D. (2007). *Information slicing: Anonymity using unreliable overlays*. Academic Press.

Kelly, D., Raines, R., Baldwin, R., Grimaila, M., & Mullins, B. (2012). Exploring extant and emerging issues in anonymous networks: A taxonomy and survey of protocols and metrics. *IEEE Communications Surveys and Tutorials*, *14*(2), 579–606. doi:10.1109/SURV.2011.042011.00080

Levine, B. N., & Shields, C. (2002). Hordes: A multicast based protocol for anonymity. *Journal of Computer Security*, *10*(3), 213–240. doi:10.3233/JCS-2002-10302

Li, N., Li, T., & Venkatasubramanian, S. (2007). t-closeness: Privacy beyond k-anonymity and l-diversity. In *Data Engineering, 2007. ICDE 2007. IEEE 23rd International Conference on*. IEEE.

Lin, J., Yu, W., Zhang, N., Yang, X., Zhang, H., & Zhao, W. (2017). A survey on internet of things: Architecture, enabling technologies, security and privacy, and applications. *IEEE Internet of Things Journal*, *4*(5), 1125–1142. doi:10.1109/JIOT.2017.2683200

Liu, Y., Han, J., & Wang, J. (2011). Rumor riding: Anonymizing unstructured peer-to-peer systems. *IEEE Transactions on Parallel and Distributed Systems*, *22*(3), 464–475. doi:10.1109/TPDS.2010.98

Machanavajjhala, A., Gehrke, J., Kifer, D., & Venkitasubramaniam, M. (2006). l-diversity: Privacy beyond k-anonymity. In *Data Engineering, 2006. ICDE'06. Proceedings of the 22nd International Conference on*. IEEE.

Martin, E. A. (2009). *A dictionary of law*. OUP Oxford.

Maslow, A. H. (1950). *Self-actualizing people: a study of psychological health*. Personality.

Molnar, C. (2020). *Interpretable machine learning*. Lulu. com.

Moreham, N. (2008). *Why is privacy important? privacy, dignity and development of the New Zealand breach of privacy tort*. Academic Press.

Nair, M. M., & Tyagi, A. K. (2021). Privacy: History, statistics, policy, laws, preservation and threat analysis. *Journal of Information Assurance & Security*, *16*(1).

Nour, B., Sharif, K., Li, F., & Wang, Y. (2019). Security and privacy challenges in information-centric wireless internet of things networks. *IEEE Security and Privacy*, *18*(2), 35–45. doi:10.1109/MSEC.2019.2925337

Ozturk, C., Zhang, Y., & Trappe, W. (2004). Source-location privacy in energy-constrained sensor network routing. In *Proceedings of the 2nd ACM workshop on Security of ad hoc and sensor networks*. ACM. 10.1145/1029102.1029117

Perera, C., Zaslavsky, A., Christen, P., & Georgakopoulos, D. (2014). Context aware computing for the internet of things: A survey. *IEEE Communications Surveys and Tutorials*, *16*(1), 414–454. doi:10.1109/SURV.2013.042313.00197

Pfitzmann, A., & Hansen, M. (2008). *Anonymity, unlinkability, undetectability, unobservability, pseudonymity, and identity management-a consolidated proposal for terminology*. Version v0.

Pfitzmann, A., & Hansen, M. (2010). *A terminology for talking about privacy by data, minimization: Anonymity, unlinkability, undetectability, unobservability, pseudonymity, and identity management*. Academic Press.

Pfitzmann, A., & Waidner, M. (1987). Networks without user observability. *Computers & Security*, *6*(2), 158–166. doi:10.1016/0167-4048(87)90087-3

Rabin, M. O. (1989). Efficient dispersal of information for security, load balancing, and fault tolerance. *Journal of the Association for Computing Machinery*, *36*(2), 335–348. doi:10.1145/62044.62050

Raymond, J.-F. (2001). Traffic analysis: Protocols, attacks, design issues, and open problems. In *Designing Privacy Enhancing Technologies* (pp. 10–29). Springer. doi:10.1007/3-540-44702-4_2

Reed, M. G., Syverson, P. F., & Goldschlag, D. M. (1998). Anonymous connections and onion routing. *IEEE Journal on Selected Areas in Communications*, *16*(4), 482–494. doi:10.1109/49.668972

Regulation, P. (2018). General data protection regulation. *InTouch*.

Reiter, M. K., & Rubin, A. D. (1998). Crowds: Anonymity for web transactions. *ACM Transactions on Information and System Security*, *1*(1), 66–92. doi:10.1145/290163.290168

Riazi, M. S., Rouani, B. D., & Koushanfar, F. (2019). Deep learning on private data. *IEEE Security and Privacy*, *17*(6), 54–63. doi:10.1109/MSEC.2019.2935666

Rivest, R. L., Shamir, A., & Tauman, Y. (2001). How to leak a secret. In *International Conference on the Theory and Application of Cryptology and Information Security*. Springer.

Roman, R., Najera, P., & Lopez, J. (2011). Securing the internet of things. *Computer*, *44*(9), 51–58. doi:10.1109/MC.2011.291

Roman, R., Zhou, J., & Lopez, J. (2013). On the features and challenges of security and privacy in distributed internet of things. *Computer Networks*, *57*(10), 2266–2279. doi:10.1016/j.comnet.2012.12.018

Sahai, A., & Waters, B. (2005). Fuzzy identity-based encryption. In *Annual International Conference on the Theory and Applications of Cryptographic Techniques*. Springer.

Samarati, P. (2001). Protecting respondents identities in microdata release. *IEEE Transactions on Knowledge and Data Engineering*, *13*(6), 1010–1027. doi:10.1109/69.971193

Schwartz, B. (1968). The social psychology of privacy. *American Journal of Sociology*, *73*(6), 741–752. doi:10.1086/224567 PMID:5695022

Shamir, A. (1979). How to share a secret. *Communications of the ACM*, *22*(11), 612–613. doi:10.1145/359168.359176

Shamir, A. (1984). Identity-based cryptosystems and signature schemes. In *Workshop on the theory and application of cryptographic techniques*. Springer.

Solove, D. J. (2005). A taxonomy of privacy. *U. Pa. L. Rev.*, *154*(3), 477. doi:10.2307/40041279

Solove, D. J. (2007). *The future of reputation: Gossip, rumor, and privacy on the Internet*. Yale University Press.

Subhedar, M. S., & Mankar, V. H. (2014). Current status and key issues in image steganography: A survey. *Computer Science Review*, *13*, 95–113. doi:10.1016/j.cosrev.2014.09.001

Taddicken, M. (2014). The 'privacy paradox'in the social web: The impact of privacy concerns, individual characteristics, and the perceived social relevance on different forms of self-disclosure. *Journal of Computer-Mediated Communication*, *19*(2), 248–273. doi:10.1111/jcc4.12052

Tao, F., Fei, X., Ye, L., & Li, F. J. (2015). Secure network coding-based named data network mutual anonymity communication protocol. *Proceedings of International Conference on Electrical, Computer Engineering and Electronics (ICECEE)*, 1107–1114.

Tikkinen-Piri, C., Rohunen, A., & Markkula, J. (2018). Eu general data protection regulation: Changes and implications for personal data collecting companies. *Computer Law & Security Review*, *34*(1), 134–153. doi:10.1016/j.clsr.2017.05.015

Tyagi, A. K., Nair, M. M., Niladhuri, S., & Abraham, A. (2020). Security, privacy re-search issues in various computing platforms: A survey and the road ahead. *Journal of Information Assurance & Security*, *15*(1).

Westin, A. F. (1968). Privacy and freedom. *Washington and Lee Law Review*, *25*(1), 166.

Wolford, B. (2019). What is gdpr, the eu's new data protection law. *GDPR. eu*, 13.

Xiao, X., & Tao, Y. (2007). M-invariance: towards privacy preserving re- publication of dynamic datasets. In *Proceedings of the 2007 ACM SIGMOD international conference on Management of data*. ACM. 10.1145/1247480.1247556

Chapter 2
Industry 4.0:
Design Principles,Technologies, and Applications

Sheetal Zalte
Shivaji University, India

Smita Deshmukh
Vishwakarma College of Arts, Commerce, and Science, Pune, India

Prajkta Patil
Vishwakarma College of Arts, Commerce, and Science, Pune, India

Minal Patil
Vishwakarma College of Arts, Commerce, and Science, Pune, India

Rajanish K. Kamat
Shivaji University, India

ABSTRACT

The fourth technological revolution, which is widely called Industry 4.0, works by incorporating the critical features like physical (object in existence), digital, and biological worlds. The attributes related to Industry 4.0 are more important as they change from producing a large amount of standardized products by using manual assembly, semi-automated assembly, or fully automated assembly with customization based on different product manufacturing. The fourth technological revolution is not progressing to modification; however, "it can modify us" and revolutionize societal life. The chapter elucidates the essential technologies behind Industry 4.0 and how they are shaping smart manufacturing and digital supply chain management. It also throws light on the policy frameworks required to be adopted to inculcate Industry 4.0 in the walks of societal life and reviews the upcoming trends.

DOI: 10.4018/978-1-6684-5250-9.ch002

INTRODUCTION

Over the past hundred years, Industrial Revolution has increased productivity by rapidly and significantly, especially in logistics organizations. The third industrial revolution is from the 1950s and 1970s and refers to the digital revolution that has arisen due to the shift from analog mechanical systems to digital ones. This is due to the impact of immense development in computer, information and communication technologies. The automation of manufacturing processes is shifted to the next level by introducing suitable and adaptable mass production technologies in this fourth industrial revolution.

Industry 4.0 involves Cyber-physical systems (CPS), hyperactive connections, the Industrial Internet of Things (IIoT) and the Internet of Services (IoS) that shape the way services and values are used across supply chains. Thus, Industry 4.0 is a concept or process in the current manufacturing and automation industry that focuses on digital data transformation. The main goal is to empower monitor assets, self-directed decision-making processes, processes in a real-time environment. Priorinvolvement of stake-holders and vertical-horizontal integrationcan create real value networks. In chronological order, the 3 most essential throughput factors are steam moving manufacture lines, industrial control-monitoring systems and automation.

As briefly, covered in this chapter, the 4thIndustrial Revolution which is essentially an orientation toward automation and data transfer or exchange across manufacturing processes and techniques, including cloud computing, cyber-physical systems (CPS), IIoT (Industrial Internet of Things), intellectual or simulative computing and artificial intelligence. Virtual, structured and intelligent factories governingand controlling the substantial activity, it creates an imaginary world that will be helpful to make decentralized decisions. This revolution is said to be behind the widespread dependence on technologies such as 3D printing technology.

Industry 4.0 provides six design principles to provide clear guiding principles for those companies or industries, who want to get knowledge, recognize, identify, and develop the projects or services.

It involves large data transfer and automation in the manufacturing work environment, including the systems as a cyber-physical system, cloud computing, Big-Data, IoT, IIoT, Smart Factory. All these systems aim at the integration of computation and physical processes (Kicińsk & Chaja, 2021).

The 4thIndustrial Revolution and Industry 4.0 is the progressive automation of old manufacturing and industrial processes through recent intelligent technologies. The term "Industry 4.0" itself is a broad term encompassing the range of modern automation or computerization, data transfer and exchange and manufacturing technologies.

This chapter presents current advances in design and technology in the phase of Industry 4.0. It is inspired by the tendency toward smart plants (workplace) and the forthcoming of the 4th Industrial Revolution, which will enable better use of people's skills and resources, cyber and physical production environments. The evolving paradigms of the industry 5.0 present innovative system design issues or problems at the edge between intelligent manufacturing or processing, robust and adaptable automation, scattered and reconfigurable production systems, industrial IoT and supply chain integration.

DESIGN PRINCIPLES

As portrayed, with the previous section, Industry 4.0 refers to a next level of industrial evolution that emphasis on networked, computerization or automation, machine learning, and realworld data. It includes

IIoT and smart manufacturing systems combining the actucal production and operation with smart digital technologies, machine learning and big data to build or create a complete, connected ecosystem for businesses that are focused on manufacturingi.e.productive and supply chain management.These technologies are innovative and exciting, but according to automation solutions provider Swisslog, they are only part of the picture. Upcoming new information and communications technologies, like CPS (cyber-physical systems), big data and cloud computing can help to predict the opportunities for increasing productivity, superiority and flexibility in the manufacturing industry which is helpful to understand the benefits of competition. A latest article recommends that Industry 4.0 will be advantageous and affect developing countries such as India. The integration of such technologies allows objects to work together to solve problems. The critical role IoT plays in Industry 4.0 is industrial IoT. IoT has a lot of IoT stack components, platforms, gateways, devices and so on. So many modern technologies as process automation, Artificial Intelligence, machine learning, virtual conference, chat-boat and pop-up software in information enterprise management, business process management and application source markets naturally show how IoT supports industrial and manufacturing applications and how IoT is a manufacturing platform.

The 4thIndustrial Revolution took the manufacturing automation processes to a next level by providing the tailor-made, configurable, and flexible mass production technologies. Machines became self-governing units that could gather, analyze and decide or advise data. This means that machines can work independently or work with people to create a customer-oriented production field that works and maintains itself. The Internet of Things (IoT) allows enitiy and machines like smartphones and digital devices like sensors to communicate that is transfer the data with each other and people to collaborate on solutions or output. This helps an industry to integrate the real world with the virtual world by enabling machines to collect, analyze, and make decisions based on live data. The key role that the IoT plays in Industry 4.0 is industrial IoT, as it has many stack components of IoT; it is a platform for industrial IoT, a gateway device and more.

Figure 1. Design principles

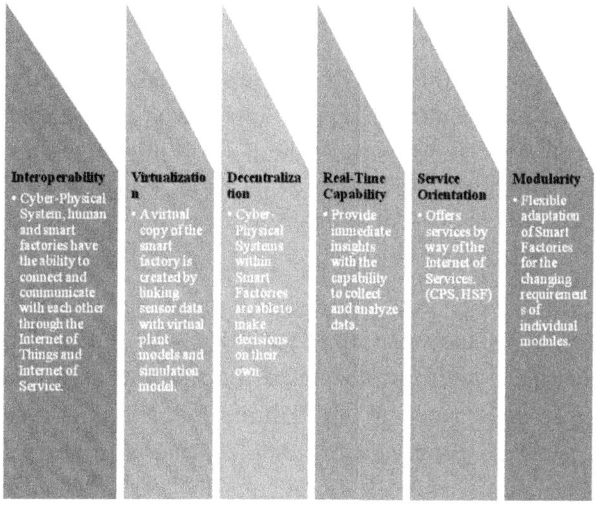

In this scenario, to gain useful insights, factory management must obtain the correct content of data and processes and develop tools and analytical algorithms to generate meaningful information. In Industry 3.0, for example, machines may predict system failures, trigger or monitor maintenance processes, organize logistics themselves, respond to unexpected behaviour or changes in production, and are networked. Manufacturing is now undergoing massive changes as one of the world's most important economic forces that will have a long-term impact on the methods and technologies used to produce things and the people involved. This leap will be much harder for many manufacturers, but significant key benefits will convince policymakers to begin the transition. Let us look at the industry 4.0 few design principles and the technologies they address as shown in Figure 1.

Interoperability

Interoperability means to the connectivity between machines and human beings, in a business or in the process to communicate, transferring / exchanging data, and co-ordinate and monitor activities over the IoS and IoT. This is the capability to connect every entity in anorganization, at any time, anywhere is essential to benefit from aperception provided by data to enhance efficiency and advancese processes.

If the product or system cannot exchange environmental data with other products or systems, then building new technology will provide the limited capacity to work with it. Similarly, the communication between man and machine remains restricted to straightforward and clear scenarios without interoperability.

Without connectivity, one may not ensure interoperability, so that as a first stage, industries essentially digitize their operations and procedures by utilizing cloud computing technique for the software services and data information storage. The next stage is to start with combiningan open-source platform and software into business operations and procedures (Luenendonk, 2019; Kiciński & Chaja, 2021). Accessing the open-source platforms to exchange of data between the system and business decreases the outlays. On information gathering and management, unnecessary replication and control of third-party applications as and when it is required. The connected databases, connected devices, communication techniques, people connected and communicated with machines using Internet, machines communicate with machines through networks, and all these will be considered as an Interoperability, i.e., Interconnection + Communication.

Virtualization

Virtualization is creating a virtual instance that simulates things with a real-world entity, e.g., Operating System, Server, Networking, etc. In Industry 4.0, virtualization refers to making a virtual copy of the real or physical world that monitors all the processes as humans handle it. While creating virtual copies of physical world objects, digital models will be created by collecting sensors and interconnected devices.

Decentralization

Decentralization is the concept where the systems can make their decision on their own. So, our CPS systems come with their set of decisions to perform dedicated functions or tasks assigned to them. Only in case of conflicting situations, interferences, or any failures concerning proposed goals will it be handled at a higher level. For the system's proper functioning, continuous assessment and tracking have to be done to get quality assurance (Kiciński & Chaja, 2021).

Real-Time Capability

It is the ability to collect, store and analyze data in real-time that allows making decisions immediately as per changes observed. With the help of the above principles, i.e., Interoperability, Virtualization, and Decentralization, we collect data in real-time. Then the analysis of data will be performed to find what's happening in the business, such as in production or manufacturing industries, logistics sectors, educational sectors, to improve their productivity (Kiciński, & Chaja, 2021). In general, to work with real-time data collection and storage, a cloud system is more advantageous since it provides data access faster at any time and anywhere with many embedded services.

Service Orientation

The system gives the production of products or services it should be customer-oriented rather than what industry/business wants to produce or serve the service. Real-time data analysis and interoperable systems (for collecting data) make it easier to find customers' current needs. Here the smart devices/object and people should be interconnected through the Internet of Services. This will provide the information about what customer exactly wants and their expectations, with the help of this industries/business adopting the changes to provide the personalized services to the customer. It is focused on customers rather than mass production. During finding customer needs, industry/business must identify and remove repeating and non-core tasks that can divert the focus on critical industry/ business functionality.

Modularity

With the changing environment or requirement in the business/industries, they have to modify new changes, which are essentials. It can be achieved in two ways; one is a business partitioned into small parts that will be focused on the particular task of business. The other is implementing modular systems that will make expertise in it to provide efficient products/services. This allows businesses/ industries to adopt dynamic changes as per market trends and better understand where we can improve efficiencies and optimize resources (Kiciński, & Chaja, 2021).

INDUSTRY 4.0 TECHNOLOGIES AND APPLICATIONS

Theprinciple idea behind implementing business 4.0 solutions is to empower producing firms to boost collaboration among varied departments, creating the correct information out there to the correct individuals on the real-time basis. The main goal is to simplify the applicable decision-building at the exact or correct time or point, thereby growing potency and production (Kiciński, & Chaja, 2021), (Arcot, 2021). Figure 2 describes the various sectors which involve Industry 4.0 technologies.

Internet of Things

With the history of IoT, the concept or term IoT was defined in 1999 by Kevin Ashton, although the actual implementation of connection between physical objects and the internet started between 2008 and 2009 (Pastas et al., 2022).

Figure 2. IoT and its Applications

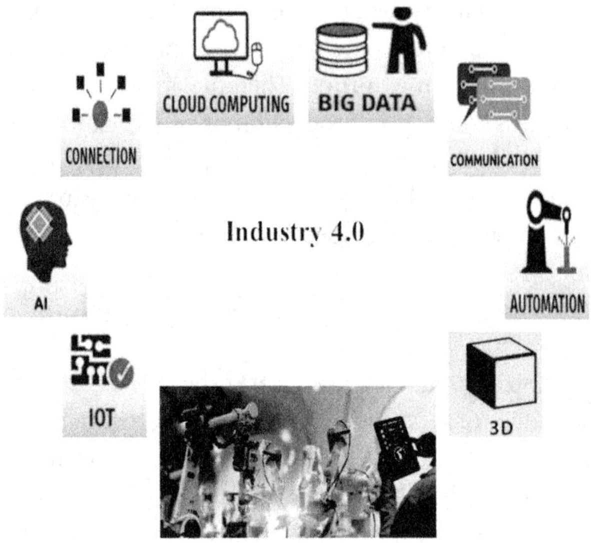

The term IoT refers to the network formed between physical objects using sensors, software, and other components to exchange or collect real-time data. These connected devices collect all data, which are further analyzed to take proper decisions to improve productivity, efficiency, services and many more (AMFG, 2019).

A wide range of applications uses IoT that can be broadly classified into commercial, consumer, industrial, manufacturing, and infrastructure. Here are some typical applications of IoT covered in brief, detailed in (Pastas et al.,2022) .

Industrial Applications (which also refers as Industrial IoT - IIoT)

It extends IoT by extending the working in Manufacturing, Supply Chain Monitoring, and Management systems. Using it will provide quick decision-making to reduce the time and money for repair and another failure.

Manufacturing

Manufacturing devices are interconnected IoT, allowing monitoring network control and management to run the manufacturing process smoothly.

Smart Home Application

In the current world, every electronic device will play a vital role in our life. IoT-enabled systems such as lighting, heating, conditioning, multimedia, security systems are part of Smart Home. These Smart devices or appliances are more often controlled by smartphones, tablets, laptops, or other devices without Wi-Fi connectivity.

Transportation

IoT provides tremendous application in the transport sector, such as traffic monitoring, smart parking, Toll collection, logistics, road safety, road assistance, and vehicle control. Using IoT systems, this vehicle to any/every communication (V2X) leads the automatic transportation connected with road infrastructure (Zalte et al.,2021).

Health Care (Internet of Medical Things - IoMT)

IoT can be used for various purposes; which collects data, analyzes it for research and patients' health monitoring? It is also referred to as the Smart HealthCare System, which provides real-time assistance by connecting to the resource provided by smart devices such as smartwatch that derives basic medical information of person based on their physical activity done daily. A digitized health care system monitors all patient data collected through the remote network to diagnose the diseases and find risk factors; some practitioners may use this data to apply algorithms for research finding and provide new findings to improve medical history. Furthermore, this system is used in the Health Insurance industry to track customer data and provide precise policy models to customers.

Environmental Monitory Systems

Various factors under the environment can consider where IoT-enabled systems work better to collect data. The collected data can be further used for monitoring natural disasters like earthquakes or tsunamis, which help in emergencies to save the life of living things and limit the damage of objects.

Big Data and Analytics

Big Data, the term indicates a tremendous and composite or complicated data collection done mainly through the Internet of Things (IoT) and the Internet of Services (IoS). The Big Data Analytics is the process of extracting valuable data, finding hidden patterns or uncovered data by analyzing unstructured or structured data that will be helpful for industries to make a different decision as shown in Figure 3.

Here data is considered structured, semi-structured, or unstructured because data collection is done from various points such as websites, sensors, cameras, smart applications, and much more, storing data in different formats and using different protocols (Davenport & Dyché, 2013). Using Big Data analytics software or tools, businesses/industries make data-driven decisions to improve the product or services related outcome. Faster and better decision making by industries/businesses leads to fulfilling customer needs, gains the higher profit, efficiency in operations/process, new product or services finding (AMFG, 2019).

Big Data Analytics will be used in various sectors to analyze data and improve the productivity of services or products by making faster decisions as shown in Figure 4. There are multiple areas where Big Data is used, but we will see some of them here (Cheung et al., 2019).

Figure 3. Important in Big DataAnalysis

Figure 4. Big DataApplications

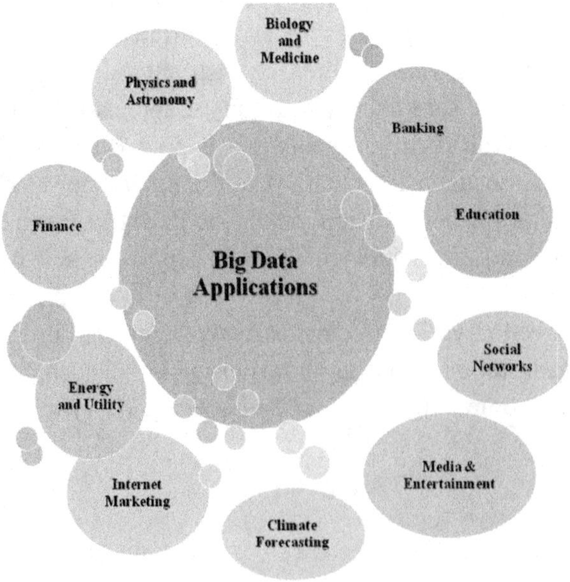

Banking and Securities

In the Banking sector, Big Data will be useful for monitoring the financial market activity. This analysis is used to find trade analytics for pre-trade decision support, predictive analysis, risk analytics – including money laundering, fraud mitigation (Cheung et al., 2019).

Education

These days to get a progress report of a student in education, the analysis is made based on how much time students use the resources, how actively participated in events, when he/she logs on to the system to access the resource. On the other end, Big Data is helpful to find effectiveness to ensures teachers' teaching skills, teacher's feedback, or performance can be measured based on many students, subject content, information delivery, and many more factors (Cheung et al., 2019).

Energy and Utility

The energy consumption was measured using an old meter that may recognize incorrect results, giving unexpected predictions. However, by using smart meters that provides operational data after some specific time interval opposed on it. The data collected by smart meters are further analyzed to get proper consumption and correct pricing of consumed data by industries/businesses/the public. That will be better to get improved feedback from customers and have control over the utility's usage (Cheung et al., 2019).

Simulation

The simulation techniques are well utilized in the operation to understand the information in real-time to copy the physical surrounding data into video games. This can embody machineries, merchandise yet similar to groups of people. It will provide an easier method for distinguishing the machinery at the threat just about beforehand getting it in reality, affecting smart quality (Mobinius, 2020).

Autonomous Robots

Though, robots are getting used during this time, not as extensively as they will be in later years. The robots can eventually upgrade into human action with them and work safely around humans. It will even have a lesser value and immense quality within the returning future (Mobinius, 2020). While advanced robots utilized in production for many years, Industry 4.0 has given new life to the current technology. With recent advancements in technology, a brand-new generation of advanced AI is rising, capable of acting challenging and delicate tasks. Powered by the latest code and sensors, they will recognize, analyze and affect data they receive from the setting and even collaborate and learn from humans.

One space of advanced robots gaining significant traction is cooperative robots ("cobots"), designed to figure safely around individuals, releasing employees from repetitive and dangerous tasks (AMFG, 2019).

As robots become lot autonomous, versatile, and cooperative, they will be ready to tackle many complicated assignments, relieving the employees from monotonous tasks and increasing productivity on the manufacturing plant floor.

Cyber Security

The goal of cybersecurity is vital in Industry 4.0 and concerns defensive structure parameters. It is very usually concerned with protecting a personal network. The strategies that want to stop breaches embody the utilization of firewalls, anti-virus and anti-malware software systems, IDS (intrusion detection systems) among others. Even though, this cybersecurity methods are turning a lot obsolete day by day, particularly in the industrial context. Industry 4.0 aims to reduce the boundaries between the digital and real or physical worlds.

With a property of knowledge on an outsized measure, there are continuous intimidations within the industrial software systems, to beat these intimidations, cybersecurity comes into the picture. It obeys the business protocol and provides knowledge precautions (Mobinius, 2020).

Cyber Physical System

Cyber-physical systems are sensible systems that embody designed interacting networks of physical and processing or computational parts as shown in Figure 5. These systems with an embedded software system (as a part of a devices, making, means that of transport, routes, production process systems, medical procedures, logistical processes, coordination-monitoring processes and management processes), which:

§ Directly record real physical information with the help of sensors and have an effect on real physical processes using actuators

§ Assess then save recorded information and activelyact each with the real/ physical and digital world

§ Systems are connected through internet networks via data communication features (wireless and/ or wired, native and/or global)

§ Use universally accessible information and service processes

§ They have a sequence of devoted, multimodal human-machine interfaces to interact and communicate.

The results of an association of the embedded system with the internet may be affluence of comprehensive solutions and an application for all parts of our daily life. Later on, innovative business choices and paradigms are developed based on a platform and an organization network (AMFG, 2019).

Cyber-physical systems are merely replacement generations of combining all three physical processes, computations, and networking. Internet and the physical world are integrated with the help of CPS. Cyber-Physical Systems (CPS) has a variety of applications within the following sectors: production, energy, infrastructure setup, communication, military, robotics, good buildings, healthcare, and transportation. Communications in the above systems happen using the internet network. It means that connectivity is provided using a standard set of protocols, specifically Internet Protocol (IP) and Transmission Control Protocol (TCP) (Ayuya, 2020).

For example, the Cyber-Physical System in Network Movement: the mobility section, i.e., transportation, intensive networking of the various field of transportation is the only possible victimization of CPS. This applies to individual vehicles and road users, in addition to the complete transportation infrastructure. Networking using cyber-physical systems creates a new method of avoiding or preventing accidents, use oflimited energy, and reducing pollution (Hellinger, & HSeeger, 2011).

Figure 5. Cyber-Physical System

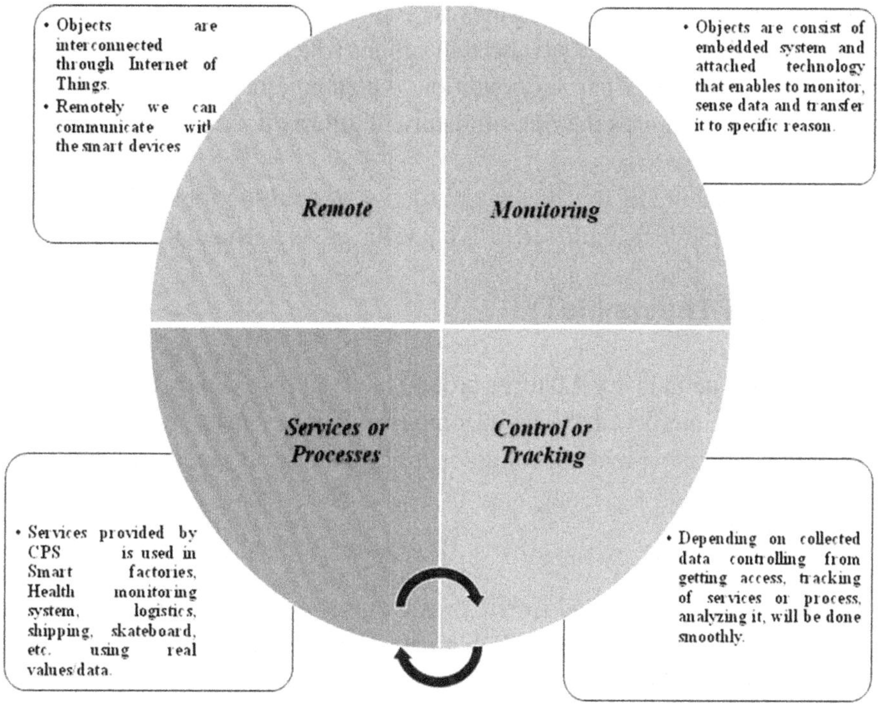

Artificail Intelligence

Artificial Intelligent is the science and engineering of making intelligent machines, brilliant computer programs (McCarthy, 2007). Artificial Intelligence transformed our lives because this technology is used in an extensive range of areas of everyday services. It is not regarded to develop machine slaves for rushing up to our work by fastening correct results by reducing human effort. On the contrary, it is a field of applied science that tries to simulate human intelligence and human capabilities with the assistance of machines, software, and our platforms. It uses digital technologies that have created us smarter and a lot of productive remodeling; however, we tend to communicate, learn, look and play. Advances in artificial intelligence give rise to computing systems that may see, hear, learn, and reason, making new opportunities to enhance education and health care, address poverty, and sustainable future. Artificial intelligence is taking part in a significant role in transportation service, Healthcare, Financial, Insurance, Retail, High-Tech, Telecommunications, Utilities, Energy Resources, production, Assembly manufacturing, Agriculture, Mining, client grocery, Social Services, and Construction (Gaikwad,2019)

Application areas for AI cover a huge spectrum considering e-Commerce by providing a recommendation engine for customers to engage in between browsing new products or customized filters applied for searches. A personnel chatbot/ shopping assistant will be provided to get more details about products or services. Based on digital transactions, fraud detection and prevention techniques are also implemented by using AI.

One More common example that all might be used that Navigation: GPS technology can give accurate, detailed, timely, and accurate information about places for which a search has been done. This navigation facility is primarily used in all transportation sectors to find out the person who books cab or products delivered by courier etc. Here AI may use various Neural Network algorithms to get the correct result.

AI is also used in healthcare to create advanced machines which will discover diseases and determine cancer cells. AI facilitates analysis of chronic conditions with laboratory and different medical knowledge to confirm early diagnosing. AI uses the mix of historical information and medical intelligence for the invention of the latest medicine.

Like this, AI can be used in HR for the hiring process, agriculture for finding defects and nutrient deficiency in the soil, automobiles to build self-driving vehicles, social media, marketing, and many more.

Industrial Internet of Things (IIoT)

Internet of Things (IoT) in an industry 4.0 turns around the featuresgiven by the technologies and types of machinery wherever an internet of things encompasses a major part. Machines produce work at a faster rate. It gives quick decision-making solutions for critical assets, advanced data analytics, etc.

Cloud Technology

For decades, makers are assembling and stored knowledge aiming to upgradethe data storing and accessing operations (Mobinius, 2020). Though, with the presence of an IoT and industry 4.0, a result is, knowledge will beproducedby staggering speed and huge volumes, creating it is not possible to handle manually, which creates a requirement for an infrastructure that may store, control and manage this knowledge efficiently. Cloud computing provides the facility to users, to store and manage huge amounts of knowledge on the remote servers (Zalte et al.,2022). It permits organizations to use computing services like servers, database storage, software, networking, etc. without developing a computing infrastructure on-premises.

Cloud computing is defined asthe data being kept on the "cloud" and it is accessed from anywhere via internet connections. Cloud scalability concerning cloud computing is the ability to control the growing or shrinking usage of resources to achieve the business demands as per the capacity of supply.

Augmented Reality

Augmented Reality may be considered a specific kind of technology that will put a computerized image on the top surface of the user's view in the real world, by making a composite view of the globe that merges the real (Reality) with one thing is not (the generated image). This technology has created its method into video games, testing things for extreme jobs, and now, it is in the user's pocket (Rasoo, 2018). Augmented Reality (AR) bridges the real-world entity and digital world entity. For instance, Augmented Realitymight be utilized with a physical toy/objectwith the help of an application on a tablet/ smartphone / smart device that canread or view or examines a real-world object (flashcard or image of a tiger). This scan can concern with a wealth of data about the thing in real-time. The ability of AR lies in creating a toy/object an interactive and immersive those will make a significant roleplay experience for youngsters (Goyal, 2018).

The world of augmented reality is rapidly advancing, and companies are beginning to notice this advancement happening around it. In the marketing sector, virtual reality technology will be used as, wherever everything a user sees could be a virtual atmosphere, AR augments a consumer's physical surroundings with digital elements. For instance, customers may use their phone to see; however, a settee may look in their lounge. The couch is digital; however, everything else is real. Augmented Reality may be with success accustomed build brands, generating client experiences, increasing conversion in online and brick-and-mortar retail environments, and style advertising campaigns that maximize client engagement and influence buying selections or choices (Titone, 2020).

With the ability to reinforce Reality and machines, AR is an excellent solution for companies wanting to modify instrumentation maintenance and increase their growth. Well-maintained machines or equipment help achieve three critical factors for producing goods: Cost, quality, and Product. So it will reduce the scrap and rework (Girish, 2019).

The distinction between augmented and virtual Reality is seemingly small, however necessary. Augmented Reality is tiny changes to the globe imposed on the real world. Simply pictures created to seem like they are somewhere they are not. a Virtual Reality, however, is a whole new 'Reality' created and meant to be used other than the real world (Rasoo, 2018).

Additive Manufacturing

Additive production has been started, and therefore the most used technology in its 3D printing is employed to create sample prototypes of the ultimate model beforehand to glance at what the result is going to be and what necessities square measure required (Mobinius, 2020).

Alongside artificial intelligence and intelligent systems, additive producing or 3D printing may be a key technology driving business 4.0. Additive producing works by mistreatment digital 3D models to make elements with a 3D printer layer by layer.

Within the context of business 4.0, 3D printing is rising as a valuable digital-producing technology. Once entirely a speedy prototyping technology nowadays, Additive Manufacturing offers an enormous scope of potentialities for producing from tooling to mass customization across just about all industries.

It allows elements to behold on as style files in virtual inventories, so they will be made on-demand and nearer to the purpose of want — a model referred to as distributed producing.

Such a decentralized approach to producing will cut back transportation distances, and therefore prices, similarly as change inventory management by storing digital files rather than physical elements (AMFG, 2019).

AFFORDABILITY ISSUES IN INDUSTRY 4.0 APPLICATIONS

Industry 4.0, the technologies gather factory data and surface knowledge, enabling manufacturers to identify the causes of problems that lead to poor quality and machine failures. Simply put, the answers lie in the data, and manufacturers can make better decisions through data analysis. The potential cost of this information to improve decision-making and support a data-rich digital production environment is enormous. Since the manufacturing businesses approach the execution of the 4thIndustrial Revolution, adaption and changes in planning, production planning, control system, and cost-accounting are needed in all departments. There is a general notion that the industry 4.0 paradigm is as much the future of manufacturing as the present, but the simple truth is that manufacturing will require the future.

However, there are various cost-efficient ways to turn these ideas into reality for those who wish to take their first steps towards Industry 4.0, for example by modernizing production lines. However, many industry players believe that while advanced industrial technology can provide valuable cost savings in the long term, it is also an expensive investment. The Industrial Manufacturing industry is expected to spend $175 billion on Industry 4.0 by 2020. Many manufacturers shy away from the imaginary costs and complexity of deploying "smart factories" that are more efficient, productive, flexible, and tailored to their factories "customers (Fauzdar et al., 2022; White). However, it is now increasingly realized that the Industry 4.0 technology enables cost reduction without having to lay off employees or implement drastic cost-cutting measures.

Industry 4.1 technology gives companies a competitive advantage over companies that do not use it. Manufacturers are running against time to gain a competitive advantage by investing in Industry 3.0. In the year 2007-09 Great Recession and the Global Pandemic of 2020 have made companies aware of the importance of planning and assessing technology spending to quantify returns, create a sustainable environment and promote efficiency and positive outcomes. Traditional financial accounting and reporting models were not designed for this task and cannot be defined. The digital age requires new approaches to financial decision support and modeling. In the backdrop of this, as we can imagine, we have to compromise between creating high-quality products and what is good in today's market, even if it is not the best. Industry 4.0 technology makes it cost-effective and easy to manufacture high-quality products. By introducing digital manufacturing solutions, you can reduce the cost of quality (COQ) and achieve a higher return on investment (ROI).In general, it is evidenced that Smart industrial plant managers struggling with outdated infrastructure and tighter budgets are looking for more cost-effective ways to modernize a growing number of competitors investing in the large Industry 4.0 factory architecture. Retrofit options can make an important contribution to better communication and optimized manufacturing, resulting in cost and energy-efficient results.

EFFECT OF GLOBAL PANDEMIC ON ADOPTION OF INDUSTRY 4.0

Research in many areas has shown that knowledge gaps exist when investigating the relationship between concepts such as collective creativity in connection with the Fourth Industrial Revolution. Digital tools developed since the advent of Industry 4.0 can equip manufacturers with the vigilance and resilience they need to recover from COVID 19 crisis and deal with other future incidents. Despite limited conceptual knowledge, they can help entrepreneurs face crises, trade disruptions, and external forces such as the pandemic. The primary aim of this study is to explain how collective creativity and Industry 5.0 technologies can be used to reduce the negative impacts of COVID and how local entrepreneurs can develop a framework for preparation. After the turbulence of spring and the rebalancing of the summer, companies are entering a period of deep uncertainty caused by the pandemic. Companies that survived the initial effects of pandemics now face difficult questions about their overall spread and resilience. The path to the future with the myriad technologies that Industry 4.0 provides is difficult. However, the uncertainty created by the COVID 19 pandemic has made the universe of viable options smaller and more manageable and the business models more evident. Supply chain managers who want to maintain the momentum of their Industry 4.0 efforts should look ahead despite the pandemic and have room to build compelling business models. With a confident view of future market margins, many companies are scaling back their capital investments. In the wake of the pandemic, a key trend is emerging towards developing technology-based platforms that combine supply and demand and disrupt existing industry structures as we see them in share-and-demand economies. Technology platforms that are easier to use by smartphones bring people, assets, and data together to create new ways to consume goods, services, and processes. There is a major shift on the demand side as increasing transparency in consumer engagement, new patterns in consumer behavior, and integrated access to mobile networks and data forces companies to adapt how they design, market, and deliver products and services. In this context, we are increasingly feeling that we are on the verge of a technological revolution that will fundamentally change the way we live, work, and interact. The COVID 19 pandemic is steering the world towards the next industrial revolution to create a society where 50% of the information cannot be processed without Industry 4.0 technology. The focus is on enabling sustainability in Industry 3.0 through the development and exchange of information between companies, machines and people. It paves the way for more ROI-based Industry 4.0 initiatives that focus on efficiency, such as automated trucks, logistics automation, co-bots, etc. The transformative effects of COVID-19 will be immense, but they will not all be negative. The inclusion of Covid-19 in society will have a positive impact on the development of industrial communities. New paradigms such as Society 5.0 and Medical 4.0are carved given the effects of the COVID 19 pandemic according to the considered and applied technological strategies. It has been demonstrated that the application of advanced information technologies, including AI, BD, information technology, IoT, and healthcare, Medical 4.00 stands for the application and support of microsystems of information technology, high-level automation, personalized therapies, artificial intelligence, and intelligent devices made possible by the Internet of Medical Things (IOMT) an offshoot of Industry 4.0 (Spiegel, 2021).

Thus, the impact and role of Industry 4.0 are increasing as the world goes into a new phase due to the Coronavirus Pandemic (COVID-19) 2019. A recent BDO survey of 100 manufacturers shows that the pandemic has accelerated adoption in industry 4.0. The survey shows significant changes in the manufacturing sector over the past year. At the time of the coronavirus outbreak, many people and companies were reluctant to implement Industry 4.0 technologies comprehensively because the capacities and framework conditions for these technologies were not perfect. It was a question of survival to innovate and try new ways of working to serve customers and stakeholders, which had not been adopted in the past for one reason or another. Recent digital tools and techniques have shown promising results in dealing with occurrences of infection. Digital companies have been able to manage their supply chains better than traditional companies. As individuals and businesses seek solutions, Industry 4.0 technologies will become an integral part of whether we survive the pandemic or not or whether we will exist in a post-pandemic world. Imagine we are living in our reality of 2020, rather than the 1980s, with connected devices, the ability to video conferencing, and artificial intelligence to support these efforts (Sarfraz, 2021).

URGENT NEED TO REFURBISH NATIONAL STRATEGIC POLICY FRAMEWORKS FOR GLOBAL ADOPTION OF INDUSTRY 4.0

Beyond automation and remote work, business models need to evolve, retrain and retrain workers. For countries such as South Africa, the manufacturing companies, the introduction of I40 will impact their workforce, so the learning experience is paramount. Innovation is achieved by implementing various strategies such as automating routine functions, providing time for creativity and problem solving, absorbing more content, introducing outsourced functions, leveraging the capabilities of the Industry 4.0 technology, focusing on technologies that expand people, and increasing competitiveness and productivity through internal retraining/retraining.

Various companies, organizations and governments encourage training as well as retraining tohelp people, to prepare for and avoid a dual-level work environment where some of the workers are ready for changes, and remainings are not. Individuals are essentialto take responsibility for their upgrading skills in development to remain competitive in a rapidly changing labor marketplace. The WEF predicts the need for an average of 101 days of retraining and retraining of workers by 2022, with some skills lasting up to five years and soft skills foreseen as the future skills that are irreplaceable due to AI, automation, and digitization. (Orsolya, 2019; Editorial team, 2020). This contradicts many current trends in education that promote specialization and generalization. To be at the forefront of this issue, people need an education that enables them to remain agile and make the most of their training initiatives. If on-the-job training is to be crucial to Industry 4.0, we need to change our approach to education.

Global influencers are forecasting an exciting change in the skills to fill innovativeroles as more companies adopt Industry 4.0 and automation strategies to raise productivity, diminish costs and advance a competitive advantage. Workers need to combine knowledge of specific processes such as working with robots and modifying apparatuses and machinery with IT skills ranging from essential spreadsheets and access to interfaces to more advanced and applied programming and analysis skills. The ideal initial point for assessing the skill gap is to decide what new roles it needs in the upcoming future. However, the employees must be ready to change, have great opportunities to adapt to new roles and working culture, and be used to continuous inter-disciplinary learning. To succeed in Industry 4.0, the employee needs to spread a variety of hard skills. The necessity of various hard skills and the extraordinary scale of change in the workshop mean that the soft skills will become increasingly significant. Technology and new working styles are the disruptors of the current crisis arising due to recession and challenges arising out of the adoption of new technology. The increase in automation and networkedsystems indicates the transformation or changes of the workforce. Manufacturers must attract tech-savvy talent and redeploy and redefine existing resources to connect the power of new disruptive manufacturing technologies. Thus, the fourth industrial revolution will affect the skills needed to create jobs. The resulting displacement and lack of talent will inevitably affect business dynamics and social cohesion, as automation affects the labor market.

The integration of technology leads to changes in business models and new types of jobs. Workers will have to adapt to a dynamic labor market, and businesses will have to figure out how to reconcile it with new jobs and roles. Organizations must take responsibility for firing their employees, rather employees must be eager to learn new skills no matter how many years they have expended in their existing roles. Upskilling is the best and only worthwhile option for organizations, employees, andsociety. Dismissing present employees simply because they do not have the essential and latest skills is not a solution. It is not acceptable that groups of unemployed struggle to feed them and for their families while fighting for a dignified life, this approach isn't feasible with the point of an economic, social or humanitarian. Investments can come from in-house training, digital learning programs such as Autodesk's free online course on generative design, MOOCs certifications on basic manufacturing processes, and online certifications in additive manufacturing, as well as innovative design and production. The message comes from technology giants and educational institutions and the manufacturing industry: SMEs and the Industry 4.0 ecosystem will enable companies to focus on current demand.

A small number of organizations dedicated to training and retraining are equipping their current workforce with the skills needed for production in the region. Japan is accelerating the education of young engineers by organizations such as Kojima Industries Corporation, an automotive supplier and one of Toyota's partner companies, and Technohama, its sister company that specializes in injection molding, and measurement of materials. Another strategy is to engage small businesses specializing in 3D printing, cobots, and collaborative robots to train employees. The Society 50 Plan a high level of skills that will enable Japanese citizens to promote future industries' development and strengthen the foundations of nations' research, technology, and innovation. The plan's new manufacturing capacity covers many areas, but we will continue to focus on manufacturing. Big data, the Industrial Internet of Things (IIoT), Artificial Intelligence (AI), and Robotics will be integrated into various production levels involving machines and processes. The future emphases on the key Industry 4.0 technologies, such as the Internet of Things (IoT), Big Data, Cloud Computing, Systems Integration, collaborative robots, modeling, and simulation.

INDUSTRY 4.0: FUTURE TRENDS AND CHALLENGES AHEAD

In the age of digital transformation, which is the ultimate goal for most companies, it makes sense for manufacturing technology to evolve and include automation and information and data exchange. Cyber-physical systems, augmented reality, Industrial Internet of Things (IoT), and cloud computing work in harmony with the limits Industry 4.0 sets for the factory environment. Many manufacturing companies that have already used Industry 3.0 technologies do not face these challenges. New challenges will arise as Industry 4.0 continues to transform how we interact with the world around us. Many companies are already struggling to succeed in adoption; according to Industry Week, for example, two out of three companies testing digital manufacturing solutions are making progress with large-scale rollouts. As the industry gathers to compete in tomorrow's world, technology companies will evolve.

As depicted in this chapter, Industry 4.0 refers to the new era of the industrial revolution that is going to be focus on networking, automation, machine learning and real-time data analysis. The Internet of Things (IoT) and networked machines and systems enable seamless data transfer between departments and workplaces and open up opportunities for new business models in manufacturing, computing, and many other industries. The industry includes IoT and smart manufacturing, which combine physical production with intelligent digital technologies such as machine learning with the help of big data to create a complete, interconnected environment for the companies which is focusing on manufacturing and supply chain management. Thus Industry 4.0 is the current trend in manufacturing technology by using complete automation and data exchange.

Technological challenges with the reference to Industry 4.0 include standardizing interfaces, improving autonomous decision-making systems, developing infrastructure around big data and strengthening cybersecurity. New regulatory challenges include creating new forms of governance around data security, ownership of new labor market activities, intellectual property, national security, digital currencies and bioethics. Socio-economic challenges include:

- § Avoiding the concentration of new technologies in a handful of companies,
- § Ensuring universal digital skills,
- § Developing workers' skills to meet new demands,
- § Monitoring the impact of changes in the labor market, with a particular focus on the inequality of income between men and women, and
- § Reducing the digital gender gap.

With a deeper understanding of how to harness the unique potential of Industry 4.0 technologies, we can begin to see how seamless integration, real-time communication, and the ability to create virtual, interchangeable, decentralized, and modular production environments have the potential to transform the industrial landscape. Take a closer look at some of the current trends and advancements in Industry 5.0 that will shape the months and years to come if we look at the bigger picture. In this backdrop, the present chapter presented the most essential best practices, challenges and opportunities related to the paradigm of Industry 4.0.

From the facts and figures depicted in this chapter, it can be concluded that to remain competitive, systems and processes must be in place to offer the customers and customers the same service they receive from companies like Flipkart, Amazon, etc. As the result, these companies are continuing to optimize logistics work and supply chain management needed to invest more in technological solutions that improve the processes. As technology has matured in recent years, more and more companies have realized that it is not enough to invest a lot of time and money in installing smart sensors and new systems and also to take the time to ensure that they are smart and strategic.

By 2020, we have witnessed that industrialization, digitization, and the development of nuclear technologies have been accelerated in key areas to strengthen competitiveness and reduce industrial pollution. The second stage, foreseen for 2025, will focus on improving the quality of all aspects and bringing information technology to an advanced level to reduce pollution to global standards, and Industry 4.0 will be a key enabler to achieve the same.

CONCLUSION

As reviewed in this chapter, the 4thIndustrial Revolution takes the automation of manufacturing processes to a new hipe by introducing tailor-made, flexible, and mass-production technologies. Rapid advances in information and communication technology (ICT) have broken down the limits between virtual reality and real-world entities. The chapter showcased that the Fourth Industrial Revolution is built on the digitization andautomation of factories, companies using the Internet of Things (IoT), and cyber-physical systems (CPS). These techniques are self-sufficient systems with the ability or capability to make self-decisions through machine learning, and by collecting the real-time data which is analyzed and stored in the cloud that is accessible from anywhere with the help of a network connection.

As exemplified in this chapter, Industry 4.0 is the digitization of the manufacturing, production, and related industries and value-added processes. It enables the use of components such as the Internet of Things (IoT), Big Data, Data Analysis, Augmented Reality (AR), Virtual Reality, Real World representation, Cybersecurity, collaborative robots (Crowd-powered), additive manufacturing, cloud computing, artificial intelligence, and 5G networks. Intelligent factories are not just about digitizing processes connected with efficient energy use, process optimization and reducing environmental pollution.

As covered in the introductory part of the chapter, the phrase "fourth industrial revolution", was used by the team of scientists who developed a high-technological strategy for the Government of Germany. The 4th Industrial Revolution (Industry 4.0) is the progressive automation of old way manufacturing and industrial processes using modern intelligent technologies. The term is often used alternatively with the "fourth industrial revolution" and denotes a new stage in an organization and the control of industrial value chains. Industry 4.0 is an information-intensive transformation of manufacturing and it's related industries into an inter-connected environment where huge amounts of data, people, processes, techniques, services, and systems (which are IoT) enable the creation of industrial assets and use the actionable data and information in a way that implies the realisation of a smarter ecosystem for industrial innovation and collaborative. Enabling a more direct model of personalised production and maintenance through the customer to consumer interactions, including an actual product used data in the real-time, decreasing inefficiencies, in-appropriateness and costs of inter mediators and digitized supply chain models is predictableto make the new customer-centric industry in terms of customer worth, speed, cost efficiency and value creation through innovative and attractive services.

A destructive effect on manufacturing companies is made possible by the paradigm of the intelligent production ecosystem based on Industry 4.0. Industrial plants can communicate with other machines and users, self-regulate and automate processes that require minimal human intervention, dynamic communication and control of automated modules in the workshop and on the market, generating a new manufacturing paradigm.

In the Large-scale, machine-to-machine communication (M2M) and the Internet of Things (IoT) will be combined into the industrial process to increase automation, improve communication, monitor production and deploy intelligent machines to analyze and diagnose problems without human intervention. It includes IIoT and smart manufacturing factories for combining physical production and operations with smart digital technologies such as machine learning and big data to create a completely connected ecosystem for businesses that are focused on manufacturing and supply chain management. Industry 4.1 is a turning point that puts an end to conventional centralized applications.

The chapter emphatically concludes that manufacturers will be forced to introduce technologies that support individualization, product development, sales, services, and more for meeting growing demand. If the technologies of the Fourth Industrial Revolution and Industry 5.0 are not adopted, companies will fall behind if their business is not digitized to compete with those of their competitors.

Industry 4.0 is unquestionably aninnovative approach for producing new techniques. Thought can force international manufacturers to a brand-new phase or stage of optimization and productivity. Not solely that, however customers will relish a brand-new level of in-person customizable products which will not be out there before. As stated as, higher than, the economical rewards are huge. However, there are several challenges present that require be handling or tackling consistently to confirm the sleek conversion. This is the main focus of huge firms and governments alike. Assertive analysis and experimentation in such fields is important. While assumptions relating to confidentiality, safety, and employment would like additional study, the general image is promising. Such a method to produce industry is revolutionary.

CONSENT FOR PUBLICATION

We, the author, the undersigned, give our consent for the publication of identifiable details, which can include a photograph(s) and/or videos and/or case history and/or details within this chapter to be published by Bentham Science.

CONFLICT OF INTEREST

We, the authors do not have any conflict of interest concerning research, authorship, and/or *publication*of this book *chapter.*

ACKNOWLEDGMENT

We, the authors want to thank all the Anonymous Reviewers, Publishers and Editors of this project for their speedy response.

REFERENCES

AMFG. (2019). *Industry 4.0: 7 Real-World Examples.* AMFG.

Arcot, R. V. (2021). *Cyber-Physical Systems: The Core of Industry 4.0.* Academic Press.

Ayuya. (2020). *Industry 4.0 and Cybersecurity.* Academic Press.

Cheung, K. S., Leung, W. K., & Seto, W. K. (2019). Application of Big Data analysis in gastrointestinal research. *World Journal of Gastroenterology, 25*(24), 2990–3008. doi:10.3748/wjg.v25.i24.2990 PMID:31293336

Davenport, T. H., & Dyché, J. (2013). Big data in big companies. *International Institute for Analytics, 3*, 1–31.

Fauzdar, C., Gupta, N., Goswami, M., & Kumar, R. (2022). MICMAC Analysis of Industry 4.0 in Indian Automobile Industry. *Journal of Scientific and Industrial Research, 81*(08), 873–881.

Gaikwad. (2019). *Artificial Intelligence And It's Impacts On Industry 4.0.* Academic Press.

Girish, R. (2019). *Augmented reality used to maintain equipment.* Academic Press.

Goyal. (2018). *What are Augmented Reality toys? How are they useful for children?* Academic Press.

Hellinger & Seeger. (2011). *Cyber-Physical Systems-Driving force for innovation in mobility, health, energy and production.* Acatech Position Paper.

Kiciński, J., & Chaja, P. (2021). Industry 4.0—The Fourth Industrial Revolution. In *Climate Change, Human Impact and Green Energy Transformation* (pp. 115–140). Springer. doi:10.1007/978-3-030-69933-8_10

Kovács-Ondrejkovic. (2019). Decoding Global Trends in Upskilling and Reskilling. Academic Press.

Luenendonk, M. (2019). *Industry 4.0 definition,Design,Principles,Challenges, and the Future of employment.* Cleverism.

McCarthy, J. (2007). *What is artificial intelligence?* Academic Press.

Mobinius. (2020). *Industrial Revolution 4.0: Top 9 Technologies in Detail.* Academic Press.

Pastas Pastaz, J. S., & Pujos Tualombo, J. F. (2022). *Estado del arte utilizando mapeo sistemático de la seguridad del internet de las cosas para infraestructuras en hogares inteligentes* (Bachelor's thesis).

Rasoo. (2018). *What is Augmented Reality in Smartphones?* Academic Press.

Sarfraz, Z., Sarfraz, A., Iftikar, H. M., & Akhund, R. (2021). Is COVID-19 pushing us to the fifth industrial revolution (society 5.0)? *Pakistan Journal of Medical Sciences*, *37*(2), 591. doi:10.12669/pjms.37.2.3387 PMID:33679956

Titone. (2020). *Brock augmented reality marketing*. Academic Press.

Zalte, Patil, & Tone. (2022). Edge Computing Technology: An Overview. *AJOMC*, 96-99.

Zalte, S. S., Patil, P. N., Deshmukh, S. N., & Kamat, R. K. (2021). Data Packet Security in MANET and VANET. *BBRC, 13*(15), 271-274.

Chapter 3
The Role of the Trucking Industry in the Pre-/Post-COVID-19 Environment for Modern Industries

Alan D. Smith
Robert Morris University, USA

ABSTRACT

Various economic, social, and environmental developments are converging to create an uncertain future for the U.S. trucking industry. These include, but are not limited to, the continuing truck driver shortage, an increased concern about environmental sustainability, and the industry volatility brought on partly by the effects of the COVID-19 pandemic, which includes consumers pivoting to online shopping in never previously seen before numbers. On the horizon, technologies, such as IoT and autonomous vehicle technologies, have the potential to provide supply chain managers with information and services needed to enact positive change and solve existing logistics problems. This chapter is an examination of the issues currently surrounding the trucking industry in the U.S., with a particular focus on the two compelling topics of the truck driver shortage and autonomous vehicle technology. For the purpose of context, two Pittsburgh-area trucking companies were examined to gain a better understanding of how small- to medium-sized trucking-based logistics companies are currently operating in this space.

INTRODUCTION

Covid-19, Trucking Industry

The trucking industry in the U.S. has been at a crossroads for some time. The global pandemic has laid bare many of its inequalities and shortcomings. Numerous economic, social, environmental, and technological developments are converging to create an uncertain future. The truck driver shortage continues, the rise of ecommerce as a result of the Covid-19 pandemic increased industry volatility.

DOI: 10.4018/978-1-6684-5250-9.ch003

Sustainability continues to be an issue for a global industry (Sharma & Joshi, (2018) that contributes over 23% of greenhouse gas emissions (Kite-Powell, 2020), with 5% produced by large and medium-weight trucks in Canada and the U.S. alone (Barla, 2010). Most notably, new technologies, especially IoT and autonomous vehicle technologies, are poised to further disrupt the industry but also provide supply chain managers with the tools needed to tackle existing issues, such as the current truck driver shortage and sustainability concerns.

Purpose

This research effort provides a scholarly examination of the current status of trucking in the U.S. and a discussion of driving forces that are affecting the industry, with a particular focus on the truck driver shortage and autonomous vehicle technology. Additionally, two Pittsburgh-area trucking companies were examined in order to gain a better understanding of how these macro industry forces are shaping small-medium sized trucking-based logistics companies. Pitt-Ohio is an example of a successful traditional trucking operation while Locomation is a technology start-up aiming to disrupt the current trucking industry through the introduction of long-haul autonomous trucking technology. Based on these analyses, a discussion of managerial implications is presented, which supply chain managers can use to improve trucking operations in the short and long terms.

BACKGROUND

Brief Overview of the U.S. Trucking Industry

Trucking is a global industry and a necessary component of almost all supply chains. While sea, rail, and air can move items to specified locations such as ports, stations, and airports, trucks have the flexibility to move items over both long and short distances to a wide variety of locations, including last mile delivery directly to the customer. Trucks can also move different quantities of goods ranging from a full truckload (FT) or truckload (TL) and less-than-truckload (LTL). Currently, the U.S. trucking industry is comprised of approximately 75,000 companies which includes smaller single location and larger multi-location entities. The combined annual revenue is approximately US$190 billion (Dun & Bradstreet, 2021). Recent changes in consumer behavior have altered demand. As a result of the Covid-19 pandemic, online shopping has increased while demand from struggling businesses has declined. As a result, more emphasis has been placed on LTL hauls, medium-duty commercial vehicles that are more flexible for short-haul, and last-mile transportation needs.

The U.S. trucking industry has been very competitive and, as with any sustainable business enterprise, profitability of these transportation companies depends on efficient management, cost containment, and operations. While larger companies can take advantage of account relationships, bulk-fuel purchasing, fleet size, and accessibility to drivers, small-medium compete by the ability of quick turnarounds, serving niche markets, and/or transporting irregularly sized goods. Net margins are very low at less than 1% while bankruptcies are common. Additionally, the industry is considered "fragmented" with the 50 largest companies only accounting for 40% of total revenue. Revenue and bankruptcies are correlated directly to the cost of fuel. Additionally, all companies in this industry must adhere to a variety of government regulations surrounding emissions, safety, the transportation of hazardous materials, and commercial trucker licensing. Despite these issues, the industry is projected to grow at a compounded rate of 7% annually for the near future (2020 - 2024). Technology in the form of the connected truck, which uses the interconnectivity of the Internet of Things (IoT) technology, as well as autonomous trucking technology, is expected to contribute to industry efficiency and sustainability.

Truck drivers are a very important component of the trucking industry. Drivers are required to have a commercial driver's license (CDL) and be properly trained. They must adhere to federal regulations, which determine hours-of-service (HOS). Employee turnover rates at trucking companies is typically high (Hossain & Hossain, 2018; Smith, 2020a). Currently, the U.S. is experiencing a driver shortage, which adversely affects U.S. trucking operations specifically as well as supply chains overall.

Introduction to the Problem

The unknown can be rather intimidating, especially whenever the prospects of what is to come sounds like it could potentially put hundreds of thousands of people out of work. Truck driving is the primary occupation in over 50% of the some of the individual states, so whenever autonomous trucking is mentioned, it can come with a bit of a negative connotation. Perhaps these concerns may be overblown as there is room for much innovation and technologic improvements in the trucking industry. There is already a large shortage of truck drivers across the U.S., and this shortage is primarily concentrated in the long-haul sector of the industry. The autonomous trucks will first take hold in this sector of the field, which actually means that a large portion of the routes that will become autonomous were being unfilled anyways.

Traditionally, two-thirds of all goods in the U.S. are shipped via truck (Washburn, et al., 2021). Working on autotomizing this massive industry is going to take decades (and for some sectors it may never get there). However, autonomy for some standardized routes will pay massive dividends whenever they are able to work, especially in risk reduction (Franca, et al., 2010; Gaudenzi, et al., 2006; Goh, et al., 2007; Kumar Dadsena, et al., 2019). It was estimated that autonomy will bring operating costs down by a staggering 45%, or roughly 85-125 billion US$ (Kumar Dadsena, et al., 2019). Of course, these new toys will cost a pretty penny to bring into the fleet, so the balance sheet will begin to look different as well, with a substantial drop in operating costs, but an increase in capital expenditures.

The inevitable wave of advancement is slowly but surely making its way through each and every aspect of life whether it is welcomed or not. The trucking industry will be no different. Data and analytics have already begun to shape the way decisions are being made and the way transportation routes are being designed and implemented (Gothwal & Raj, 2018; Hossain & Hossain, 2018; Jain & D'lima, 2018). Constant improvement is on the forefront of everybody's mind, and the trucking industry will be no different.

Truck-Driving Jobs: Are They Headed for Rapid Elimination?

As mentioned in the introduction, the common connotation that comes along with the growing reality of automation (Giannakis & Papadopoulos, 2016; Goel & Irnich, 2016; Gouda & Saranga, 2018; Govindan & Chaudhuri, 2016), is certainly one of negativity in regards to the possibility of losing truck-driver jobs. However, the above case study attempts to fully investigate this assertion, and get to the bottom of exactly how the impending growth of automation in the trucking industry will impact the number of truck driving jobs available. The argument posed by this study is that the automation of the trucking industry will not dramatically eliminate jobs for three primary reasons. In support of this proposition, the actual number of drivers working today is greatly inflated due to occupational classification system in federal statistics. Next, the actual occupation of truck driver includes far more than just driving. Lastly, automation stands to really only take hold of the long-haul aspects of the trucking field (at least initially, not concentrating on the last-mile operations at they are still very complex and personalized). The large majority of trucking routes that remain unfilled are in this sector, which means that a large portion of the routes that will be filled due to automation are going largely unfilled anyways.

First, the reasoning for why the number of drivers is inflated must be explained. The federal statistical system relies on uniform classification systems for industry and occupational surveys of households and establishments. Many articles claim that the number is close to three million, however according to the article, there are far fewer. The reason for the ambiguity is the way that occupations are classified. The actual group classification name is "Driver/ Sales Workers and Truck Drivers." This actually covers three separate occupational codes. This count does not include self-employed owner-operators, which is estimated to make up about 10-25% of all heavy truck drivers. Due to these classification discrepancies, the estimated number of truck drivers is somewhere closer to two million, rather than three.

The second factor is the simple fact that the occupation of truck driver does not simply entail of 100% driving. Autonomous technology can substitute for certain tasks that a driver will need to complete throughout their day, of course, but not every task can be explicitly programmed. Using the Occupational Requirements Survey (ORS), these tasks can be analyzed. The ORS collects elements in four separate categories: educational, experience requirements, mental and cognitive demands, physical demands, and environmental working conditions. The data used for this analysis was collected from May 2015 to July 2017 and contains roughly 48,000 observations. The five most engaged in tasks for drivers that do not include driving are: freight handling, safety, equipment operation, paperwork, and customer service. These activities will require much more time to become automated than the driving part of the job. The most important activity that stands out from this group is the safety aspect. Sensors can detect whenever tire pressure may be low, but to actually fix the problem, human intervention is required. Of course, the most important factor when deciding if fully automated trucks will be able to be on the road is going to be safety. Are they going to be able to detect whenever a small car is going to cut them off to get to their exit?

The third factor that is listed is that the type of truck driving job is quite important to the story. There is a shortage of drivers across the country for all types, yes, however whenever a deeper look is taken at the situation, there is a concentration in a certain field of the industry. The long-haul routes within the industry are where a large majority of the shortages can be found, due to the simple fact that these are the routes that can be most taxing for drivers. Along with new restrictions on hours, these jobs are flat out becoming less and less desirable, but at the same time, even more important. The autonomization of the trucking industry will come in waves as mentioned earlier, but the wave of complete autonomization will first crest at the long-haul sector of the field. These routes that are having trouble being filled anyways will begin to be filled by autonomous trucks, which in the long run will actually ease some of the burden felt by overworked drivers.

To bring these concepts together, ultimately, nobody knows exactly what the future holds, the best way to make decisions about the future is to take the information that is available at the time and use that to form a conclusion. Using the information displayed in this analysis, we can conclude that no, not all truck drivers are going to lose their jobs to automated trucks within the decade. The actuality of the situation is that there will be a specific subset of drivers that will be impacted by the automated trucks.

Some drivers will undoubtedly be displaced and lose their jobs, but it will not be a mass elimination of the truck driving occupation. This is the way of the world, technology does not stop for anybody, and it will certainly not stop on the open road either.

CASE STUDIES

Overview

Considering the vital role trucking plays in the supply chain and the challenges the industry currently faces, it is necessary and helpful to examine real world scenarios in order to better understand how these challenges can be overcome. Below, two local companies, one traditional and one modern, will be examined to see how they have handled the current situation as well as how they can improve their operations to adapt to future trends in the industry.

Company Description: Pitt-Ohio

Founded in 1979 by three brothers, Chuck, Bob, and Ken Hammel, Pitt-Ohio started as a simple company with three trucks and a one-door warehouse in East Liverpool, Ohio. Their primary route was transporting less than truckload (LTL) shipments between Ohio and Pittsburgh, Pennsylvania which led to the naming of Pitt-Ohio Express. Pitt-Ohio Express quickly built a reputation for outstanding customer service—winning its first of forty-one Quest for Quality Awards from Logistics Management Magazine in 1993—as well as prompt and precise delivery, becoming the first regional carrier to offer an expedited service in 1999 while maintaining a 98% on-time delivery record (*History of Pitt-Ohio*, n.d.).

By the early 2000s, Pitt-Ohio Express had expanded its footprint into Illinois, Indiana, Kentucky, Maryland, Michigan, New York, North Carolina, Virginia, and West Virginia. Additionally, Pitt-Ohio Express had acquired a partnership interest in ECM Transport giving it access to another 300 tractors and 1,200 trailers. On top of that, it joined five other carriers to form The Reliance Network which spans all of North America. As a result of this growth, Pitt-Ohio Express was no longer just an LTL company. In 2011, Pitt-Ohio Express officially changed its name to Pitt-Ohio "to better reflect the transportation solutions provider it has evolved to" but it still maintained its commitment to its core services of supply chain management, ground transportation, LTL and truckload (TL) (History of Pitt-Ohio, 2021).

Company Description: Locomation

Pittsburgh-based start-up Locomation was founded in 2018 with the intention of relieving trucking industry strains as a result of the increased demand for truck freight and the driver shortage. Comprised of colleagues from the prestigious Carnegie Mellon National Robotics Engineering Center (NREC), Locomation's technical team has an extensive understanding of autonomous vehicles and artificial intelligence (Locomation - About, 2021). As essentially one of the world's largest and leading robotics R&D center, the NREC has given Locomation founders the opportunity to cut their teeth developing government and commercial concepts, with some career highlights including working on the U.S. Army Autonomous Ground Resupply contract and winning the DARPA Urban Challenge, a 60-mile test course race for fully autonomous vehicles. Currently working with Wilson Logistics, Locomation's initial phase of autonomous trucks is a convoy style system where a manned vehicle will be followed by an unmanned drone though future goals include fully autonomous driving (Rosenblatt, 2021).

Supply Chain Operations

Supply Chain Operations – Pitt-Ohio

Throughout its evolution, as Pitt-Ohio has expanded its services, it has always viewed these expansions through the lens of its company's commitment to its customers, employees, sustainability, safety, and security. Even at its inception, Pitt-Ohio has been committed to building long-term, customer-centric partnerships through the help of its most valuable resource, its employees. These services started out as regional LTL shipments but have since expanded to TL shipments as well while offering consultive services to increase supply chain efficiency.

Just recently, Pitt-Ohio has begun a new venture, warehousing and distribution services. Utilizing and combining several supply chain operations grants Pitt-Ohio a competitive advantage against other companies unable to offer all of these services and its customers with a consolidated point of contact for all of their logistics needs. With warehouse and distribution centers strategically located next to Pitt-Ohio terminals, they are able to offer next day delivery up to 250 miles from the following cities even with a notice late in the day: Cleveland, OH, Grand Island, NE, Pittsburgh and Harrisburg, PA, Indianapolis, IN, Rock Island, IL, and Roseville, MN. As a result, its customers in these service areas can combat common supply chain problems that occur due to forecasting uncertainty and lack of suitable warehousing space. Now clients can better handle demand surges without the need for unnecessary safety stock on hand. It grants them the flexibility to receive either finished goods or raw materials just as they are needed. Also, it passes the inventory management function on to a different channel participant. While there are costs associated with this service, it can lead to greater efficiencies as it allows the customer to focus on their core competencies which are not likely warehouse management. Reducing or eliminating these activities for the client can have secondary cost savings and result in better overall inventory management (Berman, 2021).

Supply Chain Operations – Locomation

Locomation's supply chain operations specialties differ from Pitt-Ohio's but they are equally as important. Primarily, the adoption of autonomous trucking can help the industry manage costs and create a competitive advantage through material handling functions. Achieving these costs savings and competitive advantages is a two-pronged strategy. First, the average truck driver in Pennsylvania makes an annual base salary of US$68,035 according to Indeed.com which is based off of 19,100 reported salaries. This figure is 10% higher than the national average (*How much does ...*, 2021). Second, autonomous convoy relays can create fuel efficiencies that would be challenging and unsafe to try to achieve with two manned vehicles. Because the drone truck can operate much closer to the lead, manned truck, better aerodynamics are created which means a fuel cost savings which can reduce the total cost of ownership of each truck by 1% (Chottani, et al., 2020). Focusing on these analytical factors is key to managing costs for logistics companies that Locomation partners with. Based on certain elements of the case analyses, Pitt-Ohio and Locomation have many complementary operations. A very basic summary comparison of their supply chain operations can be found in Table 1.

Table 1. Comparison of supply chain operations (Pitt-Ohio and Locomation).

Pitt-Ohio Operations	*Locomation Operations*
Supply Chain (Ground Logistics) Trucking (TL and LTF) Warehousing and Distribution	Material Handling Data Analytics Cost Management

Supply Chain Problems

The U.S Bureau of Labor Statistics indicated that in 2019 there were 2,029,000 heavy and tractor-trailer drivers (*Heavy and tractor-trailer truck ...*, 2020). While that may seem substantial, the stark reality is that it is not. In 2018, the trucking industry "was short roughly 60,800 drivers, which was up nearly 20% from 2017's figure of 50,700." If the current trends hold true, over the next decade, the trucking industry will need to hire an additional 1.1 million drivers to meet demand. The nation's highways account for 71.4% of all freight tonnage (Costello & Karickhoff, 2019) and that volume is only expected to increase as the American Trucking Association anticipates volume to grow 36% by 2031 (McNally, 2020). Additionally, the median age of all truck drivers is 46 compared to 42 for all U.S. workers and that some sectors of the trucking industry such as private fleet drivers have a median age of 57 years old. Add in the requirement that the current age to drive a tractor trailer across state lines is 21 years old and a situation arises where the average age of a new driver being trained is 35 years old (Costello & Karickhoff, 2019). What this means is that an already underserved industry is facing an increase in demand coupled with a reduction in supply.

Driver turnover in the industry continues to be an issue. While it was originally feared that this would have safety implications, research shows that high rates of turnovers do not have a linear correlation with high rates of safety issues, which is a good thing (Miller, et al., 2017), but what these high-turnover rates mean from a managerial perspective is that while a driver shortage exists, this issues becomes extrapolated by the fact that turnover in the industry is a result of churn amongst fleet operators. Because of this shortage, operators are continually poaching drivers from other operators with enticements of various sign-on bonuses, potential for higher wages, more modern trucks and equipment enhancements, and preferred routes (Costello & Karickoff, 2019). Management at Pitt-Ohio prides the company's reliance on shorter routes so that more truckers can be with family at nights. Of course, with warehouse utilization at near capacity (Maiden, 2021), this may be a more difficult option to quarantine for all short-haul drivers. All of these factors result in increased costs from an operator's standpoint.

Another issue facing the trucking industry is that of sustainability. Again, accounting for over 70% of all freight tonnage moved in the U.S., doing that in a way that minimizes one's carbon footprint is not only environmentally responsible but also fiscally responsible as well. This usage accounts for the annual consumption of over 50 billion gallons of fuel and the emission of 402 million tons of CO_2 (Carbon War Room, 2012). In North America, medium and heavy-duty trucks are responsible for producing 5% of the total greenhouse gas emissions (GHG) in the entire world and the rate with which GHG emissions by trucks are increasing is twice that compared to total emissions (Barla, 2010).

These problems together pose a serious threat to an essential industry. A need exists for more drivers and more sustainable practices. Driver wages, bonuses, and benefits are the greatest expense for motor carriers, accounting for 43% of the costs per mile with fuel consumption coming in second at 24%, and both costs are expected to increase. Though fuel costs do not contribute as proportionally to total costs as they once did, as more fuel is consumed, the total cost will climb (Murray & Glidewell, 2019). Steps need to be taken to find alternative solutions to the shortage of drivers as well as the consumption of nonrenewable energy.

Supply Chain Solutions

Supply Chain Solutions - Locomation

Focusing first on the driver shortage issue, Locomation, by design, is built specifically to address this problem. In its current state, each truck in the relay convoy has a driver though the lead truck acts as the master. While this does not inherently address the driver shortage problem, what it does currently address is issues surrounding driver regulations. Federal regulations limit drivers to 14 hours per day with only 11 of those hours allowed for active driving (Federal Motor Carrier ..., 2020). By no means should those regulations be reduced, but what Locomation's current setup allows is near round the clock transportation. As the technology matures, the drone truck's driver would be able to get their required rest while the master truck's driver operates the convoy. Once the master truck's driver reaches his daily limit, the drivers can switch off rather than stopping for the day.

Because it is still in its infancy, Locomation cannot make the driver shortage problem go away overnight, but its next goal is to eliminate the need for a secondary driver in the drone truck. While this again results in issues with federal driving regulations, it will help curb the increased demand for drivers. Now one driver can transport twice the cargo it was once capable of, therefore anyone employing Locomation technology essentially doubles their workforce without incurring additional costs for drivers. This can be substantial considering that drivers' costs account 43% of the costs per mile (Murray & Glidewell, 2019). With time, Locomation's ultimate goal is to have completely unmanned fleets though they have no specific timeframe for when that goal can be achieved.

Supply Chain Solutions – Pitt-Ohio

Turning to sustainability, in the past decade, Pitt-Ohio has turned its attention to reducing its carbon footprint. In October 2014, Pitt-Ohio opened the first LEED Gold Certified trucking terminal in Western Pennsylvania and in May 2017, received its second LEED Gold certification for a newly constructed Pittsburgh terminal. In all, Pitt-Ohio has 5 LEED Certified buildings (Sustainability – Green Fleet ..., *2021*). Through the use of recycled building materials, low flow faucets and waterless urinals, and solar panels and vertical wind turbines, Pitt-Ohio has helped achieve its focus on people, planet, and profit (3 Ps). Pitt-Ohio's concerted efforts to increase sustainability does not stop at its terminals though. They have achieved a 20% reduction in carbon emissions through various techniques including technological innovations in integrated engine components, switching to compressed natural gas in some vehicles, diesel exhaust fluid system implementation in select vehicles, and converting to electronic forklifts instead of fossil fuel powered (Cybator, 2017). All of these sustainability efforts have resulted in them receiving numerous recognitions including the SmartWay Excellence Award from the U.S. Environmental Protection Agency, the Inbound Logistics Top Green Supply Chain Partner, the Top Green Fleet by Heavy Duty Trucking, and a Supply & Demand Chain Executive Green Supply Chain awardee (History of Pitt-Ohio, 2021).

Many of Pitt-Ohio's efforts are taken in their terminals, and while the steps they have taken to reduce their environmental impact are admirable, further steps could be taken, largely with the help of Locomation. Autonomous vehicles are expected to improve transportation efficiency as a whole, but the benefits that impact commercial transportation in particular include the reduction of roadway congestion, better aerodynamics especially for highway driving, and smoother driving operation which increases fuel efficiency. In 2014, it is estimated that 3.1 billion gallons of fuel were wasted in the U.S. as a result of sitting in congestion. Overall, platooning typically leads to better aerodynamics and can save an estimated 3-25% in fuel consumption (Williams, Das, & Fisher, 2020). Lastly, monitoring driving speed can help increase fuel efficiency. Currently speed governors and cruise control are used to maintain efficient driving speeds. Operators that set predetermined speed governors on their trucking fleet encounter almost one MPG fuel efficiency improvement (from 5.6 MPG to 6.4 MPG) (Murray & Glidewell, 2019). As fully autonomous vehicles become available, these limitations can be programmed so that these trucks operate at the most fuel-efficient level.

No one person or organization is going to correct the issues facing the trucking industry. Pitt-Ohio has taken efforts to reduce their carbon footprint but that is just one company. Locomation has the technology to combat the driver shortage problem as well as sustainability issues, but trucking companies need to adopt the use of the technology. Where the greatest implications can occur is when partnerships form between organizations such as Pitt-Ohio and Locomation so that the future of trucking can be observed from different perspectives and a collaborative approach can be taken to make the industry more efficient, sustainable, and profitable.

MANAGERIAL IMPLICATIONS

Supply Chain Challenges

In order to thrive in the changing trucking industry, supply chain managers must meet current challenges but also focus on efficiency and sustainability for future success. Current challenges include maintaining supply chain agility by continuing to adjust to a highly volatile Covid/post-Covid shipping environment as well as protecting against the driver shortage. While managing these issues, supply chain managers must also look for and create opportunities to increase operating efficiency, which includes the adoption of technologies, and achieve higher levels of sustainability.

Uncertainties Associated Covid-19 Impacts

Like most industries, the trucking industry has been uncertain during the Covid-19 pandemic. Online shopping and other ecommerce are on the rise. In the last quarter of 2020, consumers spent US$245.28 billion in online shopping. This was a 31.2% increase over the same period the previous year (Young, 2021) and proved overwhelming for many supply chain channel members, which led to significant bottlenecks and delays (Murphy, 2020). However, other industries, such as restaurants, retail stores, etc. have suffered and, as a result, slashed transportation demands (Trinity Logistics, 2020). Post-Covid could see a sharp increase in transportation demand as previously closed businesses come back online before settling into a "new normal." However, experts predict that "digital shopping is here to stay" and current customers report they will continue online shopping post-pandemic (Charm, et al., 2020). Supply chain managers must, therefore, remain adaptable to the changing competitive terrain in order to be successful. This may include, but is not limited to, complete restructuring management's orientation and performance model towards smaller pockets of growth that are greater profit potential in the near future by shifting now to take advantage of those smaller venues of opportunity faster than their competitors (Arora, et al., 2020).

The shortage of qualified truck drivers was an issue pre-Covid (Costello & Karickhoff, 2019) and the pandemic exacerbated the issue with a 4.4% decrease in drivers from June 2020 - November 2020 (Cassidey, 2020). Truck drivers are a necessary part of the motor transport supply chain. While autonomous vehicle technology is in its infancy and expected to have a paradigm shifting impact on motor vehicles, it is not yet available and might not be for years to come. Additionally, once the technology is adopted, truck drivers will still be needed to oversee larger autonomous highway vehicles, manually operate both the drones and autonomous vehicles (when they are off-highway), as well as manually operate the traditional last-mile vehicles (Gittleman & Monaco, 2020). As a result, managers must find ways to recruit and retain drivers despite the shortage, if they want to remain in business now and be successful long-term strategy. Possible ways to accomplish this include, but are not limited to, adopting an hourly pay model over the traditional per-mile pay model, creating financial incentives for drivers reaching fuel efficiency and safety goals, and providing more benefits (RTS Financial ..., 2020).

Renewed Focus on Efficiency

Longer term managerial strategies for continued success focus on efficiency and sustainability. As supply chains increasingly become more global in nature, companies that have more control over more aspects of their supply chain are able to better implement efficiency changes, which save costs and benefit customers. Pitt-Ohio's recent expansion into warehouses and distribution centers is a good example of how trucking companies can claim additional margins by taking on the responsibilities of other channel members and also better serve their customers as a result.

Companies that control large portions of the supply chain are able to better plan for efficiency. They can adjust transportation routes and better schedule intramodal transfers, which allow the companies to move items more quickly through the supply chain while using less fuel and labor. By making trucking less labor intensive, supply chains would be less vulnerable to driver shortages. When companies control more aspects of the supply chain, they can incorporate more flexibility and adaptability, which allows the supply chain to adjust more easily to external forces, such as weather. Additionally, companies who control the supply chain are able to better implement technology seamlessly along the entirety of the supply chain. For example, companies can utilize AIDC technologies more effectively, if the same technology is used throughout an item's movement through the supply chain process and . This would provide both the company and the customer with real-time, accurate item location data, which quickly alerts all stakeholders to any issues, allows the supply chain managers to quickly mitigate the situation, and creates customer value. The same can be said for sensors and other IoT technologies on connected trucks as well as the associated data analytics, which supply chain managers can use to better understand what is occurring during transport and make improvement via data-driven decision-making. Already, some third-party logistics (3PL) firms similar to Locomation have found that "new routing powered by connectivity and analytics can produce efficiencies up to 25%" (Chottani, Hastings, Murnane, & Neuhas, 2018). In order to accomplish this, managers must be open to partnering with and/or acquiring other supply chain channel members and logistics companies in order to gain the expertise needed to gather data, understand patterns, and make the changes needed to increase efficiency.

Sustainability

Another driving force of supply chain management is sustainability. Through efficiency and technology, the trucking industry will become more sustainable. While trucking's adverse impact on the environment has been known for over a decade (Barla, 2010) and the industry has responded, there is still much work to do in this area. Pitt-Ohio is a good example of this. The company has made great strides in applying sustainability principles to their LEED certified terminals, but has yet to apply the same innovative thinking to their transport activities. Locomation's fuel sensor technology would be a potential avenue for Pitt-Ohio to start analyzing transportation data in order to make sustainable changes in their trucking activities.

Sustainability is not only an ethical goal, this is also a solid business practice. Through the use of technology and innovative lean thinking, supply chain members are able to become more efficient, use less fossil fuels, and produce less CO2, which, in addition to being good for the environment, is a cost-savings (Kim, et al, 2011; Kroes & Ghosh, 2010; Laroche, et al., 2001; Mainieri & Barnett, 1997; Sahu, et al., 2014). Many eco-friendly consumers are demanding business use more sustainable business models and are scrutinizing supply chains as a result (Sharma & Joshi, 2018; Smith, 2020a, 2020b). Supply chain managers in the trucking industry must make sustainability a priority to ensure future success. They can decrease their company's environmental footprint in a number of ways including, but not limited to, the use of alternative fuel vehicles (AFVs), using full truckloads (FTL) thereby reducing empty miles, investing in autonomous vehicles, and using IoT technology for maximum efficiency (Sporrer, 2020).

One area of expertise traditional trucking managers will need to somehow acquire is autonomous trucking technology. This burgeoning technology has the potential to help supply chain managers increase supply chain efficiency, address the current truck driver shortage, and achieve sustainability goals. While the true implementation of this technology is projected to be years in the future, the potential of this technology is game-changing. Traditional trucking companies, such as Pitt-Ohio, would be advised to partner with technology companies working in this arena such as Locomation, in order to ensure long-term profitability and success. The following comparison table (Table 2) shows the overlap between each company's operating strategies and illustrates the potential for collaboration.

GENERAL CONCLUSIONS

Uncertainty is present both in the current U.S. trucking industry and its near future. The financial impacts of the Covid-19 pandemic, a sustaining truck driver shortage, the meteoric rise of online shopping, and concern over global CO2 emissions all contribute to a general state of unease. However, with all of this uncertainty comes opportunities for growth for supply chain managers willing to make the changes needed in order to ensure an efficient and sustainable supply chain. While supply chain goals of efficiency and sustainability are lofty, new and potential disruptive technologies are emerging that can assist managers in reshaping their operations to thrive in this new environment. Current connected truck IoT and future autonomous vehicle technologies will allow managers to better assess the current supply chain, use data analytics to make efficiency improvements, and operate in ways that decrease dependence upon human labor and fossil fuels, which address both the driver shortage and trucking's large environmental footprint. Finally, implications and recommendations are presented, which supply chain managers can use to improve trucking operations now and prepare for the future.

Table 2. Comparison of operating strategies and recommendations

Operational Strategy	*Pitt-Ohio (Current Operating Strategies)*	*Pitt-Ohio (Recommendations for Future Initiatives)*	*Locomation (Current Operating Strategies)*	*Locomation (Recommendations for Future Initiatives)*
Efficiency	Expanded control over supply chain activities to include warehousing and distribution centers Must abide by trucking regulations, which include how long a trucker can drive before resting.	Continue to investigate opportunities to gain more control over the supply chain	R&D autonomous truck technology	Partner with local companies, like Pitt-Ohio to implement the technology via the autonomous truck retrofit
Sustainability	LEED certification for terminals	Route planning for less fuel consumption	Current IoT technology captures data, which allows traditional trucking companies like as Pitt-Ohio, make route adjustments that lower fuel consumption	Future autonomous truck technology would allow traditional trucking companies like Pitt-Ohio to move more freight using less fossil fuel.
Technology	Standard trucking and warehousing technology including the use of AIDC technology. No evidence of IoT technology use.	Partner with technology companies such as Locomation to implement their IoT and autonomous driving technology to achieve greater efficiency and meet sustainability goals	R&D for autonomous trucking technology	Partner with local companies, like Pitt-Ohio to implement the technology via the autonomous truck retrofit

FUTURE RESEARCH DIRECTIONS

The mini-case studies of Pitt-Ohio and Locomation illustrated how small-medium trucking-related companies are making significant changes in these areas but will have to continue to innovate and potentially partner in order to thrive. The managerial implications of this analysis include making short-term adjustments to enquirer the Covid and post-Covid environments as well as making long term investments in technologies that will help managers achieve supply chain efficiency and sustainability in the long-term. There will eventually be a post-Covid environment and much research needs to examine these new normal realities. Both practitioner and academic research initiatives will be need to unravel its mysteries.

REFERENCES

Arora, S., Murnane, J., Bhattacharjee, D., McConnel, S., & Panda, A. (2020). *US freight after COVID-19: A bumpy road to the next normal.* McKinsey & Company. Retrieved December 31, 2021 from https://www.mckinsey.com/industries/travel-logistics-and-infrastructure/our-insights/us-freight-after-covid-19-a-bumpy-road-to-the-next-normal

Barla, P. (2010). Greenhouse gas issues in the North American trucking industry. *Energy Efficiency*, *3*(2), 123–131. doi:10.100712053-009-9066-6

Berman, J. (2021). Pitt-Ohio rolls out new warehouse and distribution service for in Mid-Atlantic and Midwest regions. *Supply Chain Management Review.* Retrieved December 31, 2021 from https://www.scmr.com/article/pitt_ohio_rolls_out_new_warehouse_and_distribution_service_for_in_mid_atlan/news

Carbon War Room. (2012). *Road Transport: Unlocking Fuel-Saving Technologies in Trucking and Fleets, November 2012* [Report]. Retrieved December 31, 2021 from https://rmi.org/wp-content/uploads/2017/04/Unlocking-Fuel-Saving-Technologies-in-Trucking-and-Fleets-Carbon-War-Room_0.pdf

Cassidey, W. B. (2020). US truck driver shortfall steeper than expected. *Journal of Commerce.* Retrieved December 31, 2021 from https://www.joc.com/trucking-logistics/labor/us-truck-driver-shortfall-steeper-expected_20201125.html#:~:text=A%20growing%20deficit&text=That's%20an%20improvement%20from%20the,all%20of%202019%20and%202018

Charm, T., Coggins, B., Robinson, K., & Wilkie, J. (2020). *The great consumer shift: Ten charts that show us how US shopping behavior is changing.* McKinsey & Company. Retrieved December 31, 2021 from https://www.mckinsey.com/business-functions/marketing-and-sales/our-insights/the-great-consumer-shift-ten-charts-that-show-how-us-shopping-behavior-is-changing

Chottani, A., Hastings, G., Murnane, J., & Neuhaus, F. (2018). *Distraction or Disruption? Autonomous trucks gain ground in US logistics.* McKinsey & Company. Retrieved December 31, 2021 from https://www.mckinsey.com/industries/travel-logistics-and-infrastructure/our-insights/distraction-or-disruption-autonomous-trucks-gain-ground-in-us-logistics

Costello, B., & Karickhoff, A. (2019). *Truck driver shortage analysis.* American Trucking Association. Retrieved December 31, 2021 from https://www.trucking.org/sites/default/files/2020-01/ATAs%20Driver%20Shortage%20Report%202019%20with%20cover.pdf

Cybator, C. (2017). *Pitt-Ohio to be first trucking company with two LEED Gold Certified terminals.* Pittsburgh Green Story. Retrieved December 31, 2021 from https://pittsburghgreenstory.com/pitt-ohio-first-trucking-company-two-leed-gold-certified-terminals/

Dun & Bradstreet. (2021). *Trucking industry insights from D&B Hoovers.* Retrieved December 31, 2021 from https://www.dnb.com/business-directory/industry-analysis.general_freight_trucking.html

Federal Motor Carrier Safety Administration. (2020). *Summary of hours of service regulations.* Retrieved December 31, 2021 from https://www.fmcsa.dot.gov/regulations/hours-service/summary-hours-service-regulations

Franca, R. B., Jones, E. C., Richards, C. N., & Carlson, J. P. (2010). Multi-objective stochastic supply chain modeling to evaluate tradeoffs between profit and quality. *International Journal of Production Economics, 127*(2), 292–299. doi:10.1016/j.ijpe.2009.09.005

Gaudenzi, B., & Borghesi, A. (2006). Managing risks in the supply chain using the AHP method. *International Journal of Logistics Management, 17*(1), 114–136. doi:10.1108/09574090610663464

Giannakis, M., & Papadopoulos, T. (2016). Supply chain sustainability: A risk management approach. *International Journal of Production Economics, 171*, 455–470. doi:10.1016/j.ijpe.2015.06.032

Gittleman, M., & Monaco, K. (2020). Truck-driving jobs: Are they headed for rapid elimination? *Industrial & Labor Relations Review*, *73*(1), 3–24. doi:10.1177/0019793919858079

Goel, A., & Irnich, S. (2016). An exact method for vehicle routing and truck driver scheduling problems. *Transportation Science*, *51*(2), 737–754. doi:10.1287/trsc.2016.0678

Goh, M., Lim, J. Y. S., & Meng, F. (2007). A stochastic model for risk management in global supply chain networks. *European Journal of Operational Research*, *182*(1), 164–173. doi:10.1016/j.ejor.2006.08.028

Gothwal, S., & Raj, T. (2018). Prioritising the performance measures of FMS using multi-criteria decision making approaches. *International Journal of Process Management and Benchmarking*, *8*(1), 59–78. doi:10.1504/IJPMB.2018.088657

Gouda, S. K., & Saranga, H. (2018). Sustainable supply chains for supply chain sustainability: Impact of sustainability efforts on supply chain risk. *International Journal of Production Research*, *56*(17), 5820–5835. doi:10.1080/00207543.2018.1456695

Govindan, K., & Chaudhuri, A. (2016). Interrelationships of risks faced by third party logistics service providers: A DEMATEL based approach. *Transportation Research Part E, Logistics and Transportation Review*, *90*, 177–195. doi:10.1016/j.tre.2015.11.010

Heavy and tractor-trailer truck drivers. (2020). *Occupational Outlook Handbook*. Retrieved March 8, 2022 from https://www.bls.gov/ooh/transportation-and-material-moving/heavy-and-tractor-trailer-truck-drivers.htm

History of Pitt-Ohio. (2021). Retrieved December 31, 2021 from https://pittohio.com/myPittOhio/corporate/about/history-of-pitt-ohio

Hossain, M. S., & Hossain, M. M. (2018). Application of interactive fuzzy goal programming for multi-objective integrated production and distribution planning. *International Journal of Process Management and Benchmarking*, *8*(1), 35–58. doi:10.1504/IJPMB.2018.088656

How much does a truck driver make in Pennsylvania? (2021). https://www.indeed.com/career/truck-driver/salaries/PA

Jain, N., & D'lima, C. (2018). Organisational culture preference for gen Y's prospective job aspirants: A personality-culture fit perspective. *International Journal of Process Management and Benchmarking*, *7*(2), 262–275. doi:10.1504/IJPMB.2017.083122

Kim, J. H., Youn, S., & Roh, J. J. (2011). Green Supply Chain Management orientation and firm performance: Evidence from South Korea. *International Journal of Services and Operations Management*, *8*(3), 283–304. doi:10.1504/IJSOM.2011.038973

Kite-Powell, J. (2020). Using machine learning to reduce carbon emissions in the trucking industry. *Forbes*. Retrieved December 31, 2021 from https://www.forbes.com/sites/jenniferhicks/2020/09/29/using-machine-learning-to-reduce-carbon-emissions-in-the-trucking-industry/?sh=3145bfc1a9e6

Kroes, J. R., & Ghosh, S. (2010). Outsourcing congruence with competitive priorities: Impact on supply chain and firm performance. *Journal of Operations Management*, *28*(1), 124–143. doi:10.1016/j.jom.2009.09.004

Kumar Dadsena, K., Sarmah, S. P., & Naikan, V. N. A. (2019). Risk evaluation and mitigation of sustainable road freight transport operation: A case of trucking industry. *International Journal of Production Research, 57*(19), 6223–6245. doi:10.1080/00207543.2019.1578429

Laroche, M., Bergeron, J., & Barbaro-Forleo, G. (2001). Targeting consumers who are willing to pay more for environmentally friendly products. *Journal of Consumer Marketing, 18*(6), 503–520. doi:10.1108/EUM0000000006155

Maiden, T. (2021). Transportation, warehouse capacity lacking, costs soar in November: Logistics Managers' Index shows supply chain tightens further. *FreightWaves*. Retrieved March 8, 2022 from https://www.freightwaves.com/news/transportation-warehouse-capacity-lacking-costs-soar-in-november

Mainieri, T., Barnett, E., Valdero, T. R., Unipan, J. B., & Oskamp, S. (1997). Green buying: The influence of environmental concern on consumer behaviour. *The Journal of Social Psychology, 137*(6), 189–204. doi:10.1080/00224549709595430

McNally, S. (2020). *ATA freight forecast projects continued long-term growth in volumes*. American Trucking Associations. Retrieved December 31, 2021 from https://www.trucking.org/news-insights/ata-freight-forecast-projects-continued-long-term-growth-volumes

Miller, J. W., Saldanha, J. P., Rungtusanatham, M., & Knemeyer, M. (2017). How does driver turnover affect motor carrier safety performance and what can managers do about it? *Journal of Business Logistics, 38*(3), 197–216. doi:10.1111/jbl.12158

Murphy, N. (2020). Santa's got shipping issues: Why retailers are worried about gifts stuck just beyond the last mile. *Forbes*. Retrieved December 31, 2021 from https://www.forbes.com/sites/niallmurphy/2020/12/08/santas-got-shipping-issues-why-retailers-are-worried-about-gifts-stuck-just-beyond-the-last-mile/?sh=18c5dd406a9c

Murray, D., & Glidewell, S. (2019). *An Analysis of the Operational Costs of Trucking: 2019 Update*. American Transportation Research Institute. Retrieved March 8, 2022 from https://truckingresearch.org/wp-content/uploads/2019/11/ATRI-Operational-Costs-of-Trucking-2019-1.pdf

Rosenblatt, L. (2021). No driver needed: Self-driving trucks are starting to move cargo on the nation's highways. *Pittsburgh Post-Gazette*. Retrieved December 31, 2021 from https://www.post-gazette.com/business/tech-news/2020/03/30/self-driving-trucks-autonomous-cars-Locomation-Wilson-Logistics-Maven-Machines-Idelic/stories/202003290032

RTS Financial and RTS Carrier Services. (2020). *Best practices for hiring and retaining drivers*. Retrieved December 31, 2021 from https://www.rtsinc.com/articles/best-practices-hiring-and-retaining-drivers

Sahu, A. K., Datta, S., & Mahapatra, S. S. (2014). Green supply chain performance benchmarking using integrated IVFN-TOPSIS methodology. *International Journal of Process Management and Benchmarking, 3*(4), 511–551. doi:10.1504/IJPMB.2013.058272

Sharma, A., & Joshi, S. (2018). Green consumerism: Overview and further research directions. *International Journal of Process Management and Benchmarking, 7*(2), 206–223. doi:10.1504/IJPMB.2017.083106

Smith, A. D. (2020a). Online vehicle purchase behavior and analytics among supply chain professionals: An exploratory study. *World Review of Intermodal Transportation Research*, *9*(3), 264–296. doi:10.1504/WRITR.2020.108229

Smith, A. D. (2020b). Being green and social responsibility: Basic concepts and case studies in business excellence. *International Journal of Sustainable Entrepreneurship and Corporate Social Responsibility*, *5*(2), 34–54. doi:10.4018/IJSECSR.2020070103

Sporrer, A. (2020). 5 trucking sustainability trends for 2021. *FreightWaves*. Retrieved March 8, 2022 from https://www.freightwaves.com/news/5-trucking-sustainability-trends-for-2021

Sustainability – Green fleet & LEED certified buildings. (2021). *Pitt-Ohio*. Retrieved December 31, 2021 from https://pittohio.com/myPittOhio/corporate/about/sustainability/planet/green_fleet_and_LEED_certified_buildings

Trinity Logistics. (2020). *Assessing Covid-19's impact on trucking companies*. Retrieved December 31, 2021 from https://trinitylogistics.com/assessing-covid-19s-impact-on-trucking-companies/

Washburn, C., Murray, S., & Kueny, C. (2021). Electronic Logging Device System: Early outcomes of use in the trucking industry. *Professional Safety*, *66*(11), 26–30.

Williams, E., Das, V., & Fisher, A. (2020). Assessing the sustainability implications of autonomous vehicles: Recommendations for research community practice. *Sustainability*, *12*(5), 1902. doi:10.3390u12051902

Young, J. (2021). Pandemic causes ecommerce to surge north of 32% in Q4. *Digital Commerce 360*. Retrieved December 31, 2021 from https://www.digitalcommerce360.com/article/quarterly-online-sales/

Chapter 4
Unmasking the Masked:
Face Recognition and Its Challenges Using the Periocular Region – A Review

Sheela R.
https://orcid.org/0000-0001-8924-0008
Department of BCA, School of CS&IT, Jain University, India

Suchithra R.
School of CS&IT, Jain University, India

ABSTRACT

Today, COVID-19 is one of the most severe issues that people are grappling with. Half of the faces are hidden by the mask in this instance. The region around the eyes is usually the sole apparent attribute that can be used as a biometric in these circumstances. In the event of a pandemic, the three primary biometric modalities (facial, fingerprint, and iris), which commonly enable these tasks, confront particular obstacles. One option that can improve accuracy, ease-of-use, and safety is periocular recognition. Several periocular biometric detection methods have been developed previously. As a result, periocular recognition remains a difficult task. To overcome the problem, several algorithms based on CNN have been implemented. This chapter investigated the periocular region recognitions algorithms, datasets, and texture descriptors. This chapter also discuss the current COVID-19 situation to unmask the masked faces in particular.

INTRODUCTION

Biometrics is a field that looks at a person's biological characteristics that are unique. Biometrics methods used to determine the distinctive behavioural and physical characteristics of humans. It is the preferred means of identification, outperforming traditional methods such as passwords and PINs (*G. Liu, at al, June 1997*). Biometric devices aid biometric system authentication and identification by utilising a number of unique human attributes such as fingerprints, vein patterns, DNA sequencing, hand geometry, iris pattern, voice pattern, face detection, and signature dynamics (*Kumari P, Seeja KR., 6 June 2019*). The

DOI: 10.4018/978-1-6684-5250-9.ch004

fingerprint, which is a physical characteristic, is the first and most common thing that comes to mind when discussing distinct features (*U.J. Gelinas,at al, 2004*) (*N. Osifchin and G. Vau, 1997*). In our day-to-day uses for biometrics as a way of authentication, there are a variety of biometric traits that can be utilized to identify humans (*K. Kimura and A. Lipeles, 1996*). Biometric-based authentication is more secure than any other technique since it binds an identity to a specific person rather than a password or a code that anybody could use.

One of the most fundamental aspects in facial computation is the classification of certain facial traits from photos and videos. (https://www.koreatimes.co.kr/www/nation/2019/01/371_262460.html,2019*)*. These significant traits, such as the distance between the eyes and the relative placements of the nose, chin, and mouth, are combined to generate a facial profile that aids in the identification of each individual.

Face biometrics stand out among other biometrics because they do not demand an individual's active engagement *(H. Zhang, 1997)*. Many scientists are interested in face recognition, and as a result, it has become a gold standard in the field of human recognition. It has been the most exhaustively investigated field in computer vision for more than four decades *(J. M. Smereka and B. V. K. V. Kumar, 2013)*. Face recognition is a widely used biometric that works well in a controlled environment. Face recognition systems, on the other hand, perform worse when the face is partially obscured. Surveillance videos frequently do not show the entire face of crooks. Helmets, hair, glasses, and skiing masks are used to conceal the face in various settings. Furthermore, women in other nations conceal their faces partially owing to cultural and religious reasons. Face recognition suffers from a loss of accuracy and reliability when persons wear surgical masks *(L. Bass,at al, 2003)*, despite being unexpectedly accurate and reliable in the presence of partial facial occlusions.

Therefore, in this chapter we have discussed the various challenges in facial recognition research, different algorithms researched and developed for recognition of face. Mainly, the current situation of covid-19, has been discussed on unmasking the masked face. Section 2 briefs the challenges in facial recognition systems. Section 3 describes the social consequences of wearing a mask. Section 4 explains the emotional recognition of its valence and context. Section 5 explains the consequences of face masks that affect facial recognition. Section 6 brief about the periocular biometrics. Section 7 clarifies about the databases available for periocular biometrics. Section 8 describes the pre-processing of periocular images. Section 9 elaborates the detection and segmentation techniques involved in the periocular region. Section 10 is detailed on feature encoding and comparison. Section 11 explains about the various classification methods. Section 12 brief about the comparison of periocular with other modalities. Finally, Section 13 summarizes the chapter with future scope in periocular research area.

CHALLENGES IN FACIAL RECOGNITION SYSTEM

Illumination- Illumination is the term for light fluctuations. The tiniest change in lighting conditions can make automatic facial recognition extremely difficult and have a major impact on the results. If the lighting changes and the same individual is taken with the same sensor and in a nearly same facial expression and attitude, the results can be drastically different. The illumination variation of face and periocular region is given in Figure-1. The effect of illumination on the appearance of the face is dramatic *(P. H. C. Eilers and J. J. Goeman, r, 2004)*.

Pose- Differences in posture are quite sensitive to facial recognition algorithms. The stance of a person's face changes as their head moves and their viewing angle changes. Intra-class variations are always

Figure 1. Illumination variations

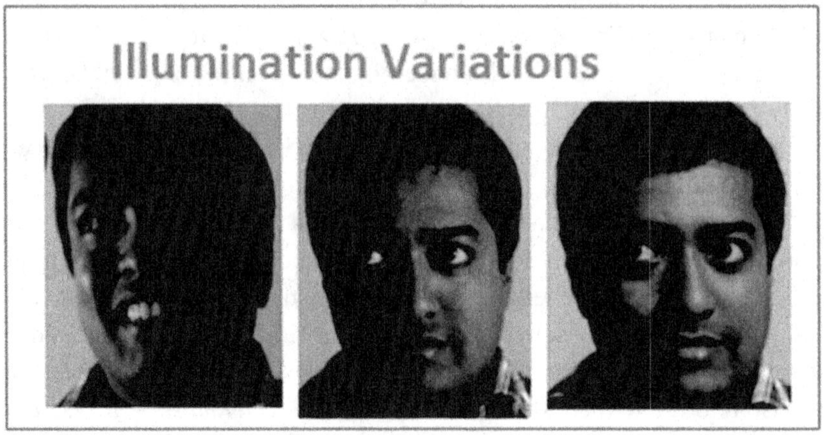

produced by changes in face appearance induced by head motions or multiple camera POVs, decreasing automated face recognition rates considerably. When the rotation angle is increased, identifying the true face becomes more difficult. If the database just contains a frontal image of the face, recognition may be faulty or non-existent (*P. H. C. Eilers and J. J. Goeman, r, 2004*). The different pose variation of the face of a person wearing spectacles is given in Figure-2.

Figure 2. Pose variations

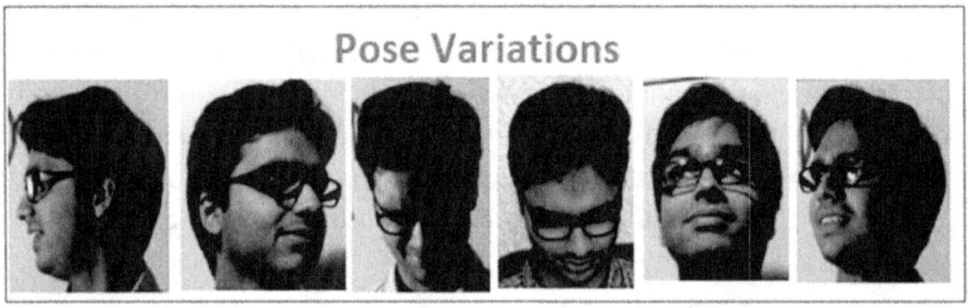

Occlusion- The full face cannot be utilised as an input image when one or more sections of the face are blocked. Occlusion is one of the most difficult problems to solve in a face recognition system. It's induced by beards, moustaches, and other accessories in real-life circumstances. The presence of such components adds to the complexity of the subject, making computerised facial recognition a tough nut to crack (*P. H. C. Eilers and J. J. Goeman, r, 2004*).

Expressions- It is the distinctive quality that is fundamental in determining human identity and emotions, the face is one of the most important biometrics. Various circumstances result in a variety of moods,

Figure 3. Expression variations

which in turn result in a variety of emotions and, finally, variations in facial expressions. Another crucial factor to examine is the person's various expressions. Human expressions include macro-expressions such as happiness, sadness, fury, disgust, fear, and surprise. Involuntary facial patterns known as micro-expressions display rapid facial patterns (*P. H. C. Eilers and J. J. Goeman, r, 2004*). In Figure-3, the different facial expression is shown for a person wearing spectacles.

Low Resolution- A common image should have a resolution of 16*16 pixels at the very least. An image having a resolution of fewer than 16*16 pixels is considered low-resolution. These low-resolution images can be obtained from small-scale standalone cameras such as street CCTV cameras, ATM cameras, and supermarket security cameras *(Walid, Hariri., 2020).* These cameras can only record 16*16 facial regions because the camera is not very close to the face. In such a low-resolution photograph, the bulk of the pixels are destroyed, therefore it doesn't transmit much information. Recognizing people's faces might be incredibly tough *(J. M. Smereka and B. V. K. V. Kumar, 2013).*

Ageing- The appearance of a person's face varies with time and reflects their age, making facial recognition systems more difficult to use. As people become older, their facial characteristics, shapes/ lines, and other features change. The dataset for a separate age group of persons over a period of time is calculated for reliability verification. The feature extraction approach is used to identify wrinkles, marks, brows, haircuts, and other basic characteristics *(P. H. C. Eilers and J. J. Goeman, r, 2004).*

THE SOCIAL CONSEQUENCES OF MASK-WEARING DURING COVID-19

Face masks are one of the most effective COVID-19 defences, but their widespread use is having an unforeseen consequence: they are weakening facial recognition algorithms *(CDC. Cases in the U.S. June 2020).* The facial signature is well defined, with essential features such as the nose, lips, and chin visible. Anything that makes crucial features less visible is interfering. In the context of a pandemic, all three popular biometric modalities (face, fingerprint, and iris), which commonly empower these tasks, present particular obstacles (*Huang C, et al, 2020).* Iris identification cannot be done using visible light cameras and must instead rely on near-infrared sensors, which are difficult to scale up and aren't always compatible *(Global cases of covid 19, 2019), (Kandasamy M., 2020).*

To determine the mask-emotional wearer's, an observer can only see the upper portion of the face *(Lauer SA, at al, 2019)*. Even if the mask-grin wearer's is perceived as a frown and the brows are drawn together as a scowl, the viewer is left with only half information, and the presupposed emotion is unlikely to be as convincing as a full frown or smile (*Huang C, et al, 2020*). It's also likely that these partially visible facial expressions will be misinterpreted as an incorrect one. Squinting without revealing the mouth, for example, could be mistaken for scepticism rather than a smile. Masks have been demonstrated to increase negative emotion perception while lowering positive emotion perception *(Markus HR, Kitayama S., 1991)*.

EXPLORING EMOTIONAL VALENCE AND CONTEXT

The valence of the target's emotion in combination with a face mask modifies the observer's notions of trustworthiness, likability, and intimacy, in addition to the major effects of face masks on social judgments.

Observers judge features based on the valence of facial emotional expressions, according to the emotion-as-social-information concept (*Elfenbein, at al, 2002*). In general, pleasant emotions like happiness indicate a social engagement approach, whereas negative emotions like wrath indicate a social disengagement avoidance attitude *(Franklin, at al, 2013)*. To put it simply, the emotional valence of a target's display can influence observers' social assessments. Face masks have a lot of significance and can thus influence inferential processes. Compulsion of face masks in public, on the other hand, has resulted in a partial restoration to pre-pandemic life *(Carbon, Claus-Christian., 2020)*. As a result, face masks may also represent a greater sense of personal freedom and potential.

The proper perception of emotions is essential for effective human communication. People's emotional impressions, for example, influence how they connect with one another. According to the emotion-as-social-information theory *(McArthur, at al 2002)*, *(Elfenbein, at al, 2002)*, an emotional expression might prompt inferential processes, which then inform cognitions and actions.

Emotion recognition is critical because different emotions send different forms of information. Interaction partners may act incorrectly if emotion recognition fails, jeopardising the interaction's success *(Dimberg, at al, 2000)*.

Face coverings increase the ambiguity, making it more difficult for older target faces to recognise emotions *(Ruffman, at al, 2008)*. The amount of available facial cues may be insufficient for successful emotional interpretation since both age-related changes in face morphology and face masks reduce facial signals *(Hess, at al, 2013)*.

As a consequence, when people meet for the first time, being able to accurately analyse an interaction partner's emotional expression is very important *(Ekman, Paul, 1993)*. People utilize a variety of tactics, including their expressions, to express their feelings. Face muscles are stimulated in unique ways by emotions, making the face a particularly valuable source of emotional information *(Shiota,, et al, 2003)*. As a result, viewers must decode information communicated by facial clues in order to infer others' emotional experiences.

The eyes, nose, and mouth are all information-rich locations. Importantly, by covering the lips and a portion of the nose, traditional face masks restrict the quantity of available facial clues (when worn correctly). As a result, they may impair observers' capacity to correctly recognise emotions portrayed on the face of a target individual *(Guo,, at al, 2019)*. Adult participants did, in fact, have reduced accuracy rates for faces with covered mouth regions. In addition to face masks, previous research has identified demographic characteristics that (may) influence emotion recognition accuracy *(Carbon,Claus-Christian,2020)*. Emotion recognition is hypothesised to be influenced by changes in brain activation *(Joseph, at al, 2010)*. When target people wear face masks, age disparities in emotion identification may be substantially more obvious since the lack of facial cues makes the work more challenging. According to research, the gap between younger and older persons' performance on cognitively demanding tasks widens as task complexity increases *(Carbon, Claus-Christian., 2020)*. Also, there is proof that increases in task complexity have a negative impact on older individuals' emotion perception. As a result, when demands are high, neurological aging-related changes may be especially important *(Ruffman, at al, 2008)*.

The target's age is another age-related element that influences emotion recognition accuracy. With increasing age, skin tautness decreases, making emotional expressions more ambiguous and thereby altering emotion perception *(Guo,, at al, 2019)*.

FACE MASK AND FACE RECOGNITION CHALLENGES

The corona virus has recently been examined, and it has been discovered that wearing a face mask by both healthy and sick persons inhibits the virus's transmission significantly. However, wearing a mask to the face has the following drawbacks such as fraudsters and thieves use the disguise to steal and commit crimes without revealing their true identities *(Franklin, at al, 2013)*.

Face masks have posed a considerable challenge to existing face recognition algorithms as a result of these issues. To overcome these challenges, two distinct tasks, mask recognition and masked face recognition, have been proposed. The first checks to see if the person is wearing a mask *(Markus HR, Kitayama S, 1991)*. When wearing a mask is needed in public, this will be utilized. Face detection with a mask focused on the eyes and thus the forehead regions, on the other hand, attempts to recognise a face using a mask focused on the eyes and thus the forehead regions. As a result, wearing a mask, which covers a substantial section of the face, including the nose, is regarded as the most difficult facial occlusion issue. A number of approaches have been proposed to address this problem. Using the ocular region of the face, also known as periocular biometrics *(Hareli S, at al, 2013)*, is one possible option.

PERIOCULAR BIOMETRICS

According to the study, ocular and facial biometrics are the most prevalent among other biometric qualities such as fingerprints, ears, sclera, retina, and face. However, each has its own set of disadvantages.

Facial biometrics frequently fails due to ageing, location, illumination, and expression concerns, whereas ocular biometrics necessitates a high level of user interaction and a decent camera stand-off distance for obtaining the photos. To tackle these issues, researchers proposed that the periocular region, which surrounds the eye, be used for recognition. The actual periocular region is detected, and it is demonstrated in Figure-4.

The eyelids, eyelashes, eyebrows, tear duct, eye shape, skin tone, and other elements around the eye are all part of the periocular region. Periocular region-based authentication systems are a good trade-off between face and iris-based biometric authentication systems since they require high user collaboration.

Figure 4. Periocular Region Demonstration

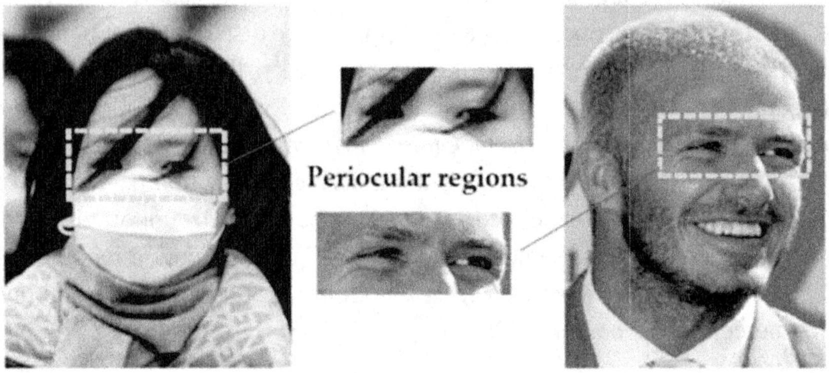

Figure 5. Periocular Region and Its Features

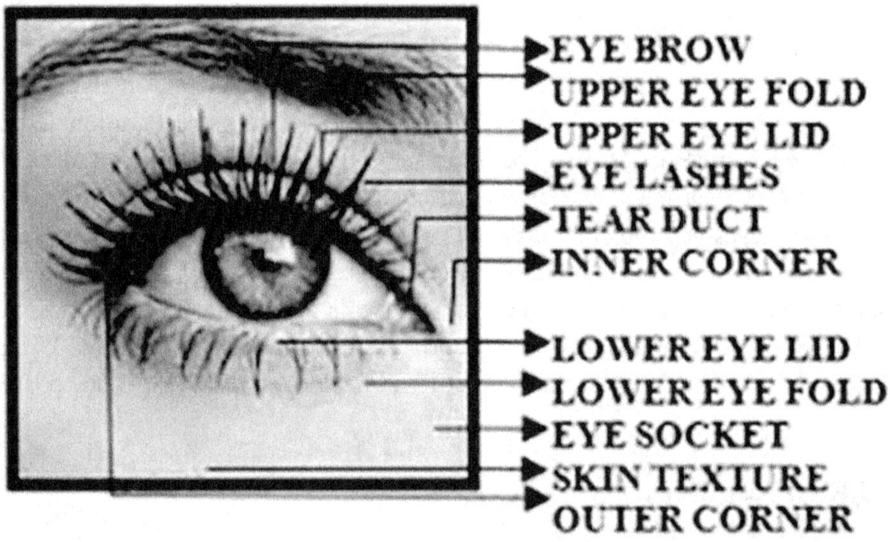

For soft biometric categorization and matching of medically transformed face photographs, such as gender alteration before and after surgery, recognition of surgically altered faces, and human shots before and after cataract surgery, the periocular region is very important. Figure-5 depicts the various features of the periocular region.

DATABASES OF PERIOCULAR REGION

The CASIA Iris Database v.1 was the first publicly available database, created by the National Laboratory of Pattern Recognition, Institute of Automation, CASIA. The authors used a custom-built NIR camera to manually analyse the images in the database, replacing the pupil area with a constant intensity value. This database should not be used in iris biometrics research *(P.J. Phillips, at al, 2007)* because the manual participation oversimplified the problem and has misleading outcomes. CASIA-Iris-Lamp (CASIA Iris Database V4,, 2018) (16,212 photos and 819 classes), CASIA-Iris-Twins, CASIA-Iris-Distance, cross-sensor compatibility, ageing influence, and CASIA-Iris-Mobile-V1.0 are only a few of the updated version's features that make it easier to examine the impact of diverse impacts. CASIA-IrisV4-Interval (CASIA Iris Database V4,, 2018) (2,639 photos and 395 classes) and CASIA-IrisV4-Thousand (CASIA Iris Database V4,, 2018) (20,000 shots and 2,000 classes) were taken indoors with the lights turned on and off using a bespoke NIR camera. This was the first publicly available iris database, with over 1,000 individuals. In 2007, the IIT Delhi Iris Database (CUHK Iris Image Dataset,*IIT Delhi Iris Database* 2018), *(A. Kumar, A. Passi,, 2010)* was established. It contains 1,120 NIR pictures (224 classes) taken in a restricted environment and is limited to Indian subjects. There are 254 photos in the CUHK Iris Image Dataset *(C.-N. Chun, at al, 2004),(CUHK Iris Image Dataset,, 2020)* that were collected in the near-infrared spectrum (36 classes). Due to considerable changes in the anatomy of the face, plastic surgery has a negative impact on facial recognition performance. The periocular region, on the other hand, is prone to minor alterations due to the low frequency of procedures conducted there. The negative impact of plastic surgery on face recognition ability can be mitigated by combining face and periocular region information *(R. Jillela and A. Ross, 2012)*.

Facial cosmetic makeup for aesthetic purposes has also been shown to reduce face recognition performance *(A. Dantcheva, at al, 2013)*. Detecting facial cosmetics automatically is a difficult task. While there hasn't been any research on periocular recognition under makeup, look at the eye region's performance in makeup detection *(C. Chen, at al, 2013)*.

It was discovered that the periocular region can behave similarly to the face when it comes to automatic makeup detection. Transgender identification: According to Mahalingam and Rickaneck *(G. Mahalingam and K. Ricanek, 2013)*, when photographs of persons who have undergone gender alteration are used, face recognition performance is lowered. It was determined that using the periocular region outperforms facial recognition performance in such photographs.

8. ACQUISITION AND PRE-PROCESSING OF PERIOCULAR IMAGES

In the field of iris recognition, researchers have experimented with a variety of acquisition strategies. The immediate neighbourhoods of the eye surround the face area. Periocular biometric is predicted to need less subject participation than traditional ocular biometric while providing for a substantially greater depth of field.

Periocular Biometric systems are used to determine a person's unique identity by evaluating one or more genetic characteristics. The ability to extract features and match corresponding areas of two different images while maintaining consistency is aided by defining a region of interest.

The iris and sclera areas have been regarded as a part of the periocular region in the majority of research studies *(R. Jillela, at al, 2013)*. The iris and sclera of the eye, on the other hand, are biometric

Figure 6. Workflow of Periocular Recognition

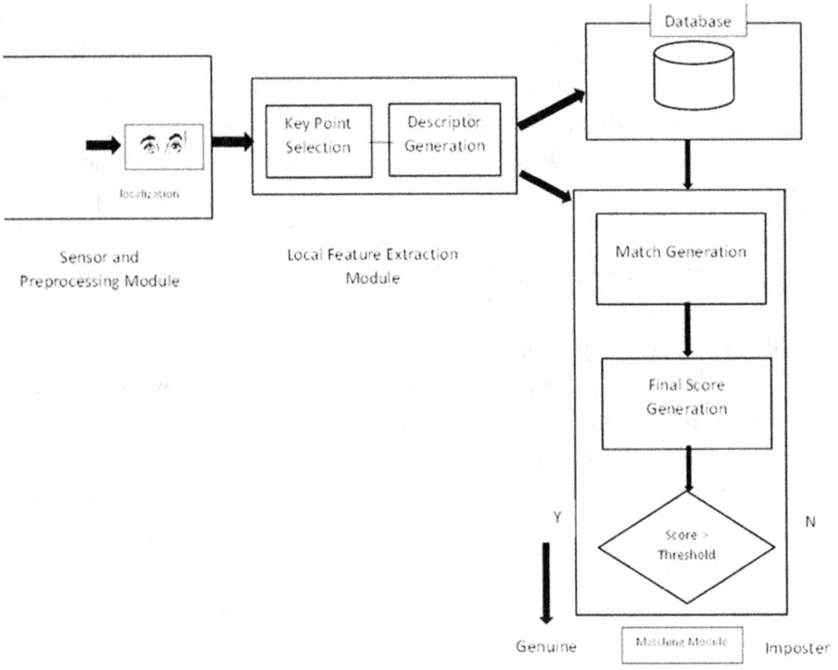

traits in and of themselves, according to certain studies *(P. Miller, at al, 2010)*. The automatic localization and image enhancement routines are part of the periocular recognition pre-processing technique.

In automatic localization, the ROI is often located using the iris location. The iris can be easily recognised due to its roughly spherical form and noticeable contrast from the sclera. The periocular region has been identified using the inner and outer corners of the eye, as well as the iris *(C. Padole and H. Proenca, 2012)*.

Prior to feature extraction, most periocular recognition methods incorporate an image enhancing stage. This phase allows for dramatic changes in lighting or imaging spectrum to be addressed.

To smooth the fluctuation across local pixel intensities, Gaussian blurring was used *(U. Park, R, 2011)*. Filtering with morphological operations or 1D rank filters *(F. Alonso-Fernandez and J. Bigun,, 2015)* can be used to remove small line edges in images, such as eyelashes.

DETECTION AND SEGMENTATION OF THE PERIOCULAR REGION

For a long time, image segmentation analysis has been a high level of thought. There are numerous different segmentation systems on the market at the time of writing, however there isn't a single strategy that may be regarded as beneficial for numerous images, and all methods aren't equally used for a specific type of image.

The choice of one segmentation approach over another, as well as the level of segmentation, are determined by the type of image and characteristics of the object under consideration.

Face databases are used in most periocular biometrics research projects; however, in uncontrolled environments, the periocular region must first be cropped from the face region. Manual segmentation and automatic segmentation are the two main methods for accomplishing this. There are various types of detection and segmentation techniques, some are Viola-Jones (VJ) algorithms *(P. Viola and M. J. Jones,, 2004)* which is the face detector to detect the face. The precision of the face detector determines the overall performance of periocular recognition *(F. Alonso, at al, 2016)*. The second way is to use the iris, pupil, or eye corners to directly detect the eye in the image. Eye corners were detected using Canny edge detectors, morphological procedures, and the Harris corner detector *(D. Ambika, at al, 2016)*, while pupil centres were found using Haar features via weak classifiers followed by binarization and contour processing *(M. Uzair,, at al, 2015)*. In Figure-6, the workflow of periocular region recognition is demonstrated.

The periocular region is established by the position of the iris in the iris segmentation method. The eye centre is detected using correlation filters *(R. Jillela, at al, 2013) (G. Mahalingam, at al, 2014)*. Gabor filters *(F. Smeraldi, at al, 2002)* or convolutions with 1D filters tailored to identify circular symmetries *(F. Alonso-Fernandez, at al, 2014)* could also be used to detect eyes.

Finally, subface parts such as the eyebrow, sclera, or VJ sub-part detectors could be used to identify the periocular region. Using the Local Eyebrow Active Shape Model (LE-ASM) and graph-cut based segmentation, the eyebrow could be recognised directly from a facial image *(T. H. N. Le, at al, 2014)(F. Juefei-Xu, at al, 2012)*. After iris segmentation, the sclera region was recognised using the HSV/YCbCr colour spaces *(H. Proença, 2014)(K. Oh, at al, 2014)*. Region Growing is a technique for dividing pixels in an image into sub-districts or bigger areas in the absence of a preset foundation *(H. Cao, at al, 2012)*. It is usually prepared in four stages: select a group of seed pixels within the distinctive image *(S. Karkra, at al, 2015)*, select a briefing of similitude live, for example, dim level power or shading and begin a halting gospel, develop districts by adding to each seed those neighbouring pixels that have predefined properties like seed pixels, and stop district development once you have a lot of pixels met the live for thought in this scene. Estimate, resemblance between a competition constituent and a constituent developed thus far, and the current status of the district under development.

FEATURE ENCODING AND COMPARISON

Every feature extraction methodology uses its unique way to convert a 2-D image into a 1-D feature vector. Because the periocular portion of the face is a subsection of the face, it stands to reason that common facial feature representations would be beneficial in classifying persons who suffer from it.

Face feature representations are classified as native look, key point-based, and holistic. Local Appearance-Based Feature Extraction methods are a type of feature extraction technique that collects data at regular intervals around each component of a photograph's local neighborhood. These statistics, which include the occurrences of various textures, patterns, and data, are often kept in a one-dimensional feature vector.

Native Binary Patterns, orienting Gradient bar graphs, native component quantization, and Weber native Descriptors are all employed to extract native appearance-based features in these studies. In biometric applications, such as hostile texture categorization, there are some changes in how these parameters are applied.

Local phase quantization (LPQ) is a texture analysis method that uses the discrete Fourier transform's (DFT) quantized phase spectrum feature to accomplish texture classification that is insensitive to centrally symmetric blur such out-of-focus blur, motion blur, and atmospheric turbulence blur.

The image's 2-D DFT was computed first using a NxN window (N=3,5...) kernel, and then the four low-frequency coefficients for the real and imaginary sections of the transform were quantized and concatenated into an 8-bit binary code to produce the LPQ code. A histogram of codes, or LPQ code, is created by concatenating the codes from all pixels.

By treating an image's pixels as an array of particles, each of which generates a spherically symmetric force field on other pixels in the array, the inverse square law of gravitational force is applied to it. This force is treated as a vector based on pixel intensity and position. The transform is an effective averaging method for reducing image noise effects *(D. J. Hurley, at al, 2005)*.

The Weber local descriptor (WLD) was inspired by Weber's theory of human perception, which states that perception is influenced by the size or intensity of the original stimulus as well as changes in that stimulus. The ratio of the change in intensity to the original intensity is hence the Weber constant *(M. Castrillón, at al, 2016)*. WLD is thus a measure of intensity change with respect to a central pixel and the gradient orientation *(N. Aginako, at al, 2017)*.

The Local Color Histogram (LCH) is a description that depicts the distribution of colors in an image. Each color dimension is quantized into discrete ranges, the number of ranges representing the color histogram's bin, and a count of the pixels that fall within the ranges is computed *(C. Gode, at al, 2014)*.

Ojala et al. *(T. Ojala, M, at al, 2000)* created a texture categorization algorithm called Local Binary Patterns (LBP). LBP creates a feature vector from texture data in a picture. This is performed by marking components with a binary variety, which is the result of placing a threshold on the neighbourhood around each pixel. The LBP are critical for texture recognition since they can recognise edges, line endings, corners, spots, and other patterns. It is calculated for each pixel in a picture by taking into account a 3x3 neighbourhood around it. The intensity of each pixel's eight neighbours is assigned a '0' or a '1' depending on whether that neighbour's intensity is lower or higher than the reference pixel. A number of scholars have looked at the use of LBP *(A. H. T. Ahonen, at al, 2006)* to define the texture of the periocular region.

Miller et al. *(P. Miller, at al, 2010)* classified LBP features using city block distance. Using evolutionary algorithms to choose the optimal subset of LBP features, they discovered their findings in *(J. Adams, at al, 2010)*. They employed periocular data manually extracted from a selection of high-resolution frontal photographs of FRGC *(P. Phillips, at al, 2005)* with neutral expression, little appearance fluctuations, and controlled illumination.

LBP characteristics and colour histograms were employed to depict the periocular area's local appearance in *(D.Woodard, at al, 2010)*. Using the FRGC v2 face *(P. Phillips, at al, 2005)* and MBGC v1 NIR video (*NIST, Multiple Biometric Grand Challenge (MBGC) dataset.* https://face.nist.gov/mbgc/, *2008.*) datasets, they enhanced their results by matching LBP features with city block distance and colour histograms using the Bhattacharya coefficient. All of the films were not included in the MBGC NIR dataset. The test was made up of periocular regions extracted manually from the first two frames of the film, whereas the gallery was made up of periocular regions retrieved from a random frame. There were no differences in scale or appearance in the periocular areas. Because BRIEF (Binary Robust Independent Elementary Features) is sensitive to rotation, Oriented FAST and Rotated BRIEF (ORB) is a feature extraction that improves the BRIEF (Binary Robust Independent Elementary Features) descriptor by integrating it with the FAST corner detector.

In this collaborative effort, the dominant rotation of the key point is initially calculated using first order moments, and the BRIEF descriptor is then steered accordingly *(F. Alonso-Fernandez and J. Bigun, 2016)*. SIFT locates crucial points in a picture by utilising a difference of Gaussian (DoG) function to filter the image with two different scales for a few octaves and detecting where the extrema are discovered. Scaling, translation, and rotation have no effect on it (*C. N. Padole and H. Proenca, 2012*). The coordinates, scale, and orientation of each extracted point are used to represent it. After that, the array of data is normalised using an affine transformation and processed with the picture to provide a feature descriptor *(S. Bakshi, at al, 2015) (Ş. Karahan, at al, 2014)*. Adaptive thresholding was used to apply SIFT iteratively. The effects of blurring, image resolution, and lighting conditions on the robustness of appearance-based periocular recognition *(P. Miller, at al, 2010*). According to their findings, the biggest performance reduction owing to blurring was recorded for neutral expressions, which ranged from 94.10 percent to 54.49 percent across sessions.

In contrast, when the photos are down sampled to 40% for alternate expressions captured across sessions, the performance does not suffer significantly, dropping from 94.90 percent to 84.70 percent. In *(R. O. Duda, at al, 2001)*, they investigate the impact of distortion in dealing with quality fluctuation using the Globally Coherent Elastic Graph Matching algorithm. On their own gathered dataset Face-ExpressUBI, they show an improvement in recognition. Histogram of Orientation Gradients (HOG) as a grip and gradient-based feature descriptor for studying humans in photos. HOG could be a method for counting the occurrences of distinct gradient orientations in specific sections of a photograph based on natural look. Spite of the fact that HOG was created to detect objects, it has been used to identify people's faces and *eyes (U. Park, at al, 2011) (U. Park, at al, 2009)*

CLASSIFICATION PROCESS

Deep learning's application to periocular has yielded intriguing results. Deep learning models, on the other hand, are hampered by the fact that they require a substantial amount of training data, which is rarely available in the public domain. The ability to incorporate human-expert knowledge into the design process and applicability to tiny dailies are two advantages of employing hand-designed feature representations. The k-Nearest Neighbour (k-NN), Support Vector Machine (SVM), Artificial Neural Network (ANN), and Gaussian Mixture Model (GMM) are some of the classification algorithms *(R. O. Duda, at al, 2001)*. SVM is a supervised classification algorithm that aims to increase the margin between classes as much as possible. This classification method looks for a classification hyperplane with the shortest distance between it and the nearest data point on each side. SVM is widely used in pattern recognition applications like text and hypertext categorization, image classification, remote sensing, biology, and other sciences (D. Jianxiong, 2008) .

Convolutional Neural Networks (CNNs), the most prevalent type of neural networks, were used in a preliminary investigation by Ahuja et al. The authors first used the pre-trained CNN models in OpenFace *(T. Baltrusaitis, at al, 2016*) and the VISOB database *(A. Rattani, at al, 2016)* to perform transfer learning. For supervised learning testing, employed a four-layer stacked convolution network, a 512-dimensional feature vector, and cosine similarity.

The usefulness of CNN feature learning for the periocular recognition problem is demonstrated by the fact that both models from transfer learning and training from scratch outperform handcrafted features *(K. Ahuja at al, 2016)*. The authors later demonstrated that the same technique may be applied to smartphones *(K. Ahuja, at al, 2017)*. Eduardo et al., on the other hand, used another CNN architecture called VGG to execute transfer learning and showed competitive performance on multiple periocular datasets *(E. Luz, et al, 2017)*. To strengthen matching accuracy, *(Z. Zhao and A. Kumar, 2017)* added semantic information to automatically retrieve entire periocular characteristics.

This technique allows for greater matching accuracy with a lesser number of training samples when several biometrics are used, which is occasionally a concern. To improve the CNN feature learning process by implicitly recognizing the privileged regions-of-interest in the input data *(H. Proenca and J. C. Neves, 2018*). In *(Z. Zhao and A. Kumar, 2018)* they have proposed explicitly focusing on crucial periocular regions and adding higher weights to allow those critical regions to have a greater impact on the identification process. It's worth noting that CNN-based periocular recognition has been tested in the context of horse periocular recognition, with encouraging results *(M. Trokielewicz and M. Szadkowski, 2017)*. Raghavendra et al. looked into deeply coupled autoencoders instead of CNNs for smartphone-based robust periocular verification. Despite the fact that there are numerous architectures in CNNs and Autoencoder, the community has only looked into the performance of a small number of them.

The most recent, such as ResNet (*K. He at al, 2016*), DenseNet *(H. Gao, at al 2017)*, MobileNet *(A. G. Howard et al, 2017),* and others, require additional investigation. An in-depth analysis of the performance differences between various architectures is necessary. In addition, the community must concentrate on determining the optimal method to construct the architecture of deep networks (CNNs and Autoencoders). Stacking numerous layers without a thorough understanding of each layer's role and modelling capability would result in sub-optimal structures and accuracy.

Human performance on the periocular recognition test was studied in (*A. Kumar and A. Passi, 2010), (J. Xu, 2010)*. Researchers also calculated the results of the periocular recognition test to compare human and machine performance.

COMPARISON OF PERIOCULAR WITH OTHER MODALITIES

Biometrics, a crucial identity component of science which is frequently employed to provide a reliable technique of identifying people in many large-scale county-wide programs. Iris, periocular, retina, and eye movement are ocular biometric traits that have recently attracted a lot of interest among existing modalities.

To create a multimodal biometric system, iris recognition will be integrated with periocular data. By merging the information offered by numerous biometric modalities in different stages, the predicted benefit of combining multiple data (two in this example) is to address the drawbacks of each particular technique. Hence this system increases the overall performance of the recognition process (*M. K. Bhowmik et al, 2012)*.

Multibiometric systems have a number of advantages over typical unimodal systems, including a greater population coverage, improved anti-spoofing, increased robustness to noisy data in a single modality, continuous monitoring when a single characteristic is insufficient, and fault tolerance. When specific biometric sources become unreliable owing to sensor or software failure, or willful user manipulation, and when a single attribute is insufficient, continuous monitoring is required.

SUMMARY AND FUTURE TRENDS IN PERIOCULAR RESEARCH

In highly secure identity recognition systems, periocular biometrics have shown to be critical in coping with the rising occurrence of fraud problems. This chapter looks at how periocular biometrics and its different properties are used in face identification, as well as some other fields of research. Due to its robustness and high discriminative properties, the periocular region emerged as the most beneficial property. In forensic science, it can be used to identify criminals whose faces are obscured and only the periocular region is visible. This chapter also covered periocular databases and attributes. This chapter discusses the use of fusion modalities for face recognition as well as the periocular region in other applications. The effects of wrinkles, cosmetics, spectacles, and skin color can all be studied in the future. Periocular can also be utilized in conjunction with deep neural networks to uncover essential features in vital periocular areas and to improve accuracy in the situation of occlusion and low-resolution images. There is no large-scale, real-life periocular recognition competition like there is for other modalities in terms of future work for periocular recognition. Researchers would be able to evaluate their ideas in the same benchmark, ensuring that the comparison is compatible and fair, in a large-scale competition with real-life data collected. This would have a big impact on practical research in linked domains.

CONSENT FOR PUBLICATION

We, the author, the undersigned, give our consent for the publication of identifiable details, which can include photograph(s) and/or videos and/or case history and/or details within this chapter to be published by IGI Global Publishing

CONFLICT OF INTEREST

We, the authors do not have any conflict of interest with respect to research, authorship and/or publication of this book chapter.

ACKNOWLEDGMENT

We, the authors, want to thank all the Anonymous Reviewers, Publishers and Editors of this project for their speedy response.

REFERENCES

Adams, J., Woodard, D., Dozier, G., Miller, P., Bryant, K., & Glenn, G. (2010). Geneticbased type ii feature extraction for periocular biometric recognition: Less is more. *International Conference on Pattern Recognition*, 205–208.

Aginako, N., Castrillón-Santana, M., Lorenzo-Navarro, J., Martínez-Otzeta, J. M., & Sierra, B. (2017). Periocular and iris local descriptors for identity verification in mobile applications. *Pattern Recognition Letters*, *91*, 52–59.

Ahonen, A. H. T., & Pietikainen, M. (2006). Face Description with Local Binary Patterns: Application to Face Recognition. *IEEE Transactions on Pattern Analysis and Machine Intelligence*, *28*, 2037–2041.

Ahuja, K., Islam, R., Barbhuiya, F. A., & Dey, K. (2017). Convolutional neural networks for ocular smartphone-based biometrics. *Pattern Recognition Letters*, *91*, 17–26.

Ahuja, K., Islam, R., Barbhuiya, F. A., & Dey, K. (2016). A preliminary study of CNNs for iris and periocular verification in the visible spectrum. *2016 23rd International Conference on Pattern Recognition (ICPR),* 181-6.

Alonso-Fernandez, F., & Bigun, J. (2015). Near-infrared and visible-light periocular recognition with gabor features using frequency-adaptive automatic eye detection. *IET Biometrics*, *4*, 74–89.

Alonso-Fernandez, F., & Bigun, J. (2016). A survey on periocular biometrics research. *Pattern Recognition Letters*, *82*, 92–105.

Alonso-Fernandez, F., & Bigun, J. (2014). Eye detection by complex filtering for periocular recognition. *IWBF 2014–2nd International Workshop on Biometrics and Forensics 2014*.

Ambika, D., Radhika, K., & Seshachalam, D. (2016). Periocular authentication based on FEM using Laplace–Beltrami eigenvalues. *Pattern Recognition*, *50*, 178–194.

Bakshi, S., Sa, P. K., & Majhi, B. (2015). A novel phase-intensive localpattern for periocular recognition under visible spectrum. *Biocybernetics and Biomedical Engineering*, *35*, 30–44.

Baltrusaitis, T., Robinson, P., & Morency, L. P. (2016). OpenFace: an open source facial behavior analysis toolkit. *2016 IEEE Winter Conference on Applications of Computer Vision (WACV)*.

Bass, L., Clements, P., & Kazman, R. (2003). *Software Architecture in Practice* (2nd ed.). Addison Wesley.

Bhowmik, M. K., De, B. K., Bhattacharjee, D., Basu, D. K., & Nasipuri, M. (2012). Multisensor fusion of visual and thermal images for human face identification using different SVM kernels. *Systems, Applications and Technology Conference (LISAT), 2012 IEEE Long Island*, 1-7.

Cao, H., Deng, H.-W., & Wang, Y.-P. (2012). Segmentation of M-FISH images for improved classification of chromosomes with an adaptive Fuzzy C-Means Clustering Algorithm. *IEEE Transactions on Fuzzy Systems*, *20*, 1–8.

Carbon, C.-C. (2020). Wearing face masks strongly confuses counterparts in reading emotions. *Frontiers in Psychology*, *11*, 2526.

Castrillón-Santana, & Lorenzo-Navarro, & Ramón-Balmaseda. (2016). On using periocular biometric for gender classification in the wild. *Pattern Recognition Letters*, *82*, 181-189.

CDC. (2020). *Cases in the U.S.* https://www.cdc.gov/coronavirus/2019-ncov/casesupdates/ cases-in-us.html

Chandra & Bedi. (2018). Survey on SVM and their application in image classification. *International Journal of Information Technology*.

Chen, C., Dantcheva, A., & Ross, A. (2013). Automatic Facial Makeup Detection with Application in Face Recognition. *International Conference on Biometrics*.

Chun, C.-N., & Chung, R. (2004). Iris recognition for palm-top application. In D. Zhang & A. K. Jain (Eds.), Biometric Authentication (pp. 426–433). Springer.

Dantcheva, A., Cunjian, C., & Ross, A. (2012). Can Facial Cosmetics Affect the Matching Accuracy of Face Recognition Systems? *International Conference on Biometrics: Theory, Applications and Systems*, 391–398.

Decor, K. (n.d.). Available online: https://kitchendecor.club/files/now-beckham-hairstyle-david.html

Delhi Iris Database, I. I. T. (Version 1.0). (n.d.). http://www4.comp.polyu.edu.hk/csajaykr/IITD/Database_Iris.htm

Dimberg, U., Thunberg, M., & Elmehed, K. (2000). Unconscious facial reactions to emotional facial expressions. *Psychological Science*, *11*(1), 86–89.

Duda, R. O., Hart, P. E., & Stork, D. G. (2001). Pattern classification (2nd ed.). Wiley.

Eilers, P. H. C., & Goeman, J. J. (2004, March). Enhancing scatterplots with smoothed densities. *Bioinformatics*, *20*(5), 623–628.

Ekman, P. (1993). Facial expression and emotion. *The American Psychologist*, *48*(4), 384.

Elfenbein, H. A., & Ambady, N. (2002). Predicting workplace outcomes from the ability to eavesdrop on feelings. *The Journal of Applied Psychology*, *87*(5), 963.

Franklin, R. G., & Zebrowitz, L. A. (2013). Older adults' trait impressions of faces are sensitive to subtle resemblance to emotions. *Journal of Nonverbal Behavior*, *37*(3), 139–151.

Gao, H., Zhuang, L., Van Der Maaten, L., & Weinberger, K. Q. (2017). Densely connected convolutional networks. *2017 IEEE Conference on Computer Vision and Pattern Recognition (CVPR)*, 2261-9.

Gelinas, U. J. Jr, Sutton, S. G., & Fedorowicz, J. (2004). *Business processes and information technology*. South Western/Thomson Learning.

Global cases of covid 19. (n.d.). https://www.google.com/search?q=global+cases+of+covid+19&rlz=1C1CHBF_enUS779US779&oq=global+cases+&aqs=chrome.0.0j69i57j0l6.2899j0j7&sourceid=chrome&ie=UTF-8

Gode & Ganar. (2014). Image retrieval by using colour, texture and shape features. *International Journal of Advanced Research in Electrical, Electronics and Instrumentation Engineering, 3*.

Guo, K., Soornack, Y., & Settle, R. (2019). Expression-dependent susceptibility to face distortions in processing of facial expressions of emotion. *Vision Research*, *157*, 112–122.

Hareli, S., David, S., & Hess, U. (2013). Competent and Warm but Unemotional: The Influence of Occupational Stereotypes on the Attribution of Emotions. *Journal of Nonverbal Behavior*, *37*, 307–317.

He, K., Zhang, X., Ren, S., & Sun, J. (2016). Deep residual learning for image recognition. *29th IEEE Conference on Computer Vision and Pattern Recognition, CVPR 2016*, 770-778.

Hess, U., & Fischer, A. (2013). Emotional mimicry as social regulation. *Personality and Social Psychology Review*, *17*(2), 142–157.

Howard, A. G., Menglong, Z., Bo, C., Kalenichenko, D., Weijun, W., & Weyand, T. (2017). MobileNets: Efficient Convolutional Neural Networks for Mobile Vision Applications. Academic Press.

Huang, C., Wang, Y., & Li, X. (2020). Clinical features of patients infected with 2019 novel coronavirus in Wuhan, China. *Lancet*, *395*(10223), 497–506.

Hurley, D. J., Nixon, M. S., & Carter, J. N. (2005). Force field feature extraction for ear biometrics. *Computer Vision and Image Understanding*, *98*, 491–512.

Iris DatabaseC. A. S. I. A. V4. (n.d.). http://biometrics.idealtest.org/dbDetailForUser.do?id=14

Iris Image Database VersionC. A. S. I. A. 1.0. (n.d.). http://biometrics.idealtest.org/dbDetailForUser.do?id=1

Iris Image DatasetC. U. H. K. (n.d.). http://www.mae.cuhk.edu.hk/~cvl/main_database.htm

Jianxiong, D., Suen, C. Y., & Krzyzak, A. (2008). Effective shrinkage of large multi-class linear SVM models for text categorization. *19th International Conference on Pattern Recognition, ICPR 2008*.

Jillela, R., & Ross, A. (2012). Mitigating Effects of Plastic Surgery: Fusing Face and Ocular Biometrics. *International Conference on Biometrics: Theory, Applications and Systems*, 402–411.

Jillela, R., Ross, A. A., Boddeti, V. N., Kumar, B. V., Hu, X., & Plemmons, R. (2013). Iris segmentation for challenging periocular images. In Handbook of Iris Recognition. Springer.

Joseph, D. L., & Newman, D. A. (2010). Emotional intelligence: An integrative meta-analysis and cascading model. *The Journal of Applied Psychology*, *95*(1), 54.

Juefei-Xu, F., & Savvides, M. (2012). Unconstrained periocular biometric acquisition and recognition using COTS PTZ camera for uncooperative and non-cooperative subjects. *Applications of Computer Vision (WACV), 2012 IEEE Workshop on*, 201-208.

Kandasamy M. (2020). Perspectives for the use of therapeutic Botulinum toxin as a multifaceted candidate drug to attenuate COVID-19. *Med Drug Discov*.

Karahan, Ş., Karaöz, A., Özdemir, Ö. F., Gü, A. G., & Uludag, U. (2014). On identification from periocular region utilizing sift and surf. *Signal Processing Conference (EUSIPCO), 2014 Proceedings of the 22nd European*, 1392-1396.

Karkra & Patel. (2015). Atlas based medical segmentation techniques-A review. *Geinternational Journal of Engineering Research, 3*(5).

Kimura, K., & Lipeles, A. (1996). *Fuzzy controller component*. U.S. Patent 14,860,040.

Kumar, A., & Passi, A. (2010). Comparison and combination of iris matchers for reliable personal authentication. *Pattern Recognition*, *43*(3), 1016–1026.

Kumar, A., & Passi, A. (2010). Comparison and combination of iris matchers for reliable personal authentication. *Pattern Recognition*, *43*, 1016–1026.

Kumar, M. A., & Gopal, M. (2010). An Investigation on Linear SVM and its Variants for Text Categorization. *2nd International Conference on Machine Learning and Computing (ICMLC 2010)*, 27-31.

Kumari, P., & Seeja, K.R. (2019). Periocular biometrics: A survey. *Journal of King Saud University-Computer and Information Sciences*.

Lauer, S. A., Grantz, K. H., & Bi, Q. (2020). The Incubation Period of Coronavirus Disease 2019 (COVID-19)From Publicly Reported Confirmed Cases: Estimation and Application. *Annals of Internal Medicine*, *172*(9), 577–582.

Le, T. H. N., Prabhu, U., & Savvides, M. (2014). A novel eyebrow segmentation and eyebrow shape-based identification. *Biometrics (IJCB), 2014 IEEE International Joint Conference on*, 1-8.

Liu, G., Lee, K. Y., & Jordan, H. F. (1997, June). TDM and TWDM de Bruijn networks and shufflenets for optical communications. *IEEE Transactions on Computers*, *46*(6), 695–701. doi:10.1109/12.600827

Luz, E., Moreira, G., Zanlorensi, L. A. Jr, & Menotti, D. (2017). Deep periocular representation aiming video surveillance. *Pattern Recognition Letters*.

Mahalingam, G., & Ricanek, K. (2013). Article. *EURASIP Journal on Image and Video Processing*, *36*. Advance online publication. doi:10.1186/1687-5281-2013-36

Mahalingam, G., Ricanek, K., & Albert, A. M. (2014). Investigating the periocular-based face recognition across gender transformation. *IEEE Transactions on Information Forensics and Security*, *9*, 2180–2192.

Markus, H. R., & Kitayama, S. (1991). Culture and the self: Implications for cognition, emotion, and motivation. *Psychological Review*, *98*, 224–253.

McArthur, L. Z., & Baron, R. M. (1983). Toward an ecological theory of social perception. *Psychological Review*, *90*(3), 215.

Miller, P., Rawls, A., Pundlik, S., & Woodard, D. (2010). Personal Identification Using Periocular Skin Texture. *ACM Symposium on Applied Computing*, 1496–1500.

NIST. (2008). *Multiple Biometric Grand Challenge (MBGC) dataset*. https://face.nist.gov/mbgc/

Oh, K., Oh, B.-S., Toh, K.-A., Yau, W.-Y., & Eng, H.-L. (2014). Combining sclera and periocular features for multi-modal identity verification. *Neurocomputing*, *128*, 185–198.

Ojala, T., Pietik¨ainen, M., & M¨aenp¨a¨a, T. (2000). Gray scale and rotation invariant texture classification with local binary patterns. *Proceedings of the European Conference on Computer Vision*, 404–420.

Ojansivu, V., & Heikkilä, J. (2008). Blur insensitive texture classification using local phase quantization. *International conference on image and signal processing*, 236-243.

Osifchin, N., & Vau, G. (1997). Power considerations for the modernization of telecommunications in Central and Eastern European and former Soviet Union (CCE/FSU) countries. *Second International Telecommunication Energy Special Conference Special Conference*, 9-16. 10.1109/TELESC.1997.655690

Padole, C., & Proenca, H. (2012). Periocular Recognition: Analysis of Performance Degradation Factors. *International Conference on Biometrics*, 439–445.

Padole, C. N., & Proenca, H. (2012). Periocular recognition: Analysis ofperformance degradation factors. *Biometrics (ICB), 2012 5th IAPR International Conference on*, 439-445.

Park, U., Jillela, R., Ross, A., & Jain, A. (2011, March). Periocular biometrics in the visible spectrum. *IEEE Transactions on Information Forensics and Security*, *6*(1), 96–106.

Park, U., Ross, A., & Jain, A. K. (2009). Periocular biometrics in the visible spectrum: A feasibility study. *Proceedings of the IEEE International Conference on Biometrics: Theory, Applications, and Systems*, 1–6.

Phillips, P., Flynn, P., Scruggs, T., Bowyer, K., Chang, J., Hoffman, K., Marques, J., Min, J., & Worek, W. (2005). Overview of the face recognition grand challenge. *IEEE International Conference on Computer Vision and Pattern Recognition*, 1, 947–954.

Phillips, P. J., Bowyer, K. W., & Flynn, P. J. (2007, October). Comments on the casia version 1.0 iris data set. *IEEE Transactions on Pattern Analysis and Machine Intelligence*, *29*, 1869–1870.

Proença, H. (2014). Ocular biometrics by score-level fusion of disparate experts. *IEEE Transactions on Image Processing*, *23*, 5082–5093.

Proença, H., & Briceño, J. C. (2014). Periocular biometrics: Constraining the elastic graph matching algorithm to biologically plausible distortions. *IET Biometrics*, *3*, 167–175.

Proenca, H., & Neves, J. C. (2018). Deep-PRWIS: Periocular Recognition Without the Iris and Sclera Using Deep Learning Frameworks. *IEEE Transactions on Information Forensics and Security*, *13*, 888–896.

Rattani, A., Derakhshani, R., Saripalle, S. K., & Gottemukkula, V. (2016). ICIP 2016 competition on mobile ocular biometric recognition. *2016 IEEE International Conference on Image Processing (ICIP)*, 320-4.

Ross, A., Nandakumar, K., & Jain, A. (2006). Handbook of Multibiometrics. Academic Press.

Ruffman, T., Henry, J. D., Livingstone, V., & Phillips, L. H. (2008). A meta-analytic review of emotion recognition and aging: Implications for neuropsychological models of aging. *Neuroscience and Biobehavioral Reviews*, *32*(4), 863–881.

Shiota, M. N., Campos, B., & Keltner, D. (2003). The faces of positive emotion: Prototype displays of awe, amusement, and pride. *Annals of the New York Academy of Sciences*, *1000*(1), 296–299.

Smeraldi, F., & Bigun, J. (2002). Retinal vision applied to facial features detection and face authentication. *Pattern Recognition Letters*, *23*, 463–475.

Smereka & Kumar. (2013). What is a 'good' periocular region for recognition? *IEEE Comput. Soc. Conf. Comput. Vis. Pattern Recognit. Work.*, 117–124. doi:10.1109/CVPRW.2013.25

The Korea Times. (n.d.). Available online: https://www.koreatimes.co.kr/www/nation/2019/01/371_262460.html

Trokielewicz, M., & Szadkowski, M. (2017). Can we recognize horses by their ocular biometric traits using deep convolutional neural networks? Photonics Applications in Astronomy, Communications, Industry, and High Energy Physics Experiments 2017.

Uzair, M., Mahmood, A., Mian, A., & McDonald, C. (2015). Periocular region-based person identification in the visible, infrared and hyperspectral imagery. *Neurocomputing*, *149*, 854–867.

Viola, P., & Jones, M. J. (2004). Robust real-time face detection. *International Journal of Computer Vision*, *57*, 137–154.

Walid, H. (2020). *Efficient Masked Face Recognition Method during the COVID-19 Pandemic.* . doi:10.21203/rs.3.rs-39289/v1

Woodard, D., Pundlik, S., Lyle, J., & Miller, P. (2010). Periocular region appearance cues for biometric identification. *IEEE International Conference on Computer Vision and Pattern Recognition Workshops*, 162–169.

Xiuming, J., & Jing, W. (2011). Research of remote sensing classification about land survey based on SVM. *2011 2nd International Conference on Artificial Intelligence, Management Science and Electronic Commerce (AIMSEC 2011),* 3230-3.

Xu, J., Cha, M., Heyman, J. L., Venugopalan, S., Abiantun, R., & Savvides, M. (2010). Robust local binary pattern feature sets for periocular biometric identification. *Biometrics: Theory Applications and Systems (BTAS), 2010 Fourth IEEE International Conference on*, 1-8.

Yu, W., Liu, T., Valdez, R., Gwinn, M., & Khoury, M. J. (2010, March 22). Application of support vector machine modeling for prediction of common diseases: The case of diabetes and pre-diabetes. *BMC Medical Informatics and Decision Making*, *10*, 16.

Zhang, H. (1997). *Delay-insensitive networks* [M.S. thesis]. University of Waterloo, Waterloo, Canada.

Zhao & Kumar. (2018). *Improving Periocular Recognition by Explicit Attention to Critical Regions in Deep Neural Network.* Academic Press.

Zhao, Z., & Kumar, A. (2017). Accurate Periocular Recognition under Less Constrained Environment Using Semantics-Assisted Convolutional Neural Network. *IEEE Transactions on Information Forensics and Security*, *12*, 1017–1030.

Chapter 5
The Impact of the COVID-19 Pandemic on Manpower (Labor) and the Supply Chain

Alan D. Smith
Robert Morris University, USA

ABSTRACT

The COVID-19 pandemic of 2020 has changed everything on a global scale. The lockdowns and general fear of the unknown caused a dramatic increase in ecommerce as buyers turned to the internet to get the goods and products they wanted. Many businesses had to close during this time due to lack of customers, lack of workers, and due to staffing issues due to the virus. As things started opening back up the demand for goods and services has been overwhelming to many industries. Ships are waiting off the coast for months to be unloaded, shelves are empty, the next day deliveries are taking days and weeks as the transportation system is overwhelmed. High demand and a lack of workers in every industry has led to a major global supply chain disruption that has not been experienced before. These disruptions affect every part of the supply chain from manufactures, warehouses, shipping, rail, truck, down to the retail level. This chapter will look at two companies in the Pittsburgh area (i.e., FedEx Ground and Ensinger, Inc.).

INTRODUCTION

COVID-19 Economic Impacts

Walk into almost any store and you find empty shelves. Order something online from any of the major retailers and what used to be next day delivery may now be a week later and sometimes a month later. The shortages that are seen everywhere are painting a bleak picture for the holiday season. The labor shortages have been linked to the disruptions in the supply chain. This labor shortage comes at a time of high demand and effects every part of the supply chain. "Companies are facing sharply higher demand for goods and services, with sharply less labor availability, and substantial uncertainty about their ability to pass cost on their customers." (Conerly, 2021, p. 4). With all parts of the supply chain impacted by

DOI: 10.4018/978-1-6684-5250-9.ch005

this labor shortage the effects are widespread. The Global supply chain woes all point back to the lack of labor (Caminiti, 2021). Shipping cost have increased four to five times and transit times have increased three to four times longer than usual. (Caminiti, 2021). There are many reasons for the labor shortage but its impact on the supply chain is long lasting and impactful.

BACKGROUND

Agility in Supply Chains

In an uncertain environment, it is critical that the supply chain management adopts different, and more innovative strategies that support a better response to customer needs. They must be able to respond rapidly and in a cost-effective way both in terms of volume and variety. Supply chains are unfortunately vulnerable to disruptions which makes risk to business continuity very high and continuing to get higher. There are many changes that businesses are constantly dealing with in regard to customer service to relationship management, forecasting to end-casting, functional integration to process integration, and share of information among supply chain entities. These changes have been stimulated by restructuring to drive down costs, the increasing importance of reverse logistics to manage waste and protect the environment, and constant search for cheap manufacturing labor. Businesses are forced to be reactive, and need to find ways to become proactive. Agile supply chain management refers to, "the degree of flexibility, velocity, responsiveness, competence, visibility and collaboration will influence the supply chain behavior supporting the quick response to changes in demand," (Agile and resilient …, 2012).

An agile supply chain management approach depends on market sensibility, customer satisfaction, quality improvement, delivery speed, data accuracy, new product introduction, and much more. This approach helps the supply chain respond quickly and pursues responsiveness of the supply network. Having this type of supply chain skill will influence the supply chain performance and increase competitiveness. As suggested by Kim and Davis (2016), sustainability can be enhanced by utilizing an agile approach. They conducted an analysis of conflict minerals reports submitted to the Securities and Exchange Commission (SEC) by directive of Section 1502 of the Dodd-Frank Act 2010. This section of Dodd-Frank required firms to determine and report whether product contained conflict minerals from the Democratic Republic of Congo (DRC) geographic area benefitted armed militia groups. In their narrative, the authors analyze and critique data that is required to show the origin of their products. As the operations of any give firm become more complex, the control over their supply chain operations is lessened to the point that a firm may not be aware of the source of their end products. Kim and Davis (2016) found that by identifying the organizational factors that enable a firm to vet their supply chain versus factors that hinder their ability to provide effective governance of their supply chain can be a very effective supply chain strategy in adverse environmental conditions.

According to Carvalho, et al. (2012), the 6 main characteristics of the supply chain. Flexibility refers to the ability of a supply chain to adjust its speed, destinations, and volume in response to changes in demand. It is critical for the supply chain to be consistent with the demand of its customers. As customer needs change, the product or service changes in regard to what will make their customers happy. Velocity refers to the ability to complete an activity as quickly as possible. As disruptions in the supply chain occur, recovery needs to happen instantly. Responsiveness is the ability to identify changes in demand and responding quickly. This relates to market sensitivity and response to real demand. It is better for a supply chain to be proactive, not reactive. Competence is the ability to efficiently and effectively respond to market changes. Visibility is capturing data on demand and sharing between buyers and suppliers. This creates a virtual supply chain and keeps information flowing amongst everyone in the supply chain. Good communication results in a smoother and more efficient supply chain. Lastly, collaboration is when all in the supply chain members discuss specific issues on the demand and supply side. The demand side issues can be related to quality or cost, while the supply side has to do with buyer-supplier relations and information sharing. Operational levels, including inventory, delivery, and time, help the supply chain tremendously. Without the inventory constantly being supplied, how can we sell the product? If delivery speed is not up to customer expectations, they will order elsewhere. "According to some studies, almost no performance measurement systems are adjusted to the actual supply chain necessities," (Agile and resilient Approaches to Supply Chain Management, 2012). Adjusting the evaluation of the supply chain performance to focus on these key points will ensure a successful supply chain, which is what the agile approach does.

Perhaps, supply chain performance focuses too much on logistics and not enough on how key business practices have been performed or how well customer needs were met (Verma, et al., 2018; Xu, et al., 2018; Yazdi & Esfeden, 2018). Purchasing and Supply Management (PSM), which was originally a sub-discipline of manufacturing and operations management, has only recently gained recognition as a separate discipline. This new focus on PSM can be attributed to: Outsourcing, globalization, and e-business. For example, Van Weele and Van Raaij (2005) go into much detail about the 6 aspects or dimensions of SC in order to pave a path for the future of PSM. They argue that both relevance and rigor in terms of academic research are necessary in order to define a clear theoretical underpinning for the subject of PSM and in order to help those outside of the PSM community to recognize and utilize it. Instead of researchers scouring to find new theories, they should focus more on researching topics that revolve around strategic priorities and a limited number of management theories: Stakeholder theory, network theory, the Resource-Based View of the Firm, dynamic capabilities theory, and relational view are all identified by Van Weele and Raaij as interesting candidates. Not only is relevance important, but so is the rigor. Instead of 'one-shot' studies, researchers should focus more on replication studies, longitudinal studies, and meta-analytical studies.

So, what is PSM? PSM can be defined as the discipline that is concerned with the management of external resources - goods, services, capabilities and knowledge - that are necessary for running, maintaining and managing the primary and support processes of a firm at the most favorable conditions. In short, PSM is a vendor-manufacturer connection that results in a mutually beneficial relationship. The traditional problem is that many applications of SCM (Jain & D'lima, 2018; Kailash, et al., 2018; Oey & Nofrimurti, 2018; Rego, et al., 2018), the primary focus of PSM is typically on cost reduction, especially through competitive contracting. This is easily understandable when one considers that PSM has its roots in Transaction Cost Economics (TCE). It is important to understand where a philosophy comes from and what it traditionally focuses on in order to fully understand its implications and how it will evolve in the future. In more recent decades PSM has focused on strategic relationships with suppliers and research has focused on: supplier relationship management, collaborative networks, and early supplier involvement in new product development. It's interesting to note the applicability of some of these ideas; for example, my own company has recently involved itself in a specific supplier relationship known as Vendor Managed Inventory (VMI) (Smith, 2021a). A supply chain performance measurement system needs to include productivity, quality, and customer satisfaction (Bhurjee, et al, 2018; Chaturvedi & Chakrabarti, 2018; Gothwal & Raj, 2018; Hossain & Hossain, 2018; Kim & Davis, 2016).

With these aspects being the supply chain's competitive priorities, it is important that the previous characteristics of the supply chain are met along with operational levels (Smith, 2021a). Customers are becoming a lot more demanding of new products and features and if the business cannot give them these in a reasonable amount of time, business will be lost. Customers will find anything to complain about, which is why keeping up with these complaints and responding to customer complaints can help maintain future business. Using the agile approach on supply chain performance ensures all characteristics are maintained. The agile approach also reduces development cycle times (Oey & Nofrimurti, 2018; Rego, et al., 2018). This often means, "service levels can be improved by reducing delivery lead times due to shorter product/process design and development time (Agile and resilient …, 2012). It also reduces the time to market. The agile approach facilitates rapid decision-making by building stronger relationships with its suppliers. When all strategic partners in the supply chain has a strong relationship, it will make its supply chain performance more effective and efficient, which as explained, leads to happy customers. Product customization is able to happen using the agile approach which gives company a one up. They can listen to the wants and needs of customers and respond by producing customized goods. Producing customized goods results in economies of scope being achieved, at low cost, in order to gain from economies of scale. It is a no brainer to use the agile approach because everything in the supply chain flows smoother, in a more beneficial way for the business.

Covid-19 and Supply Chain Instability

In 2009 the unemployment rate was 10% in the United States. Fast forward to 2019 and the unemployment rate in the U.S. was reduced to 3.5%. In the span of a decade, the labor market improved from the lowest numbers since the great depression to one of the strongest labor markets in the world (Levannon, et al, 2020). In 2020 the labor market fell off a cliff with unemployment immediately skyrocketed to 14.8% at the end of April 2020 which signified the peak of the recession (Falk, et al, 2021). Covid-19 and the calamity to follow was obviously a major contributor to the drastic shift in the labor market (Smith, 2021b). Covid-19 and its economic disruptions have instilled a lot of fear and uncertainty amongst government, nations, and businesses resulting in many "knee-jerk" reactions were made and the effects of which are still being felt, especially in the health sector (Smith, 2022).

Setting Covid-19 and the slew of geopolitical and world events to follow aside, there were a handful of other factors setting the stage for a potential labor shortage. First, unemployment rate was at an all time low for all demographics and job functionalities. While this is excellent for the economy of a nation, an item that was overlooked was how this compared to the growth rate of the blue-collar workforce. Many of the jobs being created where blue collar jobs either being brought back from overseas or from companies breaking ground on new facilities. When one considers how this compares to the diminishing growth rate of blue-collar working-class individual there is a large disparity. The baby boomer generation which made up an overwhelming fraction of the blue collar workforce is at retirement age and while generation X and the millennials began to backfill these positions in the workforce, the ratio of those in blue collar positions has slowly been decreasing over time (Moore et al, 2014).

A disruption to the global supply chain at the level we are seeing was inconceivable in the global economy. Covid-19's impact on the supply chain is still relatively new and not much research has been conducted in how the supply chain should and must adapt to the new challenges especially in the area of labor shortage. The supply chain used to be the low-cost part of the equation. How to move products from point a to b as economically as possible. Now the disruption has made the supply chain a costly and ever rising expense in the equation. The global pandemic has and will change forever the way supply chains do their work. (Flynn, et al, 2021, Smith, 2022). Instead of looking at the supply chain on a cost basis it must be looked at in an organic system that constantly adapts and changes. The research is just starting in this field as the current state of supply chain disruptions have caused everyone to rethink the supply chain.

CASE STUDY

In the following sections, two Pittsburgh, PA-based corporations to uncover their actions and reactions to the green movement, and their current and future plans to remain viable, respected corporate citizens as it pertains to their eco-friendly strategic initiatives. The large companies are FedEx Ground, a global provider of logistics services and manufacturer, and Ensinger Group, a large region-based manufacturer. Through a closer examination of these two companies this chapter will look at how the labor shortages, pandemic, and supply chain disruptions have impacted their operations and what these companies are doing to overcome the challenges. A qualitative business case study approach was used in research supply chains and their responses to the current labor shortages. The basic structure of this section is to have a company description of both companies, followed by supply chain operations, supply chain problems, then potential supply chain solutions.

Company Description

FedEx Ground

FedEx Ground is a subsidiary of FedEx Corporation specializing in ground transportation of small packages to commercial and residential locations. Based in Moon Township, PA, FedEx Ground started as Roadway Package Systems in 1985 and pioneered the use of barcoded packages to be able to scan and trace packages at all points in the distribution system. 9 years after its creation it exceeded US$1 billion in annual revenue. FedEx acquired RPS in 1998 and it became FedEx Ground in 2000. Today FedEx Ground has over US$22 Billion in annual revenue.

Ensinger Inc.

The Ensinger Group, founded in 1966 in Nufringen, Germany, is engaged in the development and manufacture of high-performance plastics. It has over 2,690 employees. Ensinger Inc., located in Washington, PA, has an area-wide reputation of high quality and reliability in its manufacturing and delivery processes.

Supply Chain Operations

FedEx Ground

FedEx Ground handles more the 12 million package every day. The network is comprised of over 39 hubs and 600 operating facilities employing over 225,000 team members (Company structure and facts, 2021). The FedEx Ground network is built on a hub and spoke network model. In 2019 FedEx rolled out

7-day residential deliveries to adapt to the rising demands of ecommerce. With this rapid growth FedEx has continually invested in new facilities and emerging technology and has the industries most automated hub network. FedEx Ground is an integral part in the supply chain by partnering with major retailers to distribute their packages to stores and homes across the country in 1-4 days. With the Pandemic rise in ecommerce demand FedEx Ground package volume and revenues have grown over 25%.

Ensinger Inc.

Ensinger Inc., located in Washington, PA extrudes semi-finished stock shaped product comprised of both engineered and high-performance plastics. This process, though plastic extrusion, is analogous to steel casting processes such that steel manufacturers cast solid billets and slabs that later get machined into finished goods. Ensinger Inc. sources various plastic resins both domestically and internationally. Plastic resins are another by-product of the oil and gas industry. Plastic resins are produced from the cracking process where hydrocarbons are heated until they "crack". After which, the by-products are collected and further processed to make specific plastics, such as polyethylene (PE) and polypropylene (PP). These plastics resins are then supplied as raw materials to compounding facilities where they are running through extruders and mixed with other ingredients to make a unique plastic resin. Both the raw materials and finished good form these compounding facilities are in the form of plastic resin, with the exception being that the finished good contained unique properties relative to how it was formulated. Another source of the plastic resin is from various chemical reactions which highlight different forms of polymerization reactions. Here, similar to how the PE and PP are produced, more specialty plastic resins are made such as Acetal based products, PEEKs, Ultems, and Nylons. Often, these specialty resin operations are contained in the same facilities that compound them for ease of logistics and regulatory requirements. Once Ensinger Inc. receives the resin, they begin processing it until the plastic is in its finished form.

Supply Chain Problems

FedEx Ground

With over 25% increase in packages the demand has exceeded capacity. The increased volume was more than double and almost triple what the original forecast were prior to the Pandemic of 2020. Plans for this volume level were not addressed for another 2-3 years. How to add capacity in existing facilities quickly to meet the Christmas peak demands were top priority. Many new solutions were looked at too quickly open new sort facilities across the network to deal with rising demand. 7-day operations became the norm and many facilities operate and 100% plus capacity 24/7. With the new facilities and additional sorts more people are needed, and this is where the labor shortage has been seen. Throughout the country many buildings were not able to operate at full capacity. In most recent earnings for Quarter 1 ending August 31 FedEx reported US$450 million dollars in higher cost due to overtime, higher wages, and extra spending on transportation. Chief Operating Officer Raj Subramaniam said "The impact of constrained labor markets remains the biggest issue facing our business." (Ziobro, 2021). He went on to point out that one hub in Portland OR had 65% of the workers needed to hand the volume. As a result, FedEx was having to divert 25% of the volume to other locations and using third-party transportation companies to move the freight around the country to be sorted. Salaries and benefits have risen over

13% in an effort hire enough workers in a tight labor market. Service has also seen sharp decline due to the demands exceeding capacity. Ontime performance dropped to 86.4% in August according to Ship Matrix (Ziobro, 2021). FedEx service levels prepandemic were above 98%. Ship matrix estimates that shipping demand exceeds capacity by 4.7 million packages a day in November and December for the market. FedEx needs to hire over 90,000 workers for the holiday peak season which will be a challenge in an already tight market.

Ensinger Inc.

Ensinger Inc., like many other businesses is facing major supply chain challenges. Raw material lead times keep getting extended and demand is greater than ever. Coupled with a national labor shortage and it is the perfect storm for a major supply chain dilemma. As a result of supplier lead times getting longer and less predictable, Ensinger Inc. has had to adapt their own purchasing behavior to keep the shop floor stocked with raw materials and like many others, extend some its lead times as well. A major factor in the state of Ensinger Inc.'s supply chain challenges can be traced back to labor shortages. Whether it was workers getting sick, finding employment elsewhere, or simply quitting for unknown reasons, labor shortages have hit the plastics industry hard. Ensinger Inc. witnesses the blowback of labor shortages firsthand within its own operation however farther up the supply chain, the labor shortage impacts many other players in the industry besides Ensinger Inc. The root cause of the supply chain issues, though centrally a by-product of the labor shortage, is more predicated in the bulk chemical industry and largely stems back further into the oil and gas industry. To repair the plastics industry, oil and gas companies are going to need to invest time and resources (both labor and fiscal) into oil and natural gas extraction infrastructure. From here, the industry will need to look towards repairing oil and gas refining and processing plants. Lastly, they will then need to ramp up production to deliver the large volumes of feedstock chemicals that many companies, including the plastic resin compounders rely on (Williams, 2021).

As a result of the bulk chemical shortage, demand has begun to greatly outpace the available supply, causing everything to rise in price. For example, common commodity chemicals such as PVC containing compounds which includes but not limited to pipes, medical devices, and credit cards are up nearly 70% from March 2020 as of September 2021. Epoxy resin are up nearly 170% and Ethylene, one of the most commercially used chemicals is up nearly 43% both over the same time span (Wiseman, 2021). During the summer of 2020, amidst Covid related lockdowns, companies began to deplete their finished goods inventories in order to keep up with the massive ramp up in demand. Following, when hurricane Laura hit Texas and Louisiana, it forced a handful of petrochemical plants to close, essentially knocking out 10-15% of the U.S. PE and PP supply overnight (Vakil, 2021). Massive chemical and polymer producing companies such as Lyondelbasell and Chevron Phillips were among the slew of companies that ended up filing force majeure claims.

Supply Chain Solutions

FedEx Ground

The solutions to the huge demand are to add capacity. The capacity can be adding sorts, adding more workers, and adding more sorting facilities. Another thing FedEx is doing to offset the higher cost is raising rates to customers. In a recent statement rates will be increasing an average of 5.9% the largest increase in more than 8 years. FedEx is also focusing on more profitable customers at the expense of losing some low margin customers. Higher pay, weekend bonuses, increased health benefits, and tuition assistance are all being rolled out to attract and retain workers in the tough labor market. FedEx has increased hourly pay by as much as 25% from a year ago. In Q1 FedEx spent US$85 million in ground network by adding 16 new automated facilities and expanding 100 others. (Garland, 2021). This adds more than a million packages to capacity compared to last peak.

Ensinger Inc.

There are a handful of solutions that can and were implemented within Ensinger Inc. Ensinger Inc. took both internal and external approaches to the matter and though it didn't solve all their supply chain issues, it greatly improved the situation at hand. Ensinger Inc. is a lean enterprise and as such, has adopted a continuous improvement culture that was quickly able to discern which variable where within their control to invest resources to alleviate their supply chain dilemmas. Since many of the factors affecting the Ensinger Inc. supply chain were external and outside of their control, they immediately began to investigate what could be done internally to improve their processes. Without going into too much detail for the sake of proprietary information, various avenues were explored. These ranged from process control initiatives, process optimization tactics, material handling flows, and even how the product order were fulfilled. Another method Ensinger investigated was challenging the quality and regulatory compliance to quickly qualify alternative raw materials. This way should a different supplier then Ensinger Inc. would typically use have excess resin available, they would be prepared to purchase and run it. All of these in combination allowed Ensinger to remain competitive with their lead times when faced with increased supplier lead times for their raw materials. Granted Ensinger was not able to improve everything across the board in such a short period of time, they were able to improve enough lead times so that their customers did not experience the full brunt of what they were experiencing in terms of lead time delays from the upstream resin suppliers.

In parallel with the internal process improvements, Ensinger Inc's purchasing, and logistics departments began working towards possible solutions for the difficulty to receive materials in a predictable manner. Though there was not a ton of negotiation that could be down from the purchasing department perspective given the situation, what they did do was open communications and introduce a level of transparency to the situation. In doing so, Ensinger Inc and their suppliers were able to manage expectations better and mitigate unfavorable surprises.

Managerial Implications

As evident from today's headlines and the case studies contained within this chapter, the current labor shortage has impacts upon every part of the supply chain. From truck drivers, warehouse workers, workers in manufacturer, even to the ones placing orders and keeping inventory. What we are seeing is the labor shortage has put workers in the driver's seat. Higher pay, better benefits, better work-life balance, and opportunities to expand skills have become the selling points to attract new workers in the high demand fields. In addition to increased benefits for direct labor positions, many indirect labor positions were relied upon heavily to improve production and fulfillment operations. When capacities were immediately reduced due to high turnover, it can often take months before a replacement can be found and

Table 1. How labor shortage has affected each operation.

FedEx Ground	Ensinger, Inc
Higher cost for transportation	Higher cost of raw materials
Increased cost for wages	Increased costs for wages
Short staffing equal less capacity	Short staffing equal less capacity

adequately trained to fill the void. In the meantime, increased automation and internal process improvements centered around critical value add operations can maintain or even increase capacities with fewer laborers. Historically, this philosophy has been applied to reduce the number of laborers required to perform a certain set of tasks. Nowadays, these continuous improvement initiatives are sought after not to reduce the number of employees, rather to reduce the number of laborers required for various functions such that resources can be redistributed and the current workforce can achieve greater outcomes than the previous workforce. Table 1 depicts a comparison of the largest problems each company faced as a direct result of the labor shortage.

Though FedEx Ground and Ensinger Inc. serve two entirely different sectors, they faced very similar problems as a result of the labor shortage. Both companies experienced increased in their variable costs. For FedEx Ground this was observed in their transportation costs whereas Ensinger Inc. felt the affects in their raw material prices. In addition, both companies saw diminishing capacities as result of not having the manpower to fully operate. Historically, capacity constraints are felt from worsening performance and quality and an increase in unplanned maintenance. These issues are typically resolved through capital investments such as upgrading or replacing legacy systems and equipment which results in less unplanned maintenance, higher throughput (increased performance), and greater product quality (Waddill, 2020). The labor challenge however is a lot less black and white as the issue isn't obsolete equipment or legacy systems not performing up to par, rather simply not having the manpower to utilize the maximum availability for equipment, process lines, and overall facilities. Table 2 states the various solutions both companies employed to address the problems.

Table 2. Solutions implemented at each operation.

FedEx Ground	Ensinger, Inc.
Higher pay	Higher pay
Bonus programs/ Increased benefits	Various performance-based incentives
Increase automation	Internal process improvements
New Facilities	Qualified new raw material suppliers

To address the labor shortage directly, both companies increased wages for employees and devised performance-based incentive bonus programs to promote retention. FedEx Ground, in order to hedge some capacity constraints due to the labor shortage invested in newer, more automated facilities that operated more efficiently to maintain fulfillment capacities. In a similar fashion, Ensinger Inc. began qualifying alternative raw material suppliers which allowed them to maintain upstream flexibility in the wake of waning supplier predictability.

FUTURE RESEARCH DIRECTIONS

It is true that in a competitive market, demand changes very frequently. With that being known, as competition increases, firms need to apply a more approach to their respective supply chains. If the business is unable to respond rapidly, and in a cost-effective way, to unpredictable changes in markets then management has setup their firms fail. However, a customized strategy that balances the need for being flexible with the capital needed will be necessary if this strategy is to be successful and sustainable. Most businesses say that customer satisfaction is important to them, but saying it is a lot easier than proving it when it comes to pleasing its stockholders who want a healthy return on their investment, especially during these troubling times. An agile approach ensures that companies are following up with customer complaints and closely monitoring customer needs. Much research is needed to find ways to incentivize customer satisfaction is the number one way to keep a business afloat. An agile approach supports that a performance-measurement system is being utilized to evaluate virtually all aspects of the supply chain. Using this performance measurement system shows the company their strengths and weaknesses throughout the supply chain pointing out areas of improvement. There is always room for improvement and future research needs to empirically test those assumptions. One cannot assume a supply chain will functioning in the way it needs it to by simply responding to market forces. It requires close monitoring to reassure a firm's customers, suppliers, and various other stakeholders are adapting to the myriad of environmental conditions that supply chains are currently enduring.

CONCLUSION

This chapter presented a non-empirical or business-practices case study suggesting that management must deploy agile and resilient approaches in order to increase supply chain performance and competitiveness in the wake of supply chain disruptions. High inflation, geopolitical conflict, and supply chain imbalances have left their mark in global commerce. Reduced delivery time, reduced cycle time, increasing frequency of new product introductions, and rapid decision-making are proven responses to such times of instability. Being agile and implementing such practices on supply chain performance have never been more in need than in today's difficult environment. An agile approach influences supply chain's performance regarding customer satisfaction, on-time delivery fulfilment, and ratio of annual sales to average total stock. There are many unpredictable changes in markets that supply chains need to respond rapidly to, and the agile approach helps to deal with these changes.

Companies are finding ways to adapt to the growing labor shortage as it does not appear to be slowing down any time soon. Since waiting for the labor shortage to improve itself organically is not a sustainable solution for businesses, companies are getting creative in their solutions. Companies are investigating methods for hiring, onboarding, and retaining both direct and indirect labor. Most of which is centered around benefit packages, total compensation, and work-life balance to motivate and incentivize either joining or staying with an organization. In addition to addressing the labor problem directly, companies are also pursuing options to improve internal processes and continue operations at near or greater capacities compared to before the labor shortage. The future supply chain will be different than pre-Covid. No longer will it be seen as the low-cost component in the process, the supply chain of the future will be a hybrid of more automation, higher-paid workers, and more information technology and sharing of data to ensure no or minimal supply chain disruptions. Shorter supply chains may also come out as a short-term solution to the supply chain disruptions with less moving components that are closer together.

REFERENCES

Bhurjee, A. K., Kumar, P., & Padhan, S. K. (2018). Solid transportation problem with budget constraints under interval uncertain environments. *International Journal of Process Management and Benchmarking*, *7*(2), 172–182. doi:10.1504/IJPMB.2017.083104

Caminiti, S. (2021). Lack of workers is further fueling supply chain woes. *CNBC*. Retrieved October 18, 2021 from https://www.cnbc.com/2021/09/28/companies-need-more-workers-to-help-resolve-supply-chain-problems.html

Carvalho, H., Azevedo, S., & Cruz-Machado, V. (2012). Agile and resilient approaches to supply chain management: Influence on performance and competitiveness. *Logistics Research*, *4*(1-2), 49–62. doi:10.100712159-012-0064-2

Chaturvedi, S., & Chakrabarti, D. (2018). Operational efficiency in manufacturing process using design of experiments. *International Journal of Process Management and Benchmarking*, *7*(2), 249–261. doi:10.1504/IJPMB.2017.083111

Company structure and facts. (2021). Retrieved October 22, 2021 from https://www.fedex.com/en-us/about/company-structure.html

Conerly, B. (2021). The labor shortage is why supple chains are disrupted. *Forbes*. Retrieved on October 19, 2021 from https://www.forbes.com/sites/billconerly/2021/07/07/the-labor-shortage-is-why-supply-chains-are-disrupted/?sh=45a33476301d

Falk, G., Romero, P. D., Nicchitta, I. A., & Nyhof, E. C. (2021). *Unemployment rates during the COVID-19 pandemic - fas*. Retrieved October 23, 2021, from https://sgp.fas.org/crs/misc/R46554.pdf

Flynn, B., Cantor, D., Pagell, M., Dooley, K., & Azadegan, A. (2021). From the Editors: Introduction to managing supply chains beyond COVID-19- Preparing for the next global mega-disruption. Journal of Supply Chain Management, 57(1), 3-6.

Garland, M. (2021). FedEx Diverts packages as labor shortage bits into service levels. *Supply Chain Dive*. Retrieved October 18, 2021 from https://www.supplychaindive.com/news/fedex-earnings-labor-shortage-peak-season-capacity/606988/

Genovese, D. (2021). FedEx rerouting more than 600k packages a day because of labor shortages. *Fox Business*. Retrieved on October 19, 2021 from https://www.foxbusiness.com/lifestyle/fedex-rerouting-packages-daily-labor-shortage

Gothwal, S., & Raj, T. (2018). Prioritising the performance measures of FMS using multi-criteria decision making approaches. *International Journal of Process Management and Benchmarking*, *8*(1), 59–78. doi:10.1504/IJPMB.2018.088657

Hossain, M. S., & Hossain, M. M. (2018). Application of interactive fuzzy goal programming for multi-objective integrated production and distribution planning. *International Journal of Process Management and Benchmarking*, *8*(1), 35–58. doi:10.1504/IJPMB.2018.088656

Jain, N., & D'lima, C. (2018). Organisational culture preference for gen Y's prospective job aspirants: A personality-culture fit perspective. *International Journal of Process Management and Benchmarking*, *7*(2), 262–275. doi:10.1504/IJPMB.2017.083122

Kailash, Saha, R. K., & Goyal, S. (2018). Systematic literature review of classification and categorisation of benchmarking in supply chain management. *International Journal of Process Management and Benchmarking, 7*(2), 183-205.

Kim, Y., & Davis, G. (2016). Challenges for global supply chain sustainability: Evidence from conflict materials reports. *Academy of Management Journal*, *59*(6), 1896–1916. doi:10.5465/amj.2015.0770

Levannon, G., Crofoot, E., Steemers, F., & Erickson, R. (2021). *Labor shortages - the Conference Board.* Retrieved October 23, 2021, from https://www.conference-board.org/topics/labor-shortages

Moore, S. Y., Grunberg, L., & Krause, A. J. (2014,). The relationship between work and home: Examination of white and blue-collar generational differences in a large U.S. organization. *Psychology.* Retrieved October 23, 2021, from https://www.scirp.org/html/7-6901275_50892.htm

Oey, E., & Nofrimurti, M. (2018). Lean implementation in traditional distributor warehouse - a case study in an FMCG company in Indonesia. *International Journal of Process Management and Benchmarking*, *8*(1), 1–15. doi:10.1504/IJPMB.2018.088654

Rego, S., Kumar, N., & Mukherjee, P. N. (2018). Impact of policy implementation on telecommunication diffusion in India. *International Journal of Process Management and Benchmarking*, *8*(1), 16–34. doi:10.1504/IJPMB.2018.088655

Smith, A. D. (2021a). Vendor managed inventory and strategy: Case study of global supply chains. *International Journal of Sustainable Economies Management*, *3*(1), 1–20.

Smith, A. D. (2021b). Updating an empirical investigating risk perceptions associated with national ID cards in the wake of the global Covid-19 pandemic. *Health Marketing Quarterly*, *38*(2-3), 70–90. doi: 10.1080/07359683.2021.1980841 PMID:34554045

Smith, A. D. (2022). Exploring opioid addictions and responsibilities: Almost lost in the midst of the Covid-19 pandemic. *International Journal of Human Rights in Healthcare*, *15*(1), 41–74. doi:10.1108/IJHRH-03-2021-0067

Sozzi, B. (2021). Fedex just painted a disturbing picture of the job market. *Yahoo News.* Retrieved October 19, 2021 from https://news.yahoo.com/fed-ex-just-painted-a-disturbing-picture-of-the-job-market-160422695.html

Vakil, B. (2021). The latest supply chain disruption: Plastics. *Harvard Business Review*. Retrieved October 22, 2021, from https://hbr.org/2021/03/the-latest-supply-chain-disruption-plastics

Van Weele, A., & van Raaij, E. (2005). The future of purchasing and supply management research: About relevance and rigor. *The Journal of Supply Chain Management, 50*(1), 56–72. doi:10.1111/jscm.12042

Verma, P., Sharma, R. R. K., & Kumar, V. (2018). The sustainability issues of diversified firms in emerging economies context: A theoretical model and propositions. *International Journal of Process Management and Benchmarking*, *7*(2), 224–248. doi:10.1504/IJPMB.2017.083107

Waddill, C. (2020). *The importance of OEE in ROI analysis for manufacturers*. Evocon. Retrieved October 23, 2021, from https://evocon.com/kb/why-oee-roi-provide-value-to-management/

Williams, S. (2021). Plastics shortage hits plastic parts supply chain. *Industrial Specialties Mfg*. Retrieved March 9, 2022, from https://www.industrialspec.com/about-us/blog/detail/plastic-raw-material-shortages-rising-prices-delivery-delays-early-2021/

Wiseman, P. (2021). From paints to plastics, a chemical shortage ignites prices. *AP News*. Retrieved October 22, 2021, from https://apnews.com/article/coronavirus-pandemic-technology-business-health-hurricanes-46bce9cc36dab2b330309dae0354cf53

Xu, Y., Tiwari, A., Chen, H. C., & Turner, C. J. (2018). Development of a validation and qualification process for the manufacturing of medical devices: A case study based on cross-sector benchmarking. *International Journal of Process Management and Benchmarking*, *8*(1), 79–102. doi:10.1504/IJPMB.2018.088658

Yazdi, A. K., & Esfeden, G. A. (2018). Designing robust model of Six Sigma implementation based on critical successful factors and MACBETH. *International Journal of Process Management and Benchmarking*, *7*(2), 158–171. doi:10.1504/IJPMB.2017.083103

Ziobro, P. (2021). FedEx earnings reflect labor shortage, supply-chain woes. *Wall Street Journal*. Retrieved October 19,2021, from wsj.com/articles/fedex-lowers-forecast-as-labor-shortage-supply-chain-woes-sap-results-11632256848

Chapter 6
The Role of Wireless Sensor Networks in Detecting and Predicting COVID-19 Using ML Algorithms

Sujatha Kesavan
Dr. M. G. R. Educational and Research Institute, India

Janaki N.
Vels Institute of Science, Technology, and Advanced Studies, India

Bhavani N. P. G.
Saveetha School of Engineering, India

Kavitha T.
Dr. M. G. R. Educational and Research Institute, India

Kirubakaran D.
St. Joseph's Institute of Technology, India

Su-Qun Cao
Huaiyin Institute of Technology, China

ABSTRACT

An embedded system is a specialized computer that is resource constrained to sense and controls its environment. Embedded systems usually consist of hardware and software. The most used hardware materials are processors, peripheral communication devices, actuators, sensors, power supplies, and memory storage. The application-specific algorithms, device drivers, and operating systems are typically used in software section. Normally there is a standard protocol to communicate the particular type of embedded system; for example, nodes in sensor networks are the specialized embedded systems for detecting COVID-19. Sensor nodes with wireless communication capabilities can form wireless sensor networks (WSN).

DOI: 10.4018/978-1-6684-5250-9.ch006

INTRODUCTION

Embedded System

An embedded system is a specialized computer that is used to sense and control its environment. Embedded systems usually consist of hardware and software. The hardware materials include processors, peripheral communication devices, actuators, sensors, power supplies and memory storage. The application specific algorithms, device drivers and operating systems are included in the software part. Normally a standard protocol is needed to communicate to the particular type of embedded system. The nodes in sensor networks are specialized embedded systems. Sensor nodes with wireless communication capabilities can form Wireless Sensor Networks (WSN) (Al-Aubidy et al., 2017; Alagoz et al., 2018; Han et al., 2019; Mahajan et al., 2018).

Normally two types of wireless networks are used namely Personal Area Networks (PAN) and Wireless Sensor Networks (WSN). The WSN can contain hundreds or even thousands of sensor nodes. The WSN are used in industrial applications and can be deployed in hazardous environments, such as battlefields, volcanoes and wildfires. Personal area networks usually require measurement and minimization devices that are implemented in small numbers. PAN devices are designed for Wi-Fi and Bluetooth common-use technologies and standard protocols such as web browsing, file transfer application, audio, and video streaming applications. Today's research in WSN focuses on generating large-scale network systems of electricity using very specialized algorithms. They usually feature exhibits for science, hospital based on COVID-19, military and professional usage scenarios (Karsmakers et al., 2016; Li et al., 2019; Lombardo et al., 2012; Sarkar & Misra, 2016).

Therefore, in this research, the hybrid method is used to reduce the power consumption of WSN used in hospitals based COVID-19 for the patient healthcare monitoring system. Tremendous efforts have been taken to reduce the power consumption in Wireless Sensor Networks (WSNs) for healthcare systems in recent years. In any case, in a large portion of these Investigations, sensor information handling assignments, such as health decision-making and emergency reaction, are sent by the remote server. Launching and handling of large volumes of data sensors require many more communication resources, bringing in a remote server issues and delaying the decision time notification time. This work uses a hybrid technique (direct power management method for base station and self-executing path resource allocation method for server section) to reduce power consumption based on embedded system (Ge et al., 2013; Jiang et al., 2016; Sun et al., 2018; Yue et al., 2016; Zuhairy & Al Zamil, 2018).

In any case, in a large portion of these investigations, sensor information handling assignments, for example, health decision making and emergency reaction the message is sent by the remote server. Launched and handed over large volumes of data sensors use a many more communication resources, bringing a remote server issue and delaying the decision time notification time (Tyagi et al., 2022; Pal et al., 2022; Nair & Tyagi, 2021; Nair et al., 2021).

Patient Healthcare Monitoring System for COVID-19

Patient monitoring system is the most important diagnostic system in the hospital's based COVID-19 Intensive Care Unit (ICU), providing continuous display and interpretation of the patient's vital functions. Patient monitoring systems utilize telecommunications technology, medical diagnosis, treatment and COVID-19 patient care. It can be divided into two modes of operation: real-time mode, where the patient data at the remote terminal can be collected immediately and stored and forward mode involves accessing the data later for COVID-19.

Patient monitoring systems have mainly dealt with various measurement techniques and low-level signal processing algorithms in the past. However, the quality of such a real-time system is also determined by many other factors, too. They are: application software technology, communication technology, data representation methods, high-level signal processing algorithms and signal representation to help automate human diagnosis. There are at least four types of patients who need continuous monitoring. If the patients are affected by COVID-19, then there is a need for remote monitoring system facilitated using WSN technology (Al-Aubidy et al., 2017; Alagoz et al., 2018; Mahajan et al., 2018).

- Patients are at high risk of developing a life-threatening disease; for example, patients undergo open heart surgery, or premature babies, whose heart and lungs are not fully developed
- The patient is in unstable physiological regulatory systems; for example, patients whose respiratory systems are inhibited by overdose or anesthesia
- Patients those who are suspected to have acute myocardial infarction (heart attack)
- The patient is in a critical physiological state; for example, suffering from multiple trauma or septic shock

Patient monitoring is an important part of many medical services. It can reduce the number of unnecessary COVID-19 hospitalizations while increasing healthcare services for those who need these services. Patient monitoring systems are used to collect health data at home and in some cases, outdoor scenes, which are beneficial for disease management, diagnosis, and prediction and follow-up. Recent advances in developing smaller and more accurate sensors that do not require gels which have made it possible to apply a wide range of wireless remote patient monitoring systems in natural environments.

Remote Patient Monitoring System

Remote physiological monitoring (remote patient monitoring) is a form of telemedicine computerized technology used to track patient vital signs and health without face-to-face contact. Physiological parameters such as heart rate, body temperature, blood pressure, electrocardiogram, oxygen saturation and glucose levels are measured. The data is then sent to the physician. Doctors use smart tools for further analysis and follow-up with COVID-19 patients as needed. By remotely monitoring patient parameters, the remote COVID-19 patient monitoring system allows doctors to use emergency room utilization or intervene before hospitalization, preempting unnecessary costs. Remote patient monitoring systems must serve to COVID-19 patients and doctors' potential and while keeping patients at home, it should allow doctors and nurses and resources to use their time more effectively. The typical remote COVID-19 patient monitoring system is shown in Figure 1

The remote patient monitoring system is combined with computer hardware to customize medical software and medical diagnostic instruments at each location. The use of these technologies has greatly increased the costs and convenience associated with long-term outpatient monitoring. It has the potential to extend surveillance to a wider range of healthy people for preventive diagnosis and alerting. The remote patient monitoring system also enables medical doctors to watch patients' real-time health status from remote sites and allows them to give some suggestions for emergency treatment via the Internet.

Figure 1. Remote COVID-19 Patient Monitoring

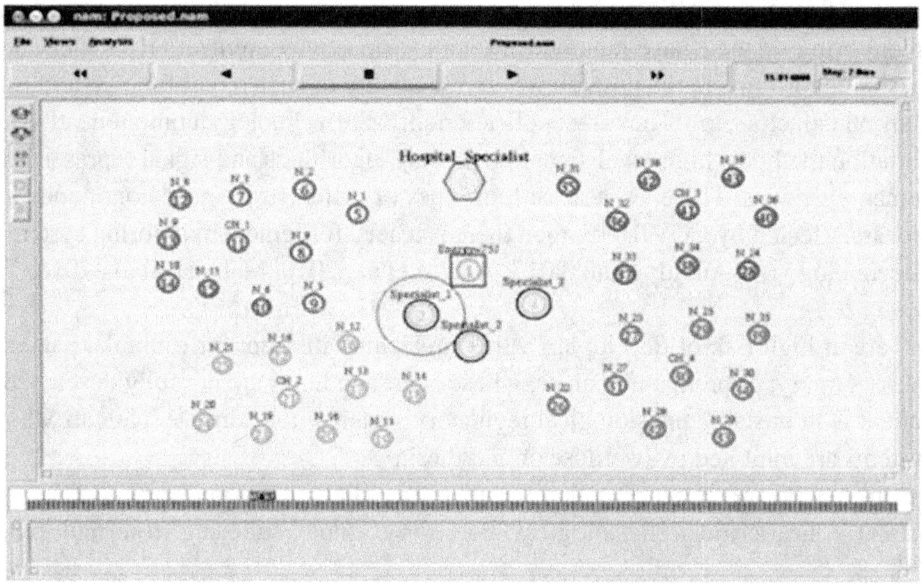

Applications of Remote COVID-19 Patient Monitoring System

The following are the significant applications of remote patient monitoring system.

COVID-19 Home Health Care

In the home health area, a remote patient monitoring system can be used.

- As alternatives to home care visits
- as means to maximize limited nursing resources
- to formulate Strategies for better management of risky and costly patients, such as those with congestive heart failure

Disease Management

As part of a disease management plan, remote patient monitoring systems have the potential to help limit patient costs by

- Equipping caregivers who need information to detect health management issues as early as possible
- Providing patients with the feedback they need for informed self-management

Hospitals based on COVID-19

In addition to the two aforementioned applications, preliminary research indicates that a remote patient monitoring system can provide continuous patient management in the Intensive Care Unit (ICU). Also, hospitals based on COVID-19 can use remote patient monitoring systems to automatically measure the process of vital signs.

Contribution of this Work

To reduce the power consumption in Wireless Sensor Networks (WSNs) for healthcare systems, researchers have generated tremendous efforts in recent years. In any case, in a large portion of these investigations, sensor information handling assignments, such as health decision-making and emergency reaction, are sent by the remote server. For launching and handing of large volumes of data, sensors use many communication resources, bringing in a remote server issues and delaying the decision time notification time.

This work uses a hybrid technique (direct power management method for base station and self-executing path resource allocation method for server section) to reduce power consumption based on embedded system. In this work, ARM Cortex-A72 controller presents a prototype of the implemented smart gateway. Gateway is an interconnection and service management platforms, especially in the home environment WSN health care system.

Motivation of the Proposed Work

Following points motivate us to work on the proposed work

- This proposed research work's main motivation is to find out the optimal solution with the newly developed algorithm's help. The proposed work motivates us to improve the performance of execution time as compared with existing and also reduces the power utilization and end-end delay response
- An electronic medical document is a convenient way to exchange patient medical information between different medical providers. These records of the patient contain the confidential information required on a mandatory medical document to protect patient privacy and prevent unauthorized access
- Because the proposed work is patient-centric and can be used by multiple patients, a huge amount of data will be shared between the system's various entities. So, this prompted us to propose such a bandwidth efficient solution that would reduce bandwidth requirements and increase data rates

Objectives

- This research work mainly reduces the power consumption in wireless sensor network using embedded system. This system automatically disables the function of unused nodes. Here the application of patient health monitoring system is used with various sensor nodes, such as temperature, hear beat and pressure, etc.
- The main concern of this research work is to reduce power consumption and power management for a total of WSN node in such a way as to increase the lifetime
- Develop an improved adaptable routing that suites for high dimensional network by flooding sequence demands to the particular region in the network
- The recognition system must create less start to finish delay, routing overhead and crash rate and it must improve identification proportion and throughput in various situations

- Improve the way assumed by performing location-based sequence disclosure and adaptable routing in a work network

Organization of the Chapter

The objective of the study is to introduce the suggestion architecture for WMSNs to reduce the power consumption. This research work is organized into five chapters were the section **1** gives a brief introduction to wireless medical sensor networks, section **2** **p**resents a detailed literature review, section **3**: Presents the working function of proposed hybrid technique, section **4**: summarizes the performance analysis and finally the section **5** consists of conclusion and the future work.

LITERATURE SURVEY AND PROBLEM STATEMENT

Introduction

Low-power embedded devices are called low-power sensor terminals. Sensor nodes generate more data on environmental sensor temperature, pressure, movement, fire and humidity. Transmission at the sensor node of the base station's data is done by an intermediate sensor node in a multi-hop environment. The energy-controlled environmental sensor network television network takes the energy from transmission time to the energy efficient routing protocol. The data of the base station must arrive in a reliable path. Reliable path significantly reduces traffic flow and reduces the amount of data supply to reduce energy consumption. Therefore, the sensor node needs a reliable path for its energy efficiency and data transfer. It gives the requirements specified by the cluster-based multiple routing protocol. In wireless sensor networks, methods are developed to reduce network data traffic congestion. This network helps reduce energy consumption. Multi-channel routing can increase network reliability through multiple routes. If the sink fails to find the path between the source nodes, the path is selected from the available source nodes. The package multicast method improves network reliability and fuel-efficiency for COVID-19 (Al-Aubidy et al., 2017; Mahajan et al., 2018).

Information-Based Sensor Ranking Mechanism Finite Capacity

Syed Muhammad Haider Aejaz et al. (2016) chose the right mixer partner to increase a wireless sensor network's lifecycle. In this paper, the IEEE study was conducted. 802.15.4 cooperative mixed focus effectiveness is the ideal wireless sensor network query. First a profit-based partner selection algorithm meets the problem-free criteria provided by poor link coding and applies a broadcast power level together for the error rate estimated. Cooperation as compared to any other coherence has to be significantly reduced in terms of time constraints and has been done through simulations that can provide error rates. This reduced power 103 to 102 increases the lifespan of any given network of sensible nodes where practical wireless sensor networks energy supply is limited. Wireless sensor networks approximation effectiveness is based on the CG comparison of wolf partner selection algorithm arrays for mixed AF IEEE 802.15.4. This has been shown to give the algorithm network a lifetime improvement for COVID-19. Mario Demaria et al. (2016) the smart farming CMOS camera is a specific ware design integrated into a multimedia wireless sensor node. Together with the efficient image acquisition CMOS camera functions, better images are taken. Moreover, integrating all hardware components into a compact PCB allows the detection of non-compact and small form-component sensor nodes. Prototypes growing season 2015 three vineyards are under construction and tested. All devices show energy efficiency, radio propagation, efficiency and reliability for image quality. The number of pesticides suppressed can reduce lung surveillance, which is widespread in the cultivated area. Nowadays, large portions of satellite and aerial photography are allowed for detailed representation of plants health status and COVID-19 on maps. However, high cost and long operating times have affected the complexity, although this method has already proven effective. These barriers limit the frequency of monitoring of COVID-19, as well as the large-scale exploitation (Alagoz et al., 2018; Han et al., 2019).

FayazAkhtar and Mubashir Husain Rehmani (2017) described that uninterrupted medical and non-medical monitoring (and other repairing) applications requiring mini hybridization of electronic devices require considerable attention. This wireless sensor has led to advances in the development of Wireless Body Area Networks (WBAN). These include implantable sensor rods that deliver a wide range of power supply, low power, wearableand provides silent data over a monitored session to store data in remote locations. With various applications including health monitoring, these nodes can be exploited with living, telemedicine and exercise tracking. These devices have low compliance and are traditionally equipped with limited power sources and rechargeable batteries with limited capacity. The performance of these batteries is not only marshy but also likely to be regularly lowered, thus limiting service availability. In most cases, these batteries may be inoperable because the sensor devices must be autonomous (Li et al., 2019; Lombardo et al., 2012).

Shuo-Han Chen et al. (2016) a Wireless Sensor Network (WSN) is a collection of low-power sensor nodes that collect environmental information and transmit wire information to a base station. However, the degree of communication with the sensor nodes is limited and the relay nodes must be present throughout the connection. Relay common sensor nodes are more advanced and more expensive nodes. Therefore, effective NP is difficult to develop strategies to reduce the number of relay nodes and deploying relay nodes has always been a hot research topic and according to previous work, it is known that the tree problem, which is set by the minimum number of points, is proved. With this in mind, the 3-star approximate equivalent performance ratio O (n log) reduces the time complexity from O (n3) and improves the algorithm. Experiments of this algorithm require proper testing. The number of relay nodes has reduced this problem and the worms are kept under a limited transmission range to maintain global connectivity (Karsmakers et al., 2016).

AbdallahA Alshehri et al. (2018) described that pressure, temperature, fluid composition and real-time information are relevant, for example, in the optimal development of oil and gas fields. Therefore, it is necessary to develop new designs to extract more oil to achieve the reservoir's real-time overall satisfaction. One technique called hydraulic fracturing mapping to monitoring unconventional investments is a developing technique for measuring wellbore parameters. NFC/MI technology has been used to quantify refractory methods, overcoming the challenges of the Wireless Underground Sensor Network (WUSN) inter-node communication key in an underground environment. This paper describes the performance evaluation of air, sand and stone media NFC/MI antennas at the frace bot node. The main result is that sandstone and media ultimately reduce the transmission and humiliation of MI signals, affecting NFC antennas' performance. The development of hardware and antennas allows us to understand the challenges to improve electronic sensitivity and optimize the most resource-rich fracebot to reduce hardware (Jiang et al., 2016; Sarkar & Misra, 2016).

SourabhBharti et al. (2019) Wireless Sensor Networks (WSN) service studies problem with service characteristics in ranking for effective resource allocation. The existing sensor service ranking system cannot continuously meet the application requirements and significantly reduce network consumption trade-off. Furthermore, the sensor data sensors are calculated during the ranking of various application queries in the usual usage context. This service's needs are caused by many applications that cannot see their particular quality. This paper models information-based sensor service information attribute as a value and ranking the power of a sensor service while considering its application context and energy-aware value of that system. Network gateway service providers used the ranking system integration for application-specific quality which refers to its ability to maintain trade-offs between total energy consumption. Simulation results system service ranking systems show the current sensor service in terms of requirements and quality of data for COVID-19 patients (Ge et al., 2013; Yue et al., 2016).

Marco Carminati et al.(2019) described that environmental monitoring is now important for several purposes, including safety, monitoring hazardous environments, and farming efficiency. These application fields will meet them with many specific requirements. Therefore, many of the challenges that can be effectively controlled by applying an interdisciplinary approach can be addressed. The purpose of this survey article is to promote each other's electronics, aerospace community concepts and perspectives beyond the state-of-the-art sensors for traditional navigation or flight-line control. Miniaturization and sensor highlighting are done for low-power design and fixed-mobile dual-core architecture. The challenge of getting the combined data is getting harder and harder, thus allowing more of the solution. Practical space professionals need integrated software tools, including sensors, low-power circuits and mesh wireless transmission to applications for finding COVID-19 (Sun et al., 2018; Zuhairy & Al Zamil, 2018).

Signal Reconstruction of Enhanced Perception Data

Patrick Eugster et al. (2015) described that the Internet of Things (IoT) for humans is to interact more closely with their physical environment and lead a new practice. Computer devices' miniaturization supports many machines' visions in the smart grid, smart building, or entire smart city. Through networked computer systems, AHTOs will identify devices in the eco market including their interactions. They will then take action to improve the physical context in real time. Improvements and physical well-being will range from health to reduced energy (Tyagi et al., 2022; Nair et al., 2021).

Antonio Frezzetti and SabatoManfredi(2015) Random Sensor Compressive Sensing (RSCS) is a popular Wireless Sensor Network (WSN) because it reduces the number of samples required to produce a signal significantly. This improves the life cycle of the network but can introduce uncertainty in signal reproduction. In this two-layer controller, the key is to ensure efficient signal reconstruction (ie, low to reconstruction error) and high network life cycle. Controlling the global controller and Fusion Center (FC) layer is practically mastered on each node layer developed by two local controllers. Errors are used to reconstruct the values required by the front cradle, while the latter is implemented to reduce each node's energy consumption. The control scheme is developed on two levels: 1) The global controller of the FC layer's dynamic layer, which targets the error to reconstruct the dynamically desired value CS. 2) Decentralized local laws on the target node layer conserves two battery energy. As a result, the two-layer controller can generate both the required reconstruction error and extend the network lifetime. Simulation results of two-layer controller provide more network lifetime to rebuild error control. At the same time, the other two receivables' strategies show outer performance (Pal et al., 2022; Nair & Tyagi, 2021).

Roisin Howard (2016) sports performance is a very popular measure of sports biomechanics. It is important for an athlete to always look for ways to improve performance. This can be achieved in many ways, from movement prevention to improving movement patterns or rehabilitation. It can be very beneficial to know exactly how muscle activation occurs in different parts of the body in joint movements. The use of a wireless multichannel sensor can allow the athlete to replicate the athlete's performance, data training or performance as he / she does in his / her natural environment rather than recreate the movements in a laboratory control. Analyzing aspects of the human movement may require varying degrees of performance, injury prevention or rehabilitation (Al-Aubidy et al., 2017; Alagoz et al., 2018).

KanchanDhote and Asutkar(2017) inventions and applications in the electronics and communications industries, where they still exist, are chosen as routing algorithms. The use of wireless sensor networks has rapidly increased. Existing routing protocols, such as energy consumption and service parameters, face many problems and limitations in quality, while latency, volatility is high and throughput and packet transfer rates are low. Safe and wise, they are very unsafe. We have decided to overcome the limitations of existing routing protocols. Developing a secure, energy efficient, high speed routing protocol can solve this problem. This paper describes the utility of wireless communication sensor network applications using QoS parameter optimization in routing techniques (Tyagi et al., 2020).

Therefore, optimization of service variables leads to optimizing wireless communication sensor network systems for power efficient applications. This paper focuses on the performance improvement of QoS variables with traffic queue management for routing protocols. The routing protocol is analyzed based on the following QoS parameters: throughput, latency, packet transfer rate and energy consumption. With the help of improved graphics and simulation results, the queue management curve is below. This paper describes the work of routing quality QoS parameters for wireless communication quality protocols (Li et al., 2019).

WalidElgenaidi et al. (2017) monitoring wireless sensor networks based on marine environments is challenging for studying water environments' characteristics. Therefore, there are some design and considerations, network architecture and data security management that need to be considered as remote sensor data. The system changes the query and response to which the environment sensor nodes network must configure its sensor members. Advanced encryption-based wireless sensor networks, such as the number of data security and security algorithms, do not provide algorithms for message consumption, as any end user via authentication and sensor node travel source data. The leader of this work, node introduces a new method of recommendation mixer due to network stability. This node is designed to monitor all network members' behavior and abnormal members' behavior in a modified network topology. Only two neighboring countries (cancel/plus) must have regeneration and keys to their nodes in any network members' changes. These keys are only superseded by each other. This approach will result in an increase in the lifetime of the node as well as the entire shelf as it communicates with its authenticated neighbors (Lombardo et al., 2012).

Christos N Efrem and Athanasios D Panagopoulos (2018) energy sensitive resource allocation battery strike Wireless Sensor Network (WSN) is an indispensable role in improving energy efficiency, improving network performance and network lifetime. At the same time, there is a central access point sensor node that sends their data to sleep mode (repeating the process), and a work cycle method, each cycle of which is the back side. In particular, the allocation of an integrated Quality of Service (QoS) requirements, energy consumption, and quality-of-Service (QoS) for a maximum transmission time of the algorithm reduces cost and energy. This problem takes into account the energy consumption of each sensor node circuit. Finally, the numerical results of the method provide significant performance compared with the basic plan. In this paper, duty-cycle WSNs is used to the transmission and distribution of learning time and cost. These data repositories can lead to significant failure to manage a sudden emergency. These issues and the division of a district-based information collection algorithm resolve the competition's dynamic event. In this algorithm, the value of the packet header of the information determines its transmission priority. The sink area is determined by the mobile navigation's spatial location and responsibility for each area's row(Karsmakers et al., 2016).

PROPOSED MODEL FOR EMBEDDED SYSTEM BASED POWER MANAGEMENT IN WSN FOR HEALTH CARE APPLICATIONS

Introduction

Wireless Sensor Networks (WSNs) are crucial systems because they are widely used in various applications, such as hospitality, military, industrial processes and Wireless Sensor Networks (WSN). Data is sent via a wireless sensor network node. To build these networks, the nodes capture information about the environment and communicate with the end users. Each node of the WSN has a microprocessor, Memory type, RF thresholder, various sensors and electricity (EN, batteries, solar) cells. Dense deployment in the WSN environment often characterizes the Control resources, processing power, storage and most importantly, energy equipment components. That is why they usually use power batteries. Due to the rechargeable battery in the sensor network, it is sometimes impossible to assign a Body Area Network (BAN) position to a body-like area. Despite quality performance, the quality of the service depends on many conditions. An essential role of power consumption management in sensors plays this domain using core performance scale in the lifetime network.

In contrast, the purpose of a Wireless Sensor Network (WSN) is for users to access information of interest from data collected by spatially distributed sensors. In most applications, users only need to summarize some of the features for this distributed data. An example of a temperature sensor network is a specific trigger in an average temperature alarm network or event location. All data related to the central collector node has been communicated in the end-to-end information flow mode. Simultaneously, despite serious limitations on energy, memory, and bandwidth, worms are a very capable solution for limited cleaning and latency. An alternative is the network calculation of the solution.

Self-Executing path Resource Allocation (SERA) is to combine different clustering decisions and achieve the best accuracy for any individual cluster. Examples of known methods are the feature-based approach that shows that clustering data (i.e., cluster labels) changes the cluster ensemble problem. The direct approach is to find the final partition through the base clustering results relabeling.

RESULTS AND DISCUSSION

Methodology

Network Simulator (NS-2) tool is used for the implementation of this work. Programming problems are solved in a familiar mathematical, illustrative and easy-to-use environment by integrating computation.

Figure 2. Connection Establishment between the Base Station and Hospital based COVID-19 Server

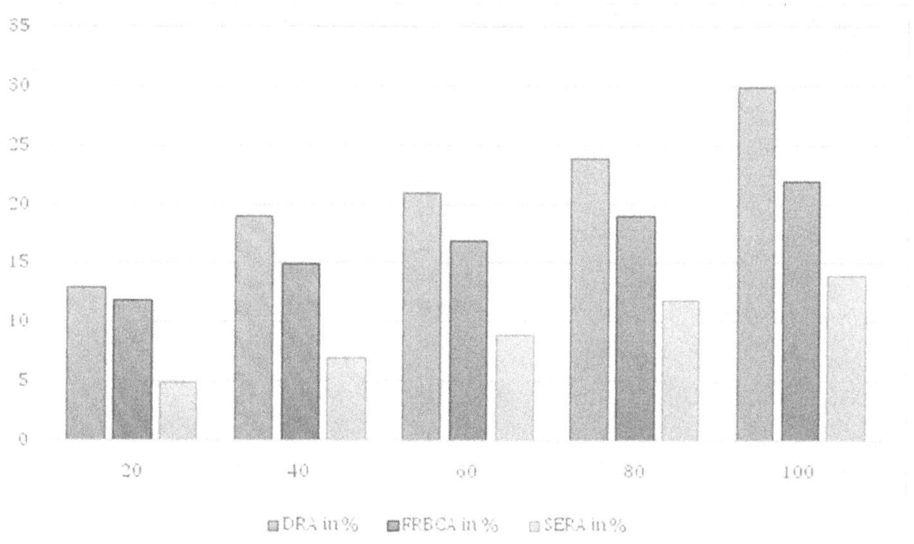

NS-2 toolboxes have a family of application-based solutions. Toolkits are a comprehensive collection of NS-2 functions (Tcl file) that solve specific classes' problems and extend the simulation environment.

Simulation Results and Discussion

Every technique has considered different measurements and diverse issues were recognized in each area of the paper. For identified problems, appropriate practical arrangements have been proposed and conventions can be reproduced to use the leading network test system NS-2. In this section, a similar examination of results is performed for the proposed plans with the standard directing convention. The proposed algorithms' performance for the given input is evaluated based on the delivery Ratio, time complexity, delay ratio, energy efficiency, and link stability. The proposed algorithm states the process of inter and intra cluster communication. In this section, simulation results and performance analysis of proposed system are discussed.

Here, the number of mobile sensor nodes is available in the medical field organization to determine the symptoms of patients' disease level. The connection between base station and hospital based COVID–19 server to be covered in this wireless sensor network is shown in Figure 2.

The base station is to be covering each mobile sensor nodes to form the cluster group. There are some distance ranges to be covered from the base station to the cluster group formed uniquely identified by different colors in the network as in Figure 3.

Each mobile sensor nodes are forwarding their disease symptoms to the elected cluster head and cluster head forwards to the base station to get the result of the specified symptoms disease from each cluster group level as shown in Figure 4.

Here, patients' disease is identified based on assigned energy level and each disease status is received by the cluster head and then it is forwarded to the base station from the separate cluster group as in Figure 5.

Describe the general perspective of the chapter. End by specifically stating the objectives of the chapter.

Figure 3. Cluster Group Formation

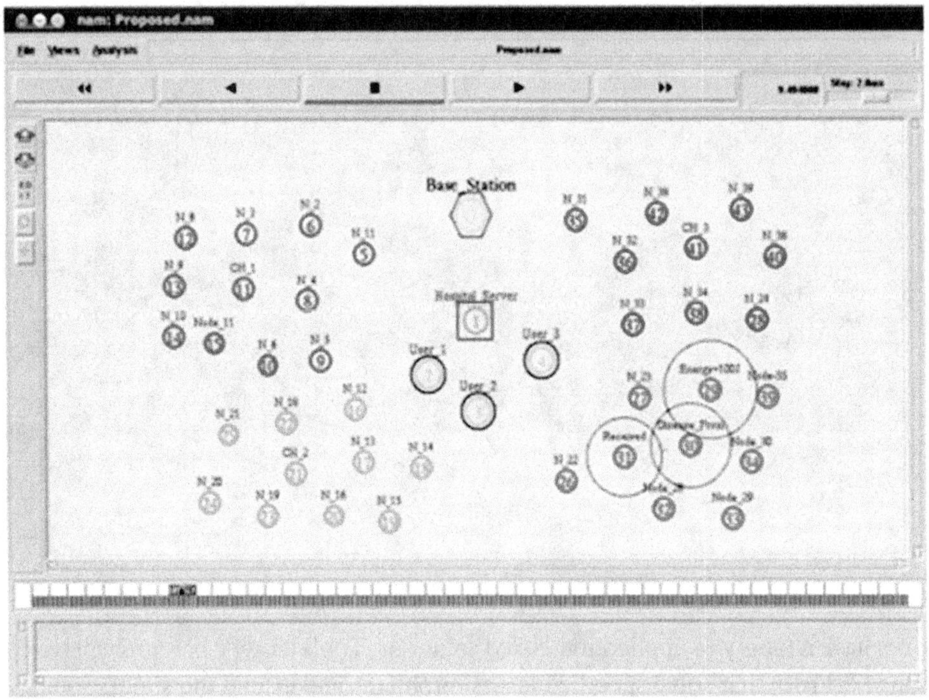

Figure 4. Assignment of Initial Energy Level

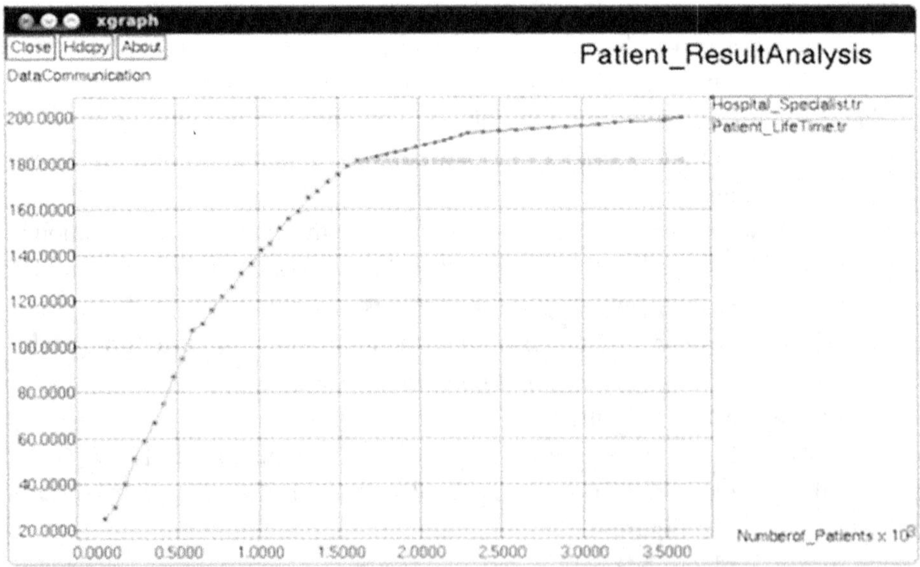

Figure 5. Energy Level Identification in Each Group

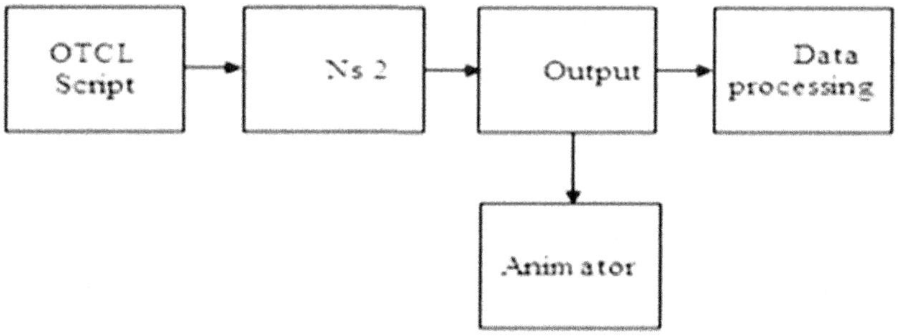

Once received the symptoms, then it should be forwarded to the base station to get the prescription of the medicine from the hospital based COVID-19 server in this organization field as shown in Figure 6.

After receiving the symptoms level based on the energy status, it forwards to the hospital based COVID-19 server with collected disease of symptoms level in the medical field organization as shown in Figure 7.

Here, the energy level status is received based on filtering the disease status symptoms and getting the result of specific disease medicine from the hospital specialist and it is forwarded back to the base station in the medical organization as shown in Figure 8.

Here, the specialist's specific symptoms disease medicine is received, and it is forwarded to the hospital based COVID-19 server from the base station. All the disease symptoms of the medicine received from the hospital based COVID-19 server to the base station with prescription of the medicine is forwarded to the related patients based on energy level as shown in Figure 9.

Figure 6. Symptoms Received from Cluster Head

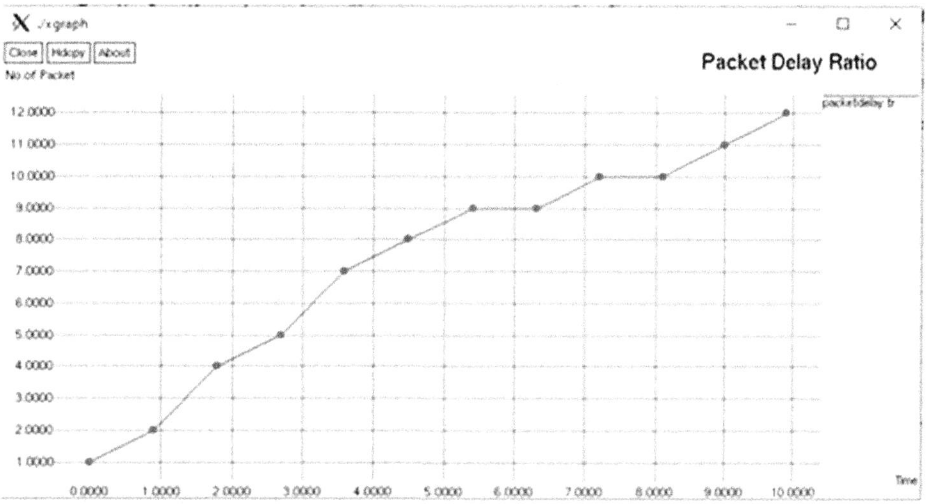

Figure 7. Symptoms Sent to Hospital based COVID-19 Server

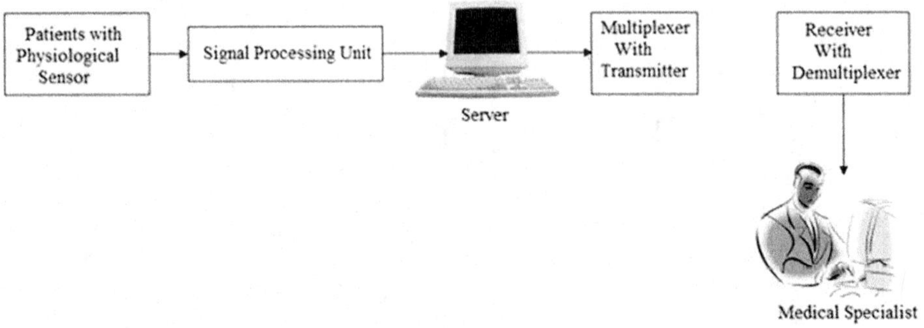

Here, the received medicine symptoms are forwarded to the related patient with their specific cluster group level in the network organization as shown in Figure 10.

Number of Patients Vs Packet Delivery Ratio

The X-axis is the number of patients and Y-axis is the packet delivery ratio or data communication for lifetime of the patient status are calculated to increase the hospital COVID-19 specialist status level as in Figure 11.

Figure 8. Symptoms Sent to Hospitals with COVID-19 Specialist

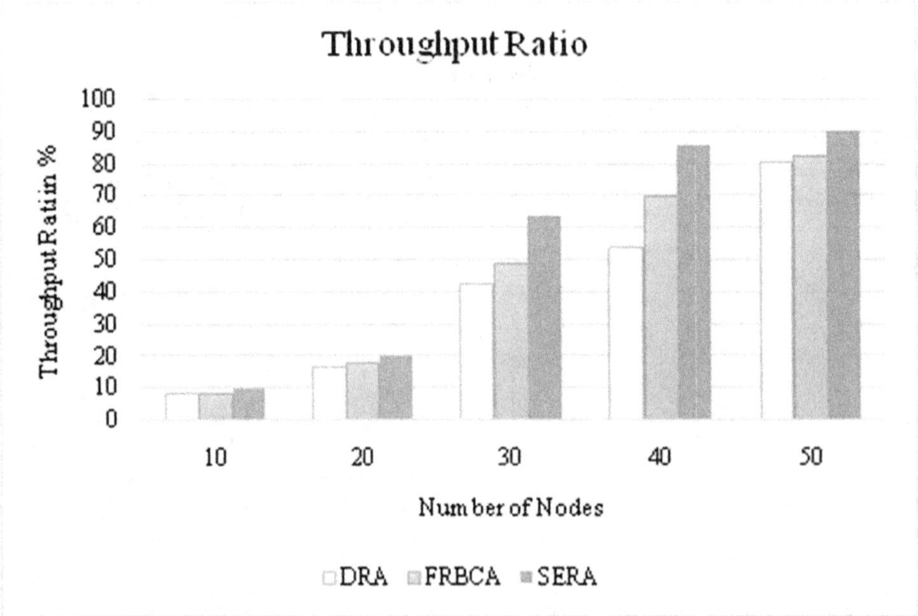

Figure 9. Medicine Received from the Hospital based COVID-19 Server

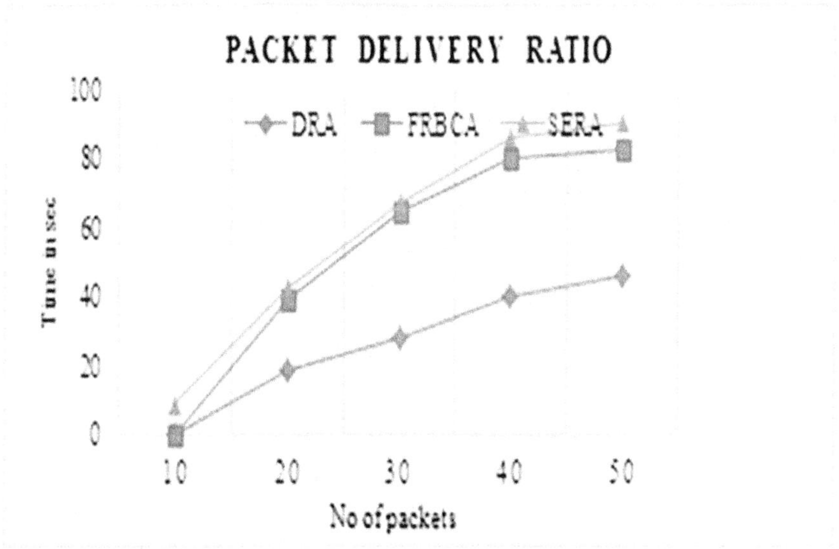

Figure 10. Retrieving Medicine from Base Station

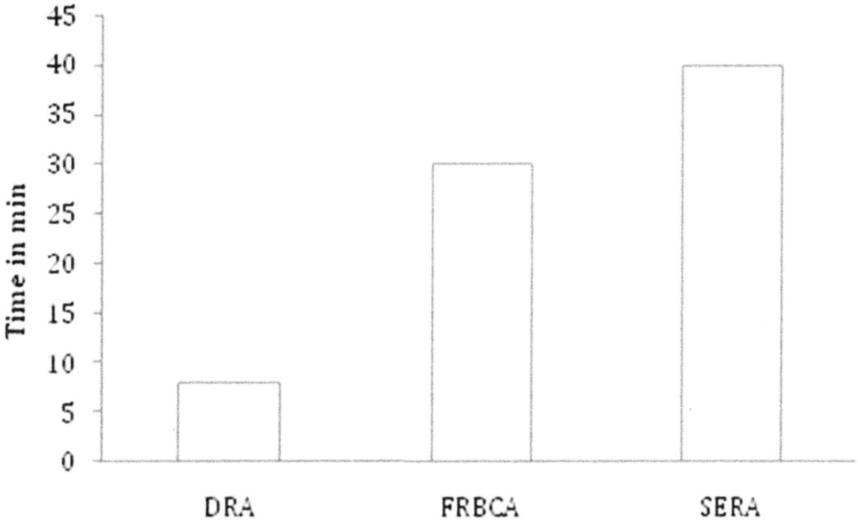

Figure 11. Status – Lifetime for patients

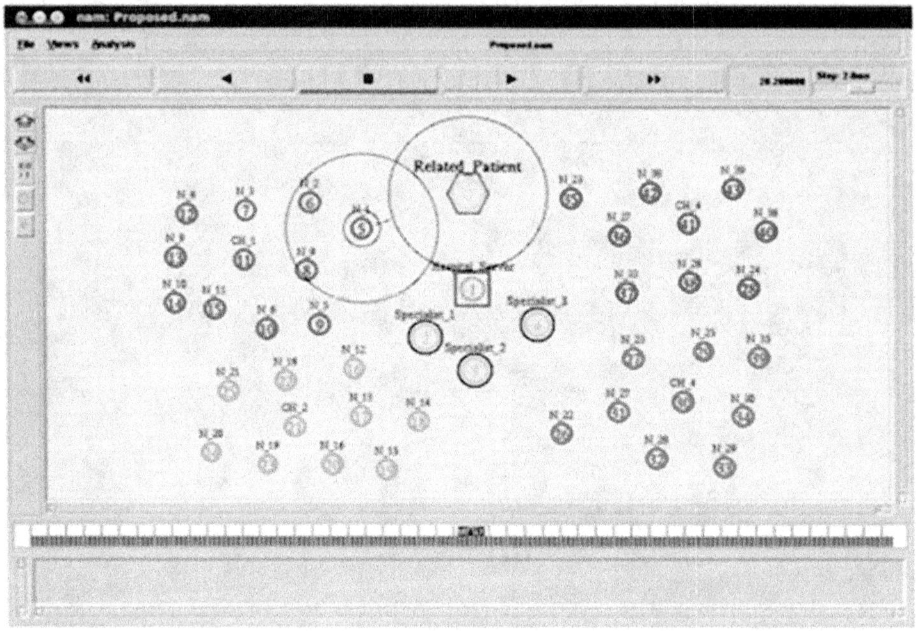

Number of Patients Vs Network Performance

In X-axis, the number of patients and Y-axis, the cluster connection establishment for improving network performance in the medical field is shown. There are increasing cluster formation level to identify the

Figure 12. Network Performance

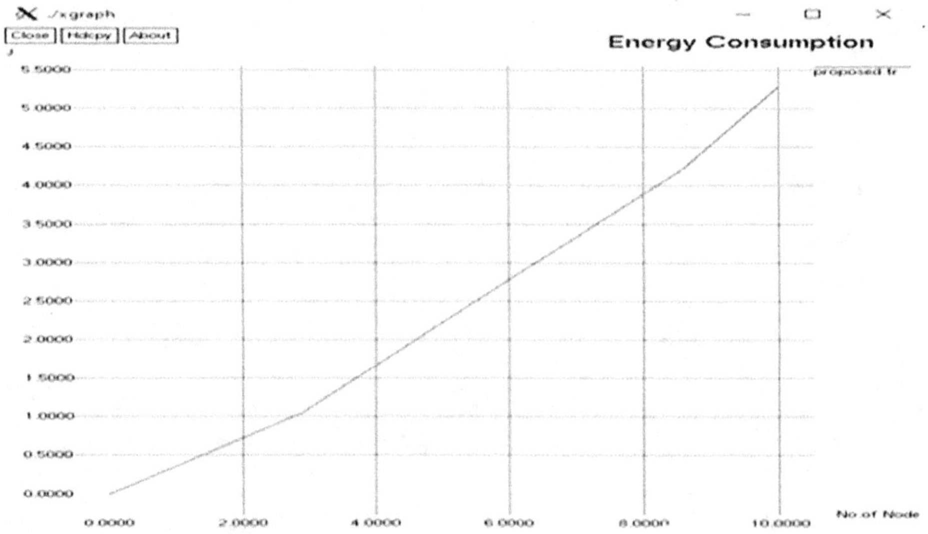

symptoms of patient disease level when the patient's failure cases decrease and delay of cluster connection to be obtained as in Figure 12.

Figure 13. Energy Consumption

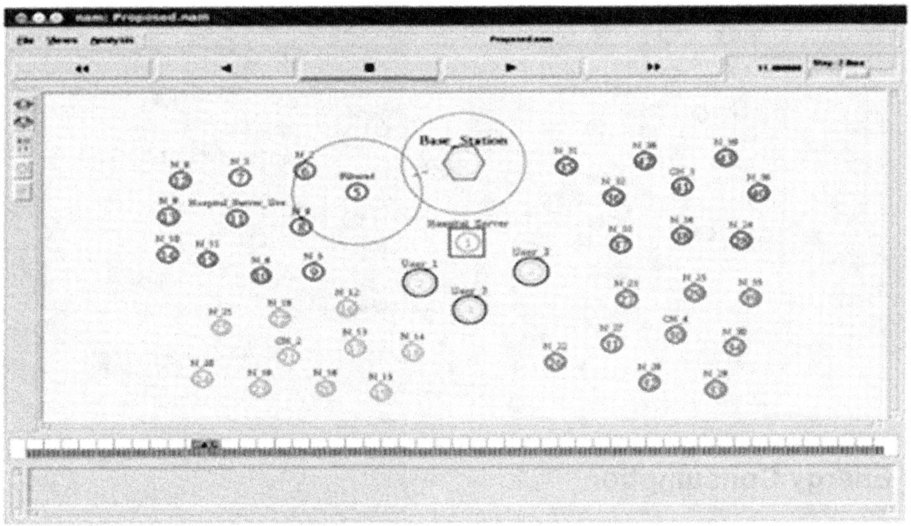

Figure 14. Throughput Analysis

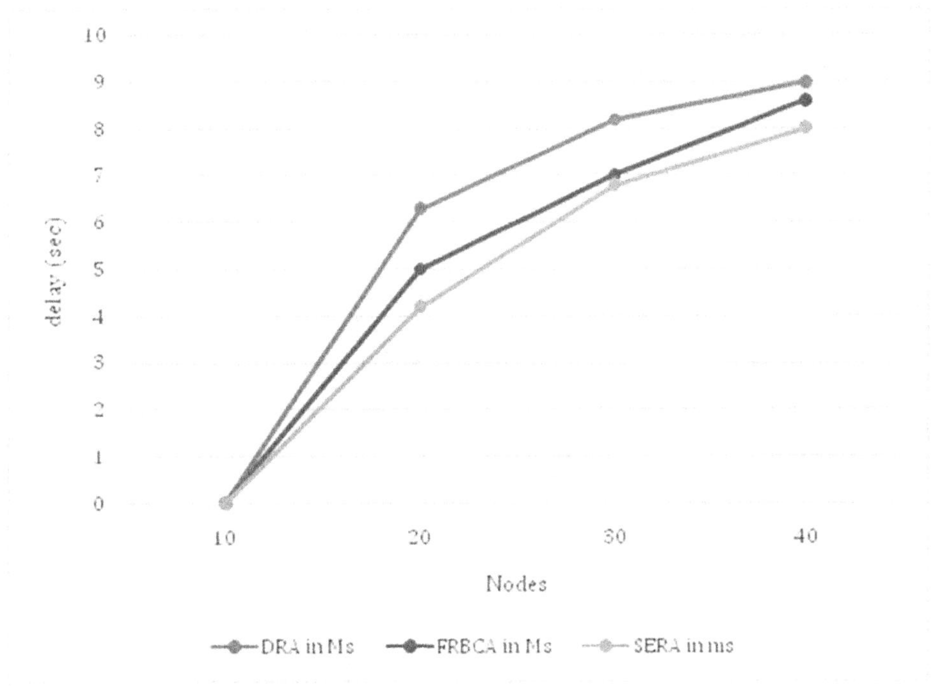

Figure 15. Packet Delay Analysis

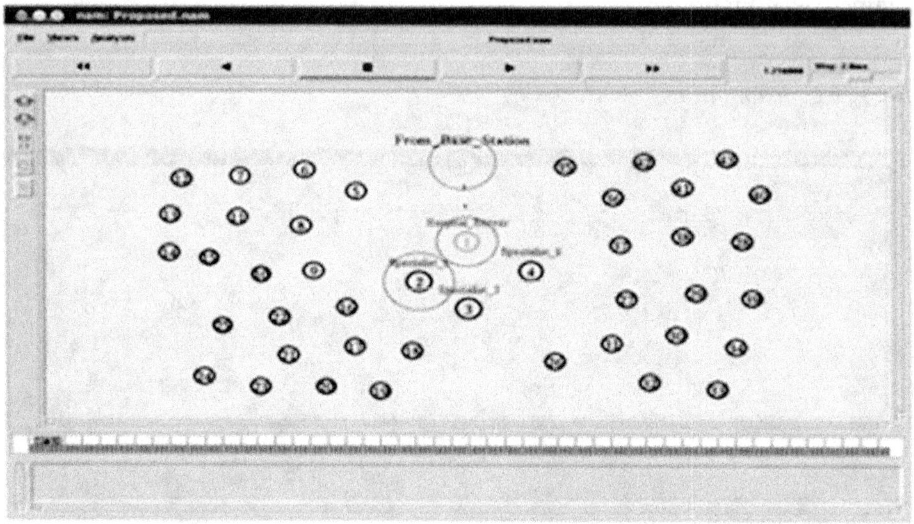

Result of Energy Consumption

In the above graph Figure 13, red color represents the number of packets archives the energy consumption. Every two packets are shown to save their relative energy. 97.5MJ of energy is saved when sending 10 packets per second.

The proposed method network throughput analysis is shown in Figure 14. Shows the total number of packets sent to the end time destination. It has sent 140 number of packets at 10 mins.

Figure 16. Packet Delivery Ratio Analysis

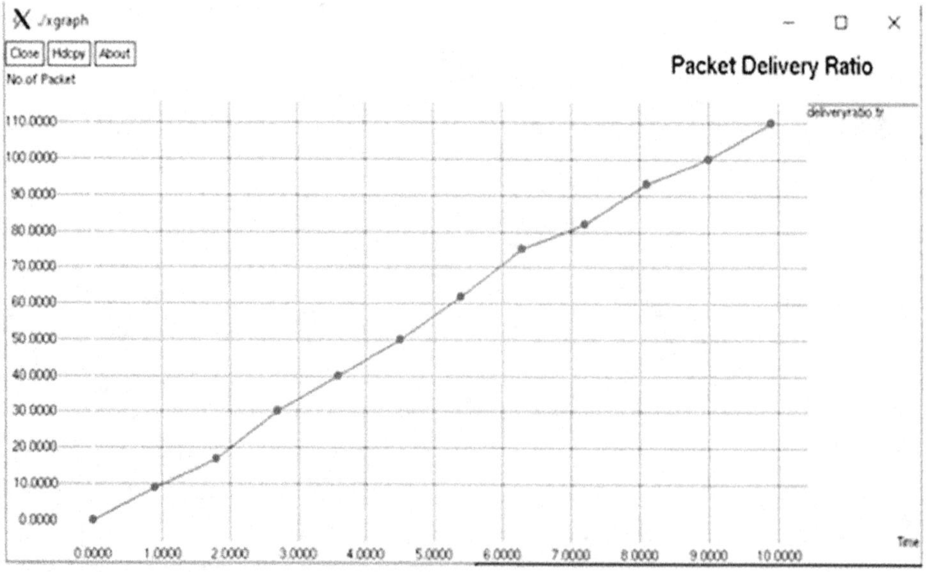

Figure 17. Network Simulator Processing

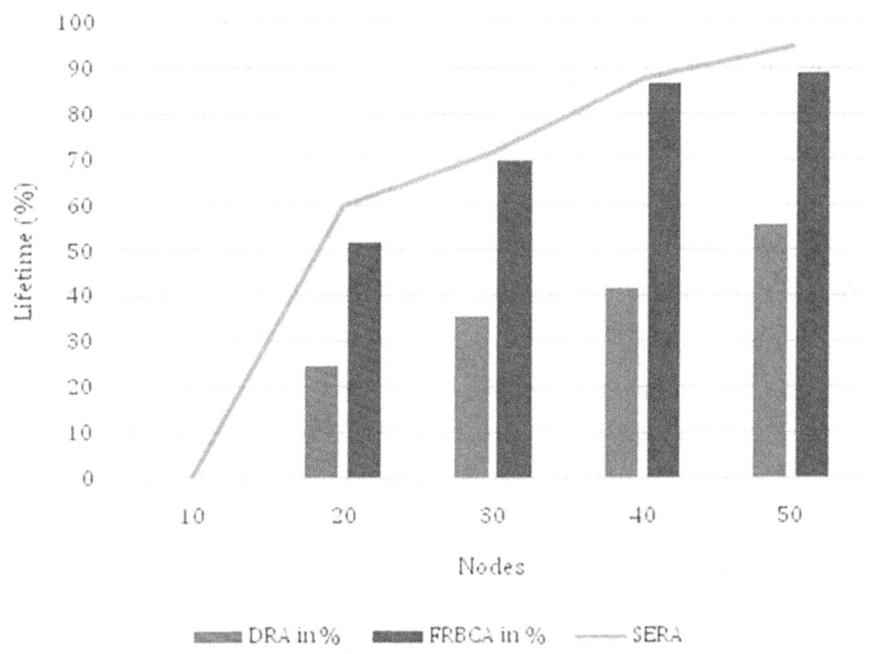

Figure 15 above shows the number of packet delay sent to the destination.

The proposed method packet delivery ratio is shown in Figure 16. In this delivery analysis source, each node delivers 110 packets at the end of time.

Simulation Analysis

Every technique has considered different measurements and diverse issues were recognized in each area of the paper. For identified problems, appropriate practical arrangements have been proposed and conventions can be reproduced to use the leading network test system NS-2. In this part, a similar examination of results is performed for the proposed plans with the standard directing convention. The proposed algorithms' performance for the given input is evaluated based on the delivery ratio, time complexity, delay ratio, energy efficiency, and link stability.

To evaluate the performance of the program, the NS-2 simulator was used (Figure 17). The adhoc environment is created and the mobile node is free to move in a specific geographic area. The TCL script is used to code the network environment. The following scenario is considered.

In this work, a 150 m × 150 m is considered to the destination in the experiments. The node communication range is 50m and their sensing range is 10m. To consider all sensors, 20j have the same hardware capabilities and initial power. The proposed SERA algorithm gets a better network lifetime than other existing algorithms like FRBCA and DRA.

- Flexible Route Based Congestion Avoidance (FRBCA)
- Distributed Route-Aggregation (DRA)

Packet Delivery Ratio

The target will be notified from the source on the network of their packets. It defines the ratio between messages generated by the destination packet source. It can be used in AWK scripts to generate trace file results. The state of this completed message has been the amount of the bundle specified by the completion partition in the network obtained from the starting point.

PDR = (Pr/Ps)*100

Packet Delivery Ratio (PDR) is used to assess network quality.

Table 1. Packet Delivery Ratio Evaluation Table

No of Nodes	DRA in %	FRBCA in %	SERA in %
10	0	0	9
20	19	39	43
30	28	65	67
40	40	80	86
50	46	83	90

PDR = Received packets/ Generated packets * 100

Figure 18. Packet Delivery Ratio in Percentage

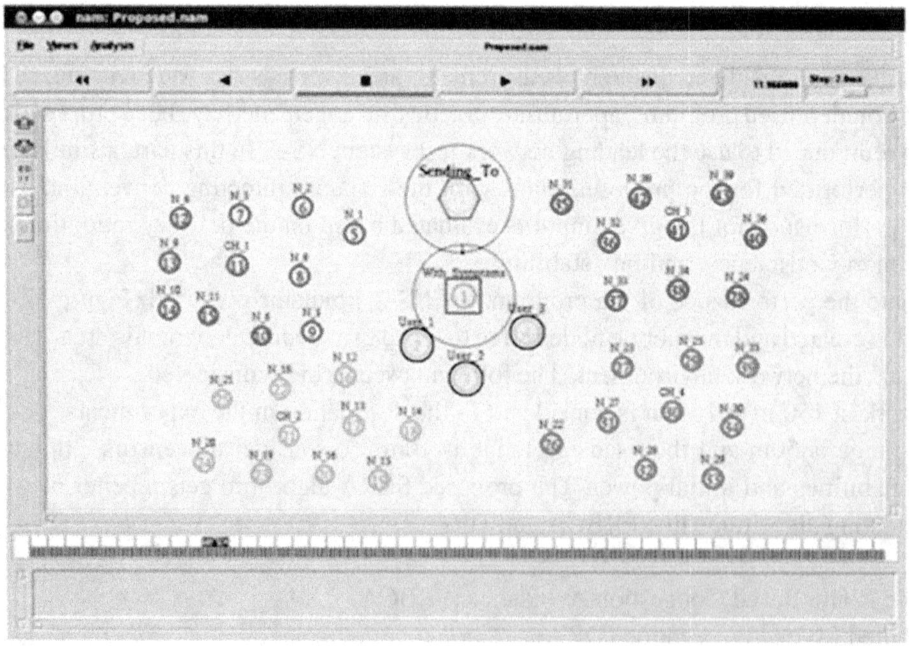

Table 2. Throughput Evaluation Table

No of Nodes	DRA in %	FRBCA in %	SERA in %
10	8.4	8.6	9.8
20	16.2	18.1	20.1
30	42.4	49.0	63.5
40	53.6	69.8	85.5
50	80.2	82.5	90.0

The Table 1 and Figure 18 discuss the performance evaluation of packet delivery ratio. The proposed algorithm may be detrimental to find the given weighted system in graph weight. All high energy neighbor chooses node's neighbor as nodes. In intermediate nodes receiving fast cause, data transfer in dynamic network makes their energy.

Throughput Ratio

The number of packets generated by the source node in a specified period and received through a destination can be defined by the data packet rate.

Throughput = Received data * 8 / Data transmission period

Figure 19. Throughput Ratio Analysis

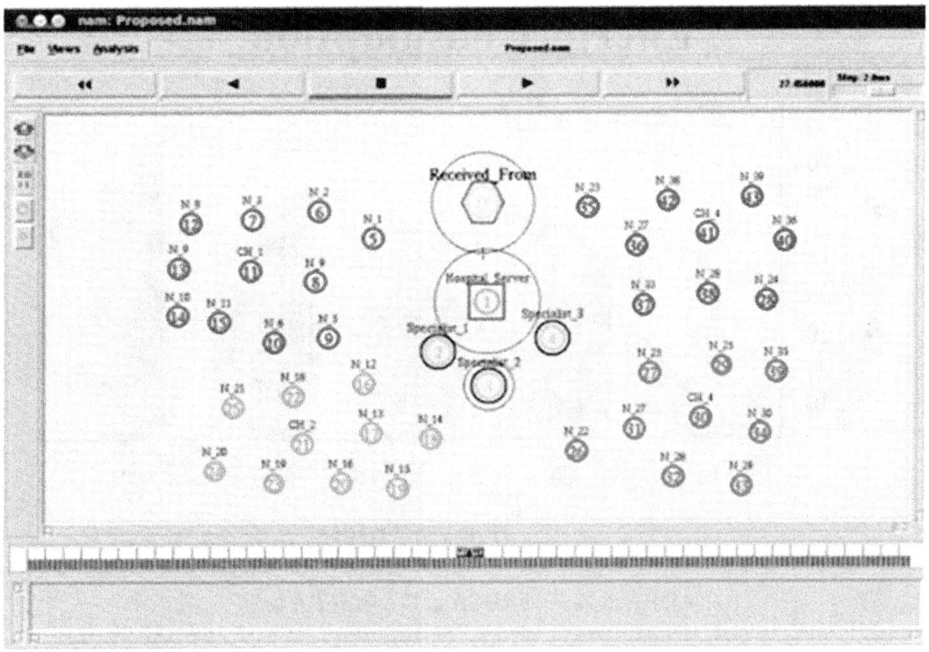

Table 2 shows the analysis of current systems and forward system throughput ratio. The table demonstrates the throughput assessment contrast with the current technique. Our proposed strategy has created the dynamic and high throughput proportion contrast. The analysis clearly shows that the specified SERA has 90% better throughput ratio than the existing system.

Table 3. End to End Evaluation Table

No of Nodes	DRA in Ms	FRBCA in Ms	SERA in ms
10	0	0	0
20	6.3	5	4.2
30	8.2	7	6.8
40	9	8.6	8
50	11	10.2	10

D = (Tr-Ts),

The performance analysis of throughput ratio is discussed in Figure 19. Pattern utility methods are frequently based on a comparison of time complexity, which attempts to transform the original features into an appropriate time complexity. For pattern utility, the original meaning of the elements is generally lost.

Figure 20. End to End Delay

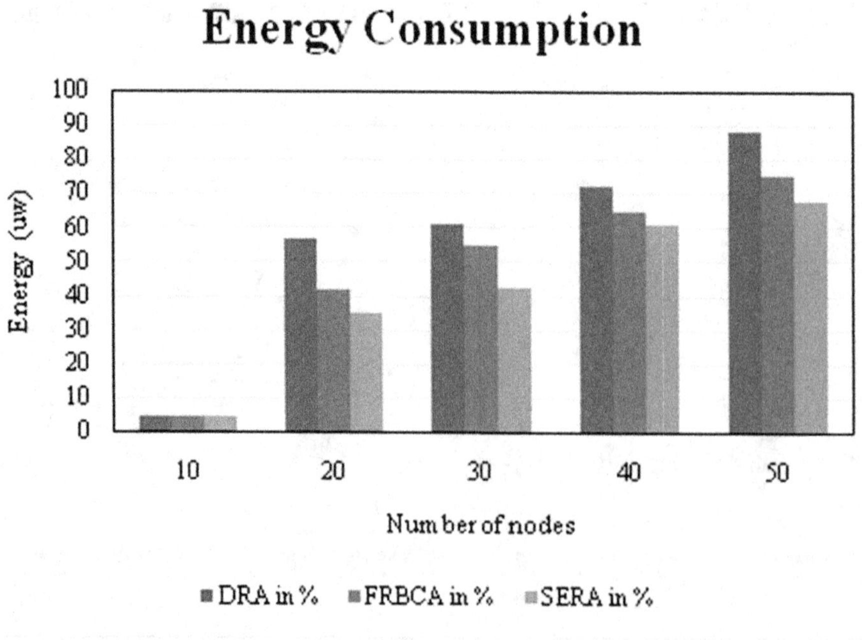

Table 4. Energy Consumption

No of Nodes	DRA in %	FRBCA in %	SERA in %
10	0	0	0
20	57	42	35
30	61	55	42.3
40	72	65	61
50	88	75	68

End-to-End Delay

They must verify the normal number of deactivation settings on the network. All hypothetical interruptions should be discovered by routing the domain name as the edge line of the mobile buffer and the intermediate access control eliminates the retransmission delay and the time of the hacker.

Where Tr gets Time and Ts is sent to Time

The Table 3 and Figure 20 shows the performance evaluation of end delay based on the destination and the time. It is measured from the time received by the transmission source. The difference between the two-time values defines the value end-to-end delay or latency.

Figure 21. Evaluation of Energy Consumption

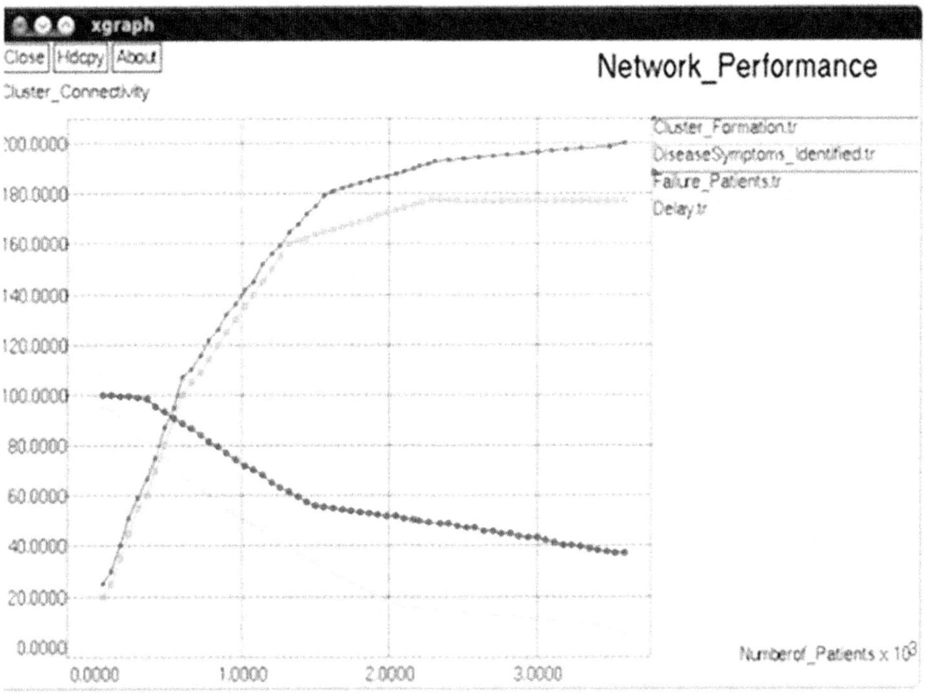

Table 5. Lifetime Evaluation Table

No of Nodes	DRA in %	FRBCA in %	SERA in %
10	0	0	0
20	25	52	60
30	36	70	72
40	42	87	88
50	56	89	95

Energy Consumption

Each area in the progressive multicast information system reports to the sink along the multicast chain of its importance. Any information in the middle of its locale can be summed up from ordinary details.

The performance analysis of energy consumption is shown in Table 4. It is the proportion of the standard measure of a control message dealt with by the node and the ratio of information packets gotten by the sinks. There are many routing plans accessible to every one with an unmistakable procedure. If a network is critical, it must have more significant measures of trade of control representing messages to be equipped for finding and making more routes.

Figure 21 describes the construction of different energy performance methods, which indicate that the project has increased the energy period.

Network Lifetime

The network is an essential trademark for estimating lifetime sensor networks. The term network lifetime alludes to the sensor scope, the presence of nodes and its industrious availability.

Figure 22. Average Network Lifetime

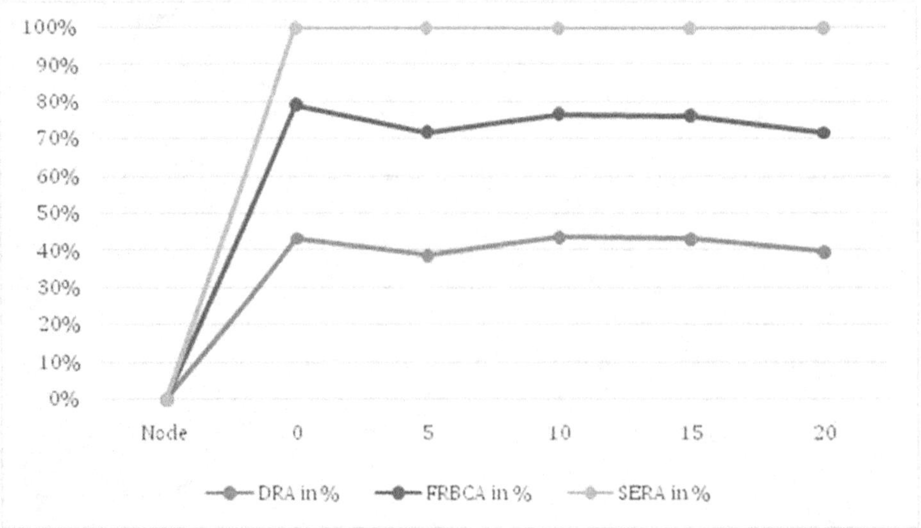

Table 5 and Figure 22 discuss the performance evaluation of average network lifetime. To assess the impact of the number of sensors in the maximum network life cycle, the SERA algorithm's performance is presented.

Link Stability Estimation

They have calculated an average no of nodes grouped into a single link in a particular time for all packet transfer in the source to destination in WSN.

It's calculated by

LSE= (No. of node/single link) *multi hop

Table 6. Link Stability Estimation

Methods	Link Stability in %
DRA	8
FRBCA	30
SERA	40

Figure 23. Performance of Link Stability

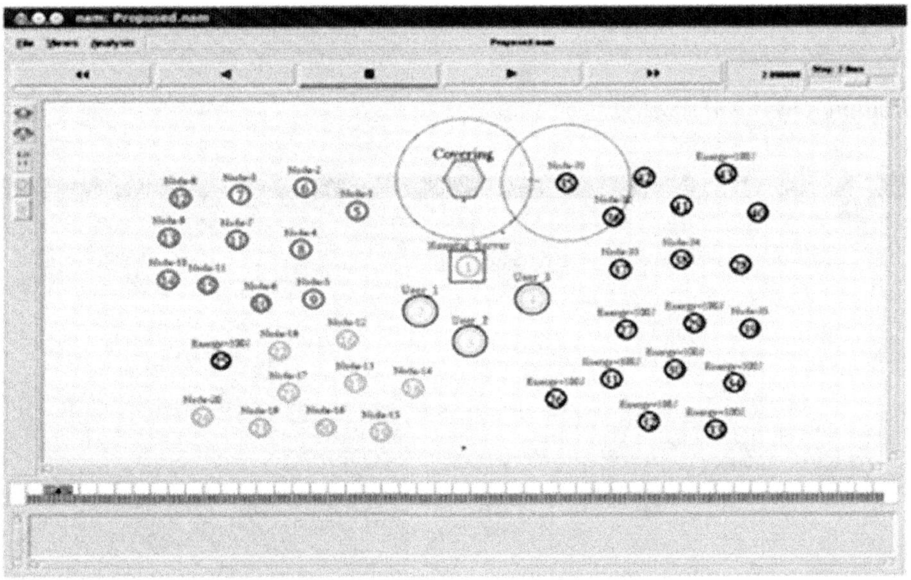

The above Table 6 and Figure 23 show the performance of link stability of the whole network at a particular time and our proposed system gives efficient results compared to other methods.

Table 7. Analysis of Routing Overhead

No. of. Node	DRA in %	FRBCA in %	SERA in %
0	0.52	0.43	0.25
5	0.66	0.57	0.48
10	0.79	0.60	0.42
15	0.82	0.63	0.45
20	0.95	0.76	0.68

Routing Overhead

This measure represents the proportion of control packet transfers or quantities associated with instruction-finding for less data communication. The nodes are mobile nodes that cause continuous moving of mobile nodes, which leads to link breakage and failure in the frequent paths. So, there is a need for route discovery, and broadcasting is a productive tool for route discovery.

Routing Overhead = (Total number of monitoring packets)/(Total number of the data packet)

Table 7 shows the experimental results of the routing cost of the secure network exchange distribution key, distributed secret key sharing based management, and the density-based network node key exchange for no nodes which increased from 0 to 42% at a fixed speed.

Figure 24. Routing Overhead Analysis

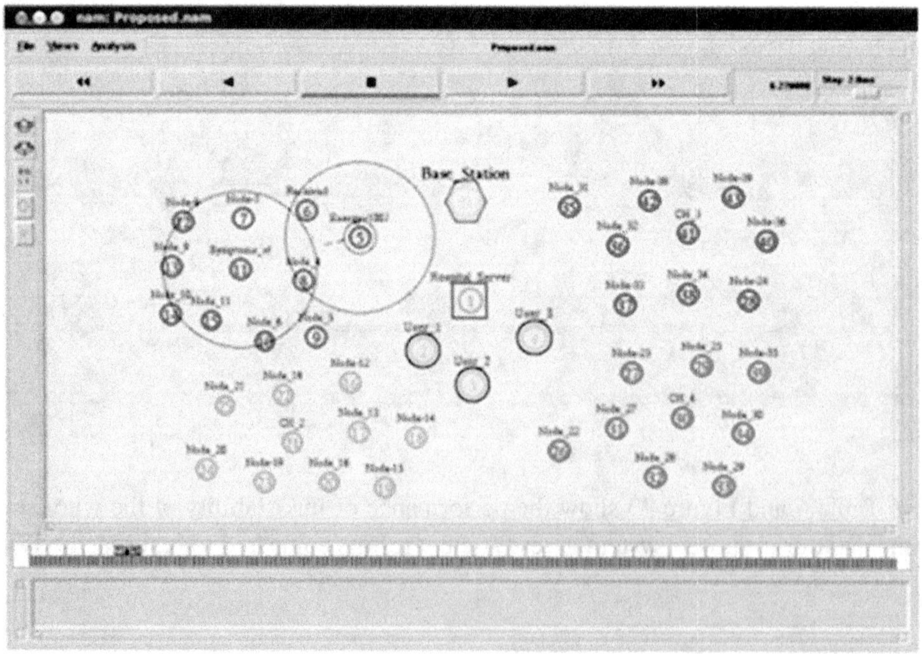

Figure 24 shows the routing overhead. Compared to all other methods, the DRA and FRBCA method gives a routing overhead ratio in graph on orange and grey which is better than the existing method which provides low overhead ratio as mentioned in blue color.

Packet Drop Ratio Impact

Packet drop ratio is measured from the source network with the packet. Normally it will drop in between the transmission

Packet Drop = Packets received - Produced packets * 100

Table 8. High-Speed Data Pack Drop

Nodes	DRA in %	FRBCA in %	SERA in %
20	13	12	5
40	19	15	7
60	21	17	9
80	24	19	12
100	30	22	14

Table 8 shows the packet drop ratio with different methods in which the data pack drop node to node send the data passing the test is carried out with an unrelated service probability packet of service result.

Figure 25. Comparative Analysis Packet Drop

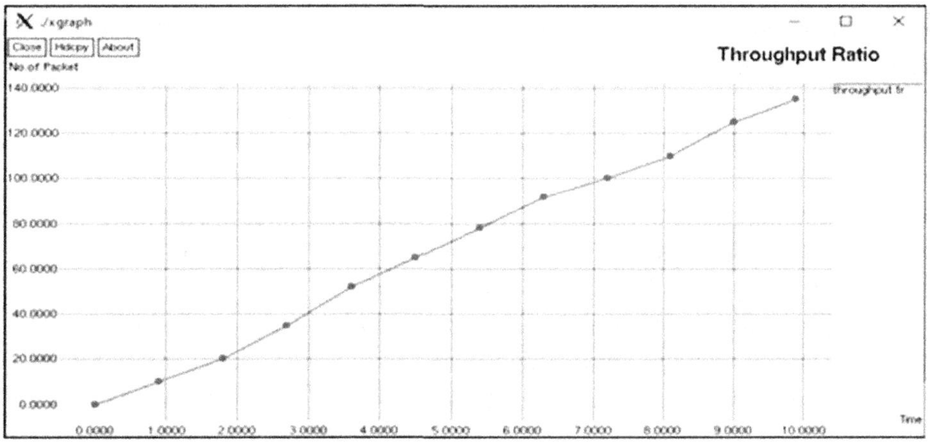

Comparative analysis packet drop is discussed in Figure 25. Earlier network protocols were often built for wireless Local Area Networks (LANs), where containers can be moved from one end of the network to other operations in milliseconds.

In this section, by creating a node to optimize the forwarded list, the decision is made based on receiving the intermediate forwarding node's message. The proposed algorithm is compared based on NS-2 different schemes under different conditions. From the simulation results, well-known evaluation parameters such as packet transfer rate, throughput, and end-to-end delay are achieved for better performance evaluation. The proposed method improves network performance by a lot. The proposed model approximately achieves the overall throughput performance of 90.01%, by increasing the energy consumption by 4.07%. Finally, our proposed model gives the better result compared all another methods in the network.

CONCLUSION AND FUTURE SCOPE

Conclusion

An embedded system is a specialized computer that is resource-constrained to sense and control its environment. Embedded systems usually consist of hardware and software. The most used hardware materials are processors, peripheral communication devices, actuators, sensors, power supplies and memory storage. The application specific algorithms, devices drivers and operating systems are typically used in software section. Normally, a standard protocol is needed to communicate the particular type of embedded system, for example nodes in sensor networks are the specialized embedded systems. Sensor nodes with wireless communication capabilities can form Wireless Sensor Networks (WSNs) for finding COVID-19.

Normally two types of wireless networks are used namely Personal Area Networks (PANs) and Wireless Sensor Network (WSNs). The WSN can contain hundreds or even thousands of sensor nodes perform better on COVID-19. The WSNs are used in industrial applications and can be deployed in volatile environments, such as battlefields, volcanoes and wildfires. Personal area networks usually require measurement and minimization devices which are implemented in small numbers. PAN devices are designed for Wi-Fi and Bluetooth common-use technologies and standard protocols such as web browsing, file transfer application, audio, and video streaming applications. Today's research in WSN focuses on generating large scale network system of electricity using very specialized algorithms for COVID-19. They usually feature exhibits for science, hospital based COVID-19, military and professional usage scenarios

Therefore, in this research, the hybrid method has been introduced to reduce the power consumption in WSNs used in COVID-19 hospitals based on the patient healthcare monitoring system. Reducing the power consumption in Wireless Sensor Networks (WSNs) for healthcare systems has generated tremendous efforts in recent years. In any case, in a large portion of these investigations, sensor information handling assignments, such as health decision-making and emergency reaction, are sent by the remote server.

Launching and handing over large volumes of data sensors need many communication resources, bringing a remote server issue and delaying the decision time notification time. This work uses the hybrid technique (direct power management method for base station and self-executing path resource allocation method for server section) to reduce power consumption based on embedded system for COVID-19. This research work has been organized into four parts.

At the start, the first section discusses the Knowledge of Wireless Sensor Networks (WSNs), energy consumption, routing systems, routing algorithms, robustness, efficiency and more active areas of scene research. Despite the open complexity of the worms, there are already a large number of applications. When designing any application, the main objective is to keep a log alive and well by forming a network of components. This survey presents the latest creation strategies and WSN methods.

Second section gives a clear-cut information about the current WSN implementations in the health care monitoring and power management domain. It provides a systematic review of the use of WSN in health applications, power management applications and presenting current WSN research implementations. It compares issues and arguments surrounding the different approaches and describes recent research in the field.

The third part of this chapter discusses the working procedure of proposed power management technique in wireless sensor networks in the field of hospital based COVID-19 power management system. This work uses a hybrid technique (direct power management method for base station and self-executing path resource allocation method for server section) to reduce power consumption based on embedded system. In this work, ARM Cortex-A72 controller, a prototype of the implemented smart gateway. Gateway is an Interconnection and service management platforms, especially in the home environment WSN health care system.

The proposed system consists of sensor nodes, central processing control module and transmitter with indicator and receiver module. In this research work, Directed Power Management (DPM) technique has been used to control the base station to disable the working of unused nodes and Self-Executing path Resource Allocation (SERA) method is used to detect the active nodes through WSN in receiver side.

The Directed Power Management (DPM) technique reduces the power consumption in sensor nodes for base station. The DPM has the effect of initializing each sensor node's energy without significantly degrading performance with reduced system power consumption. The basic idea is to turn off sleep mode devices and wake them up when needed. Supposing that the energy and performance overhead of the sleep state transition is negligible, in that case, the genetic algorithm is executed so that the idle speed will be perfect when the system enters deep sleep state. A Large sensor networks environments also require the deployment of many sensors for intelligent patient monitoring, object tracking and low power consumption or high battery life using energy efficient cluster formation algorithms.

Once the design time parameters are fixed, dynamic power management strategies are attempted to minimize the system's power consumption by dynamically defining the most economical operating conditions. This situation considers the requirements of the topology of the network and the task arrival rate of different subsystems.

In receiver side, each node is dependent on event sensitivity rate, node distance and the location of each node's location factors, such as the power rate changes. This imbalance in WSN energy consumption causes an imbalance in the node power level. The protocol performs three-levels namely synchronization node selection, fixing another standard for authentication and cluster head range and optimize path selection are controlled using self-executing path resource allocation method. This approach is used to networks where the path is disconnected due to optimize track discover done by a transfer without losing data of COVID-19. Multiple monitoring routing path and node information of the data and any lost routing are detected before the transfer data. This increases the lifetime of the sensor node by reducing the power required for information exchange.

The Proposed wireless sensor network system using Self-Executing path Resource Allocation (SERA) strategy is used to implement the hardware implementation using ARM Cortex-A 72 controller. This implements an analysis of the energy consumption of the system. The proposed system's experimental and simulations results show low power energy-efficient data transmission with security, reduced packet losses, and improved throughput ratio.

In this section, the performance analysis of proposed hybrid technique (direct power management method for base station and self-executing path resource allocation method for server section) with some other existing methods (Flexible Route Based Congestion Avoidance (FRBCA) and Distributed Route-Aggregation (DRA)) have been discussed.

This section clearly states that the proposed method gives the best response against all working conditions as compared with existing power management methods. For example, the proposed Direct Power Management (DPM) method with Self-Executing path Resource Allocation (SERA) method utilizes only 51.575% power consumption but the existing flexible route based congestion avoidance and distributed route-aggregation methods consume 69.5% and 59.25% respectively.

Finally, the power management technique greatly circulates nature. It gives expanded goals and adaptation to the sensor hubs' non-critical failure with sparing vitality improved in the hospitalization condition. Those systems depend on the bunch arrangement under the remote sensor hub is battery worked with vitality compelled. The proposed system completely determines the areas of daily peak power consumption levels. It is equipped with solutions that allow us to reduce consumption during peak hours and improve resources that are already very limited for better utilization. This research aims to obtain the consumer's response to smart wireless sensor network technology, its advantages and disadvantages, possible concerns, and overall perceived utility responses.

Future Work

Location-based optimized clustering: Rather than having a CH node selection based on probability of clustering, if each node specifies its location (using GPS) and energy level to the BS (Base Station), BS can run an optimization algorithm to determine the CHs for that round and hence uniform distribution of cluster heads throughout the network can be done which improves performance of the network for maintaining data of COVID-19 patients.

- Low computing data encryption can be used as part of the future to secure a higher amount of data transfer process for COVID-19.
- In the future, we intend to elaborate and analyze complex issues related to connection routing, such as responding to transient (restricted) properties of packet flow (i.e., state full Russia levers).
- The time consumption and the data delivered in the system are improved by increasing the number of multiplexes for maintaining data of COVID-19 patients
- Multi-hop routing through border nodes: In cluster-based routing protocol like Multi-hop-LEACH, after the clustering operation, if the optimal path between cluster heads is set, cluster border nodes energy can be still minimized.
- Secured clustering with a multi-hop routing can be provided to meet the fundamental requirement of security in certain applications where more security is required for protecting data of COVID-19 patients.

REFERENCES

Al-Aubidy, K., Mutairi, A.W., & Derbas, A. (2017). Real-time healthcare monitoring system using wireless sensor network. *International Journal of Digital Signals and Smart Systems, 1*(1), 26-42.

Alagoz, Ozger, & Akan. (2018). Clustering In Multi-Channel Cognitive Radio Ad Hoc And Sensor Networks. *IEEE Communications Magazine, 56*(4), 156-162.

Ge, Y., Cao, B., Feng, G., Tan, H. P., Kim, C. W., & Li, Y. (2013). An Experimental Study for Inter-User Interference Mitigation in Wireless Body Sensor Networks. *IEEE Sensors Journal, 13*(10), 3585–3595. doi:10.1109/JSEN.2013.2267053

Han, Tang, He, Jiang, & Ansere. (2019). District Partition-Based Data Collection Algorithm with Event Dynamic Competition in Underwater Acoustic Sensor Networks. *IEEE Transactions on Industrial Informatics, 15*(10), 5755-5764.

Jiang, T., Wang, Z., & Liu, G. (2016). Qos-Aware Throughput Maximization In Wireless Powered Underground Sensor Networks. *IEEE Transactions on Communications, 64*(11), 4776–4789. doi:10.1109/TCOMM.2016.2602863

Karsmakers, P., Mercuri, M., Vanrumste, B., Leroux, P., & Schreurs, D. (2016). Biomedical Wireless Radar Sensor Network For Indoor Emergency Situations Detection And Vital Signs Monitoring. *IEEE Topical Conference on Biomedical Wireless Technologies, Networks, and Sensing Systems (BioWireleSS), 32-35.*

Li, Pirbhulal, Wu, & Sangaiah. (2019). Medical Information Security For Wearable Body Sensor Networks In Smart Healthcare. *IEEE Consumer Electronics Magazine, 8*(5), 37-41.

Lombardo, Camarero, Valverde, Portilla, de la Torre, & Riesgo. (2012). Power management techniques in an FPGA-based WSN node for high performance applications. *7th International Workshop onReconfigurable Communication-centric Systems-on-Chip (ReCoSoC)*, 1-8. 10.1109/ReCoSoC.2012.6322888

Madhav, A. V. S., & Tyagi, A. K. (2022). The World with Future Technologies (Post-COVID-19): Open Issues, Challenges, and the Road Ahead. In A. K. Tyagi, A. Abraham, & A. Kaklauskas (Eds.), Intelligent Interactive Multimedia Systems for e-Healthcare Applications. Springer. https://doi.org/10.1007/978-981-16-6542-4_22.

Mahajan, Pandey, & Hegde. (2018). Joint Localization And Data Gathering Over Small World WSN With Optimal Data Mule Allocation. *IEEE Transaction on Vehicular Technology, 67*(7), 6518-6532.

Mishra, S., & Tyagi, A. K. (2022). The Role of Machine Learning Techniques in Internet of Things-Based Cloud Applications. In S. Pal, D. De, & R. Buyya (Eds.), Artificial Intelligence-based Internet of Things Systems. Internet of Things (Technology, Communications and Computing). Springer. https://doi.org/10.1007/978-3-030-87059-1_4.

Nair, M. M., & Tyagi, A. K. (2021). Privacy: History, Statistics, Policy, Laws, Preservation and Threat Analysis. Journal of Information Assurance & Security, 16(1), 24-34.

Nair, M. M., Tyagi, A. K., & Sreenath, N. (2021). The Future with Industry 4.0 at the Core of Society 5.0: Open Issues, Future Opportunities and Challenges. *2021 International Conference on Computer Communication and Informatics (ICCCI)*, 1-7. 10.1109/ICCCI50826.2021.9402498

Sarkar, S., & Misra, S. (2016). The Evolution of Wireless Sensor-Based Health Care. *IEEE Pulse*, *7*(1), 21–25. doi:10.1109/MPUL.2015.2498498 PMID:26799723

Sun, Z., Liu, G., & Jiang, T. (2018). Joint Time and Energy Allocation for QoS-Aware Throughput Maximization in MIMO-Based Wireless Powered Underground Sensor Networks. *IEEE Transactions on Communications*, *67*(2), 1400–1412.

Tyagi, A. K., Nair, M. M., Niladhuri, S., & Abraham, A. (2020). Security, Privacy Research issues in Various Computing Platforms: A Survey and the Road Ahead. Journal of Information Assurance & Security, 15(1), 1-16.

Yue, Li, Fan, & Qin. (2016). Optimization-Based Artificial Bee Colony Algorithm for Data Collection in Large-Scale Mobile Wireless Sensor Networks. *Journal of Sensors,* 1-12.

Zuhairy, R., & Al Zamil, M. (2018). Energy-efficient load balancing in wireless sensor network: An application of multinomial regression analysis. *International Journal of Distributed Sensor Networks, 14*(3), 1-13.

Chapter 7
The Role and Impact of Federal Learning in Digital Healthcare:
A Useful Survey

Rajasree R. S.
New Horizon College of Engineering, India

Gopika G. S.
Sathyabama Institute of Science and Technology, India

Sree Krishna M.
Sathyabama Institute of Science and Technology, India

Carlos Andrés Tavera Romero
Universidad Santiago de Cali, Colombia

ABSTRACT

During the COVID-19 pandemic, IoT and machine learning played a very important role in assisting doctors by remote patient monitoring. Machine learning and deep learning algorithms are used to process the data that are generated by IoT devices. However, there was major concern about the privacy of the patient data that is generated. The data that has been generated by the devices was sent to central servers which may cause data privacy issues. FL (federated learning), a type of machine learning, was created to address this problem. It provides a solution for data governance and privacy by processing the data rather than transferring the data to another location. The performance of FL models is better when compared to the models that are trained on datasets maintained centrally. In this work, certain insights are given on some of the challenges faced by the healthcare industry while employing digital healthcare techniques and how FL (federated learning) can improve the digital healthcare as well as how patient data can be preserved.

DOI: 10.4018/978-1-6684-5250-9.ch007

INTRODUCTION

Machine learning is considered a science exposed and developed in the 1950s as a subset of artificial intelligence. The first steps in deep learning date back to the 1950s, and there have been no significant advances in this field. However, studies in this domain were revived, extended, and continued throughout the 1990s. It's a technology that'll keep progressing. This pattern is due to the difficulties of interpreting and analyzing the continuously rising data. Machine learning is predicated on accumulating more data to discover the best model-based approach knowledge among previously collected data. As a corollary, computer vision innovation will keep pace with the expanding volume of information. As a consequence, supervised learning work will proceed at the same time as the massive data grows. The objective of this research would be to help educate experts about machine learning as well as its tools, but has become progressively prevalent. The impact of machine learning, the procedures used in machine learning, its specific uses, and the main objective of this survey is to help educate scientists about machine learning and its apps that became popular recently.

Machine Learning and Artificial Intelligence are extensively used these days in different sectors like educational sector, business sector, sports, industry healthcare sector, e-commerce and many more. Health care sector demands quality treatment and health care services. The application of ML in healthcare sector increases day by day.

According to Deloitte, AI will enable major scientific breakthroughs and accelerate creation of new therapies and vaccines to fight against the diseases. AI-enabled digital therapeutics and personalized recommendations will empower consumers to prevent health issues from developing. AI-generated insights will influence diagnosis and treatment choices, leading to safer and more effective treatments. Additionally, intelligent manufacturing and supply chain solutions will ensure the right treatments and interventions are delivered at the exact moment needed by the patient.

Telemedicine

Telemedicine is a broad term that encompasses all of the aspects you and ones doctor can interact using advanced technologies while not even in the same room. During the Covid -19 pandemic, telemedicine has got a wide popularity where examination of the patients and consultation are performed through communication devices. Patients can consult the physician by using a mobile application or through a video conferencing and discuss about their health conditions. It is a boon to elderly patients who are unable to reach hospitals. Telemedicine can be classified into different categories

Interactive Telemedicine

In an interactive telemedicine, patients who seek medical attention are given immediate advice in video conferencing software's and phone calls. The software's that are used for interactive telemedicine must protect patient privacy. The patient protection policies are defined by The Health Insurance Portability and Accountability Act (HIPAA) was enacted to make health insurance more Health Insurance Portability and Accountability Act of 1996 (HIPAA) is a federal law that mandated the construction of global regulations to prevent important patient data from it being divulged without the prior consent of the customer.

Remote Patient Monitoring

Remote monitoring employs a set of self-monitoring technological devices to monitor the health of the patients. The devices that are used in self-monitoring facilitate interaction between the patient and the clinician. This method is cost-effective. Moreover, remote patient monitoring is also an efficient method for chronic disease like diabetes, asthma, cardiovascular disease.

Store and Forward Medicine

In store and forward method, the data about the patient like the demographic details about the patient, laboratory test details, medical images (CT, MRI scans, etc.), bio-signals like cardiovascular, respiratory dataset is stored and then forwarded to a clinician through an expert system. The disadvantage of store and forward medicine method is as patient is not monitored physically, there are chances of misdiagnosis.

BACKGROUND

The authors in (McMahan et al., 2016) have suggested an approach in which federal learning was employed in deep neural networks. They have done their experiments on four different datasets and have applied five methods on these datasets. An iterative federated model averaging was proposed. In the first model, a simple multilayer perceptron that has 2 hidden layers are applied MNIST dataset with ReLU activation. In the next method CNN method having 5×5 convolution network, fully connected layer having 512 units ReLU activation and a final softmax output layer. The data of MNIST is distributed over the clients using IID and Non IID methods. In the IID method, the data is first shuffled and then the data is partitioned. In the non-IID method, the data sorted using a digital label and then divided into shards and distributed to clients. A character level LSTM model was trained on this dataset. The experimental results showed that CNN applied to the MNIST dataset achieved an accuracy of 99%, character level LSTM with Shakespeare works dataset achieved 54%. CIFAR-10 dataset that consists of 10 classes and 32×32 images achieved an accuracy of 96.5%for the model architecture that consists of two convolution layers followed by two fully connected layers with a linear transformation layer to produce light.

Experiments were also performed on real world social media dataset that consists of 10 million posts. Huang and D. Liu say that the FedAvg achieved an accuracy of 10.5% with learning rate 9.0 and 35 communication rounds. FedSGD also achieved an accuracy of 10.5% with learning rate 18.0 and 820 rounds. From the results, it can be concluded that federal learning can be used to train high quality models with a few rounds of communication.

The authors of (2) have proposed new algorithm for federated optimization or distributed optimization with a goal to minimize the number of rounds for communication. Some of the existing algorithms for federated optimization are Stochastic Variant Reduced Gradient (SVRG) and Distributed Approximate Newton (DANE). The authors claim that some of the challenges that have to be addressed by distributing optimization are massively distributed, non-IID, unbalanced and sparse properties of federated optimization. The proposed method FSVRG handles federated optimization, which the existing methods could not handle.

Federated Learning on a software engineering perspective was performed by the authors of (Lo et al., 2021). The study covers the life cycle federated learning system that involves background understanding, requirement analysis, architecture design, implementation, and evaluation. Data used in this study is extracted from 231 primary studies. The study made in this work clearly states that the two motivations behind selecting federated learning is communication and data privacy. As the data does not move out of the local device data privacy is conserved. Only model parameters are transferred communication efficiency is achieved. The study also states that data privacy and efficient communication promote scalability. The data types that are handled by federated learning is also clearly enlisted in this study. Graph data, Image data, Sequential data, structured data, Text data, Time-series data are some of the data types that are handled by federated learning. The model performance in federated learning is also impacted by client data distribution. Some of the client data that are used are Non-IID, IID.

Some of the approaches that are proposed by the researchers to address the challenges of federated learning are model aggregation, training management, incentive mechanisms, privacy-preserving mechanisms, decentralized aggregation, security management, resource management, communication, coordination data augmentation, data provenance, model compression, feature selection, auditing mechanisms, evaluation, and anomaly detection.

In the healthcare field collecting the data, organizing the data and maintaining the data requires time and effort. Federal learning addresses the problem of data governance by building models of localized devices without sharing the data. Hospitals can have full control over the data and can minimize the risk of misuse of data. A protocol that is failure robust, secures multiparty computation protocol and aggregates user models and is suitable for mobile devices was designed in (4). This protocol also handles dropping of users by informing the existing users about the dropouts. Moreover, threshold secret sharing scheme is used to handle dropping of users and seed sharing during dropouts. The limitation of this work is that it does not protect when any attacked client prevents the server from learning the same. Moreover, the clients can send any arbitrary values. It does not check whether the user values are within the bounds.

ML algorithms need ample amount of data for developing the model with full potential. The authors of (Rieke et al., 2020) have given some insights on the use of federal learning in health care, the challenges that are faced while using federal learning and the problems that need to be addressed. Data pooling is demanded by AI algorithms for model development. But health care data often has license restrictions which make it tedious for collecting and using the data. Federal learning overcomes this issue wherein it works with decentralized data and thus by preserving privacy. In an FL environment, data controller has their own data privacy and governance policies. Some of the challenges that are identified for FL are Data heterogeneity, Privacy and security, Information Leakage, Traceability and Accountability, System architecture.

The authors of (Topaloglu et al., 2021) in their work has addressed three main aspects of federal learning in healthcare such as privacy of the data, ethics in using the medical data and legal considerations that are to be taken care. Breast cancer dataset with 569 records was given to two different institutions and a horizontal FL operation was carried out. The evaluation of the dataset was done with Sorensen-Dice model. Feature importance and Shapley values were calculated for institution 1 and institution2. Feature importance's and the levels varied for both approaches.

Some of the evolving applications of FL are health data management, remote health monitoring, medical-imaging and COVID-19 detection. Health care projects that employ federal learning are investigated in (Nguyen et al., 2023). Some of the limitations in the current AI based health care systems are data privacy and security issues, lack of sufficient medical datasets, efficient training models, communication overhead in data transfer. Resource management is one of the important aspects in FL. A solution to reduce the training time and training loss is to use multi-armed bandit (MAB) theory. To ensure security, and to prevent unreliable updates, reputation is introduced for healthcare systems that use FL.

In (Xu et al., 2021) the authors have explored some of the issues that make a path to further research, such as Data Quality, Incorporating expert knowledge, Incentive mechanisms, personalization and model precision. In FL the data is collected from different hospitals, devices, etc.So, the quality of data which is uniform is a major concern, which directly affects the performance of the model. This problem can be solved to a certain extent by incorporating expert opinion along with the model prediction. A communication overhead is experienced by the communication devices that are involved in the FL learning process. An effective contract theory-based incentive design was proposed in (Xu et al., 2021) that accelerates the mobile devices to participate in the FL learning process. The task publisher designs different contracts for different data owners. For eg: the publisher assigns rewards (RN (fn), fn) for different data owners with different computational resources. Herr, RN is the reward that is assigned by the publisher for the data owner and finishes the computation resource of type n for a data owner. The data owner with good computational resources receives more rewards. If the data owner cannot complete the learning task, the task publisher puts the data owner in the blacklist. Data quality of the data owner and also defines as

$$\Theta(n) = \psi /\log(1 /\varepsilon n) .$$

Ψ is the coefficient about the number of local iterations.

The data owners are sorted in ascending order based on the data quality available ($\theta 1 < \theta 2 < \theta 3 < \ldots \theta m$), where $\theta(m)$ refers to high quality data with higher accuracy and m€ {1, 2…M}(Nishio&Yonetani, 2019).

IOT DEVICES AND DATA GENERATION

Internet of Health Thing is extensively used in healthcare. IoT devices are highly used for health monitoring in remote patient monitoring. These devices are often referred as IoMT (Internet of Medical Things). Emit is a boon to elderly patients and people who cannot travel on their own and reach the health care centers for their medical checkups. It devices in healthcare come in the form of wearable bands, glucometer, blood pressure and heart rate monitoring devices etc. These devices collect data like heart rate, temperature, blood pressure, etc. from the patients and send it to health care professionals through software. The data thus collected and received from the patients are analyzed by various algorithms and suggests treatments. Alerts can also send to family members or healthcare providers if there are sudden changes in the readings like blood pressure, heart rate, etc. These devices reduce human intervention and workload in giving care to patients. For e.g.: smart bed is an application of it which sends alerts when the patient sleeps in a dangerous posture. Ensuring the privacy and confidentiality of the patient data is a very big challenge. Some of the IoT Devices that are used in health care are,

IoT Sensors

Sensors are commonly found in the architecture of IoT devices. Sensors can detect objects and devices, among other things. The sensor is the component that responds to the assessment by producing a usable signal. The sensor collects physiological parameters and transforms it to a response that is used to analyze the properties of any object or substance is designed to check the existence of a certain physical amount. The control output is a message that is transformed into a human-readable language, such as variations in traits, impedance, voltage, resistance, and so on. Here the IoT sensors collect the data about the patient. Doctors collect the data from the cloud, analyzes it recommends treatment for the disease.

IHoT Services

Services and ideas have transformed the medicine business by providing answers to a variety of healthcare issues. More programs are offered on a continuous basis to meet higher healthcare demands and technical advances. Many more are playing an increasingly important part in the growth of IoT systems. Each provision in an IHoT setting provides a set of healthcare systems. These ideas/services aren't specified in any particular way. IHoT systems are distinguished by their uses. As a result, defining each concept in a broad sense is difficult

Wearable Devices

Patients and healthcare professionals can handle with a number of health conditions more easily and affordably with smart watch. Multiple units might be combined with human-wearable items like as wristbands, bracelets, brooches, clothing, sandals, purses, hats, and so on to produce these non-intrusive gadgets. The linked signal contains environmental and patient health data. The content is then uploaded to the azure. Some smart watches are indeed offered as mobile phones using health apps.

Glucose Monitoring

Diabetes is a metabolic condition in which the blood sugar levels in the body stay abnormally high over long periods of time. It is among the most frequent illnesses in humans. The three common kinds of insulin are type I diabetes, type 2 diabetes, and gestational diabetes. To establish the ailment and its forms, three parameters can be used: a random plasma glucose test, a fasting plasma glucose test, and a plasma glucose. However, "clawhammer style" diabetes screening, followed monitoring blood glucose level analysis is likely the much more widely utilized health and general. The most it breakthroughs have already been leveraged to build a multitude of unobtrusive, ergonomic, effective, and efficient self - monitoring blood glucose wearable technology.

Prescription Management

Early treatment is a major issue in the medical business. If individuals do not take their drugs on time, their medical problems may become worse. Drug non-adherence is particularly frequent among the elderly, who suffer clinical disorders such as mental impairment, psychosis, and so on as they age. As a result, completely following doctor's prescriptions is tough for them. Employing it to monitor a patient's prescribing has been the subject of several research in the past. So the smart medical box is used to remind people to take their medication.

Rehabilitation System

Physical medicine, particularly combined with psychotherapy, can help a patient retain their functional ability. The objective of the training is to confirm the diagnosis and help people return to their regular lifestyles. In restoration, the Internet of Things is employed in a number of ways, such as the treating cancer, physical injury, strokes, as well as other physical impairments.

COMMUNICATION TECHNOLOGY IN IOHT

Communication technologies allow different organizations in an IHoT network to communicate with one another. Short-range and medium-range communication systems are the two examples of different systems available. Low transmission strategies are used to link things within a restricted range or in a Body Area Network (BAN), whereas medium-range communication devices provide long-distance communication, including information exchange between an access point and a BAN's root controller. The connection closeness in quick transmission can extend from a few millimeters to many meters. Like most IHoT deployments, quick communication technology is utilized. RFID, Wi-Fi, Zigbee, Bluetooth, and other telecommunication are only a few of the most popular.

RFID

RFID (Radio-Frequency Identification) is a process of detecting a person using radio waves (RFID). RFID can be used for short-range transmission (10 cm–200 m). It consists of two components: a label and a scanner. The tag is made up of a microchip as well as an antenna. It is used to define a particular object or technology in the IoT ecosystem. The scan transmits or gathers signals from the object by interacting with a tag through radio waves. RFID may be used by healthcare practitioners to swiftly find and track medical equipment. The primary benefit of RFID is that it does not require any external power. Nevertheless, it is a very vulnerable method that might lead to inconsistencies for use with a Cell phone.

Bluetooth

Bluetooth low energy connectivity method that uses infrared waves at ultra-high frequencies (UHF). This function facilitates wireless communication between the two or more medical equipment. The sampling rate of Bluetooth is 2.4 GHz. Bluetooth can communicate over a distance of 100 m. Bluetooth uses encryption to keep data safe.

Zigbee

Zigbee is just a usual procedure for integrating medical equipment and exchanging data. The frequency range of Zigbee appears to be similar to those of Bluetooth (2.4 GHz). Yet, it has a greater communication range than Bluetooth devices. The mesh network topology is used in this technology. End nodes, routers, and a processing centre make up the system.

Satellite

In remote and widely separated geographical areas where other methods of communication are difficult to reach, satellite communication has proven to be more effective and beneficial. The satellite picks up signals from the ground, amplifies them, and sends them back to earth. High-speed data transfer, instant broadband connections, innovation, stability and interoperability are all advantages of satellite communication technology. However, when compared to certain other methods of communication, satellite uplinks have very high energy consumption.

In communication technology, both the Deep learning and Machine Learning algorithms are extensively used in the field of healthcare. Deep learning models require an abundance of data to work with. Also, it is well suited for models that require working with large number of image datasets. (Zech et al., 2018) in his work has demonstrated a deep learning model to detect pneumonia with chest radiographs. The work shows that when the model was trained with data from a single institution, it created a biased model with high accuracy. Moreover, this model did not work well with data collected from different institutions. RFID tags are incorporated with IoT devices for healthcare monitoring (Zech et al., 2018). The patient's data can be secured using cryptographic algorithms (Naresh et al., 2020). RFID tags help the doctors to recognize the patients, whereas wearable WBAN sensors, monitors the information about the patient like ECG, blood pressure etc. The patient information server will provide information about the patient to the authorized user when requested. Data privacy is ensured by using HECC (Hyper Elliptic Curve Cryptography).

Privacy of data and security is a big concern while using these IoT communication devices and transferring data over a network. Unauthorized access to patient data and misusing personal information of patients is a primary issue that needs to be addressed. When a youth device used to get patient data compromises security or if the data is transferred over an unsecure network, the intruder can get access over the network and can control these devices. This type of attacks can lead to fatal accidents. Intruders can get access to private information such as location information, account numbers and other health information. So these devices become insecure for elderly patients who reside alone. In order address these privacy issues and security issues; a new decentralized concept of learning called federal learning was introduced.

Federated learning is a concept in which ML models runs on local devices for the locally available data. The results of these local models are transferred to the central server. This central server aggregates the data that is obtained from all the local devices.

In this concept of federal learning, user data is processed in the local devices itself, which in turn protects the privacy of the data. Hence federated learning is one of the significant concepts that can be used in digital healthcare where privacy of data is a serious concern. The leading research in federated learning is carried out by Google, IBM and WeBAnk (Konečný et al., 2016).

Some of the components of federated learning on the client side are data collection and preprocessing, feature extraction, training the model and inference. The components on the server side are aggregating the models and evaluating the models.

The authors of (McMahan et al., 2016) has done a survey on federated learning. In this work, the authors have categorized federal learning according to privacy mechanism scale of federation, motivation of federation.

Some of the areas of federated learning where research is being carried out are communication efficiency, system and statistical heterogeneity, scalability, model performance. But there are many other aspects of federal learning that are left unexplored. Federal learning is widely known for its communication efficiency (Lo et al., 2021) as it transfers only model parameters and data privacy as client data is stored in local devices. Digital Healthcare is a field where data privacy of patients is one of the primary goals. FL has a great impact on clinicians, patients, hospital and practices, researchers and AI developers, health care providers, manufacturers and many more (5).

In this work, we discuss some basic algorithm of the federated learning and the work that has been carried out in the field of digital healthcare using federated learning and impact of FL in digital healthcare.

FEDERAL LEARNING

Recently Federal Learning has been used in Medical Imaging which allows individual sites to train an overall model in a mutual effort. Federated learning is the process of combining training results from various sites to establish a new model without communicating datasets directly. This virtually guarantees that the anonymity of patients is protected across all sites. Several reports have shown proof of concept of federated learning in the context of real-world medical imaging. In 2018, Intel collaborated with the University of Pennsylvania's Centre for Biomedical Image Computing and Analytics to test its use Federal Learning for brain-image segmentation for that they have used the public dataset BRATS 2018 is taken. The BraTS investigations showed that the federalized semantic segmentation models' grades on brain MRI scans were comparable to those inferred from models trained on the entire dataset. The similar work is carried out by King's College London collaborated with Nvidia Corporation Training in federated learning was carried out for brain tumor segmentation using the same BRATS 2018 dataset without sharing the patient data. In a federated learning environment, they repeatedly tried to use the differential-privacy approach to safeguard patient records. This method encrypts each information about patients before sharing it with other customers. To protect reverse engineering and the restoration of the entire dataset, complex mathematical algorithms are used. Using the federated learning model, Nvidia could achieve similar segmentation results without instantly sharing data.

In order to reduce the communication overhead in a centralized federal learning, a peer to peer Federated learning was adopted in which all the nodes communicate with each other (Behera & Otter, 2021). Here node can act as a leader, follower and a candidate node. The leader is elected only for a specific duration of time. To show the existence of the leader, a heartbeat message is broadcasted over the network within a particular frequency of time. When the heartbeat message is not received for a particular period, the next candidate becomes a leader. Here all the participating nodes become an aggregator. Unlike the centralized server model all the nodes participating in a P2P network must be homogeneous. As aggregation is distributed over all the participating nodes, there is a need for maintaining security over all these communication networks.

The performance of an FL algorithm relies on the parameters and hyper parameters used in the models. The authors of (Mulay et al., 2021) has undergone an empirical study to study the effect of FL parameters (datasets, data partitioning, data variety, data schemas, data distribution heterogeneity, communication, number of clients, stragglers, ML models, Synchronicity, client fairness, computational power) on the performance of the model, a single metric that can evaluate the performance of the FL models, best performing FL algorithm for a given federal learning system parameters. The work was carried out on a LEAF dataset with five different FL algorithms FeddAvg, FedProx, FSVRG, CO-OP, -FedAvg. A schematic Diagram of FL framework is shown in figure1.\

Figure 1. Federated Learning Framework

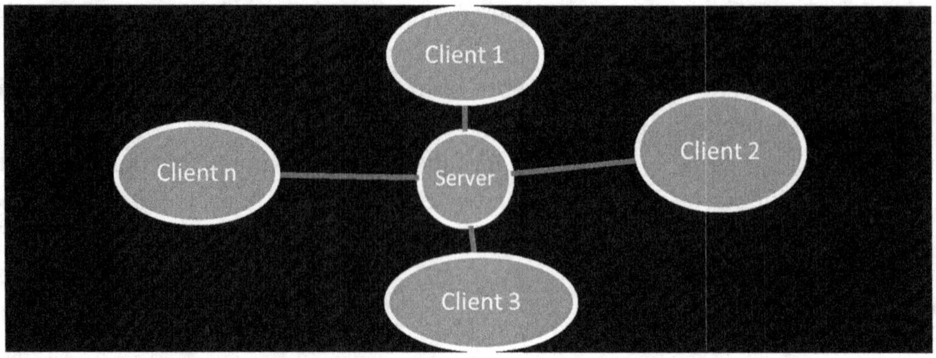

Integrating Block chain with Federal learning avoids the need for centralizing the data. A block chain FL system consists of the following stepsa) Local Training b)Model Broadcasting and Verification c) Mining d)Block Validation e)Local Model Updating

Workflow and Topologies in Federal Learning

Some of the topologies used in federal learning are a) Centralized b) Decentralizedc) Hierarchicald) Hybrid

a) Centralized Server Topology

In this type of FL topology, the central server collects the model from each node, aggregates it and distributes the updated model to the training nodes(Li et al., 2019).As the number of client nodes increases, there is a computational bottleneck for the server system.

b) Decentralized or Peer to Peer topology

In this type of FL topology, training nodes are connected to more than one per node. Aggregated models are created in each of the peer nodes. All the nodes perform training multiple times to train a common model. Later a common model can be created by taking an average weight of all associated models without having the need to share actual weights. As peers communicate with their neighbors, a need for centralized server is eliminated.

c) Hierarchical

This type of FL is a combination of both peer-to-peer model and aggregation model.

Research findings from (Li et al., 2019) shows that using P2P topology requires more communication costs than a centralized server model to achieve a specified accuracy. In terms of scalability, peer to peer models can add a greater number of clients or highly scalable as compared to a centralized server. In a P2P, topology the node can take the roles of a leader who aggregates all the models, a follower who is a participant in the network and a candidate node who participates in the election for the next leader (Behera & Otter, 2021).

Figure 2. Centralized Topology

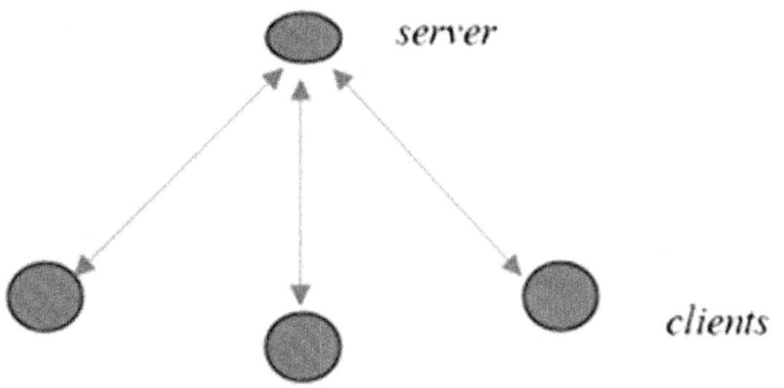

TYPES OF FEDERATEDLEARNING

Based on the distribution of data and sample space, Federated learning can be classified into three categories

a) Horizontal Federal Learning

Horizontal Federal learning or homogeneous federal learning is a type of learning, in which different samples of data with same characteristics is used. This is similar to the traditional supervised ML.To train the model, the data from different users with same characteristics is used. This type of learning can be used where a greater number of similar features reused and different samples are used.

Figure 3. DecentralizedTopology

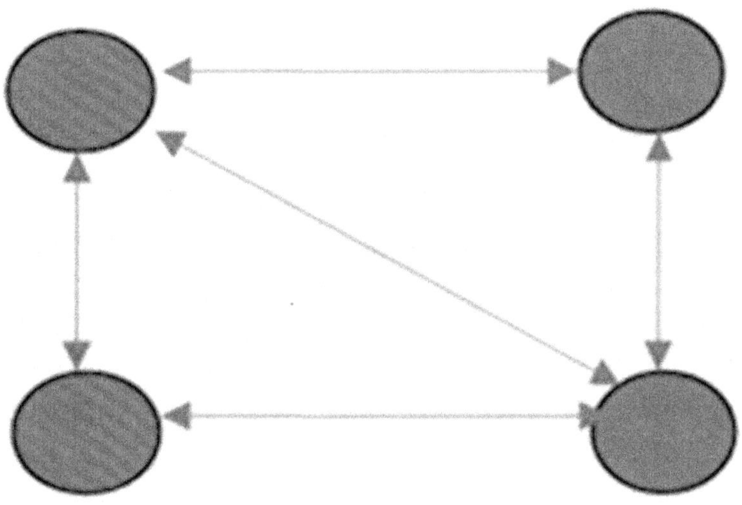

Figure 4. Hierarchical Topology

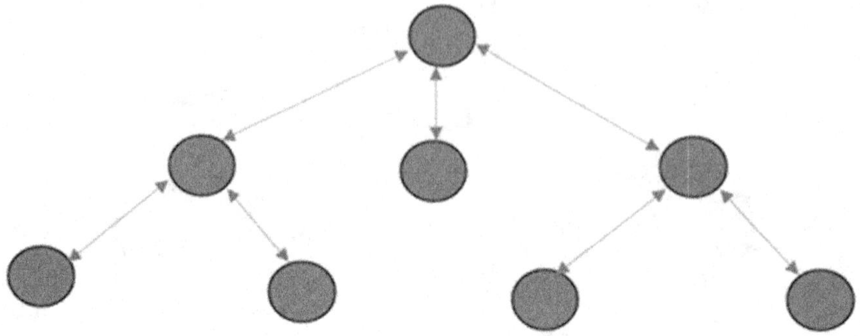

Figure 5. Data of Party A

	Feature 1↓(Cholestrol)	Feature 2↓(Blood pressure)	Feature n↓(Blood Glucose level)	Label (Heart disease)
Sample 1->				
Sample 2->				

Sample n->				

Figure 6. Data of Party B

	Feature 1↓(Cholestrol)	Feature 2↓(Blood pressure)	Feature n↓(Blood Glucose level)	Label (Heart disease)
Sample A->				
Sample B->				

Sample N->				

Table 1. Data of Party A

	Feature 1¯(Height)	Feature 2¯(Weight)	Feature n¯(Blood Glucose level)	Label (Diabetes)
Sample 1->				
Sample B->				
Sample C->				

Sample n->				

Feature spaces are same and the labels are different. In the above example, Figure 5 denotes the features like height, weight, and blood glucose level of different subjects. The label for the first party is Diabetes.

Figure 6 considers the features like cholesterol, blood pressure and blood glucose level for the subjects and the label is heart disease.

In the above figures, the blood glucose level is a common feature for different sample space and different labels. This type of learning is particularly used for business applications where a company has different branches in different locations etc.

b) Vertical Federal Learning

In vertical learning or heterogeneous federated learning, same data samples with different characteristics are used.

Table 2. Data of Party B

	Feature 1¯(Cholestrol)	Feature 2¯(Blood pressure)	Feature n¯(Blood Glucose level)	Label (Heart disease)
Sample A->				
Sample B->				
Sample C->				
Sample D->				

Sample N->				

Same users but different feature is used

FEDERATED TRANSFER LEARNING

When the data characteristics and the overlap of data samples are relatively small, we use Federated Transfer learnings. Y. Qu et al., recommends ML algorithms assume that the distribution of training and test data set is uniform. As well as ML algorithms assume that the data is from the same feature space.

But this assumption does not hold in most of the practical applications. Transfer learning addresses this issue by training the model in one data and use again in another data (Saha& Ahmad, 2021).

Different approaches are adopted for transfer learning (Nishio&Yonetani, 2019)

1. **Instance Transfer:** The labeled data is assigned new weights and is used in the target domain
2. **Parameter Transfer:** Parameters are shared between the source and target domain
3. **Feature-representation Transfer**: Finds a feature representation so that it decreases the difference between source domain and target domain.
4. **Relational Knowledge transfer:** Y. Chen et al., suggests how to build a mapping of relational knowledge between source and target domain.

Steps involved in Smart health care using FL are

a) Task Identification, Client Selection and Initialization of Learning Parameters

This is the first step in FL. The server identifies the task that is to be accomplished e.g.: classification task or prediction task. It also identifies the learning parameters and the number of clients that must be involved in this process. FedCS is a client selection protocol proposed by Nishioet al. (12). It analyzes the resource conditions of clients. The clients are selected based on the following condition. The client who can complete the distribution, model upload and update within the specified deadline will be selected.

b) Distributed Model Training on Local Data

The data is then trained on the local devices based on the initial model that is sent by the server to all the local devices and this local model is then updated. In this phase a distributed training happens. These updated models are then sent to the central server for aggregation. The central server aggregates these models.

c) Model Aggregation

An aggregation algorithm is applied over the received models and these models are then aggregated. After aggregation, the server creates new models and distributes to all the clients that are involved in this learning process. This new model is again updated in the next round. This process will be repeated until a desired accuracy is achieved.

CHALLENGES

Data Distribution: Medical data is unevenly distributed (non-IID) over different clients. This is a great challenge to FL algorithms, as they assume the data is IID (Identically distributed). Data for the same protocol will be collected by different devices as well as different modalities will be used in the dataset. T. Li et al., gives the algorithms that can handle data that are heterogeneous, more research has to be carried out to address this challenge.

1. **Privacy and Security:** Although FL algorithms ensure privacy of the data, there is a tradeoff between privacy and performance of the model. In(JEAN-F. TOMB et al., 1997) there were different cryptographic primitive discussed like secret sharing, key agreement, authenticated encryption etc. To ensure the privacy of data. Still there are threats to the server by an adversarial client which can be considered for future research.
2. **Information Leakage:** In FL learning, model changes over time. The adversary can observe the model updates that happen over a period which may lead to data leakage.
3. **Traceability and Accountability:** Multiparty communications happen over a network with variety of hardware, software and networks. The constraint for the researchers here is investigations cannot be carried on the training data that lead to unexpected results.
4. **System Architecture:** Ensuring data integrity while communication with nodes that are powerful is a big challenge. Appropriate data encryption methods must be employed in such architectures. In an environment where data privacy is stringent, Trusted Third Party (TTP) can be used as a mediator for exchange of data. But this requires extra computation and dependency on the TTP.
5. **Model Aggregation:** The model that is created by different devices must be aggregated at the central level. A secure aggregation method must work with high-dimensional updates, must be communication-efficient, must be robust to user dropping-out, ensure security under unfavorable conditions (6). Aggregation of weights in deep learning models, uneven distribution of data, differences in the hardware platform used, difference in image acquisition protocol and labeling methods are some of the challenges faced by FL (9). Deep learning model uses back propagation for optimization. During aggregation, weights updating is one of the challenge that is faced by federal learning, as the central server needs to aggregate all the weights that comes from hospitals (9).So weighting during back propagation is an area of research under Federal Learning. One of the other challenges faced by FL is the uneven distribution of data by different institutions participating in the learning process.

FL IN SMART HEALTH CARE

AI-based approaches have been extensively used in smart healthcare to learn health data and improve healthcare services. W. Zhang et al.,The privacy issue induced by public data exchange with the cloud or base station for data training is a key issue in such a traditional AI model. In healthcare settings in which different parties, such as hospitals and insurance companies, have access to healthcare databases as a part of their employment requirements, such as information analysis and processing, removing information such as patient records are insufficient to protect patient privacy. H. Zhusuggested the recent research has shown that FL can be used in the smart healthcare industry with complex features. In this paper, we examine the roles of FL in healthcare through two scenarios: EHR manager and healthcare collaboration.

FL for Digital Health Records

FL for allowing healthcare processes to manage DHRs in a flexible and privacy-preserving manner. For example, introduces a group learning protocol based on FL for an DHRs system involving several hospital organizations along with a cloud service. M. Aledhariet al., suggested using its own DHRs, each hospital runs a NN with the support of a cloud server. The inconsequential data perturbation scheme is

Table 3. Confusion matrix

		Predicted class	
Actual class	*P*	*P*	*N*
		True Positive	*False Negative*
	N	*False Positive*	*True Negative*

well thought-out to agitate the training-related statistics with the purpose of ensuring privacy for design variables in the FL process, which can thus defend prototype memorization attacks in the teaching. Although attackers can obtain tampered data, obtaining or recovering the actual data is difficult.

FL predicts ADR with a similar level of accuracy without jeopardizing user data privacy. In the FL architecture, which consists of secret providers, DHRs owners, and a central server, the authors suggest removing inappropriate updates while exploring the significance of local notifications using a sign technique at each DHRs owner to improve the accuracy rate and speed it up the generalization ability for FL in DHRs studying. Furthermore, for a FL-based medical imaging processing architecture, security and privacy are taken into account. Hospitals, healthcare providers, and patients work together to build a secure multi-party computation prototype for image analysis tools by a computation entrepreneur at a therapeutic centre using a secure FL prototype with secret sharing support.

FL for Healthcare Cooperation

FL can enable safe healthcare cooperation for enhanced medical service delivery because to its dispersed and privacy-protected nature. FL enables a proactive healthcare environment among clinical IoT devices. Q. Li et al., Smart phones were utilized to impose a FL methodology for federated global healthcare, with the purpose of alleviating the sluggish reply condition caused by some smart applications' slow data production and production process during the shared FL process. Block chain technology has evolved as a feasible solution for major healthcare cooperation, and it may be combined with FL to develop autonomous healthcare systems including many medical bodies functioning as administrative workers. D. Vermaet al., shows the traditional FL architecture's central authority is removed by using block chain, which seeks to promote networking access and speeds up the learning process in a large-scale healthcare system.

FL's potential to aid in the fight against infectious diseases such as COVID-19 has only recently been discovered. Several hospitals use the block chain to interact with one another and run DL algorithms locally to identify CT scans of COVID-19 patients. A deep capsule network is built at each hospital to improve image classification performance, while FL provides guidance for model update data transmission in order to perform design accumulation at a familiar hospital.

PERFORMANCE MEASURES

Some of the performance measures that can be used to evaluate the performance of the FL models are explained with the help of a confusion matrix

A confusion matrix has the TP (True Positive), TN(True Negative),FP(False Positive)and (FN)False Negative entries of sample data.

True Positive (TP) is the number of positive samples correctly classified as positive.True Negative(TN) is the number of samples correctly classified as negative.False positive(FP) is the number of negative samples incorrectly classified as positive.False Negative is the number of positive samples incorrectly classified as negative.

Accuracy

Accuracy is one of the significant measures in finding the performance of the model. Accuracy is the measure of how many numbers of predictions made by the model is correct.

Accuracy = (TP+TN)/ (TP+TN+FP+FN)

But accuracy is not a correct measure for classes that have skewed distribution(Nilsson, 2018).

Precision

Precision is defined as the number of true positives to the total number of positive predictions.

Precision= TP/ (TP+FP)

Recall

Recall is the number of true positives to the total number of positive samples. It is also called as True Positive Rate.

Recall = TP/ (TP+FN)

F-Score

Precision and recall are used combined and used as a single value called as F-Score. It is the harmonic mean of precision and recall.

F-score = 2 (Precision*Recall)/ (Precision+Recall)

The above measures accuracy, precision, recall and F-score are well suited for models whose output is a class label. Apart from these measures we have other performance measures like ROC and AUC that can be used for probabilistic models also.

ROC Curve

ROC Curve (Receiver Operating Characteristics Curve) shows the relationship between TPR (True Positive Rate) and FPR (False Positive Rate). This method is widely used to test the accuracy of medical diagnostic systems. ROC is plotted between TPR (sensitivity) and FPR(1-specificity) across threshold values.

AUROC Curve

AUROC (Area Under Receiver Operating Characteristics Curve) calculates the Area Under the ROC from (0, 0) to (1, 1). The value of AUC ranges from (0,0) to (1,1). An AUC value of 1 indicates that the model prediction is 100% accurate and an AUC value of 0.0 indicates that the model predictions are 100% incorrect.

Real World Research in Federal Learning for Health Care

A real-world experiment was carried out at the University of Pennsylvania and 19 other institutions globally as part of the co - creative healthcare effort to examine the feasibility of FL in medical imaging. By exploiting the capabilities of Intel Xeon Scalable processors and Intel Software Guard Extensions (Intel SGX) for performing FL operations at institutions and the cloud server, that Intel Corporation has supported the FL-health initiative. Additionally, this business supports powerful hardware resources and sophisticated DL techniques to speed up learning. Preliminary real-world experiments conducted at the University of Pennsylvania's Centre for Biomedical Image Computation and Insights demonstrate that the FL-based approach can train image datasets with an error rate of up to 90%, which really is competitive with the centralized system.

In 2020 Rajesh Kumar et al used the power of Deep learning, Block chain and Federal learning technology to detect the COVID-19 cases when its spread was in a peak. The major obstacle in diagnosing the COVID cases was the shortage of testing kits and the reliability of test results that were provided by the kits. The authors have proposed a model framework that incorporates block chain and federal learning. As the data is collected from various hospitals, data privacy preservation is a major challenge. To address this privacy issue federal learning is used. A deep learning approach is used to identify the patterns of lung CT scans.

As the data is obtained from different sources, there is a need to normalize the data. Spatial and signal normalization was carried out to handle the dimensions, resolutions and intensity of the voxels. To identify the COVID-19 cases, a capsule network that contains Primary Caps layer and Digit Caps layer in addition to convolution layer and hidden layer which improves the performance of deep learning framework was employed.

In this block chain based federated learning patient data is stored in the hospitals. This is a collaborative approach where the weights that are obtained from the locally trained model is combined using federated learning and dta privacy is also ensured.

CONCLUSION

Digital health care played a significant role in healthcare industry during COVID-19 pandemic. Irrespective of age most of the population depended on telemedicine facilities for their routine checkup and other health related issues. Studies from Precedence Research project shows that digital healthcare will grow by 27% from 2020 to 2027.Innovations in IOT, AI, and block chain technologies will ease the use of digital health care. AI and ML in medical field is a growing field of research. In this review the impact of Federal learning in digital healthcare is discussed. The needs of Federal learning, the research that has been conducted in federal learning and the challenges that are to be addressed when federal learning is employed are widely discussed. Privacy and confidentiality of patient data is a major concern in existing digital healthcare technologies that can be addressed by Federal Learning by having a distributed processing of data in local devices without a need to share data in central server. From the review it is understood that FL is an area that needs to be explored and it opens door to wide research in collaborating health industry and AI/ML technologies.

REFERENCES

Aledhari, M., Razzak, R., Parizi, R. M., & Saeed, F. (2020). federated learning: A survey on enabling technologies, protocols, and applications. *IEEE Access: Practical Innovations, Open Solutions*, *8*, 140699–140725. doi:10.1109/ACCESS.2020.3013541 PMID:32999795

Behera, M. R., & Otter, R. (2021). Federated Learning using Peer-to-peer Network for Decentralized Orchestration of Model Weights. doi:10.36227/techrxiv.14267468

Chen, Y., Qin, X., Wang, J., Yu, C., & Gao, W. (2020). Fed Health: A federated transfer learning framework for wearable healthcare. *IEEE Intelligent Systems*, *35*(4), 83–93. doi:10.1109/MIS.2020.2988604

Goyal, D., & Tyagi, A. (2020). *A Look at Top 35 Problems in the Computer Science Field for the Next Decade*. . doi:10.1201/9781003052098-40

Huang, L., & Liu, D. (2019). Patient clustering improves efficiency of federated machine learning to predict mortality and hospital stay time using distributed electronic medical records. arXiv preprint arXiv:1903.09296.

Konečný, J., McMahan, H. B., Ramage, D., & Richtárik, P. (2016). Federated Optimization: Distributed Machine Learning for On-Device Intelligence. https://arxiv.org/abs/1610.02527

Kumar, Khan, Kumar, Zakria, Golilarz, Zhang, Ting, Zheng, & Wang. (2021). *Blockchain-Federated-Learning and Deep Learning Models for COVID-19 Detection Using CT Imaging*. Academic Press.

Li, Q. (2020). A Survey on federated learning Systems: vision, hype and reality for data privacy and protection. arXiv preprintarXiv:1907.0969.

Li, T., Sahu, A. K., Talwalkar, A., & Smith, V. (2020). Federated learning: Challenges, methods, and future directions. *IEEE Signal Processing Magazine*, *37*(3), 50–60. doi:10.1109/MSP.2020.2975749

Li, W., Milletarì, F., Xu, D., Rieke, N., Hancox, J., Zhu, W., Baust, M., Cheng, Y., Ourselin, S., Cardoso, M. J., & Feng, A. (2019). Privacy-Preserving Federated Brain Tumour Segmentation. Lecture Notes in Computer Science, 11861, 133–141. doi:10.1007/978-3-030-32692-0_16

Lo, S. K., Lu, Q., Wang, C., Paik, H. Y., & Zhu, L. (2021). A Systematic Literature Review on Federated Machine Learning: From a Sofware Engineering Perspective. *ACM Computing Surveys*, *54*(5), 1–39. Advance online publication. doi:10.1145/3450288

Madhav, A. V. S., & Tyagi, A. K. (2022). The World with Future Technologies (Post-COVID-19): Open Issues, Challenges, and the Road Ahead. In A. K. Tyagi, A. Abraham, & A. Kaklauskas (Eds.), *Intelligent Interactive Multimedia Systems for e-Healthcare Applications*. Springer. doi:10.1007/978-981-16-6542-4_22

McMahan, H. B., Moore, E., Ramage, D., Hampson, S., & Arcas, B. A. y. (2016). *Communication-Efficient Learning of Deep Networks from Decentralized Data*. https://arxiv.org/abs/1602.05629

Mishra, S., & Tyagi, A. K. (2022). The Role of Machine Learning Techniques in Internet of Things-Based Cloud Applications. In S. Pal, D. De, & R. Buyya (Eds.), *Artificial Intelligence-based Internet of Things Systems. Internet of Things (Technology, Communications and Computing)*. Springer. doi:10.1007/978-3-030-87059-1_4

Mulay, A., Gaspard, B., Naidu, R., Gonzalez-Toral, S., Semwal, T., & Manish Agrawal, A. (2021). FedPerf: A Practitioners' Guide to Performance of Federated Learning Algorithms. *Proceedings.Mlr. Press*, *148*(NeurIPS), 302–324. http://proceedings.mlr.press/v148/mulay21a.html

Nair, M. M., Tyagi, A. K., & Sreenath, N. (2021). The Future with Industry 4.0 at the Core of Society 5.0: Open Issues, Future Opportunities and Challenges. *2021 International Conference on Computer Communication and Informatics (ICCCI)*, 1-7. 10.1109/ICCCI50826.2021.9402498

Nair & Tyagi. (n.d.). Privacy: History, Statistics, Policy, Laws, Preservation and Threat Analysis. *Journal of Information Assurance &Security*, *16*(1), 24-34.

Naresh, V. S., Reddi, S., Murthy, N. V. E. S., & Guessoum, Z. (2020). Secure Lightweight IoT Integrated RFID Mobile Healthcare System. *Wireless Communications and Mobile Computing*, *2020*, 1–13. Advance online publication. doi:10.1155/2020/1468281

Nguyen, D. C., Pham, Q.-V., Pathirana, P. N., Ding, M., Seneviratne, A., Lin, Z., Dobre, O., & Hwang, W.-J. (2023). Federated Learning for Smart Healthcare: A Survey. *ACM Computing Surveys*, *55*(3), 1–37. doi:10.1145/3501296

Nishio, T., & Yonetani, R. (2019). Client Selection for Federated Learning with Heterogeneous Resources in Mobile Edge. *IEEE International Conference on Communications*. 10.1109/ICC.2019.8761315

Qu, Y., Pokhrel, S. R., Garg, S., Gao, L., & Xiang, Y. (2021, April). A block chained federated learning framework for cognitive computing in industry 4.0 networks. *IEEE Transactions on Industrial Informatics*, *17*(4), 2964–2973. Advance online publication. doi:10.1109/TII.2020.3007817

Rieke, N., Hancox, J., Li, W., Milletarì, F., Roth, H. R., Albarqouni, S., Bakas, S., Galtier, M. N., Landman, B. A., Maier-Hein, K., Ourselin, S., Sheller, M., Summers, R. M., Trask, A., Xu, D., Baust, M., & Cardoso, M. J. (2020). The future of digital health with federated learning. *NPJ Digital Medicine*, *3*(1), 1–7. doi:10.103841746-020-00323-1 PMID:33015372

Saha, S., & Ahmad, T. (2021). Federated transfer learning: Concept and applications. *IntelligenzaArtificiale*, *15*(1), 35–44. doi:10.3233/IA-200075

Tomb, J-F., White, O., Kerlavage, A. R., Clayton, R. A., Sutton, G. G., Fleischmann, R. D., & Ketchum, K. A. (1997). Enhanced Reader. Nature, 388, 539–547.

Topaloglu, M. Y., Morrell, E. M., Rajendran, S., & Topaloglu, U. (2021). In the Pursuit of Privacy: The Promises and Predicaments of Federated Learning in Healthcare. *Frontiers in Artificial Intelligence*, *4*(October), 1–10. doi:10.3389/frai.2021.746497 PMID:34693280

Tyagi, A. K., Fernandez, T. F., Mishra, S., & Kumari, S. (2021). Intelligent Automation Systems at the Core of Industry 4.0. In A. Abraham, V. Piuri, N. Gandhi, P. Siarry, A. Kaklauskas, & A. Madureira (Eds.), *Intelligent Systems Design and Applications*. Springer. doi:10.1007/978-3-030-71187-0_1

Tyagi, A. K., Nair, M. M., Niladhuri, S., & Abraham, A. (2021). Security, Privacy Research issues in Various Computing Platforms: A Survey and the Road Ahead. *Journal of Information Assurance &Security*, *15*(1), 1–16.

Verma, D., White, G., & de Mel, G. (2019), Federated AI for the enterprise: a web services based implementation. *2019 IEEE International Conference on Web Services*, 20-27.

Xu, J., Glicksberg, B. S., Su, C., Walker, P., Bian, J., & Wang, F. (2021). Federated Learning for Healthcare Informatics. *Journal of Healthcare Informatics Research*, *5*(1), 1–19. doi:10.100741666-020-00082-4 PMID:33204939

Zech, J. R., Badgeley, M. A., Liu, M., Costa, A. B., Titano, J. J., & Oermann, E. K. (2018). Variable generalization performance of a deep learning model to detect pneumonia in chest radiographs: A cross-sectional study. *PLoS Medicine*, *15*(11), 1–17. doi:10.1371/journal.pmed.1002683 PMID:30399157

Zhang, W., Lu, Q., Yu, Q., Li, Z., Liu, Y., Lo, S. K., Chen, S., Xu, X., & Zhu, L. (2021, April 1). Block chain-based federated learning for device failure detection in industrial IoT. *IEEE Internet of Things Journal*, *8*(7), 5926–5937. Advance online publication. doi:10.1109/JIOT.2020.3032544

Zhu, Zhang, & Jin. (n.d.). From federated learning to federated neural architecture search: a survey. *Complex & Intelligent Systems*. . doi:10.1007/s40747-020-00247-z

Chapter 8
Obstacles in Female School Education:
The Importance of Online Learning During the COVID-19 Pandemic

Divya Budhia
Lovely Professional University, India

Tushinder Preet Kaur
Lovely Professional University, India

ABSTRACT

The importance of female education is gaining popularity among individuals, societies, and nations. They are getting full support from their families and society members as well. Government has also initiated many schemes to encourage female education, but still girls face many obstacles in their attainment of school education. The present study aims to bring to the fore the problems faced by girls while pursuing school education. A survey was conducted in which data were collected from 20 students and 10 parents with the help of interview schedules, and a qualitative study was undertaken. The results show that the main challenges faced by girls relate to adverse financial condition of their families, anomalies in school infrastructure, and lack of awareness of various government schemes. Moreover, online learning due to COVID-19 has added to these troubles. These results offer useful policy implications and can go a long way in removing the constraints in the way of female education.

INTRODUCTION

Education is the transfer of information from one person to the other though spoken words, gestures, audio or visual medium. According to EU Commission (2016), education refers to any act or experience that has a formative effect on an individual's mind, character, or physical ability. In its technical sense, education is the formal process by which society, through schools, colleges, universities and other institutions, deliberately transmits its cultural heritage and its accumulated knowledge, values and skills

DOI: 10.4018/978-1-6684-5250-9.ch008

to the next generation (UNESCO). It is vital for the overall well being of the people as it makes one knowledgeable, independent and capable of taking care of oneself. Not only at the individual level, but it also plays a dominant role in laying down the foundation of a society and in determining economic development of an economy. Education increases stock of skills and productive knowledge embodied in people, and educated people create new ideas. There is wide acceptance in the literature that education contributes considerably to economic growth and development of nations (DiCorrado et al., 2015; Pegkas, 2014; and Hanushek, 2013). But, many individuals are denied access to education across the globe on grounds of region, religion, gender, caste, etc. but the bigotry on the basis of one's sex is the most prevalent one. Female education is all the more important as it not only adds to economic development, but also brings about equality in the society and improves quality of life of masses. It leads to better health and education levels of their children, and also lower mortality rates (Kumar & Sangeeta, 2013). Women with higher levels of educational attainment almost universally have fewer children than women with lower levels of education (Economic Growth in Developing Countries: Education Proves Key, 2008). In addition, female education promotes economic growth (Salatin & Shaaeri, 2015; Self & Grabowski, 2004; and Benavot, 1989) and it leads to their empowerment (Sundaram et al., 2014; Yadav et al., 2011; and Al Riyami et al., 2004). Research conducted in a variety of countries and regions has established that educating girls is one of the most cost-effective ways of spurring development. Further, studies have shown that giving women more access to education, markets, new technology, and greater control over household resources, mostly translates into greater well-being for the household. Indeed, when women are educated and empowered, the benefits are enormous. Researchers in various studies concluded that gender inequality in education greatly hampers economic growth of nations (Ali 2015; Chaudhry, 2007; and Klasen, 2002). Importance of education in general and female education in particular cannot be highlighted more for developing countries, where dearth of skilled human resource is still a major obstacle in the path of accelerated growth of the economy. Besides, equal access to education is one of the basic human rights which everyone should get but, gender discrimination in education is a global phenomenon.

Gender Discrimination in Education

The word 'gender' is generally looked at from different perspectives and is therefore used in more than one sense. Biologically-oriented theories attribute gender differences to the different biological and genetic roles played by males and females while sociological theories focus on the socio-structural determinants of gender (Hameed & Shukri, 2014). In simple terms, generally it is used to mean 'sex' of a person i.e. male, female, etc. but, actually it means the different roles, activities and responsibilities assigned to men and women on the basis of their perceived association with masculinity or femininity respectively. The term gender is becoming more common to describe biological variation traditionally assigned to sex and this has led to the misuse of this term (Torgrimson & Minson, 2005). According to Merriam Webster Dictionary, sex (noun) is the sum of the structural, functional, and sometimes behavioural characteristics of organisms that distinguish males and females. It is a natural phenomenon acquired at birth and cannot be changed, but gender is a supposed notion evolving with wisdom and experience and therefore, it can change with acquirement of more knowledge. Gender can be understood as a framework encompassing the expected behaviour from men and women as per socially prescribed guidelines and in this framework, women have been assigned lower status. This inequality in status of female's vis-a-vis males, is termed as gender discrimination, and generates quite harmful psychological, societal and economical effects (Pokharel, 2008). Women face discrimination against at all stages and in all fields in life s. a. health, education, employment, politics, etc. There are ample reasons for the existence of gender gap, some of these are:

a) Patriarchal structure of the society and deep-rooted culture of son preference since time immemorial are the main culprits in bringing down the stature of the women in the communities.
b) Social customs, beliefs and practices are so designed to subjugate women in every way. Like at the time of marriage, generally women have to leave their house and go to stay at their husband's place; women are natural caregivers so responsibility to look after family members falls on them; etc.
c) Poverty and illiteracy among people are other major causes of gender discrimination.
d) Lack of awareness of their rights among women also serves as a great platform for germination of this disease.
e) Lack of ownership of assets is also responsible for bringing about gender biasness.

For the survival of society, there must be homogeneity. Achievement of homogeneity in society will eradicate gender discrimination. Homogeneity can be achieved only through education. Thus, awareness about the importance of girls' education among the members of society is important (Singh & Rabindranath, 2020). There are many challenges arising due to the presence of gender discrimination in the society which should serve as motivation for the people and the government to work for its exclusion:

a) First and foremost, it leads to occurrence of higher rate of sexual assault and gender-based violence in the community.
b) It also leads to high incidence of unpaid work such as doing household chores, taking care of children or sick relatives, etc.
c) According to some experts, the main cost is considered to be the inefficient or under utilization of women in production (Jacobsen, 2011).
d) In a prejudiced society women are either unaware or are prohibited from attaining the knowledge of their rights, which leads to lesser political representation of them.
e) Women are more often than not paid unequal (i.e. lesser) pay for equal work. Moreover, they are subjected to harassment at the workplace as well.
f) Gender discrimination results in low level of health among women. Moreover, it affects the mental health of women and raises the level of stress.
    e) In such a society, women also face biasness in the availability of educational opportunities. Main reasons for gender gap in education are difficulties in accessibility, economic hardships, social issues and cultural viewpoints and perspectives of individuals, families and communities regarding education of the girl child (White et al., 2016).

Bringing about gender equality specifically in education can accelerate the pace of economic progress (Klasen & Lamanna, 2009) because huge benefits can accrue to a developing economy which does not neglect its girls and women while investing in education (Balatchandirane, 2007). Some approaches are available to address the gender-related barriers to girls' school education, but there still exist gaps as these either do not separate results for males and females or fail to give individual effects of each intervention component (Psaki et al., 2022).

Gender Discrimination in Education in India

Disappointingly, educational gap between males and females is astounding in our country due to patriarchal structure of the society and the consequent occurrence of gender discrimination. An account of literacy rates in various census years after independence has been given in following table.

Table 1. Total Literacy Rate in India during 1951-2011. Source: (Census of India website censusindia.gov.in)

Year of Census	Total Literacy Rate	Year of Census	Total Literacy Rate
1951	18.33	1991	52.21
1961	28.3	2001	64.83
1971	34.45	2011	74.04
1981	43.57		

Note: Literacy Rates for 1951, 1961 and 1971censuses relate to population aged five years and above and for the years 1981 onwards relate to population aged seven years and above.

It is evident from table 1 that since independence India has come a long way in terms of literacy rate. Total literacy rate was just over 18 per cent in 1951 and continuously increased after that so that more than 50 per cent of the population (aged above 7 years) was literate by the year 1991 and nearly 75 per cent by the year 2011. Also, according to World Bank data, adult literacy rate (% of people ages 15 and above) was around 18 per cent in 1951, 61 per cent in 2001 and 69 per cent in 2011. However, as per Census 2011, the female literacy level in the country was just 65.46 per cent whereas the male literacy rate was over 80 per cent. These data corroborate the occurrence of gender discrimination in education in our country. Gender inequality is prevalent quite strongly across India because of patriarchal nature of its society. Therefore, women suffer from discrimination in every sphere of life, including education. India ranked at 114th place among 156 countries in Gender Gap Index for Educational Attainment in 2021 whereas Sri Lanka ranked 88th and China 103rd (Global Gender Gap Report, 2021). Adult female literacy rate (population 15+ years) in India in 2011 was 59.28 per cent. At the same time, it was 91.63 per cent in Brazil, 92.05 per cent in South Africa and 94.07 per cent in Singapore. Also, mean years of schooling (ISCED 1 or higher) for male population 25 + years were 6.65, but these were just 4.11 years for females (World Bank Database). Gender Parity Index for adult literacy rate was 0.75 in India while it was 0.985 in Bangladesh, 1.005 in Brazil, and 0.976 in South Africa. Also, as per Census 2011, the female literacy rate was 65.46 per cent whereas the male literacy rate was over 80 per cent. Table 2 gives account of male and female literacy as well as gender gap in literacy in India since independence.

Table 2 shows that just 8.86 per cent of the female population (aged 5 years and above) was literate at the time of independence as against 27.16 per cent of the male population, resulting in a gender gap of as high as 18.30 per cent. Gender gap in literacy, instead of falling, rose to 25.05 per cent in 1961 and then to 26.62 per cent in 1981, indicating a neglect of this aspect of education by the government. After the introduction of National Policy on Education in 1986, gender differences in literacy came down to 24.84 per cent in 1991 because this policy shifted focus towards education of women. As a result, subsequent decades registered double digit increase in female literacy rates. Government has been actively

Table 2. Male and Female Literacy Rates in India during 1951-2011. Source: (Census of India website censusindia.gov.in)

Year of Census	Male Literacy Rate	Female Literacy Rate	Gender Gap in Literacy Rate
1951	27.16	8.86	18.30
1961	40.4	15.35	25.05
1971	45.96	21.97	23.98
1981	56.38	29.76	26.62
1991	64.13	39.29	24.84
2001	75.26	53.67	21.59
2011	82.14	65.46	16.68

Note: Literacy Rates for 1951, 1961 and 1971censuses relate to population aged five years and above and for the years 1981 onwards relate to population aged seven years and above.

pursuing the cause of female education since then, but there still exists huge gender gap in literacy rates. Gender gap in literacy was 16.68 per cent in 2011, which is not significantly lower than 18.30 per cent that existed in 1951. Such stark presence of gender inequality may have an adverse impact on a number of valuable development goals such as, reduction in poverty, fertility, child mortality, etc. Literacy rates are also not uniform across Indian states as some states boost of high literacy rates (like Kerala, Maharashtra, etc.) others have low rates (like Bihar, Rajasthan, etc.) while some others have managed to achieve mediocre levels (like Punjab, Haryana, etc.). Same is the case with female literacy levels as states like Kerala, Himachal Pradesh, etc. have female literacy greater than 74 per cent (which is national average of overall literacy rate), while states like Punjab, Odisha, etc. have achieved lesser than that.

Gender Discrimination in Education in Punjab

Punjab is infamous for imbalance in the structure of its population, which is inclined more towards males due to its culture of son preference. It is quite evident from the sex-ratio in the state, which is one of the lowest in the country. An account of gender discrimination in the state can be had from the following table depicting sex-ratio in the state vis-a-vis sex-ratio in India.

Table 3. Sex-Ratio (Females per 1000 Males) of Total Population for the Period 1961-2011. Source: (Gender Statistics of Punjab, 2012)

Year	India	Punjab	Year	India	Punjab
1951	946	844	1991	927	882
1961	941	854	2001	933	876
1971	930	865	2011	943	895
1981	934	879			

Table 4. Child Sex-Ratio (0-6 years) in Punjab and India for the period 1961-2011. Source:(Gender Statistics of Punjab, 2012)

	Sex-Ratio in India		Sex-Ratio in Punjab	
Year	**Total**	**Child**	**Total**	**Child**
1961	941	976	854	901
1971	930	964	865	901
1981	934	962	879	908
1991	927	945	882	875
2001	933	927	876	798
2011	943	914	895	846

As per table 3, sex-ratio in Punjab has been on the rise since independence, yet it was still very low at 895 in 2011 when compared to all India average of 943 in the same year. It is also to be seen from the table that sex-ratio in Punjab has throughout been lower than sex-ratio in India during the period considered. A lower sex-ratio depicts lesser number of females per 1000 males in the state in relation to the national average which is indicative of the higher gender discrimination in the state as compared to the country average. The situation seems to be even grimmer when child sex-ratio is also taken into account. Child sex-ratio gives the number of females per 1000 males in the 0-6 year age group.

We already know from table 3 and now also from table 4 that sex-ratio in the country is quite low and even lower in Punjab. In addition, table 4 shows that the discrimination against female sex is growing with the years instead of falling because child sex-ratio at national as well as at the state level is even lower than the total sex-ratio. In India, the child sex-ratio was 976 in 1961 as against total sex-ratio of 941 but it fell down to 914 in 2011 against total sex-ratio of 943. Also in Punjab, the child sex-ratio was 901 in 1961 against total sex-ratio of 854 but it declined to 846 in 2011 against total sex-ratio of 895. This indicates that the preference for male child has increased during the period 1961-2011 thereby leading to enhanced discrimination against the female child. Further, like total sex-ratio, child sex-ratio is also lower in Punjab than in India, implying greater discrimination towards female child in the state than in the rest of the country.

Total population in the state of Punjab is 27.7 million, where 14,639,465 are males and 13,103,873 are females. Out of this, 10,436,056 males are literate, whereas only 8,271,081 females are literate (Census of India, 2011). In 2011, male literacy rate was 81.48 per cent while that for females was 71.34 per cent. Thus, the state doesn't score so well when it comes to education in general and female education in particular. Total number of schools in Punjab in 2016 was 28,962 with total 54.91 lakh students studying in them, in which girls formed a very low percentage of just 44.98. Girls formed 45.62 per cent of the total students at primary level, 45.08 per cent at upper primary level, and 43.93 per cent only at secondary level (GOI, 2017). Gross Enrolment Rate was 103.99 per cent for girls at primary level, 102.92 per cent at upper primary level, 86.97 per cent at secondary level, and 71.69 per cent at higher secondary level. Dropout rates for female students in 2014 were 3.25 per cent and 3.55 per cent at primary and upper primary levels, and these were 8.39 per cent and 3.67 per cent at secondary and higher secondary levels. Thus, number of girl students receiving upper primary and secondary education is far less than that getting primary education.

Ignoring the education of women, who make up nearly half of the total population, does not auger well for the growth of any nation., as per World Bank Report, female labour force participation rate in Punjab was just 27 per cent in 2012. It was 18 per cent in urban areas (as compared to 78 per cent for males) and 32 per cent in rural areas (against 79 per cent for male population), which is quite low as compared to other states. Inadequacy of female education serves as a hindrance towards gender equality, greater women participation (in society, economy and polity), and women empowerment. Despite varied attempts of the central and state governments and numerous NGOs operating in the field of education, the statistics for women's education leave a lot to be desired. So, it is essential to bring to the fore the challenges that girls have to face while pursuing school education.

BACKGROUND

Women education and development does not receive the attention it deserves. However, developed nations had long ago achieved much success in this respect. Jacobs (1996), in a study related to U.S.A., found out that women fared relatively well in the area of access to and experience of college education. But they were relatively disadvantaged with respect to outcomes of schooling. In developed countries, gender differentials in education have started to show an opposite trends as female educational attainment has surpassed, or is about to surpass, male educational attainment in most industrialized countries (Pekkarinen, 2012). Gender inequality manifests itself in various fields (education, health, employment, etc.) in developing countries. Chances of girls being out-of-schools are at least 16 percent higher than for boys and these chances are even higher for Muslim girls and girls belonging to backward castes, scheduled tribes and rural areas (Mitra et al., 2022). So, it is essential to analyse the factors that are responsible for slow growth of female education. Numerous studies at international and national level have identified a variety of constraints in the way of education attainment by females. The hurdles range from budgetary constraints to safety issues, dowry problem to low academic performance, *purdah* system to bonded labour and hygiene issues to traditional mores (Singh, 2016; Meera & Jumana, 2015; Barriers to Girls' Education, Strategies and Interventions, 2005; Strategies for Girls' Education; and Rena, 2004). Many of the researchers asserted that economic condition of the household was the main determinant of child schooling in India (Misra et al., 2017; Sharma & Ng, 2014; Malik, 2013; and Basumatary, 2012). Marwaha (2018) and Yadav et al. (2011) found that issues related to parents like, parental illiteracy, discord, parents doing job, denial of school for girls, and gambling/alcoholism in father, etc. were also prominent reasons of dropout, along with poverty. Gender bias, early marriage and financial issues were the prime problems in way of girls' education (Chauhan & Kumar, 2022). Apart from these the study found household chores at home, transportation, co-education and physical harassment also to be affecting female education. Changing the mindset of people and creating more job opportunities, apart from providing financial help and concessions can play a positive role in this regard. Sharmila and Dhas (2010) however, countered that rural poverty actually acted as a push factor for women's education rather than as an obstacle to women's education. Samudra (2014) found male literacy and age at marriage to have positive effect on female literacy while female work participation rate and number of females headed households had a negative impact

Many studies in India and the world have also identified school related factors such as distance from school, lack of facilities, school violence and safety issues, etc. also to be hindrances in the way of education of the girl child (Jain et al., 2016; Bhattacharjee, 2015; King & Winthrop, 2015; Yadav et al., 2011; and Rena, 2004). Some researchers have also recognized factors related to school's academic environment such as attitude of teachers, pedagogy, etc. to be responsible for low girl education or high drop out among them (Sampath, 2016; Singh, 2016; and Sharma & Ng, 2014). Meera and Jumana (2015) cite inadequate teaching amenities, teaching competencies, and female teachers, lack of proper monitoring, and gender bias in curriculum as barriers to girl education in India. Besides these, reluctance to acquire western education, misunderstanding on the part of the girls themselves about the values of the acquisition of formal education, traditions and culture, inadequate facilities, conflicting societal role expectations, government policies and lack of political will power to implement the entire educational programme are also the contributing factors towards low female education in the country (Ahamad & Narayana, 2015). Nair (2010) points out that issues related to women's access to education are not uniform along the varying levels. While the sociological and psychological barriers prevent girls from attending primary schools, engagement in other work and safety issues prompt them to drop out at secondary level. Further, gender stereo-typing and low economic value attached to their education, restrict them from opting for or completing higher education. Though the country is advancing well in terms of school enrolments, the retention rate (especially at secondary level) is still poor and girls are more prone to dropout at every level (Malik, 2013). Covid-19 has exacerbated the difficulties in the spread of education. It has led to accessibility, security, privacy, network issues, etc. (Madhavan & Tyagi, 2022; and Nair & Tyagi, 2021) and at the same time widened the gender gap in education (UNICEF, 2020). A case study of India on gendered impacts of school closures during Covid-19 by GIRL Center (2022) also found that there was a significant digital divide among boys and girls in access and usage. The study also reported an increased burden of household chores on girls due to their staying at home.

MAIN FOCUS OF THE CHAPTER

Research Gap, Objectives & Methodology

Several studies have been taken up at the national level to explore the factors underlying low female educational attainment. But there is severe dearth of literature in this field in Punjab. The few studies which took up the topic are quite limited in their scope. Therefore, a need is felt to fill the gap as it will contribute to the education literature. At the same time, it will go a long way in generating policy implications for government. Thus, the main objective of the study is to find out the challenges that girls have to face while pursuing school education. Here, a targeted survey of school going girls has been undertaken. Also, data have been gathered from parents of school going girls to verify the information. Further, a qualitative type of study has been undertaken where data has been collected from 10 parents and 20 girl students of selected government schools in Jalandhar & Hoshiarpur districts. Sample size has been selected on the basis of judgement of the researcher regarding reaching the saturation point in additional information sought. Also, it supports the arguments of Sandelowski (1995) that "An adequate sample size in qualitative research is one that permits-by virtue of not being too large-the deep, case-oriented analysis that is a hallmark of all qualitative inquiry, and that results in-by virtue of not being too small-a new and richly textured understanding of experience." Sample was selected on the basis of purposive sampling method. Data has been collected with the help of semi-structured interview schedules and was subjected to extensive qualitative analysis and interpretation.

Table 5. Construct for the Interview Schedule. Source: (Developed by Author from Review of Literature)

<table>
<tr><th>(1)</th><th>(2)</th></tr>
<tr><td>Personal Issues
• Self Issues
• Parental Issues
• Household Issues</td><td>School Related Issues
• Infrastructure Issues
• Other Issues (safety, bullying, teacher behaviour, etc.)</td></tr>
<tr><td>(3)</td><td>(4)</td></tr>
<tr><td>Societal Issues
• Negative attitude</td><td rowspan="3">Covid-19 Related Issues
• Online Learning Issues</td></tr>
<tr><td>(5)</td></tr>
<tr><td>Government Related Issues
• Government support and schemes</td></tr>
</table>

Conceptual Framework

Qualitative research study things in their natural settings, attempting to make sense of, or interpret, phenomena in terms of the meanings people bring to them. Qualitative research involves the studied use and collection of a variety of empirical materials –case study, personal experience, interview, observation, etc. –that describe routine and problematic moments and meanings in individuals' lives (Denzin and Lincoln, 2005). Five features of Qualitative Research, as described by Yin (2011) are:

1. Studying the meaning of people's lives, under real-world conditions;
2. Representing the views and perspectives of the people in a study;
3. Covering the contextual conditions within which people live;
4. Contributing insights into existing or emerging concepts that may help to explain human social behaviour; and
5. Striving to use multiple sources of evidence rather than relying on a single source alone.

Qualitative research allows researchers to expand the array of variables that may contribute to the production of specific outcomes across multiple settings. Careful qualitative research which is done principally by continued personal observation and interviewing can make valuable contributions to educational research (Kozleski, 2017). Much qualitative research provides valuable and trustworthy accounts of educational settings and activities, the contexts in which these are situated, and the meanings that they have for participants i.e., students (Maxwell, 2012). Educational research desperately requires qualitative approach to credibly identify the actual causes underlying a problem. Therefore, in this study, girl students have been interviewed in their natural setting i.e. schools. To ensure validity of the information and give robustness to the results, data has also been collected from parents of the school going girls. A construct was developed from review of the literature and interview schedule was framed around this construct.

Table 6. Demographic Profile of the Respondents. Source: (As per survey conducted by the Author)

Respondents	Rural	Urban	Gen	SC/ST/OBC		
Students	12	08	8	12	Literate	Not Literate
Parents	6	4	4	6	9	1

Results

First of all, it is important to know the characteristics of the participants of the study to have a better understanding of their situations, thoughts and problems. Therefore, the demographic profile of the respondents is discussed in the following table.

Table 6 reveals that there was good representation of respondents both from rural as well as urban areas. 60 per cent of the respondents, both students and parents, belonged to rural area whereas 40 per cent belonged to urban area. Further, majority of the respondents belonged to SC/ST/OBC categories and 40 per cent belonged to General category. As the districts chosen for the study (Jalandhar & Hoshiarpur) are among the ones having highest literacy rates in the state, almost all of the parents were literate and only one parent was illiterate.

Personal Issues

The review of literature revealed that lack of interest or understanding in classroom study can act as a major deterrent in the way of school education for girls. But, our survey results suggested that none of the girl students reported any such issue. All of them showed a keen interest in their studies and all liked going to school and moreover, all were regular in going to school except only one case where the girl was irregular due to her disturbed medical condition. Not all were exceptionally good in studies, but still they liked to study and going to school. Also, they were getting full support from their parents in their education and they did not discriminate between their sons' and daughters' education. They helped them with their studies, supervised them and some parents had even arranged for additional coaching for their children. Even when some parents were facing financial difficulties, they supplied their daughters with necessary school related accessories like, school bags, uniforms, books, stationery, etc. Some parents had even bought cycles for their daughters so as to make their journey to and from school convenient. Parents took serious interest in their daughters' school education and kept themselves updated about their performance at school by regularly visiting school and attending Parent-Teacher-Meetings (PTMs). When asked as to whether they considered girls' and boys' education to be equally important, one of the mothers replied,

"I think it is more important to educate girls today so that they become independent, unlike us, who are less educated and therefore have to look towards others for provision of resources. If girls are educated, they can take care of themselves." (Translated from Punjabi)

On another occasion, when one mother, who had two daughters and a son, all studying in same school was asked as to what was more important for her: to educate their girl children or to save for her marriage, she replied,

"We are not thinking about their marriage as of now, education is our priority... if they are well educated then they shall become independent in life and can get married themselves." (Translated from Punjabi)

Though parents did not want to marry their girls off early, yet they wanted them to learn household chores along with their studies and involved them in such activities. But, there was no pressure or compulsion for them to do such work on daily basis. They were entitled to devote their time solely towards their studies during assessments or exam time. Here, it is to be noted that though around the globe the responsibility to do household chores is associated with the females but this mentality is very strongly and rigidly present in Indian society and more so in Punjab, and becomes evident in a few cases. One such incident was when mother of 10 years old Jaspreet, who was studying in 4th standard, passed away and her father failed to send her to school thereafter as the responsibility to manage the entire house fell on her tiny shoulders.

School Related Issues

Access to school and school infrastructure play a significant role in boosting female school education. A greater distance to school acts as an obstacle in the way of education of girls as an increase in distance leads to increased risk in going to and coming from school. Numerous cases of kidnapping and molestation fuel this fear. Our survey revealed that school fell within a comfortable distance fo all the participants. Moreover, they went to school in a group either with their siblings or with friends so that the journey was safe. Students and parents alike found school infrastructure to be good and sufficient. The building, classrooms, benches, etc, were in good shape and there was uninterrupted availability of study resources s. a. chalks, duster, etc. Playground, laboratories, library, etc. were in good condition and were put to regular use. Mid-day meal was hygienic and cooked properly; was cooked under a shed and was served in clean utensils. Therefore, students did not hesitate to eat mid-day meal in school. Drinking water was clean and available all the time. Keeping in mind the requirements of girl students, they were provided with separate toilets but one of the girls pointed out that she tried to avoid using them as those were not very clean. There was no separate common room for girls, but most of the girl students did not find it to be much required. However, one or two girls just said that it would have been better if it was there, but it doesn't make any big difference. One important thing that was found missing was the "Napkin Dispenser". Under a scheme of the state government, every school has to have a napkin-dispensing machine for the benefit of adolescent school girls, but the schools did not have it. Both students as well as parents were very much impressed by the teachers of the schools and appreciated their efforts in teaching the students. As per our survey, the teachers were seriously doing their duty, worked to make students understand the concepts, took care of their problems and spoke well. Moreover, teachers' behaviour towards male and female students was same and they did not indulged in any kind of discrimination between their pupils. While talking about teachers, one of the students remarked,

"I like to study and I like going to school and I think it is mainly because our teachers are very good. They teach very well and are always ready to listen to our problems."

(Translated from Hindi)

Societal Issues

Society has a strong bearing on almost all aspects of our daily lives, and more so at places which are still predominated by orthodox ideas and attitudes s. a. Punjab. So, in survey it was also tried to gauge as to how much influence is exerted by the society in decision-making of the parents regarding their daughters' school education. But it was surprising to know that none of the parents reported any positive or negative influence being exerted on them. They said they were solely responsible for every decision they took and were not open to any suggestion by any outsider either. Similar comments were made by school girls themselves. They were not told by any relative or neighbour or any member of their society to forgo education and get married or anything of that sort. In this regard, one father said,

"No one approaches me with any suggestion to marry my daughter off rather than give her education. People here are literate and understand the importance of girl education." (Translated from Punjabi)

Covid-19 Related Issues

World over, Covid-19 pandemic has caused havoc and affected many spheres of human life like, health, work, education, sports, etc. and freedom. Schools are forced to shut and students are compelled to attend online classes through digital learning apps like, Zoom, WhatsApp, Google Meet, etc. All these applications require a laptop or a smart phone to function which are not readily available to school going students, especially in rural areas. Our survey revealed that online learning system prevented education from halting in times of Corona. Also, there were no problems in understanding the concepts in online class but students still liked physical classes better than online classes because they regularly faced connectivity issues and also because they preferred to have face-to-face contact with the teacher. As the education shifted to online platforms, a lot of data was being generated through these websites, which created several problems like that of security, privacy, network connectivity, etc. during the process of cleaning or analyzing of such large amount of data (Madhav & Tyagi, 2022). Moreover, students missed their school and other school related activities and most importantly the company of their friends. It is important to mention here that arranging for smart phone to attend online classes was the major difficulty faced by students and their parents, especially where more than one child was to attend these classes. In such cases, either children attended classes by rotation, which led to missing of the classes by the other ones or by borrowing phones of the relatives, which also were not available daily during the school time. About her difficulty in attending online classes, one girl student said,

"I have a younger brother and a sister studying in same school and we all have classes on same time but we have just one phone to attend them. So, we attend our classes by rotation. One day I attend my classes, second day my sister and next day my brother attends... we have to miss our classes, but what else can we do as we have only one phone."

(Translated from Punjabi)

In such cases, though girls were not discriminated against knowingly or purposefully, but in some households the discrimination was hidden and the girls were unaware of it. In the houses with a boy child and one or more sisters, sometimes the boy child was given preference in providing with the mobile phones for his classes solely and the daughters shared the mobiles with parents, cousins or other relatives. If the son was elder to sisters, it was argued that his classes were more important and if he was younger, his careless attitude became the excuse, that is, if he was not given the mobile phone solely for his classes then he would get an opportunity to miss them on purpose. Thus, on one pretext or the other, some girl children faced this unfairness in times of Covid-19. Also, one of the girl students reported of enhanced financial difficulties due to Covid-19 occurrence as her father lost his job of school bus driver and had to shift to driving a commercial bus on casual basis. When asked about online classes, one girl stated,

"No doubt online classes have helped in continuing our education and there is no difficulty in understanding as such, but I miss my school, my teachers and my friends. I desperately want to go back to my school." (Translated from Hindi)

Government Related Issues

Government has initiated many policies and schemes to support education of the girl child, and these have helped masses a lot in furtherance of the education of their daughters. Schemes s. a. Mid-day Meal has proved to be path-breaking in the field of school education. In our survey, we asked students and parents about the functioning of the ongoing schemes as well as their suggestions regarding any new schemes which would help them in pursuing their road to knowledge. Of the ongoing schemes, mostly were running properly except that of installation of "napkin dispensers" as mentioned earlier. Also, students and parents showed complete ignorance regarding various scholarship and financial aid schemes being run by the central and the state governments to promote the birth and education of girl child under the broad policies of "Beti Bachao Beti Padhao", "Nanhi Chhaan", etc. Therefore, they were not availing the benefits of these schemes. Also, most of the parents suggested that government should provide enhanced financial aid in terms of free education, free books and other required material during entire school education.

SOLUTIONS AND RECOMMENDATIONS

The results of the survey highlight that student understood the importance of education and took their school education seriously. They were regular in going to school. Also, parents were providing all the required support: moral as well as financial. They took interest in studies of their daughters, kept record of their performance at school and attended PTMs regularly. They did not put any unnecessary burden on their daughters regarding household work. Society was also in the support of girl education and members of the society did not put hurdles in the way of it. This means that girls did not face any challenges on account of their own lack of interest, or lack of support from parents and society.

Girls felt safety in school and also on their way to school, as distance to school was not much and also because they went to school in groups. School infrastructure was found to be good. However, a few things were either missing like, "napkin dispensers" and "girls' common room" or needed improvement like, girls' toilets. Also, people were unaware about various ongoing government schemes of providing scholarships and financial aid to girl child. In addition, parents wanted government to subsidize entire school education of the girl child so to assist them in their financial troubles. Difficulties related to girls' school education enhanced during Covid-19 due to financial troubles and online learning. Thus, it can be said that school infrastructure, financial difficulties, online learning in Covid-19 and lack of awareness about and weak implementation of government schemes are acting as hurdles in the way of school education of girl child.

Figure 1.

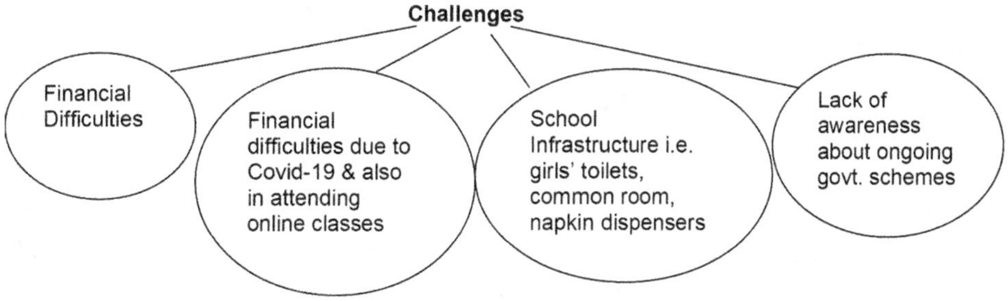

FUTURE RESEARCH DIRECTION

This research has been carried out among a sample of 10 parents and 20 girl students of government schools in Jalandhar and Hoshiarpur districts of Punjab state. Further research with wider scope is required to obtain better perspectives in this direction.

CONCLUSION

Importance of girl education is gaining popularity among individuals, societies and nations. They are getting full support from their families and society members as well. Government has also initiated many schemes to encourage female education, but still girls face many challenges in their attainment of school education. Mainly these relate to adverse financial condition of their families, anomalies in school infrastructure and lack of awareness of various government schemes. Moreover, online learning due to Covid-19 has added to these troubles. These results offer useful policy implications and can go a long way in removing the constraints in the way of female education.

REFERENCES

Ahamad, T., & Narayana, A. (2015). Girl education: A lifeline to rural transformation in India. *International Journal of Applied Research*, *1*(6), 84–87. https://www.researchgate.net/publication/290691308_Girl_education_A_lifeline_to_rural_transformation_in_India

Al Riyami, A., Afifi, M., & Mabry, R. M. (2004). Women's Autonomy, Education and Employment in Oman and Their Influence on Contraceptive Use. *Reproductive Health Matters*, *12*(23), 144–154. doi:10.1016/S0968-8080(04)23113-5 PMID:15242223

Ali, M. (2015). Effect of Gender Inequality on Economic Growth (Case of Pakistan). *Journal of Economics and Sustainable Development*, *6*(9), 125–133. https://www.iiste.org/Journals/index.php/JEDS/article/view/22620/23290

Balatchandirane, G. (2007). *Gender Discrimination in Education and Economic Development: A Study of Asia*. Retrieved from https://www.ide.go.jp/library/English/Publish/Download/Vrf/pdf/426.pdf

Basumatary, R. (2012). School Dropout across Indian States and UTs: An Econometric Study. *International Research Journal of Social Sciences, 1*(4), 28-35. Retrieved from www.isca.in/IJSS/Archive/v1/i4/5.ISCA-IRJSS-2012-061.pdf

Benavot, A. (1989). Education, Gender, and Economic Development: A Cross-National Study. *Sociology of Education*, *62*(1), 14–32. doi:10.2307/2112821

Bhattacharjee, K. (2015). *Women's Education in Rural Bihar: Issues and Challenges*. Retrieved from https://www.researchgate.net/profile/Kishore_Bhattacharjee/publication/318080118_Women%27s_Education_in_Rural_Bihar_Issues_and_Challenges/links/5958d5d4aca272c78abf033b/Womens-Education-in-Rural-Bihar-Issues-and-Challenges.pdf

Census data: Government of India. (n.d.). Retrieved September 7, 2022, from https://censusindia.gov.in/census.website/data/

Chaudhry, I. S. (2007). Gender Inequality in Education and Economic Growth: Case Study of Pakistan. *Pakistan Horizon, 60*(4), 81-91. Retrieved from https://www.jstor.org/stable/41500094

Chauhan, A., & Kumar, S. (2022). A Study on Problems and Challenges Faced by Girl Students in Higher Education. *Philosophical Readings*, *13*(4), 130–135. doi:10.5281/zenodo.5833619

Denzin, N. K., & Lincoln, Y. S. (Eds.). (2005). *The Sage handbook of qualitative research* (3rd ed.). Sage Publications Ltd.

DiCorrado, E., Kelly, K., & Wright, M. (2015). *The Relationship between Mathematical Performance and GDP per Capita*. Retrieved from https://smartech.gatech.edu/bitstream/handle/1853/54222/the_relationship_between_mathematical_performance_and_gdp_per_capita_1.bk-2.pdf

GIRL Center (2022). *Gendered Effects of Covid-19 School Closures: India Case Study*. popcouncil.org

GOI. (2012). *Gender Statistics of Punjab*. Retrieved from: http://www.pbplanning.gov.in/pdf/Gender%20Statistics%20%202012%20final.pdf

GOI. (2017). *Statistical Abstract of Punjab*. Retrieved from Economic & Statistic Organisation of Punjab website: https://www.esopb.gov.in/

Hameed, N., & Shukri, A. M. (2014). *The Concept of 'Gender' According to Different Approaches*. Retrieved from: https://www.researchgate.net/publication/332289875_The_Concept_of_%27Gender%27_According_to_Different_Approaches

Hanushek, E. A. (2013). *Economic Growth in Developing Countries: The Role of Human Capital*. Retrieved from https://hanushek.stanford.edu/sites/default/files/publications/Education%20and%20Economic%20Growth.pdf

Jacobs, J. A. (1996). Gender Inequality and Higher Education. *Annual Review of Sociology*, *22*(1), 153–185. doi:10.1146/annurev.soc.22.1.153

Jacobsen, J. P. (2011). Gender Inequality A Key Global Challenge: Reducing Losses due to Gender Inequality. Assessment Paper, Copenhagen Consensus on Human Challenges, Wesleyan University.

Jain, P., Agarwal, R., Billaiya, R., & Devi, J. (2016). Women education in rural India. *International Journal of Advanced Education and Research*, *1*(12), 27–29. http://www.alleducationjournal.com/archives/2016/vol1/issue12/1-12-19

King, E. M., & Winthrop, R. (2015). *Today's Challenges for Girls' Education*. Retrieved from https://www.brookings.edu/wp-content/.../Todays-Challenges-Girls-Educationv6.pdf

Klasen, S. (2002). Low Schooling for Girls, Slower Growth for All? Cross-Country Evidence on the Effect of Gender Inequality in Education on Economic Development. *The World Bank Economic Review*, *16*(3), 345–373. doi:10.1093/wber/lhf004

Klasen, S., & Lamanna, F. (2009). The Impact of Gender Inequality in Education and Employment on Economic Growth: New Evidence for a Panel of Countries. *Feminist Economics*, *15*(3), 91–132. doi:10.1080/13545700902893106

Kozleski, E. B. (2017). The Uses of Qualitative Research: Powerful Methods to Inform Evidence-Based Practice in Education. *Research and Practice for Persons with Severe Disabilities*, *42*(1), 19–32. doi:10.1177/1540796916683710

Kumar, J., & Sangeeta. (2013). Status of Women Education in India. *Educationia Confab, 2*(4), 162-176. Retrieved from https://slidex.tips/download/status-of-women-education-in-india

Madhav, A. V. S., & Tyagi, A. K. (2022). The World with Future Technologies (Post-COVID-19): Open Issues, Challenges, and the Road Ahead. In A. K. Tyagi, A. Abraham, & A. Kaklauskas (Eds.), *Intelligent Interactive Multimedia Systems for e-Healthcare Applications*. Springer. doi:10.1007/978-981-16-6542-4_22

Malik, B. K. (2013). Child Schooling and Child Work in India: Does Poverty Matter? *International Journal of Child Care and Education Policy*, *7*(1), 80–101. doi:10.1007/2288-6729-7-1-80

Marwaha, S. (2016). A compositional analysis of life events leading to apprehension of School Dropout in Mohali. *Australian Journal of Science and Technology*, *2*(1), 40–45. www.aujst.com/vol-2-1/06_AJST.pdf

Maxwell, J. A. (2012). The Importance of Qualitative Research for Causal Explanation in Education. *Qualitative Inquiry*, *18*(8), 655–661. doi:10.1177/1077800412452856

Meera, K. P., & Jumana, M. K. (2015). Empowering Women through Education. *International Journal of Humanities and Social Science Invention*, *4*(10), 58–61. http://www.ijhssi.org/papers/v4(10)/Version-3/H04103058061.pdf

Misra, L., Misra, S. N., & Mishra, S. (2017). A survey on women's education and their economic condition in Odisha. *The Clarion (Guwahati)*, *6*(2), 113–121. doi:10.5958/2277-937X.2017.00038.7

Mitra, S., Mishra, S. K., & Abhay, R. K. (2022). Out-of-school girls in India: A study of socioeconomic-spatial disparities. *GeoJournal*. Advance online publication. doi:10.100710708-022-10579-7 PMID:35261431

Nair, M. M., & Tyagi, A. K. (2021). Privacy: History, Statistics, Policy, Laws, Preservation and Threat Analysis. *Journal of Information Assurance & Security*, *16*(1), 24–34.

Nair, N. (2010). Women's education in India: A situational analysis. *Indore Management Journal, 1*(4), 100-114. Retrieved from www.iimidr.ac.in/wp-content/.../Womens-Education-in-India-A-Situational-Analysis.pdf

Pegkas, P. (2014). The Link between Educational Levels and Economic Growth: A Neoclassical Approach for the Case of Greece. *International Journal of Applied Economics*, *11*(2), 38–54. https://www2.southeastern.edu/orgs/ijae/index_files/IJAE%20SEPT%202014%20PEGKAS%207-30-2014%20RV.pdf

Pekkarinen, T. (2012). Gender differences in education. *Nordic Economic Policy Review*, 1. Retrieved from ftp.iza.org/dp6390.pdf

Pokharel, S. (2008). Gender Discrimination: Women Perspectives. *Nepalese Journal of Development and Rural Studies*, *5*(2), 80–87.

Psaki, S., Haberland, N., Mensch, B., Woyczynski, L., & Chuang, E. (2022). Policies and Interventions to remove Gender-related Barriers to Girls' School Participation and Learning in Low- and Middle-income Countries: A Systematic Review of the Evidence. *Campbell Systematic Reviews*, *12*(1), e1207. doi:10.1002/cl2.1207

Rena, R. (2004). Gender Disparity in Education - An Eritrean Perspective. *USA: The Global Child Journal, 2*(1), 43-49. Retrieved from https://mpra.ub.uni-muenchen.de/10315/1/MPRA_paper_10315.pdf

Salatin, P., & Shaaeri, H. (2015). Impact of Gender Inequality on Economic Growth. *China-USA Business Review*, *14*(12), 584–591. doi:10.17265/1537-1514/2015.12.002

Sampath, G. (2016, December 11). Why children drop out from primary school. *The Hindu*. Retrieved from: https://www.thehindu.com/news/national/Why-children-drop-out-from-primary-school/article16792949.ece

Samudra, A. (2014). Trends and Factors affecting Female Literacy-An inter-district study of Maharashtra. [Retrieved from http://ijgws.com/journals/ijgws/Vol_2_No_2_June_2014/17.pdf]. *International Journal of Gender and Women's Studies*, *2*(2), 283–296.

Self, S., & Grabowski, R. (2004). Does education at all levels cause growth? India, a case study. *Economics of Education Review*, *23*, 47–55. https://www.csus.edu/indiv/l/langd/self_grabowski.pdf

Sharma, U., & Ng, O. (2014). *What has worked for Bringing Out-of-school Children with Disabilities into Regular Schools? A Literature Review*. doi:10.5463/dcid.v25i2.355

Sharmila, N., & Dhas, A. C. (2010). *Development of Women Education in India*. Retrieved from https://mpra.ub.uni-muenchen.de/20680/

Singh, A.K., & Rabindranath, M. (2020). Gender Divide In Education In India: A Critical Study Based On Functionalist Theory Of Education. *Journal of Critical Reviews*. DOI: doi:10.31838/jcr.07.02.105

Singh, K. (2016). Importance of Education in Empowerment of Women in India. *Motherhood International Journal of Multidisciplinary Research & Development, 1*(1), 39-48. Retrieved from https://motherhooduniversity.edu.in/images/papers/Khushboo%20Singh .pdf

Strategies for Girls' Education. (n.d.). UNICEF. Retrieved from https://www.unicef.org/sowc06/pdfs/sge_English_Version_B.pdf

Sundaram, M. S., Sekar, M., & Subburaj, A. (2014). Women Empowerment: Role of Education. *International Journal of Management and Social Sciences*, *2*(12), 76–85. http://www.indianjournals.com/ijor.aspx?target=ijor:ijmss&volume

Torgrimson, B. N., & Minson, C. T. (2005). Sex and gender: What is the difference? *Journal of Applied Physiology (Bethesda, Md.)*, *99*(3), 785–787. doi:10.1152/japplphysiol.00376.2005 PMID:16103514

UNESCO. (1993). The Education of Girls: The Ouagadougou Declaration and Framework for Action. *Pan-African Conference on the Education of Girls*. Retrieved from http://www.unesco.org/education/pdf /OUAGAD_E.PDF

UNICEF. (2005). *Barriers to Girls' Education, Strategies and Interventions- A UNICEF Report*. UNICEF. Retrieved from https://www.unicef.org/teachers/girls_ed/BarrierstoGE.pdf

UNICEF. (2020). *COVID-19 and Girls' Education in East Asia and Pacific*. unicef.org

White, G., Ruther, M., Kahn, J. R., & Dong, D. (2016). *Gender inequality amid educational expansion in India: An analysis of gender differences in the attainment of reading and mathematics skills*. Academic Press.

World Economic Forum. (2021). *Global Gender Gap Report*. Retrieved from: https://www.weforum.org/reports/

Yadav, S. B., Vadera, B., Mangal, A. D., Patel, N. A., & Shah, H. D. (2011). A Study on Status of Empowerment of Women in Jamnagar District. *National Journal of Community Medicine*, *2*(3), 423–428. http://njcmindia.org/uploads/2-3_423-428.pdf

Yin, R. K. (2011). *Qualitative Research from Start to Finish*. The Guilford Press.

KEY TERMS AND DEFINITIONS

Education: The world 'education' comes from the Latin world e-ducere, meaning "to lead out" (Harsha, 2017). According to EU Commission (2016), education refers to any act or experience that has a formative effect on an individual's mind, character, or physical ability. In its technical sense, education is the formal process by which society, through schools, colleges, universities and other institutions, deliberately transmits its cultural heritage and its accumulated knowledge, values and skills to the next generation (UNESCO).

Gender: The word 'gender' is generally looked at from different perspectives and is therefore used in more than one sense. Biologically oriented theories attribute gender differences to the different biological and genetic roles played by males and females while sociological theories focus on the socio-structural determinants of gender (Hameed & Shukri, 2014).

Gender Discrimination: Gender can be understood as a framework encompassing the expected behaviour from men and women as per socially prescribed guidelines and in this framework, women have been assigned lower status. This inequality in status of females vis-a-vis males, is termed as gender discrimination, and generates quite harmful psychological, societal and economical effects (Pokharel, 2008).

Gross Enrolment Ratio: As per the World Bank, Gross enrolment ratio is the ratio of total enrolment, regardless of age, to the population of the age group that officially corresponds to the level of education shown. Gross enrolment ratios indicate the capacity of each level of the education system, but a high ratio may reflect a substantial number of overage children enrolled in each grade because of repetition or late entry rather than a successful education system. Gross enrolment ratio, for instance, in case of primary school is calculated by dividing the number of students enrolled in primary education regardless of age by the population of the age group which officially corresponds to primary education and multiplying by 100.

Illiteracy Rate: Percentage of persons who cannot read and write with understanding in any language. It can either be calculated as dividing the number of illiterate persons by the total number of persons and then multiplying the result by 100 or by subtracting the literacy rate from 100.

$$Illiteracy\ Rate = (Maximum\ Achievable\ Literacy\ Rate\ i.e.100) - (Literacy\ Rate):$$

Literacy: A person aged seven and above who can both read and write with understanding in any language, is treated as literate. "Literacy means a person who can read and write a simple message in any language with understanding is considered literate" (Census of India, 2011).

Literacy Rate: Literacy rate describes percentage of people (age 7 years and above) who can read and write with understanding in any language.

$$Literacy\ Rate = \left(\frac{Number\ of\ Literate\ People}{Total\ Number\ of\ People}\right) * 100:$$

According to the World Bank: literacy rate is an outcome indicator to evaluate educational attainment. It can be also used as a proxy instrument to see the effectiveness of education system; a high literacy rate suggests the capacity of an education system to provide a large population with opportunities to acquire literacy skills.

School Enrolment: Total number of students registered and/or attending classes at a school in different grade levels (data.gov.in). Enrolment indicators, however, are based on annual school surveys, but do not necessarily reflect actual attendance or dropout rates during the year (the World Bank).

Sex Ratio: Sex ratio depicts number of females per thousand males. A lower sex-ratio depicts lesser number of females per 1000 males and therefore, is indicative of the higher gender discrimination and vice-versa.

Chapter 9
Industry 4.0 Revolution and Its Impact on Society

Sheetal Zalte
Shivaji University, India

Smita Deshmukh
Vishwakarma College of Arts, Commerce, and Science, Pune, India

Prajkta Patil
Vishwakarma College of Arts, Commerce, and Science, Pune, India

Minal Patil
Vishwakarma College of Arts, Commerce, and Science, Pune, India

Rajanish Kamat
Shivaji University, India

ABSTRACT

The term "fourth industrial revolution" is used as a framework for analyzing the influence of coming technologies on the full range of societal impact on the current generation, evolving cultural laws, governmental view, economical growth, and foreign affairs. The fourth industrial revolution idea confirms that technological change is the engine of change in relevant sectors and elements of society. It underscores the theme that many technologies have emerged at some point in history that has been combined in ways that have had an impact on incremental efficiency gains. This chapter introduces how this new revolution has brought great opportunities; the core potential of this industrial revolution is to increase manufacturing output globally to meet social needs and to enhance the capacity across all the different current systems. The chapter focuses on various novel techniques that sustain this ultra-modern era and delineates the influence, prospects, desires, and acclimation of Industry 4.0 from the social viewpoint.

DOI: 10.4018/978-1-6684-5250-9.ch009

Figure 1. Advancement from industry 1.0 to 4.0

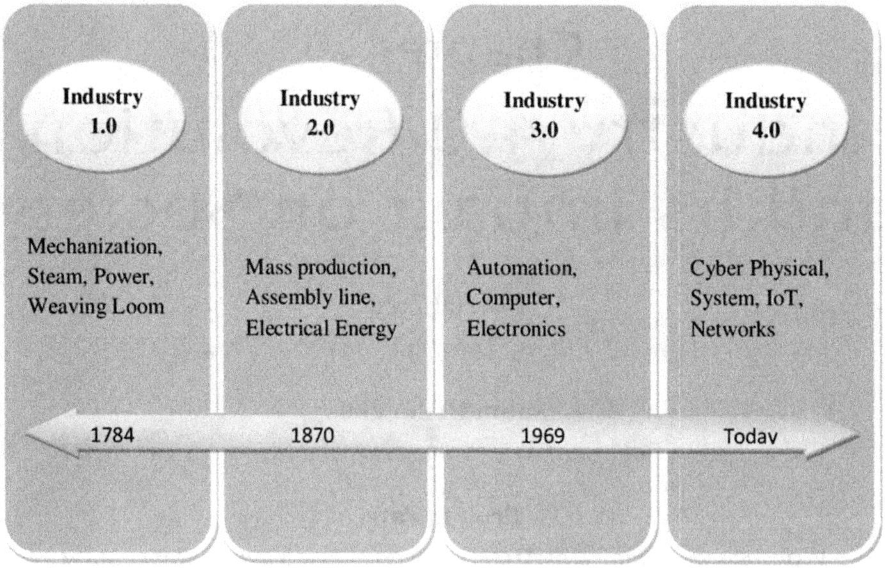

INTRODUCTION

The 21st century, marked by a knowledge explosion, has witnessed a surge in various trends, technology, and Innovations that are rapidly evolving Industry incubators that plan to grow budding ideas. "Manufacturing intelligentization and digitalization" is the core technology of the new industrial revolution (Vaidya, S., Ambad, P., & Bhosle, S, 2018). To increase productivity, so many industries are putting effort into the customization of production. The advancement from industry 1.0 to industry 4.0 implies a complete transition in the industrial epoch as shown in Figure 1.

Industry 4.0 revolution, popularly known as the 'fourth industrial revolution, is a novel trend of smart automation in the industry that brings complete administration of product's life cycle. Industry 4.0 includes various technologies like the Industrial Internet, Internet of Things, Smart Manufacturing, and Cloud-based Manufacturing. In Industry 4.0, the entire globe has faced a series of novel technologies linking the physical and virtual worlds. Adaption of modern techniques and tools results in improving production efficiency and revolutionizing the way the entire organization works and grows. The technologies enabling this revolution grip existing data and extensive supplementary data sources, containing data from associated assets, to enhance efficiency at multiple levels, convertcurrentproduction processes, create conclude information flows along the value chain, and generatecontemporary services and business prototypes. It is worthwhile to glance at the prior industry revolutions to appreciate the significance of Industry 4.0.

Industry 1.0

The use of 'Water and steam-powered machines' started in the 18th century to help employee's mass production of goods, as shown in Figure 1. Way back in 1784, the weaving loom was pioneered. While increasing the production capabilities, the business also grew from small-scale businesses to large-scale business organizations (Meindl et al., 2021). Industry 1.0 can also be considered the foundation of the industry culture that is attentive to equality on efficiency, quality, and scale (Vuksanović et al, 2016).

Industry 2.0

Industry 2.0 started with the 20th century itself, discovering assembly line production (Iyer, 2018). he primary giver in Industry 2.0 was the implementation of 'electrical machines'. Compared to the water and steam-based machines, electrical machines were more effective to operate and maintain from the point of effort and cost. Optimum allocation of resources, working protocols, and jobs enhancement of worker introduced in [(Meindl et al., 2021).

Industry 3.0

The 1990s and 2000s marked the next industrial revolution, with the invention and manufacture of semiconductor devices, including transistors and integrated circuits. By using electronic devices, automated machines are built, resulting in reduced efforts, greater accuracy, increased speed, and replacement of human resources in a few situations. In this phase, software development exploited on an electronic device is produced.

It is an automated, integrated system where enterprise resources planning tools were used for material requirements planning, execution of plans, time management, and monitoring the product cycle.

Industry 4.0

Figure 2 depicts information technology communication and its application to the industry is also referred to as 'Industry 4.0'. Currently, Industry 4.0 is implemented which links the Internet of Things IoT) and production technology to allow contribute and direct intelligent activities.

Also, according to a Deloitte University press article 'Industry 4.0 and the Manufacturing Ecosystem', manufacturing, robotics, artificial intelligence, and other intelligent technologies digitize, smart exotic materials, virtual/ It also includes advanced technologies such as augmented reality, etc. Expansion of novel technologies has been a major goal of the migration to Industry 4.0. Few programs such as smart manufacturing technology, ground-level management, product lifecycle management, etc. were developed in the sophisticated phases of the 20th century, such as smart manufacturing technology, ground level management, product lifecycle management, etc. Did the concept of a vision of the technology needed to enable its implementation? Currently, Industry 4.0 will help meet the requirements for these activities to attain their bursting potential.

(C.V.Bidnur, 2020).

Technical components of these requirements are addressed via the utility of the established principles of intelligent systems, better known as 'Cyber-Physical Systems (CPS)', along with the 'industrial internet of things (IIoT)' to the economical manufacturing structures. The enterprise 4.0 'execution device'

Figure 2. Industry 4.0 impacts on society

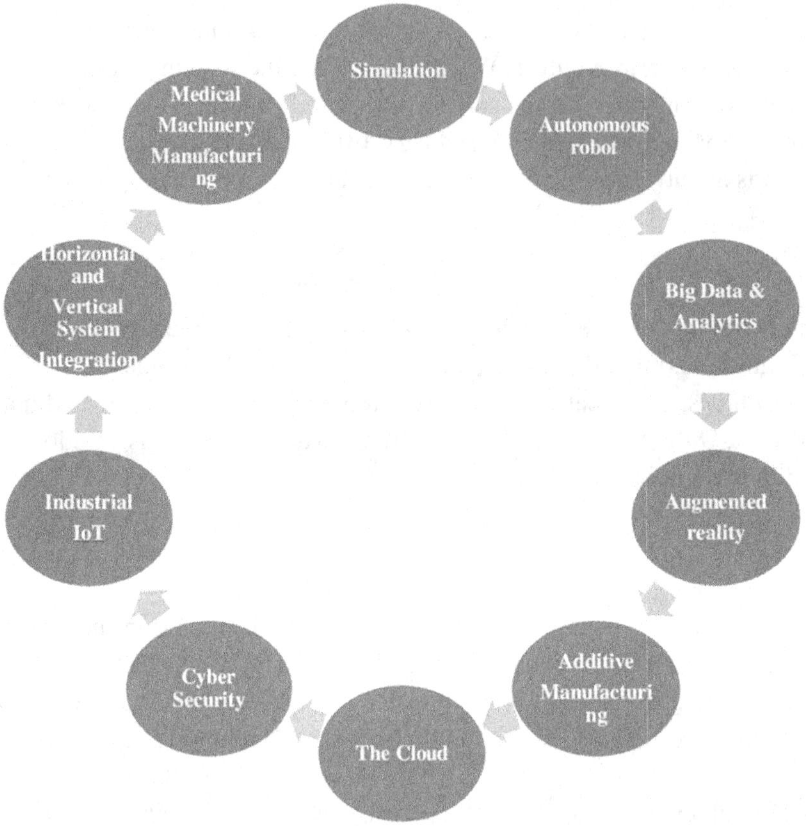

is therefore established on the links of CPS constructing sections. These sections are ingrained systems with a lack of authority management and superior connectivity accumulating and changing actual-time statistics to identify, find, track, monitor, and optimize manufacturing techniques. Furthermore, an in-depth software program aid established on distributed and tailored versions of 'manufacturing Execution systems (MES)' and business resource-making plans (ERP) is wanted for an unbroken integration of manufacturing and enterprise methods (Rojko, 2017).

INDUSTRY 4.0 IMPACTS ON SOCIETY:

Impact of industry 4.0 on different verticals of society is depicted in Figure 2

Simulation

Industry 4.0 is a novel paradigm for the structure, making plans, and execution of manufacturing tactics using contemporary IT and conversation strategies. It is far yielding completely new ideas and ideas in which IT answers are crucially blazing the trail from principal views.

First, 3D -based simulation software permits visualization and validation of tactics and manufacturing tasks. This is crucial because manufacturing plant life is seldom mounted from scratch but is frequently replanted at the same time as production is running. That in itself is not anything new — appropriate solutions for the digital manufacturing facility have long been in use. However, the novelty lies in converting the thoughts and ideas of Industry 4.0 into reality. Digital factories and version flowers must now be a genuine representation of the existing manufacturing systems. This is expected not only geometrically and kinematically but also regarding the logical conduct and management of the producing devices. They consequently constitute a sort of virtual dual or shadow factory. This is the handiest way to get from stiff, prescribed procedures to agile, self-organized production units.

A virtual factory lets implement the latest manufacturing approaches, plant concepts, and technologies that would be too high-priced or even impossible without simulation-based solutions. The extra robotic applications that are used are no longer the handiest for easy handling responsibilities. However, for complex manufacturing steps, the more the need will be for programming and simulation gear. IT answers are the leading way to these complicated programs. They deliver the operator the necessary programming and simulation surroundings to make packages that have been previously represented through a manual education-in or might now not show the essential method excellent (Uriarte, 2018).

Autonomous Robots

An essential attribute of industry 4.0 is self-governing manufacturing techniques powered by a concept different to as the "internet of things" (IoT) — the concept that is harnessing a related mesh of items, gadgets, and computer systems, machines can communicate with each other. Autonomous robots are a seminal instance throughout endless industries, inclusive of manufacturing. You can connect to servers virtually, databases or programmable logic controllers to direct and automate robot activity at a higher level than ever before. They'd be able to accomplish assigned tasks intelligently and in a well-coordinated manner with little human intervention. Independent cellular robots (AMRs) can transfer materials around the industrial facility floor, avoiding limitations, correlating with navy friends. Due to the fact they are connected digitally, their bodily actions are as well.

Meeting and production people can detect real-time assembly and production — no longer the details of internal logistics — since AMRs like TUG robots integrated with Aethon's common sense OS allow automation gadgets, gear and sensors to communicate with each other and monitored percent (Melanson, T., 2018).

Big Data Analytics

Big Data Analytics is a superior computing technology that examines the big statistics to find meaningful correlations, market patterns, developments, and alternatives for industries to form higher decisions. In industry fourth revolution, analysis of big data contributes vital a role in some regions, such as in smart activities in industry, where IoT device information from manufacturing machinery is examined to be expected. At the same time, protection and repair operations may be wished. Through its utility, producers experience manufacturing efficiency and recognize their actual-time facts with autonomous systems, forecast renovation optimization, and production control automation (Velásquez, 2018).

Producers in industry use big Data Analytics to maximize productivity and exploit a new focus on insights. They gather large quantities of statistics from digital IoT devices like sensors through cloud to discover styles that aid them to enhance the performance of deliver chain control. It can assist them in discovering hidden players imposing unknown bottlenecks in the manufacturing process. After identifying the source of the hassle, manufacturers use focused facts analytics to recognize the underlying reason for bottleneck variables better. This enables producers to progress output even by lowering value and removing waste.

Performance of manufacturing process and property are the main asset of the production industry. It can suggest the difference between good and bad reputation, as well as the possibility of a manufacturer thatcan maintain the means of production and keepit tight. Big Data Analytics uses about 25% to reduce breakdowns and unplanned downtime. Big Data Analytics includes overall actual performance, supply chain optimization, cost optimization, defect prediction, product up gradation, and clever manufacturing unit layout (Bonnard, 2019).

In the industrial area, it may optimize manufacturing first-rate, keep the electricity and enhance the carrier of gadgets. Inside the context of Industry 4.0, which has to combine information from one-of-a-kind systems, many distinctive manufacturing assets and structures, in addition to establishments and client control systems, turn into popular to support real-time decision making (Moraes, E. C., & Lepikson, H. A., 2017) .

Augmented Reality

Infusing Industry 4.0 Augmented Reality isinfull compliance with the principles of the FourthCommercialRevolution begins with the accessibility of information. AR is revolutionizinghow data is accessed, used, and exchanged. Theaugmented truth itself is data that widens users' insights. This technique maximizes the fun of ourperceptionsandallows us to interact with facts.

These days, we frequently speak about smart industries in shrewd manufacturing based on factors and significant statistics. Such context fits perfectly with augmented fact. AR generation, in truth, can actively make contributions to the fulfillment and transformation of commercial manufacturing approaches. One-of-a-kind research shows the impact of AR in the industry. The researchersexamined the performance of business groups that support AR and the business groups without AR support (Masood, T., & Egger, J., 2019) .

Researchers have found that business groups that support AR performed 50% better than other business groups without AR support. It is evident that AR helps in the industry to:

- Speed up business operations.
- Grow production method performance.
- Reduce error incidence.
- Downtime is reduced.
- Surplus and faults were kept to a minimum.
- Insightful ideas

Additive Manufacturing

Additive Manufacturing (AM) broader and more comprehensive term. Generally, it is associated with the production of prototypes of industrial applications andfeatures. AM includes additional abandonment such as mass production of parts.

Company's commenced undertaking additive production, especially 3D printing, offers prototypes and human add-ons. Throughexcellent manufacturing, this manufacturing method can be widely used to produce short batches of customized products that offer manufacturing incentives, including complicated and lightweight design. With the rise of 3D printing, different type of materials is generated with high capability and reduced time. For example, aeronautical companies uses 3D printing to use new design patterns and reduce the weight of airplanes by reducing spending on damp materials and titanium.

Horizontal and Vertical Integration Systems: Hope to do more operations with more statistics, for efficient technology through good manufacturing, digital devices, machinery, parts, computer system infrastructures, will be connected at some stage in the enterprise's cost chain and beyond a single company (Moraes, E. C., & Lepikson, H. A., 2017).

Additive Manufacturing (AM) endows digital flexibility and performance to the manufacturing process. Some applications like CAD software or 3D scanner make hardware to set fabric, convert it into specific shapes to create items. Employing comparison, when the user creates an object using the traditional method, it is far regularly essential to cast off cloth via milling, machining, carving, shaping or different methods (Chen et at.,2020).

Cloud Computing

Cloud computing facilitates various services like data storage, program, data retrieval over the network instead of your drive on the computer (Masood, T., & Egger, J., 2019). The use of clouds makes life easier. For the governance and venture application, cloud computing companies provide a modern way of manufacturing and sharing product-related real-time information.

Concomitantly, Fast response within milliseconds can improve the performance of cloud technology. The data and functionsof the computer will be slowlymoved to the cloud as a sequel, allowing more data-based services to the operating system. Systems that control and monitor processes can also be cloud-based (Atobishi, 2018).

Cyber Security

In Industry 4.0, machines are interconnected. Data that is transferred from machine to machine must be secured. Data privacy should be maintained. Whichever, the data that is transmitted must be trustable? Security, trust, and privacy all are related to each other (Zalte et al.,2021). We must know the need for cyber security and the different threats that can occur in Industry 4.0. There might be some attacks that can be done that damage physical devices/software or that steal the data. When we are dealing with cyber security, hardware, software, and data should be protected. Various components of cyber security are elaborated below:

Components of Cyber Security

Application Security: It ensures the protection of applications from other threats. For protection, some software, hardware and procedural methods are used. Certifying application security necessitates some actions that need to be taken as countermeasures. Software countermeasures and hardware countermeasures are the two types of countermeasures. Application firewalls are used for software countermeasure. Routers or proxies are used for hardware countermeasures.

Information Security: It is a subset of cyber security. In this, a set of strategies deals with some policies or tools that filter the threats based on some rules. This will help to maintain the availability, integrity, and confidentiality of data. It will protect the data from attackers.

Network Security: Network security protects the network architecture. It protects unauthorized access and damage to existing network architecture. It combines multiple layers of defense at the edge and in the network. The network is a potential through which attackers can get in and damage the system.

Operational Security: It is a process that mitigates social sensitive activity that could be beneficial for an adversary if adequately decrypted to reveal sensitive information. To defend against malicious exploitation, OPSEC uses countermeasures (Prinsloo, 2019).

End-User Education Security: The end-user is the first one who compromises the security. It might be possible that the end-user accidentally introduces a virus or does not follow good security policies. End-user education includes finding and deleting suspicious emails and attachments, not plugging unidentified USB drives, and other important good security practices of any organization (Ervural & Ervural, 2018).

Types of Cybersecurity Threats:

There are different threats. Following is the list of somethreats:

1. Ransomware
2. Malware
3. Phishing
4. Denial of Service Attack or Distributed Denial of Service Attack(DDoS) (Zalte et al,2020)
5. Attackson IoT Devices
6. DataBreaches
7. MalwareonMobileApps

Enhanced properties and common communication protocols must beused to protectcritical industrial systems and createdefense systems against cyber attacks. Reliable secure communication and precise authenticity and user access levels are therefore essential. Thereality-enhancing system supports a variety of services, including component selectionin the warehouse, and deliveryof repairordersvia mobile devices. The zonal units of these systems arecurrently in their early stages;

However, going forward, businesses could build on many widespread uses of augmented reality to generate workers using timely data to enhance decision-making and procedures. Industrial Web and CPS: Cyber Physical Systems (CPS) will move with victimization protocols supporting the web commonplace. Advanced producing can build it is attainable together and analyze information between entirely different machines, letting quicker, other versatile and additional economic processes to supply higher quality merchandise at reduced prices and enhance productivity. The Hertz topic is going to be more careful in topic 2.5. in keeping with the 'Gartner cluster (GROUP, 2015) report' that enlists technological and strategic trends, in the year 2013, over five-hundredths of web connections return from sensible devices (called "things"). By 2011, over fifteen million such devices were online with over 50 billion intermittent connections. By 2020, over thirty billion devices connected with over two hundred billion with intermittent connections (Moraes, E. C., & Lepikson, H. A., 2017).

Industrial IoT

Internet of Things or "Internet of Things" (IoT) may be a novel archetype that's quickly gaining ground within the business at giant. In keeping with Giusto (2010), the basic plan of this idea is that the hypothesized existence around the US of a spread of things or objects like Radio-Frequency Identification (RFID), sensors, actuators, mobile, and so on. Through distinctive addressing schemes, area units can move with one another and collide with their peers to achieve their aim. These devices can have additional applications in our day to day. Particularly for the industries, where a larger chance of product chases, repose, and intra-industry interaction, and machine-controlled management of the systems proved to be a boon. They are especially helpful in a very mechanical system, where simultaneous data acquisition and analysis are required. This will cut back the utilization of resources; as a result, you will have additional period data regarding utilization of resources and timely performance, with stress on energy consumption. This idea is essential during this process and its various alternative paradigms; methodologies and processes need to match (Moraes, E. C., & Lepikson, H. A., 2017).

The Industrial Internet of Things (IIoT) focuses on intended goals and scenarios in various modern industries and companies worked with artificial intelligence. IIoT, used among the contexts of trade 4.0, is thought to be a fancy system of various systems and devices. Precisely, with a scan to produce a system that functions extra (expeditiously) than the addition of its elements, IIoT integrates several up to this point key technology (Georgios, 2019). Furthermore, the IIoT will improve the design and facilitate robust solutions for many practical programming, by connecting a variety of networked devices that may interact and move with one another as well as with additional centralized controllers.Consequently, the general portability and maintainability of businesses are strengthening. In addition, their operational efficiency in terms of productivity has risen, which is an additional benefit (Georgios, 2019).

Horizontal and Vertical System Integration

The terms "horizontal integration" and "vertical integration" unit are being acquainted with various backdrops. From an operational perspective, horizontally integrated enterprises are forming an end-to-end value chain of associate degrees by focusing their work aroundtheir core competencies and building cooperative relationships. On the other hand, a vertically integrated company keeps the most quantity of its value chain in-house; as a result, it can— from development to manufacturing, marketing, sales, and distribution.

Acquisitionof acompany that serves the same customer base fora corresponding product or service, butis distinct from the consolidation of a business growth strategy. In this way, deed organizations are inflating their market share or diversifying the offerings they offer. Mean while, vertical growth strategies include certificatefirms offering new capabilities, such as reducingproduction costs, gaining access to large suppliers, and responding quickly to novel market alternatives. Integration is also talking with fully integrated processes at the production floor level when production comes to be involved. In contrast, integration means that the assembly layer is working closely with higher-level business processes suchas acquisition and management.

In this chapter, we further amplify the importance of horizontal integration and explore Business 4.0, builtat theheart of a hugeplant.

HORIZONTAL/VERTICAL INTEGRATION IN TRADE 4.0: REVIEWING CHALLENGES

Breaking Down Silos

Industry 4.0 levels of horizontal integration want breaking down information and knowledge silos; that is seldom a straight forward goal. It begins from the assembly siteitself, where instrumentation and manufacturing departments from numerous dealers offer variable levels of automation area units furnished with an oversized variety of sensors and usefully discrete communications protocols. In different languages, they sometimes do not "speak the identical language," and it is necessary to build ameta-network that can close these communication gaps.

Many units of information silos and databases in an exceedingly large corporation need to be determined to realize these enlarged phases of blending. But the difficulty is, rarely concerning ability and extra concerning dynamic structure culture. Information from departments and divisions that are unit accustomed strictly monitoring their information and guarantee of quality product, engineering, legislative, marketing department, and elevating, and more—have to be collective smartly, and flawlessly thus manufacturing processes are unit whole associated with the organization's dynamic business desires.

Knowledge Security and Privacy

Horizontal combination in trade 4.0 desires the sharing of data exterior the companies with stakeholders, contractors, associates, and suppliers in many cases, clients to boot. This level of transparency is hugely permitting regarding production lightness and acceptableness. However, it raises the challenge of constructing abound. All stakeholder geo-level data is secure and fully accessible a sneeded.

Scaling IT Systems and Infrastructure

Industry 4.0 remarkably can increase the number and rate of data accumulation and scrutinize to carry enlarged levels of horizontal integration. In many scenarios, the ITsystem-related infrastructure will uegency to make fundamental changes to support acompany's digital transformation path.The implementation of Industry 4.0 canbe a convincing stimulant for mobile databases and loads to the cloud. Thecloud isalsoonlyaccessedby a very diverseset of stakeholders. This move to cloud-based IT will help cleanup yourinterdisciplinary team. A real possibility is to start decomposing down silos. Cloud-based deployments address data security concerns, individual concerns are already being addressed, and organizations are funding cloud service providers within the scope of the implemented ongoing security and access control capabilities.

Robust Orchestration

Organizations' computerized systems and manufacturing processes become moreconsolidated and modernized, orchestration platforms provideend-to-end visibility and unfair perception over many distributed systems and entities.

These platforms integrate semi-structured data from many current business systems to capture unfair information in specificareas. They can provideend-to-end product analytics solutions, qualitative and updated information for analysis in each manufacturing company and its vendors. Its essence is the vision of horizontal integration of the production process itself, enabling them to learn, heal, and agile themselves. In Trade 4.0, jointintegration means creating a fluid network of cooperation, focusing ondata and the entire organization's supply chain. Integration can identify the problemsof the organization's business departments, and ensure that theconsistency between the production process and the corebusinessreaches an unprecedentedlevel. The measurable advantages of this integration include reduced product price and the capability to produce manageable batches and make-to-order more cost-effectively, allof whichdo not diminish from the entire good quality standards (Pérez-Lara,2020).

Bottom of Form

Given the challenges covered above it would be worthwhile to have a look at one of the domains which is significantly affected by Industry 4.0 evasion. The medical machinery manufacturing is presented below to appreciate the consequence of Industry 4.0 as a representative case.

MEDICAL MACHINERY MANUFACTURING & ALLIED TRENDS

The industry 4.0 revolution is already re-addressed; however, we tend to manufacture 'things' nowadays. It lays out smart ideas for how the business process may innovate more quickly and boost efficiencies across the value chain. What would business 4.0 mean in the medical instrument production field, which is beset by a stringent compliance and is still mostly dominated by paper-based processes? Can it, however, assist manufacturers in meeting a desire for more refined, higher-quality medical devices? And on the far side, that extremely individualized custom device?

The way they convey worth is dynamic; instruments are mobile lot of and using cutting-edge chipsets, processing capabilities, and sensors, into the world of the IoT They're more volatile and linked than ever before, producing solutions in cutting-edge new areas including patient-specific gadgets and electronic diagnostic testing using 'Lab on a Chip.' What will the long-term cost of creating medical devices be in terms of efficiency and productivity? Alternatively, if you want to be more formal, you can say:

Industry 4.0 encompasses a wide range of automation, data interchange, and production techniques that are altering the landscape of how we tend to manufacture products and expanding the bounds of inventive, novel manufacturing possibilities. It's based on a value Chain Organization, which combines the actual and imaginary globe, victimization of the Internet of Things (IoT), and Internet services.

It equips industries with real-time intelligence, permitting them to quickly produce high-quality, completely customized products. The medical device property market was not demanding five years ago; but, by influencing IoT capabilities, in the next few years market demand will be increased by 38%.

The Internet of Things (IoT) links jointly tangible things that have embedded hardware, software programs, sensors, and internet connectivity, allowing them to gather and exchange data with one another. Including ML, machine-to-machine interaction, and amalgamation of current automation techniques inside the production territory, this creates the industrial internet of things (IIoT).

Intelligent machines are equipped to precisely collect time information and share as well as the product or materials they are processing to create the most basic manufacturing options. This will not only raise production, but it will also detect any unproductiveness, improve superiority, and minimize waste by maximizing the utilization of machinery and reducing scrap. Industry4.0 provides new openings about speedy competitiveness, gearing up innovation, endorsing new products quickly, adding the ability to simply customize separate orders, and sanctioning quick response, in addition to improving existing manufacturing processes.

Industries manufacturing medical equipment are facing more hurdles in terms of value and profit pressure, speed to market, difficulties toenhance production, and more rigorousmonitoring conformance. Cutting out taxes and rising prices of satisfying new regulatory measures are causing concern about the value of medical products. Hospitals are dynamic environments in which patients can be treated.

These things are paired with increased product complexity, create more risks to quality, and necessitate higher technology and a deeper examination of product knowledge to improve processes. Patients, more willingly than the number of test cases, visits, or procedures performed, are the focus of value-based care, which proposes a shift in monetary inducement for caretakers as stipendiary support. Medical equipment can produce an ecosystem of Systems in which the value of data from sensors among the devices outweighs the value of the devices themselves.

Patient data gleaned via device sensors or self-examining will lower general care model costs by focusing on anticipation and disclosure of disease. Desegregation of cardiogram capability or force per unit area cuffs, for example, will raise the price of an instrument. However, to connect across a caring environment or a period of illness, all of this requires a single platform. The Internet of Medical Things (IoMT) links technology, medical instruments, and applications to modifypatients' personal information and data.

Mobile devices that track polygenic disorder could be a fast-growing market segment that responds to the IoT's properties. Contact lenses that identify aldohexose levels and gadgets that monitor heat intake are two examples of gadgets. A new area of bioelectronics pharmaceuticals is also developing, aided by the miniaturization of physical science. By manipulating electrical signals in nerve pathways, miniature devices constructed within the body could help treat ailments like inflammatory sickness, polygenic disorder, and respiratory illness. Other areas of the inventionencompass robotic-assisted surgery, the phase of sensitive inhalators that track inhaler use, prevent triggers, and alert patients to respiratory illness attacks, and biomimetics stamps like 'lab on a chip' (LOC) with millions of dollars rate in 2020 (Lobo, 2020) .

To respond to an ever-changing apache marketplace, medical device manufacturers will need to be innovative and agile in the future. The time it takes for manufacturers to obtain appropriate office device certifications has an impact on how quickly they can get a replacement product to market. Restrictive approval necessitates the accimalation massive volume of data throughout the product flow.

The complete development cycle will turn out difficult and frail if design, method engineering, and manufacturing systems are fragmented. This additional impact on the potency of the latest product liberates will make the complete development cycle clumsy and unreliable. Because of the market's strong competitive forces, any unharnessed product delay could result in astonishing options and market status may be lost.

Even though severe rules define that variations in the medical markets may take longer than in other industries, I4.0 provides medical instrument producers such incredible benefits that it is inevitable. It paves the way for more cost-effective production of innovative items while also gathering and evaluating data flows to aid in regulatory compliance and technique up-gradation (Javaid & Haleem,2019).

A modern Manufacturing Execution System (MES) with redistributed logic demonstrates how to vertically connect systems such that business processes become unavoidable. For example, quality or reliability checks in the process may require that a tool undergo extravalidation steps before it can be included in a featured sampling strategy.

This necessitates interaction to comply with business regulations; so, quality procedures do not appear to be skipped prior the device proceeding through its manufacturing operations. The MES also serves as a platform for the aggregation of statistical process management (SPC) knowledge, which is frequently triggered and verified against limitations set by SPC rules at regular intervals.

The smart shop floor can leverage the Internet of Things as a transmission channel, aided by technologies such as Cloud computing, which can provide "anytime, anywhere" capability and storage for vast volumes of data created.

Society's acceptance of advanced technology is truly important for its easy penetration amongst the masses at large. The present book chapter aims at the same in the true spirit and therefore the remaining part is devoted to the issues arising out of the conflict of interests of the society with the prevalence of Industry 4.0.

SOCIETY RESISTANCE AGAINST INDUSTRY 4.0

In their study (Yang, F., & Gu, S., 2021) Frey and Osborne confirmed that 47 percent of jobs in the US are shortly at risk of automation. (Hussain, 2019) concluded that the automation wave affecting the 45% and 60% re-adaptation jobs proportionally varies in European countries.

This means that companies need to monitor much more potential origin of risky data, especially social websites and media ((Mikescott, 2020), (Zervoudi, 2020). The discussion on Industry 4.0 impacts at the 2016 World Economic Forum in Davos concluded that over the next five years, up to 7 million jobs will be at risk with women being the hardest hit. Since 2010, the effects of "Industry 3.0" have been visible in some areas of the German industry. The distinctive example is the ICT sector, which is a major driver of economic growth in the 'OECD countries' and shows an employment growth of 22% in 2013 (Zervoudi, 2020), (Polat, 2020). Automation, digitalization, and other information technologies increase productivity and disrupt existing value chains. The rapid pace of progress in these technologies, coupled with all kinds of cross-sectoral innovation, has led to growing concern about negative social consequences such as rising inequality and job disappearance. Although we cannot be sure what impact profound changes in the world of work will have on the nature of society, we can discuss some of the relevant trends (Polat, 2020).

Industry 4.0 has profound implications for the functioning of economic sectors. While it has brought enormous benefits, it has also created new challenges for which many companies are unprepared. Understanding the influence of robotics and AI on industries and the economy, as well as adopting business models to the needs of customers, is a key issue for the economy in 5.0. ((Mikescott, 2020), (Hussain, 2019).

Without any hesitation we believe that novel technologies have a pragmatic influence on social life. Various Tools like AI and ML are driving progress in health care that save lives globally. They and other technologies make workflows more efficient and create new and interesting career opportunities for those who choose to do so. However, in its 'Global Trends in Reputation 2020 report', the institute found that 30% of executives consider the impact of these technologies to be a risk to their reputations, and classify them as the highest reputational risk, even ahead of privacy technology, which itself is a risk (Mikescott, 2020). New technologies contribute to reducing unemployment, combating poverty, improving the living standard of humans by offering qualitative services and final products. The exciting competitiveness at home is emblematic of a country's global competitiveness (Hussain, 2019), (Zervoudi, 2020), (Bongomin, 2020).

Sustainable manufacturing merges with Industry 4.0 technologies. Intelligent factories, coupled with dynamic production systems that use big data, and market demand, will create a production revolution that will give traditional manufacturers a huge competitive advantage (MacDougall, 2014; Sjodin and coll., 2018). Despite progress, nations need to correlate their strategies and instruments to take advantage from Industry 5.0 technology (Sony, 2020), (Bongomin, 2020).

No doubt Industry 4.0 continues to improve people's standard of living by providing consumers with tailor-made, high-quality products and by creating a better working environment for employees. The Fourth Industrial Revolution includes new technological advances to improve the industry and address global challenges. Industry 4.0 has experienced three revolutionary phases: the three industrial revolutions (Kang et al., 2016).

Though there has been a mixed reaction as far as the pervasiveness of Industry 4.0, it is without any doubt that the shaping of the digital society is emerging at a rapid pace. The following section throws light on the same.

EMERGENCE OF DIGITAL SOCIETY WITH INDUSTRY 4.0

The time is ripe for the Industry 4.0 revolution, which is advancing at an unprecedented rate driven by smart and integrated technologies are rising exponentially. IoT, Artificial Intelligence (AI), 6G, cloud are novel solutions to the future challenges in the manufacturing process. These technologies are like fuel and accelerate a new era of digital business transformation. Like the first three, Industry 3.0 will transform and redefine industries. While the first two were built on standardization, productiveness, computers, and robotics, the third combines physical and digital technologies (Susanne, 2018).

Allaspectsofproduction are becoming more mobile, digitized, and networked, as the lessons of the COVID 19 pandemic show. The fundamental question is how to ensure the integrity and trustworthiness of such complex systems while focusing on human needs - an aspect that has been neglected in industrial development (Martynov, 2019).

As reviewed in this chapter, Industry 4.0 enables an era of industrial assets and uses operational data and information in a way that implies the realization of a smarter ecosystem for industrial innovation and collaboration. The industry is customer-centric in terms of the customer benefit, speed, cost-efficiency, and value creation through inventive services and enables a more direct model of personalized production and maintenance through consumer-customer interactions, including timely data on real product utilization and inefficiencies and inapplicable costs of intermediate digital supply chain models as much as posible (AI,2022).

Wehaveseen in this chapter that Industry 4.0 refers to a new phase of the industrial revolution focusing on networking, automation, machine learning, and timely data. It encompasses IoT and smart manufacturing, combining physical production and operations with smart digital technologies such as Machine learning and big data create a globally connected ecosystem of enterprisesfor manufacturing and supply chain management. Industry 4.0, the digital transformation of manufacturing, production, related industries, and value-added processes (Morrar, 2017), (Lasi, 2014).

Thus, TheFourth Industrial Revolution and Industry 4.0 is the progressive automation of traditional manufacturing and industrial processes using modern intelligent technologies. This is essentially a trend of automation and data exchange in manufacturing technologies and processes, including cyber-physical systems (CPS), IIoT (Industrial Internet of Things), cloud computing cognition, and artificial intelligence. Large-scale machine-to-machine communication (M2M) and the Internet of Things (IoT) are integrated to improve automation, improve interaction, and monitor production. Intelligent machines analyze and diagnose problems without human intervention (AI,2022). The Fourth Industrial Revolution encouraged so-called smart factories. Modular and structured intelligent factories are CPS that control physical processes, make an instance of the real world, and build solid decisions (AI,2022). Combining this with the approach of sectors involved in cutting-edge techniques like big data, IoT and blockchain will increase the security of manufacturing processes. Further contributions from different sectors are needed to continue political support for Europe to remain in the premier league of digital change, with a safety net to provide sufficient comfort and confidence to contain fears (Lasi, 2014). By 2020, it has boosted industrialization and digitalization by developing technologies in central areas to accelerate competition and make it eco-friendly in terms of pollution. The next phase, prediction for 2025, will target upgrading the quality aspects and bringing information technology to an advanced stage to reduce pollution to global standards. In 2015, Thirty Japanese companies initiated the Industrial Value Chain Initiative. It follows the German Industry 4.0 plan, which amalgam production process and information technologies to encourage industrial cooperation (Yang, 2021).

As a result, the 10-year vision helps to measure the scale of the challenge and design the steps to address it. One company has called this transformative development better, which begins with consumer mobility services and makes digital transformation one of four priorities: core activities, customer focus, empowerment, and simplification (Fathi, 2019).

General Electric pioneered the theme of the IIoT in the coming years, aiming at the consolidation of AI, analytics, and connected people [38]. After the Third Industrial Revolution, manufacturers underwent a transformation that relied less on analog mechanical technologies and digital technologies, automation, and software. In the last twenty years, a fourth industrial revolution has developed, known as Industry 4.0. (Lasi, 2014), (Fathi, 2019).

Industry 4.0 takes digital technologies of the past decade to a whole new level by bringing the Internet of Things (IoT) to a whole new level, accessing real-time data, and introducing cyber-physical systems. Disturbances are caused by agile and innovative competitors who crowd out incumbents and improve quality, speed, price, and value thanks to accessing universal digital platforms (Lasi, 2014), (Klaus, 2016).

A strong trend is developing technology-based platforms that join supply and demand to interruptcurrentorganization structures as we see them in the shared and demand economy. Technology platforms that are user-friendly by smartphones bring human, resources, and data together to create new ways to consume goods, services, and processes. Withgreater liquidity in customer engagement and novel structures of customer behavior depending on access to mobile network data, businesses are experiencing significant demand-sidechanges to accommodate how they design, market, and deliver their productsor services. (Klaus, 2016).

CONCLUDING REMARKS

As reviewed in this chapter, the Internet 4.0 paradigm has facilitated the convergence of people, assets, and data to establishnovel paths to consume goods, services, and processes. The appearance of universal platforms and other new business prototypes means that talent, culture, and industrial forms need to be rethought. Given the paceof innovation and disorganization in the world of customer experience data-based service asset and performance analytics, new forms of collaboration are needed.

As evidenced from the finding in this chapter, today's world ofextraordinary change in diverse industries is characterized by progressive digital transformation and the creation of connections and networks across products, value chains, and business models. The unstoppable simple digitization of the ThirdIndustrialRevolution to a fusion of innovation-based technologies of the fourth industrial revolution forces companies to rethink how they do business. Today's competitive advantage creates unprecedented flexibility for businesses. The chapter covered the trend towards different synergizing technologies. Data analysis and business intelligence have shown that they requirea cultivatedunderstanding of information technology, mathematics, and statistics. AI and machine learning algorithms can be automated and optimize analysis processes that create transformative business insights. Understanding the impact of robotization and artificial intelligence on the industry and economy and adapting business models to customer needs is a crucial theme for Economy 4.0. Predictive analytics and real-time data from connected machines and automation can help manufacturers proactively address and resolve potential maintenance and supply chain management issues. Big data enables massive data management and interpretation for business purposes relevant to the development of business strategies and decision-making. It is also evident that Industry 4.0 technologies can help control and optimize every aspect of the manufacturing process and supply chain. They give access to the real-time data and insight needed to make smart and quick decisions for the business and increase the efficiency and profitability of the whole operation.

Thus, Industry 4.0 is the ingenious automation of conventional production processes by modern intelligent technologies, shaped like the fourth industrial revolution. Large-scale machine-to-machine communication (M2M) and Internet of Things (IoT) will be incorporated to accelerate automation, supervise the production cycle with intelligent machines that can diagnose problems and analyze robotically. Industry 5.0 encompasses IoT and smart manufacturing and combines physical production with smart digital technologies, ML, and big data analyticsto build an aggregated, connected environs system for industries focused on manufacturing and supply chain management.

CONSENT FOR PUBLICATION

We, the author, the undersigned, give our consent for the publication of identifiable details, which can include a photograph(s) and/or videos and/or case history and/or details within this chapter to be published by Bentham Science.

CONFLICT OF INTEREST

We, the authors do not have any conflict of interest concerning research, authorship, and/or *publication*of this book *chapter.*

ACKNOWLEDGMENT

We, the authors want to thank all the Anonymous Reviewers, Publishers, and Editors of this project for their speedy response.

REFERENCES

AI. (2022). *The fourth industrial revolution*. Presented at the American Psychological Association in Minneapolis.

Atobishi, T., Gábor, S. Z., & Podruzsik, S. (2018). *Cloud computing and big data in the context of industry 4.0: opportunities and challenges*. Academic Press.

Bidnur. (2020). A Study on Industry4.0 Concept. *International Journal of Engineering Research & Technology,* 613-618.

Bongomin, O., Nganyi, E. O., Abswaidi, M. R., Hitiyise, E., & Tumusiime, G. (2020). Sustainable and dynamic competitiveness towards technological leadership of industry 4.0: Implications for East african community. *Journal of Engineering*.

Bonnard, R., Vieira, K. M. M., Arantes, S., Lorbieski, R., Nunes, C., & Mattei, A. P. (2019). A big data/ analytics platform for industry 4.0 implementation in SMEs. *Cigi Qualita*.

Chen, C., Wang, X., Wang, Y., Yang, D., Yao, F., Zhang, W., & Hu, D. (2020). Additive manufacturing of piezoelectric materials. *Advanced Functional Materials, 30*(52), 2005141. doi:10.1002/adfm.202005141

Ervural, B. C., & Ervural, B. (2018). Overview of cyber security in the industry 4.0 era. In *Industry 4.0: managing the digital transformation* (pp. 267–284). Springer. doi:10.1007/978-3-319-57870-5_16

Fathi, M., Khakifirooz, M., & Pardalos, P. M. (Eds.). (2019). *Optimization in large scale problems: Industry 4.0 and Society 5.0 Applications* (Vol. 152). Springer. doi:10.1007/978-3-030-28565-4

Georgios, L., Kerstin, S., & Theofylaktos, A. (2019). *Internet of things in the context of industry 4.0: An overview*. Academic Press.

Horváth, D., & Szabó, R. Z. (2019). Driving forces and barriers of Industry 4.0: Do multinational and small and medium-sized companies have equal opportunities? *Technological Forecasting and Social Change, 146*, 119–132. doi:10.1016/j.techfore.2019.05.021

Hupfer & Louks. (2018). *Succeeding in the age of digital transformation*. Deloitte.

Hussain, A. (2019). Industrial revolution 4.0: Implication to libraries and librarians. *Library Hi Tech News, 37*(1), 1–5. doi:10.1108/LHTN-05-2019-0033

Iyer, A. (2018). Moving from Industry 2.0 to Industry 4.0: A case study from India on leapfrogging in smart manufacturing. *Procedia Manufacturing, 21*, 663–670. doi:10.1016/j.promfg.2018.02.169

Javaid, M., & Haleem, A. (2019). Industry 4.0 applications in medical field: A brief review. *Current Medicine Research and Practice, 9*(3), 102–109. doi:10.1016/j.cmrp.2019.04.001

Kang, H. S., Lee, J. Y., Choi, S., Kim, H., Park, J. H., Son, J. Y., ... Noh, S. D. (2016). Smart manufacturing: Past research, present findings, and future directions. *International Journal of Precision Engineering and Manufacturing-Green Technology, 3*(1), 111-128.

Lasi, H., Fettke, P., Kemper, H. G., Feld, T., & Hoffmann, M. (2014). Industry 4.0. *Business & Information Systems Engineering*, *6*(4), 239–242. doi:10.100712599-014-0334-4

Lee, C., & Lim, C. (2021). From technological development to social advance: A review of Industry 4.0 through machine learning. *Technological Forecasting and Social Change*, *167*, 120653. doi:10.1016/j.techfore.2021.120653

Lobo, F. (2020). *Industry 4.0–manufacturing and the future of medical things*. Academic Press.

Martynov, V. V., Shavaleeva, D. N., & Zaytseva, A. A. (2019, September). Information technology as the basis for transformation into a digital society and industry 5.0. In *2019 International Conference Quality Management, Transport and Information Security, Information Technologies (IT&QM&IS)* (pp. 539-543). IEEE.

Masood, T., & Egger, J. (2019). Augmented reality in support of Industry 4.0—Implementation challenges and success factors. *Robotics and Computer-integrated Manufacturing*, *58*, 181–195. doi:10.1016/j.rcim.2019.02.003

Meindl, B., Ayala, N. F., Mendonça, J., & Frank, A. G. (2021). The four smarts of Industry 4.0: Evolution of ten years of research and future perspectives. *Technological Forecasting and Social Change*, *168*, 120784. doi:10.1016/j.techfore.2021.120784

Melanson, T. (2018). *What Industry 4.0 means for manufacturers*. Available online: https://aethon. com/mobilerobots-and-industry4-0/

Moraes, E. C., & Lepikson, H. A. (2017, October). Industry 4.0 and its impacts on society. In Proc. Int. Conf. Ind. Eng. *Open Management*, *2017*, 729–735.

Morrar, R., Arman, H., & Mousa, S. (2017). The fourth industrial revolution (Industry 4.0): A social innovation perspective. *Technology Innovation Management Review*, *7*(11), 12–20. doi:10.22215/timreview/1117

Narvaez Rojas, C., Alomia Peñafiel, G. A., Loaiza Buitrago, D. F., & Tavera Romero, C. A. (2021). Society 5.0: A Japanese concept for a superintelligent society. *Sustainability*, *13*(12), 6567. doi:10.3390u13126567

Pérez-Lara, M., Saucedo-Martínez, J. A., Marmolejo-Saucedo, J. A., Salais-Fierro, T. E., & Vasant, P. (2020). Vertical and horizontal integration systems in Industry 4.0. *Wireless Networks*, *26*(7), 4767–4775. doi:10.100711276-018-1873-2

Polat, L., & Erkollar, A. (2020, September). Industry 4.0 vs. Society 5.0. In *The International Symposium for Production Research* (pp. 333-345). Springer.

Prinsloo, J., Sinha, S., & von Solms, B. (2019). A review of industry 4.0 manufacturing process security risks. *Applied Sciences (Basel, Switzerland)*, *9*(23), 5105. doi:10.3390/app9235105

Rojko, A. (2017). Industry 4.0 concept: Background and overview. *International Journal of Interactive Mobile Technologies, 11*(5).

Sony, M. (2020). Pros and cons of implementing Industry 4.0 for the organizations: A review and synthesis of evidence. *Production & Manufacturing Research, 8*(1), 244–272. doi:10.1080/21693277.2020.1781705

Uriarte, A. G., Ng, A. H., & Moris, M. U. (2018). Supporting the lean journey with simulation and optimization in the context of Industry 4.0. *Procedia Manufacturing, 25*, 586–593. doi:10.1016/j.promfg.2018.06.097

Vaidya, S., Ambad, P., & Bhosle, S. (2018). Industry 4.0–a glimpse. *Procedia Manufacturing, 20*, 233–238. doi:10.1016/j.promfg.2018.02.034

Velásquez, N., Estévez, E. C., & Pesado, P. M. (2018). Cloud computing, big data and the industry 4.0 reference architectures. *Journal of Computer Science and Technology, 18*(03), 18. doi:10.24215/16666038.18.e29

Vuksanović, D., Vešić, J., & Korčok, D. (2016). *Industry 4.0: The Future Concepts and New Visions of Factory of the Future Development.* . doi:10.15308.Sinteza-2016-293-298

Yang, F., & Gu, S. (2021). Industry 4.0, a revolution that requires technology and national strategies. *Complex & Intelligent Systems, 7*(3), 1311–1325. doi:10.100740747-020-00267-9

Yang, F., & Gu, S. (2021). Industry 4.0, a revolution that requires technology and national strategies. *Complex & Intelligent Systems, 7*(3), 1311–1325. doi:10.100740747-020-00267-9

Zalte, S. S., Kamat, R. K., & Ghorpade, V. R. (2020). Mitigation of DDoS Attack in MANET. *IJEAT, 9*, 410-413.

Zalte, S. S., Patil, P. N., Deshmukh, S. N., & Kamat, R. K. (2021). Data Packet Security in MANET and VANET. *BBRC, 13*(15), 271-274.

Zervoudi, E. K. (2020). *Fourth industrial revolution: opportunities, challenges, and proposed policies.* Industrial Robotics-New Paradigms.

Chapter 10
Preserving Privacy of Social Media Data Using Artificial Intelligence Techniques

Dhriti Rajani
Vellore Institute of Technology, Chennai, India

Sanjana Chelat Menon
PSG Institute of Technology and Applied Research, India

Shruti Kute
Vellore Institute of Technology, Chennai, India

Amit Kumar Tyagi
https://orcid.org/0000-0003-2657-8700
Vellore Institute of Technology, Chennai, India

ABSTRACT

Social media has a huge volume and variety of big data, which has enabled machine learning (ML) procedures and artificial intelligence (AI) frameworks. A few types of research have featured the dangers of revealing large amounts of information at various stages. The main aim is to connect the exploration and normalisation edge to build the consistency and proficiency of AI framework advancements ensuring user loyalty and moving towards a serious level of reliability. User security insight and the standards of its administrative assurance decide how the tech field works. It also introduces ways to deal with AI while demonstrating distinctions that are a result of comprehension of security, increasing user data privacy concerns and guidelines identified with information protection. The effect of AI systems on the relationship between clients and organisations has been stressed and examined concerning guidelines and client impression of security. With the rise of big data and AI, this issue of privacy of data has become significantly important.

DOI: 10.4018/978-1-6684-5250-9.ch010

INTRODUCTION

Social media and Big Data have changed our reality through the interconnection of the internet and real space. Map makers would now be able to follow, screen, and guide the spread of social developments, illness flare-ups, nature perils, and mainstream occasions by carefully gathering web-based media and Big Data with locational substance, for example, worldwide situating framework labels and client area profiles. The unique attributes of web-based media and Big Data give incredible examination freedom to map makers to plan and break down human practices, correspondences, and developments. There arise various difficulties and complexities in resolving affairs of cartographic examination concerning examining the connection between online media substance and Big Data through a spatiotemporal lens (Dilmaghani et al., 2019). The most well-known use of predictive analytics is recommendation systems, which are frequently utilised by eCommerce sites such as Amazon and Etsy to recommend goods to clients based on their purchasing habits. Based on our interests, Facebook suggests friends, destinations to explore, and even film recommendations.

Nevertheless, disclosing user behaviour data could lead to inference attacks, such as gender identification as per the user's behaviour. We looked into a variety of confidentiality protection techniques that are currently being used to defend from data breaches. Each one of these methods seems to have its own set of advantages and disadvantages. This paper will also examine and address significant exploration difficulties which appear in the field, along with noteworthy freedoms usable by map makers to measure and imagine Big Data and online media.

Smart Information Systems

Smart Information systems are a prominent example of a combination of Artificial Intelligence and Big data. There are many to a great extent covering banters about the moral and social results of fake insight—that is, the utilisation of equipment, programming, and applications to perform examinations of big data and to copy human psychological abilities. These advancements have pushed progress in ICT as of late. We chose to utilise the term brilliant data frameworks as a shorthand for advances that include man-made brainpower, machine learning, and big data because these are generally pertinent for the comprehension of the social results of these advances (Mazurek & Małagocka, 2019). They are framed and created in an environment of what we call "enabling technologies". The social and moral significance of these innovations emerges from a more extensive socio-economic environment that one requires to comprehend why SIS merit has extensive reflection and oversight. In the political scenario, it outlines science, innovation and research and advancement as a method for tending to social difficulties like financial development, natural maintainability, segment advancements, security, and social consideration. The political way of talking is for the most part acknowledged and duplicated by organisations and exploration associations (Tom et al.,2020; Stahl & Wright, 2018). It lays the right foundation for positive assumptions for SIS, which, by and by, have dull shadows identifying with moral issues and concerns. Fig1 summarises the relationship between SIS and both technical key drivers AI and Big data.

Organisation of the Work

Section 2 discusses

Figure 1. Relation of SIS with AI and Big data

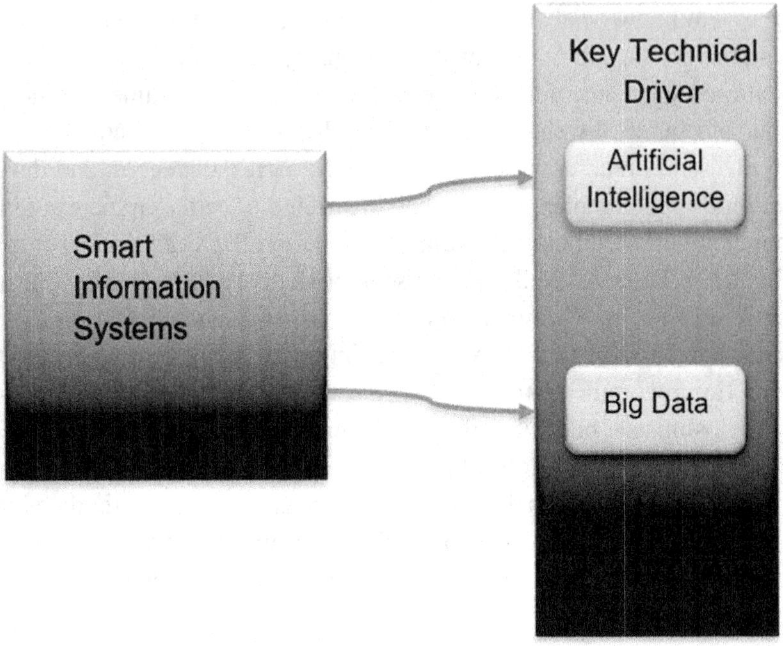

CLOUD ARCHITECTURE AND APPLICATION PROGRAMMING INTERFACE

With very much planned connecting layers, the cloud can gather a wide range of information from confided-in starting points and can put them together depending on needs. After the examination, results could be envisioned to uncover the significant data mentioned and sent back to its objective. Additionally, the cloud guarantees the vital administration and control instruments underlining the (administrative) administration rules while satisfying the necessities of global ventures. There are three primary known cloud structures: Peer to Peer (P2P), United and centralised.

Centralization: is more reasonable for applications that require low correspondence postponements and it is utilised in the processing bunches and data centres of many cloud suppliers by utilising this methodology, customers are being attached to the nearest server farm to stay away from high correspondence dormancy since cloud assets are geologically parcelled over wide distances.

Federated cloud: Is utilised to develop huge mists by combining numerous more modest mists. United engineering is valuable when customers attempt to guarantee a significant degree of secrecy while disseminating information geographically.

Peer to Peer (P2P): Depends on expanding the unified idea by constructing the cloud without utilising explicit parts for centralization and checking. Its cloud engineering comprises free companions and assets, and asset provisioning is directed for a genuinely minimal price because of negligible administration.

Big data development proceeds with analysis that lies on cloud and porfigu distributed computing (Figure 2). Data-driven applications are gaining traction faster than ever before, as the benefits and usability they provide in fields such as marketing, management, AI, automation, etc become increasingly more evident. In any case, the worth of big data analytics doesn't come solely from the tremendous volume of data being analysed, but rather more importantly from the capacity to transform, refine and co-relate a lot of seemingly disconnected and disjoint sets of information (Tawalbeh, & Saldamli, 2021). This pattern can additionally be called data insight, and would greatly prosper with help from experts in distributed computing and portability fields.

The force of big data examination is generally valued whenever information is broken down and significant outcomes are conveyed to requesters. As a rule, distributed computing is considered the most financially savvy answer for big data examinations. Other than putting away the information, the distributed computing climate furnishes the customers with a few advanced devices in AI, man-made brainpower, and numerous others (Vennila & Priyadarshini,2015). Utilising these high-level strategies, clients can investigate and dissect all arrangements of information including recordings, pictures, messages, and so on. Nonetheless, when managing such colossal volumes of data, the conventional data set methodologies probably won't suit well. The information base inquiries could get muddled and exorbitant when many credits must be taken care of (Tsou, 2015; Kevin et al., 2019). On top of these versatility issues, there are security issues identified with the information proprietorship and control.

EVIDENCE OF THREATS OF PRIVACY

A user's ability to decide what information is accessible and use access control is referred to as privacy. Because the data is kept by the data bearer, if the information is in the public digital realm, it poses a threat to personal privacy. Networking site applications, webpages, smartphone applications, online businesses, banks, and healthcare institutions are all examples of data holders. The information holder indeed should ensure that the data of the users is kept private. Except for data in the public sphere, users, whether consciously or inadvertently, contribute to data leakage. For instance, most phone applications request permission to access our contacts, emails, camera, and other personal information, and we consent to all user agreements without reviewing the privacy policy at any time, adding to data leakage. Some of the key threats include: -

Surveillance

Several businesses, such as commercial and online merchandise, research their consumers' purchasing behaviour and start coming up with different offers and real-worth services. Social networking sites like Facebook make suggestions for new acquaintances, locations to visit, individuals to follow, and other things based on subjective data and prediction. This is only possible if they keep a close eye on their clients' movements. This poses a severe danger to confidentiality because no one wants to be watched.

Disclosure

Assume a healthcare facility that stores patient information such as (zip code, sex, and age) The data owner has sent personal information to an external analyser for evaluation after anonymizing vulnerable individual data so that the individual cannot be identified. An external data analyst can combine this knowledge with publicly released independent outside-based data sources such as census data to

Figure 2. Cloud architecture and API

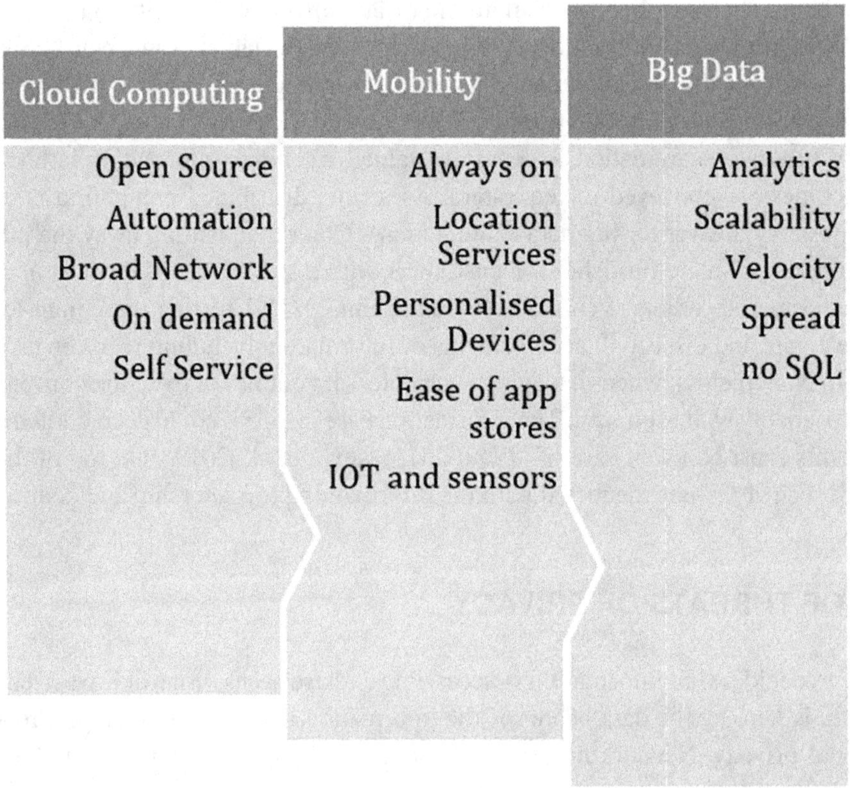

identify people who are afflicted with a disease. This is how a person's details might be revealed, which is traditionally taken into account as a privacy violation.

Discrimination

Discrimination is the prejudice or inequity that might occur when an individual's personal information is revealed. An analytical examination of election results, for example, revealed that members of one congregation were fully opposed to the organization that established the administration. Now the authorities have the power to ignore or discriminate against that society.

Personal Abuse

When an individual's personal information is revealed, it might result in personal abuse. For instance, an individual was discreetly receiving treatment for a specific illness and purchasing medications from a medical store on a routine basis. The pharmaceutical shop might send some reminders and offers connected to these drugs over the smartphone as part of a regular business strategy. If a member of the family notices, it will result in personal embracement, if not outright abuse. The use of big data analysis will have an impact on data confidentiality. Privacy rules are being enforced in a lot of nations. Privacy breaches are frequently caused by a lack of knowledge and understanding.

A new Ovum's Consumer Insights of 11,000 respondents from 11 nations makes it evident that purchasers are worried about protection issues in the period of Big Data. 68% of these respondents demonstrate that they favour a "don't follow" (DNT) include if accessible Envisioned by the idea of the "Web/Internet of Things'' (IoT), information created from clients' cell phones gives significant bits of knowledge into continuous buyer practices Location-based administrations and gadgets empower publicists and advertisers to offer profoundly setting mindful and customised administrations through clients' portable specialised gadgets Some instances of profoundly designated area based versatile vital correspondence exercises incorporate remote coupons, advertising alarms and advancements, client notifications and distinguishing pieces of proof for retailers, among others. Albeit key correspondence experts joyfully embrace the chances given by Big Data to work with their mission arranging, customer security has gotten insignificant consideration. A broad writing search utilising the catchphrases, "vital correspondence" and "purchaser protection" create a couple of exchange distributions. Generally speaking, there is an absence of methodical blended technique research that incorporates both quantitative and subjective ways to deal with looking at portable web-based media clients' day-by-day experience and their interests in protection because of portable informal communication applications. This investigation means comprehending portable online media clients' interests in security as advertisers progressively depend on Big Data to plan and execute their essential interchange crusades. Given the worldwide dissemination of these contemporary interchange innovations, this examination utilised a culturally diverse setting to inspect clients from both Taiwan and the United States, which have a high entrance of versatile online media.

EXISTED WORKS FOR PRESERVING PRIVACY

L Diversity

The first method commonly used to preserve privacy is an approach termed L diversity has been proposed to combat homogeneity attacks. Every equivalence class must have L well-indicated values for the sensitive property (disease) according to L diversity. Due to the obvious range of data, integrating L diversity is not always feasible. Skewness attacks can also affect L diversity. Attribute disclosure cannot be guaranteed when the broad distribution of data is biased through a few equivalence classes. If all of the data are divided into only three equivalence classes, for instance, the semantic similarity between such values could contribute to attributing disclosure. L diversity could also result in a similarity attack. Figure 3 shows that if Levi is 23 years old and resides in the 45103-zip code, he is most likely a minimal-income individual as for wages of all three people in the 451** zip code are low in comparison to everyone else in the tabular column. The technique is known as a similarity attack.

T Closeness

Further enhancement to L diversity is the T closeness measure, which states that an equivalence class has 'T closeness' if the distance between the distributions of sensitive attributes in the class is less than a threshold and that all equivalence classes have T closeness (Rubner & Tomasi,2001). Concerning the

Figure 3. L diversity privacy preservation technique

S NO	POSTAL NUMBER	AGE	SALARY	MEDICAL CONDITION
1	451**	>20	4K	Cancer
2	451**	>40	4K	Back pain
3	451**	>50	4K	Stomach pain
4	4587*	>30	7K	Cancer
5	4598*	>70	8K	Skin Allergy
6	4564*	>56	50K	Backpain
7	457AD	>40	10K	Skin Allergy
8	459DF	>20	20K	Food Poisoning
9	452DS	>50	10K	Stomach pain

sensitive attribute, T closeness can be calculated on any attribute. Figure 4 shows that even if we know Levi is 23 years old, it will be hard to determine if Levi has a cardiac condition or not and whether he corresponds to the low-income category or not. T closeness may assure attribute disclosure, although it is possible that T closeness will not always result in optimal data distribution.

Cryptographic Technique

Before actually providing data for analytics, the data owner could encrypt it. However, encrypting massive amounts of data employing traditional encryption algorithms is extremely challenging and should

Figure 4. T closeness privacy preservation technique

S NO	POSTAL NUMBER	AGE	SALARY	MEDICAL CONDITION
1	451**	>20	4K	Cancer
2	451**	>20	5K	Back pain
3	451**	>20	10K	Stomach pain
4	4587*	>30	7K	Cancer
5	4598*	>70	8K	Skin Allergy
6	4564*	>56	50K	Backpain
7	457AD	>40	10K	Skin Allergy
8	459DF	>20	20K	Food Poisoning
9	452DS	>50	10K	Stomach pain

only be used when collecting data. Differential privacy approaches have been used before, in which certain aggregate computations on the data are performed without any of the inputs being shared. If a and b are two data elements, for instance, a function F (a, b) will be constructed to obtain some aggregate information from both a and b without sharing x and y. If a and b are held by different parties, such as in vertical distribution, this could be used. Differential privacy cannot be used if the data is housed in a single location under the control of a single organisation. A similar technology termed secure multi-party computation was used, however, it was found to be insufficient in terms of privacy preservation. If encryption is used during data analytics, the value of the data will be reduced. As a result, encryption is not only challenging to implement but also lowers the usefulness of data (Jiang, et al.,2018).

Data Distribution Technique

The data is dispersed across numerous locations using this method. The data can be distributed in one of two distinct ways:

i. Horizontal Data distribution
ii. Vertical Data distribution

Horizontal Distribution

When data is dispersed across multiple places with the same qualities, it is referred to as a horizontal distribution, as illustrated in Fig. 5. Only whenever some operations are to be conducted on the data while not sharing the information may horizontal distribution of data be used. For instance, if a store wishes to examine sales across multiple locations, it can use analytics to do calculations on aggregate statistical information. Nevertheless, as a requirement for the analysis of data, the data owner may be required to disclose the data to an external analyst, which could result in an invasion of confidentiality. On distributed data, classification and clustering methods can be used, however, they cannot guarantee confidentiality. Whereas if data is disseminated over different sites belonging to different companies, aggregate function outcomes may aid one side in discovering data recorded by others. We anticipate all cooperating sites to be forthright with each other in these kinds of instances (Aggarwal et al.,2008).

Vertical Distribution

Vertical Distribution Vertical distribution is defined as the spread of individually distinct information across several places under the custodianship of different organisations, as seen in Fig. 6.

Not all of this data may be provided on one website. Vertical distribution is one in which each location has a small collection of a user's attributes. When performing analytics, data from each of these sites must be gathered together, posing a risk of violation of privacy. It is extremely difficult to safeguard confidentiality if datasets are shared when performing analysis on vertically distributed data, in which the entities are scattered over numerous locations under the custodianship of various entities. For instance, in the course of a legal inquiry, the lead investigator may seek data about the suspect from his workplace, health authority, or financial institutions to learn further about his or her personality.

Figure 5. Horizontal Distribution

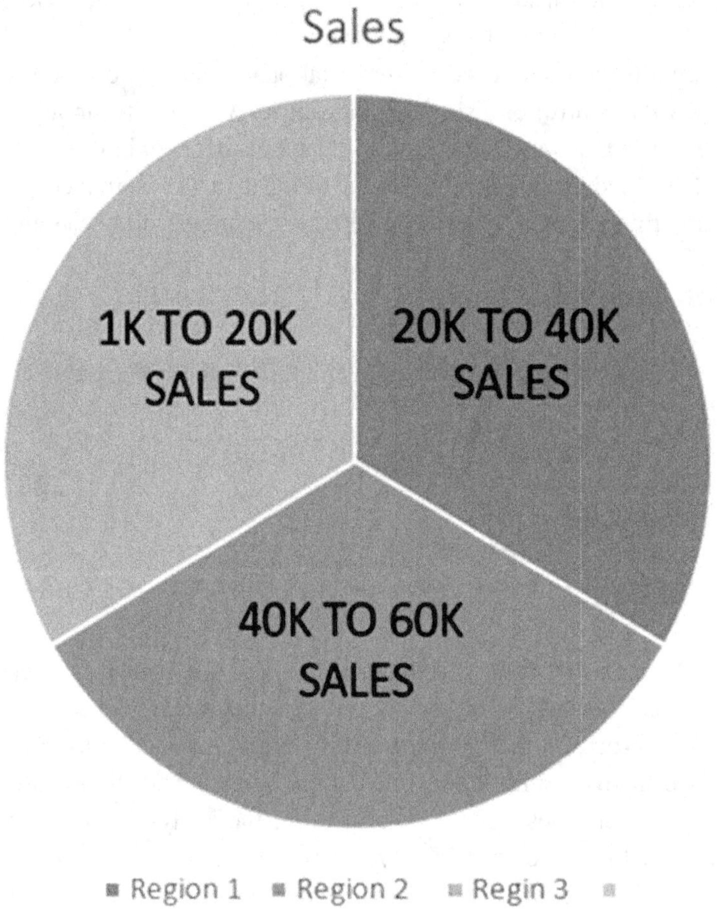

PROPOSED MODEL BASED ON ANONYMITY

K Anonymity

Anonymization is the method of altering data before it is delivered to data analytics (Iyengar,2002), such that recognition is impossible. If an individual is trying to de-identify the anonymized data by mapping it along with external data sources, this should result in K indistinguishable records. K-anonymity is a fundamental framework developed to reduce the possibility of re-identification of anonymized data when it is linked to other datasets. Latanya Sweeney proposed the k-anonymity privacy model in her paper 'Protecting privacy when disclosing information: k-anonymity and its enforcement through generalisation and suppression in 1998. To attain k-anonymity, the dataset must contain a minimum of k people who have a similar set of characteristics that could be used to detect each subject. The homogeneity attack, as well as the background knowledge assault, are two types of attacks that can be used against K anonymity. Incognito (LeFevre et al., 2005) and Mondrian (LeFevre et al.,2006) are two of the algorithms used to

Figure 6. Vertical Distribution

assure anonymity. Also, on medical data in Figure 7, K anonymity is implemented. Before anonymization, the data is shown in the column. While attempting to locate a specific individual's data, the K anonymity method is used with the value of k set as 3 to ensure three indiscernible records. Figure 8 shows the outcome of applying anonymization to postal numbers and age characteristics.

To accomplish anonymization, the aforementioned technique utilizes generalisation (Samarati & Sweeney, 1998). However, after anonymization, if we know Levi is 21 years old and resides in the 45956 postal codes, we may deduce Levi has Food Poisoning, as shown in Figure 8. This is alluded to as a homogeneity attack. If Levi is 43 years old and has never been diagnosed with cancer, then Levi is most likely suffering from a Skin Allergy. Background knowledge attack is the term for this type of attack. K anonymity can also be achieved via either generalisation or suppression (Chung et al., 2021; Sweeney, 2002). If the smallest generalisation could be performed without causing significant data loss, K anonymity can be improved (Sweeney, 2002). The most serious threat to privacy is identity exposure, which is not protected by K anonymity (Meyerson & Williams,2004). Individual privacy is more crucial when it comes to personalised privacy (Machanavajjhala et al.,2006).

Figure 7. Medical data, before anonymization

S NO	POSTAL NUMBER	AGE	MEDICAL CONDITION
1	45103	23	Cancer
2	45607	45	Back pain
3	45321	54	Stomach pain
4	45876	32	Cancer
5	45987	76	Skin Allergy
6	45643	56	Backpain
7	45743	43	Skin Allergy
8	45956	21	Food Poisoning
9	45225	55	Stomach pain

Multidimensional Sensitivity Based Anonymization (MDSBA)

The traditional approaches of anonymization, bottom-up generalisation (Xiao & Tao, 2006) and top-down generalisation (Ke et al., n.d.), were used on well-represented organized data records. Nevertheless, implementing the same to huge data sets is incredibly challenging, resulting in scalability and information loss constraints. Multidimensional Sensitivity Based Anonymization is a superior kind of anonymization that has been shown to be even more successful than those traditional methods.

Figure 8. After implementing anonymization on Postal numbers and age

S NO	POSTAL NUMBER	AGE	MEDICAL CONDITION
1	451**	2*	Cancer
2	456**	4*	Back pain
3	453**	5*	Stomach pain
4	4587*	>30	Cancer
5	4598*	>70	Skin Allergy
6	4564*	>50	Backpain
7	457AC	4*	Skin Allergy
8	459AC	2*	Food Poisoning
9	452AC	5*	Stomach pain

Multidimensional Sensitivity Based Anonymization is an enhanced Anonymization (Fung et al., n.d.) approach that can be implemented on big data sets with minimal data leakage and predetermined quasi-identifiers. The Apache MAP REDUCE (Zhang, et al.,2013) framework was utilised to manage huge data sets as the basis of this methodology. In a traditional Hadoop Distributed Files System, data is partitioned into blocks of 64 MB or 128 MB and disseminated across multiple nodes sans regard for the data contained within the blocks. The data is separated into distinct bags according to the probability distribution of the quasi-IDs using filters in the Apache Pig scripting language as an element of the Multidimensional Sensitivity Based Anonymization (Satpathy & Patnaik, 2021) approach.

Bottom-up generalisation is used in Multidimensional Sensitivity Based Anonymization, although on a set of characteristics with specific class values, wherein class denotes a sensitive attribute. Especially when compared with the traditional method of blocks, data dissemination was more successful. Employing Apache Pig, four quasi-identifiers were used to anonymize the data. If the bag comprises only a couple of parameters, the data can be protected from background knowledge attacks because it is vertically segregated into diverse factions. This strategy also makes it impossible to map the data with external sources to reveal any personal details.

The execution of this technique was accomplished with Apache Pig. Because Apache Pig is a scripting language, it requires minimal development time. Nevertheless, as contrasted to Map Reduce jobs, Apache Pig's code efficiency is lower so that every Apache Pig script must eventually be transformed into a Map Reduce job. Multidimensional Sensitivity Based Anonymization (Xuyun et al., 2014) is better for huge data sets, but only until they are at rest. Streaming data can't be anonymized using Multidimensional Sensitivity Based Anonymization.

Figure 9. Comparison between K Anonymity and Multidimensional Sensitivity Based Anonymization (MDSBA)

CHARACTERISTICS	K ANONYMITY	MDSBA
Appropriateness for unstructured data	No	Yes
Preserving attributes	No	Yes
Data utility is compromised.	No	Yes
Complexity of Implementation	No	Yes
Reliability of data analytics findings	No	No

Based on the conclusions drawn we decided to implement Multidimensional Sensitivity Based Anonymization (MDSBA).

ISSUES AND CHALLENGES FACED WHILE MAINTAINING PRIVACY BY SECURING SOCIAL DATA

Data privacy preservation is one of the dynamic topics that are frequently affected and impacted by the evolution of the digital era innovation and new corporate practices innovation. The adoption of Technology exemplifies the laws for the confidentiality of data organisation and modifies the comprehension of local data definition, cross-border data transfer administration, user anonymity in the electronic era, privileges, and data controller responsibilities (Al-Zobbi et al.,2017). According to a poll taken up by Netizens, more than 70% of European Union residents think that private data discovery is becoming an escalating important component of the online realm. While on the other hand, just around a third of social computing users and around 15 per cent of online remote consumers assume that they have complete control over their details. Queries have been raised about where and how everyone's data is located, which can be accessed by whom, who is concerned with data preservation, what strategy is in place to store individual data and maintain their privacy and security, and what guarantees are in place to ensure that data is transferred correctly among both nodes through the worldwide network (Al-Zobbi et al.,2017).

The Challenges of Social Computing (SoC)

It is well recognized that this system enables the organisation of a dialogue among specific computer users over the Internet utilizing various environments referred to as Social Networking Sites – SNS In practice, the SoC is a great tool for connecting people and transmitting content, but it presents a threat to private data security because information may be shared with an unauthorised individual. It can have serious economic and psychological effects on the data holder in various instances. The following is a concise explanation of the SoC negatives for user privacy.

1. Throughout many circumstances, webpages serve as an "unlocked door" - visitors can approve the Privacy Statement only with a single "click" at initial enrolment or on their first visit, without needing to read the content. As a consequence, the user accepts all terms without even being cognizant of them. In this instance, she or he has no idea what would happen to her or his private details in the newly established person's profile.
2. Through other circumstances, the person's private details are only saved for one visitation and then transmitted to the centre without any of the person's permission or agreement. The reality that just only less than 55 per cent of netizens believe they are notified about the terms of data collection and subsequent use when they log in to a social media platform or enrol for a web-based service is noteworthy.
3. In certain situations, a networking site may fail to give details about the Confidential Statement or may request excessive personal details when a user registers for something that goes beyond the media's stated aim.
4. Further issue is the whereabouts of private information that has been preserved in the worldwide network. When hunting for a suitable job, it may be possible to maintain multiple versions. This is against the GDPR's objective of storing and processing personal information as few as possible. The decision taken by the National Consumer Agency of Germany for the infringement of confidentiality by a social media website with the propagated data that now the adverts are free to the

public is an instance of this approach. The justification given is that the sns earns a lot of money by gathering private information and storing it in numerous locations across the world.

5. The aforesaid issue has a detrimental impact on the GDPR's "right to be erased " provision in the event of denial of continued usage. The user cannot be certain that all versions of private information have been destroyed across the social media network's nodes. A graduate law student from Europe, for illustration, sought all of the data about a person's profile that a social media website (SNS) had kept for them. They received about 1000 pages of documentation in return, including images, conversations, and articles from years in the past, including some that he thought, were lost. The service appears to have gathered far more confidential information than the individual anticipated, but also collected irrelevant and erased data.

Cloud Computing (CC) Challenges

CC is a distributed framework that provides cloud facilities to clients by connecting virtual computers and establishing variable connectivity amongst them (users). Infrastructure as a service (IaaS), Platform as a Service (PaaS), and Software as a Service are the three main cloud services specified by NIST (National Institute of Standards and Technology) (SaaS). These solutions could be supplied by a variety of cloud types, namely public, community, private, and hybrid clouds, as well as using the Cloud Computing technology that is mobile based, which combines the three components of mobile devices, mobile internet, and cloud computing. According to the Thales research for 2020, more than 80 per cent of enterprises utilise more than 10 or more SaaS providers, and less than 50 per cent of corporate data on the cloud is sensitive, but only less than 60 per cent of it is encrypted. Cloud computing does not breach data protection standards, but it can pose a threat to cross-border transferring data. In practice, there have been no special regional laws for protecting private data when using cloud services; nonetheless, to satisfy GDPR e-privacy standards, a paper containing rules and regulations for proper cloud computing service use was prepared and released. According to CISCO, close to 60 per cent of businesses have confirmed their GDPR preparedness, with the remaining approx. of 30% expecting to be ready in early 2020.

The Internet of Things (IoT) Based Challenges.

The phrase implies a collection of objects and gadgets that are interconnected to transmit and receive data collected by using sensors that can detect selected features and capture and analyse measured values to control procedures spaces such as the residence, metropolitan area, and general wellbeing. Linked devices will likely intrude on people's confidentiality, undermining customer trust. Two major features of IoT for the protection of personal data could be defined in this context:

a) Confidentiality – this could be jeopardised because any physical and logical object or entity could be assigned a globally unique code and convey information over the Internet. Although not all data supplied from endpoints are subject to strict secrecy, the statistics of data that is often received by multiple points may be containing personal information for an individual. On the other hand, as the number of sensors grows, so does the amount of data collected, raising privacy and security issues. When accessing and hacking the details from smart sensors, for example, obtaining the acquired data can contribute to the identification of particular habits, illness and lifestyle information, and more.

b) IoT security - typical credentials are used to establish a collection of different internet and computer devices, and the objects could be the target of various assaults. The assaults hunt for vulnerabilities to hacking and manipulation in equipment with a low level of security. An additional issue with IoT security is identity verification; in most cases, a conventional approach is utilised, which scarcely offers the amount of network security that is required. It's also feasible to utilise gadgets with non-changeable default passcode. According to research findings, IoT devices are vulnerable to cyberattacks. To illustrate, less than 60 per cent of risk caseworkers don't maintain track of IoT devices, while an approximate 65 per cent say they don't keep track of IoT apps. The remaining believe that cyber-based breaches will most likely be carried out via IoT.

Challenges Due to Big Data (BD) and Big Data Analytics (BDA)

The terminology "big data" refers to vast quantities of content recorded and stored from various sources in various locations for some more analysis for almost any cause. This data could be in a variety of formats. The fundamental premise is that "the more data, the better," yet this has privacy implications and goes against the GDPR policy of processing private data as little as possible. BD are gathered from a variety of resources for even more assessment (BDA) to make inferences, choose alternatives, or examine patterns in object conduct, especially for people. In this sense, BD does not pose a threat to confidentiality, but BDA might lead to undesirable consequences for users, such as inaccurate inferences regarding their personal lives.

The prevalence of potential detrimental privacy issues in BD is explored, with "big data storage, processing, sharing, and management essential procedures" being exposed to major attacks and resulting in privacy infringement. Particular aspects of the BD/BDA, which can be characterised as follows, can have unintended detrimental consequences when it comes to privacy.

- The processed BD could be acquired for a range of functions, which is a violation of the fundamental data accuracy concept of "Defining the Goal."
- The vast amount of data gathered breaches another GDPR data accuracy standard – "data minimization";
- It is conceivable for a user's "big data" to be misinterpreted, causing problems for the individual's connection with the company and with his or her household. The wrong judgments can lead to ethical lapses or prejudice.
- Employing BDA in company consumer analysis might lead to inaccurate inferences and jeopardise the person's reputation, such as when hiring staff.
- BDA is unable to meet the GDPR's criteria for anonymization and pseudonymization of private information;
- The reliability of the BDA could not be fully insured since it is unclear what techniques and approaches (algorithms, software, programmes, etc.) were utilised in the evaluation, which would violate the GDPR obligation for computational accountability.

CASE STUDY OF PRIVACY TECHNIQUES EMPLYED IN SOCIAL MEDIA PLATFORMS

Privacy concerns and customer alienation are crucial precursors to information security knowledge. It is also discovered that the requirements for privacy management and self-disclosure, respectively, are privacy concerns and customer alienation (Mishra & Tyagi, 2022). This demonstrates that in the context of social media users, the user's understanding of information security is tied to the user's concern about their privacy or whether they agree or disagree with the platform (Nair & Tyagi,2021) Practical recommendations for social media include keeping the platform trustworthy, continuing to offer good services, enhancing users' feeling of identity, reducing the distance between platforms and users, and fostering users' trust. Based on their understanding of personal information security, users on different platforms have diverse degrees of privacy concerns, according to the research findings (Tyagi et al., 2020). However, more steps will be made to restrict acts on private privacy, and even protection behaviour, when social media users have been impacted by privacy concerns and consumer alienation the steps adopted by various companies will be analysed in detail in the below-mentioned case studies.

Twitter

Twitter's default setting is to keep the user's tweets public. However, they can make it private by enabling it in their settings. Via the JSON API all public tweets will be made available. There are two kinds of API mainly search and streaming API that is employed to retrieve tweets and allow data to be accessed. Both the Search API and the Streaming API may be used to obtain batches of historical data. Whereas Search API is used for past data and Streaming API is used for real time data.

Facebook

Facebook has more complicated privacy concerns when compared to Twitter, many status updates are more difficult to access than Tweets and require users to set their status to "open authorisation." Facebook features a number of APIs, including the Public Feed APIs as well as the Keyword Insight API, and presently saves all data as objects. Making the API request requires knowing an object's specific ID in order to access its attributes.

Wiki Based Media

Academics have access to sizable open-source archives of user-generated content thanks to Wikipedia (and wikis in general). Wikipedia has HTTP-based APIs that enable programmatic access and searching that returns data in a number of forms, including XML, which is something that is not well recognised. The HTTP-based API for the wiki functions by receiving requests with one or more input arguments and returning text, sometimes in XML format, that the requesting client may read and utilise. JSON, or PHP serialised are some more formats that are supported.

Other Platforms like Foursquare

Foursquare has teamed up with Gnip to deliver a steady flow of anonymized check-in data after announcing that it will no longer permit individual check-ins on iOS 7. The information is offered in two packages: a filtered version through Gnip's Power Track service, and the full Firehose access level.

CONCLUSION AND FUTURE WORK

There are many figuring patterns offering helpful types of assistance to improve people's lives and expand the association's effectiveness. These patterns incorporate cloud and portable distributed computing yet alongside these advancements many related difficulties ought to be taken into consideration like client's protection and information security. In this analysis, we considered the re-penny arising advances. Cloud frameworks, portable cloud computing, P2P cloud frameworks, big data and capacity arrangements. Likewise, we addressed existing and noteworthy security and data protection issues related to implementations of the aforementioned technologies and introduced the significant assaults and threats which can have a major impact on distributed computing frameworks with the customary existing countermeasures used to overcome these attacks. Moreover, we examined the layered P2P CS engineering and its importance in big data analysis. After this, we examined the feasibility of applying more advanced countermeasures to counter the prevalent security threats we face. Specifically, we introduced a total of four non-customary encryption techniques and broke down the perceivable difficulties and hurdles of utilising them as far as performance parameters to get big data in cloud conditions.

As of today, a wide variety of safety approaches and methods are accessible for obscuring and anonymizing nearby recordings, which utilise separate strategies and tactics. Just with a set number of confirmations and actions, big data approaches are accessible and practical. There is no system check for big data utilising programming models such as MapReduce, data preparing, collection and securely saving analysed data for worldwide recording anonymization. The proposed work conspires new calculation for MapReduce in big data for worldwide anonymization reduction. If the mix of MapReduce, an instrument for security safeguarding, for the data analysis is utilised, it will give better protection in versatile big data during questionable conditions.

REFERENCES

Aggarwal, C. C., & Yu, P. S. (2008). A general survey of privacy-preserving data mining models and algorithms. *Privacy-Preserving Data Mining*, 11-52. doi:10.1007/978-0-387-70992-5_2

Al-Zobbi, M., Shahrestani, S., & Ruan, C. (2017). Implementing a framework for big data anonymity and analytics access control. *2017 IEEE Trustcom/BigDataSE/ICESS*. doi:10.1109/Trustcom/BigDataSE/ICESS.2017.325

Al-Zobbi, M., Shahrestani, S., & Ruan, C. (2017). Improving MapReduce privacy by implementing multi-dimensional sensitivity-based anonymization. *Journal of Big Data*, *4*(1), 45. Advance online publication. doi:10.118640537-017-0104-5

Chung, K., Chen, C., Tsai, H., & Chuang, Y. (2021). Social media privacy management strategies: A SEM analysis of user privacy behaviors. *Computer Communications, 174*, 122–130. doi:10.1016/j.comcom.2021.04.012

Dilmaghani, S., Brust, M. R., Danoy, G., Cassagnes, N., Pecero, J., & Bouvry, P. (2019). Privacy and security of big data in AI systems: A research and standards perspective. *2019 IEEE International Conference on Big Data (Big Data).* 10.1109/BigData47090.2019.9006283

Fung, B., Wang, K., & Yu, P. (n.d.). Top-down specialization for information and privacy preservation. *21st International Conference on Data Engineering (ICDE'05).* 10.1109/ICDE.2005.143

Iyengar, V. S. (2002). Transforming data to satisfy privacy constraints. *Proceedings of the eighth ACM SIGKDD international conference on Knowledge discovery and data mining - KDD '02.* 10.1145/775047.775089

Jiang, R., Lu, R., & Choo, K. R. (2018). Achieving high performance and privacy-preserving query over encrypted multidimensional big metering data. *Future Generation Computer Systems, 78*, 392–401. doi:10.1016/j.future.2016.05.005

Kevin, M., Ana, F., & Alexey, K. (2019). Smart information systems in cybersecurity. *The ORBIT Journal, 2*(2), 1–26. doi:10.29297/orbit.v2i2.105

LeFevre, K., DeWitt, D., & Ramakrishnan, R. (2006). Mondrian multidimensional K-anonymity. *22nd International Conference on Data Engineering (ICDE'06).* 10.1109/ICDE.2006.101

LeFevre, K., DeWitt, D. J., & Ramakrishnan, R. (2005). Incognito. *Proceedings of the 2005 ACM SIGMOD international conference on Management of data - SIGMOD '05.* 10.1145/1066157.1066164

Machanavajjhala, A., Gehrke, J., Kifer, D., & Venkitasubramaniam, M. (2006). L-diversity: Privacy beyond K-anonymity. *22nd International Conference on Data Engineering (ICDE'06).* 10.1109/ICDE.2006.1

Mazurek, G., & Małagocka, K. (2019). Perception of privacy and data protection in the context of the development of artificial intelligence. *Journal of Management Analytics, 6*(4), 344–364. doi:10.1080/23270012.2019.1671243

Meyerson, A., & Williams, R. (2004). On the complexity of optimal K-anonymity. *Proceedings of the twenty-third ACM SIGMOD-SIGACT-SIGART symposium on Principles of database systems - PODS '04.* 10.1145/1055558.1055591

Mishra, S., & Tyagi, A. K. (2022). The role of machine learning techniques in internet of things-based cloud applications. *Internet of Things,* 105-135. doi:10.1007/978-3-030-87059-1_4

Nair, M. M., & Tyagi, A. K. (2021). Privacy: History, Statistics, Policy, Laws, Preservation and Threat Analysis. Journal of Information Assurance & Security, 16(1), 24-34.

Rubner, Y., & Tomasi, C. (2001). The earth mover's distance. *Perceptual Metrics for Image Database Navigation,* 13-28. doi:10.1007/978-1-4757-3343-3_2

Samarati, P., & Sweeney, L. (1998). Generalizing data to provide anonymity when disclosing information (abstract). *Proceedings of the seventeenth ACM SIGACT-SIGMOD-SIGART symposium on Principles of database systems - PODS '98*. 10.1145/275487.275508

Satpathy, S., & Patnaik, S. (2021). Role of artificial intelligence in social media and human behaviour. *International Journal of Engineering and Advanced Technology*, *11*(1), 207–210. doi:10.35940/ijeat.A1926.1011121

Stahl, B. C., & Wright, D. (2018). Ethics and privacy in AI and big data: Implementing responsible research and innovation. *IEEE Security and Privacy*, *16*(3), 26–33. doi:10.1109/MSP.2018.2701164

Sweeney, L. (2002). Achieving K-anonymity privacy protection using generalization and suppression. *International Journal of Uncertainty, Fuzziness and Knowledge-based Systems*, *10*(05), 571–588. doi:10.1142/S021848850200165X

Sweeney, L. (2002). K-anonymity: A model for protecting privacy. *International Journal of Uncertainty, Fuzziness and Knowledge-based Systems*, *10*(05), 557–570. doi:10.1142/S0218488502001648

Tawalbeh, L. A., & Saldamli, G. (2021). Reconsidering big data security and privacy in cloud and mobile cloud systems. *Journal of King Saud University - Computer and Information Sciences, 33*(7), 810-819. doi:10.1016/j.jksuci.2019.05.007

Tom, E., Keane, P. A., Blazes, M., Pasquale, L. R., Chiang, M. F., Lee, A. Y., & Lee, C. S. (2020). Protecting data privacy in the age of AI-enabled ophthalmology. *Translational Vision Science & Technology*, *9*(2), 36. doi:10.1167/tvst.9.2.36 PMID:32855840

Tsou, M. (2015). Research challenges and opportunities in mapping social media and big data. *Cartography and Geographic Information Science, 42*(sup1), 70-74. doi:10.1080/15230406.2015.1059251

Tyagi, A. K., Nair, M. M., Niladhuri, S., & Abraham, A. (2020). Security, Privacy Research issues in Various Computing Platforms: A Survey and the Road Ahead. Journal of Information Assurance & Security, 15(1), 1-16.

Vennila, S., & Priyadarshini, J. (2015). Scalable privacy preservation in big data a survey. *Procedia Computer Science*, *50*, 369–373. doi:10.1016/j.procs.2015.04.033

Wang, K., Yu, P., & Chakraborty, S. (n.d.). Bottom-up generalization: A data mining solution to privacy protection. *Fourth IEEE International Conference on Data Mining (ICDM'04)*. 10.1109/ICDM.2004.10110

Xiao, X., & Tao, Y. (2006). Personalized privacy preservation. *Proceedings of the 2006 ACM SIGMOD international conference on Management of data - SIGMOD '06*. 10.1145/1142473.1142500

Zhang, X., Yang, C., Nepal, S., Liu, C., Dou, W., & Chen, J. (2013). A MapReduce based approach of scalable multidimensional Anonymization for big data privacy preservation on cloud. *2013 International Conference on Cloud and Green Computing*. 10.1109/CGC.2013.24

Zhang, X., Yang, L. T., Liu, C., & Chen, J. (2014). A scalable two-phase top-down specialization approach for data Anonymization using MapReduce on cloud. *IEEE Transactions on Parallel and Distributed Systems*, *25*(2), 363–373. doi:10.1109/TPDS.2013.48

Chapter 11
Privacy and Security Concerns During the COVID-19 Pandemic:
A Mixed-Method Study

Poonam Sahoo
https://orcid.org/0000-0001-7762-3570
National Institute of Technology, Karnataka, India

Pavan Kumar Saraf
National Institute of Technology, Karnataka, India

Rashmi Uchil
National Institute of Technology, Karnataka, India

ABSTRACT

The study's objective is to ascertain healthcare personnel's perspectives and experiences on information privacy and security during the COVID-19 pandemic. Despite the abundance of research on privacy and security issues, this study focuses on the elements that influence privacy concerns in volatile, unpredictable, complicated, and ambiguous situations, which in the current scenario might include the COVID-19 pandemic. Three levels of coding were applied to all interview transcripts using the qualitative technique. The pandemic of COVID-19 has raised various concerns about technology, data privacy, and protection. The study's objective is to find, extract, summarize, and evaluate trends in a list of privacy threats associated with the COVID-19 pandemic. Participants were healthcare practitioners who worked closely with COVID-19 cases during the COVID-19 pandemic.

INTRODUCTION

The Severe Acute Respiratory Syndrome Coronavirus-2 (SARS-Cov-2) outbreak began in humans in

DOI: 10.4018/978-1-6684-5250-9.ch011

2019 (WHO,2020). As the COVID-19 influenza pandemic swept over the world, it accelerated the use of digital technologies, mostly for communication and commerce, and the growth of these technologies resulted in technological risks (Li, 2020). Almost every gadget is interdependent and networked, raising concerns about data privacy and protection. Since the outbreak, several incidents of healthcare fraud have been documented, and one of the major concerns across the board is data privacy (Mason & Williams, 2020; Viaene & Dedene, 2004). It is critical to have access to healthcare professionals' perceptions and experiences during pandemics in order to take control of the situation (Liu et al., 2020). Numerous academics and healthcare professionals have stressed the privacy and security concerns that have arisen as a result of the evolution of healthcare technology (Chung & Hershey, 2012; Ermakova et al., 2013; Parks et al., 2011). Healthcare organizations manage a large volume of electronic medical records created by their employees and have access to sensitive and important patient information, making it critical to throw light on healthcare staff (Kaplan, 2016; Rahim et al., 2017). The three most distinguish concept in healthcare setting to protect the healthcare information is privacy, confidentiality, and security (Thomas Rindfleisch, 1997).Privacy protection not merely depends on deidentification and anonymization, but on the transparency of how actually data is utilized (Kaplan, 2016). According to Rahim et al., (2017), Support from top management may lead to educating their employees about the importance of privacy and can be done by creating a personalized and classified privacy policy that outlines the methods for implementing adequate privacy controls to mitigate potential risks. Electronic health records (EHR) and health data networks provides a wealth of public data. Data can be used for variety of objectives, ranging from comparative research to design clinical trial and various monitoring purpose (Kaplan, 2016).

Although many researchers have investigated the deployment of blockchain technology and AI in dealing with the COVID-19 crisis (Nguyen et al., 2021). These studies largely concentrated on the deployment of blockchain for the storage of data, data management, and privacy, healthcare staff reported a significant degree of concern about privacy and security, and protecting healthcare professionals is a critical principle when dealing with pandemics such as COVID-19. Examining how healthcare staff handles privacy and security concerns during a pandemic is critical for improving healthcare organizations' capacity to continue dealing with emergencies (Dopelt et al., 2021; Mabrouk et al., 2016; Parks et al., 2011). Healthcare professionals will require training on how to use digital platforms. There are huge challenges to overcome to continue using this digital base healthcare platform and training is one of the keys to achieving the objective (Bouabida et al., 2022).In the healthcare setting, effective training and education about privacy can help healthcare professional users to have a better understanding of information privacy concerns (IPC) and to acquire better judgment, preventing privacy violations (Rahim et al., 2017). Businesses are putting a lot of effort into building privacy policies and measures to combat these threats of security concerns (Meingast et al., 2006; Parks et al., 2011; Thomas Rindfleisch, 1997). Prior to the deployment of digital technologies in the healthcare system, healthcare professionals should have sound knowledge of these technologies. Many professionals proclaimed positive experiences in online consultations, but online consultations performance in terms of relational aspects and in relation to privacy and security of software was found to be key impediments to deployment (De Witte et al., 2021; Lenert & McSwain, 2020). Doctors have always valued their privacy, before the advent of technology in the medical industry (Alhasan et al., 2020). According to Earp & Payton (2006), a Substantiated amount of awareness of privacy orientations among healthcare employees plays a significant role. Wilkowska & Ziefle (2011) investigates the perceived importance of security and privacy concerns in separate groups and evaluates the predictive value of these features on medical technologies and E-health technologies uptake found that, the more users' cognitions are integrated into sensitive information concepts, the more likely new E-health technologies will be widely accepted and adopted.

According to Mohamed & Ahmad (2012), healthcare professionals will be more apprehensive about adopting electronic emphatical records if they believe it is subject to privacy concerns and risks. The degree to which healthcare professionals perceives the possible threats in the use of electronic medical record, there is a risk of compromising patients' privacy. Privacy control is defined as employees' perceptions and their ability to protect electronic medical records, it demonstrates employees' belief in their abilities to defend electronic medical reports (Alraja et al., 2019; Dehling & Sunyaev, 2014; Rahim et al., 2017). Despite various obstacles to telemedicine, such as worker training, and broadband access cost, telemedicine has thrived during the pandemic (Solimini et al., 2021; Valentino et al., 2020). Thus, the study's objective is to conduct a comprehensive examination of healthcare professionals' experiences and perspectives about privacy and security concerns during the COVID-19 crisis.

Problem Statement and Motivations for Research

Several factors motivated this study. To date, no study experimentally investigates the various theoretical reasons weighing the privacy implications in the healthcare sector during Covid-19. This research aims to bridge the gap and contributes to the literature on information privacy. Furthermore, various research investigated focus on a specific area, such as social networks, and e-commerce (Chen et al., 2009; Tsai et al., 2007). During the COVID-19 pandemic, healthcare organizations needed immediate action to stop the virus from spreading and to protect health workers in maintaining appropriate workplace safety and information privacy and understanding the healthcare worker experiences during pandemic is critical (Bouabida et al., 2022; Eftekhar Ardebili et al., 2021; Ventrella, 2020). Hence, this study tries to understand healthcare professional perception regarding information privacy and security issues at the workplace.

Based on the above considerations, the following objectives are being considered in this study:

RO1. To investigate the privacy and security concerns of the healthcare professionals during the Covid-19 pandemic.

RO2. To bring insight into the digital health platform for healthcare professionals.

The remaining sections of the study are as follows: The review of literature is covered in section 2. The proposed approach is presented in section 3. The analysis of data is covered in section 4. The conclusion and scope of future study are explained in section 5.

LITERATURE REVIEW

Healthcare and COVID-19

The Covid-19 pandemic triggered an unanticipated crisis in health, educational, social, economic, and sports systems. This pandemic is linked to people and progression which is heavily influenced by people's behaviour and government policies of each country (Bratianu, 2020; T. Sharma et al., 2021). Healthcare professionals are critical resources for the whole nation. Employee health and safety are critical not just for continued patient care, but also for preventing disease outbreaks (Liu et al., 2020). During the initial months of the pandemic outbreak, healthcare employees were exposed to a plethora of novel and unprecedented events and experienced a range of emotions concealed behind masks. Because health employees lived through the COVID-19 pandemic, it was the only way to comprehend and focus on what they endured (Mehrdad et al., 2021), and could provide valuable insights for future preventive measures. Many cyber hazards exist during the pandemic as a result of people's actions and technological system failures. Cyber-attacks pose a threat to IoT and telework-based applications (L. Wang & Alexander, 2021). With the advent of digital technologies, cybersecurity turns out to be very challenging. The COVID-19 pandemic situation is being used by bad actors all over the world as a tool for cyber-attacks through hacking, scamming, and attacking (Khan et al., 2020). The worldwide healthcare community faces huge hurdles as a result of the COVID-19 pandemic. Transition to the digitalization of the health system is well means to offer innovative answers to this public health crisis, this includes novel diagnostic systems, surveillance systems, decision-making techniques, etc (Kapoor et al., 2020). A video conferencing of telemedicine sessions could contain sensitive information that the patient wishes to keep private. Furthermore, without the knowledge of owners, automatic contact tracing tools accumulate critical location data, which is a major privacy infringement to share personal and sensitive data with unauthorized third parties (Hall & Mcgraw, 2014; Siriwardhana et al., 2021).

Technology like RFID (radio frequency distribution) is a valuable technology with a wide range of implications and applications in industries like retail, healthcare, and manufacturing settings. It has the potential to scan nearby devices and send the information to the systems connected with information technology. In the healthcare setting, RFID raises security concerns for the people especially healthcare personnel (Rosenbaum, 2014; Winston et al., 2016). Government officials and policymakers face significant privacy threats in ensuring the safe application of technologies like artificial intelligence and telehealth for the general public. The present Coronavirus pandemic has hastened the integration of AI, blockchain and other cloud technologies in healthcare settings to reduce risk among healthcare professionals (Cresswell et al., 2021; Dagher et al., 2018; El-Sherif et al., 2022; Gerke et al., 2020). The major roadblocks to digital healthcare development are privacy and security breaches. Medical equipment issues are the most common sources of digital security concerns, it has enhanced the medical care quality and accessibility (Q. Wang et al., 2021). The electronic health record is a digital record that contains patents medical reports and history, it has resolved numerous data security issues (Reegu et al., 2021; Wu & Tsai, 2018). Electronic health services are built on the foundation of EHR (electronic health records), EPR(electronic patient records), and EMR (electronic medical records), and the information contained in all these records including patient healthcare data must be passed across multiple healthcare professionals and practitioners, privacy concerns of these records is a major roadblock to all EHR, EMR, and EPR implementation (Ermakova et al., 2015). Perceived privacy plays a major role in explaining the variance of acceptance when it comes to the perceived utility of electronic health technologies and in explaining how this differs depending on the diversity of users (Harman et al., 2012; Keshta & Odeh, 2021; Shi et al., 2020; Wilkowska & Ziefle, 2011). However, adopting a unified standard for electronic health data privacy and security is a difficult task (Sahama et al., 2013). Healthcare organizations will need the signing a contract or trust agreement(Ray & Wimalasiri, 2006).

Digital Health Technology and Privacy and Security

During the Coronavirus pandemic (Covid-19) pandemic digital technology transformed the healthcare settings to keep track on all activities of hospitals. According to the WHO health technology is describe as application and implementation of knowledge and skill in different form of devices vaccines, medicines, telemedicine to solve health related issues and to improve the life quality (Haverinen et al., 2019;

Jääskelä et al., 2022;Mahoney, 2020;Salam & Bajaba,2021).The successful implementation of these technologies (IoT),artificial intelligence, blockchain, robotics will require safe, dependable, and smart infrastructures to be effective (Fusco et al., 2020; Porambage et al., 2016; Vargo et al., 2021; Xu et al., 2019).In the realm of healthcare IT, research on information privacy can be divided into four categories: healthcare consumers, public policy, healthcare providers, and inter-organizational (Appari & Johnson, 2010; Meingast et al., 2006). Privacy frameworks for technologies like Internet of things (IoT), big data, blockchain, and e Health apps to be visible and open to them, to explains the clarify the basis for collecting and gathering necessary health data, to preserve updated data and to protect the records of patient (Chenthara et al., 2020; Gupta et al., 2011; Miller & Tucker, 2009; Nageshwaran et al., 2021; Porambage et al., 2016). The continuous shift from traditional legacy of paper records of medical to e-medical records will give biomedical researchers unprecedent volumes of data, potentially catalysing important improvements in medical understanding (Kaiser et al., 2021). However, this potentiality will be fully realised if the researchers have access to entire population of patient. As a result, enabling individual patients opt out of sharing their health information, as per traditional concepts of inform consent, may jeopardise the research and medical benefits it generates (Hoffman & Podgurski, 2012; Xing et al., 2021).On the other hand according to the study by Aultman & Dean (2014) delineate that electronic health systems were not much secure as they supposed to be, despite safety measures like password protections. Important digital health innovations have begun to blur the line between licensed and unlicensed devices, so the goal of digital health system is to create a circulation of patient data to health professional devices who can make sense of the information gathered, and finally back to initial stage of device that offer the patient information (Kalla et al., 2020; Vayena et al., 2018). Precision medicine uses data from different means through omics, medical records, insurance claims, lifestyle, and environment to provide tailored care and anticipate sickness, and precise therapies. It makes substantial use of sensing and communication technologies like electronic monitoring devices, machine learning (Alshalali et al., 2018; Lorenzen-Huber et al., 2011; Park & Shin, 2020). Because health data consists of sensitive personal information such as the name and additional information about the patients' health conditions, it must be handled with caution at all period. Leakage of this sensitive information in ones' personal life such as bullying increased insurance premiums, and job loss owing to medical history. Online businesses rely on the ability to acquire enormous volume of personal information and data about users (Y. Sharma & Balamurugan, 2020; Son & Kim, 2008). As a result, data security, privacy and trustworthiness are critical (Fox & James, 2021; Mendelson & Wolf, 2017; Thapa & Camtepe, 2021; Townsend & Bennett, 2003).

Grounded Theory and Employee Experience

A grounded theory method is particularly beneficial in explaining the phenomenon and producing a description that is context-based (Orlikowski, 1993). It takes into account previously unrecognized organizational activity. The study's focus on healthcare information and on comprehending privacy problems within healthcare necessitates a qualitative method based on grounded theory (Foley and Timonen, 2015). Quantitative studies have shown that frontline healthcare workers who serve COVID-19 patients are more susceptible to mental stress, anxiety, and depression, and have encountered extra problems while working in a new setting (Mehrdad *et al.*, 2021). Healthcare employees' experiences were described as having faith in advanced monitoring systems, seeking system convenience of use, and being aware of their own performance. As a result, the fundamental category of learning to engage with new advanced technology emerged, which was characterized as the primary method for leveraging E- monitoring sys-

Table 1. Description of the data collection for the study

		Number (Responses)	Percentage (%)
Gender	Male Female	26 23	53 46
Age	20-25 26-30 31-35 36-40 Above 40	6 5 13 20 5	12 10 26 40 10
Work experience	<5 5-10 >10	5 17 27	10 35 55
Job positions	Hospital Emergency Services Physicians Hospital Managers Nurses	13 11 14 11	26 22 28 22
Mode of interview	In-person interview Telephonic interview	18 31	37 63

tems in clinical set-up (Alsunaidi et al., 2021; Granqvist et al., 2021).In the past two decades research in information security has emerged as a well-established area in the Information system literature (Appari & Johnson, 2010).The goal of this work is to provide a plausible response by utilizing grounded theory's ability to analyse complicated phenomena by gradually integrating qualitative evidence.

MATERIALS AND METHODS

The research collected data from healthcare personnel using a semi-structured interview style. The study's objective was to ascertain healthcare personnel's perceptions of privacy concerns regarding patient information. The study used a grounded theory approach as it focuses on social processes and interactions (Madlen et al., 2022). Grounded theory is ideally suited to the present study since it aims to collect respondents' experiences and generate thorough explanations through theory building. It is effective for gaining insight into the previously undiscovered area since it allows researchers to evaluate areas from various perspectives (Granqvist et al., 2021). According to Martin & Turner (1986), the grounded theory implies an ongoing and appropriate interaction between data gathering and interpretation. NVIVO 12 software was used for data analysis. Cluster analysis was used to display the pattern among transcripts that share comparable words, properties, values, or node-coded similarities. It includes a schematic of graphical representations of sources and nodes to make comparisons and distinctions simple. The nodes that show close together in the cluster analysis diagram are more similar to those that appear far away (Mabrouk et al., 2016). Table 1 contains a summary of the data obtained.

Semi-structured and telephonic interviews continued till the saturation point was reached. Sample size consideration in qualitative research is adequately relative in nature of judging a sample, the size of the sample should not be very small that it becomes unachievable to reach its impregnation, at the same time it should not be too large that is difficult to undertake a detailed analysis (Sandelowski, 1995). Data were collected through interviews, out of 49 respondents involved,31 were over the telephone and 18 in person-over a period of five months periods lasting from Dec to May 2021. Due to covid-19 emergency, only few interviews took place in person. the remaining ones were conducted via-telephonic. According to Holt et al., (2007) use of telephonic interview can be considered as an alternative to face to face interviews. Therefore, in the present study face to face and telephonic interview both was conducted for data collection.

After then, all of the respondents' interviews were transcribed and examined. During the process of the interview, the following interview questions were evaluated to achieve the study's major goal:

1. What are the privacy and security concerns of healthcare employees during the Covid-19 pandemic?
2. What will be the role of digital health technology in privacy and security in a healthcare setting?

RESULTS

A word cloud was created using transcripts of respondents' interviews, which were then transcribed into written order for cluster analysis. When dealing with verbal data, such as an interview, the material must be transcribed into written form for analysis (Braun and Clarke, 2006). In Figure 1, text mining findings indicate health care personnel' perspectives and experiences about privacy problems during the first wave of the COVID-19, which may be interpreted as technological and physical protections, patient information, and resources that may be subject to privacy concerns. It is clear that the bulk of healthcare professionals operating during the pandemic period had access to encryptions and audit controls, posing a significant privacy risk. Perceived privacy in general, refers to the perception regarding individual identical information on the communications network, it arises when individuals lack confidence in the proper functioning of technology. Protection of data ultimately relies on organizations and employees as individuals who deal with personal data. Healthcare employees are unsure about their responsibilities in protecting the information of patients and privacy while yet obeying supervisory directions and providing adequate medical treatment. In terms of human life, inaccurate patient data can lead to poor medical practitioner, and nurse performance, while legal ramifications threaten to deplete organizational resources. However, the preceding findings show that healthcare employees are unconcerned about organizational practices involving the gathering of patient data. Rather, substantial concern is given to the reliability of medical records of patients and the extent to which information of patients is used without authorization.

The thematic analysis was conducted using the autocode feature of Nvivo software. To have better results both text mining and content analysis was deployed, so that thematic analysis result become more evident from the interview transcripts. Thematic analysis of both research questions revealed definitive themes connected to perceived privacy and changing nature of work environment. Only those themes were included in the final results which were having more than two frequencies. The themes were categorized as healthcare professional privacy (14%) and information transparency (12%), this signifies that healthcare professionals need to safeguard the privacy of each person's health records, including their insurance data, private information, and other medical records. This also establishes limitations how patient information may be used or disclosed to third parties. Third and fourth dominant themes identified was working environment (16%) and change management (6%) which reveals that the working environment conditions for healthcare professionals has changed with an excessive workload, lack of resources, major gap in interaction among co-workers, and patients' admission to hospitals. The change

Figure 1. Word cloud based on respondent's interview transcripts

working environment has a negative impact on well-being of healthcare professionals. Thereafter technological and physical protection (3%) also identified as theme.

Table 2. Themes identified for research questions (RQ1, RQ2)

S.No.	Themes	Frequency	Percentage
1.1	Healthcare Professional privacy	23	14
1.2	Information transparency	20	12
1.3	Working environment	16	10
1.4	Change management	10	6
1.5	Technological and physical protection	6	3

To uncover more patterns in the data derived from interview transcripts, the Pearson coefficient was used to build hierarchical clustering, as seen in Figure 2. This kind of diagram is commonly used in data mining, pattern analysis, and machine learning (Shahzad, 2020). The labelled clades of the dendrogram cluster in figure 2 represent various patterns of known information based on healthcare employees' perceptions and experiences regarding privacy concerns, which can be summarised as "privacy issues confronting healthcare employees at various levels and having a significant negative impact," and "degree of resources available to mitigate privacy issues in technical processes." Additionally, the discovery of hierarchical dendrogram clades demonstrates a focus on building privacy measures to prevent privacy concerns. The text-mining results indicate that the majority of respondents are concerned about various protections, technological, physical, and human, as well as sufficient privacy education in the healthcare business, which may assist staff in preventing privacy breaches. In the wake of the Covid-19 pandemic outbreak, it is critical to consider ways to incorporate emerging technologies like blockchain to ensure data privacy and security and it also provides appropriate tools for assessment, testing, screening, and control of patients' information (Torky & Hassanien, 2020).

Healthcare managers could revise disclosure policies to adopt appropriate solutions for data disclosure, if they have field level awareness of operational performance of information disclosure technologies (Appari & Johnson, 2010; Hussein et al., 2020; Q. Wang et al., 2021).New information communication technologies (ICT) such as Internet of things, Artificial intelligence, Big data, Cloud computing, and blockchain technology play a critical role in facilitating environmental preservation and improvement They are critical in alleviating Covid-19 pandemic related difficulties because of their capabilities for widespread health services (Kaur et al., 2018; Talal et al., 2019; Zaidan et al., 2020). Furthermore, a considerable security and privacy challenge associated with the effective and diverse deployment of resources. Traditional information technology security and privacy solutions are incompatible with the Internet of things. To overcome current vulnerabilities, numerous access points can be used(Pacheco & Hariri, 2016).

DISCUSSIONS AND CONCLUSIONS

The research adds to the growing body of knowledge on the critical significance of privacy and security concerns in healthcare data settings. The study's findings shed some insight on the reasons for various privacy and security breaches from the viewpoint of healthcare employees. Additionally, the conclusion implies that enterprises will need to upgrade and adapt current processes to battle ongoing cyber-attacks and threats in order to retain privacy and security. The future work will examine employee engagement in the formulation of a clear strategy for enhancing and adapting privacy policies and awareness among healthcare employees, which will contribute to the development of a strategic plan for a future health crisis, based on the premise that healthcare organizations facing privacy and security challenges today are not an anomaly but a new reality. Managers must influence the privacy beliefs of employees specifically those who have daily access to sensitive data of patients, to build a privacy culture within the healthcare organization. Recognizing these points of view will serve as a foundation for training staff and implementing a privacy policy in the organization. The coronavirus pandemic (Covid-19) cause enormous hurdles to the worldwide healthcare community. Digital health structure and set-up are well adapted to offer innovative solutions to this crisis. It consists of tools like novel diagnostic tools, robust surveillance system, tracking devices for physiological parameters, telehealth, and other chat services for information disseminations related to Covid -19. Electronic healthcare systems is becoming an increasingly important aspect of day to day living environment, with advantages over traditional paper based system. Privacy and security is the top most hurdle to e-healthcare implementation. To improve privacy and security systems, healthcare professionals must focus on upgrading their Internet of things (IoT) infrastructure. Attention should be given to employees for understanding the use of IoT in general, and think about ways to improve and maintain their privacy clients. Resolving privacy problems would increase future mobility, speed of deployment, and adoption of digital initiatives. Different countries can use or modify the substantial technology breakthroughs and lessons learnt to ensure preparedness for future pandemics.

Additionally, this research has significant drawbacks. To begin, the research surveyed a small sample of healthcare personnel. Second, owing to the greater infection dissemination rates associated with the number of COVID-19 cases, data collection from hospital staff was difficult. To circumvent these

Figure 2. Dendrogram of discovered employees' experiences during COVID-19 on privacy concerns

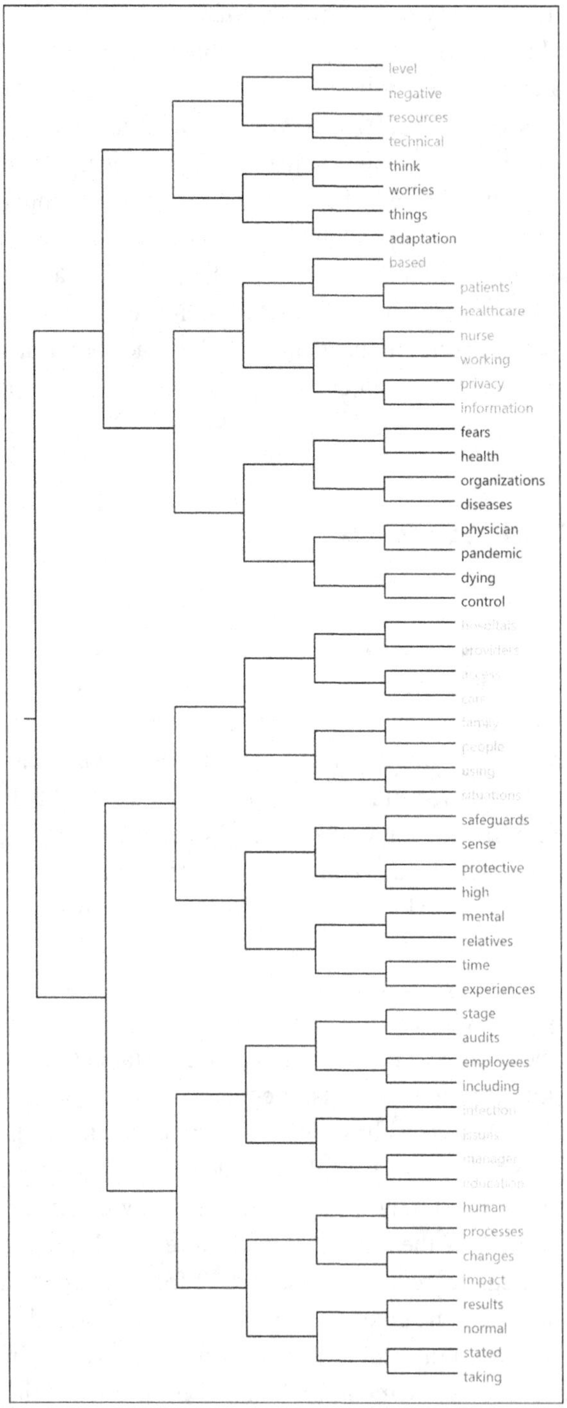

constraints, future research may examine the privacy and security concerns of healthcare practitioners using a larger sample size. In general, there is a dearth of research in this field. We recommend more research on other frontline healthcare professionals throughout the pandemic period. Finally, the most important issue in healthcare systems is that they should concentrate on training to promote acceptance and improvement of digital health platforms. This work adds to the body of information privacy and telehealth in general, and to the knowledge of the application of digital health platform settings.

REFERENCES

Alhasan, A., Audah, L., Ibrahim, I., Al-Sharaa, A., Al-Ogaili, A. S., & Mohammed, M. J. (2020). A case-study to examine doctors' intentions to use IoT healthcare devices in Iraq during COVID-19 pandemic. *International Journal of Pervasive Computing and Communications*. Advance online publication. doi:10.1108/IJPCC-10-2020-0175

Alraja, M. N., Farooque, M. M. J., & Khashab, B. (2019). The Effect of Security, Privacy, Familiarity, and Trust on Users' Attitudes Toward the Use of the IoT-Based Healthcare: The Mediation Role of Risk Perception. *IEEE Access: Practical Innovations, Open Solutions*, *7*, 111341–111354. doi:10.1109/ACCESS.2019.2904006

Alshalali, T., Mbale, K., & Josyula, D. (2018). Security and privacy of electronic health records sharing using hyperledger fabric. *Proceedings - 2018 International Conference on Computational Science and Computational Intelligence, CSCI 2018*, 760–763. 10.1109/CSCI46756.2018.00152

Alsunaidi, S. J., Almuhaideb, A. M., Ibrahim, N. M., Shaikh, F. S., Alqudaihi, K. S., Alhaidari, F. A., Khan, I. U., Aslam, N., & Alshahrani, M. S. (2021). Applications of big data analytics to control covid-19 pandemic. *Sensors (Basel)*, *21*(7), 2282. Advance online publication. doi:10.339021072282 PMID:33805218

Appari, A., & Johnson, M. E. (2010). Information security and privacy in healthcare: Current state of research. *International Journal of Internet and Enterprise Management*, *6*(4), 279. doi:10.1504/IJIEM.2010.035624

Ardebili, Naserbakht, Bernstein, Alazmani-Noodeh, & Hakimi. (2021). Healthcare providers experience of working during the COVID-19 pandemic: A qualitative study. *American Journal of Infection Control, 49*, 547–554. chrome-extension://dagcmkpagjlhakfdhnbomgmjdpkdklff/enhanced-reader.html?pdf=https%3A%2F%2Fbrxt.mendeley.com%2Fdocument%2Fcontent%2Ffde9dc97-e038-3a64-999b-8fdf1699a4b0%0Amoz-extension://49275573-6aab-4b60-a5da-2b3c5083f8bb/enhanced-reader.html?openApp&pd

Aultman, J. M., & Dean, E. (2014). Beyond privacy: Benefits and burdens of e-health technologies in primary care. *The Journal of Clinical Ethics*, *25*(1), 50–64. PMID:24779319

Bouabida, K., Malas, K., Talbot, A., Desrosiers, M.-È., Lavoie, F., Lebouché, B., Taghizadeh, N., Normandin, L., Vialaron, C., Fortin, O., Lessard, D., & Pomey, M.-P. (2022). Healthcare Professional Perspectives on the Use of Remote Patient-Monitoring Platforms during the COVID-19 Pandemic: A Cross-Sectional Study. *Journal of Personalized Medicine*, *12*(4), 529. doi:10.3390/jpm12040529 PMID:35455645

Bratianu, C. (2020). Toward understanding the complexity of the COVID-19 crisis: A grounded theory approach. *Management and Marketing*, *15*(s1), 410–423. doi:10.2478/mmcks-2020-0024

Chen, J., Xu, Y., Ping, W., & Tan, B. C. Y. (2009). Am i afraid of my peers? understanding the antecedents of information privacy concerns in the online social context. *ICIS 2009 Proceedings - Thirtieth International Conference on Information Systems.*

Chenthara, S., Ahmed, K., Wang, H., Whittaker, F., & Chen, Z. (2020). Healthchain: A novel framework on privacy preservation of electronic health records using blockchain technology. In PLoS ONE (Vol. 15, Issue 12 December). doi:10.1371/journal.pone.0243043

Chung, W., & Hershey, L. (2012). Enhancing Information Privacy and Data Sharing in a Healthcare IT Firm: The Case of Ricerro Communications. *Journal of Information Privacy and Security*, *8*(4), 56–78. doi:10.1080/15536548.2012.10845666

Cresswell, K., Williams, R., & Sheikh, A. (2021). Using cloud technology in health care during the COVID-19 pandemic. In The Lancet Digital Health (Vol. 3, Issue 1, pp. e4–e5). doi:10.1016/S2589-7500(20)30291-0

Dagher, G. G., Mohler, J., Milojkovic, M., & Marella, P. B. (2018). Ancile: Privacy-preserving framework for access control and interoperability of electronic health records using blockchain technology. *Sustainable Cities and Society, 39*(December), 283–297. doi:10.1016/j.scs.2018.02.014

De Witte, N. A. J., Carlbring, P., Etzelmueller, A., Nordgreen, T., Karekla, M., Haddouk, L., Belmont, A., Øverland, S., Abi-Habib, R., Bernaerts, S., Brugnera, A., Compare, A., Duque, A., Ebert, D. D., Eimontas, J., Kassianos, A. P., Salgado, J., Schwerdtfeger, A., Tohme, P., ... Van Daele, T. (2021). Online consultations in mental healthcare during the COVID-19 outbreak: An international survey study on professionals' motivations and perceived barriers. *Internet Interventions: the Application of Information Technology in Mental and Behavioural Health*, *25*(May), 100405. Advance online publication. doi:10.1016/j.invent.2021.100405 PMID:34401365

Dehling, T., & Sunyaev, A. (2014). Information security and privacy of patient-centered health IT services: What needs to be done? *Proceedings of the Annual Hawaii International Conference on System Sciences*, 2984–2993. 10.1109/HICSS.2014.371

Dopelt, K., Bashkin, O., Davidovitch, N., & Asna, N. (2021). Facing the unknown: Healthcare workers' concerns, experiences, and burnout during the covid-19 pandemic— a mixed-methods study in an israeli hospital. *Sustainability (Switzerland)*, *13*(16), 9021. Advance online publication. doi:10.3390u13169021

Earp, J. B., & Payton, F. C. (2006). Information privacy in the service sector: An exploratory study of health care and banking professionals. *Journal of Organizational Computing and Electronic Commerce*, *16*(2), 105–122. doi:10.120715327744joce1602_2

Eftekhar Ardebili, M., Naserbakht, M., Bernstein, C., Alazmani-Noodeh, F., Hakimi, H., & Ranjbar, H. (2021). Healthcare providers experience of working during the COVID-19 pandemic: A qualitative study. *American Journal of Infection Control*, *49*(5), 547–554. doi:10.1016/j.ajic.2020.10.001 PMID:33031864

El-Sherif, D. M., Abouzid, M., Elzarif, M. T., Ahmed, A. A., Albakri, A., & Alshehri, M. M. (2022). Telehealth and Artificial Intelligence Insights into Healthcare during the COVID-19 Pandemic. *Healthcare (Switzerland)*, *10*(2), 1–15. doi:10.3390/healthcare10020385 PMID:35206998

Ermakova, T., Fabian, B., Kelkel, S., Wolff, T., & Zarnekow, R. (2015). Antecedents of health information privacy concerns. *Procedia Computer Science, 63*(Icth), 376–383. doi:10.1016/j.procs.2015.08.356

Ermakova, T., Fabian, B., & Zarnekow, R. (2013). Security and privacy system requirements for adopting cloud computing in healthcare data sharing scenarios. *19th Americas Conference on Information Systems, AMCIS 2013 - Hyperconnected World: Anything, Anywhere, Anytime, 4*, 2937–2945.

Fox, G., & James, T. L. (2021). Toward an Understanding of the Antecedents to Health Information Privacy Concern: A Mixed Methods Study. *Information Systems Frontiers*, *23*(6), 1537–1562. doi:10.100710796-020-10053-0

Fusco, A., Dicuonzo, G., Dell'atti, V., & Tatullo, M. (2020). Blockchain in healthcare: Insights on COVID-19. *International Journal of Environmental Research and Public Health*, *17*(19), 1–12. doi:10.3390/ijerph17197167 PMID:33007951

Gerke, S., Shachar, C., Chai, P. R., & Cohen, I. G. (2020). Regulatory, safety, and privacy concerns of home monitoring technologies during COVID-19. *Nature Medicine*, *26*(8), 1176–1182. doi:10.103841591-020-0994-1 PMID:32770164

Granqvist, K., Ahlstrom, L., Karlsson, J., Lytsy, B., & Andersson, A. E. (2021). Learning to interact with new technology: Health care workers' experiences of using a monitoring system for assessing hand hygiene – a grounded theory study. *American Journal of Infection Control, 000*, 1–6. doi:10.1016/j.ajic.2021.09.023 PMID:34610392

Gupta, S., Xu, H., & Zhang, X. (2011). Balancing privacy concerns in the adoption of Location-Based Services: An empirical analysis. *International Journal of Electronic Business*, *9*(1/2), 118. doi:10.1504/IJEB.2011.040358

Hall, J. L., & Mcgraw, D. (2014). For telehealth to succeed, privacy and security risks must be identified and addressed. *Health Affairs*, *33*(2), 216–221. doi:10.1377/hlthaff.2013.0997 PMID:24493763

Harman, L. B., Flite, C. A., & Bond, K. (2012). State of the Art and Science Electronic Health Records: Privacy, Confidentiality, and Security. *American Medical Association Journal of Ethics, 14*(9), 712–719.

Haverinen, J., Keränen, N., Falkenbach, P., Maijala, A., Kolehmainen, T., & Reponen, J. (2019). Digi-HTA: Health technology assessment framework for digital healthcare services. *Finnish Journal of EHealth and EWelfare, 11*(4), 326–341. doi:10.23996/fjhw.82538

Hoffman, S., & Podgurski, A. (2012). Balancing Privacy, Autonomy, and Scientific Needs In Electronic Health Records Research. *SMU Law Review, 65*(1), 85–144.

Hussein, M. R., Apu, E. H., Shahabuddin, S., Shams, A. B., & Kabir, R. (2020). *Overview of digital health surveillance system during COVID-19 pandemic: public health issues and misapprehensions*. https://arxiv.org/abs/2007.13633

Jääskelä, J., Haverinen, J., Kaksonen, R., Reponen, J., Halunen, K., & Tokola, T. (n.d.). *Digi-HTA, assessment framework for digital healthcare services: Information security and data protection in health technology – initial experiences*. Academic Press.

Kaiser, F. K., Wiens, M., & Schultmann, F. (2021). Use of digital healthcare solutions for care delivery during a pandemic-chances and (cyber) risks referring to the example of the COVID-19 pandemic. *Health and Technology*, *11*(5), 1125–1137. doi:10.100712553-021-00541-x PMID:33875933

Kalla, A., Hewa, T., Mishra, R. A., Ylianttila, M., & Liyanage, M. (2020). The Role of Blockchain to Fight against COVID-19. *IEEE Engineering Management Review*, *48*(3), 85–96. doi:10.1109/EMR.2020.3014052

Kaplan, B. (2016). How Should Health Data Be Used? Privacy, Secondary Use, and Big Data Sales. *Cambridge Quarterly of Healthcare Ethics*, *25*(2), 312–329. doi:10.1017/S0963180115000614 PMID:26957456

Kapoor, A., Guha, S., Kanti Das, M., Goswami, K. C., & Yadav, R. (2020). Digital healthcare: The only solution for better healthcare during COVID-19 pandemic? *Indian Heart Journal*, *72*(2), 61–64. doi:10.1016/j.ihj.2020.04.001 PMID:32534691

Kaur, H., Alam, M. A., Jameel, R., Mourya, A. K., & Chang, V. (2018). A Proposed Solution and Future Direction for Blockchain-Based Heterogeneous Medicare Data in Cloud Environment. *Journal of Medical Systems*, *42*(8), 156. Advance online publication. doi:10.100710916-018-1007-5 PMID:29987560

Keshta, I., & Odeh, A. (2021). Security and privacy of electronic health records: Concerns and challenges. *Egyptian Informatics Journal*, *22*(2), 177–183. doi:10.1016/j.eij.2020.07.003

Khan, N. A., Brohi, S. N., & Zaman, N. (2020). Ten Deadly Cyber Security Threats Amid COVID-19 Pandemic. TechRxiv *Powered by IEEE,* 1–6. https://www.techrxiv.org/articles/Ten_Deadly_Cyber_Security_Threats_Amid_COVID-19_Pandemic/12278792

Lenert, L., & McSwain, B. Y. (2020). Balancing health privacy, health information exchange, and research in the context of the COVID-19 pandemic. *Journal of the American Medical Informatics Association: JAMIA*, *27*(6), 963–966. doi:10.1093/jamia/ocaa039 PMID:32232432

Li, T. (2020). Privacy in Pandemic: Law, Technology, and Public Health in the COVID-19 Crisis. SSRN *Electronic Journal, 52*(3). doi:10.2139/ssrn.3690004

Liu, Q., Luo, D., Haase, J. E., Guo, Q., Wang, X. Q., Liu, S., Xia, L., Liu, Z., Yang, J., & Yang, B. X. (2020). The experiences of health-care providers during the COVID-19 crisis in China: A qualitative study. *The Lancet. Global Health*, *8*(6), e790–e798. doi:10.1016/S2214-109X(20)30204-7 PMID:32573443

Lorenzen-Huber, L., Boutain, M., Camp, L. J., Shankar, K., & Connelly, K. H. (2011). Privacy, Technology, and Aging: A Proposed Framework. *Ageing International*, *36*(2), 232–252. doi:10.100712126-010-9083-y

Mabrouk, M., Rajan, S., Bolic, M., Forouzanfar, M., Dajani, H. R., & Batkin, I. (2016). Human Breathing Rate Estimation from Radar Returns Using Harmonically Related Filters. *Journal of Sensors*, *2016*, 1–7. Advance online publication. doi:10.1155/2016/9891852

Madlen, H., Drewitz, K. P., Piel, J., Hrudey, I., Rohr, M., Brunnthaler, V., Hasenpusch, C., Ulrich, A., Otto, N., Brandstetter, S., & Apfelbacher, C. (2022). *Intensive Care Units Healthcare Professionals ' Experiences and Negotiations at the Beginning of the COVID-19 Pandemic in Germany : A Grounded Theory Study.* doi:10.1177/00469580221081059

Mahoney, M. F. (2020). Telehealth, telemedicine, and related technologic platforms: Current practice and response to the Covid-19 pandemic. *Journal of Wound, Ostomy, and Continence Nursing*, *47*(5), 439–444. doi:10.1097/WON.0000000000000694 PMID:32970029

Martin, P. Y., & Turner, B. A. (1986). Grounded Theory and Organizational Research. *The Journal of Applied Behavioral Science*, *22*(2), 141–157. doi:10.1177/002188638602200207

Mason, P., & Williams, B. (2020). Does IRS Monitoring Deter Managers From Committing Accounting Fraud? *Journal of Accounting, Auditing & Finance*. Advance online publication. doi:10.1177/0148558X20939720

Meingast, M., Roosta, T., & Sastry, S. (2006). Security and privacy issues with health care information technology. *Annual International Conference of the IEEE Engineering in Medicine and Biology - Proceedings*, 5453–5458. 10.1109/IEMBS.2006.260060

Mendelson, D., & Wolf, G. (2017). Health privacy and confidentiality. *Tensions and Traumas in Health Law*.

Miller, A. R., & Tucker, C. (2009). Privacy protection and technology diffusion: The case of electronic medical records. *Management Science*, *55*(7), 1077–1093. doi:10.1287/mnsc.1090.1014

Mohamed, N., & Ahmad, I. H. (2012). Information privacy concerns, antecedents and privacy measure use in social networking sites: Evidence from Malaysia. *Computers in Human Behavior*, *28*(6), 2366–2375. doi:10.1016/j.chb.2012.07.008

Nageshwaran, G., Harris, R. C., & El Guerche-Seblain, C. (2021). Review of the role of big data and digital technologies in controlling COVID-19 in Asia: Public health interest vs. privacy. *Digital Health*, *7*, 1–12. doi:10.1177/20552076211002953 PMID:33815815

Nguyen, D. C., Ding, M., Pathirana, P. N., & Seneviratne, A. (2021). Blockchain and AI-Based Solutions to Combat Coronavirus (COVID-19)-Like Epidemics: A Survey. *IEEE Access: Practical Innovations, Open Solutions*, *9*, 95730–95753. doi:10.1109/ACCESS.2021.3093633 PMID:34812398

Orlikowski, W. J. (1993). CASE tools as organizational change: Investigating incremental and radical changes in systems development. *MIS Quarterly: Management Information Systems*, *17*(3), 309–340. doi:10.2307/249774

Pacheco, J., & Hariri, S. (2016). IoT security framework for smart cyber infrastructures. *Proceedings - IEEE 1st International Workshops on Foundations and Applications of Self-Systems. FAS-W, 2016*, 242–247. doi:10.1109/FAS-W.2016.58

Park, Y. J., & Shin, D. (2020). Contextualizing privacy on health-related use of information technology. *Computers in Human Behavior, 105*(October), 106204. doi:10.1016/j.chb.2019.106204

Parks, R., Chu, C. H., Xu, H., & Adams, L. (2011). Understanding the drivers and outcomes of healthcare organizational privacy responses. *International Conference on Information Systems 2011, ICIS 2011*, *1*(2), 245–264.

Porambage, P., Ylianttila, M., Schmitt, C., Kumar, P., Gurtov, A., & Vasilakos, A. V. (2016). The Quest for Privacy in the Internet of Things. *IEEE Cloud Computing*, *3*(2), 36–45. doi:10.1109/MCC.2016.28

Rahim, F. A., Ismail, Z., & Samy, G. N. (2017). Healthcare employees' perception on information privacy concerns. *International Conference on Research and Innovation in Information Systems, ICRIIS, November 2013*, 3–8. 10.1109/ICRIIS.2017.8002498

Ray, P., & Wimalasiri, J. (2006). The need for technical solutions for maintaining the privacy of EHR. *Annual International Conference of the IEEE Engineering in Medicine and Biology - Proceedings*, 4686–4689. 10.1109/IEMBS.2006.260862

Reegu, F. A., Daud, S. M., Alam, S., & Shuaib, M. (2021). Blockchain-based Electronic Health Record System for efficient Covid-19 Pandemic Management. April, 1–5. doi:10.20944/preprints202104.0771.v1

Rindfleisch, T. (1997). Privacy, Information Technology, and Health Care. *Communications of the ACM, 40*(8), 92-100. http://delivery.acm.org.sheffield.idm.oclc.org/10.1145/260000/257896/p92-rindfleisch.pdf?ip=154.59.124.32&id=257896&acc=ACTIVE SERVICE&key=BF07A2EE685417C5.33526737E11CAFEF.4D4702B0C3E38B35.4D4702B0C3E38B35&__acm__=1558621514_ee4cff6b52d7ab91993c4

Rosenbaum, B. P. (2014). Radio frequency identification (RFID) in health care: Privacy and security concerns limiting adoption. *Journal of Medical Systems, 38*(3), 1–6. doi:10.100710916-014-0019-z PMID:24578170

Sahama, T., Simpson, L., & Lane, B. (2013). Security and Privacy in eHealth: Is it possible? *2013 IEEE 15th International Conference on E-Health Networking, Applications and Services, Healthcom 2013, Healthcom*, 249–253. 10.1109/HealthCom.2013.6720676

Salam, M. A., & Bajaba, S. (2021). The role of transformative healthcare technology on quality of life during the COVID-19 pandemic. *Journal of Enabling Technologies, 15*(2), 87–107. doi:10.1108/JET-12-2020-0054

Sandelowski, M. (1995). Sample size in qualitative research. *Research in Nursing & Health, 18*(2), 179–183.

Shahzad, M. A. (2020). NVIVO Based Text Mining on COVID-19 Studies: Precision Technologies and Smart Surveillance May Help to Discover, and Coup COVID-19 Transmogrify. SSRN *Electronic Journal*. doi:10.2139/ssrn.3623499

Sharma, T., Dyer, H. A., & Bashir, M. (2021). Enabling User-centered Privacy Controls for Mobile Applications: COVID-19 Perspective. *ACM Transactions on Internet Technology, 21*(1), 1–24. Advance online publication. doi:10.1145/3434777

Sharma, Y., & Balamurugan, B. (2020). Preserving the Privacy of Electronic Health Records using Blockchain. *Procedia Computer Science, 173*(2019), 171–180. doi:10.1016/j.procs.2020.06.021

Shi, S., He, D., Li, L., Kumar, N., Khan, M. K., & Choo, K. K. R. (2020). Applications of blockchain in ensuring the security and privacy of electronic health record systems: A survey. *Computers & Security, 97*, 101966. Advance online publication. doi:10.1016/j.cose.2020.101966 PMID:32834254

Siriwardhana, Y., Gür, G., Ylianttila, M., & Liyanage, M. (2021). The role of 5G for digital healthcare against COVID-19 pandemic: Opportunities and challenges. *ICT Express, 7*(2), 244–252. doi:10.1016/j.icte.2020.10.002

Solimini, R., Busardò, F. P., Gibelli, F., Sirignano, A., & Ricci, G. (2021). Ethical and legal challenges of telemedicine in the era of the covid-19 pandemic. *Medicina, 57*(12), 1–10. doi:10.3390/medicina57121314

Son, J. Y., & Kim, S. S. (2008). Internet users' information privacy-protective responses: A Taxonomy and a nomological model. *MIS Quarterly: Management Information Systems*, *32*(3), 503–529. doi:10.2307/25148854

Talal, M., Zaidan, A. A., Zaidan, B. B., Albahri, A. S., Alamoodi, A. H., Albahri, O. S., Alsalem, M. A., Lim, C. K., Tan, K. L., Shir, W. L., & Mohammed, K. I. (2019). Smart Home-based IoT for Real-time and Secure Remote Health Monitoring of Triage and Priority System using Body Sensors: Multi-driven Systematic Review. *Journal of Medical Systems*, *43*(3), 42. Advance online publication. doi:10.100710916-019-1158-z PMID:30648217

Thapa, C., & Camtepe, S. (2021). Precision health data: Requirements, challenges and existing techniques for data security and privacy. *Computers in Biology and Medicine, 129*(October), 104130. doi:10.1016/j.compbiomed.2020.104130

Torky, M., & Hassanien, A. E. (2020). *COVID-19 Blockchain Framework: Innovative Approach*. https://arxiv.org/abs/2004.06081

Townsend, A. M., & Bennett, J. T. (2003). Privacy, technology, and conflict: Emerging issues and action in workplace privacy. *Journal of Labor Research*, *24*(2), 195–205. doi:10.1007/BF02701789

Tsai, J. Y., Cranor, L., Egelman, S., & Acquisti, A. (2007). The effect of online privacy information on purchasing behavior: An experimental study. *ICIS 2007 Proceedings - Twenty Eighth International Conference on Information Systems, 22*(2), 254–268.

Valentino, L. A., Skinner, M. W., & Pipe, S. W. (2020). The role of telemedicine in the delivery of health care in the COVID-19 pandemic. *Haemophilia*, *26*(5), e230–e231. doi:10.1111/hae.14044 PMID:32397000

Vargo, D., Zhu, L., Benwell, B., & Yan, Z. (2021). Digital technology use during COVID-19 pandemic: A rapid review. *Human Behavior and Emerging Technologies*, *3*(1), 13–24. doi:10.1002/hbe2.242

Vayena, E., Haeusermann, T., Adjekum, A., & Blasimme, A. (2018). Digital health: Meeting the ethical and policy challenges. *Swiss Medical Weekly*, *148*(34), w14571. doi:10.4414mw.2018.14571 PMID:29376547

Ventrella, E. (2020). Privacy in emergency circumstances: data protection and the COVID-19 pandemic. *ERA Forum, 21*(3), 379–393. 10.100712027-020-00629-3

Viaene, S., & Dedene, G. (2004). Insurance Fraud: Issues and Challenges. *The Geneva Papers on Risk and Insurance. Issues and Practice*, *29*(2), 313–333. doi:10.1111/j.1468-0440.2004.00290.x

Wang, L., & Alexander, C. A. (2021). Cyber security during the COVID-19 pandemic. *AIMS Electronics and Electrical Engineering*, *5*(2), 146–157. doi:10.3934/electreng.2021008

Wang, Q., Su, M., Zhang, M., & Li, R. (2021). Integrating digital technologies and public health to fight covid-19 pandemic: Key technologies, applications, challenges and outlook of digital healthcare. *International Journal of Environmental Research and Public Health*, *18*(11), 6053. Advance online publication. doi:10.3390/ijerph18116053 PMID:34199831

Wilkowska, W., & Ziefle, M. (2011). Perception of privacy and security for acceptance of E-health technologies: Exploratory analysis for diverse user groups. *2011 5th International Conference on Pervasive Computing Technologies for Healthcare and Workshops, PervasiveHealth 2011*, 593–600. 10.4108/icst.pervasivehealth.2011.246027

Winston, T. G., Paul, S., & Iyer, L. (2016). A study of privacy and security concerns on doctors' and nurses' behavioral intentions to use RFID in hospitals. *Proceedings of the Annual Hawaii International Conference on System Sciences,* 3115–3123. 10.1109/HICSS.2016.392

World Health Organization. (2020). *Covid-19 situation reports-102*. https://www.who.int/docs/default-source/coronaviruse/situation-reports/20200501-covid-19-sitrep.pdf?sfvrsn=742f4a18_4

Wu, H., & Tsai, C. (2018). Toward Blockchains for Health-Care Systems. *IEEE Consumer Electronics Magazine*, *7*(july), 65–71. doi:10.1109/MCE.2018.2816306

Xing, Y., Li, Y., & Wang, F. K. (2021). How privacy concerns and cultural differences affect public opinion during the COVID-19 pandemic: A case study. *Aslib Journal of Information Management*, *73*(4), 517–542. doi:10.1108/AJIM-07-2020-0216

Xu, J., Xue, K., Li, S., Tian, H., Hong, J., Hong, P., & Yu, N. (2019). Healthchain: A Blockchain-Based Privacy Preserving Scheme for Large-Scale Health Data. *IEEE Internet of Things Journal*, *6*(5), 8770–8781. doi:10.1109/JIOT.2019.2923525

Zaidan, A. S. A. (2020). Role of biological Data Mining and MachineLearningTechniques in Detecting and Diagnosing the Novel Coronavirus (COVID-19): A Systematic Review. *Journal of Medical Systems*.

Chapter 12
A Visualization Dashboard for COVID-19 Tweets Sentiment Analysis

Devang Pathak
Vellore Institute of Technology, Chennai, India

Ishita Kumar
Vellore Institute of Technology, Chennai, India

Maheswari Raja
Centre for Smart Grid Technologies, Vellore Institute of Technology, Chennai, India

Carol Anne Hargreaves
https://orcid.org/0000-0002-5522-4058
National University of Singapore, Singapore

ABSTRACT

The COVID-19 pandemic has compelled the world to come to a standstill. Everyone including governments, researchers, organizations were caught off-guard. Social scientists and psychologists all try to understand the sentiment of the public so that they can help social organizations and governments to avert situations that ought to become worse if a negative sentiment persists among the commonality. With government-issued lockdowns in place during the pandemic, the public was mostly confined to their homes. So, the public started to share their status updates, discussions, photos, and videos over social media. Social media became the go-to place to obtain the public's sentiments and insights on the COVID-19 pandemic. This chapter introduces the utilization of the Twitter API to obtain tweets in real-time based on hashtags relating to the COVID-19 pandemic in order to gain insights on the sentiments of people at specific times. Each tweet received will be analyzed for emotional tone and sentiment. All data is stored in a Cloudant database.

DOI: 10.4018/978-1-6684-5250-9.ch012

INTRODUCTION

COVID-19 pandemic has been a mystery and something the world never saw coming and was unprepared for. COVID-19 is caused by SARS-CoV2 coronavirus. The most common symptoms include fever, cough, tiredness and loss of taste or smell. As COVID-19 was highly infectious and somewhat deadly, governments had to quickly develop policies to contain the spread of the disease. Further, COVID-19 was a new pandemic and governments, healthcare workers and people in general didn't know what to do. An absence of established literature and research about the coronavirus added to the confusion and fear of the people. There can be riots, displeasure towards government policies, or any other kind of chaos when the public is scared. So, researchers felt that there is a need to examine how people are reacting to the pandemic more closely. Internet changed how people connected with each other and how they expressed their views. Social media websites give people the power to instantly share their views with their online friends and family groups. During times of excitement or distress the majority of people share their comments about the pandemic, phots eating in a restaurant or watching their favorite team win online. Social media means a lot to people as it gives them the power to express what they feel without filter.

SOCIAL MEDIA BIOLOGY MECHANISM

It is important to understand how social media attracts an individual because this explains one revolving the system proposed towards a social media website is valid and is a credible source to rely on when it comes to understanding the reaction of people. The social media addiction is a real thing and not totally a behavioral issue. A big reason for this addiction is two chemicals produced by one's brain: dopamine and oxytocin. Dopamine is produced at the base of the brain by the neurons present in that region. Dopamine is a feel-nice neurotransmitter that is involved in reinforcement. That is why when a person uses social media, he/she tends to come back. This intense feeling of reward produced by dopamine leads to addiction. A research team headed Wilhelm Hofmann of Chicago University's Booth Business School found out that twitter was harder to resist than cigarettes and alcohol. Then comes the other chemical, Oxytocin which is released when you kiss or hug. Neuroscientist Paul Zak discovered that social media triggers the release of generosity-trust chemicals in the person's brains. When one use social media oxytocin levels can rise up to 13% which is almost similar to the levels, one may experience on their wedding day. So, it becomes hard to resist the feeling of wanting the social media more. As a result of this addiction, the researchers can leverage social media as a place to get myriad of data to analyze and understand the emotions of people at a particular instance of time.

SOCIAL MEDIA ADDICTION

Together with the very rapid digitalization in our age, the use of social media is increasing in our country and in the world (Ersöz & Kahraman, 2020; Singh et al., 2020). Scrolling through tweets, posts, and stories have become one of the most common activities among people over the past decade. Although social media is considered a new area of socialization and that this situation is an advantage (Savcı & Aysan, 2017), it is also reported that social media has a negative effect on interpersonal relationships (Çalışir, 2015), psychological health (Chen et al., 2020) and private life (Acılar & Mersin, 2015), increases the level of depression (Haand & Shuwang, 2020) and leads to social media addiction. In fact, for adolescent users, excessive use has been found to be associated with paranoid thoughts, phobic anxiety, and feelings of anger and hostility (Bilgin, 2018).

The majority of the audience using social media is harmless, but, there is always a small section of people that become heavily addicted to these social networking sites and are investing the majority of their time browsing through these apps. Researchers claim that 5 to 10% of Americans are highly addicted to social media. Social media addiction is a behavioural addiction that can be defined as being highly anxious about social media and having an uncontrollable urge to log on or use social media and spending so much of their time and energy on social media that they stop thinking about other main areas of their lives. Social media addiction is like any other substance addiction. It may include mood swings such as anxiety, depression, excitement, etc. The person may also feel withdrawal symptoms like feeling physically and emotionally uncomfortable and irritated when they stop using social media. They may also face relapse quickly and may return to their habit of excessive usage of social media.

In a study by Drahošová and Balca (2017) that investigated the advantages and disadvantages of using social media, 97.7% of participants said that the advantages of using social media were communication and information exchange, while 72.2% said that the biggest disadvantage was the dependence on internet Dopamine is a chemical released in the brain that induces feelings of delight, contentment, and encouragement. Dopamine is released when a person feels satisfied or gets a feeling of being rewarded. It is released when a person eats delicious food, has nice sex, gets money, or even wins a game. Consumption of substances like drugs, cigarettes, and alcohol, also increases dopamine levels in a person. Hence, these substances become addictive and it becomes very hard for a person to give them up. Low levels of dopamine can make a person feel low, with no motivation to carry on with their work., and can lead to psychological issues like depression, anxiety, psychosis, etc. Too much dopamine release can cause a person to feel hyperactive, angry, and lose impulse control. It can lead to ADHD, eating disorders, and addiction. One of the most important reasons for social media addiction is that the dopamine levels go high when people are subjected to the social environments on these sites. Researchers have found out that using social media have the same effect on the brain as gambling and consuming drugs. They also claim that social media usage is the same as injecting a syringe of dopamine-inducing drugs into the body. When people receive likes, comments, retweets, etc., their brain interprets it as a reward, which induces the same effect as using drugs like morphine.

A study by Harvard has shown that around 73% of people feel panicked and stressed when they are not around their phones. It claims that they are not necessarily addicted to their phones, but they are highly addicted to apps on their phones such as Facebook, Twitter, Instagram, Snapchat, etc. have shown that the usage of social media triggers the same part of the brain that is triggered when it is subjected to consuming an addictive substance. The brain interprets these rewards as a dopamine-inducing substance, which gives them positive reinforcement. When the phone rings with a notification from any social media platform, it makes people highly curious to know what that notification is. This causes a rush of dopamine and transmits a 'reward' pathway to the brain, causing the person to feel more pleasure. Social media platforms like Facebook, Snapchat, Twitter, and Instagram, give these constant feelings of 'rewards' with minimal effort. The brain of the consumer's brain trains itself to interpret likes, comments, retweets, and reactions to the posts as a positive emotion. The major reason why people feel these feelings of 'reward' is that they talk about themselves. People love to receive, likes, comments, and retweets on their posts. It gives a feeling of validation and satisfaction. In a face-to-face conversation, an average human being talks about them only 30 to 40% of the time; on these social media platforms they have the freedom to express and talk about themselves as much as they want. It is seen that on social media, 80% of the time people are expressing their views and sharing their own stories. Receiving positive responses to their stories and posts stimulates the brain to release high doses of dopamine.

The problem with social media usage comes when people start using these sites as their coping mechanisms to deal with stress, depression, and loneliness. They find an escape through their day-to-day problems, with posts, stories, and tweets. People start ignoring their real-life relationships, work duties, school assignments, and physical activities. The person starts feeling more mood swings. The overall productivity of a person goes down significantly. When start ignoring their life activities, and start overcoming their low moods through social media, they become highly dependent on these sites for their mental peace. It becomes their only support to deal with the negatives in their life. A digital detox happens when a person decides to reduce the usage of their electronic gadgets significantly and involve more in their real-life activities. Take simple steps like turning off notifications, and using social media for small amounts of time at varying intervals. People can also, turn on the do not disturb mode, while they work, which might help them gain more focus on their work, and increase their productivity. Taking such detox helps a person overcome their dependency on social media for pleasure and feelings of contentment.

Researchers have found out that there is an unquestionable relation between degrading mental health and low self-esteem (Hou et al., 2019). Using social media can be pleasurable at times but, excessive usage of these sites can increase a feeling of isolation and misery. People portray their best versions on social networking sites, a perfect lifestyle with high-paying jobs, healthy relationships, extreme good looks, etc. The posts are far from reality. But the person viewing them gets the feeling that the people around have perfect lives while they are dealing with hardships in their lives. Studies have proved that most social media users believe that the people around them have much better lives than them. People start comparing their flawed life with flawless, filtered, and edited versions of others, which results in a feeling of low self-worth and depression. The person viewing these posts constantly starts feeling conscious and unsatisfied with their life. This can also lead to social anxiety disorder.

The constant availability of social networks provides an opportunity for a significant increase in the possibilities of connecting, sharing and experiencing experiences with acquaintances and friends (Fuster et al., 2017). "FEAR OF MISSING OUT" or FOMO is a new term introduced in the year 1996, but gained popularity over the last decade. It is a fear of not being a part of any social events or missing out on any enjoyable activity (Gupta & Sharma, 2021). Przybylski et al. (2013) linked FoMO to self-determination theory (Deci & Ryan, 1985), stating that it stems from an individual's psychological needs such as autonomy, competence, and relatedness. FoMO is defined as "a pervasive fear that others may have rewarding experiences that one is missing" (Przybylski et al., 2013, p. 1841). This anxiety creates an environment for the individual to stay in touch and interact with their social environment so as not to miss anything (Oberst et al., 2017; Wiesner, 2017). The individual constantly desires to be informed about what others are doing here and there for fear of missing out on development (Przybylski et al., 2013). The more activities or situations a person can do, the less likely they are to choose the best option. This situation causes the person to question to what extent their own choice is the "best choice" (Milyavskaya et al., 2018). Consumers viewing posts and stories of their friends having a fun party to which they were not invited, or people going on trips which they couldn't go due to work or school, induces a fear that their friends will forget about them and that no one cares if they are present or not. This causes the person to self-isolate themselves. People can have this impulse urge to constantly scroll through social media to make sure that are not missing out on any fun activities. FOMO depreciates the mental well-being of the consumer to a great extent. The negative impact of FOMO can affect a person's real-life connections and academics.

The social networking sites like Instagram and Facebook show posts and advertisements specific to the user's interests and needs. Whenever a person looks up a product or a service online, they start receiving advertisements about those products all over these sites. The algorithm is designed in such a way to show the products that are required by that particular user. Every user receives different advertisements, as the needs of every consumer are different. These algorithms are developed to attract users to use their sites more and more, which will in turn increase their revenue significantly. A study was conducted on school children's mental health and the amount of time they spend on social media apps. The study concluded that around 27% of the children who were using social media for more than 3 to 4 hours per day, showed signs of poor mental health. Social media addiction is most dangerous for children and young adults, as their brain is still developing social skills. Researchers have said that teenagers who excessively use social media platforms have poor communication skills. Though people stay in touch on social media and may chat for several hours, conversion of these online chats may not happen in real life. Surveys have shown that people who use excessive social networking sites have extreme social anxiety, a higher rate of depression, low self-esteem, and a lower level of empathy towards their fellows. The continuous editing of selfies to get a perfect and flawless picture for social media destroys a person's self-confidence. People find it hard to accept themselves as they are and are in a constant practice of enhancing their face, hair, etc on the images they post, to get more likes and comments. People are in a constant battle to match the unrealistic high beauty standards f social media. The likes and comments end up giving people validation about themselves. If a person gets fewer likes or comments, they start feeling like they are not good enough and that people do not appreciate them. This creates a negative body image in the person's mind. Young adults even go to the lengths of attempting risky challenges trending on social media, just to impress their peers, and to get the feeling that they fit in and everyone around them likes them. Many such challenges have proved fatal for many people, yet, people take part in such trends to gain more followers.

Social media creates this competition for attention that may even lead to bullying. Social networking sites are misused and young adults can be subjected to name-calling, shaming, rumour-spreading, and even harassment. The majority of the group that ends up being a victim of these are young girls. Explicit photos and videos are taken of people without their consent and posted online to make fun of them or bully them. Cyberbullying cases have surged over the last decade. This type of abuse has led to an increased suicide rate among young adults. It not only harms the self-esteem of the person but also makes them extremely anxious in social groups.

SCIENCE BEHIND SENTIMENTS

Sentiments are not just a result of the person's direct experiences. When two neurons meet or interact there is a very small gap between them. In order to bridge this gap the electrical signal that travels along the axon of the neuron must convert into a chemical signal to bridge this gap. These chemicals are called as neurotransmitters. These are the chemical messengers that are responsible for the different responses to situations. A human's emotions depend on the varying levels of neurotransmitters, which cause different parts of brain to get activated resulting into different moods, or activate parts of brain that triggers the simulation of the nervous system. Emotions are caused by complex interactions in the brain. Every time a person tends to feel something, their whole body starts a physiological transition, a chemical release or what is called as behavioral responses. Here multiple processes work together, including the main organs, limbic system and neuro-transmitters. The limbic system is that part of the brain which is involved in the behavioral responses. The limbic system is also thought to have first evolved in mammals. It has a lot of ancient pathways that activates the sentiments in response to stimulus from external surrounding. These responses have evolved as a need for one to make decisions on the basis of those sentiments.

"Sentiment analysis or opinion mining is the computational study of people opinions, evaluations, attitudes, and emotions toward entities, individuals, issues, events, topics, and their attributes" (Liu & Zhang, 2012, p. 215). The word "sentiment" represents people's feelings, such as joy, sadness, anger, and the like. With the explosive popularity of social media leading to the need to quickly process huge volumes of data, e.g. from customer reviews, traditional methodologies are manual estimation of people's opinions on product topics of interest is increasingly being replaced by automated sentiment analysis (Liu, 2012). As a result, scholarship on computer methodology and practice

Sentiment analysis is in demand and showing rapid growth. For example, the work of Bakshi et al. (2016) on using tweet sentiment analysis to predict stock price changes has been cited more than 10,000 times.

THE PROCESS OF EMOTIONS

While people debate about the sequences, there is a general consensus that sentiments comprises of three parts: subjective experiences, physiological and behavioral responses.

1. **Subjective Experiences:** The seed for all sentiments are subjective experiences also termed as stimulus. Basic sentiments are expressed by everyone irrespective of their background, but the experiences that produces them can be very subjective. No matter how powerful the experience is, it can produce many sentiments in an individual.
2. **Physiological Response:** Everyone has experienced how it feels when the heart beats fast. This physiological change or response is the result of the nervous system's reaction to the subjective experiences. The autonomic nervous system which is a part of the peripheral nervous system is the one responsible for regulating physiological processes including blood pressure, sexual arousal, heart rate.
3. **Behavioral Responses:** This part accounts for actual expression of sentiments.

BACKGROUND AND MOTIVATION

There is a new generation of communication that has taken over the lives of people. People tend to now share everything over social media websites. The lives are becoming busier. People tend to live away from each other. They commute for hours and then work for majority of their day. This leaves one with very little or no time to communicate and have in person relationships with their closed ones. But humans have a tendency to live in a social world and surround itself with people. So, the need to socialize brings everyone to social media.

In cities on metros, buses or at home or in workplaces and public parks, one can see people of all ages- young and old, males or females- completely immersed in their mobile phones. The personal preferences may vary but all focus of a person is mostly on their digital devices with all their heart and mind. A social media website nowadays is used for a myriad of purposes. People use it to create social networks or connections with people whom they share mutual connection or similar interests with. Social Media has been a key catalyst in reshaping the communication and it has completely redefined the ways in which one communicate with others. Social media has kept people constantly engaged in different exciting and trending activities. People have accepted social media so heartily that it has now became an integral part of their daily lives. Everyone from common people to governments and organizations are using social media platforms for continuously engaging with public. Almost every house has a seamless and fast internet connection. It has become an important human need which satisfies the evolutionary need to connect. Through social media people can now connect and communicate with peers and mutual friends. Information and messages can be transferred instantly. Over the past two decades social networking have seen tremendous evolution and continues to grow. So, seeing the necessity of social media the authors saw this as a gateway to understand what people feel in different situations and how they react.

SENTIMENT ANALYSIS

Sentiment analysis or sometimes called as opinion mining, is the computational assessment of people's sentiments, emotions and opinions. It is extensively used in domains of data mining, web mining and text mining. But most importantly the increasing importance of sentiment analysis coincides with the growth of social media, such as Twitter, Reddit and Facebook. The basis of most of the work in this field is based on the sentiment lexicons. Sentiment lexicon is a collection of words also called as opinion words associated with their respective sentiment orientation. Sentiment orientation can be positive or negative. Some positive sentiment words are beautiful, wonderful and amazing. Similarly some negative words are distasteful and bad. Several lexicons of sentiments have been constructed. Most sentiment-analysis works focuses on English language text therefore most of the researches are in English.

The words sentiment, opinion, view and belief are used interchangeably but there are subtle differences between them, which are important to understand in order to make the computational analysis of sentiments more accurate and valid.

- **Opinion:** It is an inference that is open to dispute. This is because different experts may have different opinions.
- **View:** It is a subjective opinion.
- **Belief:** It is a thought one deliberately accepts or have an intellectual assent to.
- **Sentiment:** It is an opinion carrying what one feel.

LEXICON BASED APPROACHES

Lexicon based method use a sentiment dictionary that contains opinion words and then it uses this dictionary of words and match them with the data provided as input to determine its sentiment orientation or polarity. They assign a sentiment score to these words and describe how positive, negative and

Figure 1. A general lexicon-based approach flow

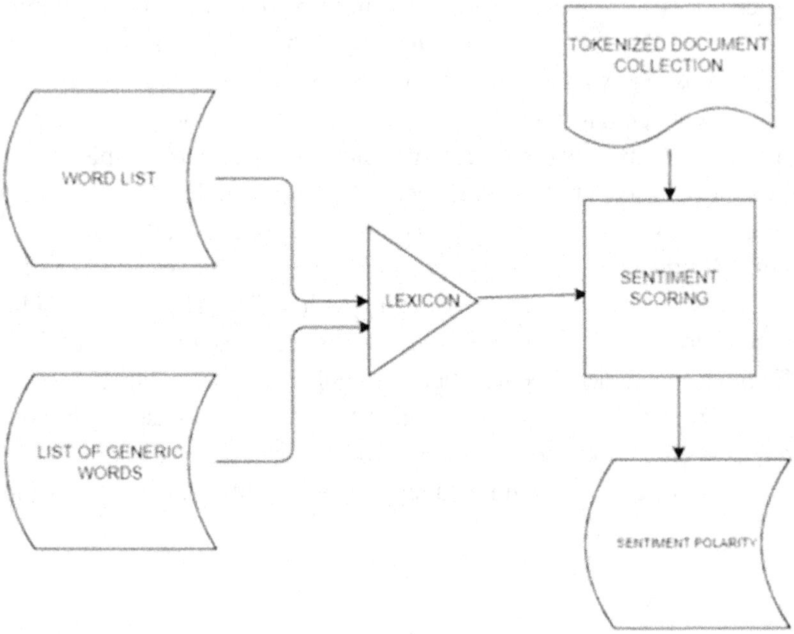

objective the words in the dictionary are. This approach is basically based on a sentiment lexicon. It is a collection of already known and precompiled terms denoting various sentiments developed for genres of communication as presented in figure 1.

There are two main sub categories of the Lexicon based approach:

1. Dictionary based: Here the terms are called seeds. This approach is based on the usage of terms which are collected manually. This set grows by searching for synonyms and antonyms of the words in the dictionary.
2. CORPUS BASED: This deals with a specific domain. Its objective is to provide dictionaries related to that domain. These dictionaries are generated from a set of terms or seed opinions and this set grows through the search of related words by using either semantic or statistical techniques.

SENTIMENT ANALYSIS TASKS

Sentiment analysis in itself is a complex task. It can be decomposed into following tasks:

1. Subjective Classification: This task involves classifying sentences based on whether they are opinionated or not opinionated. The problem that is solved here is to identify sentences used to represent subjectivity from the sentences which are used to present factual information in an objective manner.

2. Sentiment Classification: Once the sentences that carry certain kind of opinion are classified, now this task involved finding the polarity of those sentences i.e., whether it carries a positive or negative opinion. The classification can be binary or multi-class.
3. Complimentary tasks: This task depends on the application and is optional.
    a. Opinion Holder Extraction: It is about finding sources or opinion holders.
    b. Object /Feature Extraction: It is about finding the target entity.

LEVELS OF SENTIMENT ANALYSIS

The tasks mentioned in the previous heading can be performed at varying levels as shown in figure 2.

Figure 2. Different levels of Sentiment Analysis

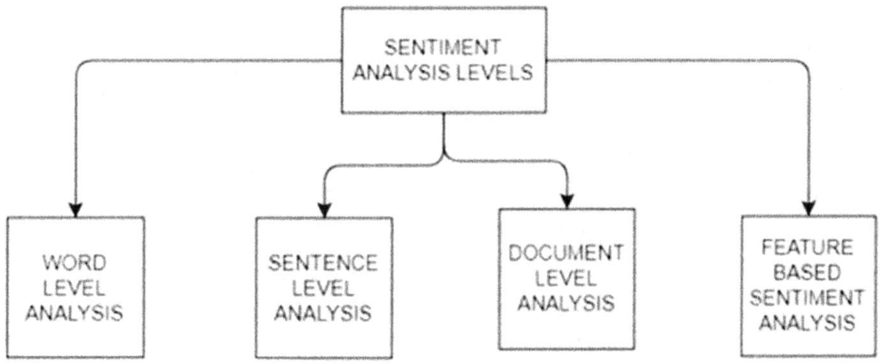

1. *Document Level*: In this level the authors have tagged entire document with a sentiment value. The whole document is classified into either positive or negative document. A general approach to do this is to find the polarities of individual words or sentences and combine them together to compute the polarity of the whole document.
2. *Sentence Level*: In this level of analysis, it deals with tagging an individual sentence with a sentiment polarity. It classifies sentences into positive, negative or neutral. A general approach for this kind of analysis is to calculate sentiment polarity for individual words and combine it to calculate polarity for the whole sentence and then tag that sentence with the calculated polarity.
3. *Feature Level*: It involves determination of two things. First, it computes the polarity of individual words and then it also identifies the entity towards which the sentiment is directed. It is majorly used for extracting features of a product from input data.
4. *Word Level*: This level of classification uses adjectives as features.

IMPORTANCE OF TRANSLATING FINDINGS INTO VISUAL CONTEXT

Representation of data through various graphs, charts, images, etc., is known as Data Visualization. It is used to communicate essential information via visuals and is a much faster way of expressing a detail without long texts. It may vary from simple hand-drawn flow charts or expertly designed interactive visual dashboards.

Sometimes reading about scientific research or a report with lots of data analysis and extensive descriptions becomes challenging for general people to understand and recognize. A graph or a simple pie chart might help people to understand the analysis in a much better way. It helps not only the common people but also, professionals to understand various data trends, which otherwise would be a tedious task. A visual presentation of data and information helps the experts to see the new patterns and analyse data in a better hassle freeway. There are extremely complicated information systems that produce large amounts of data that are being generated every second. It becomes very difficult to analyse such colossal amounts of data and use those insights for the research's benefit.

Visualizing data helps one understand data faster and in detail. It allows the person to make predictions based on the previous data trends. It allows the general public to see and understand the concepts much easier and in simple terms. Analysing the data patterns through graph helps the person understand the concept much better, which helps in making decisions simple. Watching graphs also gives the analysts a new viewpoint. The saying "A single picture can say a thousand words" holds when one talks about data and its presentation. Visuals captivate a person's attention way more than longs texts explaining data sets. They allow the message to be conveyed in a readable and understandable manner. As an example, a graph showing the rise and fall of COVID cases, helped experts to predict the next wave, and even the general public could understand when COVID was at its peak through these simple graphs. When a sales graph is made, the result might go positive or negative, which may help the analysts decipher the trend, and prevent the sales from going south.

As mentioned above, the visual representation of business trends helps in prediction. When people view these trends in such an easy and interactive form, they understand the concepts better. It also aids in analysing the prime reason for these trends, in the data sets. The experts can perform an analysis of their data, and prepare a detailed forecast of the opportunities or problems that they might come across. This way they can prepare beforehand with better knowledge and accuracy of the facts. Visualization helps in creating an interactive report, that allows investors and executives to have access to the reports of all departments at once. This way, they do not require to consult an IT expert to elaborate on the data. The analytics experts provide consultation in form of graphs and conclusions from the graphs. The entire company's data can be assembled and represented with comprehensible visuals. Decision-making is an important aspect of managing a company. It is always advised that decisions are data-driven, i.e., lead by solid data collected by the systems and interpreted through human intellect. Data analysis is made much simplified by visualization hence it enhances the decision-making process guided by data. Data visuals help in activating vision perceptive mechanisms that stimulate lateral thinking, that assist in making new points of view regarding the growth and development of the company. This way, data visualization plays a major role in contributing to data-driven innovation. Companies use data for more innovative progress regarding their products and services and new possibilities for development. The company collects data through different software that are identified via their high volume, variety, and constantly increasing variability and intricacy. Data visualizations help the brain to process large amounts of raw information and make solid conclusions out of them. Presenting the data in graphic form saves a lot of time. People could spend hours reading and interpreting long texts describing data and identifying the data trends. Visualizing makes this tedious job, much easier. It allows any person with no prior knowledge of the field to get insights into the data and what is happening in the field. As an executive, it is hard to know all the departments, but data visualization helps them understand the concepts much easier and make appropriate decisions for the company based on those reports. Data Visualization tools provide excellent analysis without much human interference. An adequate visual report is built upon the specific objectives and the purpose of the analysis in progress; the attributes of the viewers; and the communication targets according to which the report is made. The objectives of the analysis can be to evaluate the causes of stunt production growth. While the communication target depends upon how the public perceives the visual report presented to them. Data visualization also avoids incurring errors in evaluation. With advancements in data, visualization acts as a progressively demanded tool that helps in giving billions of data sets, some meaning. Visuals help in elaborating the contents and arranging data in a more comprehensible manner, which focuses on the trends and patterns. It helps in filtering out redundant data and brings out convenient information. Data analysis is a key skill that will be expected among the new generation that will enter the workforce soon. Companies are using data and data analysis more frequently to make decisions based on trends and to gain profits from the information gained through analysis. Visualization of details, facts, data, and inter-relations in a form of visual aid is a favourable approach as it allows everyone to understand the concepts. It provides professionals a key point of discussion for a brainstorming session about data trends, changes, solutions, and further enhancements.

Node-RED Visualizations

Node-red is a tool that helps users to display functions and inter-related processes with an interactive UI-Dashboard which helps in visualizing the accumulated and processed data.

Node-Red Provides the following graphs:

1. *Gauge chart*: Gauge charts are simple yet very extensive in use. It is also called a dial chart. It helps when there is a range of progressive data points that change periodically. They are extremely simple to use. It eradicates the probability of issues like parallax errors. These are user-friendly and are very understandable, and they do not require an expert to explain the chart. A variety of colours can be given and assigned to different values for a detailed presentation.
2. *Donut chart*: Donut charts are used to represent categorical data, with each section representing a category. By adding the number of categories and the number of data points for each category, one can create the donut chart.
3. *Compass chart*: It is a multi-directional gauge chart that uses animated routines to change the initial and final angles of the whole chart imitating a compass dial.
4. *Line chart*: It is also known as line plot or line chart. This graph connects discrete data points via lines. It is majorly used to present quantitative data points over a defined range of time. It consists of a horizontal axis (x-axis) and a vertical axis (y-axis). It depicts changes in values over a period of time.
5. *Bar chart*: Bar charts are used to visualize grouped data in the form of horizontal or vertical bars. The length of each bar represents the measure of data. They also have horizontal axis(x-axis) and vertical axis(y-axis). These are majorly used in data handling in statistics.

6. *Histogram*: Histograms are used to depict frequency distribution depicting how different values occur in a data set. It looks a lot like bar graph, but have key-differences. It is a continuous plotted graph that helps in analysing the process changes occurring in a period of time.
7. *Pie chart*: It is a circular statistical chart that shows the proportion of each part, as a slice of a pie. Pie charts express a part-to-whole relationship of data in form of a pie-shaped graph. The size of the slice shows the quantity of data points under it.

PROPOSED METHODOLOGY

Figure 3 illustrates the interconnection of various application components used in this work.

Figure 3. Proposed application components

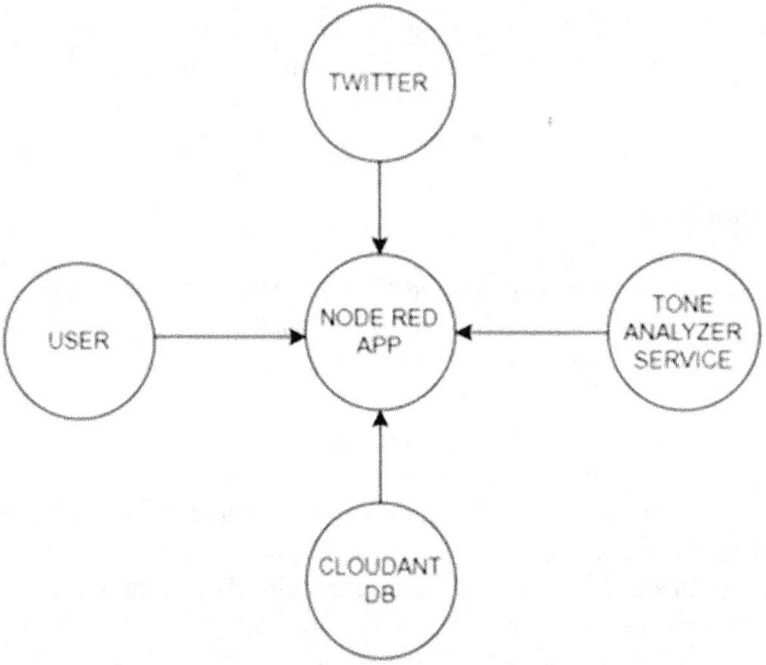

The authors have proposed to make a Dashboard to show the sentiment analysis of tweets by the public. The dashboard through use of gauges and charts will show pictorially what is the actual sentiment of the public? This work mainly focuses on people's sentiment towards the pandemic, understands the sentiments of people on government's decisions to extend the lockdown and possibility to predict riots against the government.

Application Components

1. Node-RED: Node-RED is a programming tool that helps wire together hardware devices, APIs and other online services in easy and interesting manner. It provides a browser-based flow-based editor which makes it very simple to wire the flow together using different kinds of nodes provided in a palette and can be deployed to the Node-Red's runtime in just a single click. JavaScript functions can be created inside the editor. Node-RED also provides a built-in library that allows the user to save useful functions or flows and also enables reusability. This run-time is built on Node.js, and takes complete advantage of its event-driven, non-blocking model. The flows that are created over Node-RED can be easily imported or exported using JSON.
2. Twitter API: This API allowed the authors to have a programmatic access to Twitter in several different ways. Thus, one can get access to Twitter and its endpoints and data.
3. Watson Studio: Watson Studio is one of the main services provided by IBM for Data as a Service. It provides an environment to solve business related problems by working with data. One can choose tools from a lot of options to analyze, cleanse, shape data and visualize data. It has a project which is basically a workspace where people can organize their resources and work with data. There can be three types of resources in the Project:
   § Collaborators: They are the stakeholders or people involved in the team working with the data.
   § Data Assets: These indicates the data that are either in the uploaded files or accessed by connecting to data sources of various types.
   § Operational Assets: These are the objects that the team creates, such as models, that would run the code to work with the data.
   § Tools: These are the software the team would use to work with the data.
4. Cloudant Database: It is a fully managed and distributed database developed by IBM and is optimized for a fast-growing world. It has an ability to elastically scale the storage and the database throughput.

HARDWARE/SOFTWARE DESIGN

The server application subscribes to a Twitter feed as configured by the user. Each tweet received will be analyzed for emotional tone and sentiment, all data is stored in a Cloudant database, with the opportunity to store historical data as well. The resulting analysis is presented in a Node-Red based Web UI as a series of graphs and charts. The flow of the application is as follows:

- Tweets are pushed out by Twitter based on Hashtag.
- The Watson Tone Analyzer Service /Sentiment node performs an analysis of sentiment and emotional tone.
- Tweets and metadata are stored in Cloudant database.
- The web UI displays charts and graphs.

Backend consisted of creating Twitter developers account and then get access to twitter API. Import twitter node in node-red and incorporate the API in TwitterIN node of Node Red using the specified twitter handle.

Table 1. Table contains description of all the nodes used in Node-RED for the development of the application

NODE NAME	FUNCTIONALITY
TwitterIn	This node can be used to search either: • The public or the user's personal stream for tweets containing configured search terms which are mostly hashtags. • All tweets by specific twitter handles • Direct messages by authenticated users
Debug	Debug node displays information passed onto it in the debug sidebar.
Function	Allows JavaScript node to be run against the messages that are input or passed through the node. The message is passed in form of an object called msg. By convention it will contain a msg. property which will hold the body of the message.
Delay	This node introduces a delay in the propagation of a message through a flow and to limit the rate of messages coming through the node.
Sentiment	Analyzes the sentiment of the tweets passed to it and attaches a sentiment score which is contained in the sentiment.score property and attaches it to the msg.
Switch	Switch node allows execution of one of the several possible paths depending on the rule that is specified in the node editor.
Cloudant out	Allows basic access to the Cloudant database. Allows operations like insert, delete, update and search for documents.
Text	Displays text messages in the UI dashboard.
Chart	Helps to create different types of visualizations in form of charts including line charts, bar charts, pie charts and polar area charts.
Gauge	Provides gauge shaped visualizations. The shapes can be of a Donut, Compass or a Level.

Front-end consisted of a fully functional real time dashboard the displayed the assigned polarity or tweet orientation

NODE-RED FLOW OF THE APPLICATION

Node-RED involves creation of a flow in its main editor. So, this flow consists of several nodes that help to form the application with bespoke JavaScript codes as well for different functionalities. The nodes used for the proposed system are mentioned in Table 1 and the Node-RED flows are presented in figure 4 and 5.

NODE-RED FLOW DESCRIPTION

The development of application consists of creating an IBM developer account and subscribe to necessary services the complete flow of the application is depicted in figure 6.

The development of application needs certain important services that has to be subscribed from the IBM account dashboard. The services that were subscribed to were as follows:

Figure 4. Twitter tweet processing and storage Node-RED flow

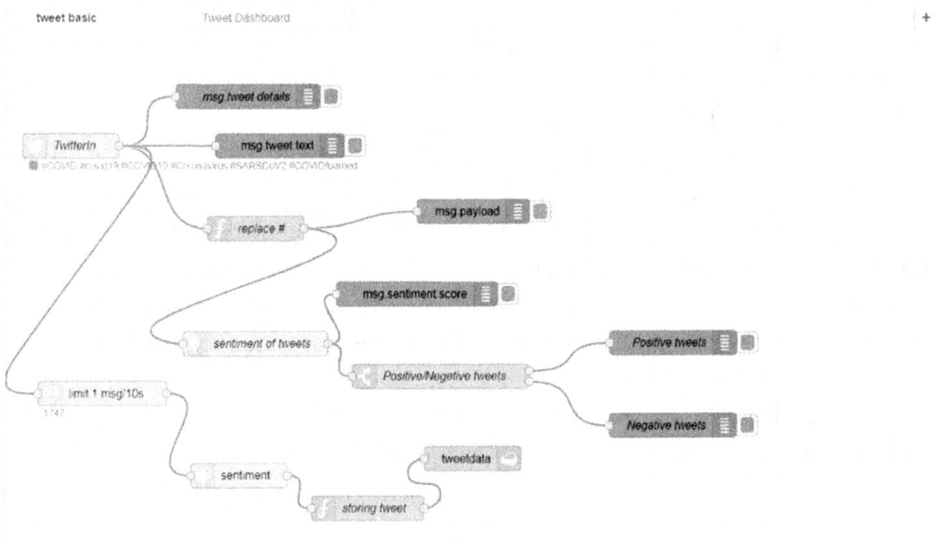

Figure 5. Twitter tweet processing and storage Node-RED flow

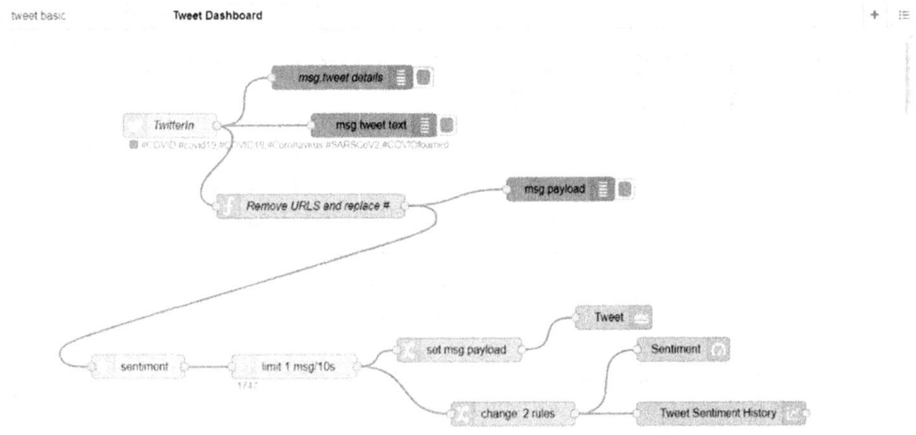

Figure 6. Block Diagram showing the Flow of the application

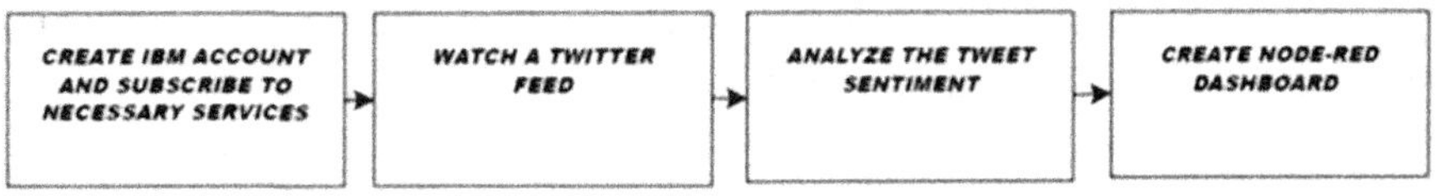

- Continues delivery service: This service includes open toolchains that helps to automate the deployment and building of applications. It allows instant startup just by simply creating a deployment toolchain that would support operational, deployment and development tasks.
- Language Translator service: This service allows translation of documents such as markup files that would be using XML or HTML, or other applications.
- Machine Learning service: IBM machine learning service put AI models to work and help the team to deploy, monitor, and update models to get useful insights about the input data from the data modeling. It has tools like AutoAI, SPSS Modeler, notebooks and Decision Optimizations to build predictive AI models. It also allows operationalization of models by making scalable, orchestrated environment spaces for deployment and run and manage online deployments or manage batches. Watson Machine Learning also allows to monitor quality, drift metrics and fairness of AI and build trust capabilities.
- Speech to Text: IBM Watson speech to Text service transcribes audio to text to provide much needed speech transcription capabilities for the application.
- Text to Speech service: This would convert text in written form to natural-sounding speech. So, it would provide speech-synthesis capabilities to the application.
- Tone Analyzer service: This service helps to analyze the input content's tone.
- Watson Assistant: This assistant helps complete tasks and get information faster from the users of the application. It may also search answers from a given knowledge base and direct the customer to a human correspondent if necessary.

CLOUDANT DATABASE CONNECTION AND IMPORTANCE OF HISTORICAL DATA IN ANALYSIS

After creating the Watson account and subscribing to services, Cloudant database subscription is required. The application's main purpose of having a database connection is to store the tweet meta data including a timestamp, actual tweet content and the sentiment score associated with the tweet. The application is storing tweets to enable future scientist to have historical data of a particular timestamp at their disposal as historical content is very important in data interpretation and analysis. Historical analysis is a systematic and clear analysis of the past. Historic Analysis can be used as a tool to challenge the current dominant assumptions and theories. Historic analysis also plays a vital role in understanding development and changes the matter being studied brought over time and what are its ripples in the present. It helps people take cues from the past and implement a nuanced solution of the problem in the present. History also helps the present intelligentsia to know how people tackled a similar problem in the past.

Subscribing to a Twitter Feed

After making an account on Cloudant Database the server application subscribes to a Twitter Feed as configured by the user. Subscribing to the tweet is done by Twitter API using a user account. Then these tweets are brought into the Node-RED flow using TwitterIn Node which watches for a tweet and sends it to the node. The configuration of the twitter node allows to have multiple options. The application can either get all the tweets, tweets only from select followers and also tweets of multiple languages as well.

Tweet Preprocessing

After receiving the tweets, they are preprocessed. Preprocessing involves directing the tweets towards a function node. This function node contains a JavaScript code that converts the symbol '#' into the text hashtag for ease of analysis. All the URL's attached to the tweets are removed so that only the main content is shown while the analysis is done and also while these tweets are shown in the dashboard window of the Node-RED UI.

Analyzing Sentiment

This is the heart and soul of the application. At this step in the Node flow, a sentiment score is attached to the tweet. The application uses Node-RED sentiment node that is a Node.js module that makes use of AFINN-165 wordlist and Emoji Sentiment Ranking to perform sentiment analysis on blocks of input text.

Sentiment node provides various functionalities like:

- Performance
- Ability to append and overwrite word pairs from the wordlist AFINN.
- The ability to add new languages for which the team needs to add the language and its associated opinion words.
- Gives ability to design and enforce bespoke strategies on the basis of languages chosen.

Sentiment node also uses Emoji Sentiment Ranking. In this new world there has been emergence of a new generation of emoticons called as emojis which are much better in graphics and thus capturing emotions in an otherwise plain text. Emojis are Unicode graphic symbols which are used to express ideas and emotions. They carry clear emotional contents. In the method of Emoji Sentiment Ranking, a sentiment map of the 751 most frequently used emojis are made. Then the sentiments of emojis are calculated.

After calculating the tweets one flow sends the tweets to the Cloudant node to be stored there for historic analysis. The other sends it to the flow which would configure the live Dashboard.

Live Dashboard Creation

Now, the other flow window of the application will handle the formation of a Live visualization dashboard which would act as the final result of the application showing the visualizations. Visualization would contain a live meter showing live tweets and the sentiment attached to it. The other visualization would be a line chart showing sentiments varying over a period of time.

In the Node-RED flow the tweets are sent to a function node where the URLs are removed and the '#' symbol is replaced with the word hashtag. Then these tweets are sent to the chart and gauge node which Node-RED provides for the visualizations as captured in figure 7 and 8.

Figure 7. Dashboard containing line chart showing sentiments varying over a period of time

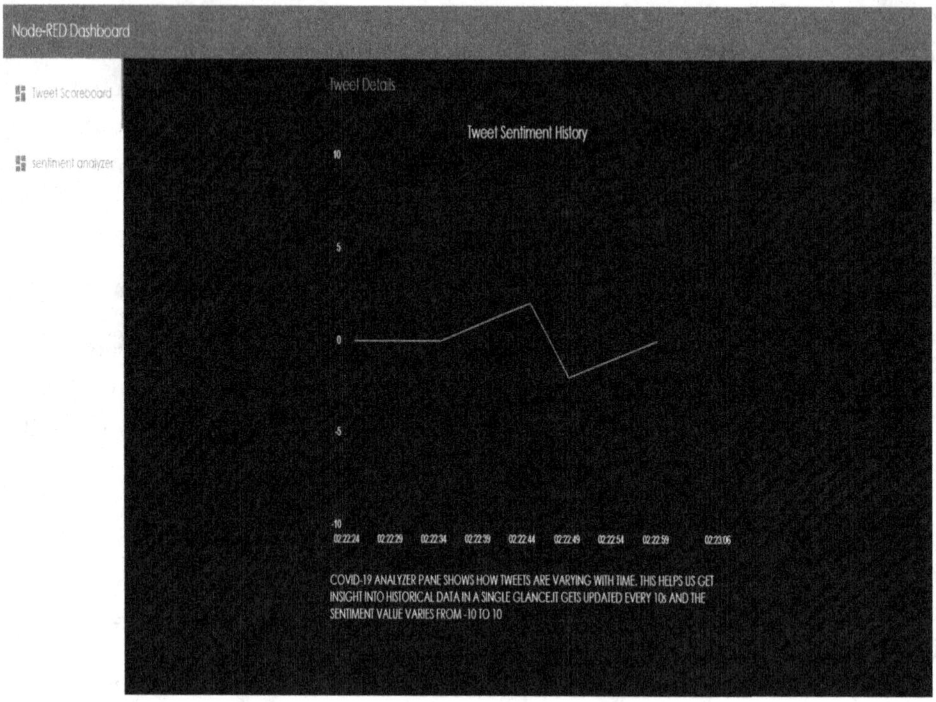

Figure 8. Dashboard containing a live meter showing tweet content and the sentiment assigned to the tweet

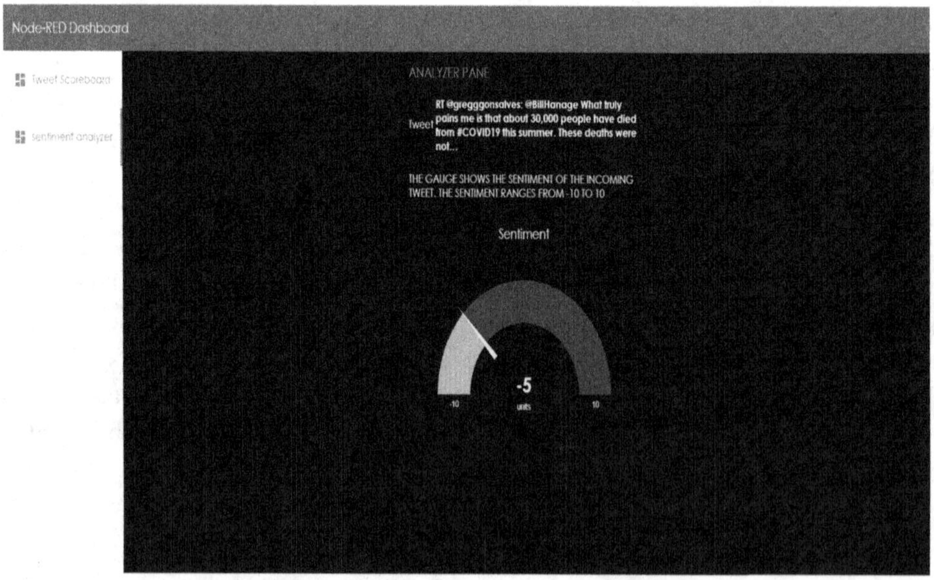

FUTURE RESEARCH DIRECTIONS

The application is highly scalable. It can be extended to having a lot more visualizations and the authors have tried to isolate its scope to a select few languages. More languages can be added to it and the application's scope can be increased accordingly. More AI capabilities can be added to it in the future.

CONCLUSION

The system introduced a way to analyze Tweets using existing efficient and better solutions provided by IBM. It tried to leverage their AI models and distributed capabilities to prepare an efficient and fast way of analyzing the tweets and tried to keep visualizations simple so that a technical inclination is not required in gaining basic insights. The dashboard watching twitter feeds in real time makes the application different from generic Tweet analysis applications. This study aimed at removing the technical aspects and steep learning curve for people who just wants to gain quick insights about what is happening around them and how people are reacting.

REFERENCES

Analytics Vidhya. (2021). *12 Data Plot Types for Visualization from Concept to code.* https://www.analyticsvidhya.com/blog/2021/12/12-data-plot-types-for-visualization/

Deniz, M. (2021). *Fear of missing out (FoMo) mediate relations between social self-efficacy and life satisfaction*. Springer Open. doi:10.118641155-021-00193-w

Hagino, T. (2021). *Practical Node-RED Programming: Learn powerful visual programming techniques and best practices for the web and IoT*. Packt Publishing.

Haynes, T. (2018). *Dopamine, Smartphones & You: A battle for your time.* https://sitn.hms.harvard.edu/flash/2018/dopamine-smartphones-battle-time/

Hou, Y., Xiong, D., Jiang, T., Song, L. & Wang, Q. (2019). Social media addiction: Its impact, mediation, and intervention. *Journal of Psychosocial Research on Cyberspace.*

IBM Cloud. (2021a). *Getting started with IBM Cloudant.* https://cloud.ibm.com/docs/Cloudant?topic=Cloudant-getting-started-with-cloudant

IBM Cloud. (2021b). *IBM Cloudant docs.* https://cloud.ibm.com/docs/Cloudant

Kerner, S. M. (2020, June 23). *IBM advances its Cloudant cloud database as DBaaS grows.* https://www.techtarget.com/searchdatamanagement/news/252485085/IBM-advances-its-Cloudant-cloud-database-as-DBaaS-grows

Lea, R. (2016, July 17). *Lecture 7- Dashboards and UI techniques for Node-RED.* http://noderedguide.com/lecture-7-dashboards-and-ui-techniques-for-node-red/

Learner, J. S. (2014). *Emotions and Decision making.* https://scholar.harvard.edu/files/jenniferlerner/files/annual_review_manuscript_june_16_final.final_.pdf

Miller, J. D. (2019, March). *Hands-On Machine Learning with IBM Watson.* Packt Publishing. https://nodered.org/docs/creating-nodes/

Open J. S. Foundation. (n.d.a). *Node-RED, Developing Flows.* https://nodered.org/docs/developing-flows/

Open J. S. Foundation. (n.d.b). *Node-RED, First Flow Tutorial.* https://nodered.org/docs/tutorials/first-flow

Open J. S. Foundation. (n.d.c). *Node-RED, node-red-contrib-graphs, Version 0.3.5.* https://flows.nodered.org/node/node-red-contrib-graphs

Open J. S. Foundation. (n.d.d). *Node-RED, node-red-dashboard, Version 3.1.6.* https://flows.nodered.org/node/node-red-dashboard

Open J. S. Foundation. (n.d.e). *Node-RED, node-red-node-sentiment Version 0.1.6.* https://flows.nodered.org/node/node-red-node-sentiment

Poller, J. (2019). *Hybrid Multi-cloud Artificial Intelligence (AI): IBM Watson Studio and Watson Machine Learning.* https://www.esg-global.com/hubfs/ibm/4761/index.html

Shaandri, B., Madara, S.R., & Maheswari, P. (2020). *IoT-Based Smart Tree Management Solution for Green Cities.* doi:10.1007/978-981-15-0663-5_9

Steer, D. (2021, Dec. 9). Visualizing Data. *Forbes.* https://www.forbes.com/sites/forbestechcouncil/2021/12/09/visualizing-data/?sh=1b0fc0a5519f

Chapter 13
A Comparative Analysis of Urban Transport Using K-Means Clustering and Multi-Class Classification

Aswani Kumar Cherukuri
https://orcid.org/0000-0001-8455-9108
Vellore Institute of Technology, Vellore, India

Karan Bhowmick
Vellore Institute of Technology, Vellore, India

Firuz Kamalov
Candian University, Dubai, UAE

Chee Ling Thong
https://orcid.org/0000-0002-5138-883X
UCSI University, Malaysia

ABSTRACT

The transportation planning process requires a comprehensive study of the regions that need development. This study is an extension of the methodology of transportation planning. The authors use real-time data from Foursquare API to map out the number of transportation facilities and infrastructure available for each city. This study will shed light on areas that need the most development in terms of intra-neighbourhood and inter-neighbourhood transportation. We use k-means clustering to organize and visualize clusters based on a calculated metric called "Availability Factor" that they have defined, and the number of transportation facilities available in each neighbourhood. Finally, they use the data at hand to create a model for multiclass classification to segregate new data into the predefined classes produced by the unsupervised learning model. The information procured in this work can be used to assess the quality of transportation available in the neighbourhoods of a location and help identify key areas for development.

DOI: 10.4018/978-1-6684-5250-9.ch013

INTRODUCTION

Mumbai is the commercial hub of India, the recent population explosion has been a boon and a bane for the residents of Mumbai. With the increasing traffic volumes as a consequence of the increasing population, the transportation infrastructure in Mumbai needs to be augmented. The problems in transportation infrastructure range from a lack of availability, increased hours of commuting, and rush hours. The congestion of traffic in Mumbai has been steadily increasing according to recent trends. Furthermore, the peak-hour crowding has also shown increasing trends. This causes major discomfort in planning trips using public transportation, and especially in increasing the difficulties faced by daily commuters, since this adds an element of unpredictability to their routines. And, longer commuting times, not to mention the environmental efficacy of the modes of transportation being used are also significant hurdles that need to be circumvented.

To tackle these issues, we plan to introduce two comprehensive models that categorize the neighbourhoods of Mumbai on the basis of the transportation infrastructure available. This will be achieved through data mining and machine learning techniques that are elaborated upon below. We use data mining and clustering techniques for this scope because of its relatively unexplored potential in targeted development for transportation infrastructure. We create two models developed by K-Means Clustering algorithm. We propose this model for analysing trends in the transportation amenities of Mumbai on a geographic scale. Data Visualization is used to present two different clustering algorithms based on the total number of transportation infrastructure and the availability factor, which is a metric introduced in the scope of this paper. The first clustering algorithm can be used as a metric to assess the inter-neighbourhood transportation. The second clustering algorithm is used as a metric to assess the fit for intra-neighbourhood transportation. We use folium maps to project the geographical trends using these metrics.

Our contributions aim to fill salient gaps in the literature survey. We use the guidelines explored in S. Na et al. (2010) and M. A. Syakur et al. (2017), and we combine elements of the methodology proposed in Jieh-HaurChen et al. (2020), Omar Elmansouri et al. (2020) and M. A. Syakur et al. (2017) to our functionality. With this exploration of various techniques in K-Means Clustering and Urban transportation analysis, we craft a new methodology which explores the classification of transportation infrastructure across two unexplored directions, namely intra-neighbourhood and inter-neighbourhood parameters. We explore the insights produced by the study in the following sections, starting with the background on which we base this study which includes the literature survey, problem statement and the objectives. Next, we explicate the proposed model through the dataset description, system architecture and methodology. We, then, explore the experimental analysis of the study. Finally, we sum up our findings in the Discussion and Conclusion sections.

BACKGROUND

In this section, we present the findings of the literature survey, research gaps and problem statements that helped inspire this study. We take a look at the Literature surveyed (2.1), the work done in the field and how it can be augmented to produce efficacious results. Next, we elaborate on the goals we have set out for this study and the problems we address (2.2).

Literature Survey

In this section, we present the articles and conference papers we have researched to tackle our problem statement. The literature ranges from the study and evaluation of the K-Means clustering algorithm to the methods used by others to classify and produce improvement in transportation systems using Machine Learning.

Paul S. Bradley, Usama M. Fayyad (1998) present a procedure for computing a refined starting condition from a given initial one that is based on an efficient technique for estimating the modes of a distribution. Highlights K-Means Clustering Algorithm's superiority in using distance metrics. However, the methods of refinement are not explored in Hierarchical or Agglomerative clustering. K. A. Abdul Nazeer, M. P. Sebastian (2009) proposes a method for making the algorithm more effective and efficient so as to get better clustering with reduced complexity. The paper emphasizes gauging the strengths and weaknesses of K-Means Clustering on the basis of computational intensity. S. Na et al. (2010) aim to resolve the problem of efficiency in K-Means Clustering. The improved method avoids computing the distance of each data object to the cluster centers repeatedly, saving the running time. It is based on the value of evaluation metric of silhouette score. However, other algorithms have mitigated this issue.

D T Pham et al. (2013) first reviews existing methods for selecting the number of clusters for the algorithm. Factors that affect this selection are then discussed and a new measure to assist the selection is proposed. It proposes new function to calculate the number of clusters to assign in K Means Clustering. However, the elbow method has been established as a standard. Abhay Kumar et al. (2014) propose a model for predicting the probability of the outcome of the Play class as YES or NO through K-means clustering on weather data. It provides pseudo-code to use k-means in a different environment, but the practical applications are not explored.

Noto G., Bianchi C. (2015) propose a Dynamic Performance Management which allowed the authors to understand who the governing players are, their roles, and how they influence the production and provision processes. The extent and impacts of this study however, are not explored. M A Syakur et al. (2017) provide a combination of K-Means method with elbow to improve efficient and effective k-means performance in processing large amounts of data. They use K Means Clustering for classifying customer profiles. The effects of the clustering analysis have not been documented.

Sciara G. C. (2017) describe contemporary urban transportation planning, three limitations are accentuated. With historical case studies to back its claims, they use data visualization to present their findings. The paper only uses data visualization to highlight the issues. Machine learning algorithms could be used to gain further insight. Kristof Van Laerhoven (2018) propose an adaptive approach that uses a Kohonen Self-Organizing Map, augmented with on-line k-means clustering for classification of the incoming sensor data. This sensor data is collected from context based features in mobile phones. The paper does not analyse the efficacy of K-Means Clustering using other algorithms. Cleophas C et al. (2018) propose a survey paper that analyses the various methods used to plan urban transportation. They emphasize on the horizontal and vertical collaboration citing articles using logistics. The survey is comprehensive but it focuses completely on logistic services.

Fränti, P, Sieranoja (2018) present two contributions. First, it introduces a clustering basic benchmark. Second, it studies the performance of K Means using this benchmark. The paper only uses K-means for benchmarking. Chunhui Yuan and Haitao Yang (2019) delve into the analysis of the methods used to detect the value of K in K Means Clustering. The silhouette score has been established for assessing quality of clustering. Omar Elmansouri et al. (2020) have aimed at providing an overview of urban transportation in Libya, in addition to some of the issues that are faced by the transportation system. This paper uses data visualization and demographic statistics to analyse issues of traffic volume, pollution etc.

Jieh-HaurChen et al. (2020) propose a practical approach to identifying the macroeconomic factors critical to air-traffic volumes from among a wide range of potential factors, using the data-mining techniques, K-means clustering and decision-tree classification. The paper does not present the possible impacts of this model on the existing system. Hamurcu M., Eren T. (2020) use the analytic hierarchy process and fuzzy technique for order preference by similarity. The fuzzy TOPSIS method has been applied for ranking the proposed alternative projects. It is a thorough article, but it does not evaluate the results of the algorithms and their significance.

In the thorough analysis of the articles presented above, we gain valuable insights into the methodology to apply with urban transportation planning in mind. From the reading above, we can see that K-Means Clustering is a popular method for unsupervised learning, producing the best efficacy. When it comes to urban transportation, little progress has been made to integrate machine learning algorithms for the development. We have taken inspiration from the work of Jieh-HaurChen et al. (2020) emulated the concepts on urban transportation analysis. The work on unsupervised machine learning hasn't been evaluated or applied to diverse scenarios. We plan to overcome these issues in this paper.

Problem Statement and Objectives

Given the chaotic public transportation facilities in most metropolitan areas, we decide to take a look at the lack of transportation facilities in the commercial hub of India (https://bitmesra.ac.in/naps/vox14/). Public transportation is the lifeline of Mumbai's daily commute.

The objectives of our study are to identify areas that need better public transportation facilities by grouping them in clusters. Next, conducting a comparative analysis of neighbourhood transportation facilities based on transportation facilities in Mumbai, India. And finally, improving the dynamism of the proposed model using Naïve Bayes Classification.

PROPOSED MODEL

In this section, we delineate the data used (3.1), detailed architecture (3.2) of the proposed model and further explore the model to achieve the objectives of the study (3.3). We use the methodology mentioned in 3.2 and 3.3 to achieve the objectives mentioned in section 2.2. We use inter-neighbourhood and intra-neighbourhood parameters for our clustering analysis. This helps highlight the neighbourhoods that need development of public transportation infrastructure. Next, we use the Silhouette score to evaluate the relevance of the model pertaining to the case study. We used the insights gained from section 2.1 to draft the architecture and functionality of the proposed model. This architecture streamlines the process used to achieve the goal mentioned.

Dataset Description

In this section, we explicate the datasets being used for the scope of this study. We have used two main datasets for the project, the first is made via web scraping and geocoder library, the second dataset has been produced using Foursquare API with cluster labels.

Table 1. Latitude-Longitudinal dataset

	Neighborhood	Latitude	Longitude
0	Aarey Forest	17.663600	75.897820
1	Agripada	18.976280	72.826150
2	Altamount Road	18.964334	72.807842
3	Amboli, Mumbai	19.129060	72.846440
4	Amrut Nagar	18.993800	73.992600
5	Antop Hill	19.026140	72.866450
6	Anushakti Nagar	19.042830	72.927340

This dataset consists of the names of neighbourhoods and their latitude and longitude coordinates. This is achieved by the geocoder library in Python. This dataset is used for the visualization of clusters across the map.

Table 2. Neighbourhood with the total number of amenities

	Neighborhood	Zoo	ATM	Airport	American Restaurant	Antique Shop	Aquarium	Arcade	Art Gallery	..... & Crafts Store	...	Tree	Vegetarian / Vegan Restaurant	Video Game Store	Waterfront	Whisky Bar	Wine Bar	Wine Shop
0	Aarey Forest	0.0	0.0	0.0	0.0	0.0	0.0	0.0	0.0	0.0	...	0.0	0.0	0.0	0.0	0.0	0.0	0.0
1	Agripada	2.0	0.0	0.0	0.0	0.0	0.0	0.0	0.0	0.0	...	0.0	0.0	0.0	0.0	0.0	0.0	0.0
2	Altamount Road	0.0	0.0	0.0	0.0	0.0	0.0	0.0	0.0	2.0	...	0.0	2.0	0.0	0.0	0.0	0.0	0.0
3	Amboli, Mumbai	0.0	0.0	0.0	0.0	0.0	0.0	0.0	0.0	0.0	...	0.0	2.0	0.0	0.0	0.0	0.0	0.0
4	Antop Hill	0.0	0.0	0.0	0.0	0.0	0.0	0.0	0.0	0.0	...	0.0	0.0	0.0	0.0	0.0	0.0	0.0
5	Anushakti Nagar	0.0	0.0	0.0	0.0	0.0	0.0	0.0	0.0	0.0	...	0.0	0.0	0.0	0.0	0.0	0.0	0.0
6	Asalfa	0.0	0.0	0.0	0.0	0.0	0.0	0.0	0.0	0.0	...	0.0	0.0	0.0	0.0	0.0	0.0	0.0
7	Badhwar Park	0.0	0.0	0.0	0.0	0.0	0.0	0.0	2.0	0.0	...	0.0	0.0	0.0	0.0	0.0	0.0	0.0
8	Baiganwadi	0.0	4.0	0.0	0.0	0.0	0.0	0.0	0.0	0.0	...	0.0	0.0	0.0	0.0	0.0	0.0	0.0
9	Ballard Estate	0.0	0.0	0.0	0.0	0.0	0.0	0.0	0.0	0.0	...	0.0	2.0	0.0	0.0	0.0	0.0	0.0
10	Bandra	0.0	0.0	0.0	0.0	0.0	0.0	0.0	0.0	0.0	...	0.0	2.0	0.0	0.0	0.0	0.0	0.0

Table 3. Transportation dataset

	Neighborhood	Total Amenities	Transport Amenities	Availability Factor
0	Aarey Forest	8.0	2.0	0.250000
1	Agripada	58.0	2.0	0.034483
2	Altamount Road	130.0	2.0	0.015385
3	Amboli, Mumbai	56.0	2.0	0.035714
4	Antop Hill	24.0	2.0	0.083333

This dataset is developed using the Foursquare API, we group the sum of each amenity on the basis of the neighbourhood name.

Here, we transform the second data set to contain only the necessary variables for the scope of this study. Now, we calculate the availability factor as another column, the second parameter used for the clustering analysis.

Detailed Architecture

The architecture presented in Figure 1, delineates the steps that we took in this paper to achieve the proposed solution. We first use Web Scraping to mine real-time geographical data of the neighbourhoods in Mumbai. We then plan to use the geocoder library in python to assign the latitudinal and longitudinal values of these neighbourhoods. Now, we use Foursquare API, Foursquare is one of the largest databases of geographical locations. They have Places API, which when called returns the amenities of a particular location based on its geographical coordinates. We merge these datasets based on the localities. Next, we convert the obtained merged data set to a pandas data frame, so that it can be used for model development. Data pre-processing is done to mitigate instances of redundant data, remove null values if any. Then, we develop the model using K-Means Clustering and evaluate said model via the standardised metric for analysis of Clustering models. This is done to compare the efficacies of both approaches and to signify the relevance of clustering. Through this, we achieve the first two research objectives of the study. Furthermore, we plot the trends obtained on the world map. This would help identify areas according to geographic location, to focus on development. Finally, we use a function to classify new neighbourhoods on the basis of their Availability Factor.

Methodology

In this section, we take a look at the methodology used for the scope of this paper.

Equation 1: Availability Factor

Availability factor = Number of transportation facilities/Total amenities in neighbourhood

We used K means clustering with two different parameters for model development. The two metrics used are the total number of public transportation amenities and the availability factor. The clusters formed via the former parameter are called Transportation clusters and the clusters formed via the latter

Figure 1. Architecture

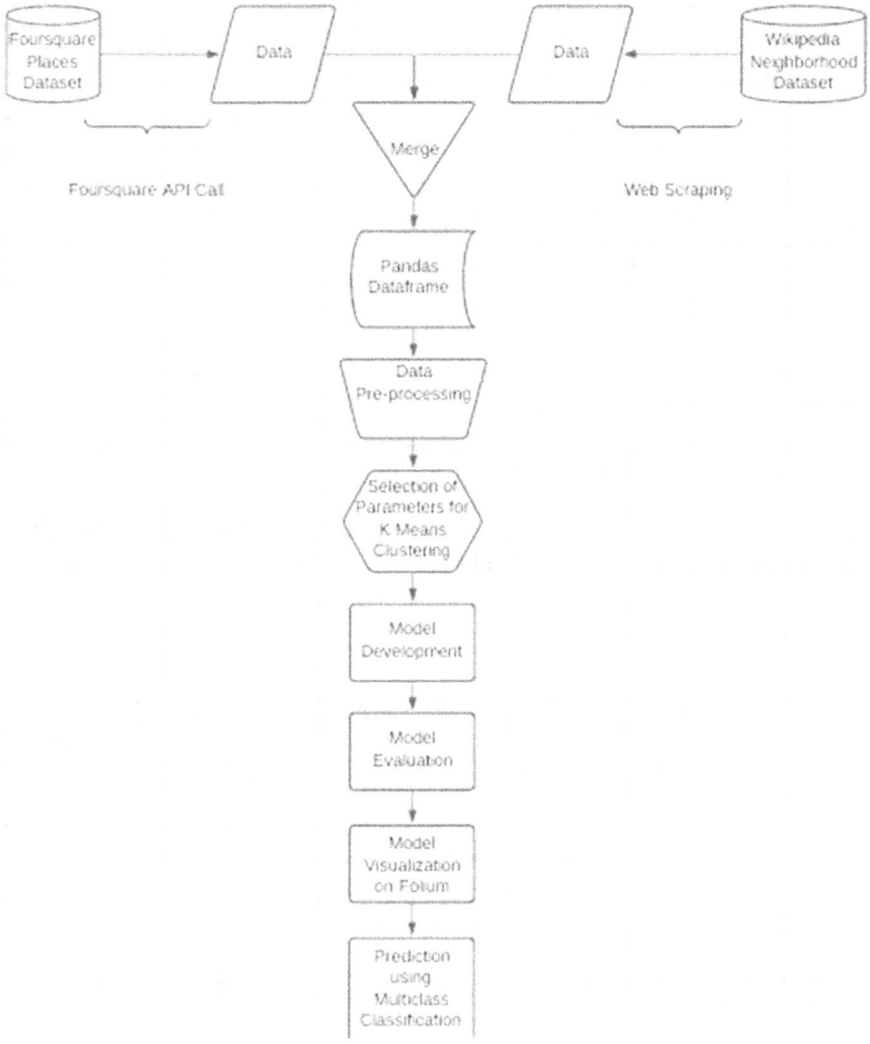

parameter are called Availability clusters. We propose the use of this equation for intra-neighbourhood transportation analysis.

Next, we use a supervised learning algorithm for the classification of new data or neighbourhoods on the basis of these factors. We train the model using the clustering labels produced by K-Means Clustering and use it to make accurate estimates of new neighbourhoods.

Now, we delineate the steps followed to achieve the aforementioned goals set in the study. For data pre-processing, we analyse the statistical quality of the data, so we can determine if the data set can be used as the foundation for the model being used. We check for inconsistencies, null values, outliers etc. This also includes feature selection, i.e., the best features to use in the model. In this case, it refers to the curated independent variable of 'Availability Factor.' After data processing, we can proceed with model development. We have established the parameters to use for development of the unsupervised learning clusters. We create two different paths for the model to proceed, one, on the basis of the total transportation amenities and the second, on the basis of the availability factor. This creates two clustering labels that correspond to the parameters used. We use the Silhouette Score to evaluate the quality of the clusters produced by the K-Means algorithm. And, finally we plot the trends of clustering on the world map using Folium. Next, the Multiclass Naïve Bayes classification algorithm is developed using the target labels of the clustering analysis. This helps classify new data into the predefined clustering labels. It makes augmentation easier and makes the model more resilient to new inputs and data.

To recapitulate, the functionality given above elaborate on the research design, in terms of the processes and functionality of the proposed work. This facilitates the classification and clustering of real-world data based on a structured algorithm implementation.

EXPERIMENTAL ANALYSIS

In this section, we discuss the results of the two clustering models that were developed. The first clustering parameter used is the number of public transportation amenities and the second clustering parameter used is the availability factor. In this experiment, we use an unsupervised learning algorithm to cluster the neighbourhoods in Mumbai. We gain insight into the transportation facilities in Mumbai. We also make use of Multiclass Classification in conjunction with K-Means Clustering for extending the application to prediction.

4.1 K-Means Clustering on the Basis of Public Transportation Amenities

K-Means Clustering was used to cluster the neighbourhoods into five clusters based on public transportation infrastructures. The variables we selected for the public transportation facilities are Metro stations, Bus stations, Bus lines, Train stations, Harbours, Airports and Rental Services.

The clusters below are formed based on the total number of transportation amenities in each neighbourhood. The "Cluster 1" column in the table is the column name for the Transportation cluster.

Transportation Cluster 0

We can see here, the Transportation Cluster 0 encompasses neighbourhoods with 2 public transportation facilities. The number of transportation amenities in each area has been given under the "Transport Amenities" column, and the corresponding cluster label in the following column.

The table given above shows the neighbourhoods that have been grouped under the zero cluster in accordance to the number of transportation amenities in the area. It groups 19 of the neighbourhoods as a high priority candidate for transportation infrastructure development.

Transportation Cluster 1

We can see Transportation Cluster 1 has neighbourhoods with 4 public transportation amenities. Similar to the format mentioned above, the number of transportation amenities an cluster have been included in the table. We can see that Transportation Cluster 1 shows a better availability of total transportation amenities as compared to Transportation Cluster 0. This signifies that areas in Transportation Cluster 0 must be given higher priority in relation to development of transportation infrastructure.

Table 4. Neighbourhoods in Transportation Cluster 0

	Neighborhood	Transport Amenities	Cluster 1
32	Dadar	2.0	0
33	Aarey Forest	2.0	0
34	Antop Hill	2.0	0
35	Tardeo	2.0	0
36	Baiganwadi	2.0	0
37	Mahalaxmi, Mumbai	2.0	0
38	Land's End, Bandra	2.0	0
39	Nepean Sea Road	2.0	0
40	Currey Road railway station	2.0	0
41	Kherwadi	2.0	0
42	I.C. Colony	2.0	0
43	Gowalia Tank	2.0	0
44	Gopalrao Deshmukh Marg	2.0	0
45	Four Bungalows	2.0	0
46	Dongri	2.0	0
47	Dadar Parsi Colony	2.0	0
48	Pali Village	2.0	0
49	Saki Naka	2.0	0
50	Koliwada	2.0	0

The table given above shows the neighbourhoods that have been grouped under the first cluster in accordance to the number of transportation amenities in the area. It groups 18 of the neighbourhoods as a mid-tier priority candidate for transportation infrastructure development.

Table 5. Neighbourhoods in Transportation Cluster 1

	Neighborhood	Transport Amenities	Cluster 1
12	Pydhonie	4.0	1
13	Matunga Road, Mumbai	4.0	1
14	Bori Bunder	4.0	1
15	Kopar Road	4.0	1
16	Maheshwari Udyan, Mumbai	4.0	1
17	Mahim	4.0	1
18	Anushakti Nagar	4.0	1
19	Princess Street (Mumbai)	4.0	1
20	Hindu Colony	4.0	1
21	Marine Lines	4.0	1
22	Umarkhadi	4.0	1
23	Marine Drive, Mumbai	4.0	1
24	Dava Bazaar	4.0	1
25	Ferry Wharf	4.0	1
26	Chandivali	4.0	1
27	Thakkar Bappa Colony	4.0	1
28	Ballard Estate	4.0	1
29	Cotton Green	4.0	1

Transportation Cluster 2

We can see Transportation Cluster 2 has neighbourhoods with no public transportation amenities. These areas and neighbourhoods are in severe need of transportation infrastructure, so they should be highly prioritized. From the trends do far, Transportation cluster 2 and Transportation cluster 0 have the least amount of transportation amenities.

Table 6. Neighbourhoods in Transportation Cluster 2

	Neighborhood	Transport Amenities	Cluster 1
65	D.N. Nagar	0.0	2
66	Kala Ghoda	0.0	2
67	Kajuwadi	0.0	2
68	Dagdi Chawl	0.0	2
69	Hiranandani Gardens, Mumbai	0.0	2
70	Bangur Nagar	0.0	2
71	Gorai	0.0	2
72	Manori	0.0	2
73	Kamathipura	0.0	2
74	Gokuldham	0.0	2
75	Kalbadevi	0.0	2
76	Lion Gate (Mumbai)	0.0	2
77	Kannamwar Nagar	0.0	2
78	Kemps Corner	0.0	2
79	Yashodham	0.0	2
80	Bandra Kurla Complex	0.0	2
81	Jagruti Nagar	0.0	2
82	Chor Bazaar, Mumbai	0.0	2
83	Lokhandwala Complex	0.0	2

The table given above shows the neighbourhoods that have been grouped under the second cluster in accordance to the number of transportation amenities in the area. It groups 19 of the neighbourhoods as an extremely high priority candidate for transportation infrastructure development. These neighbourhoods should be the first priority of any official focused on improving transportation facilities in Mumbai.

Table 7. Neighbourhoods in Transportation Cluster 3

	Neighborhood	Transport Amenities	Cluster 1
0	Mandvi, Mumbai	14.0	3

Transportation Cluster 3

We can see Transportation Cluster 3 has a neighbourhood with 14 public transportation amenities. This cluster has only one neighbourhood, and it has an astounding number of transportation amenities. The neighbourhood in this cluster does not need to be the focus for public transportation development.

The table given above shows one neighbourhood that have been grouped under the third cluster in accordance to the number of transportation amenities in the area. It consists of only one neighbourhood which can be given the last priority.

Transportation Cluster 4

We can see Transportation Cluster 4 has neighbourhoods with 6-8 public transportation amenities. These neighbourhoods have a higher frequency of transportation amenities than most of the neighbourhoods in the other clusters. It has the second lowest priority when it comes to development of transportation infrastructure.

The table given above shows the neighbourhoods that have been grouped under the fourth cluster in accordance to the number of transportation amenities in the area. It groups 11 neighbourhoods as a low priority candidate for transportation infrastructure development.

We evaluate this model by using silhouette score. Silhouette coefficient is a measure of similarity between pints in the same cluster and the difference between different clusters in a model. The values of Silhouette Score range from -1 to 1. The best value is 1 and the worst value is -1. Values near 0 indicate overlapping clusters. Negative values generally indicate that a sample has been assigned to the wrong cluster, as a different cluster is more similar. The silhouette score of the model used is given in Figure 2.

K-Means Clustering on the basis of availability factor

K-Means Clustering was used to cluster the neighbourhoods into three clusters based on the availability factor of public transportation infrastructure. Among the amenities considered for the total number, were: Recreational centres, monument/landmarks, restaurants, Fast-Food places, Stationery shops, Malls, Residential Areas and much more. The Foursquare API provided a total of 230 amenity categories. Now, we take a look at the three clusters formed on the basis of availability factor. The "Cluster 2" column name in the tables below are the cluster labels on the basis of availability factor.

Table 8. Neighbourhoods in Transportation Cluster 4

	Neighborhood	Transport Amenities	Cluster 1
1	Lohar Chawl	8.0	4
2	Zaveri Bazaar	6.0	4
3	Byculla	6.0	4
4	Churchgate	6.0	4
5	Royal Opera House (Mumbai)	6.0	4
6	Dharavi	6.0	4
7	Chandanwadi, Mumbai	6.0	4
8	Sewri	6.0	4
9	Ghodapdeo	6.0	4
10	Khotachiwadi	6.0	4
11	Thakurdwar	6.0	4

Availability Cluster 0

Availability Cluster 0 comprises of neighbourhoods that have an availability factor in the range: 0-0.1053. The number of neighbourhoods in this cluster are the most as compared to the other clusters formed. The range of availability factor is the lowest in this cluster of neighbourhoods.

The table given above shows the neighbourhoods that have been grouped under the zero cluster in accordance to the number of transportation amenities in the area. It groups 50 neighbourhoods as a high priority candidate for transportation infrastructure development. The neighbourhoods with the availability factor in the lower ranges should be treated as the top priority. This cluster overall, consists of neighbourhoods that are top priority.

Figure 2. Silhouette Score for the first Clustering Analysis

```
Silhouette Score for Cluster 1: 0.9800000000000001
```

Table 9. Neighbourhoods in Availability Cluster 0

	Neighborhood	Availability Factor	Cluster 2
18	Thakkar Bappa Colony	0.105263	0
19	Lalbaug	0.100000	0
20	Dharavi	0.096774	0
21	Antop Hill	0.083333	0
22	Thakurdwar	0.062500	0
...	...	...	...
120	Shastri Nagar, Goregaon	0.000000	0
121	Shivaji Park	0.000000	0
122	Shivaji Park Residential Zone	0.000000	0
123	Prabhadevi	0.000000	0
124	Virar	0.000000	0

Availability Cluster 1

Availability Cluster 1 comprises of neighbourhoods that have an availability factor in the range: 0.75-1.0. This cluster has the lowest number of neighbourhoods and has the highest availability factor among the other clusters.

Table 10. Neighbourhoods in Availability Cluster 1

	Neighborhood	Availability Factor	Cluster 2
0	Dadar	1.00	1
1	Sewri	0.75	1

The table given above shows the neighbourhoods that have been grouped under the first cluster in accordance to the number of transportation amenities in the area. It groups 2 neighbourhoods as a low priority candidate for transportation infrastructure development. The neighbourhoods with the availability factor in this range, should be treated as lowest priority or the last priority for a transportation infrastructure development programme.

Availability Cluster 2

Availability Cluster 2 comprises of neighbourhoods that have an availability factor in the range: 0.1111-0.3333. This cluster has a moderate range of availability factor, from approximately one in ten amenities to one in three amenities are transportation infrastructure. Out of the three Availability clusters, Availability cluster 0 has to be highly prioritised, Availability cluster 1 has the best intra-neighbourhood results and Availability cluster 2 has to be moderately prioritised.

The table given above shows the neighbourhoods that have been grouped under the second cluster in accordance to the number of transportation amenities in the area. It groups 16 neighbourhoods as a mid-tier priority candidate for transportation infrastructure development. The neighbourhoods with the availability factor in the lower ranges should be treated as high priority, whereas the neighbourhoods in the higher ranges can be given lesser priority for a transportation infrastructure development programme.

Again, we used Silhouette Score for the model's evaluation. Figure 4 shows the value obtained for K-Means Clustering.

Multiclass Classification using Naive Bayes Algorithm

We use supervised learning to predict the classes or tiers that have been produced above by the clustering algorithms. Here, we use the Naive Bayes Classifier to predict classes of randomized data based on transportation amenities and Availability Factor. We use sklearn library to import the model developer class. Next, we fit the model using the data set produced, here the independent variable is 'Availability Factor' and the dependent variable is Tier or Cluster number. 0 indicates low-level availability, 1 indicates high-level availability, and 2 indicates medium-level availability. Their corresponding ranges are given in the section above.

We use a randomized data set to test the efficiency of the classification algorithm used. First, we develop the model using the data set with the clustering labels. We use precision, recall and F1-score to evaluate the classification model. The results produced are high and they are shown below.

Here, we can see that the weighted average of precision, recall and F1-score are above 0.9 indicating an extremely high accuracy. Next, we use the model trained here, to predict the labels for new data. The data set used is shown below.

After passing the data through the function, we get the results produced as the "Tier of Availability Factor." The results produced are shown in the table below. And we can see that the availability factors correspond to the range demonstrated in section 4.2.

Data Visualization on Folium

First, we take a look at the clusters formed on the basis of public transportation infrastructure.

Table 11. Neighbourhoods in Availability Cluster 2

	Neighborhood	Availability Factor	Cluster 2
2	Kherwadi	0.333333	2
3	Anushakti Nagar	0.285714	2
4	Ferry Wharf	0.285714	2
5	Mandvi, Mumbai	0.259259	2
6	Aarey Forest	0.250000	2
7	Koliwada	0.200000	2
8	Lallubhai Compound	0.200000	2
9	Cotton Green	0.181818	2
10	Dava Bazaar	0.181818	2
11	Baiganwadi	0.166667	2
12	Pali Village	0.166667	2
13	Dongri	0.166667	2
14	Chandanwadi, Mumbai	0.142857	2
15	Ghodapdeo	0.142857	2
16	Byculla	0.125000	2
17	Kopar Road	0.111111	2

Figure 3. Silhouette Score for the second Clustering Analysis

```
Silhouette Score for Cluster 2 is: 0.8128126573589791
```

Figure 4. Classification report for Naive Bayes Classifier

	precision	recall	f1-score	support
0	1.00	0.96	0.98	72
1	1.00	0.50	0.67	2
2	0.78	1.00	0.88	14
accuracy			0.95	88
macro avg	0.93	0.82	0.84	88
weighted avg	0.96	0.95	0.96	88

Colour index

Yellow: 0-Cluster encompasses neighbourhoods with 2 public transportation facilities.

Orange: 1-Cluster has neighbourhoods with 4 public transportation amenities.

Lawn green: 2-Cluster has neighbourhoods with no public transportation amenities

Red: 3-Cluster has a neighbourhood with 14 public transportation amenities.

Sienna: 4-Cluster has neighbourhoods with 6-8 public transportation amenities.

We can see from Figure 6 that Southern Mumbai has a wide range of clusters. Ranging from red, the highest strata of transportation amenities based on availability to Lawn green, demarcating the neighbourhoods with the poorest transportation amenities based on availability. Masjid Bunder, here is the outlier as the only neighbourhood with fourteen transportation amenities. The neighbourhoods marked by orange and sienna, like Victoria Garden and Wadi Bandar, indicate a moderate level of transportation availability. Whereas the neighbourhoods with lower strata of availability, like Colaba, Malabar Hills and Tulsi Wadi are interspersed. There is no general trend or uniformity in the transportation availability of Southern Mumbai.

Next, we look at the clusters formed over Central Mumbai. Again, we see a wide distribution of clusters over the neighbourhoods of Central Mumbai. The outlier here is Dharavi, forming a sienna cluster, indicating high transportation availability. The orange and yellow clusters indicate moderate levels of availability, they are concentrated over the southern region of the figure given above. Neighbourhoods of Matunga, Bahadur Nagar and Chembur have relatively better transportation availability. Whereas, the neighbourhoods in the north show a higher proportion of neighbourhoods with low transportation availability, these include: Powai, Tunga, Andheri East and Madh among others. In this figure, we can see that as we move from south to north the availability of transportation amenities decreases.

Finally, we look at the distribution of clusters over Northern Mumbai. A major proportion of the clusters formed here are of the lower strata i.e. neighbourhoods with fewer than two transportation amenities. There are two outliers to the Southeast, namely Chandivali and Kanjurmarg East, that are denoted with orange clusters. Up north, there is a sparse distribution of yellow and green clusters, this region has the largest number of neighbourhoods with 0 transportation including Lokhandwala Complex, Goregaon West, Borivali East, and Malwani among others. As we move further North the availability of transportation amenities only decrease. Now, we take a look at the clusters on the basis of availability factor.

Table 12. Data set used for testing the classification model

	Transport Amenities	Total	AF
0	8	28	0.285714
1	15	42	0.357143
2	15	40	0.375000
3	19	40	0.475000
4	13	21	0.619048
5	4	21	0.190476
6	14	15	0.933333
7	2	25	0.080000
8	14	45	0.311111
9	5	33	0.151515
10	10	36	0.277778
11	10	16	0.625000
12	14	48	0.291667
13	5	23	0.217391
14	19	32	0.593750

Colour index

Royal blue: 0-Cluster comprises of neighbourhoods that have an availability factor in the range of 0-0.1053.

Indigo: 1-Cluster comprises of neighbourhoods that have an availability factor in the range: 0.75-1.0.

Navy: 2-Cluster comprises of neighbourhoods that have an availability factor in the range: 0.1111-0.3333

Table 13. Data set with predicted label

	Transport Amenities	Total	AF	Predicted Tier of AF
0	8	28	0.285714	2
1	15	42	0.357143	2
2	15	40	0.375000	2
3	19	40	0.475000	2
4	13	21	0.619048	2
5	4	21	0.190476	2
6	14	15	0.933333	2
7	2	25	0.080000	0
8	14	45	0.311111	2
9	5	33	0.151515	2
10	10	36	0.277778	2
11	10	16	0.625000	2
12	14	48	0.291667	2
13	5	23	0.217391	2
14	19	32	0.593750	2

Based on the calculated Availability Factor, we look at the clusters formed over South Mumbai. We can see from the figure above that most of the neighbourhoods have an availability factor between 0 and 0.105. Neighbourhoods in the South and the South-western regions of the map are denoted by royal blue, whereas the neighbourhoods on the South-eastern side have better Availability Factors.

Again, in Central Mumbai, we see a large proportion of royal blue clusters. But here there are relatively more diverse clusters representing all three clusters delineated in the colour index above.

The neighbourhood in Sewri is the outlier with the indigo cluster, denoting the highest strata of Availability Factor. We can see neighbourhoods with a good availability factor in the south and eastern regions of the map shown, marked with the navy blue hue. These neighbourhoods include Sewri, Mankhurd, Shivaji Nagar, and Anushaki Nagar. The Northern and western parts of the map have neighbourhoods with a low Availability Factor.

Figure 5. The clusters in South Mumbai

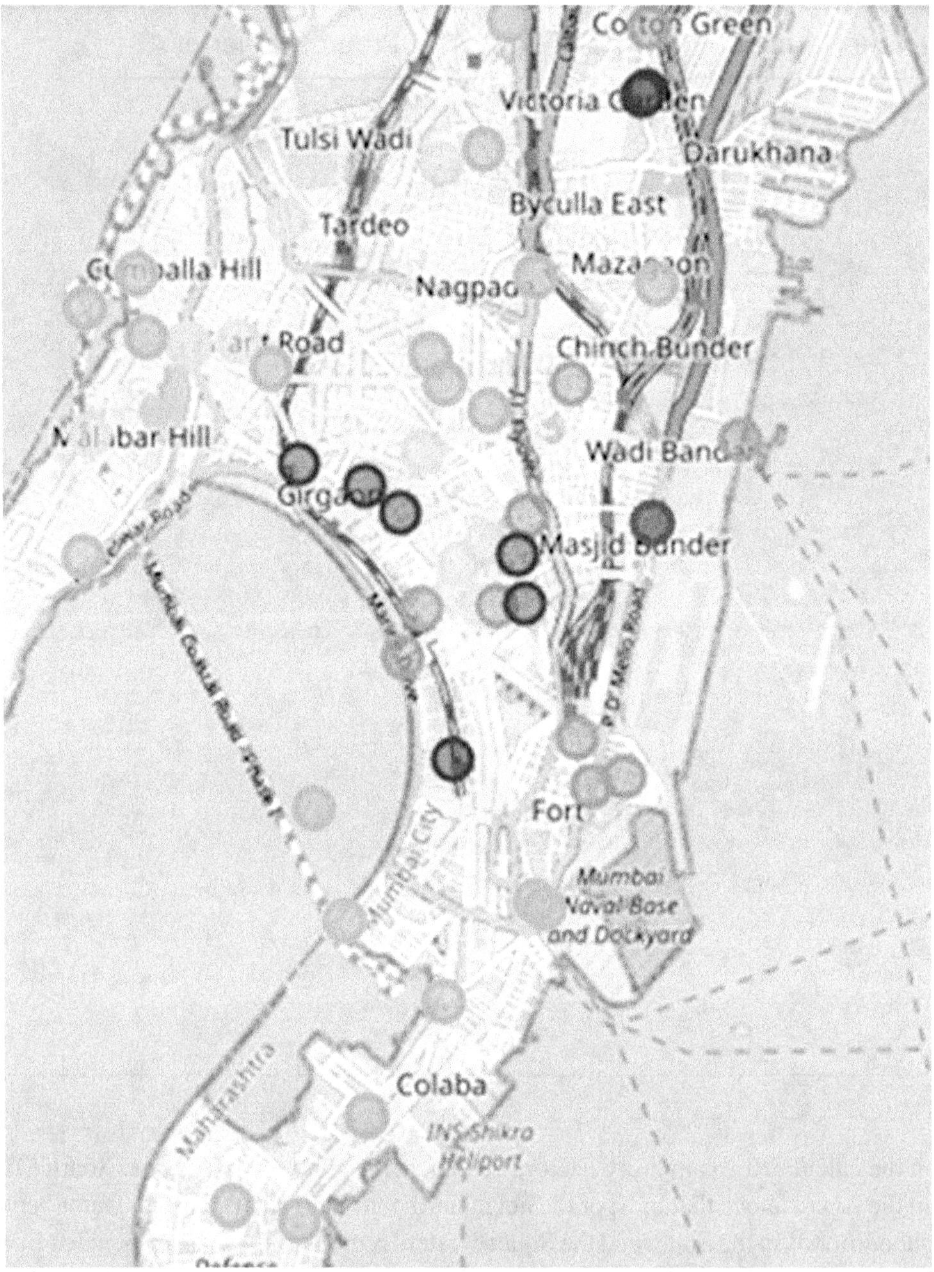

Finally, in Northern Mumbai we can see the most number of royal blue clusters indicating low Availability Factor, which supports the assertion of the first clustering model. There are only two neighbourhoods with a medium Availability Factor, Kanjurmarg East and Shivaji Nagar. The rest of the map is dominated by royal blue clusters denoting low Availability Factors.

The insights produced in this paper are quintessential to tackle the problem of public transportation problem. The application of unsupervised learning can prove highly beneficial to planning and develop-

Figure 6. The clusters in Central Mumbai

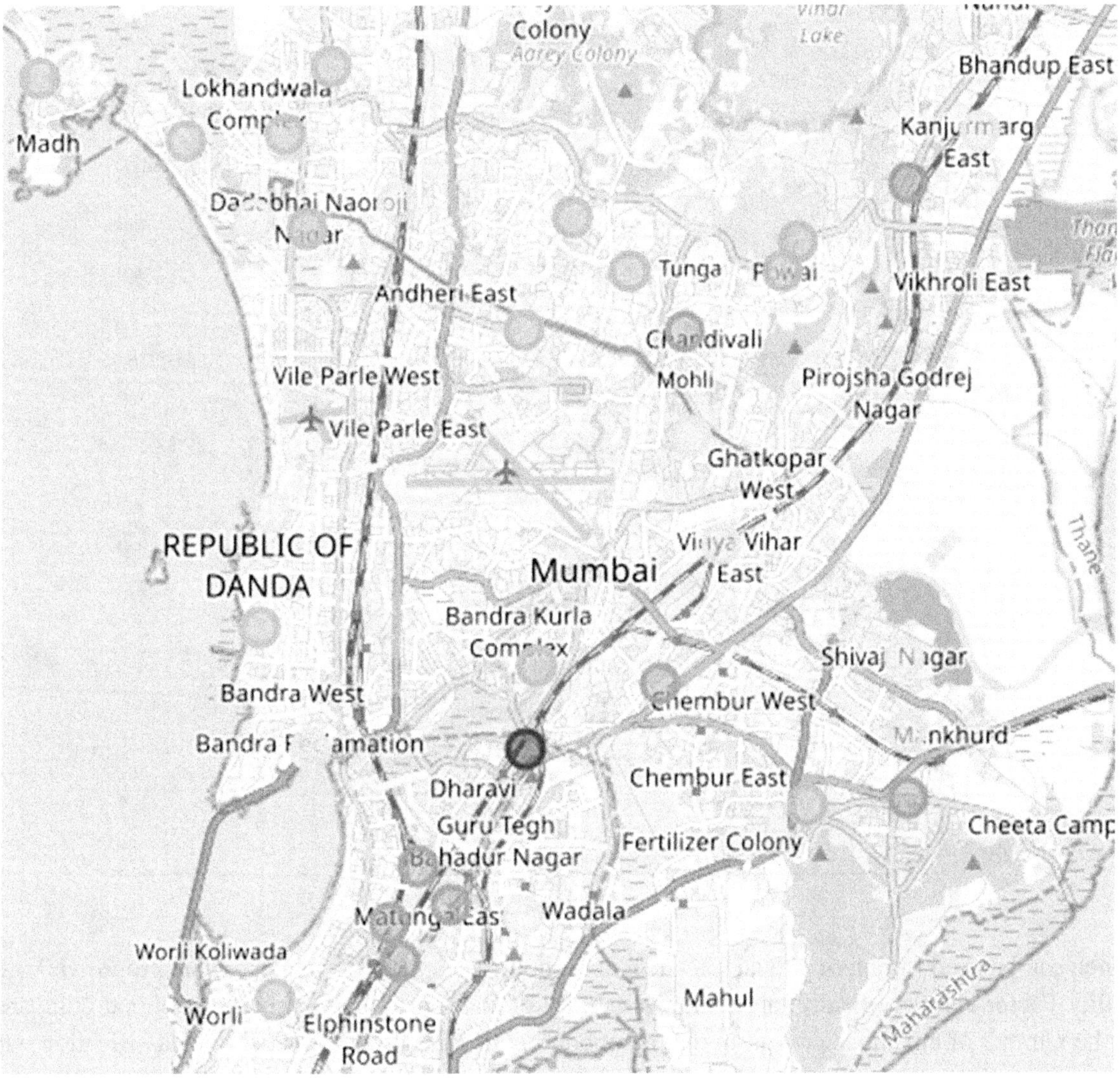

ment of infrastructure in major cities. Furthermore, we use the supervised machine learning algorithm in conjunction with an unsupervised algorithm, a novelty that has not been experimented with in our survey. This classification can help improve the dynamism of the model and accommodate new data in a streamlined manner. With real-time data available for free, these research methodologies can be extrapolated to other crucial issues.

CONCLUSION AND FUTURE WORK

The results of the chapter are the classification of neighbourhoods on the basis of public transportation amenities. It reveals insights into the quality of transportation in the commercial hub of India. This paper has used two parameters for clustering analysis: the number of public transportation infrastructure,

Figure 7. The clusters in North Mumbai

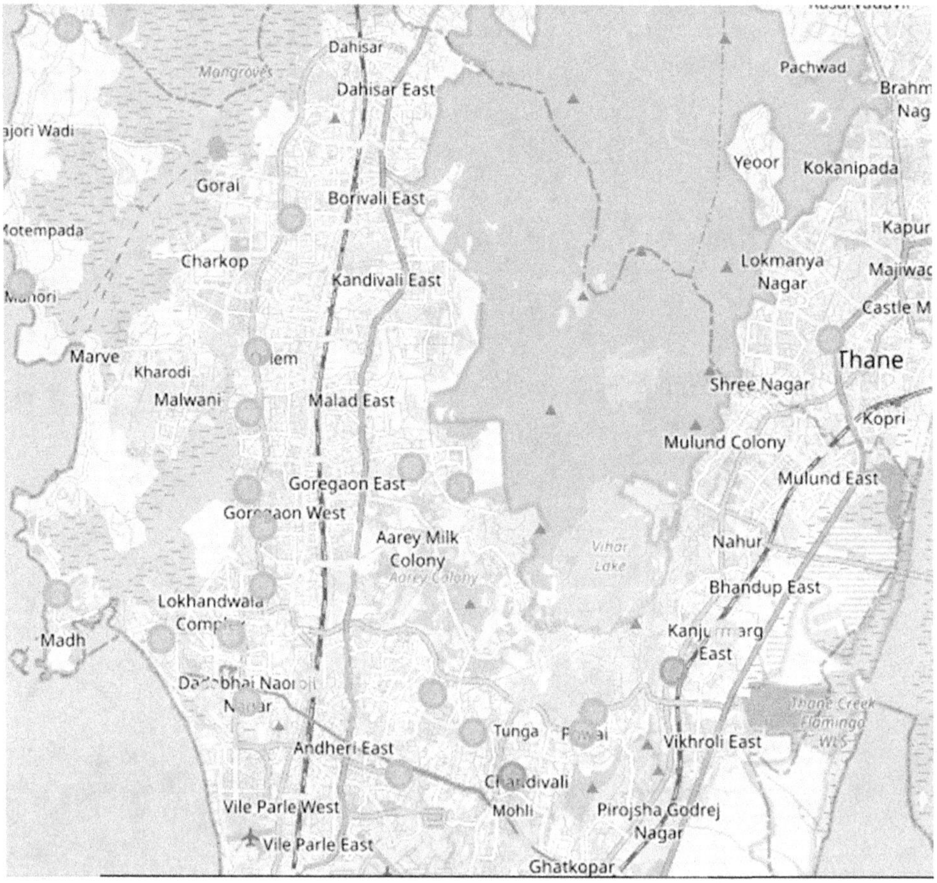

which can be used for inter-city and inter-neighbourhood transportation analysis. The proposed Availability Factor can specifically target the availability of transportation in a neighbourhood compared to the number of amenities present in that neighbourhood. We also use Multiclass Classification with Naive Bayes Classifier to predict the tiers of availability factor for new data. We test this out through a randomized data set and we get promising results as shown in the classification report. This increases dynamism and versatility of the model and streamlines the process of updating the model and data set. From the results, we can see that the neighbourhoods marked indigo and sienna or red are most developed in terms of public transportation infrastructure. Whereas the neighbourhoods marked royal blue, lawn green or yellow are in severe need of development in terms of public transportation.

From this study, we have successfully incorporated certain missing functionalities in the previous papers. We have accomplished the proposal of a new methodology for urban transportation analysis, identified the areas most in need for development and the areas in which a lesser budget for development of transportation would surmise and the use of supervised learning to classify other metropolitan cities. The organisation of these clusters makes it easier for us to concentrate on each section of the problem, its range, the consequences and the area affected. Furthermore, clustering analysis on multiple parameters is an avenue that has not been explored. It allows us to tackle the problem with different perspectives.

Figure 8. The clusters in South Mumbai

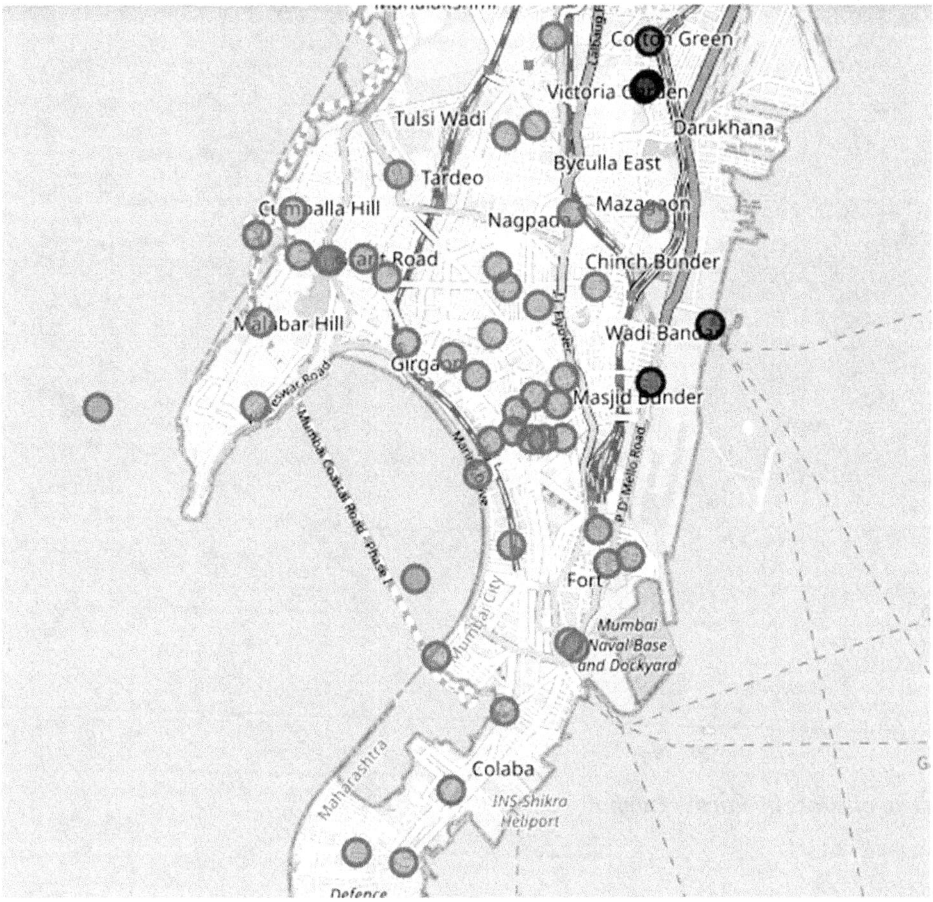

In the future, we would like to explore the applicability of other complex clustering algorithms for this scope. Next, we would like to test the scalability of the proposed model, and test more parameters for precision. Some of the parameters to augment the model could be a survey-based user score, quantitative estimates of road quality, quality of vehicles and repair needs to name a few. And finally, to further the applicability of this model to larger and diverse case studies.

Figure 9. The clusters in Central Mumbai

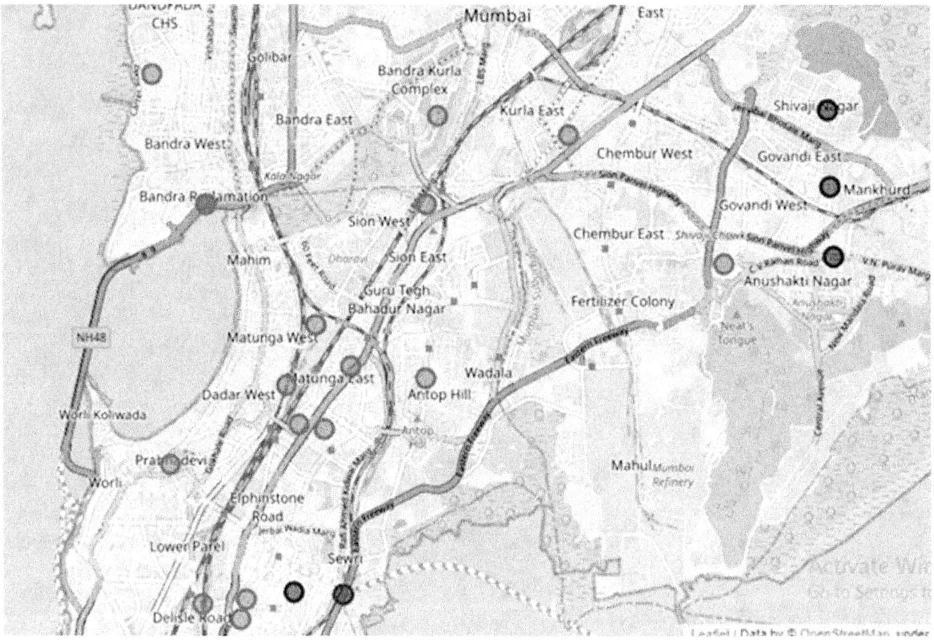

Figure 10. The clusters in North Mumbai

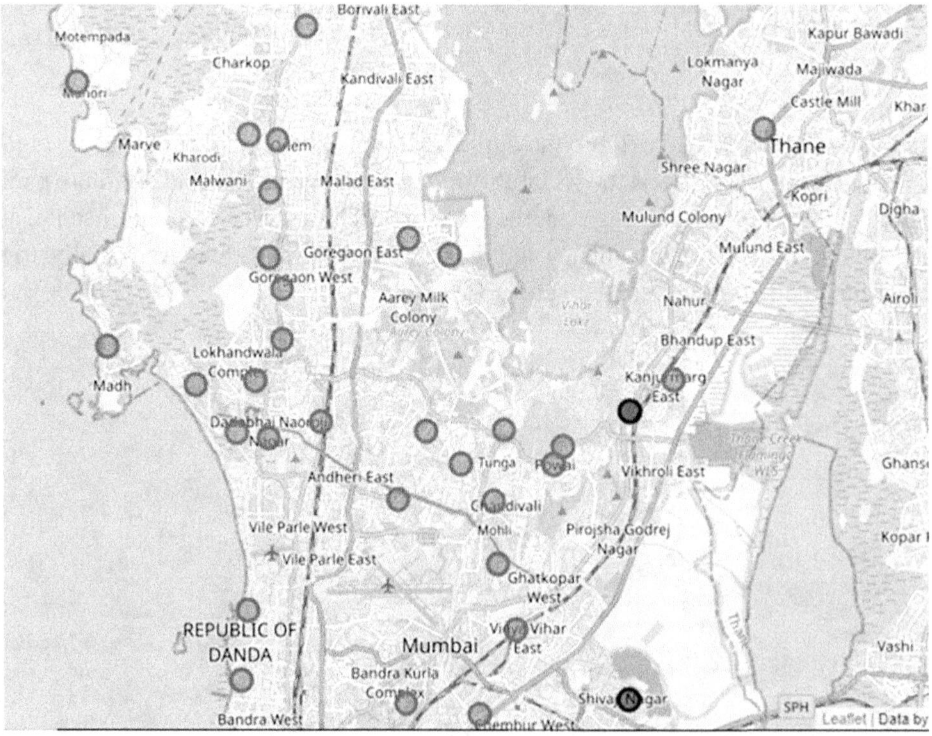

REFERENCES

Bain, K. K. (2015). Customer Segmentation of SMEs Using K-Means Clustering Method and modelling. In *LRFM International Conference on Vocational Education and Electrical Engineering*. Universitas Negeri Surabaya.

Bain, K. K., Firli, I., & Tri, S. (2016). Genetic Algorithm For Optimized Initial Centers K-Means Clustering In SMEs. *Journal of Theoretical and Applied Information Technology*, *90*, 23.

Banfield, J., & Raftery, A. (1993). Model-based gaussian and non-Gaussian Clustering. Biometrics, 49, 803-821.

Bradley, P. S., & Fayyad, U. M. (1998). Refining Initial Points for K-Means Clustering. In *Proceedings of the 15th International Conference on Machine Learning (ICML98)* (pp. 91-99). Morgan Kaufmann.

Chen. (2020). A practical approach to determining critical macroeconomic factors in air-traffic volume based on K-means clustering and decision-tree classification. *Journal of Air Transport Management*, *82*, 101743.

Chen, C., Wang, Y., Hu, W., & Zheng, Z. (2020). Robust multi-view k-means clustering with outlier removal. *Knowledge-Based Systems, 210*.

Cleophas, C., Cottrill, C., Ehmke, J. F., & Tierney, K. (2019). Collaborative urban transportation: Recent advances in theory and practice. *European Journal of Operational Research*, *273*(3), 801–816.

Cosmin, M. P., Marian, C. M., & Mihai, M. (2014). An Optimized Version of the K-Means Clustering Algorithm *Proceedings of the 2014 Federated Conference on Computer Science and Information Systems (ACSIS)*, *2*, 695.

Elmansouri, O., Almhroog, A., & Badi, I. (2020). Urban transportation in Libya: An overview. *Transportation Research Interdisciplinary Perspectives, 8*.

Fränti, P. (2018). Efficiency of random swap clustering. *Journal of Big Data*, *5*(13), 1–29.

Fränti, P., & Sieranoja, S. (2018). K-means properties on six clustering benchmark datasets. *Applied Intelligence*, *48*, 4743–4759. https://doi.org/10.1007/s10489-018-1238-7

Hamerly, G., & Elkan, C. (2002). Alternatives to the K-means algorithm that find better clusterings. *Proceedings of the 11th International Conference on Information and Knowledge Management (CIKM 02)*, 600–607.

Hamurcu, M., & Eren, T. (2020). Strategic Planning Based on Sustainability for Urban Transportation: An Application to Decision-Making. *Sustainability*, *12*(9), 3589.

Han, J., & Kamber, M. (2007). *Data mining Concepts and techniques* (2nd ed.). Morgan Kaufmann Publishers.

Huang, X., Zhang, L., Wang, B., Li, F., & Zhang, Z. (2018). Feature clustering based support vector machine recursive feature elimination for gene selection. *Applied Intelligence*, *48*, 594–607.

Jia, M., Liang, W., Xu, Z., & Huang, M. (2016). *Cloudlet load balancing in wireless metropolitan area networks*. IEEE.

K-means clustering. (n.d.). In *Wikipedia*. Retrieved from https://en.wikipedia.org/wiki/K-means_clustering

Kumar, A., Sinha, R., Bhattacherjee, V., Verma, D. S., & Singh, S. (2012). Modeling using K-means clustering algorithm. *2012 1st International Conference on Recent Advances in Information Technology (RAIT)*, 554-558.

Kumari, C. U., Jeevan Prasad, S., & Mounika, G. (2019). Leaf Disease Detection: Feature Extraction with K-means clustering and Classification with ANN. *3rd International Conference on Computing Methodologies and Communication (ICCMC)*.

Münz, G., Li, S., & Carle, G. (2007). *Traffic Anomaly Detection Using K-Means Clustering*. Academic Press.

Na, S., Xumin, L., & Yong, G. (2010). Research on k-means Clustering Algorithm: An Improved k-means Clustering Algorithm. *2010 Third International Symposium on Intelligent Information Technology and Security Informatics*, 63-67. 10.1109/IITSI.2010.74

Noto, G., & Bianchi, C. (2015). Dealing with Multi-Level Governance and Wicked Problems in Urban Transportation Systems: The Case of Palermo Municipality. *Systems*, *3*(3), 62–80.

Pham, D. T., Dimov, S. S., & Nguyen, C. D. (2003). Incremental K-means algorithm. *Proc. Instn Mech. Engrs. Part C. Journal of Mechanical Engineering Science*, *218*(7), 783–795. doi:10.1243/0954406041319509

Prabhakar &Rajaguru. (2017). PCA and K-Means Clustering for Classification of Epilepsy Risk Levels from EEG Signals – A Comparative Study Between Them. *The 16th International Conference on Biomedical Engineering,* 80-87.

Rezaei, M., & Fränti, P. (2016). Set-matching methods for external cluster validity. *IEEE Transactions on Knowledge and Data Engineering*, *28*(8), 2173–2186.

Rohr, J. R., Raffel, T. R., Romansic, J. M., McCallum, H., & Hud-son, P. J. (n.d.). Evaluating the links between climate, disease spread, and amphibian declines. *Proceedings of the National Academy of Sciences of the United States of America*, 105(45).

Sciara, G.-C. (2017). Metropolitan Transportation Planning: Lessons From the Past, Institutions for the Future. *Journal of the American Planning Association*, *83*(3), 262–276.

Sieranoja, S., & Fränti, P. (2018). Random projection for k-means clustering. *Int. Conf. artificial intelligence and soft computing (ICAISC)*.

Syakur, M. A., Khotimah, B. K., Rochman, E. M. S., & Satoto, B. D. (2018). Integration K-Means Clustering Method and Elbow Method For Identification of The Best Customer Profile Cluster. *IOP Conf. Ser.: Mater. Sci. Eng., 336*.

Theodoridis & Koutroumbas. (2009). *Pattern Recognition* (4th ed.). Academic Press Publications.

Tibshirani, R., Walther, G., & Hastie, T. (2000). *Estimating the number of clusters in a dataset via the gap statistic*. Technical Report 208, Department of Statistics, Stanford University.

Ullah, I., & Youn, H. Y. (2020). Task Classification and Scheduling Based on K-Means Clustering for Edge Computing. *Wireless Personal Communications*, *113*, 2611–2624. https://doi.org/10.1007/s11277-020-07343-w

Van Laerhoven, K. (2001). Combining the Self-Organizing Map and K-Means Clustering for On-Line Classification of Sensor Data. In G. Dorffner, H. Bischof, & K. Hornik (Eds.), Lecture Notes in Computer Science: Vol. 2130. *Artificial Neural Networks — ICANN 2001. ICANN 2001*. Springer. doi:10.1007/3-540-44668-0_65

Vijay Singh, A. K. (2017). Detection of plant leaf disease using image segmentation and soft computing techniques. *Information Processing in Agriculture*, *4*, 4149.

Welcome to BIT Mesra. (n.d.). Retrieved September 7, 2022, from https://www.bitmesra.ac.in/

Xie, S., Hu, Z., & Wang, J. (2020). Two-stage robust optimization for expansion planning of active distribution systems coupled with urban transportation networks. *Applied Energy, 261*.

Yuan, C., & Yang, H. (2019). *Research on K-Value Selection Method of K-Means Clustering Algorithm*. doi:10.3390/j2020016

Chapter 14
Identification of Subtype Blood Cells Using Deep Learning Techniques

Parvathi R.
Vellore Institute of Technology, Chennai, India

Pattabiraman V.
https://orcid.org/0000-0001-8734-2203
Vellore Institute of Technology, Chennai, India

ABSTRACT

The deep learning mechanism has indicated power in numerous applications and is recognized as a superior technique by an ever growing number of people than the conventional models of machine learning. In particular, the use of deep learning algorithms, particularly convolutional neural networks (CNN), brings immense benefits to the clinical sector, where an immense amount of images must be prepared and analyzed. A CNN-based framework is generated to automatically classify the images of blood cells into subtypes of cells. This chapter suggested the deep learning models, which are the convolutional neural network, the deep convolutional neural network, and a CNN-based model built in combination with the recurrent neural network (RNN), which is called RCNN, to identify the monocytes, lymphocytes, and types of WBCs. These are monocytes, eosinophils, lymphocytes, basophils, and neutrophils.

INTRODUCTION

A significant part of the immune system is white blood cells (WBC), also known as leukocytes. By destroying bacteria, viruses, and germs invading our bodies, these cell battle infections. In the bone marrow, white blood cells formed, yet flow through the bloodstreams. It travels from blood to tissue and provides protection against the capture, absorption, demolition of infectious agents or antibody formation of foreign microorganisms, such as germs, viruses and bacteria.

There are five types of leukocytes(WBC):

DOI: 10.4018/978-1-6684-5250-9.ch014

1. Neutrophils,
2. Eosinophils,
3. Lymphocytes,
4. Monocytes and
5. Basophils.
    - **Neutrophils -** in general, Neutrophils are numerous and are responsible for hiding tiny organisms or infectious contaminants from reaching the surface of the cell membrane.
    - **Eosinophils** have very little WBC and function on the basis of sensitivities and parasite diseases.
    - **Lymphocytes** are subject to special identification by distant specialists and eventual expulsion from the host. In the direct annihilation of pathogens and the cleaning of waste from polluted areas.
    - **Monocytes** This counter of various white platelets plays an important role in clinical identification and examination because it represents the secret contamination within the body, which is something that haematologists are aware of and treat as a warning. The abnormal disease in white blood cells is known as leukocytosis, and it is an indicator of this secret contamination. Also possible is the observation of the effectiveness of chemotherapy or radiation therapy, which is referred to as cancer, in persons who have malignant growth by physicians.
    - **Basophils** are bone marrow cells that play a role in preventing the immune system from functioning correctly. It helps to diagnose any health concerns.

The proportion of blood cells is as follows:

- Neutrophils (50-70%)
- Lymphocytes (25-30%)
- Monocytes (3-9%)
- Eosinophils (0-5%)
- Basophils (0-1%)

Identifying and distinguishing the complex WBC from other WBC, as well as quantifying the matching proportions, is critical due to the quantity of clinical significance that it carries. In order for the automated categorization based on WBC images to emerge, it is necessary to manually differentiate leukocytes under magnifying tools, which is time-consuming and of inferior quality.

For the most part, with a few simple steps, automated classification approaches are available: **preprocessing, segmentation, extraction of features, and classification.**

Preprocessing The term "preprocessing" refers to the practice of attempting to reduce noise from images or other objects in order to produce high-contrast images.

Segmentation Alternatively, segmentation may be seen as as the process of separating the WBC from the background of smear photographs or eliminating the Region of Interest (ROI) from the images again. The next step is to create an agent highlight vector for each of the WBC forms that have been identified.

Feature Extraction is the option of images that monstrously affects the execution of the classifier. For a good grouping, each WBC subtype must be identified by the highlights and must be independent of each other for better judgment and correlation.

All established image highlights can be collected into

- shape features (regions of the cell, core cell edge, minimization, roundness).
- intensity features histogram (mean, standard deviation, skewness)
- texture features (differentiate, homogeneity, connection, entropy).

The shape highlight of the object is accepted in this work because it is seen as effective in identifying the Lymphocytes from various WBC forms.

Classification Hematologists may also be interested in the identification of the features throughout these critical periods of the disease process. White blood cells are divided into two categories: granulocytes and nongranulocytes. Granulocytes are the most common kind of white blood cell (also known as agranulocytes). Neutrophils, eosinophils, and basophils are examples of granulocytes, which are cells that contain granules in their cell cytoplasm. They may also contain a multilobed nucleus, which is unusual. Agranulocytes are seen in lymphocytes and monocytes, which are cells that do not have visible granules. Images of granulocytes and nongranulocytes are shown in the section "Granules." (Pictures are inserted – processing characteristics are segmented and classified in the extraction process.)

PROBLEM STATEMENT

Counting machines that automatically count the number of samples have been available in clinical testing facilities for over 30 years. The methods utilised to do cell counts determine whether a combination of mechanical, electrical, and chemical approaches should be used. Physical WBC totaling and form organisation by a qualified pathologist, who examines the shape of the cells, including the nucleus and cytoplasm, occlusion, and degree of contact among cells, is the most widely used method across biological disciplines and the gold standard.

Regardless issue, however extensive or accurate the manual inspection procedure, there will always be three categories of faults: statistical or factual errors, distributional errors, and human errors such as poor-quality or low-magnification viewpoints on the slides.

The most common issues with the classification of various white blood cell types are:

- Manual counting is affected negatively by poor magnification and the dispersion of leukocytes, which are both factors that reduce precision of the differential count. Manual examination and physical cell tallying have been abandoned in favour of electronic methods. As an initial point of reference, the success of manual cell tallying is tremendously dependent on the image resolution.
- At higher goals, more exactness can be accomplished. However, this methodology is laborious and expensive.
- Under high goals settings, multiple images must be procured to cover the entire region.
- Second, manual techniques are likewise error-prone due to natural fatigue after hours of analysis.
- Obviously, cell attributes, for example, cell or cluster size, are hard to acquire physically.
- Third, processing images could take a long time. It takes care to analyze advanced cells that magnify lens images, which may take several rounds to verify the findings.

In contrast, the computer vision (CV) methods are promising for analyzing microscopic images, and also in this manner, they are an option for manual strategies for biological research. In reality, M. Lejeune has accomplished a semi-mechanized measurement of differing subcellular immunohistochemical markers with program Image-Pro Plus. In any case, it requires researchers to input complex commands at each progression. In the literature, image segmentation strategies, including color space, threshold, and classifiers, have been received in handling bio-medical images. Most current work basically focuses on the processing of high magnification images and the identification of WBC nuclei. A new segmentation technique that can process and analyze these images adaptively and robustly whenever needed is for images with clustered WBCs and complex backgrounds.

POST/RELATED WORK

There were two forms of post work to count the WBCs in the bloodstream: the automatic and the physical way.

The Automatic Method: Coulter Counters and Laser Flow Cytometry

The Coulter Counter, which was created in the 1950s and is still in use today, is considered the world's first automated system. When it comes to identifying and counting WBCs, a Coulter Counter takes use of the fact that they are poor electricity conductors. The counter is comprised of a conductive solution consisting of two balls, as well as a tiny channel over which a current can pass.

The current flowing via the channel drops as the cells travel via the channel, and this decrease is relative to the shape and size of the cells moving through the channel The machine determines the form of the cell by calculating the transition between two conditions. Coulter counters, which have lately gained popularity as a safer alternative to laser flow cytometers, have been developed. In this type of technology, a laser is shone through a channel, and the amount of light refracted from the laser when cells move over it is measured. The system's goal is to determine the location of the specified cell based on the refraction of light. These devices perform at a high level in comparison to Coulter Counters since they use light instead of electricity as the channel for calculating disturbances against it.

In the tens of thousands of dollars, the price of both the Coulter Counter and Laser Flow Cytometers. There is little uncertainty, however, that it has played a key role in enhancing quantitative understanding of our well being. *The manual Method: Inspecting a Sample under a Microscope*

The manual method is exactly as it sounds: a blood sample is located below a microscope, and the sum of cells in every frame is manually counted by a pathologist. The number is then determined by supposing that and multiplying the distribution over the entire blood sample is uniform.

LITERATURE REVIEW

More and more individuals consider deep learning as a better solution than conventional machine learning models. The introduction of deep learning algorithms has brought enormous benefits to the field of medicine, especially Convolutionary Neural Networks (CNN), where a large number of images are processed and analyzed. A deep learning model has evolved in this paper to diagnose blood cells. A double

Convolutional Layer Neural Network (DCLNN) CNN-based structure has been developed to classify blood cells(Shuangling).From a microscopic blood picture that uses the saturation portion of HSV (Hue, Saturation, Value) with blob examination for segmentation and CNN for total(G G Gardner) The White Blood Cells (WBC) image recognition issue is being studied. Using a feed forward back propagation neural network, five forms of white blood cells are listed(S.Roychowdhury,2014)To detect anaemia, leukaemia, and a variety of other hematologic illnesses, white blood cells are classified and tested for specific characteristics. It is especially true for uncommon types of leukocytes that the machine learning technique, which takes a significant amount of time and has a high mistake rate in recognition, is used. The techniques utilised for automatic classification include Knearest Neighbor (K=3), Support Vector Machine, Logistic Regression, Decision Tree, and CNN Model, with the greatest accuracy being Knearest Neighbor (K=3), Support Vector Machine, and CNN Model (J.Lachure,2015) .The three layers of the Artificial Neural Network (ANN) architecture are used for the best output and error for blood analysis (R.Priya,2012) Using probabilities of co-occurrence, we can quantify the grey scale image texture. We can also evaluate the characteristics of leukocyte recognition using a statistical method for characterizing the Gray Level Co-occurrence Matrices (GLCM) spatial organisation such as energy, entropy, inertia, and local homogeneity(S.Giraddi,2015).For the classification of several joint histogram-based features for the extraction of segmented blood cells, the suggested Bhattacharya kernel coefficient of a joint histogram with an aid vector machine is used (G.Lim,2014) Three types of features are extracted, i.e. geometric features, color characteristics, and LDP-based texture characteristics to segment a white blood cell from a smear picture (Winder,2009) Three Fuzzy C-means (FCM), Classic K-Means (CKM) and Enhanced KMeans (EKM) clustering techniques and Mean- shift Filtering (MSF) and Seeded Region Growing (SRG) filtering techniques are implemented (S. Ravikumar,2015).An adaptive K-Means clustering algorithm is used to apply automatic segmentation. HIS and S components in white blood cells, an approach based on a circular histogram in the iterative Otsu method for leukocyte segmentation. A technique of contrast enhancement has been developed to ease the segmentation process (Mehdi Habibzadeh,2014) Image acquisition, preprocessing, image enhancement, image segmentation, function extraction are used in the primary stages of noise and outlier removal(Thulasimani Thangamani,2020) .Picture Segmentation is a system in which blood cell types are classified irrespective of their irregular shapes, sizes and orientation. White blood cells differential counts, by using Mathematical morphology, Fuzzy C-means and Bayes classifier(Merl James Macawile,2018) .Extremely powerful learning machine When using RVM to fit the histogram, it is necessary to create sparse relevance vectors (RVs). The relevant necessary threshold value is filtered openly from the minimum RVs, and the complete connective WBC areas are segregated from the original picture using the appropriate necessary threshold value. To detect WBC, the proposed method successfully searches for the finest value of each parameter that changes its discriminating function, as well as upstream, by searching for a subset of features that feeds the RVM classifier, in order to achieve the highest possible precision of the RVM classifier, and to search for the best value of each parameter that changes its discriminating function((G Y. Rajaa Vikhram,2018), (Bambang Krismono,2017).A morphological approach to image segmentation, most efficient than the conventional algorithm focused on the watershed. Centered on opening gray scale granulometries with disk- shaped elements, flat and non-flat. A non-flat diskshaped structuring element has been used to improve the roundness and enhance the compactness of red cells.(Sankara Nayaki,2020), (Wei Yu, 2017) . Various Deep Learning Model for the Automatic Classification of White Blood Cells is discussed along with accuracy (Sarang Sharma, 2022) Automatic classification of leukocytes using deep neural network (Yu, W,2022), Efficient Classification of White Blood Cell Leukemia with Improved Swarm Optimization of Deep Features(Sahlol,2020) and

Classification of white blood cells by deep learning methods for diagnosing disease(Yildirim,2019) were discussed. White Blood Cell Leukemia classification is carried out with Improved Swarm Optimization of Deep Features(Sahlol,2020) . White blood cells detection and classification using RNN is experimented by (Kutlu H,2020) and using capsule networks (Baydilli YY,2020). Automatic classification of white blood cells using deep features using deep features are analyzed by (Meenakshi,2022) . Classification of lymphocytes, monocytes, eosinophils, and neutrophils on white blood cells using hybrid Alexnet-GoogleNet-SVM were experimented by (Çınar, A,2021)

OBJECTIVES

The key goal of this study is to create a tool to process and interpret a large number of photographs of white blood cells automatically.

- Create a classified model
- Enhance the accuracy of the work
- Enhance the response time
- Extraction and analysis of WBCs
- To provide results instantaneously
- Cheaper equipment
- Improved method than the previous approach
- The accuracy of the proposed model should be high.

Similar to other machine learning, it assures to get improved over time. If the more blood cells are given for the experimentation and classify them with increased dataset size then it will give the good results.

CHALLENGES

The challenges faced during the development of the project are:

- An issue with the quality of the image: The quality of the WBCs images is significantly worse.
- Issue in detecting the features of the images.
- Issues related to object-specific segmentation because in WBCs, the types of cells have a very minute difference.
- Study of the WBC organization from microscopic images and cell grouping into types and subtypes is difficult due to the dissimilarity of the cell form in the maturation stage and the intra-class difference in images due to the use of separate possession and staining methods. A large variety of state-of-the-art approaches in the WBC grouping task is due to the great interest in the health, hematology, and medical imaging community.
- Various measures, including image enhancement, image segmentation, extraction of features, classification and assessment,

- The method of recognizing WBC in photographs, including obtaining images, and the outcome of staining to imagine fluctuations in nucleus color and form.
- The challenges, including illustration difference, deviations in size and location,

Various maturation stages, shape, rotation, and background difference.

Features

With the automation of the classification of white blood cells, the organization can reduce human efforts, cost, and time. With this, the organization can able to implement the system of classification of WBCs. The best-in-class features of this project are:

- Time-saving: Manually classifying the blood cells can take lots of time. It will save hours that are spent on the verification and processing of blood cells.
- Improvement of accuracy of the work: More efforts can be made in a machine instead of humans, so there is less chance of error in the work.
- The analysis of the present methods with respect to the above-given challenges are evaluated.
- Cost reduction: The organization can reduce costs. There is less intervention of human power.

Data Acquisition

The images of white blood cells are taken and the segmentation of the images is done to extract the unique features to create knowledge base each and every image. A standard models developed for evaluating the classification results for each type of blood cells using CNN, DCNN and RCNN.

Preprocessing

- RGB to grayscale:

In layman terms, an RGB image is denoted as a matrix of X, Y dimensions,and depthof3planeswhereeachplanecomprisesofRed, Green, and Blue values ranging from 0 to 255. Whereas, gray image is denoted as a matrix of X, Y dimensions, and depth of only one plane. Each cell value varies from 0 to 255. Any RGB (Red, Green, Blue) image, which has to undergo Image Processing (IP) needs to be converted to a grayscale image. The computational complexity of IP decreases significantly by doing this and allows to run algorithms for image processing in a much smoother way.

Training the Model

We are using CNNs in this application. A CNN (or ConvNet) is a kind of deep, feed-forward artificial neural networks that have been used successfully for visual images analysis. Biological processes inspired CNN's, in that the communication arrangement between neurons parallel, the arrangement of the visual cortex of the animal. We use the Keras library with the Tensor Flow backend for the implementation of CNN in our work. The directory of preprocessed images is loaded and then we train the model to evaluate the output with distinct training- testing split ratios. For training images and testing images, it is spilt in the ratio of 80%-20%. The training images taken are thousand and the testing image is taken as two thousand five hundred.

Once the image is converted into the desired size then we apply the machine learning algorithm i.e. CNN and DNN. With the help of these algorithms, we compare every image with the process image, and once the process has been done then we get equal class representation by duplicating the different levels of training data. Then we get back to the

Back system once all these parts have done perfectly, then the system will create balanced classes that will tell the user what the system has been predicted. Predictions will be divided into four groups and then it will give the result to the users that the patient having the tumor in the brain or no symptoms of brain tumor disease. After which we will be able to get the visualization part of the brain MRI images which it belongs to and accuracy of the model.

PROPOSED MODEL

Recently, most image processing researchers have been increasingly interested in the advancement of machine learning techniques, particularly those using deep neural networks applied to handwritten digital identification datasets such as the MNIST dataset and IMAGENET image classification. On the basis of these major characteristics of illness severity categorization derived from blood cell images, a recommended strategy has emerged as a strong contender.

The focus is working towards these models which are as follows.

- Deep Learning Model with power of Transfer Learning to classify images of a particular class.
- Algorithm/model to extract the information out of brains.

In the proposed model for the classification of the design is simplified:

- Data Augmentation
- Preprocessing
- CNN Architecture

Data Augmentation: blood cell images were acquired using different datasets of different fields of vision, non-clearness, blurring, contrast and picture sizes, captured under different camera sets. Contrast adjustment, rotating images and brightness changes is made in data augmentation.

Preprocessing: Both snapshots have been translated for pre-processing, record augmentation, and training in a hierarchical statistical format. There were several steps involved in preprocessing: photographs were cropped using Otsu's method. Images were normalized by subtracting from each channel the minimum pixel intensity and dividing by means of the inferred pixel depth to symbolize pixels in the range 0 to 1. The use of the evaluation contrast restricted adaptive histogram equalization (CLAHE) filtering algorithm is carried out by contrast correction.

CNN Architecture: Essentially, it is a feed-forward artificial neural network in which the pattern of communication between its neurons is influenced by the arrangement of the visual cortex of animals, in which individual neurons are organized in such a way that they respond to overlapping regions of the visual field tiled together. The convolutional neural network employs a sophisticated design consisting of multiple layers in which the images are very well suited for classification in deep learning, and this architecture is particularly well suited for classification in deep learning. This sort of method is durable and adaptable to each and every brand depicted in the images for use in a multi-class arrangement.

The typical layers used in the production of CNN are:

- Convolutional Layer
- Pooling Layer
- RelU Layer
- Dropout Layer
- Fully connected Layer

Classification Model and Convolutional Layer:

Following the identification of the input image, this is the first and most important layer to be identified. Local receptive fields, as well as mutual weights, are the building blocks of a convolutional neural network's architecture. These are used to construct a deep convolutional neural network for the identification of pictures. The filter kernel or package is the building block of the convolutional layer (local receptive field). Convoluting each filter involves applying a new layer or activation map to the input picture and deleting the features from it. Each activation map contains or reflects any fundamental qualities or attributes of the input picture that were present in the original image. Convolution is achieved by convolution the NxN input neuron layer with the MxM filter in the convolution layer. The contribution of the convolution layer will thus be of the scale (N-m+1) x (N-m+1), and so on. The function of brain activity introduces nonlinearity into the system.

Pooling Details

This is one of the most important layers that support the network by decreasing parameters and calculation in the network to prevent over-fitting. This functions as a form of nonlinear down sampling. The activation maps are pooled into a collection of rectangles and the maximum value in the sub area is obtained. The pixels with features are merely a downsize. For example, if the NxN input layer is used, it will provide the N/K x N/K layer output layer. The key importance of this layer is to question if somewhere in a region of the picture a given attribute is located. It then throws the same positional data away.

ReLU Layer:

The function $f(x) = max(0, x)$ is extended by the ReLU layer to all the values in the input volume. This layer essentially changes all the negative activations to 0 in simple terms. This layer improves the model's nonlinear properties and the total network without influencing the conv layer's receptive fields.

Dropout Layer:

The parameters that are generated from each stacked layer are meticulously handled by the deep convolutional neural network's critical element, which is comprised of several layers. Over-fitting is a condition that can occur. In order to prevent such events from occurring, some neurons in the layer that transfered to the next layer were removed. Dropouts are used to prevent the creation of parameters that aren't essential, particularly near the completely linked layer. The term refers to a sort of regularisation that is commonly utilised.

Final Layer:

The Fully Linked Layer is the one that comes after the convolutional and max/average pooling layers in a cascaded fashion. This layer is responsible for the high-level reasoning that occurs during categorization. A wholly connected layer gets all neurons from max-pooling layer in the preceding layer and adds them to any neurons that the layer already has in its network. Fully associated layers are no longer spatially connected, and as a result, they are shown as a single-dimensional layer.

Classification Layer:

The final layer is constructed with SoftMax layer that is arranged at the end to identify the fundus picture after the stacked as shown in Fig. 1

Figure 1. Layer Diagram

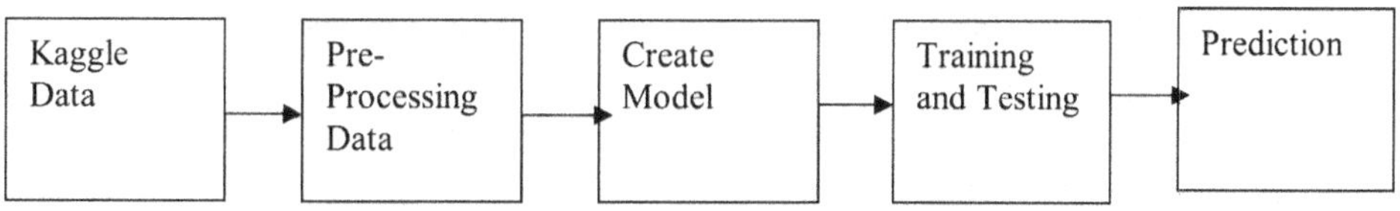

RESULTS

Once we have completed the classification and analysis of the training dataset, we will be able to extract and categorize the various entities of blood types that have been discovered within it. It is also possible to categorize images of blood cells by subtypes using CNN, which may be accomplished by classifying the different regions of an image of blood cells. Previously, it was not feasible to forecast the real problem by looking at the image directly, and even if it were possible, the findings were not sufficiently precise. As a result, several strategies are being developed in order to obtain precision. We were able to achieve an accuracy rate of 98 percent after running the classification algorithm on a large number of data sets, which we can share with the doctors so that they can begin collecting data on how our model performs in the real world.Additionally, it is intended to commercialize the technology, first cross the regulatory hurdles. As previously said, an essential contribution of this algorithm is to assist in the execution of clinical validation by contributing to a validation strategy, which is a key step in the process. It's important to remember that medical validation is taking demonstrating that our technology functions in the manner that we claim. If someone claims that their device can measure hippocampal volume, validation must demonstrate that it is capable of doing so and verify the amount to which we claim is correct, among other things. In order to verify this, our validation strategy must specify how it will do so and to what degree it will do so.

CONCLUSION

The project summarizes the key aspects and usage of machine learning in healthcare. The project provides a free and easy use of usage to the clinics and labs to detect any blood related problems and with the help of this technology, doctors can easily predict whether they are prone to disease or not. Hence, the project focused on contributing to a smart solution in the early prediction of blood disease using deep learning techniques. Even In spite of the significant influence the study approaches of deep learning techniques have had on quantitative clinical image analysis, it is still difficult to develop a standard procedure that is resilient to all differences in blood pictures from various institutions. The execution of deep learning methods is heavily reliant on a number of critical aspects, including preprocessing, initialization, and post-processing, among others. In addition, training datasets are tiny in comparison to large size ImageNet/Clinical datasets (e.g., millions of images) in order to achieve simplicity across datasets (e.g., millions of images). On top of that, existing deep learning architectures builds on supervised learning, which necessitates the creation of manual ground truth labels, which is time-consuming task when dealing with a large-scale dataset. Because of this, deep learning models that are particularly resilient to fluctuations in blood or that have unsupervised learning capabilities with lower reliance on ground truth labels are necessary to be developed. Additionally, data augmentation technologies that effectively imitate changes in blood data might reduce the requirement for a significant quantity of data, which is beneficial. As demonstrated in n, transfer learning may be beneficial in contributing to high-performing deep learning models. Figures 2 and 3 show the accuracy and loss of the model, respectively.

After performing various classifications and analysis of the training dataset we are in the position to extract and classify the different entities of blood types found in the dataset. Also, with the use of artificial intelligence we achieved a way to classify the image of the subtype of blood cells by categorizing the different portions. Earlier it is not possible to predict the actual problem by seeing the image directly and also if possible, the results are not accurate enough. So, we have developed some techniques to achieve the accuracy. After performing the numerous algorithms of classification on a large no. of data sets, we acquired the accuracy rate of 98%. Along with this, the developed AI system, and which can be used by the clinicians, so that, the technician can acquire the data and test our model performs in the real world. It is discussed in our final experimentation, the main influence of an AI expert of this work is helping perform the medical justification by contributing to a validation design. Summon up that medical authentication is all about demonstrating that our technology achieves the way we privilege it does. Our validation plan requirements to describe how we would demonstrate this and found these extents.

If we talk about the preprocessing of the medical images part where we see that first we are loading the original image of the patient eye then we

adjusting the eye with the help of estimating of the radius of the eye. Once we got the radius of the eye we are trying to resizing the image with the scale of 256 pixels so that the we get the more accurate images of brain MRI. If they want to crop the unwanted parts of the image, then we can crop the image. The best validation accuracy was achieved on the 23rd iteration.

Once everything has been done, then we will apply the Gaussian blur func- town so that we can convert the image into a gray scale image. If we see in the above image we see that there is a boundary so we remove that boundary. And then placing the image in the center of 512 pixels.

Figure 2. Model Accuracy

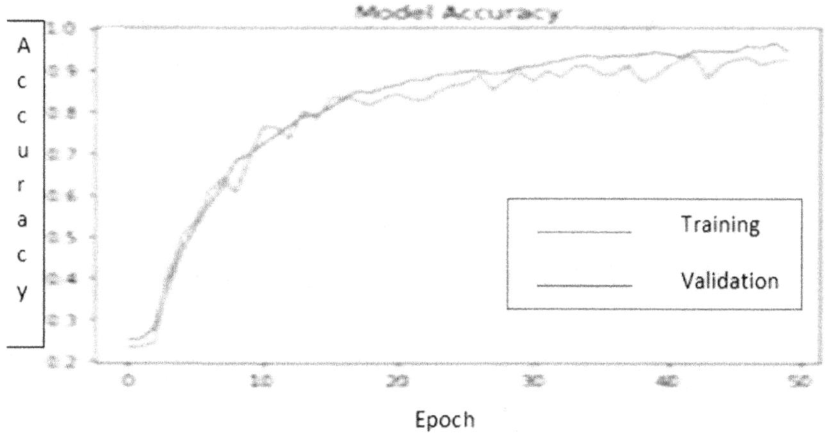

Discussions

This study has exposed that the five-elegance has lex for national screening of medical images can be analyzed using the CNN approach. Our network has exposed likely signs of being able to examine the capabilities necessary to categorize of images and appropriately categorizing the popular of proliferative cases and not using a Classification of subtype of blood. As in different studies using huge datasets excessive specificity has come with an exchange off decrease sensitivity. Our method produces comparable on sequences to those previous techniques with none feature-specific detection and the usage of a mile's trendier dataset. The prospective advantage of the use of our educated CNN is that it can classifyheaps of images, each minute allowing it for use in actual time each time a brand- new image is obtained. In exercise pictures are dispatched to clinicians for grading and now not correctly graded when the affected person is in for screening. The trained CNN makes a quick diagnosis and immediate reaction to an affected person possible. The community additionally accomplished those effects with simplest one picture in

Figure 3. Model Loss

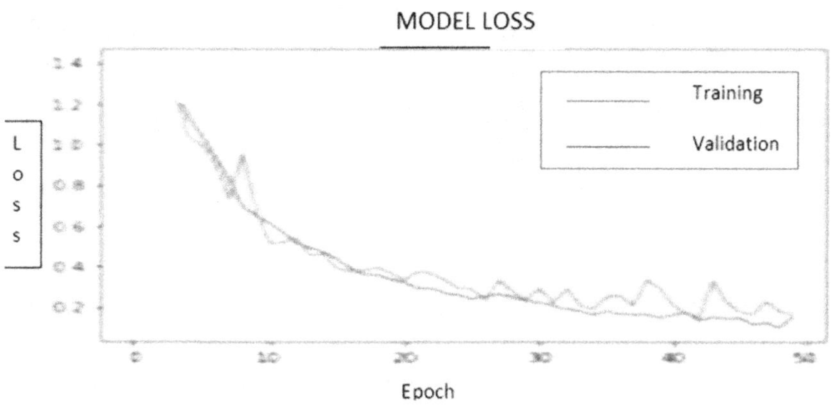

Figure 4. Result of detection of different blood types

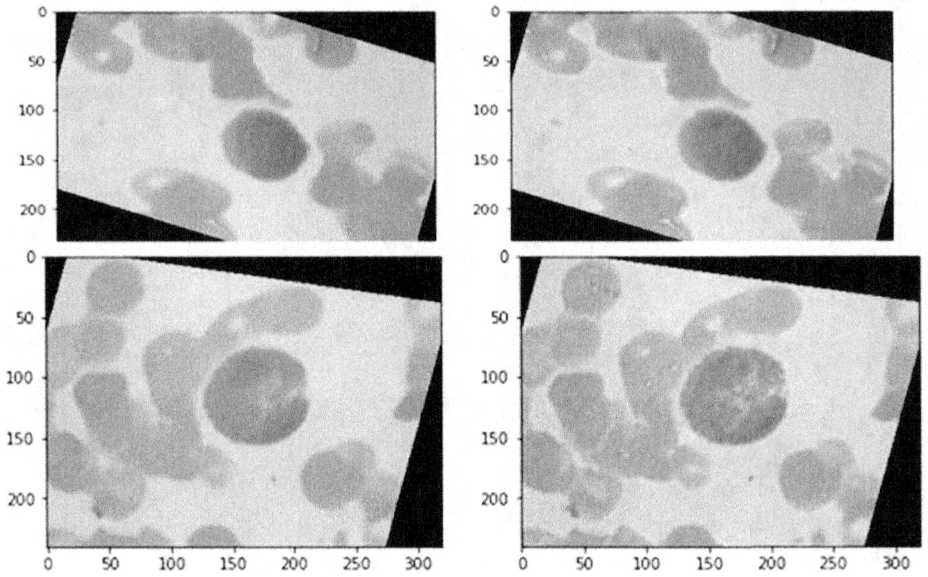

step with eye. In schooling the gaining knowledge of required to classify the photographs at the extreme ends of the scale become significantly much less. The problems derived in making the community to differentiate between the Monocytes, Lymphocytes, Eosinophils, Basophils and Neutrophils. The low sensitivity, mainly from the mild and moderate training indicates the network resisted to learn deep enough capabilities to locate some of the most problematic factors. These snap shots had been defined a class on the premise of getting at least a positive stage. This may want to have significantly hindered our consequences as the photographs are misclassified for both schooling and validation.

Figure 5. Result of detection of different blood types

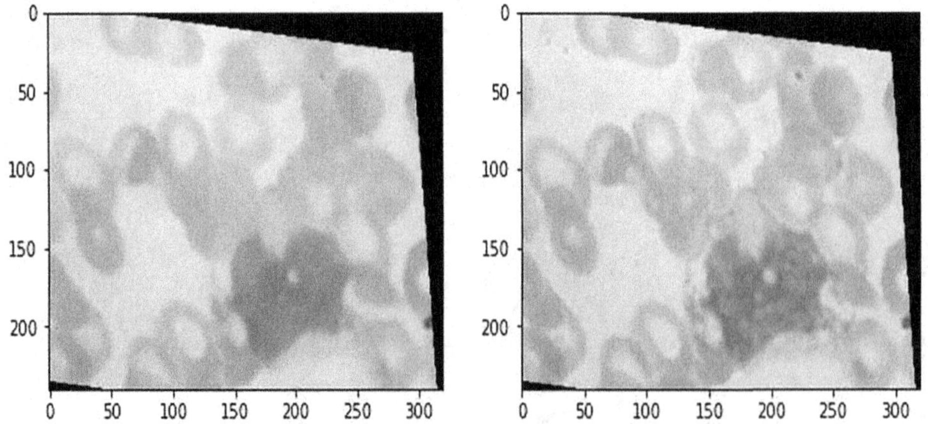

CONCLUSION

The chapter summarizes the key aspects and usage of machine learning in healthcare. The project provides a free and ease use of usage to the patients to detect any blood related problems and with the help of this technology, doctors can easily predict whether they are prone to disease or not. Hence, the project focused on contributing to a smart solution in the early prediction of blood disease using machine learning techniques. Even with the significant impact that deep learning techniques have had flagrant study tactics on quantitative clinical imaging, it is still difficult to develop a standard method that is resistant to all of the differences in blood images that are produced by various institutions. The successful application of deep learning methods is strongly dependent on a great number of important parameters, including preprocessing, initialization, and post-processing. Also, training datasets are comparatively small related to large-scale ImageNet/Clinical dataset (e.g., billions of images) to achieve simplification across datasets. In addition, the most recent generations of deep learning architectures are dependent on supervised learning and need for the creation of manual ground truth labels. This is laborious work when applied to a massive dataset. Hence, we need deep learning models that are either exceedingly strong in fluctuations of blood or have the capability of unsupervised learning with fewer dependence on ground truth labels. Both of these approaches are desirable. In addition, the use of data augmentation methods that realistically replicate variances in blood data might eliminate the requirement for a huge amount of data to be collected.Transfer learning might be useful to contribute to well-performing deep learning architectures, which are experimented on normal and pathological brain MRI data, among brain imaging research groups and enhance the standardization ability of these architectures across datasets with less work than learning from scratch.

Future Work:

Future scope of the work for improvement includes:

- This can be extended as a mobile application as well as computer soft- ware for ease use of doctors.
- Use of Sensors and Internet of Things can be extended in a real time application.
- More work needed in CNN to get better results.
- For photographs taken from different cameras with different fields of view, an additional step increase is needed.

REFERENCES

Baydilli, Y. Y., & Atila, Ü. (2020). Classification of white blood cells using capsule networks. *Computerized Medical Imaging and Graphics.*

Çınar, A., & Tuncer, S. A. (2021). Classification of lymphocytes, monocytes, eosinophils, and neutrophils on white blood cells using hybrid Alexnet-GoogleNet-SVM. *SN Appl. Sci.*, *3*, 503.

Gardner, Keating, Williamson, & Elliott. (n.d.). Deep Learning Algorithms for classing subtypes of blood. *British Journal of Opthalmology.*

Giraddi, Pujari, & Seeri. (2015). Identifying Abnormalities in the Blood cell Images using SVM Classifiers. *International Journal of Computers and Applications*, *111*(6).

Habibzadeh, Krzyżak, & Fevens. (2014). *Comparative Study of Feature Selection for White Blood Cell Differential Counts in Low Resolution Images*. Springer Science and Business Media LLC.

Kutlu, H., Avci, E., & Özyurt, F. (2020). White blood cells detection and classification based on regional convolutional neural networks. *Medical Hypotheses*.

Lachure, D., & Lachure, G., & Jadhav. (2015). White blood cell study and detection using Machine Learning. *IEEE International Advance Computing Conference (IACC)*.

Lim, Lee, & Hsu. (2014). Transformed Representations for Convolutional Neural Networks in Blood subtypes detection. *Modern Artificial Intelligence for Health Analytic Papers from the AAAI.*

Macawile, Quinones, Ballado, Cruz, & Caya. (2018). White blood cell classification and counting using convolutional neural network. *2018 3rd International Conference on Control and Robotics Engineering (ICCRE)*.

Meenakshi, Anitha Ruth, Kanagavalli, & Uma. (2022). Automatic classification of white blood cells using deep features based convolutional neural network. *Multimedia Tools and Applications*, •••, 101.

Nayaki, D., Rubeena, & Denny. (2020). Cloud based Acute Lymphoblastic Leukemia Detection Using Deep Convolutional Neural Networks. *2020 Second International Conference on Inventive Research in Computing Applications (ICIRCA)*.

Priya & Aruna. (2012). SVM and Neural Network based Diagnosis of blood cell types. *International Journal of Computers and Applications*, *41*(1).

Ravikumar, S. (2015). Image segmentation and classification of white blood cells with the extreme learning machine and the fast relevance vector machine. *Artificial Cells, Nanomedicine, and Biotechnology*.

Roychowdhury, S., Koozekanani, D. D., & Keshab, K. P. (2014). Blood subtypes detection Using Machine Learning. *IEEE Journal of Biomedical and Health Informatics*, *18*(5).

Sahlol, A. T., Kollmannsberger, P., & Ewees, A. A. (2020). Efficient Classification of White Blood Cell Leukemia with Improved Swarm Optimization of Deep Features. *Scientific Reports*, *10*(1), 2536. doi:10.103841598-020-59215-9 PMID:32054876

Sahlol, A. T., Kollmannsberger, P., & Ewees, A. A. (2020). Efficient Classification of White Blood Cell Leukemia with Improved Swarm Optimization of Deep Features. *Scientific Reports*, *10*(1), 2536. doi:10.103841598-020-59215-9 PMID:32054876

Sharma, S., Gupta, S., Gupta, D., Juneja, S., Gupta, P., Dhiman, G., & Kautish, S. (2022). Deep Learning Model for the Automatic Classification of White Blood Cells. Computational Intelligence and Neuroscience. doi:10.1155/2022/7384131

Thangamani, Prabha, & Prasad, Kumari, Raghavender, & Abidin. (2020). IoT Defense Machine Learning: Emerging Solutions and Future Problems. *Microprocessors and Microsystems*.

Triwijoyo, Budiharto, & Abdurachman. (2017). The Classification of Hypertensive Retinopathy using Convolutional Neural Network. *Procedia Computer Science*. doi:10.1109/ICIRCA48905.2020.9183249

Vikhram, Agarwal, Uprety, & Prasanth. (2018). Automatic Weed Detection and Smart Herbicide Sprayer Robot. *IACSIT International Journal of Engineering and Technology*.

Wang, Yin, Cao, Wei, Zheng, & Yang. (n.d.). *Detection of blood cells*. School of Computer Science and Technology, Shandong University.

Winder, R. J., Morrow, P. J., McRitchie, I. N., Bailie, J. R., & Hart, P. M. (2009). Algorithms for digital image processing in white blood cells. *Computerized Medical Imaging and Graphics*, *33*(8), 608–622. doi:10.1016/j.compmedimag.2009.06.003 PMID:19616920

Yildirim, M., & Çinar, A. (2019). Classification of white blood cells by deep learning methods for diagnosing disease. *Revue d'Intelligence Artificielle*, *33*(5), 335–340. doi:10.18280/ria.330502

Yu, W., Chang, J., Yang, C., Zhang, L., Shen, H., Xia, Y., & Sha, J. (2017). Automatic classification of leukocytes using deep neural network. *2017 IEEE 12th International Conference on ASIC (ASICON)*, 1041-1044.

Yu, W., Chang, J., Yang, C., Zhang, L., Shen, H., Xia, Y., & Sha, J. (2017). Automatic classification of leukocytes using deep neural network. *2017 IEEE 12th International Conference on ASIC (ASICON)*. 10.1109/ASICON.2017.8252657

Chapter 15
An Augmented Edge Architecture for AI-IoT Services Deployment in the Modern Era

Ambika N.
https://orcid.org/0000-0003-4452-5514
St. Francis College, India

ABSTRACT

The previous proposal gains prognostic and regulatory examination. It uses boundary-based AI procedures to accomplish its task. It analyzes its received transmission utilizing a set of amenities. It verifies the data packets and detects the inconsistency in them. It also encompasses choosing the appropriate procedure to evaluate the data stored in the cloud. Kubernetes cases plan handles Docker similes vigorously. The dominant point has a trustable and stable credential supply. The system aims to manage the information of various groups. The leading device has a control component that aims to supervise the well-being of the other instruments. Replica set maintains anticipated mock-up count. The endpoints component seeks to spot and watch the modifications to the approaches in the service. The proposal suggests increasing the reliability by 4.37%, availability by 2.74%, and speed by 3.28%.

INTRODUCTION

Revolution in divergent domains has grabbed the eye of the IoT-empowered (Ambika N., 2020) (Ambika N., 2019) (Dian, Vahidnia, & Rahmati, 2020) (Hassan, 2019) brilliant world by coordinating edge Artificial Intelligence (Farivar, Haghighi, Jolfaei, & Alazab, 2019) components with versatile advances. A joining of heterogeneous organizations and wearable gadgets can encourage every corner of the world. With the progression in cell phones, modern areas have changed everywhere degree. The AI-driven (Gupta, Tewari, Cvitić, Peraković, & Chang, 2022) edge registering instrument for mechanical applications is exceptionally imperative for the whole world to address the significant issues at the worldwide level. Simulated intelligence for the boundary is an examination bearing zeroing by answering compelled streamlining issues in Edge Computing with the assistance of viable AI advancements. AI (Abiodun,

DOI: 10.4018/978-1-6684-5250-9.ch015

Awotunde, Ogundokun, Adeniyi, & Arowolo, 2021) is a blessing to the edge with more knowledge and optimality. Synthetic intelligence is an investigation of how to run AI models. It is a system for running, preparing, and dedicating AI models with gadget edge-cloud cooperative energy, which targets extricating bits of knowledge from huge and conveyed edge information with the fulfillment of calculation execution, cost, security, dependability, proficiency, and so on. Monitoring in healthcare (Balandina, Balandin, Koucheryavy, & Mouromtsev, 2015), industry (Bellavista & Zanni, 2016), and military environment (Liang, Zhao, Shetty, & Li, 2017) are enabled to minimize user effort and maintain the network during critical situations.

The previous system (Debauche, Mahmoudi, Mahmoudi, Manneback, & Lebeau, 2020) uses a learning methodology to teach the modules operating on different data sets and documentation handling natural language. The modules use divergent methods to quote the instruction, decision trees, and cognition network. The modules draw out their inference from the detectors and the system guidance. The approach used is centralized. It transmits all the information to the storage system. This data train the modules and draws inferences from them. The primary device is responsible for deploying, scheduling, and providing a decision on the system. It engages itself in managing the changes applied to the design and detecting the same. This device is trustable, containing the credential paired with the solution database. The host provides the interaction happening between the endpoints. The device responsible for controlling various activities is also made accountable for monitoring and detecting the state of the different instruments. It contains the replica set that includes the replicas of the assembly. It detects and manages the modifications to the access points. The storages involve storing, providing semantics, communicating with the server, and managing different storage locations of a small collection. The proposal suggests increasing the reliability by 4.37%, availability by 2.74%, and speed by 3.28%.

The work has five sections. The various contributions summarize in section two. The proposal is detailed in segment three. The work analysis is in division four. The work concludes in section five.

LITERATURE SURVEY

The following section summarizes the contribution toward the domain. The Sensor Level (Debauche et al., 2022) contains different information makers ordered in remote and wired sensors. These sensors associated with microcontrollers can be coordinated into organizations of a couple of gadgets to many thousands, exclusively delivering modest quantities, from few bytes to few Kb, of information at ordinary spans. The handling level has three sorts of information handling with expanding limits and dormancy from sensors to the cloud. Edge Computing is accomplished on microcontrollers, while Fog figuring accumulates network components between the edge of the organization and the cloud where the limits are accessible. The cloud offers conceivable outcomes to oversee significant information measures and is expensive as far as transmission capacity because of information transfer. User-level contains wired gadgets. Coordination administration guarantees the interoperability among MEC and LPWAN to accomplish the assortment and the treatment at haze level before their transmission to the end client or activating frameworks. It permits the disclosure of sensors and Edge/Fog Computing administrations to give information required as the contribution of uses facilitated by MEC.

The AI-empowered IIoT administration (Sun, Liu, & Yue, 2019) incorporates the board's self-observing, request estimating, issue recognition, and labor force. The choice is taken back to the IIoT gadgets and executed naturally. The process engineering comprises a two-layer shrewd server farm, boundary area, and storage area. Edge and distributed computing work helpfully to serve IoT gadgets with general and brief figuring administration through the edge layer just as incredible and thorough processing administration through the cloud layer. Edge Layer obliges lightweight canny figuring administration for IIoT. They registered separately from one another by processing the application and administering the precision. The storage Layer gives ground-breaking and far-reaching processing administrations for IoT at the expense of idleness and correspondence trouble. The edge layer and cloud layer interface with one another. The edge layer may require the help of the cloud layer to prepare its AI model. The edge layer additionally functions as à hand-off to move information from IIoT gadgets to the distant Cloud. The cooperation between the edge layer and the cloud layer is at the expense of extra correspondence on the spine network. Hence, send the registering administration between the edge layer and cloud layer. It appoints the figuring errands of IoT gadgets. It indicates by their prerequisites as the qualities of heterogeneous edge workers and distant Cloud. In heterogeneous edge processing, the assurance of traffic offloading depends on the specific postponement and precision necessities of registering tasks, the heterogeneous ability, and the clogged state of the edge worker. It represents an illustration of IIoT gadgets with canny processing administration comprising edge layer and cloud layer. Every base station outfit with edge worker usefulness on AI-based figuring administration. IIoTMDs decide on the suitable edge workers as per their necessities, giving precision to the edge workers.

The creators (Singh, Rathore, & Park, 2020) propose the Block-IoT Intelligence Architecture of meeting Blockchain and AI for IoT (Nagaraj, 2021), where cloud knowledge, mist insight, edge knowledge, and gadget knowledge introduces progressively. Cloud Intelligence has a few AI-empowered server farms associated with one another utilizing Blockchain innovation to give decentralized and secure enormous information investigation. Hence, haze insight conveys to a few AI-empowered haze hubs with Blockchain innovation to move the heap of the extensive information investigation at the mist layer in a decentralized and secure way. Edge insight has a few AI-empowered base stations with Blockchain for one another. It gives the third level of decentralization and security to move the calculation and capacity at the edge layer. The gadget knowledge conveys the quantity of IoT gadgets with AI and blockchain applications to perform enormous information examinations at the gadget layer. The architecture of joining Blockchain and AI with IoT is associated with Blockchain. The AI-empowered server farm breaks down and prepares the information starting with one hub and then onto the next hub in a brought-together framework. Simulated intelligence empowered fog hubs with blockchain usage, where the hub shares the data with the next fog hub with blockchain innovation. The hub designed with AI and chain dissects and prepares the knowledge at the haze layer. The AI-empowered haze hub has assets the executives, absence of information, energy utilization, and adaptability challenges. Artificial intelligence and blockchain innovation empower base stations to give the third level of decentralization and security to move the calculation and capacity at the edge layer. The IoT stage is depicted as a mix of six layers-actual layers, the correspondence layer, connect control layer, the administration layer, the executive's layer, and the application layer. The actual layer distinguishes the information or data, for example, temperature, area, contamination, climate, movement, and farming. This data was obtained from different sensor gadgets, for example, RFID, Barcode, and Infrared.

The system (Debauche, Mahmoudi, Mahmoudi, Manneback, & Lebeau, 2020) uses a learning methodology to teach the modules operating on different data sets and documentation handling natural language. The modules use divergent methods to quote the instruction, decision trees, and cognition network. The modules draw out their inference from the detectors and the system guidance. The approach uses decentralized. It transmits all the information to the storage system. This data trains the modules and draws out inferences from them. The primary device is responsible for deploying, scheduling, and providing a decision on the system. It engages itself in managing the changes applied to the design and detecting the same. This device is trustable, containing the credential paired with the solution database. The host provides the interaction happening between the endpoints. The device responsible for controlling various activities is also made responsible for monitoring and detecting the state of the different instruments. It contains the replica set that includes the replicas of the assembly. It detects and manages the modifications to the access points. The storages involve storing, providing semantics, communicating with the server, and managing different storage locations of a small collection.

The system (Calo, Touna, Verma, & Cullen, 2017) operates in trio stages. In the discovering phase, the customer uploads the data by labeling it. He uses different machine learning module data to do this. The top-most category modules analyze the association between the test data and itself. The customer chooses among the modules. The system also provides an automation procedure where the divergent modules searches to find the fittest. This method aims to identify the potential one among the lot. In the deployment stage, the models chosen by the automated system or the user serialization and packed using the docker ampoule present in the shared storage accessing the end elements. The relevant chain system implements the flow. The flow encapsulates using wrappers by identifying the elements of the chain. The flow affixes the start map construction generated during the training stage. It also suffixes the vocabulary of training collection. The third stage is known as the operation stage. This stage runs a small service oriented with the edge devices. It installs the flow and applies the docker encapsulating the edge system as requested by the users. The modules customize themselves using relevant attribute collection. It sometimes also includes assembly and professional attributes. The retraining stage captures the data that is found effective in the flow. This methodology aims to improve the system continuously.

The centralized stockpiling houses (An et al., 2019) use divergent procedures. The methodologies provide various services with the help of IoT devices and different technologies. The provisions are predefined using divergent gateways. The system maps the functionalities to real-time functioning to make it work. They interface using a shared medium. The methods sync with divergent services and information. The activities also encompass managing the resources, enhancing network safety, and increasing stockholders' reliability. The procedures train modules using various knowledge hubs. Some smart implementation includes facial identification, intrusion notification, and circumstance analysis. The architecture consists of storing methodologies related to the scenario from different stockpiling devices. The shipped methods are isolated and accommodated. The assembly makes the intelligent network. The fog hosts are used during run-time, optimizing the usage. A service is a management tool that provides smart solutions. An adaptive knowledge-gaining method aggregates collection from the framework components, knowledge, and methodologies. The architecture provisions a dynamic division of activities and resource scalability. The resource reservation is predefined in the methods. The architecture implements specific measurements to incorporate stakeholder requests. The system uses smart procedures to choose supplement materials to find a relevant solution. The interface incorporates-common improving solutions. The dual layers analyze the scenario and make the relevant procedure available. The data available from fog undergo analysis in the top layer. The framework assembles the filmed images. These data sets are learning tool. Possibilitygrid architecture evaluate the situation. The same records are in the database.

The trio framework (Hosseini Nejad, Haddad Pajouh, Dehghantanha, & Parizi, 2019) provides security at edge area. Dual safety modules are used in the application area. The device assembles the readings of detectors using IoT devices. The varied amount of procedures enhances the reliability of the system.

A cyber-based firewall identifies intrusion. The parameters form rule collection. The network area also has a firewall that incorporates certain norms. The intrusion discovery model formulates the detection mechanism based on the intruder's travel in the network. The edge area encompasses the risk in the network installed on the end devices. The components evaluate the risk level. The trouble undergoes analysis by mapping it to the available procedures in the intelligence component. Based on the stage, the system evaluates illegitimate degrees. The passage collecting data assembles the information from various areas and feeds it into the intelligent machinery.

The instruments (Wu, 2020) collect information and process them. Theycreatedynamicedge computation. The system consists of a trio structure. The upper design supports Industrial IoT functions. The edge devices form the intermediate network. It manages to assemble the knowledge procedure from edge hubs. It stabilizes cyber, computation, and stocking reserves. The lowest design has edge machines. The boundary area (Greco, Percannella, Ritrovato, Tortorella, & Vento, 2020) has convenient pre-handling gadgets. The low-level elaborations on information gather from Wireless Body Sensor Networks. The Fog area has computers, workers/doors accumulate information from field sensor organizations to perform nearby handling storage. The storage area has cloud administrations that are called for elite processing undertakings and far-off information stockpiling. The edge hub is associated with the web and permits sending an alarm to relatives or experts. It helps in making quick changes in estimated values.

The framework (Hao et al., 2019) addresses divergent networks. It is the amalgamation of IoT devices, stockpiling for boundary devices, and unrealistic innovative methodology. The system provides a dynamic platform to supervise and alter the configuration of the system reserves. It implements information gathering of IoT devices and supports practical computing and innovative interface of divergent procedures. After computing or on-demand, the devices transmit the information using the down-connection. The uploading rate is specified. The proposal supports enormous computation.

It is a dynamic and accessible methodology (Sodhro, Pirbhulal, & De Albuquerque, 2019) that deals with the execution, season of detecting, and transmission errands in AI-based IoT gadgets for modern applications. The framework level battery model of edge AI-empowered IoT gadgets for mechanical applications inspects the obligation cycle and energy advancement. The information dependability model of IoT-based hand-held devices over hybrid transmission power control and obligation cycle network. As per the creator's information, the work enhances the force and expands the battery life with high dependability in AI-based edge processing mechanical applications. It tunes IoT gadgets' transmission power level and obligation pattern in mechanical applications by receiving item handling, vibration, and flaw conclusion stage at good dependability or bundle misfortune proportion.

The proposed design (Chen et al., 2019) principally comprises the edge organization and the edge insight. The edge network mostly gives the entrance and asset the board of different edge gadgets. The edge insight identifies with the discernment of edge information, including administration information, organization, and asset information. The edge comprehension has two center parts. In the design, the psychological engine chiefly depends on intellectual registering advancements, while the asset-intellectual motor fundamentally utilizes the connected advances of edge processing. By joining key innovations in intellectual figuring with those in edge processing, it can more readily tackle the issue of correspondence transfer speed and postponement by combining registering, communication, and capacity, and accordingly improving the organization's knowledge. The motor can get familiar with the qualities of edge distributed computing assets, ecological correspondence assets, and organization assets by continuously comprehending and inputting the coordinated asset information to the learning-subconscious machine.

Simultaneously, it can acknowledge the investigation consequence of the information-psychological motor and understand the ongoing improvement and allotment of assets.

The work (Hao et al., 2018) includes four components. The intensive control unit manages the sick and monitors in crucial conditions. The surveillance of critical health conditions and the balance of blood can aid in the prediction of urgent situations. The database and the dual cognisant module assemble the sick's information on stockpiling devices. The second component encompasses the filming monitoring device. Some critical data are captured and stored in the store. The collection is evaluated on the boundary devices and stored in the stockpile. The intelligent machines are in the environment with automatic controlling systems, sound devices, and notifying systems. The system has a voice and facial recognizer. They aid in assembling information about the sick. The involuntary device evaluates the path and gives the appropriate acknowledgment.

In the SENET (Bulaghi, Navin, Hosseinzadeh, & Rezaee, 2020), WBSN accumulates data and sends them toward their programmable devices. It can work with dissecting the got information. The gadgets modify by various AI procedures, which everyone views as a demonstrative framework. These gadgets are programmable and can be associated with the Internet. The partition has two categories. These gadgets are outfits with various indicator models which report dubious occasions to the connected specialists. A non-deterministic polynomial issue assumes a part in the WBSN complete energy utilization. It is a reasonable plan for the gadgets to cover WBSNs. The k-inclusion procedure can be fundamental for upgrading the unwavering quality of the framework. Thesecalculationsfallinto the second layer of the proposed engineering. WCC makes some potential answers called group arrangements. Then, groups are put in different gatherings and enter the opposition utilizing four administrators. The groups scored high and kept battling in the end-stage. One group member contended with another. It views as a likely response to the issue. Cloud PCs and AI strategies exist in the third layer. This layer has two fundamental assignments, including deciding the complete number of IoT-based gadgets and their situations in the 3D climate and creating ongoing models to foresee undesired occasions like estimating a decreased measure of insulin in a body. The acquired models refresh by the third layer. It implants in IoT-based gadgets.

The cluster (Flamand et al., 2018) lives on a devoted voltage, and the frequency domain is on while packages walking at the material controller offload fairly computation-extensive kernels. It includes eight RISC-V cores equal to the only one used inside the FC, permitting the SoC to run the equivalent binary code on both the material controller and the cluster. This eight-middle cluster is served through a shared L1 records reminiscence, permitting shared-reminiscence parallel programming fashions with OpenMP. Access to the L1 reminiscence supports through an optimized interconnect. It is among the cores' load/keep devices and the reminiscence banks. The shared L1 can serve all reminiscence requests in parallel with single-cycle get right of entry to latency and coffee competition rate. The cluster application cache is likewise shared to maximize performance fetching records-parallel code. Fast occasion supervision, parallel strand dispatching, and synchronization are maintained through a devoted hardware block, permitting fine-grained correspondence and excessive power competence. The HW Sync segment additionally controls the top-stage clock gating of each unmarried center inside the cluster. The kernels in GAP-eight function an in-order, 4-level pipeline, docile with the RISC-V ISA subsets. Since the RISC-V ISA is architected to be extendable, we've prolonged edit to reinforce overall performance for DSP-centric divisions, shaping actual or complicated numbers factored as vectors of short integers. The fetch level extends with zero overhead hardware loops. Efficient array manipulation supports through the post-changed load. It keeps commands, unmarried-cycle multiply and collects complicated increase, as devoted commands for green rounding, normalization, and cutting.

The exploration location (Wang et al., 2020) consists of three central hierarchical elements: standards, groups, and courses. The super network, which describes the exploration scope, can be separated into complicated degrees. Each grade settles producing system multiplied by impenetrable numbers. The progress of each course in each compact number and the associations between enigmatic numbers determines during the optimization period. Grades divide into solidified steps and searchable degrees. The beginning and the latest stages of the system fixes before hunting for the optimal arrangement structure. The operation types and connections search for new zones. The moderately small channel measurements are used for early courses to decrease the device expenditure contracted by lessening the input to size. The searchable degree consists of a measured output zone and versatile compact block. Direct joints establish from each dense cell to all succeeding dense numbers. Therefore, the manufacturing highlight outline of each number has the corresponding measurement. The output layer is a down-sampling panel for the current stage. The adjusted output channel size for the output layer eliminates the sharp increment in calculations generated by the obtuse conjunctions.

The scheme (Rego, Canovas, Jiménez, & Lloret, 2018) is for surveillance. The architecture combines two network technologies. IoT networks work as edge networks. The IoT nodes implement the functionality of the system. The SDN provides the focus system. The SDN controller, whose purpose is to guarantee the most reliable QoS, is the principal joint in the network, and it can make arrangements to interconnect the various IoT interfaces. The two tracks accompany the Network Head of each IoT system. It is an exceptional junction that maintains the IoT system connection and addresses the data within the SDN arrangement. The jobs devices outline with various intensities. The SDN controller is in charge of system administration and manages the statistics from the SDN junctions to the AI module. The AI module uses this data set to utilize the AI methods and notify the controller about the multimedia transactions moving through the system and its supply conditions. This module has two components. The transfer classifier describes whether the incoming course is significant. The estimator selects the description of movement that the SDN controller should complete confirming the QoS requirements for multimedia communication. The interaction between the SDN controller and the AI module is inside but composed of structured messages. The SDN controller implements system administration duties.

It is a Privacy-Preserving hierarchical IoT eHealth structure (Nadian-Ghomsheh, Farahani, & Kavian, 2021) and its construction pieces. End Equipment Zone contains wearable accessories and ambient sensors combined with the system by wireless/circuited technologies presenting a 360-degree aspect of individuals. The fog course is geographically divided by gateways. The purpose is to connect the gap between the endpoint IoT projects and the Cloud. It intensified by establishing data storehouse and computing supplies closer to the data-producing references. The convergence offers higher processing capabilities for complex data analytics and storage. It tackles big data created by IoT devices. The marketing design and a cost-effective solution correlate, adviser, and maintain any eHealth IoT devices from any position. The rule consists of various network concepts and ML duties that are instructed simultaneously on the end design and the cloud server to protect the separation of the user. The objective of the computer vision system is to locate the position of the markers on the hand via personalized surface exposure and Federated Learning. These tags consist of the rotating unit and two other labels chosen by the definition of the particular application. The labels produce two vectors on the 2D plane of the hand. The actual output of the vector extricates the ROM value. Misclassification of the joints or inaccurate discovery of the label space manages incorrect ROM capacity. The specific discovery and localization of labels are essential. The presented technique for tag localization is composed so that the secrecy of the users conserve by bypassing vision communication in the interface.

The proposed administration (Trakadas et al., 2020) arranged design comprises the layers. The fundamental obligation of the Communication and Information Intelligence layers is to play out every one of the required activities on the industrial facility-wide datasets. It goals that the parts of the upper layers can settle on choices given the result of AI calculations running on top of such handled information streams or bunch datasets. Crude information created by assembling gadgets is alongside any remaining applicable data of the lower layer. The correspondence and data knowledge layer likewise contain the usefulness of conveying AI calculations nearer to the sensor and identifying shifts in the dataset measurements, demonstrating a need to retrain calculations. The AI-empowered information pipelines orchestrator part empowers the creation and sending of information handling pipelines. The practical and business knowledge layer obliges all administrations. It demonstrates the assembly process's status and conduct of all capacities and resources. The human in circle layer gives imaginative devices that will work through a coordinated effort between people, machines, and AI frameworks. It allows them to exploit each other's assets for more successful agreeable, and natural errand execution and navigation. The Federated Learning part targets taking care of the issue of information assortment for taking care of or preparing AI models.

The foundation layer (Guo, Lu, Gao, & Cao, 2018) has savvy lighting frameworks, RFID-labeled things, clever vehicles, brilliant checking frameworks, brilliant clinical frameworks, wearable widgets, and cell phones are only the tip of the iceberg. The device isolates into three unique sorts. It includes sensors, actuators, and cross-breed gadgets. Sensors are principally utilized in detecting the climate and delegated to the temperature sensors, moistness sensors, light sensors, cameras, brilliant groups, and RFID perusers. The actuator makes moves when it gets a command. The administration of the executive's layer is principally liable for gadget the board, information examination, and administration arrangement. It is sent in the Cloud and the help region. It connects the client with the Cloud.

There are three significant uncoupled modules. The IoT stage is the available entry of the IoT for devices. The AI module contains five submodules- information investigation, client distinguishing proof, conduct acknowledgment, administration development, and arrangement. In the AI module, submodules can use the semantic examination connection point to conduct a semantic investigation. The IoT stage transfers the information to the AI module through the AI interface. The information investigation submodule gets and breaks down the gathered information from the foundation. In the information examination submodule, the information attributes disconnect. The information changes are mined on time series investigation for social displaying. The semantic analysis module gives essential data on semantic examination for client=recognizable proof, conduct acknowledgment, and administration development in the AI module. Semantic innovation can develop a semantic planning layer by building different semantic models. It includes the gadget, client, information, and thinking model. There are five submodules in the semantic examination module. The enlistment information matches the semantic models in the article acknowledgment submodule (On enrolling in the IoT stage). This submodule associates with the stockpile to procure the semantic model of the new gadget from the widget model supplier and build an occasion as indicated by the semantic model. The occurrences of the devices are put away in the gadget model data set. The asset arrangement layer fundamentally contains asset suppliers in the AI-IoT. Foundation and administration suppliers can offer assistance for homes, brilliant traffic, networks, and savvy clinical. Semantic model suppliers build and give semantic models in different fields for the semantic examination module, for example, the gadget model supplier, the information model supplier, and the client model supplier.

The proposed design (De Sanctis, Muccini, & Vaidhyanathan, 2020) comprises three layers. The Edge layer addresses the arrangement of IoT gadgets in the framework. Sensors send the information detected to the Fog layer given the recurrence of information move. They likewise occasionally send their QoS information to the fog tier. The Fog Layer is answerable for paying out the lightweight calculations on the detected information and further performing building variations/re-designs on the IoT gadgets. It comprises numerous Compute Node forming a Compute part and an Adapter part. The cloud layer performs heavyweight calculations. It shall consist of four top layers. Microservice Layer has the arrangement of microservices carrying out the functionalities of a given IoT system. Management Infrastructure Layer handles the disclosure of microservices, provides data on their status, manages them, and conducts variations if necessary. It comprises three principal parts. Administration Management is answerable for executing the compositional variation of the microservices. Service Mesh Control Plane routinely screens the QoS level of every microservice. Administration Discovery courses the solicitations from the API Gateway to the particular examples of microservices. The transformation Infrastructure Layer is a committed layer giving components to successfully supporting variations at various levels. It is liable for gathering the unique circumstance and QoS information from the Fog and Management Infrastructure layers.

The work (Ferrández-Pastor, García-Chamizo, Nieto-Hidalgo, & Mora-Martínez, 2018) has four phases. The examination has two sorts of clients in this stage. Master clients in agribusiness characterize the primary cycles to control. This number of issues connects with ICT specialists in a participatory plan. The aftereffects of this first methodology configure administrations and control. In this stage, a client-focused procedure catches the rancher's necessities. The model depends on engineering with three levels: edge, haze, and cloud administrations. In this stage, adjusted engineering utilizes these levels. Installation and Integration subsystems are created in this stage. Information examination configures AI administrations in light of master rules with a rancher. Test and input are sent off. The primary master rules incorporate rancher oversight. New principles have criticism processes. Programmed and adjusted rules utilize reasoning frameworks with AI stages.

The structure (Mora, Signes-Pont, Gil, & Johnsson, 2018) connects with demonstrating the appropriated framework, the correspondence conventions, access and disclosure administrations, and the plan of the booking technique for the undertakings, along with the entire system. The essential goal of the proposed circulated engineering is to exploit the sent foundation of things and the distributed computing assets to decrease the figuring costs and work on the general execution. The fundamental thought is to divide the application's responsibility among the waiter side and the remainder of things with figuring capacities, for example, cell phones, wearables, tablets, sensors, and other implanted widgets. This responsibility dividing between the things empowers a flat scaling to relieve costs, falling back on distant servers. These sorts of gadgets perform more handling errands than the server-side layer. Distributed computing is accessible to utilize just if all else fails necessary. The nonconcurrent synchronization needs between cloud server figuring and the various gadgets. The framework fosters a message pop-up-based approach. The execution units of an application connect with its ability to handle information and errands in parallel. The application utilized as a model comprises a technique for dissecting the consideration level of understudies in study hall. The mentor checks the data (As he gives illustrations to the students). The accessible processing stages conveys in a few layers. A high-goal camera outline identifies and looks for a few face elements of all understudies at once. The school could send more asset equipment to accelerate the computations. The proposed IoT engineering capitalizes on the current study hall assets. The consolidated utilization of the three processing foundations of the homeroom in a cooperative manner can decrease the application time.

The work (Abiodun, Awotunde, Ogundokun, Adeniyi, & Arowolo, 2021) proposes utilizing cryptography-put together innovation to protect data concerning the IoT-based enormous information age. Triple Data Encryption Standard gets important information created from IoT-based (Arowolo, Ogundokun, & Misra, 2022) sensors and devices. The encryption and decoding technique depends entirely on a solitary key, perceived as symmetric encryption. A similar key is part of the strategy for both the encoding and the deciphering tasks. A protected channel switches the secret key between the source and the beneficiary. The unbalanced calculation tends to the twofold code structures: block code and stream figures. Block figure works on fixed-length gatherings of pieces, called blocks, without the deviated key into transformation. A community of block figures plays out a steady structure. It includes a few indistinguishable handling steps. A substitution on one portion of the data tended to uphold a change that intermixes with the different sides. The fundamental key increased, and the system uses multi-name keys for each circle. Uneven key cryptography alludes to a cryptographic calculation that includes two separate keys: the first is confidential while the other is public.

PROPOSED ARCHITECTURE

In the previous system (Debauche, Mahmoudi, Mahmoudi, Manneback, & Lebeau, 2020), a divergent framework is suggested. The information is processed using small assistance. The doings include interpreting the content, identifying the irregularities in the system, and authenticating the same. The framework chooses relevant simulated-based astute procedures in the storage. It incorporates these procedures at the periphery systems. The present system has enhanced the previous architecture by adding some additional components to the system. The methodology aims to increase reliability. The system consists of –

Master Node

The component is responsible for deploying work, scheduling the doings, and providing decisions based on the analysis. It consists –

a. The credential-solution pairing system. The requested data is analyzed, and the relevant solution is provided by mapping it to the database.
b. The host system [server] identifies the devices requesting the information and maintains the same.
c. The schedule component chooses the node on which the processing takes place.
d. The controller managing component supervises the activities of the processing device and maintains its efficiency. It is responsible for keeping the pod duplicates of the assembly. It also manages the changes in the boundary devices.

Assistant Nodes

The system adds device components to the design for the following reasonss-

a. To have a backup in case the controller node crashes. The doings are in this device – schedule patterns, evaluation results, etc. This is stored in the admin component as the Controller node generates the key-value pair, the duplicate copies to this component
b. To assist the Controller node, if the load on the Primary node is more.
c. It also acts as a worker node in times of overload.

Figure 1 is the representation of the inner view of the Master-Assistant node. The rest of the doings are similar to (Debauche, Mahmoudi, Mahmoudi, Manneback, & Lebeau, 2020).

Figure 1. Innerview of Master-Assistant Node

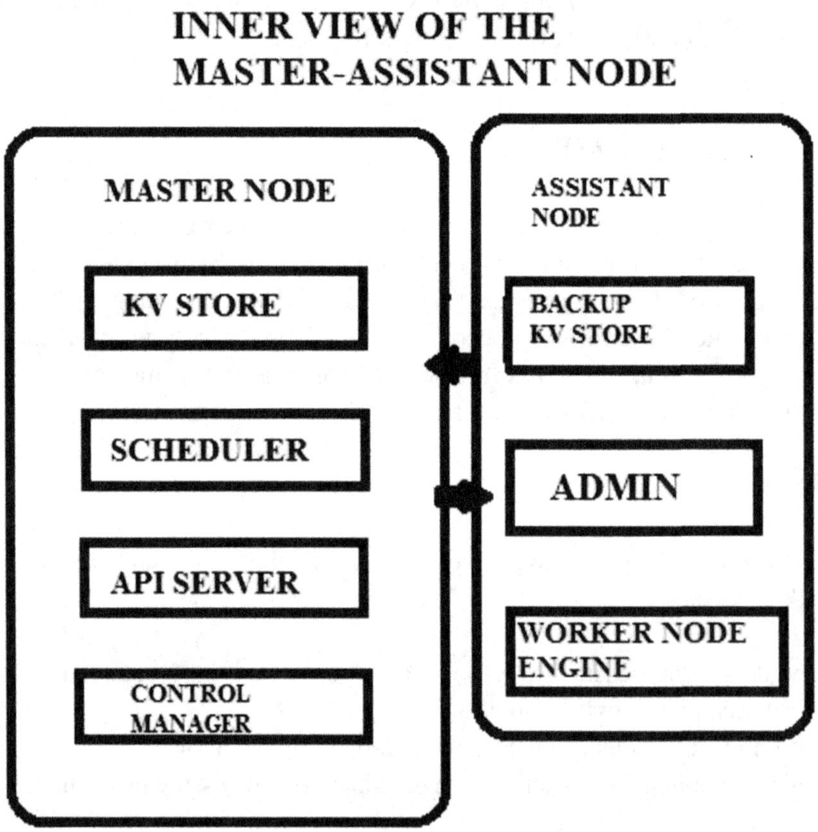

ANALYSIS OF WORK

The work is simulated in NS2. The parameters used in the work are summarized in table 1.

Table 1. Parametersused in the proposal

Parametersused	Details
No of master nodes	1
No of assistant nodes	1
No of workernodes	2
No of client requests	256
No of emergency request	12
Packet size used	214 bits
Simulated time	60 ms

Reliability

Trust is one of the critical parameters in communication. The server is always responsible for maintaining the doings of the clients according to the rules the organization offers. These details have to be very accurate to increase business. The assistant node in the cloud maintains the backup of the Controller node. Any crash or eraser in the host should be handled, and data has to be protected. Hence reliability plays a significant role in stockpiling systems. The proposal improves reliability by 4.37% compared to (Debauche, Mahmoudi, Mahmoudi, Manneback, & Lebeau, 2020). Figure 2 represents the same.

Availability

The customers avail various kinds of services based on their needs. The organization must manage to deal with low, average, and high-priority clients. If they focus on high-priority clients, the low-priority jobs often suffer. This proposal creates a balance between all kinds of clients. Compared to the previous contribution (Debauche, Mahmoudi, Mahmoudi, Manneback, & Lebeau, 2020), the enhanced proposal balances the request by 2.74%. Figure 3 represents the same.

Speed

The client chooses a particular service if the system is reliable and fast. Every client, irrespective of whatever scheme they adopt, expects good service from the system. Hence managing the client request and providing prompt service is essential. The previous work uses worker nodes to accomplish the jobs faster. The present contribution performs the assignment and processing using a fast processing system [server] by 3.28% compared with the previous assistance (Debauche, Mahmoudi, Mahmoudi, Manneback, & Lebeau, 2020). The same is represented in figure 4.

CONCLUSION

IoT is an assembly of intelligent sensors and actuators. They use their capabilities to accomplish a task. The errand is pre-defined before the deployment in the network. Thesedevicescommunicatewitheachother and transmit the processed data to the destination. Artificial Intelligence is a domain skilled in making

Figure 2. Comparison of reliability

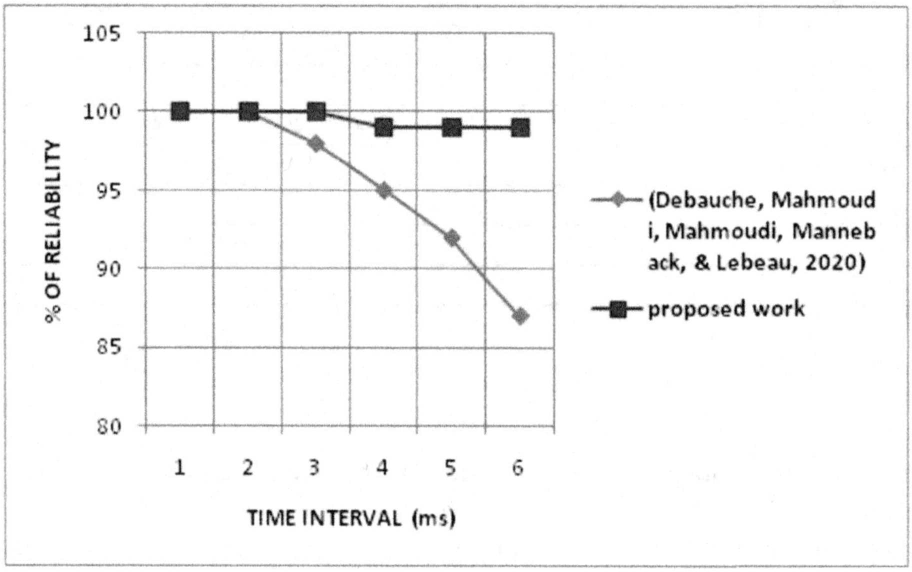

decisions based on the feed provided by the user or analysis collected by them. The devices will not be with enough memory storage. Hence stockpiling gadgets is considered.

The previous contribution uses learning methodology to teach the modules operating on different data sets, documentation handling natural language. The modules use divergent methods to quote the instruction, decision trees, and cognition network. The modules draw out their inference from the detec-

Figure 3. Comparison of bothproposal w.r.t balancing the client'srequest

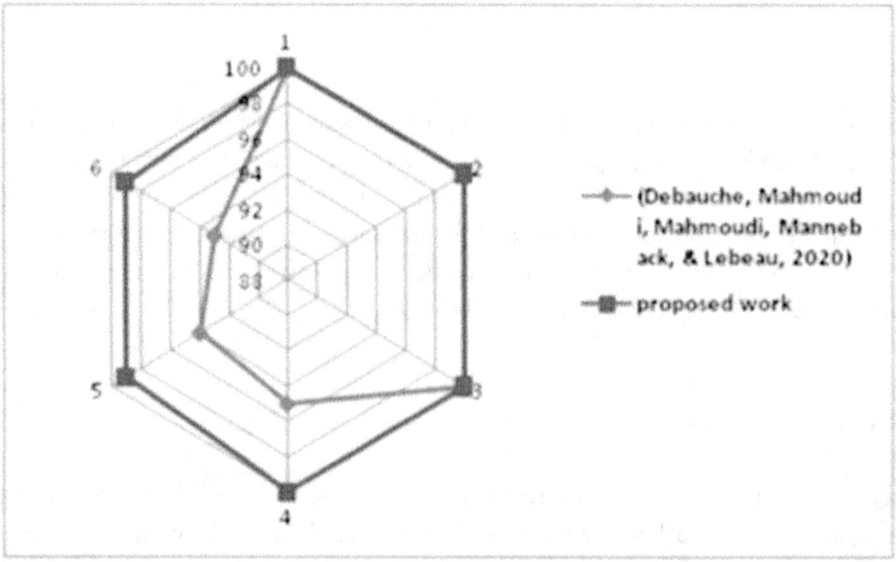

Figure 4. Depiction of acknowledging the request.

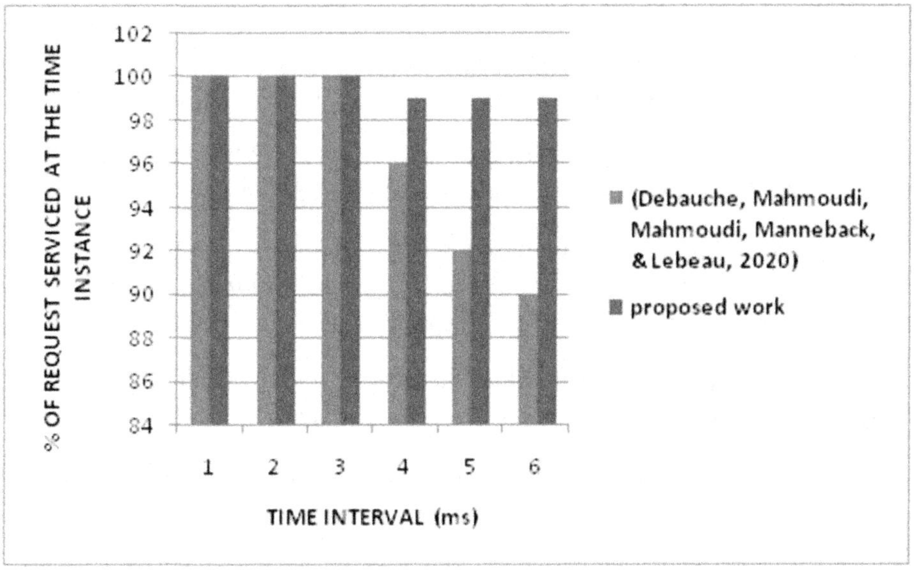

tors and the system guidance. The approach used is centralized. It transmits all the information to the storage system. This data is in training the modules and drawing out inferences from them. The primary device is responsible for deploying, scheduling, and providing decisions on the system. It engages itself in managing the changes applied to the design and detecting the same. This device is trustable, containing the credential paired with the solution database. The host provides the interaction happening between the endpoints. The device responsible for controlling various activities is also made accountable for monitoring and detecting the state of the different instruments. It contains the replica set that includes the replicas of the assembly. It detects and manages the modifications to the access points. The storages involve storing, providing semantics, communicating with the server, and managing different storage locations of minor collections. The proposal suggests increasing the reliability by 4.37%, availability by 2.74%, and speed by 3.28%.

REFERENCES

Abiodun, M., Awotunde, J., Ogundokun, R., Adeniyi, E., & Arowolo, M. (2021). Security and Information Assurance for IoT-Based Big Data. In *Artificial Intelligence for Cyber Security: Methods, Issues and Possible Horizons or Opportunities* (Vol. 972). Springer. doi:10.1007/978-3-030-72236-4_8

Ambika, N. (2019). Energy-Perceptive Authentication in Virtual Private Networks Using GPS Data. In Security, Privacy and Trust in the IoT Environment (pp. 25-38). Springer. doi:10.1007/978-3-030-18075-1_2

Ambika, N. (2020). Encryption of Data in Cloud-Based Industrial IoT Devices. In S. Pal & V. G. Díaz (Eds*IoT: Security and Privacy Paradigm* (pp. 111–129). CRC press, Taylor & Francis Group.

An, J., Li, W., Le Gall, F., Kovac, E., Kim, J., Taleb, T., & Song, J. (2019). EiF: Toward an elastic IoT fog framework for AI services. *IEEE Communications Magazine*, *57*(5), 28–33. doi:10.1109/MCOM.2019.1800215

Arowolo, M., Ogundokun, R., Misra, S., Agboola, B. D., & Gupta, B. (2022). Machine learning-based IoT system for COVID-19 epidemics. *Computing*, 1–17. doi:10.100700607-022-01057-6

Balandina, E., Balandin, S., Koucheryavy, Y., & Mouromtsev, D. (2015). IoT use cases in healthcare and tourism. *IEEE 17th Conference on Business Informatics, 2*, 37-44.

Bellavista, P., & Zanni, A. (2016). Towards better scalability for IoT-cloud interactions via combined exploitation of MQTT and CoAP. In *2nd International Forum on Research and Technologies for Society and Industry Leveraging a better tomorrow (RTSI)* (pp. 1-6). Bologna, Italy: IEEE.

Bulaghi, Z. A., Navin, A. H., Hosseinzadeh, M., & Rezaee, A. (2020). SENET: A novel architecture for IoT-based body sensor networks. *Informatics in Medicine Unlocked*, *20*, 1–9.

Calo, S. B., Touna, M., Verma, D. C., & Cullen, A. (2017). Edge computing architecture for applying AI to IoT.In *IEEE International Conference on Big Data (Big Data)* (pp. 3012-3016). Boston, MA: IEEE. 10.1109/BigData.2017.8258272

Chen, M., Li, W., Fortino, G., Hao, Y., Hu, L., & Humar, I. (2019). A dynamic service migration mechanism in edge cognitive computing. *ACM Transactions on Internet Technology*, *19*(2), 1–15. doi:10.1145/3239565

De Sanctis, M., Muccini, H., & Vaidhyanathan, K. (2020). Data-driven adaptation in microservice-based iot architectures. *IEEE International Conference on Software Architecture Companion (ICSA-C)* (pp. 59-62). Salvador, Brazil: IEEE. 10.1109/ICSA-C50368.2020.00019

Debauche, O., Mahmoudi, S., & Guttadauria, A. (2022). A New Edge Computing Architecture for IoT and Multimedia Data Management. *Information (Basel)*, *13*(2), 89. doi:10.3390/info13020089

Debauche, O., Mahmoudi, S., Mahmoudi, S. A., Manneback, P., & Lebeau, F. (2020). A new edge architecture for ai-iot services deployment. In *The 17th International Conference on Mobile Systems and Pervasive Computing (MobiSPC)* (pp. 10-19). Leuven, Belgium: Elsevier.

Dian, F. J., Vahidnia, R., & Rahmati, A. (2020). Wearables and the Internet of Things (IoT), applications, opportunities, and challenges: A Survey. *IEEE Access: Practical Innovations, Open Solutions*, *8*, 69200–69211. doi:10.1109/ACCESS.2020.2986329

Farivar, F., Haghighi, M. S., Jolfaei, A., & Alazab, M. (2019). Artificial Intelligence for Detection, Estimation, and Compensation of Malicious Attacks in Nonlinear Cyber-Physical Systems and Industrial IoT. *IEEE Transactions on Industrial Informatics*, *16*(4), 2716–2725. doi:10.1109/TII.2019.2956474

Ferrández-Pastor, F., García-Chamizo, J., Nieto-Hidalgo, M., & Mora-Martínez, J. (2018). Precision Agriculture Design Method Using a Distributed Computing Architecture on Internet of Things Context. *Sensors (Basel)*, *18*(6), 1731. doi:10.339018061731 PMID:29843386

Flamand, E., Rossi, D., Conti, F., Loi, I., Pullini, A., Rotenberg, F., & Benini, L. (2018). GAP-8: A RISC-V SoC for AI at the Edge of the IoT. In *29th International Conference on Application-specific Systems, Architectures and Processors (ASAP)* (pp. 1-4). Milan, Italy: IEEE. 10.1109/ASAP.2018.8445101

Greco, L., Percannella, G., Ritrovato, P., Tortorella, F., & Vento, M. (2020). Trends in IoT based solutions for health care: Moving AI to the edge. *Pattern Recognition Letters*, *135*, 346–353. doi:10.1016/j.patrec.2020.05.016 PMID:32406416

Guo, K., Lu, Y., Gao, H., & Cao, R. (2018). Artificial Intelligence-Based Semantic Internet of Things in a User-Centric Smart City. *Sensors (Basel)*, *18*(5), 1341. doi:10.339018051341 PMID:29701679

Gupta, B. B., Tewari, A., Cvitić, I., Peraković, D., & Chang, X. (2022). Artificial intelligence empowered emails classifier for Internet of Things based systems in industry 4.0. *Wireless Networks*, *28*(1), 493–503. doi:10.100711276-021-02619-w

Hao, T., Huang, Y., Wen, X., Gao, W., Zhang, F., Zheng, C., ... Zhan, J. (2018). Edge AIBench: towards comprehensive end-to-end edge computing benchmarking. In *International Symposium on Benchmarking, Measuring and Optimization* (pp. 23-30). Beijing, China: Springer.

Hao, Y., Miao, Y., Tian, Y., Hu, L., Hossain, M. S., Muhammad, G., & Amin, S. U. (2019, March/April). Smart-Edge-CoCaCo: AI-Enabled Smart Edge with Joint Computation, Caching, and Communication in Heterogeneous IoT. *IEEE Network*, *33*(2), 58–64. doi:10.1109/MNET.2019.1800235

Hassan, W. H. (2019). Current research on Internet of Things (IoT) security: A survey. *Computer Networks*, *148*, 283–294. doi:10.1016/j.comnet.2018.11.025

Hosseini Nejad, R., Haddad Pajouh, H., Dehghantanha, A., & Parizi, R. M. (2019). A cyber kill chain based analysis of remote access trojans. In D. A., & C. K. (Eds.), Handbook of big data and iot security (pp. 273-299). Cham: Springer.

Liang, X., Zhao, J., Shetty, S., & Li, D. (2017). *Towards data assurance and resilience in iot using blockchain. In MILCOM 2017-2017 IEEE Military Communications Conference (MILCOM)*. IEEE.

Mora, H., Signes-Pont, M. T., Gil, D., & Johnsson, M. (2018). Collaborative working architecture for IoT-based applications. *Sensors (Basel)*, *18*(6), 1676. doi:10.339018061676 PMID:29882868

Nadian-Ghomsheh, A., Farahani, B., & Kavian, M. (2021). A hierarchical privacy-preserving IoT architecture for vision-based hand rehabilitation assessment. *Multimedia Tools and Applications*, *80*(20), 1–24. doi:10.100711042-021-10563-2 PMID:33613083

Nagaraj, A. (2021). Introduction to Sensors in IoT and Cloud Computing Applications. Bentham Science Publishers. doi:10.2174/97898114793591210101

Rego, A., Canovas, A., Jiménez, J. M., & Lloret, J. (2018). An intelligent system for video surveillance in IoT environments. *IEEE Access: Practical Innovations, Open Solutions*, *6*, 31580–31598. doi:10.1109/ACCESS.2018.2842034

Singh, S. K., Rathore, S., & Park, J. H. (2020). Blockiotintelligence: A blockchain-enabled intelligent IoT architecture with artificial intelligence. *Future Generation Computer Systems*, *110*, 721–743. doi:10.1016/j.future.2019.09.002

Sodhro, A. H., Pirbhulal, S., & De Albuquerque, V. H. (2019). Artificial intelligence-driven mechanism for edge computing-based industrial applications. *IEEE Transactions on Industrial Informatics, 15*(7), 4235–4243. doi:10.1109/TII.2019.2902878

Sun, W., Liu, J., & Yue, Y. (2019). AI-enhanced offloading in edge computing: When machine learning meets industrial IoT. *IEEE Network, 33*(5), 68–74. doi:10.1109/MNET.001.1800510

Trakadas, P., Simoens, P., Gkonis, P., Sarakis, L., Angelopoulos, A., Ramallo-González, A., ... Chintamani, K. (2020). An artificial intelligence-based collaboration approach in industrial iot manufacturing: Key concepts, architectural extensions and potential applications. *Sensors (Basel), 20*(19), 5480. doi:10.339020195480 PMID:32987911

Wang, K., Xu, P., Chen, C. M., Kumari, S., Shojafar, M., & Alazab, M. (2020). Neural architecture search for robust networks in 6G-enabled massive IoT domain. *IEEE Internet of Things Journal, 8*(7), 5332–5339. doi:10.1109/JIOT.2020.3040281

Wu, Y. (2020). Cloud-Edge Orchestration for the Internet-of-Things:Architecture and AI-Powered Data Processing. *Internet of Things Journal*, 1-15.

Chapter 16
Emerging Cyber Security Threats During the COVID-19 Pandemic and Possible Countermeasures

Hepi Suthar
Rashtriya Raksha University, Gandhinagar, India & Vishwakarma University, Pune, India

ABSTRACT

The world suffering from COVID-19. In this situation, people are focusing on virtual or online modes of working, which can be done from home or anywhere. Cybersecurity has become the priority for all of us to protect data. This chapter mentions the most used cyber-attack techniques for stolen money and data from different sectors.

INTRODUCTION

A hostile Act as if aims to destroy data, steal data, or otherwise interfere with digital life is referred to as a cyber or cybersecurity threat. Cyber-threats include dangers like computer viruses, data breaches, and Denial of Service (DoS) attacks (D'Arcy J, 2020). Cyber threats and cyber-attacks are most visible in this situation because all activity takes place online, such as gaming, online certification or online course websites, payment applications, and many others. During COVID-19 situation, people want to make social distance and, because of that, only a few people move to the online platform, (Radanliev, 2020). Based on statistics, if compared to its increased usage of virtual and online application modes frequently used, the term "cybersecurity" describes a group of techniques, procedures, and procedures used to safeguard networks, devices, programs, and data from assault, deterioration, and unwanted access. Information technology security is another name for cybersecurity, (Khan, 2020). A hostile Act as if aims to destroy data, steal data, or otherwise interfere with digital life is referred to as a cyber or cybersecurity threat. Threats like computer viruses, data breaches, phishing, spamming, etc. are examples of cyber-attacks, (Partala, 2013).

DOI: 10.4018/978-1-6684-5250-9.ch016

Cyber-attacks are emerging due to more users using online platform for their work; likewise, professional meetings, online classes, online transactions, social media usage, online gaming, and many more, (Radanliev, 2020). Because of a lack of cybersecurity knowledge, cybersecurity is critical in taking lead in informing public during this pandemic situation. Using various cyber-attack techniques, data is stolen by hacker and breaches privacy policy of any company. A feature of such attacks will be that suppliers of security systems for companies, as well as organizations involved in development of control modules, will be under attack. Dozens of organizations working together can suffer at once. Another important trend in field of information security will be an increase in number of attacks on medical systems of clinics and hospitals, (Mastaneh Z, 2020). For example, in 2021, cybercriminals attacked systems that bill medical institutions and information databases containing customer medical records, (Rubí JN, 2020).

BACKGROUND

Provide In 2021, a large number of leaks of corporate data and user data were recorded. Among participants in high-profile incidents are well-known companies, and volume of lost user data is in hundreds of billions. There are different reasons, which include errors in operation of applications and protection tools, internal intruders, and actions of ransomware programs. In general, trend towards an increase in number of data leaks will continue since large amounts of corporate or personal data are always of interest to attackers due to their high cost, (Evans M, 2016). Separately, it is worth paying attention to a relatively new vector of attack propagation, namely attacks on supply chain or attacks by a third party. After attack on Solar-Winds and compromise of its Orion software, there were no less high-profile incidents, such as compromise of ASUS Live service or CCleaner program. The number of such attacks is predicted to increase in future, as corporate or private users do not expect to be attacked by trusted software or services. In same class of attacks, hacking networks of outsourcing companies and further attacks on infrastructure of their customers, as well as attacks on corporate resources through home computers of users transferred to remote work, remain relevant, (Ahmed N, 2020).

Of course, one of the most relevant cyber threats in 2022 will remain phishing attacks, in which victim receives a fake email from, for example, a search service or an online store with an offer to go to a fake website or open an email attachment that contains hidden ransomware code. According to Kaspersky Lab experts, in 2021, up to 350,000 new malware patterns were registered per day, most of which belong to ransomware class, as well as tens of millions of phishing emails. This growth is explained by fact that cyber fraud is actively developing as a separate industry, in which there are services for creating ransomware programs, distributing them, and collecting money. In addition, now, before encrypting data, ransomware will first try to find credentials to access victim's crypto wallets or other sensitive data.

Another emerging threat in 2022 will be attacks on IoT devices and process control systems. The former are usually poorly protected, latter often run on outdated operating systems and do not allow use of modern security tools. As a result, attackers have opportunity to mine cryptocurrency on any device that runs on Linux. For example, the Mirai botnet started using a Trojan for mining on video cameras back in 2017. Despite ridiculous hash rate (the computing power of farms for mining cryptocurrency), in this case, number of infected devices wins. Process control systems remain vulnerable: last spring, an attack on one of largest suppliers of gas and oil in West stopped all of its pipelines for five days.

In addition, in 2022, due to transition of many companies to remote modes of operation, personal safety of staff will decrease, (Burrell DN, 2020). Employees do not have a clearly defined motivation to master security systems; very often they neglect elementary rules of information hygiene. The reason is that ownership and individual responsibility for what happens in the company disappear, (Akhbarifar, 2020). The staff are at home. The social bonds that were formed in offices are becoming weaker. This will make it easier for hackers to break into companies' systems. Hybrid work is turning into a problem for market, which will need to be addressed as quickly as possible, (Badawy SM, 2020).

ISSUES, CONTROVERSIES, PROBLEMS

These days, the online mode of working increases in many different aspects like

- Online transaction because of social distance.
- Online game playing with a virtual room with known and unknown friends because of lockdown. People use it to spend time in a virtual world like a gaming platform and enjoy their time.
- Online education: Due to global impact of COVID-19, all universities and schools were closed for an extended period of time, forcing students to learn everything through online class mode.
- Online business because all shops and malls are closed in lockdown, so people move to online businesses, and it also indicates a huge number of smaller businesses are now online.
- Online Meetings and Conferences: As government and private sectors change their working methods, all types of meetings, conferences, ingratiation, and so on are conducted via an online platform.
- Online platform application for a movie, web series, serial, and so on. Because all of filming and new movie will not be released due to COVID-19 situation, most people will watch everything online through various applications.
    1. Online Meeting – Various platforms for online meetings and conferences are all done by various applications and they ask for a private credential. Likewise, Zoom, Google Meet, and Cisco Webex The sudden increase in an online platform possible attacks like phishing links for joining meetings may also capture video and other hidden details.
    2. Online Gaming – an online game with a virtual platform to play on in room where it's possible to steal details of device and other personal files from storage device. The number of downloads increases due to lockdown in many countries, so statistical way shows that most people use an online virtual room to play with friends.
    3. Online business – People move to enlarge or extend their business in online mode. Also, lockdown plays a role in covert business in an online way. Many threats are raised, like fake news related to tasks or supply chain processes. The process of import and export is not done on time and also delayed due to technical delay or lack of information.
    4. Education tool – Teaching online it's also a new part of changing learning in world during covid19. Online exams and lectures, which may not be as smooth as physical way or traditional way of conducting them, in this situation, many people run their own businesses. Details might leak during this online education because of all people, not being a technical person or not knowing cyber-attacks.
    5. Health-Related Applications: Health-related applications are now used for health check-ups like heart rate pulse, monitoring blood pressure, and so on, (Meghisan-Toma, 2020).

6. Money transaction – Money transactions, and as a result of COVID-19, everyone uses a digital medium to transfer money on a daily basis. People use a variety of mobile applications for transactions to avoid physical contact with currency notes.
7. News Application - Hence, many E-newspaper applications shared fake news during pandemic, also crawling details of all kinds of private information users'. The government of India launched @PIBFactCheck to verify news and release status of news.
8. Promotional Emails and Offers - User should never focus on discount offer-related emails because they may be fake, and without knowing original source of the email sender, user should never go with that deal.

Emerging Insider Cyber Threats in Covid19 & Prevention Methods

The company has a number of options for preventing systems from being exposed to insider attacks. Instead of giving each employee access to whole infrastructure, employees might be given access to just the directories and resources they need to do their task. Before granting access to company's IT systems, new recruits and contractors can be educated on policies on cybersecurity best practises and get introductory training to protect information security. Temporary credentials may be made available for contract workers and temporary employees. The access can be terminated once task is finished because it is no longer required. Requiring two-factor authentication for all company-related logins will reduce possibility of a system breach caused by an employee's account. The security team will have greater control and ability to stop any possible assaults if monitoring and regulating software is integrated into devices used by professionals for official work. The monitoring technologies may be used to deter employees from engaging in dishonest behaviour by ensuring that the workstations are running most recent software releases with most recent security updates, (Evans M, 2016).

1. Malwares - Software known as malware is purposefully created to damage the host machine and its data. Malware comes in a wide variety of forms, including worms, Trojan horses, computer viruses, ransomware, spyware, and adware. Malware can even include software that operates against user's best interests without user's awareness. One well-known instance of this was when Sony attempted to employ a rootkit programme to stop consumers of their music compact discs from forcibly duplicating material. On their music CDs in 2005, a joint venture between Sony and BMG had a digital rights management system that secretly set up a rootkit programme on user's computer, (Yallop AC, 2020). Many class action lawsuits in the US found this to be illegal, and Sony was forced to compensate and replace its consumers with new products for millions of dollars.
2. Computer viruses - Computer viruses are malicious programmes that, when run, have ability to replicate themselves without user's knowledge or agreement. By introducing their illicit code into programmes, they can alter current computer programmes and data. When a virus successfully infects a computer, it starts looking for additional computers connected to original computer over a network in order to propagate. Cybercriminals that create viruses frequently utilise social engineering or well-known operating system security holes to infect and disseminate infection. These types of malware are referred to as computer viruses because their infecting and spreading behaviours are comparable to those of biological viruses. Microsoft Windows is primary target of majority of viruses. They frequently employ complex techniques to get around antivirus protection. Viruses are used to make money, disseminate political messages, discover software flaws, make

Figure 1. Emerging Cyber Threat during Covid19 Pandemic

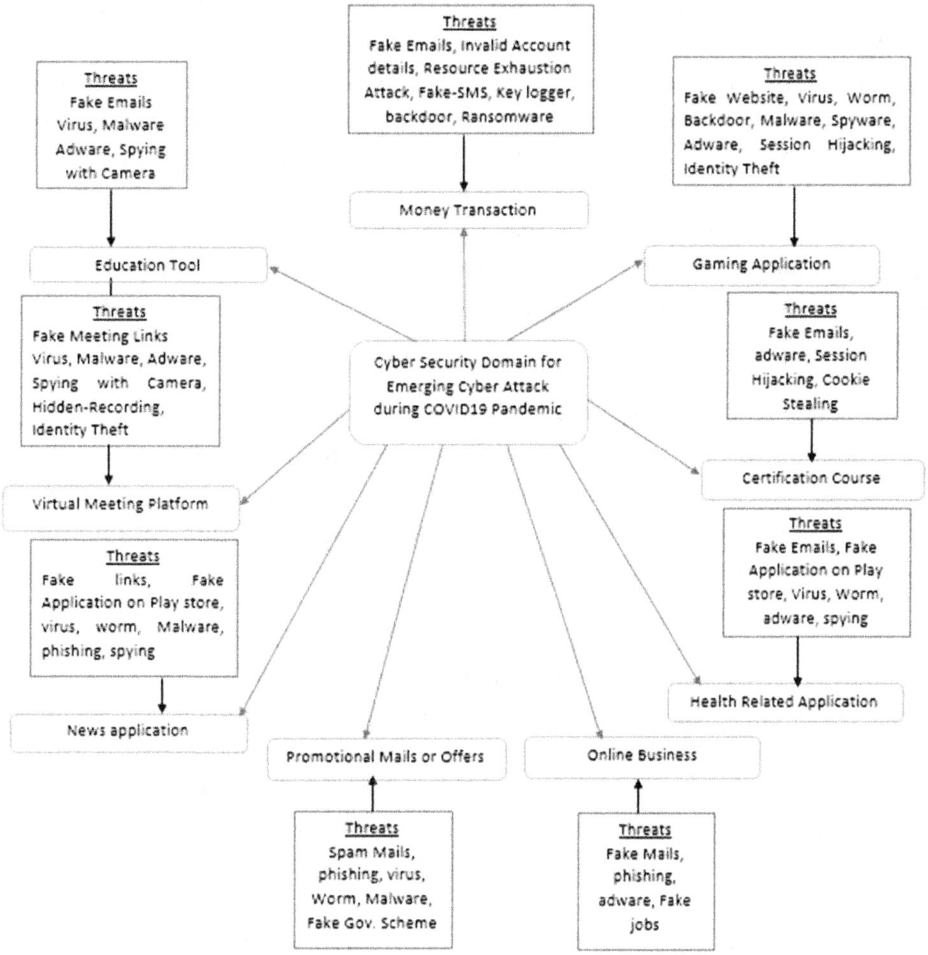

those flaws public, and simply for personal fun. Virus programmes eat up hard drive space, use CPU time, unlawfully access bank account information, contact information, email addresses, and other credentials, damage data, send pointless emails to contacts, log user keystrokes, and even completely destroy a machine.

Preventing computer viruses - To effectively address the danger of viruses, businesses and individual users alike must install antivirus software with malware protection on their computers. If they are not offered for free, virus software must be acquired and updated frequently to maintain their state-of-the-art security. By doing this, computers will be protected from further attacks. To prevent virus infections, best practises should be followed, such as not downloading and installing free software from unrecognised websites or clicking on files or links in unverified emails. Links from unknown websites, online games, and advertisements all have the potential to infect our system with viruses. When using links and webpages on internet, caution must be used.

3. Worms - Malware called "worms" is created to infect a computer, then swiftly duplicate and propagate throughout the network. In terms of behaviour, worms and computer viruses are quite similar. Worms, on the other hand, typically lack a "payload," or code necessary to alter data and applications already present on a computer. The only way it overburdens network is by utilising bandwidth. Even though they seem innocuous, worms may severely damage a network by overloading it. The Morris worm of 1988 is a well-known illustration that marked a turning point in computer security. When he was a PhD student at Cornell University, Robert Tappan Morris created a worm that duplicates itself across a network, (Naidoo R, 2020). A network overload resulted from this, affecting about 6000 PCs. An anticipated financial loss ranged from 100,000 to 1,000,000 USD as a result. The first person to be found guilty in United States under Computer Fraud and Abuse Act of 1986 was worm's inventor.

Protecting Against Computer Worms - Computer worms typically take advantage of operating system flaws on network. Most manufacturers of operating systems, including Microsoft, Apple, Ubuntu, and others, distribute patches and security upgrades on a regular basis. To avoid such attacks, users must maintain their computers updated with most recent patches. Nevertheless, zero-day attacks may take use of a system's known vulnerabilities if a fix is not yet available. Users may also add anti-virus and anti-malware software to the protection by installing it. Before installing a possible worm, they frequently search system for any dangerous programmes and look for user authentication. Users should use caution when clicking on links in emails and visiting unidentified websites. Recently, researchers have employed machine learning techniques to track a computer's network activity and the amount of scans it sends out in order to identify it as infected. The compromised PC can then be isolated from network and malware-scanned. A strong firewall will increase protection. Additionally, network administrators can confine and reduce hazards presented by worms by using Packet filters, service daemons with TCP wrappers, access control lists in routers and switches, and null route are examples of these.

4. Trojan Horses - Trojan horses are malicious programmes that conceal their actual purpose from the user by disguising themselves as innocuous applications. Typically, users are deceived using social engineering. For instance, a form that has to be completed through email can be delivered, and Trojan horses can be installed on a user's machine via bogus social media adverts. The term "Trojan horse" derives from an ancient Greek narrative in which Greeks finally defeated Troy after a protracted siege using a wooden Trojan horse. Any type of harmful programming may be payload of a Trojan horse. The majority of time, though, hackers utilise Trojan horses to open a backdoor into compromised machine. It's possible that a user will never be aware that a Trojan horse has infected their machine. The hackers will keep using backdoor to get access to the computer and take private data, including Personal data, bank account details, and credit card numbers. A well-known remote access Trojan (RAT) created by Jean-Pierre Lesueur is called DarkComet, (Burrell DN, 2020). He was a French programmer for information security. The creation of this Trojan horse began in 2008, and its widespread deployment began in 2012.

Protecting against Trojan horses - Users can increase their security against Trojan horses by using antivirus and anti-malware software. The signatures of well-known Trojan horses may be tracked and eliminated by antivirus software. Updates for antivirus software are required. Security updates for operating systems must be deployed on a regular basis. Additionally, firewalls may stop and block unauthorised connections, thwarting trojan horses. Additionally, users must use caution to avoid clicking on the links in scam emails.

5. Ransomware - Ransomware encrypts user data including files, music, video, and photos when it successfully infects a computer. The ransomware then threatens to erase files or make user's personal information publicly available online until a ransom payment is paid to attackers. Payment is frequently required using anonymous cryptocurrency like Bitcoin. Ransomware is often distributed as a Trojan horse payload. An individual with basic computer skills may be able to decrypt some ransomware assaults and get access to files. Public key encryption is used in certain ransomware operations, making it extremely hard to decrypt files without paying the attacker, (Council of the European Union, 2020). This is made worse by fact that many attackers demand payment from victims within a specific window of time. The attackers threaten to erase material if time limit has passed. Many ransomware victims choose to pay attackers rather than take chance of losing their important data. A well-known illustration is malware known as WannaCry, which attacked some 300,000 systems in 2017.

Protecting against ransomware - The current antivirus software is not particularly effective in identifying and removing ransomware threats. Even if the system is locked by ransomware, having adequate backups will let us restore prior data states. We can easily wipe everything clean and proceed. Ransomware, however, aggressively searches for and deletes backups. As a result, having offline backups is recommended. It's crucial to configure access permission for your cloud backup to append only. It is possible to prevent the exploitation of known system vulnerabilities by regularly installing security patches and updates. Additionally, users should exercise good cyber hygiene by not clicking on spam email links, segmenting their networks, and disconnecting their most crucial machines from network. Additionally, we have access to file systems like volume shadow copy and ZFS, which can defend our data against ransomware assaults. Users can establish restricted folders where alterations are controlled in some operating systems, such as Windows 10. Additionally, a known-plaintext attack can decrypt ransomware schemes that use shoddy encryption.

6. Phishing Attacks - In phishing assaults, people are misled into providing their personal information by being lead to believe an email or website is a real one. This information is then forwarded to the attacker. This is not a clever attack, but a type of social engineering. For instance, a hacker may create a website that is identical to Facebook password reset page and urge a user to change their password while sending an email from a phoney Facebook-looking email address. Unaware users that click link will give their original Facebook login information to attacker. The attacker can then log into victim's Facebook account using original credentials. Similar to this, millions of users' credit card information, bank account information, etc., can be obtained and utilised for theft and unlawful activity. The user's computer may become infected with further malware as a result of clicking on the phishing links and websites, which can worsen the attack's impact.

Preventing Phishing Attacks - Phishing attacks may be easily and effectively avoided. Users should avoid clicking links in emails from sources they don't recognise. Users should use caution when getting information and software from websites they don't trust. The risk of phishing attempts may be completely eliminated by practising excellent online safety and computer literacy.

7. DDoS Attacks - Attackers that use a large number of machines to repeatedly submit requests to a server under attack are known as denial of service attackers. Let's use a website that is hosted on a server as an example. The server and software system can deal with a maximum of 100 requests per second. The available resources will be overloaded if an attacker uses a few computers to deliver more than 100 queries per second to our web address. As a result, real users won't be able to access our web service. A massive attack may involve coordination of hundreds of thousands of computers. Distributed denial of service attacks can even leverage IOT (internet of things) devices, (Akhbarifar, 2020). Since none of these machines actively participating in attack are directly interacting with humans, they may all be considered bots. Due to fact that all of the requests sent by bots are genuine internet entries, it may be challenging to block or prevent this assault. Their requests are identical to all other valid requests in every manner. Multiple repeated queries from same IP address may be only identification. DDoS assault of enormous scope was launched against well-known software version control site GitHub. 1.35 terabits per second of traffic was generated at its peak, which is a record-breaking volume. Even though GitHub was equipped with advanced filters and enormous bandwidth to fend against assaults, many users experienced outages due to attack.

Preventing DDoS Attacks - There are several actions that businesses may take to stop or lessen the effects of a DDoS assault. Network monitoring tools with dashboards that display network traffic and system demands should be available to network administrators and system engineers. Network data may be visually analysed to detect DDoS attacks since they cause an abrupt and unusual increase in incoming traffic. To start taking action to contain assault, it is essential to understand difference between regular traffic and DDoS attack traffic. To function as a safety net in event of a DDoS assault, organisations can additionally dedicate extra servers that offer greater capacity than is typically required. It can aid in providing dependable user requests. Additionally, this will give network engineers some extra time to determine how to stop attack. Firewalls should also be updated often when new defences against such DoS assaults are introduced. Businesses should also have a solid plan in place for what to do in event of a DDoS assault, as well as exercises to evaluate how reliable their systems are.

8. Man-in-the-Middle Attacks - When hackers secretly eavesdrop on two parties' online communication, this is known as an MITM assault. Attackers have access to and can see contents of packets sent between two parties via internet. You may picture a criminal intercepting call between you and a bank representative in order to obtain your login credentials and personal financial information. Some attackers imitate responses you may anticipate from endpoint you're really trying to contact in order to spoof it. If you are connected to an unprotected WiFi network, a MITM attack may be executed with ease. By connecting to that wifi, an attacker may impersonate endpoint you're attempting to contact. The attempt to assault Organization for Prohibition of Chemical Weapons at The Hague by intelligence personnel assigned to Main Intelligence Directorate of the General Staff of Armed Forces of Russian Federation is a well-known recent incident. Although assault fell short of its ultimate goal, it is a noteworthy illustration of how even state actors may and will participate in MITM operations that aim to corrupt data transported over networks.

Preventing MITM Attacks - Over their internet connections, businesses can utilise SSL/TLS encryption protocols to encrypt communications that are being exchanged. Even if attacker is able to intercept certain packets that are being sent, contents will be encrypted, preventing him from accessing them. Today, HTTPS is protocol that is advised for all websites. Most internet browsers, including Chrome and Firefox, will flag websites without an HTTPS secure connection as insecure, which will result in less traffic and revenue for the website owner. Employees should exercise caution and refrain from utilising a public WiFi network for business or even personal network needs. Such free WiFi is vulnerable to hacking. Virtual Private Networks (VPNs) must be used to encrypt communication over public WiFi when accessing public WiFi is required.

9. Botnet - Botnets are collections of networked devices that may be incredibly diverse. As an illustration, consider computers, smart phones, web servers, and even internet of things gadgets. Even internet-connected thermostats, smart lamps, and other devices can collect data to be used in botnets. A single botnet system is often managed by a common malware, sometimes remotely from computer of an attacker. These viruses continually scour internet seeking weak PCs and infect new machines. The goal of attacker is to infect as many devices as possible with as much processing power as possible with botnet malware. In order to avoid being discovered by user, botnet malware often requires a little amount of processing power and network traffic. They typically stay latent and covert. The attacker may occasionally utilise botnet to send spam emails, engage in click fraud and click farming, as well as to produce a large number of requests for a distributed denial of service assault.

Preventing against Botnets - - Businesses may take a variety of measures to make sure that their servers and PCs are not a part of botnets. Network engineers and system administrators should periodically check network traffic and processing power utilisation for any unusual activity. If any unusual activity is noted, machine in question has to be disconnected from corporate network and properly inspected for botnet software. Additionally, it's important to keep computers' operating systems current. Additionally, all of the machine's software and firmware has to be patched for any known vulnerabilities. The company's technical personnel has to be informed about botnets and other dangers to information security, and they should be urged not to read spam emails or any links provided from unreliable email addresses. Anti-botnet tools have just been commercially accessible. Such tools can be bought and deployed in corporate equipment depending on danger level and firm's financial resources.

10. Identity Theft - Identity theft is a criminal act carried out by those who are successful in obtaining personal information about victims, including credit card numbers, usernames, passwords, identification numbers, driver's licence numbers, etc. Identity thieves attempt to enter protected networks by pretending to be someone else using these stolen credentials. This situation compromises a user who has authorised access to a secure system. As a result, system is unable to tell if a genuine user or an identity thief is attempting to login. It's possible that affected user isn't even aware that their login information and personal information have been taken. The attacker can continue to access systems up until he or she is informed of prior logins or until he or she learns of such an unauthorised login.

Protecting Against Identity Theft - The many distinct forms of assaults that we have previously examined are used to steal identity data. If attack is successful, culprit obtains credentials that they can use to carry out more identity theft attempts. Businesses need to ensure that their systems are safe and

Table 1. Telemedicine attack and description

Security threat areas	Description
WWW (Internet)	Because medical, private, and health information as well as prescriptions are communicated through the Internet, telemedicine systems are susceptible to security concerns related to sniffing, privilege escalations, and alteration/forging.
Home networks	They consist of Bluetooth, Wi-Fi, LAN, NFC, and other technologies. A telemedicine service system based on the home network is susceptible to security vulnerabilities linked to man-in-the-middle (MITM) threats and end-to-end plaintext transmission, (Hoffman, 2020).
Gateway N/W Equipment's	A gateway serves as a middleman between a patient and a telemedicine system, leaving it open to security concerns such as rogue gateway assaults, gateway theft and loss, and MITM threats.
Telemedicine devices	A device (such as a smartphone) based on a general-purpose operating system accesses external apps, making it subject to security assaults, in contrast to a telemedicine terminal based on an embedded-type real-time operating system, which is secure against unauthorized access, (Camara, 2015).
The telemedicine system	It manages patient data and could be linked to related organizations via a central government network hub. It may be used for teleconsultation via wireless connectivity between computers and patients' exercise equipment. It draws security risks from malicious code, unauthorized network access, MITM attacks, and the tampering or forging of telemedicine apps.
Patients or users	It is simple for their usage of telemedicine terminals to be subjected to security assaults owing to device loss, weak passwords, device use problems, etc. because the majority of them reside in distant areas and lack cyber security expertise or interest.
Telemedicine service providers	A telemedicine system primarily entails contacts between doctors and patients. Due to eavesdropping, data leaks, prescription changes, and incorrect device use, it is susceptible to security threats, (Kim DW, 2020).

reliable such that it will be challenging to use compromised credentials for additional attacks, even if a successful attack has already been undertaken elsewhere and identities have been stolen. One-time passwords (OTPs) provided by SMS can be used by businesses to enforce two-factor authentication, allowing users to verify themselves just by having their phone in their hands. Corporate systems also need filters that may detect possibly unauthorised login attempts during authentication process and notify authorised user via additional channels like emails or text messages. Such filters can detect unauthorised access to corporate networks using IP address, location, device type, repetitive login attempts, suspicious behaviour after signing in, etc.

Cyber Threat for Companies in this Current Year 2022

As 2021 showed, cybercriminals took full advantage of opportunities provided by coronavirus pandemic and the transition of companies to remote work. Attacks will become more and more large-scale and sophisticated, one might say "subtle", aimed at finding the most insignificant vulnerabilities in information security of companies. The number of attacks on gadgets will also increase, and ransomware will increasingly spread through them. Given the poor training of gadget users in terms of information security, the scale of hacks and losses can be enormous. Let's list the main cyber threats that security services and company management will have to face this year.

1. The number of disinformation attacks on companies will increase dramatically.

2021 has become a prime example of how fake (false) messages are spreading at great speed through information space in many countries. Some of them were custom-made in order to harm reputations of

Table 2. Technology and targeted popular brands

Various Technology (Function) types	Targeted/impersonated technology brands	Situational factors	Cybercrimes
Online payments Platforms	Paypal, Amazon Pay, Google Pay, Paytm	Small business loans	Fake website URL domain
Emails	Gmail, Yahoo	Donation/ Discount Offers/ Coupon Code	Fake emails (e.g., phishing)
Video calling / Data sharing websites	YouTube, Instagram, What's App	Entertainment	Fake Links
Social media technology	Instagram, What's App Facebook, Wechat	Social networking	Fake social media profiles / Deepfake
Cloud file hosting services	One Drive	Remote work / Online	Fake Links
Telecoms Companies with broadband and	4G (fake company)	Internet/free data	Fake Links
Video telephony and chat services online	Zoom, Webex, Google Meet, Gotomeeting	Remote Based work / Online	Fake Links
Media Streaming service (movies and television)	Netflix, Hotstar, Balaji telefilms	Entertainment Application	Fake Links

individual organizations or even states. The news will be used by hackers to commit fraudulent actions against companies in order to undermine their reputation and increase financial costs. Fake news will be used for massive phishing attacks, deceiving company customers. Most likely, they will be taken care of by cyber mercenaries working on order. They will be approached by those organizations for which it is important to remove competitors from niche where they work and take their place. Black marketing technologies will receive a new impetus for development, given well-equipped cyber mercenaries.

2. The number of large-scale attacks on supply chains will increase.

The purpose of such attacks will be to interrupt the logistics supply chains of goods for various purposes, creating chaos. Companies will be required to pay ransoms to unlock logistics to avoid even greater losses if supplies to the end consumer are interrupted. Attacks of this kind can cause huge damage to companies in the billions of dollars.

3. The number of data breaches of various natures will increase.

Leaks of sensitive data will occur more frequently and on a massive scale, (Yallop AC, 2020). Companies and governments will have to spend significant amounts to restore information bases and at same time pay larger ransoms to cybercriminals than was case in 2021, (Naidoo R, 2020). It is difficult to say exactly what amounts will have to be paid, but it is likely that we will be talking about millions and tens of millions of dollars, (D"Arcy J, 2020).

4. So-called political cyberwar will become more and more powerful and large-scale.

Table 3. Types of gadgets and description

Types	Description
Stolen device	Stolen devices, including a smartphone, laptop, hard disc, portable memory device, and data (such as private information).
Insider fraud	Someone with authorized access—such as a contractor or employee—intentionally compromises information.
Outside fraud, not device	Non-electronic data that have been destroyed, lost, or stolen include paper records; they can also include fraud involving credit or debit cards that isn't the result of hacking.
Malware or hacking	Electronic entry by an outside party, malware, spyware.
Accidental disclosure	Sensitive information that has been handled improperly, published online, or delivered by fax, email, or mail to incorrect recipient.
Linking attack	An attacker gathers supporting data on a target from several sources, merges the data, paints a complete image of the target, and then launches an assault.
Sybil attack	Attacking data redundancy mechanisms.
Spoofing attack	One object assumes the identity of another object in order to win confidence, obtain access to system, transmit malware, steal data, etc.
DoS/DDoS	Attackers employ DoS or DDoS to prevent users from accessing network services by sending out a tonne of pointless information and clogging the network.

By further developing the infrastructure of social networks, radical political groups and organized Islamist communities will be able to promote their ideology among population more quickly. Cyber wars will become part of proxy (hybrid) military conflicts in order to destabilize situation in a particular region of the planet.

5. Gadgets will be the most important targets for large-scale attacks.

With the growing number of users of mobile payment services and use of electronic wallets, hackers are adapting their methods to mobile devices. Since many of them still have weak protection against hacking, in 2022 we should expect a whole cascade of attacks on mobile devices. As a result, theft of funds from users' electronic wallets will increase. The number of hacking methods will also increase, and they will become more sophisticated and complex.

6. Deep fake will become a powerful means of attack.

Already, deep-fake technology (the development of fake video and audio clips) is beginning to be used. As it develops, it will be used for a lot of manipulation in the stock markets in order to bring down the value of companies' securities here refer (Wijayanto, 2020). Cybercriminals will use deep fakes to carry out social engineering attacks. For example, to gain access to bank accounts and private information, (Council of the European Union, 2020).

7. Cryptocurrencies will become increasingly used by hackers as a means of obtaining ransom. Cybercriminals will use cryptocurrencies, mainly Bitcoin and other altcoins, to obtain ransom. Or even anonymous tokens. They are harder to trace than fiats.
8. Micro services will be under attack.

Table 4. Social Engineering based some attack

No	Items
1	Selecting a link in an unwanted email that comes from an unknown source.
2	Using the same password across different websites.
3	Obtaining free antivirus software from an unknown source.
4	Entering into payment gateway information on a website without clear security information/ digital security certification.
5	Downloading materials/code/Application from a website on a work computer without verifying its authenticity.
6	Downloading digital media (games, Application, movies, Cloud drives and music) from unknown sources.
7	Utilizing free-to-access (Open Wifi) public Wi-Fi
8	Utilizing an online storage system to keep and exchange sensitive or personal information.
9	Saving organizations information on a personal electronic device such as laptop, tablet, or smartphone.

Today, the micro services architecture is used by cloud service vendors. Groups of hackers will look for security holes in them and launch massive attacks through them on companies that use cloud technologies in their work.

9. Ransomware will increasingly be used by cybercriminals.

According to statistics, last year ransomware attacked hundreds of thousands of companies around the world. The most common attacks were against companies that have the financial resources to pay the ransom. This year, attacks are expected to become more sophisticated, with hackers using penetration tools to set up online attacks to maliciously target company networks, (Naidoo R, 2020).

10. Increase in Cyberattacks

Every year, specific dangers intensify quickly as hackers concentrate their efforts on an especially successful or profitable attack strategy, like ransomware or crypto jacking. However, the expansion of cybercrime in general was one of most unsettling themes in 2021. Cyberattacks as a whole climbed by 50% in 2021 compared to previous year. Though certain sectors were more severely impacted than others, the majority of harm was done to fields of education, research, and healthcare, (Snell R, 2020). This suggests that cyber threat actors are concentrating their efforts on regions that are relying on technology more and more and are less equipped to defend themselves from cyber-attacks. Such a quick increase in assaults portends poorly for 2022. The frequency and severity of assaults are only going to increase as cyber threat actors hone their methods and make use of automation, machine learning, and other technologies.

11. Attacks on the Supply Chain are increasing

Supply chain assaults became more common in late 2020, increased through 2021, and are probably going to be a significant concern in 2022. This pattern started in December 2020 after the SolarWinds breach was discovered. Threat actors introduced backdoor code into SolarWinds' Orion network monitoring product while compromising the development environment. An extensive investigation that revealed specifics of the SolarWinds hack as well as several malware versions and an attack campaign that had an impact on over 18,000 public and private sector companies was launched by discovery of the Sunburst virus. Another well-known supply chain vulnerability in 2021 was the Kaseya attack, which used client and managed service provider (MSP) connections to spread ransomware through MSPs' remote monitoring and management tools, (Radanliev, 2020).

Even while the effects of these and other 2021 supply chain hacks were widespread; the most well-known incident was probably the use of the Log4j zero-day vulnerability. The widely used Apache logging library Log4j included a zero-day vulnerability that permitted remote code execution for an attacker with access to the log message's content or its arguments. The "Log4Shell" vulnerability was widely used; Many Research found over 830,000 tries within the first three days and over 40,000 attempts within two hours of it being public. Supply chain assaults of 2021 have shown that they are a practical and perhaps lucrative attack channel for cyber threat actors. In order to broaden the scope and effect of their operations in 2022, supply chain attacks will probably be used more frequently by cyber threat actors.

12. The Cyber Pandemic Continues

A significant change in corporate practises was prompted by COVID-19 epidemic. A far higher proportion of the workforce now works remotely, and this trend is anticipated to continue for the foreseeable future rather than people predominantly working from the corporate office. As cyber threat actors adjusted to and profited from changes in corporate IT operations, the pandemic started a cyber pandemic. The development of remote work made employees' computers, which were frequently personal devices, first line of defence for businesses, while the rapid uptake of cloud computing to serve the distant workforce and achieve digital transformation goals gave cyber threat actors new attack avenues. Little has changed two years after outbreak began. While number of businesses supporting a completely or mainly remote workforce is increasing, cloud adoption is not. Companies struggle to safeguard their systems and protect business and consumer data as hackers continue to take advantage of the vulnerabilities and security holes brought on by this fast IT transition.

13. Cloud Services Are a Primary Target

The shift to remote work caused by pandemic hastened adoption of cloud-based infrastructure and services. The demand for online meetings and file sharing was eliminated by Software as a Service (SaaS) solutions, and cloud-based infrastructure became more accessible and simpler for a remote workforce to administer. Companies have had the chance to address many of most significant security risks brought on by a hasty transition with little to no advance planning with the rapid move to remote and cloud in 2020. However, there are still certain security holes in the cloud, and cybercriminals keep trying to outsmart security staff in order to profit from the newly important position that cloud computing plays in contemporary industry.

Many of these attacks target holes in the cloud infrastructure itself, giving an attacker the chance to compromise numerous sites with only one flaw. The OMIGOD vulnerability was found in September 2021. Up to 65% of Azure customers might have been target of attacks due to exploitation of Microsoft's Open Management Infrastructure (OMI) software agents contained within Azure VMs before vulnerability was addressed. Not all security flaws in Azure were identified in 2021, including OMIGOD. Through a compromised key, the ChaosDB vulnerability identified in August gave full access to cloud resources used by Azure Cosmos DB clients. In the same public cloud service, Azurescape facilitated the exploitation of other customers' Kubernetes clusters while focusing on Azure's Container as a Service (CaaS) offering. Although Azurescape was patched before it was used as a vulnerability, the consequences might.

14. Ransomware Attacks Are on the Rise

As a result of the 2017 WannaCry incident, ransomware gained popularity. Since then, a large number of ransomware organisations have appeared, making it a costly and top-of-mind danger for all enterprises. Ransomware organisations showed in 2021 that they are able and willing to affect organisations than their immediate targets. The most notable instance of this is Colonial Pipeline attack, in which the Dark Side ransomware organisation shut down one of the major pipelines supplying the US East Coast for a week. Although Colonial Pipeline may be most well-known ransomware assault of 2021, it is by no means only one. The largest meat processing corporation in the world, JBS S.A., was the subject of another attack that same month. Due to attack's global effects, US facilities and Australian abattoirs were shut down, which led to cancellation of 3,000 shifts and layoff of 7,000 people. In addition to these well-known assaults, ransomware gangs also actively targeted healthcare and education industries, (Sardi A, 2020). Due to these attacks, schools had to close, vital medical and educational data was lost, and elective and non-emergency medical operations were post-poned, (Hossain MS, 2020). Iran was subject of many hacktivist assaults that disrupted the country's rail and gas systems. Attacks using ransomware have shown to be successful and profitable for the perpetrators. They will continue to be a top cyber danger to businesses unless this changes.

15. Mobile Devices Introduce New Security Risks

Bring-Your-Own-Device (BYOD) rules were widely adopted as a result of transition to remote work. Companies may have increased productivity and employee retention by enabling workers to work from personal devices, but they also lost crucial security visibility and capacity to react to infections that pose a danger to company systems and solutions. Cyberespionage tools like Pegasus have become more potent and hazardous as a result of the rise in mobile device usage. The virus, created by NSO Group, infects target devices via a number of zero-click attacks before taking control of them and gathering data from numerous sources (texts, phone, email, etc.). Pegasus has a history of being exploited to target journalists, activists, government leaders, and corporate executives while being ostensibly only available to governments, police enforcement, etc.

Cybercriminals changed their strategies in 2021 to capitalize on the rising use of mobile devices. The FlyTrap, Triada, and MasterFred Trojans are just a few examples of mobile malware Trojans that have surfaced. These mobile Trojans use similar methods to access target devices and obtain required rights, such as social media, lax app store security measures, and others. Smishing methods have been adopted by mobile malware and cyber threat actors, who now distribute phishing information via SMS messaging rather than email. This is a well-known trait of the FluBot Android botnet, which spreads itself even utilising a text message posing as a FluBot infection. Smishing attacks are popular because they are very easy to execute and cheap, with phishing kits often costing between $50 and $100 US. The battle against cybercrime is now expanding to include mobile devices. Mobile security is a crucial component of a corporate cybersecurity strategy for the modern corporation.

16. Socially engineered malware

The most popular type of attack is socially engineered malware, which is now often headed by data-encrypting ransomware. An end user is persuaded in some way to execute a Trojan horse application, frequently from a trusted and frequented website. Malware is temporarily substituted for the standard website coding on an otherwise harmless website. The criticised website instructs user to run phoney antivirus software, install new, unneeded, or harmful software, or use other "essential" applications in order to view the website, (Ahmed N, 2020). The user is frequently taught to ignore any security alerts issued by their operating system or browser and to turn off any annoying safeguards that could get in way. The Trojan malware may occasionally appear to be doing a legitimate task before beginning its nefarious activities. Each year, social engineering-based malware programmes are behind hundreds of millions of successful intrusions. The rest of the hacking kinds pale in comparison to those figures.

Countermeasure: The best way to combat socially engineered malware programmes is by constant user education that addresses current risks such as trusted websites prompting users to run surprise software. By prohibiting users from utilising elevated credentials to browse web or respond to emails, businesses may further secure themselves. A current anti-malware tool is a necessary evil, but effective end-user training offers more value.

17. Password phishing attacks

Approximately 60 to 70 percent of email is spam, and a large portion of it consists of phishing attempts to steal users' login information. Fortunately, anti-spam vendors and services have made significant progress, and the majority of us have inboxes that are rather clutter-free. I still receive a lot of spam emails every day, and at least a couple of them are really effective phishing imitations of real emails every week. An effective phishing email, in my opinion, resembles a tainted piece of art: Everything is presented beautifully, and reader is even cautioned not to fall for scam emails. The malicious link that requests private information is only thing that makes it obvious.

Countermeasure: The main defence against password phishing assaults is to use logins that are untraceable. This includes two-factor authentication (2FA), smartcards, biometrics, and other out-of-band authentication techniques (such phone calls or SMS messages). You've beaten password phishing if you can demand just more secure techniques and permit something more than simple login name/password combos. If you must utilise basic login name/password combinations for one or more systems, employ most accurate anti-phishing software or services you can find, and reduce the risk by improving end-user awareness. We especially adore browsers that draw attention to a host's actual domain name in a URL string. So, for instance, windowsupdate.microsoft.com.malware.com is more noticeable.

18. Unpatched software

Software with (available but) unpatched vulnerabilities is a close second to socially designed malware and phishing. Products that individuals frequently use to make web browsing more convenient, such as Adobe Reader, are among the most frequently abused and unpatched programmes. It's been like way for a while, yet oddly, never once has a firm I've examined had perfectly patched software. Usually, it's not even close.

Countermeasure: Make sure your patching is flawless and stop what you're doing straight away. If you can't, make sure it's ideal for things that are being used most in a particular time period, whatever they may be. Everyone is aware that improving patching is a fantastic technique to lower danger. Become one of the few companies that carry it out. Instead of futilely attempting to fully patch all software products, it is preferable to ensure that you are fully patched on the programmes that are most likely to be exploited.

19. Social media threats

Our online community is dominated by social networks like Facebook, Twitter, LinkedIn, or their localised equivalents. Social media risks typically manifest as requests to install malicious software or rogue friends. If you have misfortune of agreeing to the request, you frequently end yourself granting much more access to your social network account than you intended. The humiliation factor makes business social media accounts a favourite target for hackers who want to steal credentials that could be shared between the corporate network and the social media site. Simple social media hacking was the origin of many of today's worst attacks. Never undervalue the possibilities.

Countermeasure: End users must be educated about dangers of social media. Make sure your users are aware that they should not divulge their company credentials to any other foreign websites. Here is where employing more complex 2FA logons might also be beneficial. Last but not least, teach all social media users how to report a hacked account, either on their own behalf or another person's. Occasionally, their buddies are the ones to first identify a problem.

20. Advanced persistent threats

Only one significant company that we are aware of has not experienced a significant compromise as a result of an advanced persistent threat (APT) stealing intellectual property. Typically, phishing assaults or socially engineered Trojans are used by APTs to establish a foothold. Sending a targeted phishing campaign, also known as spear phishing, to several employee email accounts is a highly common tactic used by APT attackers. At least one employee is duped into running the Trojan attachment in the phishing email. APT attackers may compromise an entire business in a matter of hours from initial execution and first computer takeover. It's simple to complete but quite difficult to clean up.

Countermeasure: It can be challenging to identify and stop an APT, especially when up against a determined foe. The prior advice still holds true, but you also need to have an understanding of the normal network traffic patterns in your network and become vigilant for any abnormal flows. You are aware of which computers typically communicate with which other computers, however an APT is not. Spend some time right away watching your network traffic to acquire a strong understanding of what traffic should be moving where. When an APT makes a mistake, it will try to copy a lot of data from a server to a machine with which it normally wouldn't speak. Pass-the-hash attacks, SQL injection, cross-site scripting, and password guessing are other prominent attack techniques that aren't as common as the five attacks mentioned here. By safeguarding yourself against top five hazards, you may significantly reduce risk in your surroundings. Avoid investing in expensive, high-profile initiatives while the bad guys continue to enter via ways that might have simply been closed. Finally, use a tool or service that focuses on identifying APT-style assaults. These products or services either aggregate your event logs in search of indications of maliciousness or run on each of your PCs, similar to a host-based intrusion detection service. The period when it was difficult to identify APT has long gone. The prior gap has now been

Table 5. Security Key Feature & Mitigation

Security key features	Description of Mitigation
Mutual authentication	Leading security feature that protects some devices from impersonation threats.
Conditional privacy protection	The components of conditional privacy are targeted vehicle information retrieval and user privacy preservation. The VC is in charge of running the VANET system and ought to make it possible to reveal the identities of suspicious cars.
Unforgeability	The primary characteristic of safe data sharing is unforgeability against targeted message attacks.
Non-repudiation	Information that is supplied is guaranteed to be accurate.
Anonymity	Every VANET device has to maintain its anonymity.
Session key establishment	A specific car and the VANET system share a single session key. It must be made in order to follow data sharing security.

filled by a plethora of sellers that are eager to sell you protection. Decide which hazards are most likely to affect your business and focus your preparation on those. Too many businesses squander time and money focusing on unlikely, incorrect possibilities. Calculate threats for which you should be prepared the most by comparing their threat intelligence to characteristics and vulnerabilities of your environment.

SOLUTIONS AND RECOMMENDATIONS

We must conclude by stating that there will be an increase in size and sophistication of hackers' assaults. Most likely, businesses will suffer significant losses as a result of hacking and data theft. To safeguard the structure from the operations of individual hackers and organised groups, managers of businesses and security services must take a number of steps right now, (Meghisan-Toma, 2020). The year 2021 showed how cyber threat actors are modifying their methods to match a developing global environment. Cybercriminals are damaging important sectors with ransomware assaults, rather than hiding in the shadows, and adapting their strategies to a workforce that is becoming more mobile and cloud-centric. Companies should prepare for sophisticated assaults that target every aspect of their IT infrastructure in 2022, particularly weakest points. Businesses lack essential visibility and control over cloud and Bring Your Own devices, making them main targets of hackers.

The capacity to react fast and accurately to constantly developing assaults that can hit anywhere inside to protect against contemporary cyber-attack campaigns, an organization's IT infrastructure is required. Organizations demand an integrated security architecture capable of automating and coordinating threat prevention and response across the entire corporate IT infrastructure, as well as comprehensive security visibility and access to real-time threat intelligence.

FUTURE RESEARCH DIRECTIONS

Discuss future and emerging cyber threat trends. Provide insight about the future of the book's theme from the perspective of the chapter focus. Viability of cyber issues of proposed programs, etc., may be included in this section. If appropriate, suggest future research opportunities within the domain of the topic.

Table 6. Security features and Countermeasures, (Ahmed N, 2020)

Aspects	Recommendations
Authentication	Implement two-factor or multi-factor authentication. Before allowing access to a corporate network, an SMS code or a call for authentication is delivered to the employee's phone.
Management of mobile application and mobile devices	Put security measures in place, such as virus scanning and data encryption.
Security patches and virus protection	To access company networks, make sure laptops and mobile devices have virus protection and the most recent security fixes.
Implementation of policies	• Avoid the danger of accidental or unauthorized access to guarded corporate information by avoiding sharing work computers. • Avoid using a VPN to access the company's information systems while using free public WiFi • Refrain from downloading and saving sensitive company data to personal computers, thumb drives, or cloud storage services like Google Drive.
Training of employees	• Teach staff members how to protect and encrypt sensitive data at home. • Teach them how to utilize Virtual Confidential Networks (VPNs) to ensure that Internet usage is encrypted and that staff users' whereabouts are kept private when evaluating the company's network.

CONCLUSION

There are several cyber hazards during COVID-19 pandemic as a result of human behavior as well as system and technological flaws. Cyberattacks can affect applications based on telework and Internet of Things. Telehealth offers a chance to safeguard patients, doctors, nurses, and others against COVID-19 virus. Telehealth does, however, present privacy and cyber security threats. The block chain enhances privacy and security of digital health systems and aids in pandemic control. Analytics of health data, remote patient monitoring, EMR administration, control of pharmaceutical supply chain, etc. are all made possible by integration of block chain and AI. In a time when businesses are increasingly allowing their workers to work from home with no protection, COVID-19 has been released. Servers and virtual private networks (VPNs) will be key components of future cyber security. Numerous businesses throughout world are switching to work-from-home models, and thousands of these businesses are now launching and dealing with same issues. Cybercriminals are well aware of inadequate security that homeowners may offer. Finding straightforward yet safe solutions for cyber security is a new problem for those who work from home.

REFERENCES

Ahmed, N., Michelin, R. A., Xue, W., Ruj, S., Malaney, R., Kanhere, S. S., Seneviratne, A., Hu, W., Janicke, H., & Jha, S. K. (2020). A survey of covid-19 contact tracing apps. *IEEE Access: Practical Innovations, Open Solutions*, *8*, 134577–134601. doi:10.1109/ACCESS.2020.3010226

Akhbarifar, S., Javadi, H. H., Rahmani, A. M., & Hosseinzadeh, M. (2020). A secure remote health monitoring model for early disease diagnosis in cloud-based IoT environment. *Personal and Ubiquitous Computing*, *16*, 1–17. doi:10.100700779-020-01475-3 PMID:33223984

Badawy, S. M., & Radovic, A. (2020). Digital approaches to remote pediatric health care delivery during the COVID-19 pandemic: Existing evidence and a call for further research. *JMIR Pediatrics and Parenting*, *3*(1), e20049. doi:10.2196/20049 PMID:32540841

Burrell, D. N. (2020). Understanding the Talent Management Intricacies of Remote Cybersecurity Teams in Covid-19 Induced Telework Organizational Ecosystems. *Land Forces Academy Review*, *25*(3), 232–244. doi:10.2478/raft-2020-0028

Camara, C., Peris-Lopez, P., & Tapiador, J. E. (2015). Security and privacy issues in implantable medical devices: A comprehensive survey. *Journal of Biomedical Informatics*, *55*, 272–289. doi:10.1016/j.jbi.2015.04.007 PMID:25917056

Council of the European Union. (2020). *Council Resolution on Encryption – Security through encryption and security despite encryption.* White Paper, 13084/1/20 REV 1.

D'Arcy, J., Adjerid, I., & Angst, C.M. (2020). Too Good to Be True: Firm Social Performance and the Risk of Data Breach. *Information Systems Research, 31*, 1200–1223.

Evans, M., Maglaras, L. A., He, Y., & Janicke, H. (2016). Human behaviour as an aspect of cybersecurity assurance. *Security and Communication Networks*, *9*(17), 4667–4679. doi:10.1002ec.1657

Hoffman, D. A. (2020). Increasing access to care: Telehealth during COVID-19. *Journal of Law and the Biosciences*, *7*(1), 1–15. doi:10.1093/jlb/lsaa043 PMID:32843985

Hossain, M. S., Muhammad, G., & Guizani, N. (2020). Explainable AI and mass surveillance system based healthcare framework to combat COVID-I9 like pandemics. *IEEE Network*, *34*(4), 126–132. doi:10.1109/MNET.011.2000458

Khan, N. A., Brohi, S. N., & Zaman, N. (2020). Ten deadly cyber security threats amid COVID-19 pandemic. *AIMS Electronics and Electrical Engineering*, *5*(2), 146–157.

Kim, D. W., Choi, J. Y., & Han, K. H. (2020). Risk management-based security evaluation model for telemedicine systems. *BMC Med Inform Decis*, *20*(1), 1–14. doi:10.118612911-020-01145-7 PMID:32522216

Mastaneh, Z., & Mouseli, A. (2020). Technology and its Solutions in the Era of COVID-19 Crisis: A Review of Literature. Evidence Based Health Policy. *Management and Economics*, *4*, 138–149.

Meghisan-Toma, G. M., & Nicula, V. C. (2020) ICT Security Measures for the Companies within European Union Member States–Perspectives in COVID-19 Context. *Proceedings of the International Conference on Business Excellence, 14*, 362–370. 10.2478/picbe-2020-0035

Naidoo, R. (2020). A multi-level influence model of COVID-19 themed cybercrime. *European Journal of Information Systems*, *29*(3), 306–321. doi:10.1080/0960085X.2020.1771222

Partala, J., Keräneny, N., & Säreströniemi, M. (2013) Security threats against the transmission chain of a medical health monitoring system. *2013 IEEE 15th International Conference on eHealth Networking, Applications and Services (Healthcom 2013),* 243–248. 10.1109/HealthCom.2013.6720675

Radanliev, P., De Roure, D., & Walton, R. (2020). COVID-19 what have we learned? The rise of social machines and connected devices in pandemic management following the concepts of predictive, preventive and personalized medicine. *The EPMA Journal*, *30*, 1–22. PMID:32839666

Rubí, J. N., & Gondim, P. R. (2020). Interoperable internet of medical things platform for e-health applications. *Int J Distrib Sens*, *16*(1), 1550147719889591. doi:10.1177/1550147719889591

Sardi, A., Rizzi, A., Sorano, E., & Guerrieri, A. (2020). Cyber Risk in Health Facilities: A Systematic Literature Review. *Sustainability*, *12*(17), 7002. doi:10.3390u12177002

Snell, R. (2020). How Is COVID-19 Impacting Compliance Professionals across the Country? *Journal of Health Care Compliance*, 33–38.

Wijayanto, H., & Prabowo, I. A. (2020). Cybersecurity Vulnerability Behavior Scale in College During the Covid-19 Pandemic. *Jurnal Sisfokom*, *9*(3), 395–399. doi:10.32736isfokom.v9i3.1021

Yallop, A. C., & Aliasghar, O. (2020). No business as usual: A case for data ethics and data governance in the age of coronavirus. *Online Information Review*, *44*(6), 1217–1221. doi:10.1108/OIR-06-2020-0257

KEY TERMS AND DEFINITIONS

Cyber Security: Cybersecurity is the practice of protecting systems, networks, and programs from digital attacks. These cyberattacks are usually aimed at accessing, changing, or destroying sensitive information; extorting money from users; or interrupting normal business processes.

Cyber Threat: A cyber or cybersecurity threat is a malicious act that seeks to damage data, steal data, or disrupt digital life in general. Cyber-attacks include threats like computer viruses, data breaches, and Denial of Service (DoS) attacks.

Cyberattack: A cyberattack is any offensive maneuver that targets computer information systems, computer networks, infrastructures, or personal computer devices.

Malware: Malware is intrusive software that is designed to damage and destroy computers and computer systems. Malware is a contraction for "malicious software." Examples of common malware includes viruses, worms, Trojan viruses, spyware, adware, and ransomware.

Social Engineering: Social engineering is an attack vector that relies heavily on human interaction and often involves manipulating people into breaking normal security procedures and best practices to gain unauthorized access to systems, networks, or physical locations or for financial gain.

Vulnerability: Vulnerabilities are flaws in a computer system that weaken the overall security of the device/system. Vulnerabilities can be weaknesses in either the hardware itself, or the software that runs on the hardware.

Chapter 17
Computational Intelligence and Blockchain-Based Security for Wireless Sensor Networks

Renu Mishra
Department of CSE, Sharda School of Engineering and Technology, Sharda University, Greater Noida,India

Inderpreet Kaur
Galgotia College of Engineering and Technology, India

Vishnu Sharma
Galgotia College of Engineering and Technology, India

Ajeet Bharti
Galgotia College of Engineering and Technology, India

ABSTRACT

A wireless sensor network (WSN) provides the base architecture to all popular technologies like internet of things (IoT), unmanned arial vehicle (UAV), etc. Recently, a push came to make the information available to humans from the real-time environmental data collected through small sensing devices. WSN is self-organized wireless ad hoc networks to facilitate the interaction between the human and physical worlds. Rapid growth in sensing devices connected to the internet with intelligence and capabilities also opens the door because more devices connected devices means more chances of security vulnerabilities. Blockchain (BC) technology is introduced to address authentication and other security-related challanges by eliminating the role of central authority. This chapter starts with unique characteristics and security challenges in WSN and further identified different ways to apply blockchain with its potential benefits. The chapter presented the integration of blockchain in CI-enabled WSN with respect to focused sectors.

DOI: 10.4018/978-1-6684-5250-9.ch017

INTRODUCTION

These days, we are aware of the vastly useful areas that wireless sensor networks (WSNs) have captured, including the fields of natural engineering, surveillance and security, modern observation, the agricultural sector, seismic location, and the development industry. A huge number of sensors to observe the properties of an area like temperature, air quality, and pressure.The sensor is having very limited capabilities and forward the collected information to a base computer (Selmic et al., 2016)..Recently more and more new applications are being popular in the commercial sectors that are getting benefits from basic WSN. Overall prosperity depends on how it is integrated with the Internet and other advanced wireless technologies. Security threats are a significant issue in WSNs. The cause is that SNs have limited resources and are vulnerable to attack. (Verma et al., 2022). There are typically two types of attacks carried out in WSNs. Internal attacks occur when SNs act selfishly to protect their energy and storage, as opposed to external attacks, in which the attackers seize control of the SNs to carry out malicious activities. Therefore, it is essential to locate and eliminate the malicious nodes from the network(Awan et al., 2022). Still WSN, which is composed of multiple sensor always has the risk of being data tampering and can be secured with smart solutions using Intelligence computing. Presentely smart sensors are coming with high computational capacities to handle various tasks with fullflaged operating system and also web protocol stack.Such a constraintless WSN makes the decentralized operation of the data collection and management processes very efficientely with the help of Computational intelligence (Akyildiz et al., 2002).The capsule of Blockchain and CI has been gaining significant attention among sensor based business solutions to be successfully deployed and tested in real-time scenario like intelligent monitoring of temperature, criminal activity in borders and surveillance on traffic monitoring, vehicular behavioron roads, water level and pressure, and remote monitoring of patients.Sinse WSN is more vulnarable so conventional security mechanisms cannot be fully applied in WSN where sensor nodes are connected to a common link in an attack prone environment.Every node should be able to identify the other node's identity and credentials. These identities and credentials must be mutually authenticated and also shielded to avoid future questions. The identification also leads to the privacy issue, so a good security solution must cover confidentiality, availability, and integrity of information carried in packets during routing because the information may be forwarded and misused by malicious node (Tyagi et al., 2020).Blockchain (BC) technology can be introduced as part of WSN with the goal of eliminating a central server to address such security and privacy concerns. You can use blockchain technology to design an Intelligent security solution for recent networking paradigms like Content-based Networking and internet-of-Things(Martin F.R. 2018).

The chapter presented the complete view that how Computational intelligence based security solutions get benefits from BlockchainTechnology and vice verca.Second section gives the preliminiary knowledge and Fundamentals of CI and Blockchain Technology with wide coverage of the types of Computational Intelligence Techniques.Third section highlights the limitation of BT and AI.Next forth section demonstrated that both Technologies can come together as complimentary for mutual benefits. Future research directions are covered in fifth section.At last the chapter gave the conclusion that convergence of blockchain and AI may bring the new value in WSN landscape globally.

FUNDAMENTALS OF CI AND BLOCKCHAIN TECHNOLOGY

To welcome the advent of new networking paradigms, we must have some basic idea ofif various intelligent techniques and fundamentals of blockchain technology to support the smart and secure functioning of the network.

Computational Intelligence

Computational Intelligence (CI) is the most recent research area with a broad available range of intelligent paradigms such as fuzzy systems, neural networks, evolutionary computation, swarm intelligence etc (Eberhart et al.,2011)(Kacprzyk et al.,2015).Computational Intelligence tells us the possible ways to integrate different heterogeneous mentioned disciplines inside one and the same computational system with a common denominator under the CI umbrella.Computational systems mimic natural evolution-while representing humanlike intelligence with the ability to process imprecise information and seek approximate yet good-enough solutions to hard problems .One of the core CI technique,artificial neural networks(ANN) borrows inspiration from the brain's massively parallel architecture for processing their input data.

Types of Computational Intelligence Techniques

All these CI procedures for WSNs are mentioned in the below diagram with extraordinary guarantee of robustness and computational tractability.

a) **Genetic Algorithms:** GAs are one of the first and most prominent technique.A typical GA will follow the iterative process with a randomly generated population. The mutation operator slightly modifies existing solutions whereas the crossover operator generates offspring solutions that may be part of the next generation.Genetic operation and evolution operation are two kinds of calculation operation in the genetic algorithm.It covers exploration of different regions of the search space in relatively short computation time but provides only a problem-dependent framework which leads critical importance for successful use in practical problem.

b) **Fuzzy Logic:** Fuzzy logic (FL) can be a useful tool in studying natural complexity because it can show how humans make decisions in difficult circumstances. Unlike classical set theory, which simply states that an element either belongs to a concept or it does not, fuzzy logic imposes a degree of membership of an object to a concept (Balakrishnan et al., 2017).A hybrid of fuzzy logic and harmony search can be used in WSN to increase the lifetime of the network (Agrawal et al., 2021).

c) **ANN:**Technology known as artificial neural networks is based a condensed set of biological brain system ideas, these networks mimic biological neural networks. Particularly, ANN models mimic the electrical activity of the nerve system and brain. The neurodes are processing elements stacked in layers or vectors, with the output from one layer acting as the input for the following layer and maybe others. (Kordafshari et al., 2019).Weighted data signals mimic the electrical activation of a nerve cell and, in turn, the transmission of information within the network or brain by entering a neurode.

d) **SVM:** Both classification and regression are performed using the Support Vector Machine (SVM) supervised machine learning method.Although we also refer to regression concerns, categoriza-

Figure 1. Different CI Techniques

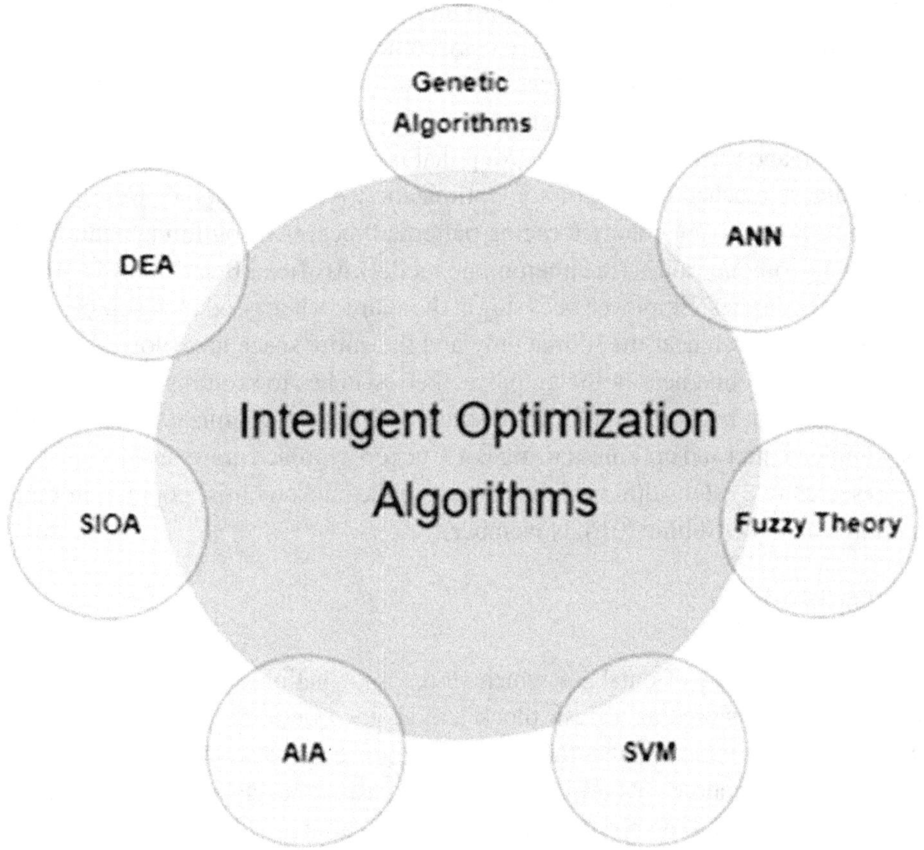

tion is the most appropriate term (Nicolas et al., 2018). Finding a hyperplane in an N-dimensional space that clearly classifies the data points is the goal of the SVM method. The number of features determines the hyperplane's size. The hyperplane is essentially a line if there are just two input features. The hyperplane turns into a 2-D plane if there are three input features.

e) **Artificial immune algorithm:** Artificial Immune Systems (AISs), which are computational techniques based on the biological immune system, are grouped with genetic algorithms, ant colony optimization, particle swarm optimization, and other meta-heuristics that draw inspiration from nature. Even though AISs are effective at tackling optimization issues, helpful elements from other approaches have been blended with a "pure" AIS to produce hybrid AIS systems that perform better.

f) **Differential Evolution algorithm:** Differential evolution (DE) is a population-based metaheuristic search technique that enhances a potential solution to a problem through iterative improvement. Such algorithms can swiftly explore very large design spaces and make few, if any, assumptions about the underlying optimization problem. One of the most adaptable and reliable population-based search algorithms with multi-modal problem resilience is DE, perhaps.

g) **Swarm Intelligence Algorithms:** Swarm Intelligence Algorithm is also the branch of nature-inspired algorithms from the collective conduct of huge creature bunches regularly alluded as swarms (Basha et al., 2008).A fitness function is used to carry out iterative optimization process. The SI based algorithms are utilizedin combinatorial and numerical problems to find the values which optimize certain fitness. In this series, Particle Swarm Optimization (PSO) and Ant Colony Optimization (ACO), BAT algorithm, Firefly algorithm etc are some landmark names (Yang et al., 2020).. PSO is frequently combined with other current algorithms and utilized for optimization. This method searches for the best solution using agents, also known as particles that are influenced by their achieved location and the position of the group that is closest to them. This cycle is repeated until a stopping point is reached.b.Ant Colony Optimization(ACO) is another well-known technique developed in response to ant colony foraging patterns.It begins by outlining a number of solution elements and pheromone values (the pheromone model).Artificial Bee Colony (ABC) mimics the behaviour of bee colonies. Employee bees stay at the source when good food sources are discovered and onlooker bees search near the source only and the entire space is explored by scout and if no other food source is found near it, the employee bee switches to scouting mode.BAT algorithmis based on the way that bats use echolocation.some well-known optimization tasks have been meticulously implemented and optimised using BA.Cuckoo approach draws inspiration from nature is the cuckoo search (CS) algorithm, which is based on the cuckoo birds' population-building brood reproduction technique(Solihin2016, November).

Blockchain Technology

Blockchain is a particular type of database which stores information in blocks that are then chained together.Every new data is stored as a fresh block and chained onto the previous block, to make the chain in distributed manner, which implies that the information entered is irreversible to achieve security and trust.Since each block contains its own mathematical hash, blockchains are immutable, unless the majority reached a consensus to do so. According to (Agrawal et al.,2020),WSN also may have their specific weakness or vulnerabilities which provide a loop hole to attackers.We studied extensively about the powerful characteristics of blockchain networks as an external component of systems with distribute databases for key storage and other security management .Vulnerability exhibits through hardware or software imperfection which opens the system for possible exploitation. The attack might be in the form of channel vulnerability which allows message misguiding and injecting false information (Nair et al., 2021). WSNs requires different security strategies at different levels because such an environment is approachable to both authorized users and attackers as well. During data exchange authentication is only achieved through the central authority. Information tampering, device spoofing, false authentication in data sharing could breach the security.With the objective of elimination of a central server, blockchain (BC) technology is introduced as a part of WSN, to address such security and privacy concerns. Blockchain technology can be used to create the node incentive mechanism for wireless sensor networks' data storage (Padalkar et al., 2020). For that, two blockchains are built, one to store data and the other to manage data access. Additionally, to substitute proof of work (PoW) for the original bitcoins' mining and storage of fresh data blocks. As a result, network nodes' storage space can be significantly reduced.

Blockchain is an innovative technology that makes it possible to create trustworthy WSN applications. Global and immutable repositories created by blockchain technology ensure the trusted key storage and other security management.Additionally, the challenge is to deal with the processing and managing large amounts of data in the blockchain.

As a result, significant advancements in machine learning and artificial intelligence techniques are giving aid to empower the next-generation networks.

Figure 2. Blockchain and AI in WSN

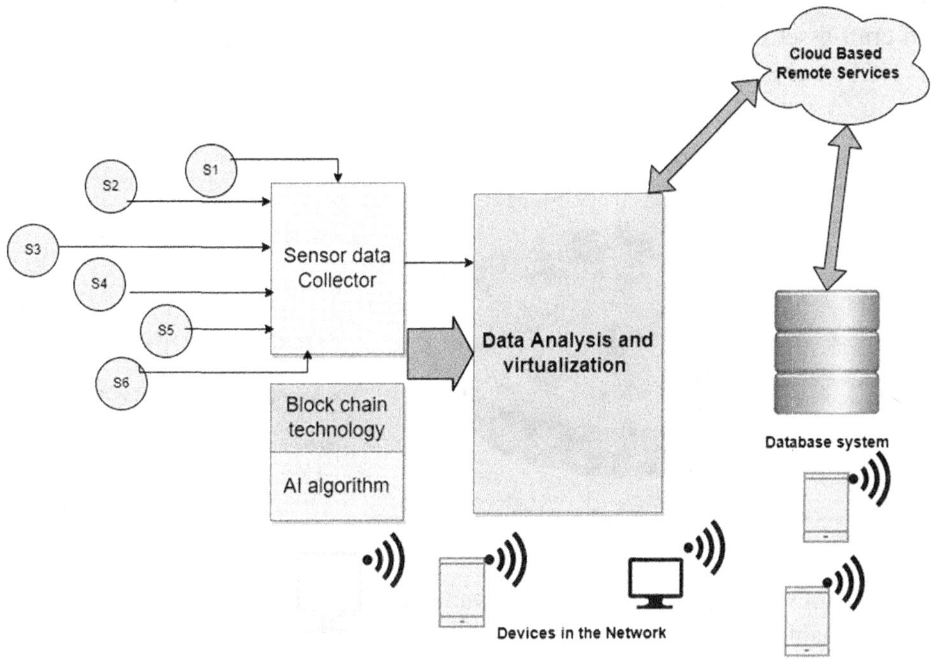

CURRENT STATE AND HURDLES IN THE ADOPTION OF BLOCKCHAIN

Industrial Revolution (IR4.0) has brought about profound changes in the Business sector (Shinde 2021). Blockchain technology combined with AI has a lot of potential to develop new business models that are made possible by digitization in different industries.

- VideoCoin and Theta Network are very popular in Entertainment industry to facilitate video encoding, video storage, and video distribution and also implemented "Proof-of-Engagement" (POE) concept to change the payments method to content suppliers with associated views and engagement times of users.
- Blockchain ensures the documentation of a product's supply chain from seed to finished product, while computational intelligence analyses crops and forecasts growing patterns.
- One aminent area of healthcare can get benefits by providing blockchain-based access to medicale experts who can use AI to personalize treatments.
- FINALIZE and NetObjex are infrastructure platform to working with connected devices to cloud-based products to improve logistics tracking, real-time failure detection and data and device authentication
- A blockchain and AI advisory, education, and marketing company is Chainhaus. The business offers a wide range of end-to-end solutions for everything from research and capital raising to teaching and app development.
- Walmart and IBM worked together to create a blockchain system that reduced the time it took to trace a product from seven days to 2.2 seconds.

- The Ethiopian Ministry of Education announced a partnership with blockchain developer IOHK in April 2021 to produce digital IDs based on the blockchain for five million students.
- Art and craft asset can be certified with Artificial intelligence and Blockchain as non fungible Tokens(NFT) and stop fraudulent copies from being sold as originals.

Figure 3. Current scenerios of blockchain based WSN applications

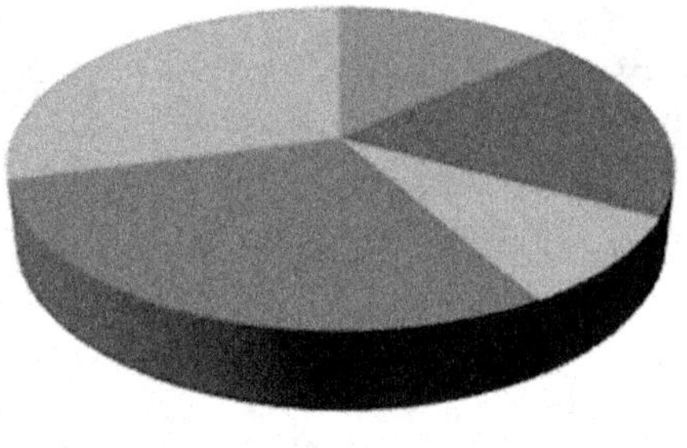

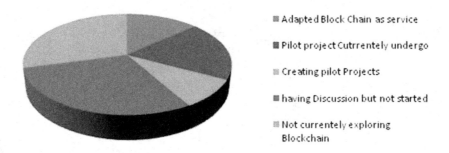

There are numerous blockchain technologies available at the moment. The most well-known ones, such as the blockchain technology used by Bitcoin, have many inefficiencies that are present in the overall system. One of the major drawbacks of blockchain is this.Indeed, blockchain is a distributed network that relies on nodes to function properly, but it does not support distributed computing system.

a. Blockchains networks are not scalable means transactions are completed depending on the network size,even in the permissioned networks.
b. Proof-of-Work consensus algorithm that relied on the Miners are dedicated nodes to solve complex mathematical problems as Proof-of-Work.In case of private blockchain, number of nodes are limited so no need for global consensus, they use efficient consensus methods to reach consensus.
c. Data immutability says that data once written cannot be removed. If a person utilizes a blockchain afterward he wants to remove its trace from the system, there is no way.
d. Size of the blockchain are growing very fastly with new transactions which makes thenetwork slow down.
e. Blockchain technology is more secure but not completely secure.blockchain network can be compromised by double-spending,DDoS's attack and other Cryptographic cracking methods.
f. Cost of implementing blockchain technology is huge even with hiring developers, managing a team of blockchain technology, licensing costs and maintenance cost
g. Blockchain technology is not enough meture mature and needs standardization. blockchain technology.Multiple types of blockchain networks needs interoperatability .

The points made above cover the drawbacks of blockchain technology, some of which can be resolved by switching to a more effective blockchain technology solution.Still, computational Intelligence may provide a way of automation to offer better solutions as discussed in the next section.

AI AND BLOCKCHAIN AS COMPLIMENTARY TECHNOLOGIES

WSN suffered from some challenges like, to share an unsafe medium, variable topology, limited energy, and bandwidth. By looking closely, one can see the contours of the security issues associated with the communication process in such networks that are still unsolved. A lot of work has been done in a different dimension for making the WSN secured, but none can be applied directly for WSNs.From the wast range of attacks,DOS attack is the most common attacks on WSNs, which goes through all the layers with the aim to disable proper functioning of the network (Mishra et al.,2022).An attackers may exhaust the channel or the node either by transmittingmany packets on the medium or by transmitting large number of packets to exhaust the battery of constrained nodes.CI based approaches has the the power of models and tools to learn and discoverto facilitate intelligence to in complex and changing environments (Bera et al.,2020).

Advancements in artificial intelligence and machine learning techniques are helping to strengthen the working of blockchain based next-generation networks. The new technologies influencing the creation of more dependable computer networks and the emergence of knowledge-driven distributed security applications and services are the subject of this section.

Blockchain Enabled Benefits for AI Modeling

For any CI based model,major challenges is the non sharable data for the model training among multiple shareholders and also impractical to deal with isolated data set.Blockchain (distributed ledger) offers the apportunity to deal with distributed data for centralized processing and training.Currentely blockchain is being utilized to facilitate AI applications by providing decentralized way of data processing while preserving data privacy, and supporting trusted AI decision and decentralized AI. Now we ll explain that how blockchain can benefit AI to ensure three essential As for trusted AI decision and decentralized AI.

Authenticity

Blockchain's digital record addresses the issue of explainable AI by providing insight into the conceptual framework and the provenance of the data it uses. This increases confidence in the accuracy of the data and, consequently, in the recommendations that AI generates. An audit trail is provided by using blockchain to store and distribute AI models, and combining blockchain with AI can improve data security.

Augmentation

A new level of intelligence is added to blockchain-based business networks by augmentation.AI, which can quickly and thoroughly read, comprehend, and correlate data. Blockchain enables AI to scale by managing data usage and model sharing, providing access to vast volumes of data from both inside and outside the organisation, and producing a reliable and open data economy.

Automation

Blockchain, AI, and automation can add new value to business processes involving multiple parties by reducing friction, boosting speed, and boosting productivity. For instance, AI models integrated into smart contracts running on a blockchain can suggest recalled products that are past their expiration dates, carry out transactions like stock purchases, payments, and reorders based on predetermined thresholds and events, resolve disputes, and choose the most environmentally friendly shipping method

AI Enabled Enhancements for Blockchain

Popular CI based algorithms can be hybridized to face security challenges in WSNs but simultaneously it is also observed that CI based solutions are not very much effective while lots of othersubsequent issues already exist with WSN. A lot of work is being done to boost the security solutions with CI encompasses techniques like neuro-computing, reinforcement learning, evolutionary computing and fuzzy computing.Biohashing is the most popular approach for human authentication in security task to enable authorized access to computer network.Artificial Intelligence can provide many improvements in multiple applications of WSN(Syarif et al., 2014). Some of the major enhancements,offered by Computational Intelligence Techniques se are given here:

1. Security: By ensuring secure future application deployments, AI-enhanced blockchain technology becomes safer. A good example of it is the increasing use of AI algorithms to determine whether financial transactions are fraudulent and should be blocked or investigated.
2. Effectiveness: AI can help calculations be optimised to lessen miner load, which reduces network latency and speeds up transactions. Blockchain technology's carbon footprint can be decreased thanks to AI. If AI machines take over the work that miners do, the cost that is imposed on them as well as the energy used would be reduced. AI's data pruning algorithms can be applied to blockchain data, which automatically prunes the data that is not needed for future use as the data on blockchains grows by the minute. AI can even introduce brand-new, highly efficient decentralised learning models like federated learning or new data-sharing strategies.
3. Trust: One of blockchain's advantage is the immutable records it keeps. When AI is used in conjunction with other technologies, users have access to detailed records that show how the system thinks. As a result, machine-to-machine interaction increases, the bots become more trusting of one another, which enables them to share information and coordinate group decisions.
4. Better Management: Human experts improve over time with practise at deciphering codes. A mining formula powered by machine learning could do away with the need for human expertise because, given the right training data, it could almost instantly improve its skills. AI thus also aids in better management of blockchain systems.
5. Privacy and New Markets: Securing private data always results in its sale, which gives rise to data markets and model markets. Markets now have simple, secure data sharing, which benefits smaller players. By using "Homomorphic encryption" algorithms, blockchain privacy can be further increased. The only algorithms that allow operations to be carried out directly on encrypted data are homomorphic ones.
6. Storage: When handled carefully by AI, highly sensitive, personal data can be stored on blockchains, adding value and convenience. A good illustration of that is smart healthcare technology that provides precise diagnoses based on medical records and scans.

Figure 4. AI Enabled Enhancements

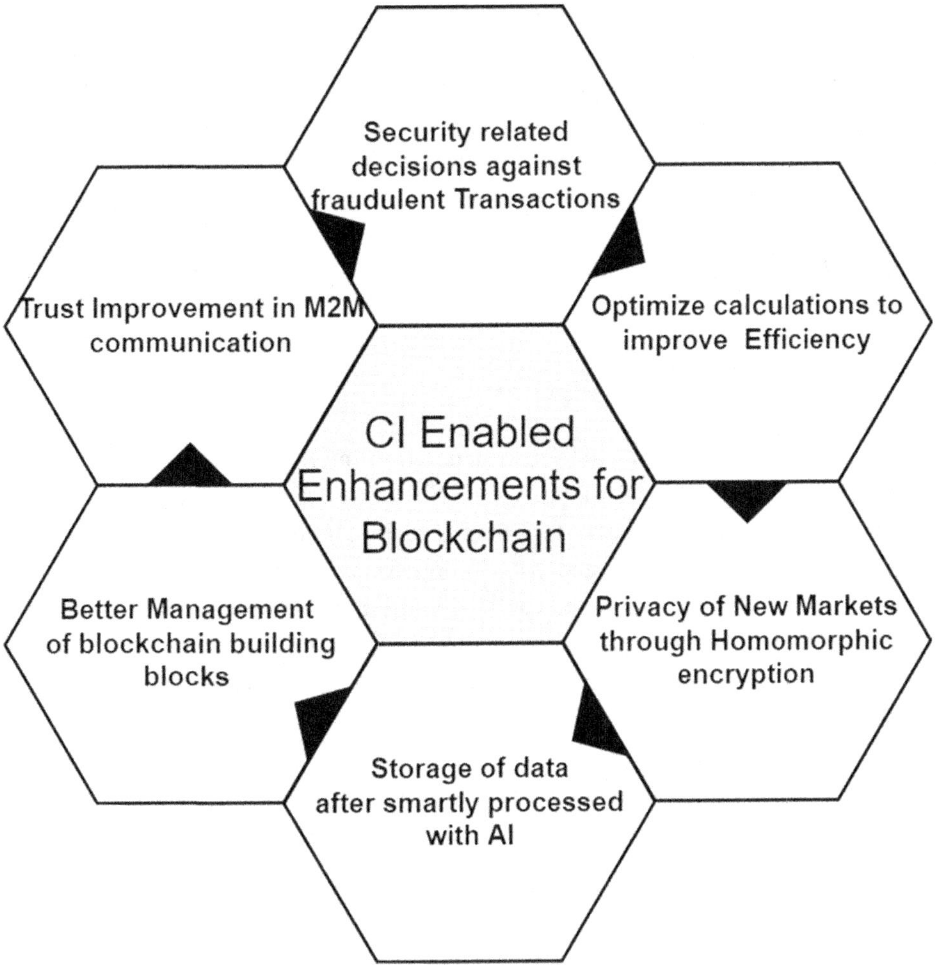

RESEARCH DIRECTIONS

Although there is research on the integration and application of AI and blockchain, our knowledge of the value of this integration for business is still fragmented. .Blockchain and Computational intelligence are paired to improve all business and industries like food supply chain logistics and healthcare, intertainment and financial security(Kumar et al., 2022).This study aims to describe the uses and advantages of integrated AI and blockchain platforms across various business verticals in order to close this gap.

- Healthcare: AI can help advance almost every area of the industry, from surfacing treatment insights and supporting user needs to identifying insights from patient data and revealing patterns. Organizations can collaborate to improve care while preserving patient privacy by using patient data on the blockchain, including electronic health records.
- Life sciences: In the pharmaceutical sector, blockchain and AI can increase the visibility and traceability of the drug supply chain and significantly boost the success rate of clinical trials. By combining cutting-edge data analysis with a decentralised framework for clinical trials, it is pos-

sible to automate trial participation and data collection while maintaining data integrity, transparency, patient tracking, and consent management.

- Financial services: By enabling trust, removing friction from multiparty transactions, and accelerating transaction speeds, blockchain and AI are revolutionising the financial services sector. Supply chain:By digitizing a largely paper-based process, making the data shareable and trustworthy, and adding intelligence and automation to execute transactions, AI and blockchain are transforming supply chains across industries and others.

Blockchain and Computational intelligence can be paired to improve overall business and industries.

CONCLUSION

Smart WSN has been acknowledged as the next-generation intelligent network that optimizes energy efficiency.Nonetheless, threaten the availability of WSN while the widespread deployment of sensors. Over the advantages of WSN, we have to design an security architectures to set the trade-off between power consumption, performance, and security.Computational Intelligence can provide a role-based secure communication and information sharing tool while incorporated with Blockchain but still industries are hesitating in adopting these new technologies. In order to close this gap, this study aims to outline the applications and benefits of combined blockchain and AI platforms across various business verticals. In this chapter, we describe an innovative combined use of CI and blockchain to realize the key potential of both the technologies as privacy-preserving decentralized approach over wireless sensor networks. This particular chapter is devoted to the emerging knowledge-driven distributed security applications and services, as well as the new technologies influencing the creation of more dependable computer networks.

REFERENCES

Agrawal, R., Chatterjee, J. M., Kumar, A., & Rathore, P. S. (Eds.). (2020). *Blockchain technology and the internet of things: Challenges and applications in bitcoin and security*. doi:10.1201/9781003022688

Akyildiz, I. F., Su, W., Sankarasubramaniam, Y., & Cayirci, E. (2002). A survey on sensor networks. *IEEE Communications Magazine*, *40*(8), 102–114. doi:10.1109/MCOM.2002.1024422

Awan, S., Javaid, N., Ullah, S., Khan, A. U., Qamar, A. M., & Choi, J. G. (2022). Blockchain Based Secure Routing and Trust Management in Wireless Sensor Networks. *Sensors (Basel)*, *22*(2), 411. doi:10.339022020411 PMID:35062371

Balakrishnan, B., & Balachandran, S. (2017). FLECH: Fuzzy logic based energy efficient clustering hierarchy for nonuniform wireless sensor networks. *Wireless Communications and Mobile Computing*, *2017*. doi:10.1155/2017/1214720

Basha, E. A., Ravela, S., & Rus, D. (2008, November). Model-based monitoring for early warning flood detection. In *Proceedings of the 6th ACM conference on Embedded network sensor systems* (pp. 295-308). 10.1145/1460412.1460442

Bera, B., Das, A.K., Obaidat, M., Vijayakumar, P., Hsiao, K.F., & Park, Y. (2020). AI-Enabled Blockchain-Based Access Control for Malicious Attacks Detection and Mitigation in IoE. *IEEE Consum. Electron. Mag*.

Eberhart, R. C., & Shi, Y. (2011). *Computational intelligence: concepts to implementations*. Elsevier.

Kacprzyk, J., & Pedrycz, W. (Eds.). (2015). *Springer handbook of computational intelligence*. Springer. doi:10.1007/978-3-662-43505-2

Kordafshari, M. S., & Movaghar, A. (2019). Multicast Routing in Wireless Sensor Networks: A Distributed Reinforcement Learning Approach. *Journal of New Researches in Mathematics*, *5*(20), 91–104.

Kumar, S., Lim, W. M., Sivarajah, U., & Kaur, J. (2022). Artificial Intelligence and Blockchain Integration in Business: Trends from a Bibliometric-Content Analysis. *Information Systems Frontiers*. Advance online publication. doi:10.100710796-022-10279-0 PMID:35431617

Martin, F. R. (2018). *Integrating AI Into Blockchain Can Help The Economy In More Ways Than You*. https://analyticsindiamag.com/

Mishra, S., & Tyagi, A. K. (2022). The role of machine learning techniques in internet of things-based cloud applications. In *Artificial Intelligence-based Internet of Things Systems* (pp. 105–135). Springer. doi:10.1007/978-3-030-87059-1_4

Nair, M. M., & Tyagi, A. K. (2021). Privacy: History, Statistics, Policy, Laws, Preservation and Threat Analysis. *Journal of Information Assurance & Security*, *16*(1).

Padalkar, N. R., Sheikh-Zadeh, A., & Song, J. (2020). *Business Value of Smart Contract: Case of Inventory Information Discrepancies*. Academic Press.

Primeau, N., Falcon, R., Abielmona, R., & Petriu, E. M. (2018). A Review of Computational Intelligence Techniques in Wireless Sensor and ActuatorNetworks. *IEEE Communications Surveys and Tutorials*, *20*(4), 2822–2854. doi:10.1109/COMST.2018.2850220

Selmic, R. R., Phoha, V. V., & Serwadda, A. (2016). *Wireless Sensor Networks*. Springer International Publishing AG. doi:10.1007/978-3-319-46769-6

Shinde, R., Patil, S., Kotecha, K., & Ruikar, K. (2021). Blockchain for Securing AI Applications and Open Innovations. *Journal of Open Innovation*, *7*(3), 189. Advance online publication. doi:10.3390/joitmc7030189

Solihin, M. I., & Zanil, M. F. (2016, November). Performance comparison of Cuckoo search and differential evolution algorithm for constrained optimization. *IOP Conference Series. Materials Science and Engineering*, *160*(1), 012108. doi:10.1088/1757-899X/160/1/012108

Syarif, M. A., Ong, T. S., Teoh, A. B. J., & Tee, C. (2014). Improved Biohashing Method Based on Most Intensive Histogram Block Location. In Neural Information Processing. ICONIP 2014. Lecture Notes in Computer Science (vol. 8836). doi:10.1007/978-3-319-12643-2_78

Tyagi, A. K., Nair, M. M., Niladhuri, S., & Abraham, A. (2020). Security, privacy research issues in various computing platforms: A survey and the road ahead. *Journal of Information Assurance & Security*, *15*(1).

Verma, P., Dumka, A., Bhardwaj, A., Kaur, N., Ashok, A., Bisht, A. K., & Gangwar, R. P. S. (2022). *Security Issues for Wireless Sensor Networks*. CRC Press. doi:10.1201/9781003257608

Yang, X. S. (2020). Nature-inspired optimization algorithms: Challenges and open problems. *Journal of Computational Science*, *46*, 101104. doi:10.1016/j.jocs.2020.101104

Chapter 18
Retrieval of Information Through Botnet Attacks:
The Importance of Botnet Detection in the Modern Era

Zahian Ismail
https://orcid.org/0000-0003-4143-6305
Universiti Malaysia Pahang, Malaysia

Aman Jantan
Universiti Sains Malaysia, Malaysia

Mohd. Najwadi Yusoff
Universiti Sains Malaysia, Malaysia

Muhammad Ubale Kiru
Universiti Sains Malaysia, Malaysia

ABSTRACT

Services and applications online involve information transmitted across the network, and therefore, the issue of security during data transmission has become crucial. Botnet is one of the prominent methods used by cybercriminals to retrieve information from internet users because of the massive impact cause by the bot armies. Thus, this chapter provides a study of Botnet and the impact of Botnet attacks especially on the security of information. In order to survive, Botnet implemented various evasion techniques, and one of the notorious ones is by manipulating an encrypted channel to perform their C&C communication. Therefore, the authors also review the state of the art for Botnet detection and focus on machine learning-based Botnet detection systems and look into the capabilities of machine learning approaches to detect this particular Botnet. Eventually, they also outline the limitations of the existing Botnet detection approach and propose an autonomous Botnet detection system.

DOI: 10.4018/978-1-6684-5250-9.ch018

INTRODUCTION

Information is an asset to many organizations. These organizations rely on the information especially for problem solving and decision making. Other organizations use information to observe the patterns and do the prediction for future exertions. For most organizations, their information is crucial and need to be protected, thus making the security of information is one of the areas that need special attention. To make things worse, recently many attackers started to use advance attacks for example the attack through Botnet, which compromised the computers in organizations and finally able to steal the organization's data.

Botnet is a vector to launch the attacks and amplify the impact of the attacks. Previously, Botnet attacks focused on the prevention of access and destruction of infrastructure through DDoS attacks, spamming and malware spreading. Nowadays, Botnet attacks mostly focusing on information stealing. Botnet itself is short for robot and networks (Jakalan et al., 2014), referring to the automated nature of Botnet operation in the network and the fact that all bots follow the instruction of the attacker (botmaster). Hence, this Botnet mechanism allows the attacker to give command through Botnet and launch the attack automatically, regardless the time and locations. In fact, if Botnet has been used to steal the information, it was in large scale and greatly affected the organizations (cloudbric, 2018).

Botnet that usually associated with information stealing mostly use encrypted channel for example SSL and TLS to launch the attacks. For instance, the attacks that targeting banking institutions, social media, and email applications (Gooley, 2017 and Desai, 2017). These applications are mostly using SSL or TLS to secure their communications and transactions. However, Botnet use the encrypted channel to hide their command and control (C&C) and to evade the detection. For that reason, this article emphasis on the discussion of the Botnet attacks over the encrypted channel.

Observing the scenario of Botnet attacks and the destructive effects cause by the attacks, the authors focus on Botnet attacks to steal the information and the detection of Botnet. The authors review the mechanism on how Botnet able to launch the attacks especially via encrypted channel and the Botnet detection techniques to suggest better detection techniques. The effective and efficient Botnet detection techniques can reduce the Botnet attacks especially the attacks targeting to steal the information. The study of Botnet detection is crucial as one of the steps for Botnet mitigation efforts. The authors study the various Botnet detection techniques and review whether the detection techniques capable to detect Botnet over the encrypted channel.

The authors organized the remainder of this article as follows. In section 2, the authors discuss the background of Botnet and possible scenarios which enable Botnet to launch the attacks over the encrypted channel. To show the severity of Botnet attacks especially for information stealing, the authors provide the example of Botnet attacks happened globally in section 3. Also in section 3, the authors are going to show Botnet variants associated with information stealing. Section 4 explains the impact of Botnet attacks to social, technical, and economy. Section 5 explains Botnet detection techniques and the limitation of Botnet detection especially for the encrypted channel. In section 6 the authors suggest the criteria for better Botnet detection system. Finally, the concluding remarks has been drawn up in section 7.

Figure 1. Coverage of encrypted channel and Botnet over the encrypted channel

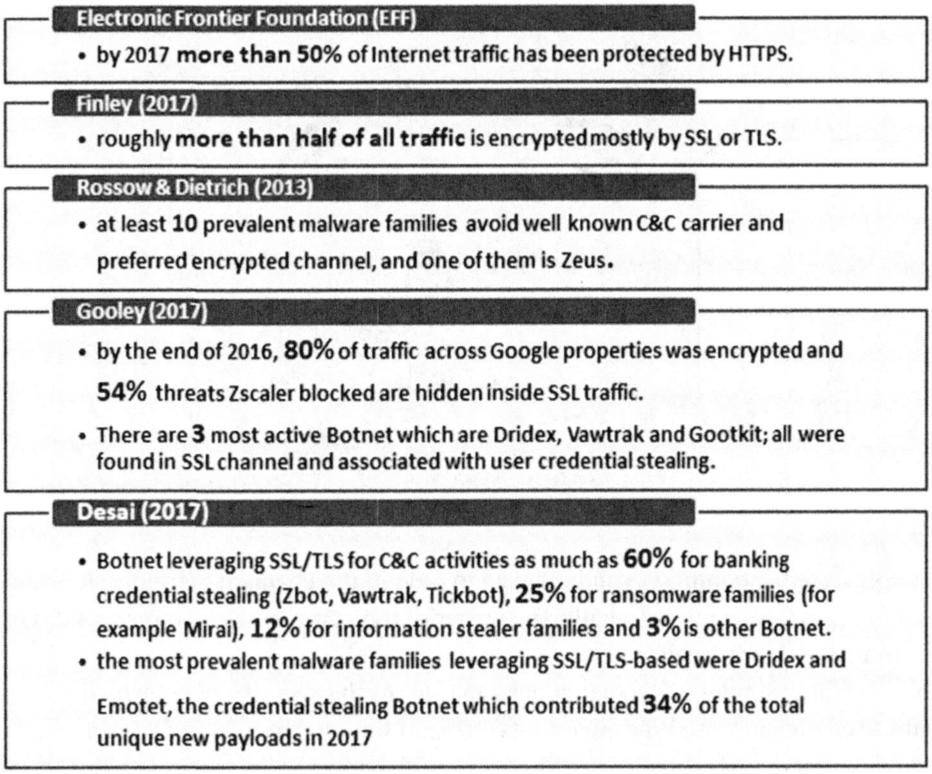

BACKGROUND

Many applications and services over the Internet are using encrypted channel, especially for critical applications or services that involving private information. Following are the statistics and the statements to show the coverage of encrypted channel over the Internet and Botnet over the encrypted channel.

According to Gooley (2017), there were three most active Botnet threats found in SSL channel that are often associated with user credential stealing; they include Dridex, Vawtrak, and Gootkit respectively. Desai (2017) states that the most prevalent malware families that leverage SSL/TLS channel for credential stealing were Dridex and Emotet, and they contributed 34% of the total unique new payloads in 2017. Desai added that the distribution of Botnets that use the SSL/TLS for C&C activities as much as 60% for banking credential stealing (Zeus, Vawtrak, and Tickbot), 25% for ransomware (Mirai), 12% for information stealer families and 3% for other attacks. The immense Botnet attacks have the huge impact on the social, technical and economy which will be further discussed in the later section.

To recruit the new hosts and turn them into the bots, botmaster initially needs to find vulnerable hosts. Scanning is the methods mostly used by botmaster to find the vulnerable hosts. After the hosts were compromised, the botmaster gives commands to the bots and they will follow the instruction given to them. Botnet common structure consists of botmaster (attacker), bots (compromised machines), C&C server (center of commands and proxies) and C&C communication channel as shown in Figure 2. Figure 2 also shows that the communication channel is encrypted. Botnet hides its commands in the packets over the encrypted traffic. In the encrypted channel, the packet binaries (content) will be encrypted. This

Figure 2. Botnet over the encrypted channel

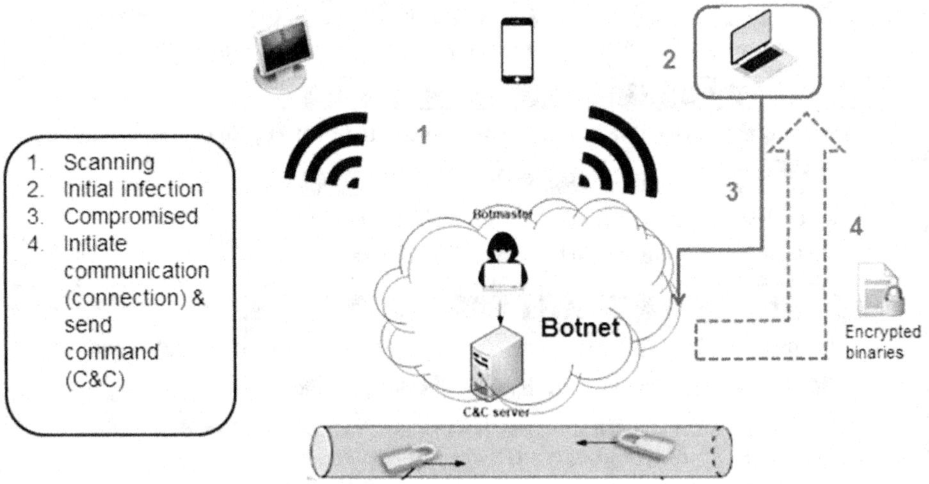

way, Botnet obfuscate the commands and manage to hide in the channel; therefore, it is a challenge to detect Botnet C&C in this channel. Usually, the owner of the compromised computers did not aware of Botnet compromising their machines.

There are several examples of Botnet attacks that harm the security of information. For instance, Botnet inquires the compromised machine (bots) to send the information to attacker and then ask the bots to delete the information. If the organizations want the information, they should pay some amount of money (ransomware attack). Other examples, the attacker may ask the bots to change the amount in the bank, transfer the money to other accounts, or retrieve the employees' information.

Given that the encrypted channel is a secure channel, Botnet has several ways to penetrate encrypted channel and compromised the machines in the network. Next the authors are going to highlight several scenarios which make the Internet infrastructure vulnerable to Botnet attacks therefore Botnet manipulates these weaknesses to enter the channel and attacks many applications that use encrypted channel.

a. Web browser

Web browsers accept new certificate from any valid certificate authorities even if the website provides the certificate which already been obtained. This allows Botnet to reuse the same certificate and disguise as legitimate.

b. Web server

Botnet manipulates the automatic open SSL channel to send it command and receive updates from its peers.

c. Digital certificate

Botnet develops its own illegal websites using the stolen or fake certificates. Botnet then use these fake websites to attract the visits from Internet users. When the users visit the websites, there are potential the machines they use will be compromised.

d. Certificate authority (CA)

CAs sold the certificate to non-existence companies. The CAs failed to verify whether the companies that they are issuing the certificates really exist or only a forgery company.

e. Encrypted applications

Botnet uses encrypted applications like social media and email. These applications mostly are encrypted by SSL or TLS and have a huge number of users. Furthermore, the web traffic is allowed almost anywhere. For instances, Botnet hides its command in social media posts, newsfeed and comments.

BOTNET ATTACKS THAT LIMIT THE INFORMATION ACCESS AND INITIATED INFORMATION STEALING

In 2000, Michael Calce from Montreal which is well-known as Mafiaboy launched a series of highly publicized DDoS attacks. These DDoS attacks were against large commercial websites such as Yahoo.com, Fifa.com, Amazon.com, Dell, E*TRADE, eBay, and CNN. The compromised machines in approximately 25 universities network and several private and company networks have been used to launch the attacks. The websites involved in the attacks have been disabled and some were shut down, making the users unable to access the websites. (Verton, 2002).

Other Botnet attacks recorded in 2008 by an unknown attacker, releasing Conficker worm targeting the Microsoft Windows operating system. There is speculation that botmaster leased the Botnet infected by Conficker to infect millions of computers and established the attacks of identity theft and other malicious activities. Conficker uses flaws in Windows operating system and dictionary attacks on administrator passwords to propagate while forming a Botnet. It infected millions of computers including government, business, and home computers in over 190 countries, making it the most massive known computer worm infection since 2003 (Rouse, 2009). Cisco Security also observed that Conficker C&C traffic was using TCP port 443 which SSL/TLS encrypted traffic typically use.

In 2009, an unknown attacker launched an attack targeting government of the United States and South Korea official websites. The investigation conducted reveals that virus has infected many personal computers which ordering them to visit official websites in South Korea and the United States at the same time, and overload the network with bogus requests, resulting to service failure. The similarity between attacks of two government website is they are launched through DDoS attacks, which involves massive, compromised computers to perform the attack commands, operate remotely by the botmaster (Weaver, 2009).

According to Nicholson (2015), the most sophisticated criminal Botnet in existence is Zeus Botnet. GameOver Zeus is a variant of Zeus family identified in September 2011. GameOver downloads the Gameover software over an SSL/TLS connection from a compromised web server. Gameover Zeus

Trojan leverages encryption for both malware distribution and C&C communications. GameOver Zeus is a credential stealing malware which primarily used by cybercriminals to harvest banking information.

GameOver Zeus also installed Cryptolocker, a type of malware known as ransomware to the infected computers. This malware encrypted computer files (for example photographs, vital business record, police investigative files) in the victims' computers and get them to pay several amounts of money, usually in between $300 to $750 before they received a decryption key. Terrifying of losing the crucial data, most of the victims directly paid, but some victims like Pittsburgh insurance company refused to pay and try to defeat the malware. They able to restore the data from the backup, but eventually losses estimated $70 000 and sending employees home during recovery. In response to the previous efforts to take down Botnet, the creators of the Zeus Botnet designed a novel and resilient structure, including three distinct layers of C&C infrastructure that rendered the Botnet particularly difficult to overcome (Homeland Security Digital Library, 2014).

A report shows that between 2012 and 2013, American banks have been targeted with massive DDoS campaign which cost the banks an estimated loss of $100 million per hour. Similarly, in March 2013, South Korea's banking industry was hit by a massive coordinated attack which caused the loss of $725 million. Within June 2014 until February 2015, Russian hackers launched attacks as many as 100 banks across 30 countries. The hackers used Botnet to send out malware-infected emails to bank employees (a tactic called spear phishing) which led to the infiltration of many employees' accounts to steal sensitive information including customer data, secret keys used by ATMs to confirm PINs, bank video surveillance, and information on security systems as well as anti-fraud measures. They also manipulated account balances and created fake accounts to move stolen money around and caused one bank to be robbed about $7.3 million after hackers reprogrammed their ATMs. Another bank's online platform was accessed, and the infiltrators took away $10 million. Till date, the authorities are unable to catch them. (Cloudbric, 2018).

In 2015 it was reported that Zeus Botnet infected more than 3.2 million computers globally within five years. From Q1 of 2018, approximately 3.2 billion Botnet attacks were detected each month at a global scale. With massive numbers of machines at hand, it also gave a great opportunity to DDoS and ransomware attacks to propagate attack campaign, which caused technical breaches and loss of money globally (Schwartz, 2015).

By the end of 2016, Mirai Botnet infected approximately 100 000 IoT device network and performed a DDoS attack on DNS provider that resulted in several website crashing, including Twitter and Netflix (Mitchell, 2017). Mirai managed to make much of the Internet unavailable for millions of people by overwhelming Dyn, a company that provides a significant portion on the US Internet backbone (Newman, 2016). IoT devices exceptionally smart home appliances are the primary target because most of them use default username and password. Mirai performs brute force using a table that contains a list of default username and password and compromised the machine to perform massive DDoS attacks. Radware Security proves that by implementing SSL channel Mirai able to cause an advance DDoS attack by stressing the servers that do not allow SSL renegotiation and rapidly establishing new TCP connection on each SSL connection.

Botnet Variants that Steal Information and Deny Access

There are special Botnet variants that associated with information stealing and limited information access. Table 1 shows some notorious Botnet variants that have been used for those purposes. Some Botnets

Table 1. Botnet Variants

Botnet (Year)	Attack
Gozi (2006)	Information stealing
Zeus (2007)	Steal bank credential info
Spyeye (2009)	Steal bank credential info
Torpig/ Sinowal/Anserin	Steal bank credential info
WireX	DDoS attack
Shylocks	Intercept network traffic and inject code into banking websites.
Ramnit	Commit financial fraud
Stuxnet (2011)	Sabotage industrial process (infect nuclear plants for the enrichment of Uranium in Iran).
Duqu (2011) - family of Stuxnet	Steal information (hide in Kaspersky network).
Flame (2012) - family of Stuxnet	Cyber espionage
Mirai (2016)	DDoS attack
Socialbot / socbot / Twitterbot	Bots that control social media accounts, performing phishing attacks, re-tweet storms, hashtag hijacks.
Koobface (2008)	Target social network (for instance Facebook, Skype, and Yahoo Messenger) and email (Gmail. Yahoo mail, AOL mail).
Dridex (2014)/ Bugat/ Cridex	Steal bank credential info
Vawtrak/ Neverquest (2013)	Steal bank credential info, descendant of Gozi
Conficker (2008)	Identity theft, phishing exploits
Kelihos/ Waledac/ Hlux (2010)	Theft of bitcoins
GameOver Zeus (2011) - family of Zeus/ Zbot/Kneber	Steal bank credential info

which have been shut down previously re-emerge and become stronger by applying encryption to mask their communication for instance Kelihos which has been shut down by Microsoft and Kaspersky in 2011. These Botnets are mostly specialized for banking credential stealing.

According to Europol (2017), Zeus is the founding father of banking Trojans and most of banking Trojans today are its descendants. Zeus builds one of the biggest Botnet in history. Zeus well-known variants include GameOver Zeus, Citadel, Ramnit, Dridex, Later Spyeye arises which is the primary competitor of Zeus.

IMPACT OF BOTNET ATTACKS

The authors study the impact of Botnet attacks in three aspects: social, technical, and economy.

a. Social

Botnet attacks have been used to steal information and this has caused loss of important data and data breaching which affecting individual and organizations. For individual, personal data in the computer can be very precious and dear to them, for instance photographs, audio, assignment etc. There are also private pictures that if they have been revealed caused them humiliation. It can be used to blackmail the victims.

For organizations, Botnet attacks able to create chaos when the information that the attacker successfully retrieved from the infected system has been altered for example employees' information and bank statement. Losing such information produces pressure and requires some effort to retrieve them back.

b. Technical

Botnet able to compromise thousands of machines leads to the creation of mass zombies' network Cleaning a Botnet infected system will be very difficult because the volume of network traffic created by bots is massive, hence, making it impossible to install updates on the infected machine. Some of the Botnets react aggressively when they notice actions have been taken to clean them and they also able to turn off the antivirus software. To clean Botnet in the system, a large amount of money has to be spent.

c. Economy

According to CyberSecurity Malaysia (2010), a large amount of money has to be spent to clean Botnet from the system. Furthermore, according to ThreatMetrix (2012), the encrypted Botnet, mostly Zeus and its variants mainly targets financial institution, merchants and online business. Recently, social media platforms also have shown increasing sophistication in monetizing their sites. Cybercriminals are seizing this opportunity to steal personal and financial information from registered users. The banking system also susceptible to Botnet attack when once compromised, the attacker can make the illegal transfer, change the amount in the account, and change the pin number. For the retail company, if their payment system has been compromised, it caused the loss of reputation and business.

BOTNET DETECTION TECHNIQUES

Botnet detection techniques have evolved through time as stated by Hyslip & Pittman (2015). The detection techniques change as the Botnet changed communication technology and infrastructure. This trend can be observed by the articles published in Botnet detection. For instance between 2000 and 2010, researchers focus on finding detection solution for IRC-based and HTTP-based (centralized) Botnet (Binkley & Singh, 2006; Strayer et al., 2008; Akiyama et al., 2007; Goebel & Holz, 2007; Gu et al., 2008; Lu & Ghorbani, 2008; Wang et al., 2009, Al-Hammadi, 2010). From 2010 and above the focus switches to decentralized architecture including P2P communication protocol (Langin et al. 2010; Liao & Chang, 2010; Liu et al., 2010; Ritu & Kaushal, 2010; Zeidanloo et al., 2010; Saad et al., 2011; Zhang et al. 2011; Yan et al. 2015; Guntuku et al., 2013; Al-Azzawi, 2014; Narang et al., 2014; Ritu & Kaushal, 2015). Apparently, a lot of P2P Botnet detection use machine learning approach. After several years, the focus of Botnet detection is to find the solution for encrypted and covert Botnet (Bortolameotti, 2014; Buriya et al., 2015; Burghouwt, 2015; Sanatinia & Noubir, 2015; Sherry et al., 2015; Tyagy et al., 2016; Jianguo et al., 2016; Cha & Kim, 2017; Zhang, 2017). 2015 onward, IoT bot becomes a hit especially after the Mirai attack (Moon et al., 2015; Angrishi, 2017; Kolias et al., 2017).

Researchers have developed many architectures and proposed different taxonomies for Botnet detection (Karim et al., 2014). Plohmann (2011) has generally classified Botnet detection into passive and

Figure 3. Basic Classifications of Botnet Detection Techniques

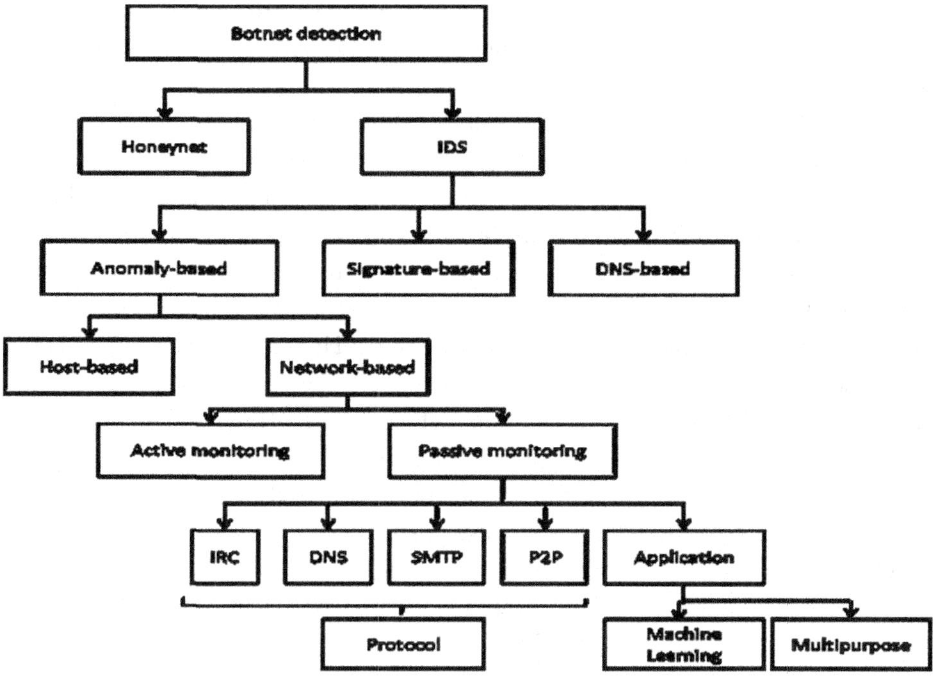

active techniques based from a survey of experts working in the field of Botnet mitigation. However, taxonomy dividing Botnet detection into Honeynet, and IDS are the common classification for detection technique (Feily et al., 2009; Zeidanloo et al., (i) 2010; Raghava et al., 2012; Silva et al., 2012; Karim et al., 2014). Even so, Honeynet did not actively involve in the individual bot detection system (Haltas et al., 2014). It is because Honeynet only collects the Botnet samples and need to be integrated with other analysis tools like antivirus and sandbox (Jakalan et al., 2014). Furthermore, Honeynet is not effective at detecting P2P and other decentralized Botnet (Hyslip & Pitmann, 2015). There is a possibility that Honeynet was not able to detect encrypted C&C. Furthermore, according to Feily et al. (2009), Honeynet is mostly useful to understand Botnet technology and characteristics, but not necessarily detects Botnet infection. Figure 3 depicts the taxonomy of Botnet detection techniques.

Other than Honeynet, IDS also has been used for Botnet detection. Referring to Figure 3, IDS was divided by signature-based, DNS based and anomaly-based detection. Signature-based Botnet detection is able of detecting Botnet immediately with low false positive rate, but only for known Botnet attack. Unknown or new Botnet cannot be detected by signature-based detection (Raghava et al., 2012). DNS based detection detect Botnet DNS traffic and detect DNS traffic anomalies (Dange & Gosavi, 2013). This detection technique is similar to anomaly detection because similar anomaly detection algorithms are applied to DNS traffic (Feily et al., 2009). Furthermore, DNS-based detection only limited to Botnet that uses DNS and does not work on non-DNS-based Botnet (Gibbs, 2014). Therefore, researchers (Arshad et al., 2011; Zhou et al., 2013) are likely to classified IDS into two broad categories; signature and anomaly-based detection. Anomaly-based detection consists of host based and network based. Machine learning is part of anomaly-based detection approach under passive monitoring.

Anomaly-based detection identifies Botnet without any prior knowledge of signatures. Therefore, this detection technique effectively detects new Botnet attack compared to known attack. Anomaly detection was based on several network traffic anomalies such as high network latency, high traffic volumes, traffic on unusual ports and unusual system behavior (Saha & Gairola, 2005) that could indicate the presence of malicious bots in the network. For example, BotSniffer (Gu et al., 2008) is an anomaly-based Botnet detection system design to detect Botnet command and control traffic. Hence this technique is suitable to detect encrypted Botnet C&C as encrypted traffic also produces anomaly which can be used for detection. Combining anomaly and signature-based algorithm able to overcome the limitation of the known attack in anomaly detection, for instance, BotHunter (Gu et al., 2007) which integrated anomaly detection algorithm into Snort.

Unlike integrated signature and anomaly techniques in BotHunter, Arshad et al. (2011) proposed a fully anomaly-based approach that requires no a priori knowledge of bot signatures, Botnet C&C protocols and C&C server addresses. They cluster bots with similar netflows and attacks in different time windows and perform a correlation to identify the bot-infected host. They developed a prototype system and evaluated it with real-world traces including normal traffic and several real-world Botnet traces. This approach produced high accuracy and low false positive rate.

There are other approaches employed by IDS-based Botnet detection as referred to Figure 3. Fedynyshyn et al. (2011) presented a host-based detection system for detecting and differentiating Botnet infections based on their C&C styles (IRC, HTTP or P2P). This host-based system focus on detecting bot on an individual host and typically use a signature or behavior-based techniques to correlate network traffic or system events with known bot signatures or behavioral information. Unlike many host-based IDS, this approach potentially discovers infections of previously unknown bots and produced best results in term of accuracy (0.929) and false positive rate (0.078).

Active bot detection involves participating in the Botnet operation, which typically involves impersonating as a component of Botnet (Khattak et al., 2014). Kanich et al. (2009) employed active Botnet detection by performing Botnet infiltration. They are insinuating into Botnet's command and control network, passively observing spam related commands and data it distributes, and where appropriate actively changing individual elements of these messages in transit. Spamming activity observed quickly led to detection and blacklisting.

Contrary to active detection, passive detection detects Botnet by silently observing and analyzing their activities without making any conscious effort to participate in the proceeding (Khattak et al., 2014). Zeidanloo et al. (ii) (2010) proposed a framework for Botnet detection based on traffic monitoring. This framework is based on finding similar communication patterns and behaviors among the group of hosts that are performing at least one malicious activity. BotMiner (Gu et al., 2008), BotSniffer (Gu et al., 2008) and BotDigger (Al-Duwairi & Al-Ebbini, 2010) exploit Botnet communication and behavior uniformity by monitoring the traffic behavior of several machines and then identifying machines which are part of Botnet when they begin to perform similar malicious actions simultaneously.

Machine learning was part of-IDS based detection. Machine learning approaches have been used extensively in analyzing various forms of network traffic data (Stevanovic & Pedersen, 2016) and machine learning has more capability to handle new variants of Botnet compared to the conventional approach. It is because machine learning mainly uses a knowledge-based approach focusing on pattern recognition, as Botnet produces distinct traffic patterns and behaviors (Roshna & Ewards, 2013). These patterns according to Stevanovic & Pedersen could be efficiently detected using machine learning algorithms (MLA). Machine learning is effective for detecting various forms of Botnet, including P2P

Botnet (Thomas & Jyoti, 2007; Guntuku et al., 2013) and other decentralized Botnet including encrypted Botnet. Furthermore, it has been proven by previous research as being able to solve many issues like accuracy (Salvador et al., 2009; Al-Hammadi, 2010; Guntuku et al., 2013; Bilge et al., 2014; Ritu & Kaushal, 2015) and real-time (Salvador et al., 2009; Guntuku et al., 2013) in Botnet detection. Table 2 summarizes various Botnet detection techniques. There are several techniques able to detect Botnet that use encrypted channel.

Even though most of the MLAs in Table 2 claims that they can detect encrypted Botnet because most of them are structure independent or HTTPS-based detection, the test that they conducted does not use appropriate datasets that include encrypted traffics. Furthermore, the results provided do not include the detection of encrypted Botnet. This section fundamentally discusses various Botnet detection techniques. An ID has been widely used to detect Botnet rather than Honeynet. Roughly IDS has been divided into signature based, DNS-based, and anomaly based. Machine learning is part of anomaly detection.

Detecting Botnet over the Encrypted Channel

Mostly Botnet detection relies on the detection features. Jianguo et al. (2016) in their experiments prove that accuracy of Botnet detection highly depends on the features extracted. There are different features used for detection as shown in Table 3. The features use for detecting encrypted Botnet might slightly differ from common Botnet, for example, encrypted Botnet produces high entropy which is used as a detection feature. There was also the algorithm available to measure the trustworthiness and reliability of the features used in detection.

Table 2 also shows the detection metrics used for detection by previous researchers. Accuracy, detection rate, and false positive rate are the standard metrics used to measure the performance of their detection approaches. These metrics are vital to prove that the proposed approaches are relevant. Therefore, it is very crucial to achieve high accuracy and detection rate while achieving a meager false positive rate to indicate that the approaches were effective. That is the issue faces by several approaches below where they can provide a high detection rate, but at the same time, the false positive rate is also very high. Relatively, common Botnet detection and encrypted Botnet detection use similar metrics to measure the performance. In detection, real-time or fast detection also is essential to measure the efficiency of the approaches.

Detecting Botnet is a challenge due to its dynamic nature but detecting Botnet in the encrypted channel is another level of challenge. Previously, detecting this kind of Botnet relies on payload analysis which requires decryption, and this leads to privacy issues. Even though Rossow & Dietrich (2013) proposed PROVEX to improve payload-based detection, their approach faces privacy issue by decrypting and inspecting the payload. Instead of payload analysis, there were also other approaches available for detecting Botnet in the encrypted channel. For example, flow analysis and machine learning approach which have become prominent. Even the approaches discussed provides a good result, there are limitations, for instance, some of them are dependable to specific Botnet structure, for example, Saad et al. (2011) and Guntuku et al. (2013) which focus on detecting P2P Botnet. It limits the type of Botnet detected. Another limitation is the insufficient alert mechanism.

There are several approaches able to detect Botnet over the encrypted channel. For instance, Khan et al. (2015) proposed a unified framework for detecting the known bots and encrypted bots using signature-based classifier and anomaly-based detection. Bots are detected based on the pattern of network flow.

Table 2. Botnet Detection Techniques

	Author	Detection Approach	Unknown Bot Detection	Protocol Structure Independent	Encrypted Bot Detection	Real-Time Detection	Low False Positive	Detection Rate (True Positive)	Features for Detection
Honeynet-based	Bhatia et al. (2011)	virtual Honeynet (Nepenthes)	X	X (IRC & HTTP)	X	X	X	X	activity and message response command sequence from payload
	Jakalan et al. (2011)	low interaction honeypot (Nepenthes)	X	X (IRC, DNS & HTTP)	X	X	X	X	source code
	Kumar et al. (2012)	virtual Honeynet (Nepenthes)	X	X (IRC, HTTP, P2P)	X	X	X	X	binaries
Signature-based	Gu et al. (2007) - BotHunter	IDS-driven dialog correlation strategy	/	/	X	/	/	99.20%	calculated value of dialog correlation
	Rossow & Dietrich (2013) - PROVEX	n-gram analysis	X	/	/	X	/	78%-100%	C&C protocol syntax
Anomaly-based	Binkley & Singh (2006)	IRC mesh detection component with TCP scan detection heuristic	/	X (IRC)	X	X	X	X	TCP work weight
	Arshad et al. (2011)	X-means algorithm and hierarchical algorithm (ML approach)	/	/	/	/	/	3 out of 4 Botnets (100%)	features associated with NetFlows
	Garcia et al. (2014)	The Cooperative Adaptive Mechanism for NEtwork Protection (CAMNEP)	/	/	/	X	/	50% (accuracy)	features associated with NetFlows
DNS-based	Choi et al. (2009) - BotGAD	Generic metric model to measure group activities	/	/	/	/	/ (0.1)	X	Botnet group activity
	Bilge et al. (2014) - EXPOSURE	J48 decision tree algorithm	/	X (DNS)	X	X	/ (0.3%)	99.50%	15 features from 4 feature set; time-based, DNS answer-based, TTL value-based, domain name-based
Mining-based / Machine Learning-based	Saad et al. (2011)	1.Nearest Neighbors Classifier, 2. Linear SVM 3.ANN, 4. Gaussian Based Classifier, 5. Naive Bayes Classifier	/	X (P2P)	/	X	X (1. NN-7%, 2.SVM-6% 3.ANN-8%, 4.GBC-20%, 5.NBC-12%)	1.NN-92%, 2.SVM-97.8% 3.ANN-94.5%, 4.GBC-96.2%, 5.NBC-89.7%	17 features (flow based and host-based features)
	Warmer (2011)	1. Adaboost, 2. Conjunctive rule, 3. J48, 4.Naïve Bayes, 5.Ripper, 6.SVM	/	X (HTTP, HTTPS)	/	X	X (Ada-5.5%, CR-5.1%, J48-3.2%, NB-44.3%, Ripper-2.9%, SVM-2.4%)	Ada-94.9%, CR-94.9%, J48-96.1%, NB-97.3%, Ripper-95.9%, SVM-96%	TLS features
	Dietrict et al. (2012) - CoCoSpot	Average-Linkage Hirarchical Clustering	/	/	/	X	88% of Botnet families have less than 0.1%	>50% of Botnet families are over 95.6%	traffic features (carrier protocol distinction, message length sequences, encoding differences)
	Guntuku et al. (2013)	Neural networks with Bayesian regularization	/	X (P2P)	/	/	X	99.2% (accuracy)	15 features selected using Information Gain Ranking Algorithm out of 44 features extracted
	Zhao et al. (2013)	Decision Tree classifier + Reduced Error Pruning Algorithm (REPTree)	/	/	/	/	/ (0.01%)	98.30%	traffic flow behavior analysis in a small-time window
	Roshna & Ewards (2013)	Adaptive Neuro Fuzzy Inference System (ANFIS)	/	X (DNS)	/	X	X	95.29%	DNS query
	Bortolameotti (2014)	Decision Tree Algorithms	/	/	/	X	/ (0)	99.96%	6 SSL features identified, only use 4 of them for detection
	Buriya et al. (2015)	Naïve Bayes	/	/	/	X	X	98.84% (accuracy)	flow duration, flow size, number of packets in flow, protocol, source IP
	Ritu & Kaushal (2015)	Nearest Neighbor, Decision Tree, SVM	/	X (P2P)	/	X	X	NN-97.10%, DT-100%, SVM-100% (accuracy)	SrcIP, SrcPort, DstIP, DstPort, Protocol, Total Packets, Total bytes and Duration
	Shanti & Seenivasan (2015)	1. Decision Tree J48 Classifier without Pruning Algorithm 2. Naïve Bayes	/	/	/	X	X (Decision Tree-13.3047%, NB-21.4592%)	Decision Tree - 86.6953%, NB-78.5408%	traffic flow characteristics based on time intervals
	Kirubavathi & Anitha (2016)	Boosted Decision Tree (AdaBoost + J48), Naïve Bayes, SVM	/	/	/	/	/ (Ada+J48-0.0813%, NB-0.0481%, SVM-0.0972%)	Ada+J48-95.86%, NB-99.14%, SVM-92.02% (accuracy)	Small Packets, Packet ratio, Initial Packet length, Bot-response_packet ratio
	Richer (2017)	SVM	/	/	/	X	X (15.1%)	100%	entropy

This approach is one of the examples of flow-based encrypted Botnet detection. Even so, this approach has an issue with detection time efficiency.

Machine Learning in Botnet Detection over The Encrypted Channel

As been discussed previously, machine learning is a promising approach to detect Botnet in the encrypted channel and solve the limitation of existing approaches in detecting encrypted Botnet. Machine learning has the goal of construction and studying of systems that can learn from data (Mitchell, 1997). Learning in this context implies the ability to recognize complex patterns and make qualified decisions based on previously seen data. According to Stevanovic & Pedersen (2016), generally, the authors can classify MLA as supervised and unsupervised based on the desired outcome of the algorithm. Kotsiantis et al. (2007) stated that supervised learning is the class of well-defined MLA that generates a function that maps input to desired output. Jain et al. (1999) stated that unsupervised learning is the class of MLA where training data consists of a set of input without any corresponding target output values.

Supervised Learning

Ericson et al. (2017) described supervised learning algorithms that make predictions based on a set of examples. Each example used for training is labeled with the value of interest. This learning algorithm looks for patterns in those value labels, and each algorithm looks for different types of patterns. Jain & Upendra (2011) generally categorized supervised learning into classification and regression. Classification is to predict the class membership as one of a finite number of discrete labels. Regression is to predict the output value as one of a potentially infinite set of real valued points. Neural Network, Expert System, Support Vector Machine, Dendric Cell Algorithm, K-Nearest Neighbors and Genetic Algorithm are the example of supervised learning algorithm.

Unsupervised Learning

In supervised learning, data points have no labels associated with them. Ericson et al. (2017) described the goal of an unsupervised learning algorithm is to organize the data in some way or to describe its structure. Unsupervised learning is categorized into clustering and association. Self-Organizing Map and K-Means algorithm are the examples of the unsupervised learning algorithm.

Machine learning has been extensively used in detecting various kind of Botnet. Stevanovic & Pedersen (2016) stated that machine learning is one of the latest trends in network-based Botnet detection for identifying patterns of malicious traffic. There are quite some research done in this area discussing different MLA; either supervised, unsupervised or semi-supervised. Later in this section is the example of various machine learning approaches which able to detect encrypted Botnet.

Some researchers performed comparative studies on different machine learning to show which machine learning provides the best performance. Saad et al. (2011) studied the ability of five different commonly used MLAs to meet online Botnet detection requirements, namely adaptability, novelty detection and early detection. All the five MLAs provide high true positive value; however Support Vector Machine got the highest true positive value which is 97.8%. Warmer (2011) compared different techniques and based on the result proposes three new techniques for detecting HTTP and HTTPS-based C&C channel. It shows Naïve Bayes got the highest true positive which is 97.3%. Ritu & Kaushal (2015) experimented to compare different supervised MLAs for determining peer to peer Botnet detection accuracy. Decision Tree and Support Vector Machine achieved 100% accuracy.

Shanti & Seenivasan (2015) proposed a detection methodology to classify bot host from the normal host by analyzing traffic flow characteristics based on time intervals instead of payload inspection. They use Decision Tree and Naïve Bayes for classification. Classification with decision tree gave better true positive of 86.69%. Kirubavathi & Anitha (2016) proposed an approach to detect Botnet irrespective of their structures. They try several MLAs to their approach, and Naïve Bayes has the highest detection rate of 99.14%.

Zhao et al. (2013) and Bortolameotti (2014) used Decision Tree to their approaches, and both provide very high detection rate which is 98.5% and 99.96% with a very low false positive rate of 0.01% and 0%. Dietrict et al. (2012) developed CoCoSpot use Average-Linking Hierarchical Clustering. 50% of Botnet families were detected by the rate of 95.6%. Buriya et al. (2015) used Naïve Bayes and achieved 98.84% accuracy. Apparently most of the MLAs discussed have very high detection rate.

Even though some techniques provide high detection rate, comparatively they also got a high false positive rate. For example, Richer (2017) proposed an approach using Support Vector Machine and got a 100% detection rate, however the false positive rate is more than 15%. The work by Shanti & Seenivasan (2015) also provided very high false positive which is more than 21%. Above all, Warmer (2011) had the highest false positive value of 44.3% by using Naïve Bayes.

Al-Hammadi (2010) presented a host-based behavioral approach for detecting Botnet based on correlating different activities generated by bots by monitoring function calls within a specified time window. Al-Hammadi used Dendric Cell Algorithm inspired by the Immune System. The evaluation shows that correlating different activities generated by IRC/P2P bots within a specified period achieves high detection accuracy (100%). In addition, using an intelligent correlation algorithm not only states if an anomaly is present, but it also exposed the source of the anomaly.

One of the most prominent MLA founds for Botnet detection is Neural Network and its distributions. Self-Organizing Map (SOM) is an unsupervised Neural Network and has been widely using in intrusion detection. Unfortunately, there are limited works discussed SOM for Botnet detection, but generally in intrusion detection. However, SOM is a promising approach especially for developing autonomous Botnet detection system. Langin et al. [i] (2009) used SOM to cluster and classify peer to peer Botnet traffic and other malignant network activity by analyzing firewall log entries. Langin et al. [ii] (2009) used Hexagonal Self Organizing Map for clustering and then used for classification of new firewall log data to look for additional bots in the network.

Guntuku et al. (2013) proposed and implemented a hybrid framework for detecting peer to peer Botnet in live network traffic by integrating Neural Networks with Bayesian Regularization for detection of newer and unseen Botnet in live traffic of a network. It was conclusively shown through the statistical tests that the trained Bayesian Regularization - Neural Network model can generalize very well and can predict the activity of unknown bots' malicious activity. Thus, Botnet detection activities successfully achieved with an accuracy of 99.2%. Nogueira et al. (2010) extended the framework proposed by Salvador and develops the Botnet Security System called BoNeSSy. Nogueira develops a Botnet detection system that is based on the collection of flow statistics using Neural Network. The results obtained shows that the system is feasible and efficient since it provides high detection rates with low computational overhead.

Many current approaches to the process of detecting intrusions utilize some forms of rule-based analysis. Expert System is the most common form of rule-based intrusion detection approaches. Most existing behavior-based approaches are not able to detect and predict the Botnet as they change their structure and pattern. Roshna & Ewards (2013) presented Adaptive Neuro-Fuzzy Inference System (ANFIS), a technique which trains the system for future prediction. However, the limitation of this work is the restriction of fuzzy rules and fuzzy sets for the comparison purpose. Therefore, the proposed work should be able to overcome the limitations by increasing the number of rules generated using the Botnet features and information gain.

Fuzzy pattern recognition proposed by Wang et al. (2011) intended to identify bot-relevant domain names and IP addresses by inspecting network traces. The algorithm developed involves traffic reduction, feature selection, and pattern recognition. Fuzziness in pattern recognition helps to detect bots which are hidden or camouflage. Performance evaluation results based on real traces show that the proposed system can reduce more than 70% input raw packet traces and achieve a high detection rate (about 95%) and a low false positive rate (0–3.08%). Furthermore, the proposed FPRF algorithm is resource-efficient and can identify inactive Botnet to indicate potentially vulnerable hosts. BotDigger proposes by Al- Duwairi & Al-Ebbini (2010) utilized fuzzy logic to define logical rules that are mainly based on some statistical facts and essential features that identify Botnet activities. The key advantage of the architecture designed in this research is that it allows the integration of a wide range of traffic specifications.

The discussion of the machine learning above mostly provides performance evaluation using the detection rate, accuracy, or false positive value. However, there are other vital metrics which are real-time and autonomous. Even the detection able to detect accurately, it is useless without fast detection or real-time detection. Researchers focus on developing real-time Botnet detection system, for example, Salvador et al. (2010), Wang et al. (2011) and Guntuku et al. (2013).

Autonomous mainly focus on self-learn and self-manage properties. Chandhankhede (2013) proposed the new autonomous model for Botnet detection using K-means algorithm, one of the most straightforward unsupervised learning algorithms that solve the well-known clustering problem. According to Khattak et al. (2014), the degree of automation can be classified as manual, semi-automated and automated. Semi-automated Botnet detection requires very little human intervention, and most of the detection is performed on automated fashion. However, fully automated Botnet detection should require no human intervention after initial development. Khattak also agreed that ideally, any detection method should be as generic and automated as possible.

CRITERIA FOR BETTER BOTNET DETECTION

For detection system, accuracy and detection time are the crucial elements and have been used to measure the performance of the detection system. However, mostly, there is always a trade-off between accuracy and detection time. Nevertheless, some researchers successfully address this issue and propose the Botnet detection system with high accuracy and real time detection. Even though accuracy and detection time are the main components to measure the detection system performance, there is another aspect that the authors need to look at, for instance the management aspect.

For system or network manager, it is a challenge to manage the system and protect them from the attack. After the Botnet detection system detects the attack, the next step is how to manage the alert generated by the detection system. By introducing the autonomous features to detection system, it helps the manager to monitor the system efficiently with less human intervention. The autonomous Botnet detection system assists the manager by providing various components for example intruder tracing, alarm strategy, protection strategy, and report generation. It should be able to alert the network manager and notify them of the severity of attacks, suggesting protection strategy, and generate a report.

It is very important to secure the system especially from Botnet attacks because of the impact of Botnet attacks can be very huge considering the massive numbers of army in the Botnet. Our system comprises of many hosts that hold many important data and information. Therefore, it is compulsory to have good Botnet detection and protection strategy to secure our system. The authors study the current Botnet detection approaches and their capability to detect Botnet over the encrypted channel in order to propose an improved Botnet detection system.

SUMMARY

The authors have seen many Botnet attacks over the year and recognize the massive impacts of their attacks for example loss of money, loss of data and a shortage of network resources; to name a few. Botnet evolves; therefore, the authors need to revise the solutions regularly in accordance to existing Botnet technology. One of advanced Botnet technology is by using an encrypted channel for their C&C communication. Botnet attacks over the encrypted channel mostly associated with information stealing and denial of access to the data. In the future, the Botnet attacks are expected to be more sophisticated, advanced, and malicious.

This article also contains a well-established literature for existing Botnet detection approaches. This knowledge is essential to understand Botnet detection technology and furthermore to find the solutions for better Botnet detection. Overall, the contribution of this article is two-fold:

a. A review of the impact of Botnet attacks over the encrypted channel.
b. A review of state of the art in Botnet detection approaches especially machine learning approaches to find the gaps in existing solutions.

The review indicates that despite the severity of Botnet attacks, there is still room for further research; especially in dealing with advanced Botnet that always tries to use existing technology to evade detection to survive. Hopefully, with the knowledge, it can help in understanding Botnet attacks and the detection system, then helps in providing the appropriate solution. Botnet detection is critical to mitigate Botnet attacks. It is hard to use single Botnet detection approach to detect all kind of Botnet. Therefore the authors observe from the study there are various approaches available to cater to a different kind of Botnet. The study provides the advantages and limitation of each approach to find the gaps for future works. By analyzing these limitations, a better solution can be proposed, and it also closes the gaps.

REFERENCES

Akiyama, M., Kawamoto, T., Shimamura, M., Yokoyama, T., Kadobayashi, Y., & Yamaguchi, S. (2007, January). A proposal of metrics for botnet detection based on its cooperative behavior. In *2007 International Symposium on Applications and the Internet Workshops* (pp. 82-82). IEEE.

Al-Azzawi. (2014). Detection of P2P Botnets Based on SVN. *Journal of Engineering & Technology*, *32*(A).

Al-Hammadi, Y. A. A. (2010). Behavioural correlation for malicious bot detection. *Doctor*. Retrieved March 22, 2019, from http://etheses.nottingham.ac.uk/1359/

Angrishi, K. (2017). *Turning Internet of Things(IoT) into Internet of Vulnerabilities (IoV) : IoT Botnets*. Retrieved April 22, 2019, from http://arxiv.org/abs/1702.03681

Binkley, J. R., & Singh, S. (2006). An Algorithm for Anomaly-based Botnet Detection. *Proceedings of the 2nd Conference on Steps to Reducing Unwanted Traffic on the Internet SRUTI'06*, 7. Retrieved from http://dl.acm.org/citation.cfm?id=1251303

Bortolameotti, R. (2014). *C&C Botnet Detection over SSL*. Retrieved from https://pdfs.semanticscholar.org/5a2e/8739648c9a8a1b57c090845df28a8ffac2b6.pdf

Burghouwt, P. (2015). *Detection of Botnet Command and Control Traffic in Enterprise Networks*. Academic Press.

Buriya, S., Patel, A. K., Yadav, S. S., Buriya, S., Patel, A. K., & Yadav, S. S. (2015). Botnet behavior analysis using Naïve Bayes classification algorithm without deep packet. *International Journal of Computer Engineering & Applications, 9*(8), 45–54.

Cha, S., & Kim, H. (2017). *Detecting Encrypted Traffic: A Machine Learning Approach*. Springer. doi:10.1007/978-3-319-56549-1_5

Cisco Security. (n.d.). https://www.cisco.com

Desai, D. (2017). SSL/TLS-based botnet attacks. *Zscaler*. Retrieved June 18, 2018, from https://www.zscaler.com/blogs/research/ssltls-based-malware-attacks

Ericson. (2019). *How to Choose Algorithms for Azure Machine Learning Studio*. Retrieved March 22, 2019, from https://docs.microsoft.com/en-us/azure/machine-learning/studio/algorithm-choice

Europol. (2017). *Banking Trojan* Retrieved March 25, 2019, from https://www.europol.europa.eu/.../banking_trojans_from_stone_age_to_space_era.pdf

Feily, M., Shahrestani, A., & Ramadass, S. (2009). A survey of botnet and botnet detection. *Proceedings - 2009 3rd International Conference on Emerging Security Information, Systems and Technologies, SECURWARE 2009*, 268–273. https://doi.org/10.1109/SECURWARE.2009.48

Goebel, J., & Holz, T. (2007). Rishi: identify bot contaminated hosts by IRC nickname evaluation. *HotBots'07 Proceedings of the First Conference on First Workshop on Hot Topics in Understanding Botnets*, 8. https://doi.org/10.1.1.177.8170

Gooley, D. (2017). The rise in ssl-based threats. *Zscaler*. Retrieved June 16, 2018, from https://www.zscaler.com/blogs/research/rise-ssl-based-threats

Gu, G., Perdisci, R., Zhang, J., & Lee, W. (2008). BotMiner: clustering analysis of network traffic for protocol-and structure-independent botnet detection. In *Proceedings of the 17th Conference on Security Symposium*. USENIX Association.

Gu, G., Porras, P., Yegneswaran, V., Fong, M., Lee, W., & Park, M. (n.d.). *BotHunter : Detecting Malware Infection Through IDS-Driven Dialog Correlation.* College of Computing, Georgia Institute of Technology.

Gu, G., Zhang, J., & Lee, W. (2008). BotSniffer : Detecting Botnet Command and Control Channels in Network Traffic. *Proceedings of the 15th Annual Network and Distributed System Security Symposium., 53*(1), 1–13. https://doi.org/10.1.1.110.8092

Guntuku, S., Narang, P., & Hota, C. (2013). *Real-time Peer-to-Peer Botnet Detection Framework based on Bayesian Regularized Neural Network.* http://arxiv.org/abs/1307.7464

Haltas, F., Uzun, E., Siseci, N., Posul, A., & Emre, B. (2014). An automated bot detection system through honeypots for large-scale. *International Conference on Cyber Conflict, CYCON*, 255–270. https://doi.org/10.1109/CYCON.2014.6916407

Holz, T., Gorecki, C., Rieck, K., & Freiling, F. C. (2008). Detection and mitigation of fast-flux service networks. In *Proceedings of the 15th Annual Network and Distributed System Security Symposium (NDSS'08).* Homeland Security Digital Library. https://www.hsdl.org

Hyslip, T., & Pittman, J. (2015). A Survey of Botnet Detection Techniques by Command and Control Infrastructure. *Journal of Digital Forensics, Security, and Law, 10*(1), 7–26. doi:10.1145/1090191.1080118

Jain, A. K., Murty, M. N., & Flynn, P. J. (1999, September). Data clustering: A review. *ACM Computing Surveys, 31*(3), 264–323.

Jakalan, A., Barazi, J., & Xiaowei, W. (2014). *Botnet Detection Techniques.* Retrieved from http://www.researchgate.net/publication/281374083

Karim, A., Salleh, R. B., Shiraz, M., Shah, S. A. A., Awan, I., & Anuar, N. B. (2014). Botnet detection techniques: review, future trends, and issues. *Journal of Zhejiang University SCIENCE C, 15*(11), 943–983. https://doi.org/ doi:10.1631/jzus.C1300242

Khattak, S., Ramay, N. R., Khan, K. R., Syed, A. A., & Khayam, S. A. (2014). *A Taxonomy of Botnet Behavior.* Academic Press.

Kolias, C., Kambourakis, G., Stavrou, A., & Voas, J. (2017). DDoS in the IoT: Mirai and other botnets. *Computer, 50*(7), 80–84. doi:10.1109/MC.2017.201

Kotsiantis, S., Zaharakis, I., & Pintelas, P. (2007). Supervised machine learning: A review of classification techniques. *Frontiers in Artificial Intelligence and Applications, 160*, 3.

Kovacs, K. (2016). *Spymel Trojan Uses Stolen Certificates to Evade Detection.* Retrieved from https://www.securityweek.com/spymel-trojan-uses-stolen-certificates-evade-detection

Langin, C., Zhou, H., & Rahimi, S. (2009). *A Self-Organizing Map and its Modeling for Discovering Malignant Network Traffic.* https://doi.org/ doi:10.1109/CI-CYBS.2009.4925099

Liao, W. H., & Chang, C. C. (2010, August). Peer to peer botnet detection using data mining scheme. In *2010 International Conference on Internet Technology and Applications* (pp. 1-4). IEEE.

Liu, D., Li, Y., Hu, Y., & Liang, Z. (2010, October). A P2P-Botnet detection model and algorithms based on network streams analysis. In *2010 International Conference on Future Information Technology and Management Engineering* (*Vol. 1*, pp. 55-58). IEEE.

Mitchell, R. (2017). *Mirai: The Program that Make IoT Botnet Zombies*. Retrieved from https://www.allaboutcircuits.com/news/mirai-the-program-that-makes-iot-Botnet-zombies/

Moon, J. G., Jang, J. J., & Jung, I. Y. (2015). Bot detection via IoT environment. *Proceedings - 2015 IEEE 17th International Conference on High Performance Computing and Communications, 2015 IEEE 7th International Symposium on Cyberspace Safety and Security and 2015 IEEE 12th International Conference on Embedded Software and Systems, HPCC-CSS-ICESS 2015*, 1691–1692. https://doi.org/10.1109/HPCC-CSS-ICESS.2015.116

Narang, P., Khurana, V., & Hota, C. (2014). Machine-learning approaches for P2P botnet detection using signal-processing techniques. *Proceedings of the 8th ACM International Conference on Distributed Event-Based Systems - DEBS '14*, 338–341. https://doi.org/10.1145/2611286.2611318

Newman, L. H. (2016). *The Botnet That Broke the Internet Isn't Going Away*. Retrieved from https://www.digitalshadows.com/about-us/news-and-press/wired-the-Botnet-that-broke-the-internet-isnt-going-away/

Nicholson, P. (2015). *What lies beneath: advanced attacks that hide in ssl traffic*. Retrieved June 16, 2018, from https://www.a10networks.com/resources/articles/what-lies-beneath-advanced-attacks-hide-ssl-traffic

Plohmann, D., Gerhards-Padilla, E., & Leder, F. (2011, March). Botnets: measurement, detection, disinfection and defence. ENISA workshop on.

Ritu & Kaushal R. (2015). Machine Learning Approach for Botnets Detection. In 3rd *Security and Privacy Symposium*. IIIT – Delhi.

Rouse, M. (2009, March). *Conficker*. Retrieved January 27, 2019, from http://whatis.techtarget.com/definition/Conficker

Saad, S., Traore, I., Ghorbani, A., Sayed, B., Zhao, D., Lu, W., . . . Hakimian, P. (2011). Detecting P2P botnets through network behavior analysis and machine learning. *2011 Ninth Annual International Conference on Privacy Security and Trust*, 174–180. https://doi.org/10.1109/PST.2011.5971980

Sanatinia, A., & Noubir, G. (2015). OnionBots: Subverting Privacy Infrastructure for Cyber Attacks. *Proceedings of the International Conference on Dependable Systems and Networks,* 69–80. https://doi.org/10.1109/DSN.2015.40

Sherry, J., Lan, C., Popa, R. A., & Ratnasamy, S. (2015). BlindBox: Deep Packet Inspection over Encrypted Traffic. *Proceedings of the 2015 ACM Conference on Special Interest Group on Data Communication - SIGCOMM '15*, 213–226. https://doi.org/10.1145/2785956.2787502

Silva, S. S. C., Silva, R. M. P., Pinto, R. C. G., & Salles, R. M. (2013). Botnets: A survey. *Computer Networks*, *57*(2), 378–403. doi:10.1016/j.comnet.2012.07.021

Strayer, W. T., Lapsely, D., Walsh, R., & Livadas, C. (2008). Botnet Detection Based on Network Behavior. *Botnet Detection*, *36*(August), 1–24. doi:10.1007/978-0-387-68768-1_1

Treat Metrix. https://www.threatmetrix.com

Verton, D. (2002). The Hacker Diaries. McGraw-Hill, Inc. doi:10.1036/0072223642

Wang, T., & Yu, S. Z. (2009, August). Centralized Botnet detection by traffic aggregation. In *2009 IEEE International Symposium on Parallel and Distributed Processing with Applications* (pp. 86-93). IEEE.

Weaver, M. (2009, July 8). *South Korea Cyber Attack*. Retrieved from https://www.theguardian.com/world/2009/jul/08/south-korea-cyber-attack

Yan, Q., Zheng, Y., Jiang, T., Lou, W., & Hou, Y. T. (2015). PeerClean: Unveiling peer-to-peer botnets through dynamic group behavior analysis. *Proceedings - IEEE INFOCOM*, *26*, 316–324. doi:10.1109/INFOCOM.2015.7218396

Zeidanloo, H. R., Shooshtari, M. J., Amoli, P. V., & Safari, M., & Zamani, M. (2010). A taxonomy of botnet detection techniques. *3rd IEEE International Conference on Computer Science and Information Technology (ICCSIT)*, 2, 158–162.

Zhang, L., Yu, S., Wu, D., & Watters, P. (2011). A survey on latest botnet attack and defense. *Proc. 10th IEEE Int. Conf. on Trust, Security and Privacy in Computing and Communications, TrustCom 2011, 8th IEEE Int. Conf. on Embedded Software and Systems, ICESS 2011, 6th Int. Conf. on FCST 2011*, 53–60. https://doi.org/10.1109/TrustCom.2011.11

KEY TERMS AND DEFINITIONS

Autonomous Detection System: A detection system which able to detect the intrusion based on the stimulus and suggest appropriate action based on the level of severity attack.

Botnet: A network of private computers infected with malicious software and controlled as a group without the owners' knowledge.

Botnet Detection: The steps involved in the detection of a botnet via correlative analysis.

Encrypted Channel: A secure channel implementing protocols/algorithms for covert communications.

Machine Learning: The use and development of computer systems that can learn and adapt without following explicit instructions, by using algorithms and statistical models to analyze and draw inferences from patterns in data.

Chapter 19
A Review on Different Encryption and Decryption Approaches for Securing Data

Udochukwu Iheanacho Erondu
Landmark University, Omu-aran, Nigeria

Nehemiah Adebayo
https://orcid.org/0000-0001-5838-8843
Landmark University, Omu-aran, Nigeria

Micheal Olaolu Arowolo
Landmark University, Omu-aran, Nigeria

Moses Kazeem Abiodun
https://orcid.org/0000-0002-3049-1184
Landmark University, Omu-aran, Nigeria

ABSTRACT

With the advancement of network and multimedia technologies in recent years, multimedia data, particularly picture, audio, and video data, has become increasingly frequently used in human civilization. Some multimedia data, such as entertainment, politics, economics, militaries, industries, and education, requires secrecy, integrity, and ownership or identity protection. Cryptology, which looks to be a viable method for information security, has been used in many practical applications to safeguard multimedia data in this regard. Traditional ciphers based on number theory or algebraic ideas, such as data encryption standard (DES), advanced encryption standard (AES), and other similar algorithms, which are most commonly employed for text or binary data, do not appear to be appropriate for multimedia applications. As a result, this research examines effective algorithms for data security.

DOI: 10.4018/978-1-6684-5250-9.ch019

INTRODUCTION

Cloud computing paradigms are becoming increasingly popular in the ever-changing technological landscape. In order to keep up with the ever-expanding possibilities of modern communications, special security measures are needed, particularly for computer networks. As the amount of data being exchanged on the Internet grows, so does the importance of network security. Protecting data from misuse and unauthorized access necessitates maintaining its confidentiality and integrity. Information hiding has grown exponentially as a result. In today's world, security measures can be broken down into a variety of subcategories, such as information concealment (Steganography), data encryption (Cryptography), or any combination thereof (Sethi & Sarangi, 2017).

People's lives have been impacted by digital technologies. Most modern electronic gadgets store their data with an external cloud service. In the cloud, people are storing a plethora of media items. A large number of individuals all over the world use these media every single second. It is imperative that these media are not accessed illegally. The user-end encryption is one of the most vulnerable points for data leaks (van Steen & Tanenbaum, 2016).

In the new computing paradigm of cloud computing, various services can be provided on demand and at a low cost. Cloud computing's primary goal is to provide fast, easy-to-use computing and data storage services to the masses. Today's computing model, called "cloud computing," makes use of a decentralized network to deliver a wide range of resources at a low cost and on demand. In addition, cloud computing's primary goal is to provide fast, easy-to-use computing and data storage services in a cloud environment (Wu & Buyya, 2015). Although the computing community has mastered the use of cloud computing services, some threats and risks do exist in this setting. Numerous techniques, such as cryptography, exist to improve the security of cloud computing and data in the cloud. Data or messages can be transferred securely while maintaining their privacy, and the cypher text used to encrypt them is only visible to the intended recipient. Data encryption, data quality assurance, and data authentication are all examples of cryptology. Cryptography provides a wide range of more secure methods that can be used to provide these services. Data that must remain private is encrypted and decrypted with the help of well-known cryptographic algorithms, such as those found in encryption protocols, digital signatures, and hash functions (Symmetric Algorithms, Asymmetric Algorithms, and Hybrid Algorithms). Protection is a problem for all of the current schemes. Cryptographic key generation, retrieval, data encoding, and decryption all take a lot of time in these schemes (Hashizume et al., 2013).

Furthermore, one of the most difficult tasks in cloud computing is safeguarding sensitive and confidential data while it is being transported and stored due to the possibility of various attacks. Using a large number of and more complex encryption keys makes the process more difficult (Al-Issa et al., 2019).

To address data security concerns, a wide range of encryption methods have been proposed for making better decisions about which encryption method to use for smart systems data security by studying a variety of techniques. Execution time, complexity, and maintainability all depend on having a thorough understanding of each technique. Some existing cloud computing security models, which use encryption algorithms to store and transmit data, have security flaws and privacy violations, which are the focus of this paper. Data security and privacy in the cloud computing environment can only be ensured by encrypting data in storage and transmission. Security policies are specified and enforced through a model used in computer science. Structured access privileges, computation models, distributed computing models, or no theoretical grounding at all can be used to build a security system (Qureshi et al., 2022).

This research provides a survey of the problem of data security through the technique of cryptography. Using cryptography, data can be scrambled or disguised in such a way that it can only be decoded by someone with the knowledge to restore the data to its original form. In today's computer systems, cryptography serves as a strong, cost-effective foundation for encrypting and verifying sensitive data.

RELATED WORKS

A simple, safe, and privacy-preserving architecture for transferring data between Clouds utilizing an encryption/decryption technique was suggested to protect data stored in the cloud from unauthorized access (Kartit et al., 2016). The enormous advantages of cloud storage are tempered by the fact that many practical security concerns persist. If we can eradicate or manage this security flaw, cloud storage solutions for large and small organizations equally will be the future. This article presents a paper presents an open cloud storage solution. Using our algorithm will protect your private information. This data is confidential and may not be shared with anyone else. If an eavesdropper (unauthorized user) obtains the data, whether by accident or design, they will be unable to read it without both keys. Some possible future developments in this field will be explored, with a focus on homomorphic encryption.

Encryption methods were proposed for use in cloud storage for smart systems (Qureshi et al., 2022). In today's rapidly evolving technological scene, cloud computing paradigms are enjoying widespread adoption. Users can access storage and computing resources on a pay-as-they-go basis with no minimum commitments. Affordable and high-quality infrastructure is a boon to small enterprises. The resource sharing property of cloud computing raises issues about the privacy and security of the data created by smart systems as it is constantly transferred to the cloud computing resources managed by a third-party provider. Concerns over data security have prompted the development of numerous encryption techniques. This document describes and provides examples of data encryption and protection techniques that use standard parameters. The purpose of this research is to assemble cloud-safety encryption methods that have been explored extensively in the literature for use with smart systems. Blowfish is unique among symmetric encryption techniques. The AES algorithm provides the maximum security among symmetric algorithms even when resources (both time and processing power) are few. The RSA technique is ideal for exchanging top-secret data due to the security provided by its usage of public-private key pairs. To cope with the ever-increasing data output at breakneck speeds from intelligent devices, researchers are working on a new encryption technique. The management of smart systems is hesitant to save their data on the cloud due to security concerns. To prevent unwanted access to authentication data, encryption and decryption keys should be more closely guarded. With this method, data modification is impossible. Even if the time spent encrypting and decrypting data slows performance, using a combination of encryption technologies can guarantee data security. If throughput needs to be maximized, parallel data encryption could be a viable solution in the future.

eHealth Cloud Security Challenges were the subject of a survey (Al-Issa et al., 2019). The healthcare industry stands to benefit greatly from the advent of cloud computing. The advantages of cloud computing are numerous, including scalability, cost and energy savings, resource pooling, and rapid deployment of new services and applications. Cloud computing in the healthcare industry and various cloud security and privacy issues are examined in this paper. For both individuals and healthcare providers, cloud-based data storage raises many security and privacy concerns. As a result of the transfer of data ownership to cloud service providers, both patients and healthcare providers have less control over their personal health information as a result of the centralization of data. As a result, concerns about cloud security, privacy, efficiency, and scalability are preventing widespread adoption. State-of-the-art solutions only address a portion of these issues, according to this research. Because of this, there is an urgent need for a comprehensive solution that addresses all of the competing demands.

A review of cloud computing security and privacy was conducted (Abdulsalam & Hedabou, 2021). Cloud computing has become increasingly popular and successful as a result of improvements in ICT usage. There are significant security and privacy issues associated with moving business information and applications to the cloud or to a third party. Numerous methods of addressing the current security flaws have been put forth by scholars and organizations that have been affected by the research. Security and privacy concerns in cloud computing are also examined extensively in the literature. Unfortunately, the literature lacks the adaptability necessary to counter diverse attacks without compromising cloud security objectives. Although security and privacy issues have been brought to light in the literature, proper technical solutions have yet to be offered. Research proposing technological countermeasures to security risks, on the other hand, has failed to explain the nature of those threats. This paper's focus on cloud security highlights the importance of an adaptive solution approach to avoiding potential conflicts with existing and developing cloud security measures. In this article, we examine a range of relevant research, with an eye toward how cloud security conflicts render the proposed models of various previous studies moot. The risks of cloud computing, from the perspective of end users, are demonstrated using the STRIDE method. This research not only recommends an adaptive cloud-based environment, but also analyzes the literature's many ineffectual solutions and gives reasons why they won't work.

It was suggested that businesses consider the benefits and drawbacks of moving to the cloud (Avram, 2014). The rapid advancement of processing and storage technology and the widespread adoption of the Internet have made today's computing resources more accessible, powerful, and cost-effective than ever before. A new computer paradigm known as "cloud computing" has arisen in reaction to this new trend in technological growth. In this model, resources are made accessible to authorized users as general utilities that can be rented and delivered over the Internet.

Cloud computing is becoming more mainstream, and businesses are shifting more of their core functions to the cloud as a result. Cloud adoption is far more difficult than we had anticipated due to the complexity of data management, system integration, and the need to manage various cloud providers. However, many companies around the world are finding that cloud computing is more expensive and more difficult to implement than they expected. Is cloud computing still able to fulfill all of its promises in this situation?

Research into the Internet of Things: Architectures, Protocols, and Applications was completed (Sethi & Sarangi, 2017). Things with sensors, actuators, and processors are referred to as "Internet of Things" (IoT) devices, and these devices can exchange data with one another in real time. An overview of current methods, protocols, and applications in this emerging field is provided in this paper. An innovative taxonomy for Internet of Things (IoT) technology is proposed, along with a look at some of the most important IoT applications that have the potential to make a significant difference in people's lives, particularly those who are differently abled or elderly. The scope of this paper is much broader than similar studies in the field, covering the full gamut of relevant technology from sensors to applications.

Enhancing the security of data using a cryptographic algorithm based on theory (Sharma & Mishra, 2021). Rapid technological development will be critical in the years to come. It is possible for attackers to intercept any type of cloud-based data and use it against the intended recipient. More and more people are demanding that the information they receive be accurate and that they be protected from prying eyes.

For enhancing data security in cloud computing applications, this paper discussed in brief the various cryptographic methods and a new cryptographic Algorithm method.

A novel strategy based on data classification, employing a number of cryptographic algorithms, has enhanced the security of cloud data (Ul Haq & Kumar, 2021). The advent of new digital technology has had a profound effect on people's daily life. The majority of today's electronic gadgets rely on external cloud storage services. Numerous thousands of media files, including movies and music, are being kept in the cloud. Tens of thousands of individuals all over the world use these outlets every single second. It's crucial that nobody gets unauthorized copies of these media. One of the most common entry points for information leaks is at the user's end of the encryption process. This study argues that combining AES with blowfish encryption/decryption can strengthen cloud data security. The first layer of the hybrid solution is an AES-256 cipher and the second layer is a blowfish cipher. The output of the first layer is processed by the second, and the combined result is assessed. The proposed method also discusses AES and other conventional algorithms, but it offers significantly better results overall.

In order to create a new method for protecting data in the cloud, researchers turned to both genetics and logical-mathematical functions (Thabit et al., 2021). The first layer is based on Shannon's theory of diffusion and confusion, and it works by dividing the original plaintext and key into equal parts and then applying logical operations like XOR, XNOR, and shifting to each of those pieces. The second layer is built on genetic structures derived from the Central Dogma of Molecular Biology and is inspired by genetic cryptography (the conversion of binary to DNA bases), transcription (the regeneration of DNA into mRNA), and translation (regeneration from mRNA to protein). The experimental findings enhanced cloud computing data security, which can be implemented to safeguard software. Experiments indicated that it provided a very high level of security, with an apparent increase in cipher size and execution time compared to the most used cloud computing methods at the time.

Recent efforts to merge Cryptography and Stratanomy were surveyed (Almuhammadi & Al-Shaaby, 2017). The proliferation of Internet-based digital communication tools is something that everyone can see and feel happening right now. Because of this, a safe method of talking to one another is essential. The importance of measuring global network security has grown in recent years. Cryptography and steganography are vital technologies for ensuring network safety. In this study, a contrast is shown between steganography and cryptography. In this work, we take a look at a wide variety of strategies that combine cryptography and steganography. An organization of various approaches was also shown, with comparisons made according to encryption algorithm, steganography method, and file type.

Based on cryptography and steganography, a dynamic four-step data security model for data in cloud computing has been proposed (Adee & Mouratidis, 2022). There has been a lot of development in the field of cloud computing recently. Without the user's intervention, administrators can control who has access to a system's resources like data storage and processing power. This work tries to create a cloud computing data security paradigm that minimizes existing security and privacy issues including data loss and manipulation by making use of cryptography and steganography. They analyzed preexisting cloud computing security frameworks to determine the root of the issue and potential solutions. This research makes use of design science research methods. Problem analysis, requirements gathering, artifact design and development, demonstration, and assessment are all part of the design science research methodology. Design thinking and Python are employed in the creation of the artifact, and histograms, tables, and algorithms are used to illustrate the explanation of the artifact's inner workings. The result of this work is a four-stage data security architecture that makes use of Rivest, Shamir, Adleman, Advanced Encryption Standard, and identity-based encryption, as well as Least Significant Bit steganography.

The four stages are: encryption methods, steganography, data backup and recovery, and data exchange. This method seeks to improve cloud redundancy, flexibility, efficiency, and security by protecting the privacy and security of cloud data.

MATERIALS AND METHODS

Several datasets exist and can be obtained from open-source datasets provided by a variety of venues, including Kaggle, Mendeley, and the UCI repository. The cryptography technology is used to achieve security, examples of dataset may be found at https://archive.ics.uci.edu/ml/datasets/MHEALTH; https://snap.stanford.edu/data/loc-gowalla.html; https://www.kaggle.com/c/ciphertext-challenge-ii/data; https://www.kaggle.com/primaryobjects/voicegender), (Kannan et al., 2021); (Kim et al., 2020); (Zhang, 2020).

Principles of the RSA (Rivest-Shamir-Adleman) Algorithm

RSA (Rivest-Shamir-Adleman) is an asymmetric cryptographic technique that modern computers employ to encrypt and decrypt messages. Asymmetric cryptography, commonly known as public-key cryptography, uses two separate keys in the encryption and decoding process. This is due to the fact that one of the two keys can be handed to anyone without compromising the algorithm's security. Both private and public keys are used in the RSA algorithm. Because it is used to encrypt messages from plaintext to ciphertext, the public key can be known and published by anybody. Messages encrypted with this specific public key, on the other hand, may only be decoded with the accompanying private key. Because of its high level of complexity compared to other cryptographic methods, the RSA algorithm's key generation process is what makes it so secure and trustworthy today (S. Li, 2017).

The RSA algorithm is primarily utilized to encrypt the Noekeon key, and its security level is mostly governed by the integer factor decomposition level. The RSA algorithm has three primary components in terms of design and implementation: key generation, information encryption, and information decryption. The RSA algorithm necessitates a vast number of primes, all of which are 2048 bits long. As a result, a huge number of complex big numerical operations must be performed when employing the RSA algorithm for information encryption. As a result, while the RSA method can successfully improve the security of hospital financial data information, its operational efficiency is invariably lower than that of other encryption algorithms. As a result, the hospital financial data encryption transmission system should continue to employ the Noekeon method, with the encryption of the Noekeon key using solely the RSA technique(Yao, 2021).

Employing the RSA algorithm to encrypt data is easier than using a symmetrical encryption scheme. Modular power multiplication is the math used for encryption and decryption. It is believed that is plaintext and is ciphertext in this case. After that, the sender can encrypt plaintext and the receiver can decrypt it. represents a very large integer, represents the public key, and represents the key(Wang et al., 2019).

Vigenère

The Vigenère Cipher is a well-known cryptographic method that is part of the symmetric key cryptography methodology (where encryption and decryption are performed with the same key). One drawback of the Vigenère Cipher is that the key will be repeated until its length is equal to the plaintext length if the

Figure 1. RSA Pseudocode Algorithm(Wang et al., 2019)

```
Input: Plaintext M
Output: ciphertext C
While(true):
  Choose two different large prime P and Q
  Calculate the time difference between P and Q
   If (time difference < limit time)
     Break
End While
 Calculate n = Q * P
 Calculate φ(n)=(p-1)(q-1)
 Choose a random integer e
Let e greater than 1 and less than φ(n) and gcd(e, φ(n)) =1
Calculate d so that d * e = 1 mod φ(n)
{e, n} is public key {d, n} is private key
use the equation C=M^e mod n to encrypt the plaintext M
Return C
```

key length is not equal to the plaintext length. The ability to undertake cryptanalysis is therefore made possible. The insecurity of the key distribution factor is a weakness of symmetric-key cryptography; if the key is known to others, the encryption is useless. The Vigenère Cipher is a time-tested method of secure communication. The symmetric key technique is a popular implementation of classic cryptography since it requires only one key for both encryption and decryption (Subandi, et al., 2017).

The Vigenère Cipher is a classic cryptographic algorithm that falls under the category of polyalphabetic substitution and is a symmetric key cryptographic algorithm that uses the same keys for encryption and decryption. Vigenère Cipher uses a table called tabula recta, which is a 26 x 26 matrix containing alphabet letters, to encrypt and decrypt data. This algorithm was discovered by Blaise de Vigenère of France in the sixteenth century, in 1586, and it took Friedman and Kasiski until 1917 to solve it. The encryption and decryption operation of the Vigenère Cipher can be represented mathematically as follows (Subandi, Meiyanti, Mestika Sandy, et al., 2017):

$$Ci = E\ pi + ki \bmod 26 \quad (1)$$

$$Pi = D/(Ci - Ki) \bmod 26 \quad (2)$$

Ciphertext (C), plaintext (P), key (K), encryption (E), and decryption (D) are the acronyms used in cryptography. To encrypt a message, each alphabet in the plaintext is joined with the alphabet keys, and the alphabet ciphertext is the alphabet that intersects (via a table) with both the plaintext and the ciphertext. Keys are repeated until the plaintext's length is equal to the length of the key alphabet, if necessary. The Vigenère cipher technique uses multiple caesar ciphers to encrypt alphabetic text based on the letters of a keyword. A shifting mechanism is used in this technique, which uses the Vigenère table to shift the characters of the plain text by varying amounts.

Blowfish

In 1993, Blowfish was born. While no actual attack against the encryption exists, it does have a 64-bit block length and was designed for 32-bit CPUs. If you're considering utilizing this algorithm, recommend switching to Twofish. Blowfish, a symmetric block cipher, can be used as a direct substitute for DES and IDEA. It's great for both domestic and foreign use thanks to its variable-length key, which may be anything from 32 to 448 bits long. Developed by Bruce Schneier in 1993, Blowfish was intended to be a fast, free alternative to previous encryption methods. Since then, there has been a lot of research done on it, and it's starting to gain traction as a reliable encryption method. (Asassfeh et al., 2018).

There are two elements to Blowfish: key expansion and data encryption. The entered key is translated into numerous sub key arrays totaling 4168 bytes during the key expansion stage. The P array is made up of eighteen 32-bit boxes, and the S-boxes are made up of four 32-bit arrays with 256 entries each. The blowfish algorithm's key expansion starts with the P-array and S-boxes, which uses numerous sub-keys and necessitates pre-computation before data encryption or decryption. The P array has eighteen four-byte sub-keys: P1, P2..., P17, P18. Blowfish transforms keys up to 448 bits in length into multiple sub-key arrays. For each of the four 32-bit S-boxes, there are 256 entries (Valmik et al., 2014).

S1, 0, S1,1,....., S1,255
S2, 0, S2,1,....., S2,255
S3, 0, S3,1,....., S3,255
S4, 0, S4,1,....., S4,255

The following are the processes for creating the subkeys:

Initialize the P-array and four S-boxes with a predefined string made up of hexadecimal digits of the first element in the P-array (P1) was XORed with the first 32 bits of the key, followed by the second element in the P-array (P2), and so on until all of the elements in the P-array were XORed with the key bits. Using the blowfish method and the sub keys described in step 1, encrypt all zero strings (1, 2). P1 and P2 should be replaced with the output of step (3). Encrypt the output of step using the changed sub keys (3). Replace P3 and P4 with the step's output (5).

The Advanced Encryption Standard (AES)

The Advanced Encryption Standard (AES) is a set of rules for encrypt, AES is an asymmetric-key block cipher technique that is used by the US government to encrypt and decrypt safe and secret material. The AES was authorized as Federal Information Processing Standards Publication (FIPS PUB) 197 by the National Institute of Standards (NIST) in December 2001, which stipulates the application of the Rijndael algorithm to all sensitive classified data. Rijndael was the initial name for the Advanced Encryption Standard. The Rijndael algorithm is a symmetric block cipher that can process 128-bit data blocks with cipher keys of 128, 192, and 256 bits, as defined by the flips standard. Rijndael was designed to accept different block sizes and key lengths, however this standard does not use them. The algorithm described here will be referred to as "the AES algorithm" for the rest of this presumption. The technique can be employed with the three key lengths listed above, and these different "flavors" are referred to as "AES-128, "AES-192," and "AES-256" respectively. Rijndael is a block cipher created by Joan Daemen and

Figure 2. Blowfish (Divya Priya et al., 2018)

```
Pseudo Code:
Step 1→Divide X in to two 32 bit.
Step 2 →XL,XR
Step 3 →For i=1 to 16;
Step 4 →XL =XL XOR Pi
Step 5 →XR=F(XL )XOR XR
Step 6 →Swap XL and XR
Step 7 →XR=XR XOR P17
Step 8 →XL =XL XOR P18
Cipher text:-concatenation of XL and XR
Divide XL in to four 8-bit parts
Step 9 →F[XL]=((s1[a]+s2[b] mod 2^32)+ S3[c])s4[d]mod 2^32
```

Vincent Rijmen as a potential AES candidate algorithm. Advanced Encryption Standard is an acronym for Advanced Encryption Standard. AES is an asymmetric key encryption method that will eventually replace the widely used Data Encryption Standard (DES) (DES). NIST adopted the Advanced Encryption Standard algorithm in December 2001, which uses 128-bit blocks (Chaudhari et al., 2017).

Triple-DES

Triple-DES is a method of making the DES encryption algorithm significantly more safe by employing it three times with three separate keys for a total key length of 168 bits. This method, sometimes known as "3DES," is commonly utilized by financial organizations and the Secure Shell program (ssh). Because of a logical plaintext attack known as meet-in-the-middle, in which an attacker simultaneously attempts to encrypt the plaintext with a single DES operation and decrypt the cipher text with another single DES operation until a match is made in the middle, simply using the DES twice with two different keys does not improve its security to the extent that one might at first suspect (Al-Hamdani, 2014).

CAST

The inventors of CAST, Carlisle Adams and Stafford Tavares, are known as CAST. CAST is a prominent 64-bit block cipher that belongs to the Feistel cipher family of encryption techniques. CAST-128 is a Substitution-Permutation Network (SPN) cryptosystem that is similar to DES. The Feistel structure is used, with eight fixed S-boxes. CAST-128 accepts keys with lengths ranging from 40 to 128 bits (Adams & Gilchrist, 1999); (Ebrahim et al., 2014).

Figure 3. The Advanced Encryption Standard (AES) Pseudocode (Bae et al., 2012)

```
state = M
AddRoundKey(state, &w[0])
for i = 1 step 1 to 9
    SubBytes(state)
    ShiftRows(state)
    MixColumns(state)
    AddRoundKey(state, &w[i*4])
end for
SubBytes(state)
ShiftRows(state)
AddRoundKey(state, &w[40])
```

Data Encryption Standard (DES)

The Data Encryption Standard (DES), a symmetric encryption method, was established as a federal standard in the United States in 1977. The Digital Encryption Standard (DES) is an asymmetric block cipher with a 56-bit key and a 64-bit block size. A symmetric block cipher is the Data Encryption Standard (DES). A stream cipher works one or more bits at a time on a digital data stream. At any given time, a block cipher operates on entire blocks of data and generates a ciphertext block of similar size. DES is a block cipher that works with data blocks that are 64 bits long. DES uses a 64-bit key, which includes one bit for parity, for a total of 56 bits. Because DES, like other block ciphers, is based on a structure known as a Feistel Lattice, it's helpful to explain how it works (Wilson, 2016).

Digital Signature Algorithm (DSA)

A standard for digital signatures is referred to as a Digital Signature Algorithm (DSA). The National Institute of Standards and Technology (NIST) introduced it in 1991 as a better way to create digital signatures. DSA, along with RSA, is one of the most widely used digital signature algorithms today. DSA, on the other hand, does not encrypt or decrypt message digests using a private key or a public key. Instead, it creates a digital signature consisting of two 160-bit values derived from the message brief and the private key using distinct mathematical methods. When compared to RSA, DSAs use the public key to authenticate the signature, but the authentication process is more difficult. Diffie-Hellman key (version 5.3) Diffie-Hellman key exchange, commonly known as exponential key exchange, is a technique of digital encryption that generates decryption keys from numbers raised to specified powers based on components that are never explicitly conveyed, making the process of breaking the code mathematically impossible. Two individuals agree on a private communication channel and two positive whole numbers p and q, where p is a prime number and q is a generator of p, to implement Diffie-Hellman. The generator q always generates a unique result when raised to a power of a positive whole number smaller than p. Though p's value can be extremely huge, q's is often very little. Alice and Bob agree in private on the prime numbers p and q, and then choose the personal keys a and b, which must be positive whole numbers and be less than the prime number modulus p. Neither user gives out their secret key, and they should memorize it rather than writing it down or keeping it in any way. (Li & Furht, 2019).

Elliptic Curve Cryptography (ECC)

Elliptic Curve Cryptography (ECC) is similar to RSA in terms of capability. In smaller devices, such as cell phones, elliptic curve cryptography (ECC) is being used (Nithiya & Sridevi, 2016). ECC is a public key encryption technique based on elliptic curve theory that can be used to make cryptographic keys that are faster, smaller, and more efficient. Instead, than using the usual approach of generating keys as the product of very large prime numbers, ECC uses the features of the elliptic curve equation to produce keys. ECC is becoming increasingly popular for mobile apps because it allows for equal security while using less computer power and battery resources. Certicom, a mobile e-business security supplier, created ECC, which Hifn, a maker of integrated circuits (IC) and network security products, recently licensed. RSA has been working on its own ECC implementation. For 150 years, mathematicians have investigated the features and functions of elliptic curves. Neal Koblitz of the University of Washington and Victor Miller of IBM proposed their usage in cryptography for the first time in 1985 (separately). An elliptic curve is a looping line connecting two axes, rather than an ellipse (oval shape) (lines on a graph used to indicate the position of a point). ECC is based on qualities of a certain sort of equation produced from locations where the line crosses the axis and derived from a mathematical group (a set of values for which operations can be done on any two members of the group to produce a third member). Even if you know the initial point and the result, finding out what number was used to multiply a point on the curve by produces another point on the curve is tough. Equations based on elliptic curves offer a highly useful property for cryptography: they are relatively simple to perform but exceedingly complex to reverse.

El Gamal

El Gamal is a digital signature and key exchange transmission algorithm. Calculating logarithms is the basis of the procedure. Its algorithm is based on the properties and calculations of logarithmic numbers. El Gamal is the basis for the Digital Signature Algorithm (DSA) (Kefa, 2005).

Metrics

Time (milliseconds), throughput (Mb/sec), and avalanche effect are performance indicators for analyzing the algorithm's performance (percent) (Quilala et al., 2018). The following is a list of the evaluation parameters:

1. Time to Generate Subkeys: The time it takes to generate the subkeys.
2. Encryption time: The time it takes to convert plaintext to ciphertext equivalent.

3. Decryption time: The time it takes to convert ciphertext to plaintext.
4. Throughput: Throughput refers to the speed with which data is encrypted. The computation for throughput is the plaintext size divided by the total time.
5. Avalanche effect: Refers to the property in which a small change in the input text causes a large change in the output, also known as diffusion, and which reflects the cryptographic strength of a cryptographic algorithm. The avalanche effect is measured by calculating the hamming distance, which is a difference measure. It's the ASCII value's bit-by-bit XOR calculation.

DISCUSSION AND CONCLUSION

The demand for cryptographic algorithms that are suitable for data-driven models to handle privacy-related challenges has surged in recent years. Nowadays, the advancement of information technology is exceedingly quick, especially with the widespread use of the Internet; the security of network communications has become a critical issue we must address. The goal of this essay is to address issues with today's data encryption techniques for network security. We analyze the implications of numerous alternative encryption approaches on strengthening network security, starting with the computer network communication security data encryption algorithm. RSA, Vigenere, AES, and DES algorithms, for example, are all fairly typical algorithms that represent many encryption systems. There are three types of encryption algorithms used in network data links: link encryption algorithm, node encryption algorithm, and end-to-end encryption algorithm.

REFERENCES

Abdulsalam, Y. S., & Hedabou, M. (2021). Security and Privacy in Cloud Computing: Technical Review. *Future Internet*, *14*(1), 11. doi:10.3390/fi14010011

Adams, C., & Gilchrist, J. (1999). The CAST-256 Encryption Algorithm. *Entrust Technologies*, 1–20. https://tools.ietf.org/html/rfc2612

Adee, R., & Mouratidis, H. (2022). A Dynamic Four-Step Data Security Model for Data in Cloud Computing Based on Cryptography and Steganography. *Sensors (Basel)*, *22*(3), 1109. doi:10.339022031109 PMID:35161853

Al-Hamdani, W. A. (2014). *Secure E-Learning and Cryptography*. doi:10.4018/978-1-4666-4486-1.ch012

Al-Issa, Y., Ottom, M. A., & Tamrawi, A. (2019). eHealth Cloud Security Challenges: A Survey. *Journal of Healthcare Engineering*, *2019*, 1–15. doi:10.1155/2019/7516035 PMID:31565209

Almuhammadi, S., & Al-Shaaby, A. (2017). *A Survey on Recent Approaches Combining Cryptography and Steganography*. doi:10.5121/csit.2017.70306

Asassfeh, M. R., Qatawneh, M., & Al Azzeh, F. M. (2018). Performance evaluation of blowfish algorithm on supercomputer IMAN1. *International Journal of Computer Networks and Communications*, *10*(2), 43–53. doi:10.5121/ijcnc.2018.10205

Avram, M. G. (2014). Advantages and Challenges of Adopting Cloud Computing from an Enterprise Perspective. *Procedia Technology*, *12*, 529–534. doi:10.1016/j.protcy.2013.12.525

Bae, K., Moon, S., Choi, D., Choi, Y., Kim, H. D., & Ha, J. (2012). A practical analysis of fault attack countermeasure on AES using data masking. *Proceedings - 2012 7th International Conference on Computing and Convergence Technology (ICCIT, ICEI and ICACT), ICCCT 2012*, 508–513.

Chaudhari, P. S., Pahade, M., Bhat, S., Sawant, T., & Jadhav, C. (2017). *A Survey on Methods of Cryptography and Data Encryption*. Academic Press.

DivyaPriya, D., Shirisha, B., & Pravallika, B. (2018). Blowfish Encryption on Cloud Data Storage. *IACSIT International Journal of Engineering and Technology*, *7*(4), 4250–4252. doi:10.14419/ijet.v7i4.15597

Ebrahim, M., Khan, S., & Khalid, U. Bin. (2014). *Symmetric Algorithm Survey: A Comparative Analysis*. https://arxiv.org/abs/1405.0398

Hashizume, K., Rosado, D. G., Fernández-Medina, E., & Fernandez, E. B. (2013). An analysis of security issues for cloud computing. *Journal of Internet Services and Applications*, *4*(1), 5. doi:10.1186/1869-0238-4-5

Kannan, C., Dakshinamoorthy, M., Ramachandran, M., Patan, R., Kalyanaraman, H., & Kumar, A. (2021). Cryptography-based deep artificial structure for secure communication using IoT-enabled cyber-physical system. *IET Communications*, *15*(6), 771–779. doi:10.1049/cmu2.12119

Kartit, Z., Azougaghe, A., Kamal Idrissi, H., El Marraki, M., Hedabou, M., Belkasmi, M., & Kartit, A. (2016). *Applying Encryption Algorithm for Data Security in Cloud Storage*. doi:10.1007/978-981-287-990-5_12

Kefa, R. (2005). Elliptic Curve ElGamal Encryption and Signature Schemes. *Information Technology Journal*, *4*(3), 299–306. doi:10.3923/itj.2005.299.306

Kim, W., Lee, H., & Chung, Y. D. (2020). Safe contact tracing for COVID-19: A method without privacy breach using functional encryption techniques based-on spatio-temporal trajectory data. *PLoS One*, *15*(12), e0242758. doi:10.1371/journal.pone.0242758 PMID:33306698

Li, S. (2017). IoT Node Authentication. In *Securing the Internet of Things* (pp. 69–95). Elsevier. doi:10.1016/B978-0-12-804458-2.00004-4

Li, X., & Furht, B. (2019). Design and implementation of digital libraries. Handbook of Internet Computing, 415–150. doi:10.1201/9781420049121.ch18

Nithiya, C., & Sridevi, R. (2016). ECC algorithm & security in cloud. *International Journal of Advanced Research in Computer Science & Technology, 4*(1), 24–27.

Quilala, T. F. G., Sison, A. M., & Medina, R. P. (2018). Modified Blowfish Algorithm. *Indonesian Journal of Electrical Engineering and Computer Science*, *12*(1), 38. doi:10.11591/ijeecs.v12.i1.pp38-45

Qureshi, M. B., Qureshi, M. S., Tahir, S., Anwar, A., Hussain, S., Uddin, M., & Chen, C.-L. (2022). Encryption Techniques for Smart Systems Data Security Offloaded to the Cloud. *Symmetry*, *14*(4), 695. doi:10.3390ym14040695

Sethi, P., & Sarangi, S. R. (2017). Internet of Things: Architectures, Protocols, and Applications. *Journal of Electrical and Computer Engineering*, *2017*, 1–25. doi:10.1155/2017/9324035

Sharma, A., & Mishra, A. (2021). *Cryptographic Algorithm For Enhancing Data Security : A Theoretical Approach*. Academic Press.

Subandi, A., Meiyanti, R., Mestika Sandy, C. L., & Sembiring, R. W. (2017). Three-pass protocol implementation in vigenere cipher classic cryptography algorithm with keystream generator modification. *Advances in Science. Technology and Engineering Systems*, *2*(5), 1–5. doi:10.25046/aj020501

Subandi, A., Meiyanti, R., Sandy, C. L. M., & Sembiring, R. W. (2017). Three-Pass Protocol Implementation in Vigenere Cipher Classic Cryptography Algorithm with Keystream Generator Modification. *Advances in Science, Technology and Engineering Systems Journal*, *2*(5), 1–5. doi:10.25046/aj020501

Thabit, F., Alhomdy, S., & Jagtap, S. (2021). A new data security algorithm for the cloud computing based on genetics techniques and logical-mathematical functions. *International Journal of Intelligent Networks*, *2*, 18–33. doi:10.1016/j.ijin.2021.03.001

Ul Haq, M. N., & Kumar, N. (2021). A novel data classification-based scheme for cloud data security using various cryptographic algorithms. *International Review of Applied Sciences and Engineering*. doi:10.1556/1848.2021.00317

Valmik, M. N., & Kshirsagar, P. V. K. (2014). Blowfish Algorithm. *IOSR Journal of Computer Engineering*, *16*(2), 80–83. doi:10.9790/0661-162108083

van Steen, M., & Tanenbaum, A. S. (2016). A brief introduction to distributed systems. *Computing*, *98*(10), 967–1009. doi:10.100700607-016-0508-7

Wang, F., Wang, Z., & Zhu, Y. (2019). Adaptive RSA Encryption Algorithm for Smart Grid. *Journal of Physics: Conference Series*, *1302*(2), 022097. doi:10.1088/1742-6596/1302/2/022097

Wilson, P. (2016). Secure Systems. In *Design Recipes for FPGAs* (pp. 135–165). Elsevier. doi:10.1016/B978-0-08-097129-2.00010-6

Wu, C., & Buyya, R. (2015). Cloud Computing. In *Cloud Data Centers and Cost Modeling* (pp. 3–41). Elsevier. doi:10.1016/B978-0-12-801413-4.00001-5

Yao, F. (2021). Hybrid Encryption Scheme for Hospital Financial Data Based on Noekeon Algorithm. *Security and Communication Networks*, *2021*, 1–10. doi:10.1155/2021/7578752

Zhang, B. (2020). Classification of Encrypted Text Based on Artificial Intelligence. *IOP Conference Series. Materials Science and Engineering*, *740*(1), 012133. doi:10.1088/1757-899X/740/1/012133

Chapter 20
Quantum-Resistant Authentication for Smart Grid: The Case for Using Merkle Trees

Melesio Muñoz-Calderón
https://orcid.org/0000-0003-1105-5157
Cupertino Electric Inc., USA

Melody Moh
https://orcid.org/0000-0002-8313-6645
San Jose State University, USA

ABSTRACT

We are currently at the beginning of a great technological transformation of our electrical power grids. These new grids will be "smart" as a result of improved communication and control systems but will also have new vulnerabilities. A smart grid will be better able to incorporate new forms of energy generations as well as be self-healing and more reliable. This chapter investigates a threat to wireless communication networks from a fully realized quantum computer and provides a means to avoid this problem in smart grid domains. This chapter examines the security, complexities and performance of device authentication in wireless mesh networks (WMN) using public-key encryption and then using Merkle trees. As a result, the authors argue for the use of Merkle trees as opposed to public-key encryption for authentication of devices in WMN used in smart grid applications.

ORGANIZATION BACKGROUND

Cupertino Electric Inc. is a private company founded in 1954 and headquartered in San José, CA. It provides electrical engineering and construction services.

San José State University (SJSU) was founded in 1857 as a normal school and has matured into a metropolitan university in the Silicon Valley. It is one of 23 campuses in the California State University system, offering more than 145 areas of study with an additional 108 concentrations.

DOI: 10.4018/978-1-6684-5250-9.ch020

INTRODUCTION

Today our modern world is not so far removed from a "simpler time" when rapid transportation was by horse, water was hauled by hand and refrigeration was a sort of science fiction. Some of us will never forget the stories told by our elders of the first time they witnessed the magic of electricity. Since those times technology has advanced quickly. Presently, as a result of political turmoil, cyber-attacks and natural disasters we see how important electric power has become to our modern societies. Electricity keeps transportation systems moving in an orderly manner. It keeps water flowing. It keeps medicines and food refrigerated. In short electric power is now fundamental to our world.

The electrical power grid forms the functional foundation of our modern societies. Born in the Victorian Era the grid has served humanity well, but as our societies continue to evolve, demands are increasing, and requirements are being put on the grid that were not there a hundred years ago. In short, this infrastructure is hitting a limit and needs to be modernized. It is expected that by 2050 worldwide consumption of electricity will triple (Kowalenko, 2010). Furthermore, power grids are still susceptible to large-scale outages that can affect millions of people (U.S.-Canada Power System Outage Task Force, 2004). These are some of the motivations for the creation of an "advanced decentralized, digital, infrastructure with two-way capabilities for communicating information, controlling equipment and distributing energy" (National Institute of Standards and Technology (NIST, 2010). This infrastructure will be better able to incorporate new forms of energy generation, as well as be self-healing and more robust. Each device in a smart grid will likely have its own IP address and will use protocols like TCP/IP for communication. Thus, they will be vulnerable to similar security threats that face present day communication networks (Yan, Qian, Sharif, Tipper, 2012); however, the stakes will be much higher. That is to say, in the information technology industry the highest priority is the confidentiality, integrity and availability of information. In the electrical power industry, the highest priority is human safety. For the smart grid cyber security measures must not get in the way of safe and reliable power system operations (NIST, 2010).

Problem Statement

In Northern California the last several years have brought the limitations of our current power grid into a clearer focus. The autumn season, once a pleasant time of less coastal fog and warmer temperatures, now appear to be drier, longer and hotter than in previous times (Deedler, 1996). In parts of California this is now being referred to as "fire season" (Sahagun, 2019). It is the combination of several factors, dried out fuels from hotter summers, a later start to the rainy season and high winds that combine to create acutely dangerous fire conditions. Electrical power lines can produce arcs and sparks when they fall, this is a basic fact of electrical power distribution. Currently, to mitigate some of the dangers of fire, utility providers are shutting down power to some of their customers during weather events. This is a disruptive, and possibly clumsy approach, but not unreasonable considering the limits of our current grid. A valid argument could be made that with real time information, self-healing automation, and the ability for fine grain controls, a smart grid could be an important tool in combating the effects of fire season in California and elsewhere.

How we extract, use and distribute energy is at the heart of some of the most important issues of our day. Renewable energy sources offer a lot of promise but are often limited by the existing electrical infrastructure. "Falling costs and growing public support for renewable power generation will require a smart grid capable of integrating these technologies" (NIST 2019). "The smart grid is a long-term and expensive resource that must be built future proof" (NIST, 2014). That is, it must be designed and implemented to be able to meet future scalability and functionality requirements. At the same time, it also needs to be able to survive future threats. With this in mind and with our knowledge of the threat posed to some types of public-key encryption from the quantum computer, it must be concluded that if the quantum computer is realized and public-key encryption is extensively used in the smart grid we will be facing a serious crisis that could have been avoided.

While many may still think that the era of quantum computing is in the far horizon, China launched the world's first quantum communication satellite in August 2016 (Wall Street Journal, 2016). While this has "set to launch Beijing far ahead of its global rivals in the drive to acquire a highly coveted asset in the age of cyber espionage: hack-proof communications," it has also shown that cyber-attacks that are based on quantum computing may be more eminent than what many initially thought. Finding alternatives to quantum vulnerable public-key encryption is therefore timely, and in line with NIST goals of making the smart grid "future proof."

This chapter looks at the threat to public-key encryption systems from the quantum computer in the context of smart grid security. The authors argue for the use of Merkle (Hash) trees as opposed to public-key on the smart grid, specifically when used to authenticate devices in WMN. Results of this chapter have been presented as a poster (Muñoz, Moh, Moh, October 2014) and a conference paper (Muñoz, Moh, Moh, December 2014). This is a continuation of our research effort in smart grid (Kapoor and Moh, 2015) and in mobile network and cloud security (Wong, Moh, Moh, 2012) (Yang, Moh, 2012) (Gaur, Moh, Balakrishnan, 2013).

For this chapter, a Merkle tree authentication scheme is implemented, and incorporated into the ns-3 Network Simulator. It is then compared to the performances of a publicly available version of RSA, a public-key encryption system. The goal is to show that Merkle trees are a reasonable alternative to public-key cryptography system for smart grid networks.

Current State of Affairs

The evolution of the power grid is already under way. Progress in the U.S. can be seen with the deployment of the Advanced Metering Infrastructure (AMI) as well as the Green Button Initiative. Started in 2011, the initiative challenged utilities across the US to give customers usage information in a secure, simple and standardized format. This gives customers the ability to make informed decisions about energy usage that will help spur innovation, e.g., consumer applications, devices (NIST, 2019).

Smart buildings are also starting to show up on the landscape. Smart buildings are defined as buildings that use technology and processes to effectively control their environments. This is accomplished through the use of IT-aided sensors and controls that allow for better building management and maintenance. These sensors and controls are developed using open systems and protocols. "All cybersecurity defense are potentially breakable," therefore, it is necessary to develop back-up plans that identify the minimum level of functionality, particularly when it comes to the safety of human life. Hardwired equipment with hands-on controls should also be a part of this functionality. "Investigating the issue of cyber threats in smart buildings is timely and pertinent" (Khaund, 2015).

The Internet of Things (IoT) has captured the attention of producers and consumers alike. Much like smart grid, real time accumulation and transmission of accurate information is critical to the overall function of the IoT. IoT communications differ from traditional smartphone communications in that their data connections shift more usage from primarily downlink transmissions to more uplink transmissions. The 5G network is being developed with IoT in mind. Our continuing work on these topics looks at increasing stability, reducing power consumption and lowering delay in 5G networks for IoT communications (Su, Moh, 2018) (Tsai, Moh, 2017).

We are now in in the era of "smart things" that are increasingly complex and interconnected. Once hypothetical situation such as DDoS attacks and botnets with and on ordinary household items are now a reality. Some of our recent works look at these situations and approaches to handle them (Kammara, Moh, 2019) (Moh, Raju, 2019).

The Samsung-owned SmartThings is an IoT framework. It is one of many including Apple's HomeKit, openHAB, Vera Control's Vera3, Google's Weave/Brillo. SmartThings is one of the more mature IoT platforms. Written in Groove, which is similar to Java, the software is event driven and lacks a main function (Schmeidl, Nazzal, Alalfi, 2019). It supports motion sensors, fire alarms and door locks. SmartThings is comprised of three main components namely, hubs, the cloud backend and a smart phone app. This work focuses on design flaw vulnerabilities, not bugs and oversights. The findings showed a number of problems related to controls, privilege and access to devices. As a result of these flaws the authors were able to steal lock pin-codes, disable vacation mode, and cause fake fire alarms. SmartApps was not *allowed* to carry out these operations, nor was physical access to the home required. This study has demonstrated how insecure smart homes can be (Fernandes, Jung, Prakash, 2016).

The study described above looked at over-the-shelf smart home appliances. In addition to the flaws demonstrated, we cannot ignore the cyber threats brought by quantum computing technologies. An evident is the recent launch of quantum satellite by China, which has shown that the era of quantum computing (and therefore its enabling of cybersecurity attacks) is no longer in a far-distant future (Wall Street Journal, August 2016).

In China, the Green Belt and Road Initiative is a global development strategy by the Chinese government involving infrastructure development and investment in 152 countries and international organizations in Asia, Europe, Africa, Middle East, and the Americas (World Bank, 2019). The initiative has a long-term goal of transferring technical standards to recipient countries. Additionally, the stated objective of the State Grid's China Electric Power Research Institute is to be the "main formulator of standards for power grid technology" (NIST, 2019). China is on track to be a formidable leader in smart grid technology.

Twenty years ago, electrical power stations were less vulnerable to cyberattacks, as were automobiles and many other products that are now connected via the internet to other computers. The connectivity that has improved their performance has also left them increasingly vulnerable to compromise. In 2016 a cyber-attack was launched against the Pivnichna power station near Kiev, Ukraine. Referred to as a "cyberweapon" CrashOverride shutdown the power station for about an hour. Technicians there took the plant offline when they noticed a problem, then were manually able to bring the plant back online. The situation could have been worse. It was modular in design and could be reconfigured for a variety of infrastructure targets (Schneier, 2018). This and other cyber-attacks lead us to conclude, that such attacks will continue and will continue to evolve, with greater sophistication and impact.

In July 2022 NIST announced it had selected four algorithms to be part of its post-quantum cryptography standard. For the public-key and key-establishing algorithm CRYSTALS-KYBER has been selected for standardization. For digital signatures CRYSTALS-Dilithium, FALCON and SPHINCS+ have been selected. All of these except SPHINCS+ are lattices based public-key encryption schemes (NIST, 2022). SPHINCS+ is a hash-based signature. Specifically, it uses Merkle trees, however Merkle trees require keeping track of state across signature which have the potential for "disastrous consequence if the states are mismanaged." Therefore, there is a requirement for this to be a "stateless" system. SPHINCS+ achieves statelessness by using one-time signatures, few-times signatures, Merkle trees and hypertrees. Hypertrees are Merkle trees of Merkle trees (Zhang, Cui, Yu, 2022). This adds complexity and slows the system down to a point where lattice based public key is faster and more efficient (NIST, 2022). However, NIST chose to standardize SPHINCS+ so that they are not totally reliant on the security of lattice-based public-key encryption, as well as the fact that SPHINCS+'s security is well understood. Although at this point it is recommending CRYSTALS-Dilithium for digital signatures (NIST, 2022).

BACKGROUND

The Threat of Quantum Information Processing

Today's computer architecture is based on the transistor and the binary number system. Invented in 1948 at Bell Labs, within 10 years the solid-state transistor completely replaced its predecessor the vacuum tube (Tanenbaum, 1990). The transistor opened the door to the modern computer age by allowing computers to do more with smaller and smaller components. In recent years the trend has been to increase computing power by increasing the number of cores on a processor, i.e., increasing computing power by adding more transistors. Multicore processors do indeed seem to be the future for computers in the near term, and the potential for greater computational power seems close at hand as a result of the progress of miniaturization, "but this trend cannot continue indefinitely" (Stajic, 2013). Yet for the security of public key there is a greater threat; namely, a fully realized quantum computer that can break the factorization and discrete log problems with a brute force attack.

The quantum computer is not bound to the limits of transistors or the binary system architecture. Quantum Information Processing (QIP) uses atoms held in a magnetic field instead of transistors. These units are called qubits. The underlying principle behind the quantum computer involves Einstein's wave-particle duality. QIP exploits the laws of quantum mechanics and as a consequence a single qubit can take infinitely many quantum states. This "allows for a much more powerful information platform than is possible with conventional components" (Stajic, 2013). It is more than just that a quantum computer would be faster, it is that in the realm of quantum physics a computer can solve the factorization or discrete log problem in polynomial time rather than exponential time (Shor, 1997).

Today the design of our modern computer closely resembles the classic conceptual model called the Turing machine. Developed by the British computer scientist Alan Turing in the 1930s, the Turing machine can effectively compute any function that is computable (Kozen, 1997). It can only have a finite amount of states and it can only read and write one symbol at a time on a one-dimensional tape (Rosen, 1995). This is how modern computers work, executing instruction after instruction, linearly on a CPU; even multicore processors work like this. The classic Turing machine can be thought of as having a single fixed state at any given time; the quantum machine on the other hand "has an internal wave function, which is a superposition of a combination of the possible basis states." Transforms of the wave function can then alter the entire set of states in a single operation (Schneier, 1996).

The quantum computer is currently in its infancy, and it will be a great challenge to get hundreds and thousands of atoms to act in unison and function correctly (Kaku, 2008). Large-scale quantum computer hardware requires that each qubit be extremely well isolated from the environment, yet precisely controlled using external fields. These problems are far from trivial (Monroe, Kim, 2013) and currently beyond our technological capabilities to overcome. That being said, "no fundamental physical principles are known that prohibit the building of large-scale and reliable quantum computers" (Rieffel, Polak, 2011).

Public-key encryption systems are secure today, but in 1994 Peter Shor of Bell Labs showed that factorization and discrete logarithm-based public-key systems could be broken with a brute force attack by a quantum computer (Kaku, 2008). Shor's algorithm attacks the problem of finding the period of a function. It uses quantum parallelism to produce a superposition of all the values of this function in a single step. It then uses a quantum Fourier transform and, measuring the yields, gives the period. This is then used to factor (Rieffel, Polak, 2011).

In 2019 a theoretical paper showed how to factor 2048-bit RSA moduli with a 20-million qubit quantum computer in eight hours (Gidney, Ekera, 2019). Advances in quantum computing involve not only getting qubits to work together, but also maintaining a stable system. The current state of the art in quantum computing belong to Google's Bristlecone, IBM Q 53, and Intel's Tangle Lake. These are all gate mode (universal) quantum processors. Annealing quantum processors are specific to a task and not a threat to quantum vulnerable public-key encryption.

Late in 2019 a team from Google claimed to have reached "quantum supremacy." Quantum supremacy is where a quantum computer overwhelmingly outperforms a classic computer on certain tasks. Documented in their article in *Nature* they use a 54-qubit processor named Sycamore. This machine performed the target computation in 200 seconds and from measurements in their experiment they determined that it would take the world's fastest computer 10,000 years to produce a similar output. The Sycamore machine is a fully programmable machine that can run general purpose quantum algorithms (Arute, Arya, Babush, et. al. 2019). Their claims are not without their opponents (Pednault, 2019). In December 2020 a team from China claimed to be the second to achieve "quantum supremacy." They claim their photonic system called Jiuzhang out performance Sycamore (Palmer, 2021). They were followed by another team in 2022 with Zuchongzhi 2.1 that has 66 qubits in a 2-dimensional array that outperforms both of the previous (Zhu et al., 2022).

Advances in quantum computing will be difficult, but it is still not clear if is on the order of "sending a man to the moon", or "faster-than-light travel" (Schneier, 2018). At this stage, it is interesting to note how far the quantum computer has come. In 2008 the most advanced quantum computer was able to compute 3 * 5 = 15 (Kaku, 2008). We can assume that the development of the quantum computer will continue full steam ahead for the foreseeable future.

Electrical Power Grid

Electrical equipment is installed with the intention that it will be in service for many years, even decades. To do otherwise would not be efficient or acceptable. Computer and communication technologies advance at a much more rapid pace. As a result, technology on the grid tends to lag. Functions in the grid today continue to use communications technologies similar to those that were used in the 1980s and 90s (IEEE-USA Board of Directors, 2010). Considering the expense, potential for disruption, and difficult to reach locations of some of this equipment, it seems clear why it is not updated with the latest trends in the computer world; the electrical power grid does not abide by Moore's Law.

In the U.S., *The Energy Independence and Security Act of 2007* established that the NIST has "primary responsibility to coordinate development of a framework that includes protocols and model standards for information management to achieve interoperability of smart grid devices and systems" (NIST, 2010). NIST is a part of the U.S. Department of Commerce, and issues standards and guidelines in the hope that they are adopted by industry. This promotes interoperability that will in turn promote economic development (Schneier, 1996).

In recent years NIST has generated many important documents related to the smart grid, particularly the *NIST Framework and Roadmap for Smart Grid Interoperability Standards*. The framework provides a common vision and vocabulary, a set of shared principles and practices as well as a collective agreement on standards and protocols. A roadmap lays out the process required to make the visions a reality, these include steps, timetables, participants, priorities and intermediate goals. Together the framework and roadmap provide a blueprint for smart grid interoperability, which allows systems and their components to work together. Version 1.0 was issued in 2008, version 2.0 in 2012, version 3.0 in 2014. Development of 4.0 is currently underway (NIST, 2016).

Wireless Mesh Networks

WMN have become popular network topologies in recent years due to their cost effectiveness and robustness. WMN are currently being used in the AMI component of the smart grid. Some smart meters currently being used in the AMI are using the ZigBee protocol to form WMN.

The ZigBee standard defines a set of communications protocols for low-data-rate short-range wireless networking. ZigBee beholds to the IEEE 802.15.4 standard, which defines the two bottom layers of the protocol, but then goes beyond that to implement two additional layers. ZigBee is well suited for controls applications because it is a low power, low data communications protocol, which can support a mesh topology. ZigBee is simple and inexpensive when compared to WiFi and Bluetooth (ZigBee Alliance, 2008).

In a WMN nodes are peers that forward messages for the network. Each node is connected to several other nodes, thus improving reliability since multiple routes exist from source to sink. WMN do have drawbacks, particularly they are vulnerable to attacks due to their dynamically changing topology, their lack of conventional security infrastructure and wireless nature (Siddiqui, Huong, 2007).

When a node joins the network establishing trust among the devices is done through the process of authentication. Authentication allows a node to ensure the identity of the peer it wants to communicate with. Public-key encryption, as well as Merkle trees, offers means by which nodes in networks can authenticate. However, the Merkle tree based scheme's security rests on the use of cryptographically secure hash functions, which we understand to be resistant to a quantum computer attack (Stallings, 1999).

Authentication Using Public-key Encryption

Public-key encryption uses a public-private key pair; one used to encrypt, the other to decrypt. This has many advantages. The strength of public-key encryption rests on difficult to solve math problems. For this chapter the authors are concerned with those based on the factorization problem and the discrete logarithms problem. The experiment will deal specifically with the factorization problem.

Public key can be used to authenticate two devices in the following manner. For clarity call one device *Alice* and the other *Bob*. *Alice* sends a message to *Bob* claiming to be *Alice*. *Bob* needs more proof than this, so *Bob* encrypts a message *R* using *Alice*'s public key. Since the public key is public, anybody can encrypt a message, but only the holder of the private key can decrypt the message. Alice receives the message *R*, decrypts it then sends it back to Bob. Since she is the only holder of her private key, she has authenticated herself (Stamp, 2011).

It is not known for certain at this point if factoring is "difficult" (Stamp, 2011). That is to say, the best factoring algorithm asymptotically is the *number field sieve*, which is an exponential-time algorithm (Shor, 1997). Solving the factorization problem in a timely manner today is beyond the reach of the most powerful computers and most efficient algorithms (Cormen, Leiserson, Rivest, 2009).

The concern with information security is not just is it safe today, but will it be safe in the future? At one time the German Enigma machine was the state of the art in data encryption; today, breaking it is a challenging graduate level homework problem.

The probability that modern cryptographic algorithms will become completely insecure in the near future is unclear. However, technological and theoretical breakthroughs are always possibilities (NIST, 2014). In 2018 the European Commission is set to start a 10-year, €1 billion effort called the Quantum Technology Flagship to support and coordinate the research and development of the quantum computer. Elsewhere governments, academia, and industry are also investing and seeking to develop this revolutionary technology (Hellemans, 2016).

RSA

This chapter focuses on factorization problem based public-key encryption systems, but several well-known and widely used discrete log problem systems are worth mentioning, namely Diffie-Hellman, El Gamal, and elliptic curve cryptography (ECC) (Rieffel, Polak, 2011). NIST approves of their use in smart grid and some are already finding use (https://www.certicom.com/index.php/device-authentication-service/smart-energy-device-certificate-service). All of these systems are vulnerable to a quantum attack.

RSA is a public-key encryption system that is based on the factoring problem. The system works with the use of public-private key pairs. To create a key pair two large prime numbers p and q are multiplied together to generate N.

That is,

$$N = pq$$

Then a value e is chosen at random that is the relative prime (i.e., their greatest common divisor is 1) of the product $(p - 1)(q - 1)$.

Then we compute the private key, such that

$$ed \equiv 1 \bmod (p - 1)(q - 1)$$

That is,

$$d = e^{-1} \bmod ((p - 1)(q - 1))$$

Note that d and n are also relative prime. At this point p and q can be discarded.

The RSA key pairs then are:

Public Key: (N, e)

Private Key: d

Now let M represent our plaintext message and let C be our cipher text. To encrypt we calculate the following:

$C = M^e \bmod N$

To Decipher we calculate:

$M = C^d \bmod N$

Here is a simple example:

$p = 47, q = 71$

Then

$N = p\, q = 3337$

$(p - 1)(q - 1) = 46 * 70 = 3220$

Choose a random number *e* (must be relative prime to 3220) say 79. Then

$d = 79^{-1} \bmod 3220 = 1019$

e and *N* are published and *d* is kept secret.
Then to encrypt a message say:

$M = 688232$

Break into blocks:

$M^1 = 688$

$M^2 = 232$

Then:

$688^{79} \bmod 3337 = 1570 = C^1$

$232^{79} \bmod 3337 = 2756 = C^2$

Then your cipher text is *1570 2756.*
To decipher:

$1570^{1019} \bmod 3337 = 688 = M^1$

$2756^{1019} \bmod 3337 = 232 = M^2$

(Schneier, 1996).

RELATED STUDIES

This section presents first related works on the justification of using WMN for smart grid, followed by a security framework of smart grid, and finally some relevant studies on using Merkle trees for smart grid authentication.

Modeling Smart Grid Using WMN

Smart grid technologies have been developing through the combined efforts of electronic control, metering, and monitoring. Early experiments used the term broadband over power lines (BPL) to represent networks that connect millions of homes via smart meters, yet researchers used the WMN technology, notably for more reliable connections to home devices as well as supporting metering of other utilities (gas, water, etc.) (Burger, Iniewski, 2012). This was partly prompted by the successful initial deployments of smart grids using WMNs, such as the 2003 implementation in Austin, Texas (Sectoral e-Business Watch, 2009).

An important work of justifying the use of WMN model for smart grid network is by Xu and Wang (Xu, Wang, 2013). Recognizing the importance of providing time-critical communications in the power system, they modeled the smart grid network as a WMN, and provided the delay analysis in typical deployment scenarios. They specified the delay bounds, which would be useful for guiding smart grid network design to meet its communication demands.

One theoretical study of using WMN as the communication environment for smart grid (Zhang, 2011), recognizing that such an environment needs to be robust, reliable, and efficient. The authors proposed a smart grid communication network, deploying WMN technologies including 802.15.4 Zigbee (Zigbee Alliance, 2008), 802.11s WLAN WMN standard (IEEE 802.11s, 2011) in different levels of smart grid networks, and verified its reliability through robust, efficient primal-dual routing.

Another study using WMN to model smart grid network is suggested using IEEE 802.11s standard (IEEE 802.11s, 2011) as the backbone for smart grid infrastructure, and analyzed the default routing protocol for the 802.11s standard, Hybrid Wireless Mesh Protocol (HWMP). They then proposed an enhancement, HWMP-RE (HWMP-Reliability Enhancement) for improving the routing reliability (Kim, Kim, Lim, Ko, Lee, 2012).

Smart Grid Security Framework

An important work on smart grid, or smart distribution grid (SDG), security was by Wang and Yi (Wang, Yi, 2011). They investigated two issues. First, they proposed a security framework for SDG based on a WMN topology and analyzed the potential security attacks and possible counter-attack measures. Next, they developed a new intrusion detection and response scheme (smart tracking firewall). They evaluated its performance and found that the smart tracking firewall can detect and respond to security attacks in real-time, and thus is a good fit for use in SDG.

The authors note that NIST guidelines document the usefulness and importance of WMN for smart grid. By their nature WMN are robust and economic so they are well suited for SDG applications. For an SDG to function properly they must meet the following requirements:

1. Collect power usage information
2. Monitor the status of electrical equipment
3. Send control messages from the control centers to electrical devices
4. Send pricing information to customers

WMN are vulnerable to signal jamming, eavesdropping and attacks from inside the network. It is argued that WMN need to cooperate with wired networks to deliver critical messages via secure and reliable paths within the shortest time. It is currently unknown if existing security of WMN can meet SDG requirements. Further research on this point is required.

Smart Grid Authentication using Merkle Trees

Merkle trees have also been evaluated as authentication schemes for multi-gate mesh network in smart grid applications (Hu, Gharavi, 2014). This work provides additional support for the use of Merkle trees in smart grid. The most recently adopted IEEE 802.11s standard supports simultaneous authentication of equals (SAE) for its security protocol. This protocol uses one password shared by all devices. The standard also offers efficient mesh security association (EMSA) as an alternative approach. Both protocols use 4-way handshaking during which a network is vulnerable to denial of service (DoS) attacks.

The first step of the four-way handshake is to use a pre-shared key (PSK) or an authentication server to establish the authentication of the server. From this a secret key is generated that is called the pairwise master key (PMK). The client and server then exchange encrypted messages and decrypt them to authenticate themselves. 4-way hand shaking is a means for the client and server to independently prove to each other that they know the PSK/PMK, without disclosing it. The PMK usually lasts the entire session, but the traffic between needs to be encrypted as well. The handshake establishes a new key called the Pairwise Transient Key (PTK). It is prior to the establishment of the PTK that a denial of service could be launched. The goal of the attack would be to prevent the establishment of the PTK key. It is assumed that the attacker can eavesdrop and is able to forge messages. The Merkle tree is used during the exchange of the first message and without the PTK information the attacker is unable to derive the Merkle tree root. By using new Merkle trees during subsequent four-way hand shakings, this scheme is also able to prevent replay attacks.

The authors used ProVerif to analyze the vulnerabilities of the network and the resilience added by use of Merkle trees to defend against DoS attacks. This work does not look at quantum computer attacks on WMN.

Additional research has been done (Li, Lu, Zhou, Yang, Shen, 2013) that uses Merkle trees for authentication to defend against message injection, message modification, message analysis and replay attacks. The work stresses the importance of authentication to the proper function of the smart grid. This work continues the discussion related to performance and security of Merkle trees in a smart grid application.

Research continues to show that Merkle trees are a good and efficient tool to be used in smart grid applications (Yan, Chang, Zhang, 2017) (Tohidi, Vakili, 2018). Their usefulness in smart grid goes beyond the focus of this work, namely quantum resistance.

Figure 1. A Merkle tree with authentication path

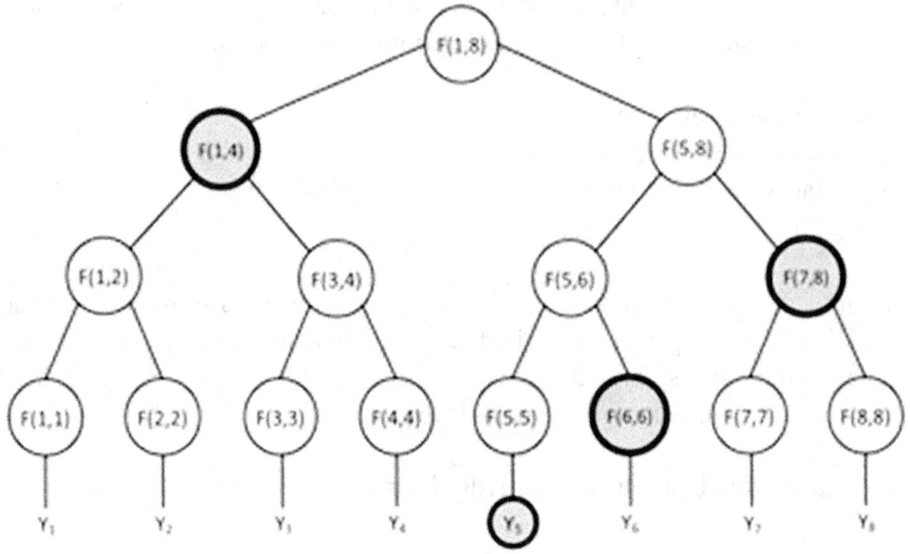

PROPOSED SOLUTION

This section describes our proposed solution. First, we will explain Merkle trees and how they constructed. As Merkle tree authentication scheme rests on a secure hash function, the second subsection explains what a secure hash function is and what their desired properties are. An important strength of hash functions is their resistance to the birthday attack, which we will illustrated in the last subsection.

Merkle Trees

A Merkle tree is a complete binary tree constructed from a set of secret leaf tokens where each internal node of the tree is a concatenation, then a hash of its left and right child. The leaves consist of a set of m randomly generated secret tokens. Since it is a complete binary tree, $m = 2^h$ where h is the height of the tree and m is the number of leaves. The root is public and is the result of recursive applications of the one-way hash function on the tree, starting at the leaves (Santhanam et al., 2008).

Merkle trees offer low-cost authentication for mesh clients. Compared to public key, they are lightweight, quick to generate and are resistant to quantum attacks (https://en.wikipedia.org/wiki/Merkle_tree). The strength of the Merkle tree authentication scheme rests on having a secure hash function and practical cryptographic hash functions do exist. The purpose of a hash function is to produce a "fingerprint" of a message, that is, a hash function *s()* is applied to a file M and produces *s(M)*, which identifies M, but is much smaller (Stamp, 2011).

Figure 1 shows a Merkle tree with 8 leaves ($m = 8$). This tree, therefore, has 8 one-time authentication tokens to offer. In a mesh application, the client generates the tree and the root of the tree is made public. The client can prove its identity to any mesh router, by comparing the published root against the root that is generated when the hash function and authentication path are provided. Note that it is computationally infeasible to determine the secret token from the published root of the tree (Santhanam et al., 2008).

Here is an example of a client authenticating itself with leaf Y_5 (referring to Figure 1):

Let F be a mapping function that we define by:

$$F(i,i) = s(Y_i)$$

$$F(i, j) = s(F(i,k), F((k+1), j))$$

where $k = \frac{i+j}{}$

1. *F(1,8)* is the root and is public, made known by the router
2. The client sends *F(1, 4)* and *F(5, 8)* and the router computes: *s(F(1, 4), F(5, 8)) = F(1, 8)*
3. The client sends *F(5, 6)* and *F(7, 8)* and the router computes: *s(F(5, 6), F(7, 8)) = F(5, 8)*
4. The client sends *F(5, 5)* and *F(6, 6)* and the router computes: *s(F(5, 5), F(6, 6)) = F(5, 6)*
5. 5. The client sends Y_5 and the router computes:

$$s(Y_5) = F(5, 5)$$

6. The router has now authenticated the client through authenticating Y_5

Note that using this method, only $log_2 n$ transmissions are required to authenticate. However, only half of the transmissions are actually required because the router is generating half of the values itself.

To recap, the client transmits to the mesh router the secret token Y_i and the path to the root. The root is public so there is no need to transmit that. The client is authenticated by the fact that the mesh router is able to regenerate the value of the root based on the hash function *s()* and the path provided by the client (Merkle, 1979).

Secure Hash Functions

Public-key algorithms use expensive modular arithmetic, exponential operations and are therefore not good fits for mesh clients (Santhanam et al., 2008). An alternative to the use of resource-hungry, quantum computer-vulnerable public-key authentication is a system based on Merkle trees. It is well known that hash based algorithms like MD5 and SHA-2 are computationally less expensive than symmetric key algorithms, which in turn are computationally less expensive that public-key algorithms.

Popular cryptographic hash functions like SHA-1 or MD5 work much like block ciphers. That is they take plain text and split them into fixed sized blocks then iterated by way of a function for some number of rounds (Stamp, 2011). They are considered secure if no collisions have been found; SHA-1 was broken in 2005 (https://www.schneier.com/blog/archives/2005/02/sha1_broken.html). Hash functions must be fast and have the effect that small changes to the input result in large changes in the output. This is known as the *avalanche effect.*

A cryptographic hash function must provide:

1. *Compression:* The input file can be of any size, but the output must always be the same size.
2. *Efficiency:* It must be relatively easy for the computer to compute the output.
3. *One-Way:* Given only y of $y = s(x)$, it must be computationally infeasible to compute x.
4. *Weak Collision Resistance:* It is not feasible to modify a message without changing its hash value. That is, given x and $s(x)$ to find any y, with $y^{1} x$ and $s(x) = s(y)$ is infeasible.
5. *Strong Collision Resistance:* We cannot find any two inputs that produce the same hash output. That is, it is infeasible to find any x and y, such that $y^{1} x$ and $s(x) = s(y)$.

The last item here refers to how resistant the hash function is to the *birthday attack* (Stamp, 2011).

The Birthday Attack

The birthday paradox is a classic topic in probability, the result being that with only 23 people in a room you have a 50% chance of having two people with the same birthday. The paradoxical part of this problem is that at first glance it would appear 23 is too small a number.

The number of comparisons required with n people in a room is:

$$\frac{n(n-1)}{2} \approx n^2$$

There are 365 days in a non-leap year and we get the following:

$$n^2 = 365$$

$$n = \sqrt{365} \approx 19$$

Appling this to hash functions, if we have $s(x)$ that has an output with n bits, then there are 2^n different possible hash values—all values being equally likely. Since

$$\sqrt{2^n} = 2^{n/2}$$

Then by the birthday problem we can expect to have a collision after $2^{n/2}$ different inputs. As a consequence, to prevent this sort of attack n must be substantially so large that a brute force attack is not reasonable (Stamp, 2011).

The goal of the birthday attack on a hash function is not to find a message x such that $s(x) = s(y)$, rather it is to find two random messages x and y such that $s(x) = s(y)$ (Schneier, 1996). "The strength of a hash function against brute-force attack depends solely on the length of the hash code produced by the algorithm" (Stalling, 1999). This is a key point; to defend against a quantum attack the hash code only needs to be increased in length.

Grover's algorithm can reverse cryptographic hash functions. Grover's search algorithm offers a quadratic speed up on unstructured search problems (Chen et al., 2016). Grover's algorithm tells us to improve the security of hash functions and symmetric cyphers increasing the key length will be enough to keep our data safe from a quantum attack (Schneier, 2018).

ANALYSIS AND PERFORMANCE EVALUATION

This section first presents the complexity analysis, which includes the analyses of time, memory, and message complexities of Merkle trees and RSA. It then describes the experiment setup, including WMN representing a smart grid network, the Merkle tree for authentication nodes, and the RSA implementation. Finally, it illustrates the experimental results consisting of build time and authentication time.

Complexity Analysis of Merkle Trees

Complexities of Build-Time and Authentication-Time

Since a Merkle tree is a complete binary tree the number of nodes at height h is 2^h. The height of the tree with n leaves is $log_2 n$. The number of internal nodes in such a tree of height h is:

$$1 + 2 + 2^2 + \ldots + 2^{h-1} = \sum^{h-1} 2^i$$

$$= \frac{2^h - 1}{2 - 1}$$

Therefore, there are $(2^h - 1)$ internal nodes (Cormen et al., 2009). To build a Merkle tree in each node we have an asymptotic upper bound of $O(2^h)$ with additional cost for the hash function.

For our experiment the *hash ()* function available with the *tr1/functional* library of *C++* was used. *C++* uses *MurmurHashNeutral2* as its hash function, which uses a "Merkle-Damgard-esque" construction for its hash (https://sites.google.com/site/murmurhash/). This has a padding scheme on the front end to make sure all input into the compression function is of the same length. The input is broken into blocks that are then compressed. The compression involves taking the result so far and combining it with the next block. Many cryptographic hash functions work this way (https://en.wikipedia.org/wiki/Merkle-Damgard_construction). We can say that asymptotically the time complexity of the hash function is $O(\beta)$, where β is the key size.

The total build time is therefore $O(2^h) + O(\beta)$. The time to authenticate is bounded by the height of the tree, as illustrated in the previous section and Figure 1, and the hash function, i.e., $O(\beta h)$.

Memory Complexity

The amount of memory a Merkle tree requires is proportional to the size of the tree and the key size. Its memory complexity is therefore:

$$\beta * (2^h + 1) = O(\beta 2^h).$$

Message Complexity

As shown in previous sections, the Merkle tree sends an authenticating path back to the request. Each entry is $O(\beta)$ and there are h entries in this path, so we have $O(\beta h)$ message complexity.

Complexity Analysis of RSA

Computational Time Complexity

Public-private key generation relies on modular exponentiation. This is when an operation is raising one number to a power modulo another number. This is resource heavy, i.e., time, power and processor resources. Assume the *public key: (N, e)* and *private key: d*, satisfy:

$\lg e = O(1)$, $\lg d \leq \beta$ and $\lg N \leq \beta$

Applying a public key requires $O(1)$ modular multiplications and uses $O(\beta^2)$ bit operations. Therefore the build time complexity is $O(1) + O(\beta^2) = O(\beta^2)$.

For authentication time, to apply a secret key requires $O(\beta)$ modular multiplications, for a total of $O(\beta^3)$ bit operations (Cormen et al., 2009).

Memory Complexity

In terms of memory consumption RSA does hold an advantage since it does not require a tree, and with one set of keys it can authenticate with an unlimited number of devices. Each node only needs to hold their own private key. Since public keys are public, the nodes do not need to retain that information. Therefore, the amount of memory used is $O(\beta)$.

Message Complexity

RSA works in three exchanges. The message complexity is therefore also $O(\beta)$.

Comparison of Complexities

Table 1 summarizes the time, memory and message complexities of Merkle tree and of RSA.

Performance Experimental Setup

The experiments were set up using ns-3, a discrete event network simulator widely used in industry and academia for the purposes of testing and evaluating networks. Both Merkle tree and RSA authentication schemes were added into ns-3. This experiment was run on a MacBook Air running OS X 10.8.5, with a 1.8 GHz Intel Core i5 and 4 GB 1600MHz DDR3 of memory.

Table 1. Complexity Analysis

COMPLEXITY COMPARISON			
		MERKLE TREE	RSA
COMPLEXITIES	BUILD TIME	$O(2^h) + O(\beta)$	$O(\beta^2)$
	AUTH TIME	$O(\beta\ h)$	$O(\beta^3)$
	MEMORY	$O(\beta\ 2^h)$	$O(\beta)$
	MESSAGE	$O\ (\beta\ h)$	$O(\beta)$

Wireless Mesh Network

In industry today we are starting to see utilization of WMN particularly in wireless lighting control systems. Currently these networks are limited to discrete sections of buildings, not entire buildings, and are often limited in size. For this reason, we defined this experiment to have a network of 64 nodes.

Merkle Trees

The Merkle tree algorithm was coded as described in the previous sections. The Merkle trees were added into the existing ns-3 node structure, which represent devices in the WMN; this would be the build time. Later when the nodes are being linked into a network, we add a functionality of authentication of nodes; this would be the authentication time.

The initial assumption was that a Merkle tree with 16 leaves (depth of 4) would be sufficient. Assuming a network of 64 devices, and if every node can authenticate with 16 other nodes around it, that should be sufficient to create a robust system. Deep trees are no more secure than shallow ones.

RSA

The RSA software used was obtained from *rsa Project* (https://code.google.com/p/rsa/). In the RSA scheme a private key is stored at the node. The public key is made public so there is no need for it to be stored in the node. This functionality was added in the same locations as the Merkle tree in ns-3.

RSA is able to use a public-private key pair to authenticate itself with any number of other nodes; this is an advantage over Merkle trees. That is, the Merkle tree scheme needs to know ahead of time how many nodes (devices) it will need to be able to authenticate with.

RSA key generation calculations depend on the length of the keys. For the sake of this test, we choose 32 bits. We also have the length of our Merkle root at 32 bits. Albeit this would not be secure in a real system, it gives us good modeling data in a reasonable amount of time. We do test larger keys to see what impact the length has on calculation times.

Performance Results

The authors wanted to evaluate how the size of a Merkle tree effected build and authentication times. A large Merkle tree offers more authentication tokens but takes longer to build and traverse. RSA on the other hand can authenticate with an unlimited number of devices, yet it requires intensive calculations

Figure 2. Build Time Comparison

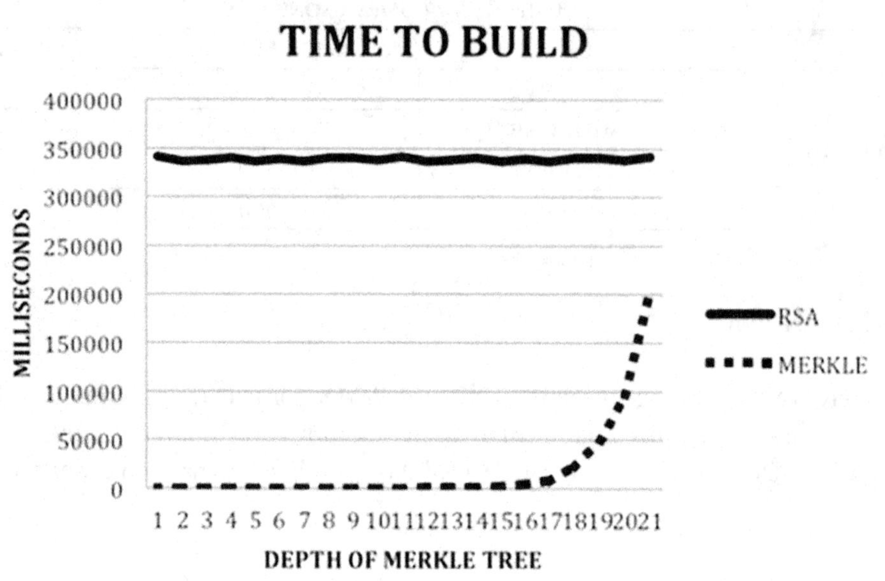

to generate and use. To evaluate the Merkle tree time measurements were taken during the construction of the node, that is, when the Merkle tree is also built. Then when the node is linked into the network, this is the authentication time.

Build Time

Figure 2 shows that RSA is very slow to build compared to Merkle, taking on the order of 350,000 milliseconds to build. When compared to a Merkle tree of shallow depth, we see the Merkle scheme has a clear advantage. The Merkle scheme does slow down as the tree grows larger. Around a depth of 16 we start to see noticeable slowing in the Merkle scheme. At a depth of 16 each node has 65,536 leaves to authenticate with.

It was not possible to see at what depth the Merkle tree equaled RSA's time because at depth 25, the computer that was running the tests started to report memory problems, then seized up. At that depth we were building a Merkle tree with 33,554,432 leaves.

Authentication Time

For the Merkle trees we can see from Figure 2 that the larger the tree the more traversing of the tree we need to do to provide our authentication path. Still Merkle continues to do better than RSA for authentication. In these plots RSA is using a 32-bit key. With the 256-bit key, RSA did much worse than the Merkle tree taking about 3 minutes to authenticate one single node. This number would then be proportional to the size of the network and number of links. What we can see from all of this is that Merkle trees are a viable alternative to the use of public key for authentication.

Figure 3. Authentication Time Comparison

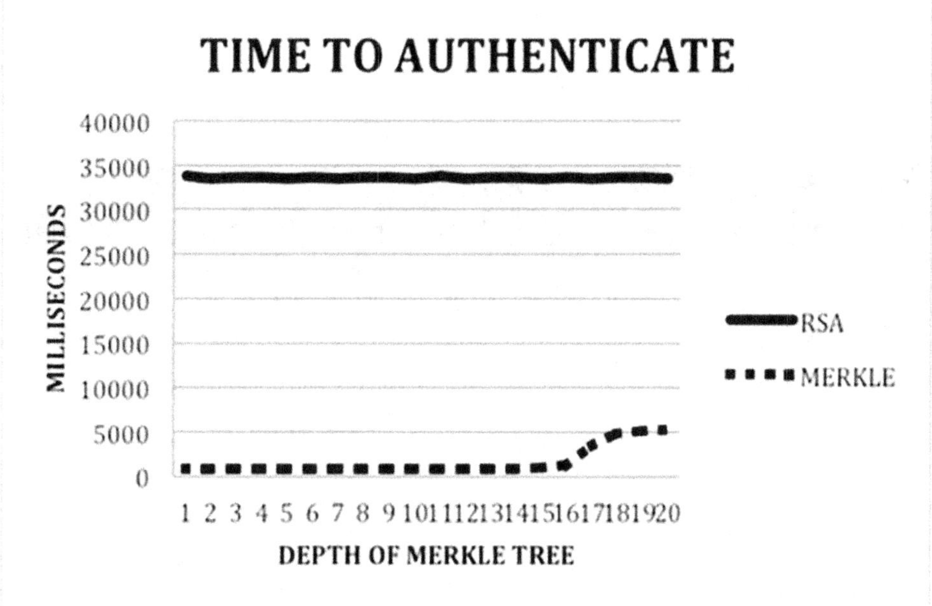

FUTURE RESEARCH DIRECTIONS

Based on the recent NIST announcement on standards there appear to be many opportunities for future studies. NIST's requirements were for the ability to securely perform 2^{64} signatures. They are asking, if a smaller maximum number of signatures would be beneficial in terms of speed and size of signatures. They also state they are seeking to diversify their signature portfolio with non-lattice-based signature schemes (NIST, 2022).

Another future direction would be to look at quantum resistant alternatives to the Diffie-Hellman key exchange. Diffie-Hellman is based on the discrete log problem and allows users to establish a shared symmetric key (Stamp, 2011). It is part of the NIST-approved cryptographic techniques, known as NSA Suite B, and is approved for use on the smart grid (NIST, 2014). Finding the pros and cons of Diffie-Hellman and providing superior alternatives would be valuable for future realization of secure smart grid systems.

Many of our most important communication protocols today rely on three core cryptographic functionalities: public-key encryption, digital signatures and key exchange. These are implemented using elliptic curve cryptosystems, RSA cryptosystems, and Diffie-Hellman, all of which are quantum vulnerable. Concern is building, and rightly so, for a world after the quantum machine is fully realized. The goal of post-quantum cryptography (also called quantum-resistant cryptography) is to develop cryptographic systems that are secure against classic, as well as quantum computers, and that can communicate using existing protocols and networks. Some of the "post-quantum primitives" NIST references are lattice-based, code-based, multivariate-polynomial cryptography and hash-based signatures. None of these primitives have been proven to be "secure against all quantum attacks," and of these only the security of hash-based signatures are well understood (Chen et al., 2016).

The table below, produced by NIST, shows the impact of quantum computing on common cryptographic algorithms.

Table 2. NIST Quantum Impact on Cryptographic Algorithms

Cryptographic Algorithm	Type	Purpose	Impact from large-scale quantum computer
AES	Symmetric key	Encryption	Larger key sizes needed
SHA-2, SHA-3	--------------	Hash functions	Larger output needed
RSA	Public key	Signatures, key establishment	No longer secure
ECDSA, ECDH (Elliptic Curve Cryptography)	Public key	Signatures, key exchange	No longer secure
DSA (Finite Field Cryptography)	Public key	Signatures, key exchange	No longer secure

The authors note that, "our understanding of quantum cryptoanalysis remains rather limited, and more research in this area is urgently needed" (Chen et al., 2016). Further research in any of these areas are worthy endeavors.

CONCLUSION

"Cybersecurity is one of the key technical areas where the state of the art falls short of meeting the envisioned functional, reliability and scalability requirements of the smart grid" (NIST, 2014). Currently, there are two paradigms of security. The first paradigm is to "get it right the first time." This is the traditional mode of designing, engineering and building, that is slow and expensive because the costs of failure are high, e.g., building a new airplane. The second, modern, paradigm is to make sure your design is agile. That is, focus on moving quickly and patch things as you go along. This is usually for applications where the costs of failure are not so high. A robust approach to smart grid security will be to integrate both paradigms (Schneier, 2018).

The main objective of this chapter is to discourage the use of discrete log and factorization-based public-key encryption in smart grid domains because of their vulnerability to quantum attacks. The build-time and authentication-time complexities, memory and message complexities of RSA, and of our proposed Merkle tree-based authentication methods were analyzed and compared based on build and authentication times. The proposed Merkle tree-based method took less time to build and to authenticate than RSA. These studies show that Merkle tree-based authentication is lightweight, secure, resistant to quantum computer attacks, and should be considered for use in smart grid applications. Although the threat of a quantum computing attack maybe low, it is understood to be a real long-term possibility (NIST, 2014).

The renowned astronomer Frank Drake has written with regards to the search for intelligent life in the universe that "our present views may be naive and will be replaced" (Drake, 2011). Trying to anticipate the future of any discipline is a venture fraught with uncertainty, but the seriousness of the power grid cannot be overstated. When we look at the security of the grid we must deal with issues as they present themselves, and we must also be looking down the road to anticipate future issues. The threat posed by a quantum attack on discrete log and factorization-based public-key encryption is known. It is therefore incumbent upon us to not allow a potentially serious design flaw to be built into our smart grids.

REFERENCES

Berger, L. T., & Iniewski, K. (Eds.). (2012). *Smart Grid - Applications, Communications and Security*. John Wiley and Sons.

Chen, L., Jordan, S., Liu, Y., Moody, D., Peralta, R., Perlner, R., & Smith-Tone, D. (2016). *NISTIR 8105 Report on Post-Quantum Cryptography*. Retrieved from https://nvlpubs.nist.gov/nistpubs/ir/2016/NIST.IR.8105.pdf

Cormen, T., Leiserson, C., Rivest, R., & Stein, C. (2009). *Introduction to Algorithms* (3rd ed.). The MIT Press.

Deedler, W. (1996). *Just what is Indian summer and did Indians really have anything to do with it?* National Weather Service. Retrieved from https://web.archive.org/web/20141009005228/http://www.crh.noaa.gov/dtx/stories/i-summer.php

Drake, F. (2011). The search for extra-terrestrial intelligence. Philosophical Transactions of the Royal Society A: Mathematical, Physical and Engineering Sciences, 369(1936), 633-643. doi:10.1098/rsta.2010.0282

Fernandes, E., Jung, J., & Prakash, A. (2016). *Security Analysis of Emerging Smart Home Applications*. Retrieved from https://cdn2.vox-cdn.com/uploads/chorus_asset/file/6410049/Paper27_SP16_Camera-Ready_SmartThings_Revised_1_.0.pdf

Gaur, S., Moh, M., & Balakrishnan, M. (2013). Hiding behind the Clouds: Efficient, Privacy-Preserving Queries via Cloud Proxies. *Proc. of International Workshop on Cloud Computing Systems, Networks, and Applications*.

Hellemans, A. (2016). *Europe Bets €1 Billion on Quantum Tech*. IEEE Spectrum. doi:10.1109/GLOCOMW.2013.6825035

Hu & Gharavi. (2014). Smart Grid Mesh Network Security Using Dynamic Key Distribution With Merkle Tree 4-Way Handshaking. *IEEE Transactions on Smart Grid, 5*.. doi:10.1109/TSG.2013.2277963

IEEE 802.11s. (2011). *Part11: Wireless LAN medium access control (MAC) (PHY) speciðcations amendment 10: Mesh networking*. IEEE Press.

IEEE-USA Board of Directors (2010). *Building a Stronger and Smarter Electrical Energy Infrastructure*. IEEE.

Kaku, M. (2008). *Physics of the Impossible*. Anchor Books.

Kammara, T., & Moh, M. (2019). Identifying IoT-based Botnets. In *Botnets: Architectures, Countermeasures, and Challenges*. CRC Press.

Kapoor & Moh. (2015). Implementation and evaluation of the DFF protocol for Advanced Metering Infrastructure (AMI) networks. *Proceedings of 11th IEEE International Conference on Design of Reliable Communication Networks*.

Khaund, K. (2015). Cybersecurity in Smart Buildings. *Frost & Sullivan Collaborative Industry Perspective*, 21. Retrieved from http://23873b0b5ea986687186-fddd749ce937721293aa13aa786d4227.r31.cf1.rackcdn.com/Documentation/Cybersecurity%20in%20Smart%20Buildings_White%20Paper.pdf

Kim, J., Kim, D., Lim, K.-W., Ko, Y.-B., & Lee, S.-Y. (2012, December). Improving the Reliability of IEEE 802.11s Based Wireless Mesh Networks for Smart Grid Systems. *Journal of Communications and Networks (Seoul)*, *14*(6), 629–639. doi:10.1109/JCN.2012.00029

Kowalenko. (2010). *The Smart Grid: A Primer.* IEEE.

Kozen, D. (1997). *Automata and Computability*. Springer. doi:10.1007/978-1-4612-1844-9

Li, H., Lu, R., Zhou, L., Yang, B., & Shen, X. (2013). An Efficient Merkle-Tree-Based Authentication Scheme for Smart Grid. *IEEE Systems Journal*, *8*(2), 655–663. doi:10.1109/JSYST.2013.2271537

Merkle, R. (1979). *Secrecy Authentication and Public Key Systems*. Information Systems Laboratory, Stanford Electronics Laboratories. Retrieved from https://www.merkle.com/papers/Thesis1979.pdf

Monroe, C., & Kim, J. (2013, March). Scaling the Ion Trap Quantum Processor. *Science*, *339*(6124), 1164–1169. doi:10.1126cience.1231298 PMID:23471398

Muñoz, M., Moh, M., & Moh, T.-S. (2014). Improving Smart Grid Security using Merkle Trees. *IEEE Conference on Communications and Network Security*, 522-523. 10.1109/CNS.2014.6997535

Muñoz, M., Moh, M., & Moh, T.-S. (2014). Improving Smart Grid Authentication using Merkle Trees. *Proc. IEEE International Conference on Parallel and Distributed Systems*.

NIST. (2016). *Framework 3.0 a Beginner's guide*. Retrieved from https://www.nist.gov/el/smartgrid/framework-30-beginners-guide

NIST. (2019). *Smart Grid Advisory Committee 2019 Report.* Retrieved from https://protect-us.mimecast.com/s/n8sWC0RXxZu2wmlXFwUuGr?domain=nist.gov

NIST 7628. (2010). *Guidelines for Smart Grid Cyber Security*. Retrieved from https://www.nist.gov/smartgrid/upload/nistir-7628_total.pdf

NIST 7628 Revision 1. (2014). *Guidelines for Smart Grid Cyber Security*. Retrieved from https://nvlpubs.nist.gov/nistpubs/ir/2014/NIST.IR.7628r1.pdf

NIST IR 8413. (2022). *Status Report on the Third Round of the NIST Post-Quantum Cryptography Standardization Process*. Retrieved from https://nvlpubs.nist.gov/nistpubs/ir/2022/NIST.IR.8413.pdf

Palmer, C. (2021). Quantum Computing Quickly Scores Second Claim of Supremacy. *Engineering*, *7*(9), 1199–1200. doi:10.1016/j.eng.2021.07.006

Raju, R., & Moh, M. (2019). Using Machine Learning for Protecting the Security and Privacy of Internet-of-Things (IoT) Systems. In Fog and Edge Computing: Principles and Paradigms. Wiley.

Rieffel, E., & Polak, W. (2011). *Quantum Computing, A Gentle Introduction*. The MIT Press.

Rosen, K. (1995). *Discrete Mathematics And Its Applications* (3rd ed.). McGraw-Hill, Inc.

Sahagun, L. (2019, June 14). One in 4 Californians live in a 'high risk' wildfire area. Is the state ready for another fire season? *LA Times*.

Santhanam, L., Xie, B., & Agrawal, D. (2008). Secure and Efficient Authentication in Wireless Mesh Networks using Merkle Trees. *33rd IEEE Conference on Local Computer Networks*. 10.1109/LCN.2008.4664310

Schneier, B. (1996). *Applied Cryptography* (2nd ed.). Wiley & Sons Inc.

Schneier, B. (2018). *Click here to kill everybody: security and survival in a hyper-connected world* (1st ed.). W.W. Norton & Company.

Sectoral e-Business Watch. (2009). *Case study: Smart grid journey at Austin Energy, Texas, USA*. In ICT and e-business impact in the energy supply industry, Bonn, Germany.

Shor, P. (1997, October). Polynomial-Time Algorithms for Prime Factorization and Discrete Logarithms on a Quantum Computer. *SIAM Journal on Computing*, *26*(5), 1484–1509. doi:10.1137/S0097539795293172

Siddiqui, M. S., & Huong, C. S. (2007). Security Issues in Wireless Mesh Networks. *International Conference on Multimedia and Ubiquitous Engineering (MUE)*, 717-722.

Stajic, J. (2013, March). The Future of Quantum Information Processing. *Science*, 1163.

Stallings, W. (1999). *Cryptography and Network Security* (2nd ed.). Prentice Hall.

Stamp, M. (2011). *Information Security Principles and Practices* (2nd ed.). Wiley & Sons Inc.

Su, G., & Moh, M. (2018). Improving Energy Efficiency and Scalability for IoT Communications in 5G Networks. *Proc. of the 12th ACM International Conference on Ubiquitous Information Management and Communication (IMCOM)*.

Tanenbaum, A. (1990). *Structured Computer Organization* (3rd ed.). Prentice Hall.

The Wall Street Journal. (2016). *China's Latest Leap Forward Isn't Just Great—It's Quantum. Beijing launches the world's first quantum-communications satellite into orbit*. Retrieved 8/17/2016 from: https://www.wsj.com/articles/chinas-latest-leap-forward-isnt-just-greatits-quantum-1471269555

Tohidi, H., & Vakili, V. T. (2018). Lightweight authentication scheme for smart grid using Merkle hash tree and lossless compression hybrid method. *IET Communications*, *12*(19). Advance online publication. doi:10.1049/iet-com.2018.5698

Tsai, C., & Moh, M. (2017). Load Balancing in 5G Cloud Radio Access Networks Supporting IoT Communications for Smart Communities. *Proc. of 2017 IEEE International Symposium on Signal Processing and Information Technology (ISSPIT).*

U.S.-Canada Power System Outage Task Force. (2004). *Final Report on the August 14, 2003 Blackout in the United States and Canada: Causes and Recommendations.* Retrieved from: http://energy.gov/sites/prod/files/oeprod/DocumentsandMedia/BlackoutFinal-Web.pdf

Wang, X., & Yi, P. (2011, December). Security Framework for Wireless Communications in Smart Distribution Grid. *IEEE Transactions on Smart Grid, 2*(4), 809–818.

Wong, R., Moh, T.-S., & Moh, M. (2012). Efficient Semi-Supervised Learning BitTorrent Traffic Detection: An Extended Summary. In *Proc. of 13th Int. Conf on Distributed Computing and Networking – ICDCN 2012.* Springer.

World Bank. (2019). *Belt and Road Initiative.* Retrieved from https://protect-us.mimecast.com/s/K-qTCgJQ3oTlZGn1SonuSv?domain=worldbank.org

Xu & Wang (2013). Wireless Mesh Network in Smart Grid: Modeling and Analysis for Time Critical Communications. *IEEE Transactions on Wireless Communications, 12*(7), 3360 – 3371.

Yan, L., Chang, Y., & Zhang, S. (2017). A lightweight authentication and key agreement scheme for smart grid. *International Journal of Distributed Sensor Networks, 13*(2). Advance online publication. doi:10.1177/1550147717694173

Yan, Y., Qian, Y., Sharif, H., & Tipper, D. (2012, January). A Survey on Cyber Security for Smart Grid Communications. *Communication Surveys and Tutorials, IEEE, 14*(4), 998–1010. doi:10.1109/SURV.2012.010912.00035

Yang, L., & Moh, M. (2011). Dual Trust Secure Protocol for Cluster-Based Wireless Sensor Networks. *Proc. IEEE 45th Asilomar Conference on Signals, Systems and Computers*, 1645-1649. doi: 10.1109/ACSSC.2011.6190298

Zhang, Y., Sun, W., Wang, L., Wang, H., Green, R. II, & Alam, M. (2011). A multi-level communication architecture of smart grid based on congestion aware wireless mesh network. *43rd North American Power Symposium (NAPS).*

Zhu, Q., Cao, S., Chen, F., Chen, M. C., Chen, X., Chung, T. H., ... Pan, J. W. (2022). Quantum computational advantage via 60-qubit 24-cycle random circuit sampling. *Science Bulletin, 67*(3), 240–245.

ZigBee Alliance. (2008). *ZigBee Specifications 053474r17.* Retrieved from https://www.zigbee.org/

KEY TERMS AND DEFINITIONS

Factor: To decompose an integer into a product of primes.

National Institute of Standards and Technology (NIST): A measurement standards laboratory and part of the U.S. Department of Commerce.

One-Way Hash Function: A function that takes a variable length input and converts it to a fixed length output.

Public-Key Encryption: Type of encryption where encrypting and decrypting are done with different keys.

Quantum Computing: A computing system that makes use of quantum mechanics to perform operations.

Ralph Merkle: Computer scientist and pioneer in the field of cryptography.

Tree: A connected acyclic graph.

Wireless Mesh Network (WMN): A wireless network topology where all nodes are peers that relay data for the network.

Chapter 21
A Close Glimpse on the Security Challenges in the Smart Era

Somya Goyal
Manipal University Jaipur, India

Ayush Gupta
Manipal University Jaipur, India

Shirisha Bansal
Manipal University Jaipur, India

Jyotir Moy Chatterjee
https://orcid.org/0000-0003-2527-916X
Lord Buddha Education Foundation, Nepal

ABSTRACT

Today the world is facing many cyber-crimes irrespective of the geographical boundaries, and privacy is being compromised all across the globe. According to some assessments, the extent and frequency of data breaches are increasing alarmingly, prompting organizations throughout the world to take action to address what appears to be a worsening situation. In today's world we cannot live without technology and cyber security is vital for keeping our personal information safe. This chapter would improve the awareness about technical, privacy, and security infringements and help in protecting data by prioritizing the most assailed sectors. It will help the key audience to learn about data leaks and other ways our privacy and security gets compromised due various challenges, diverse up-to-date prevention and detection policies, fresh challenges, favourable answers, and exciting opportunities.

INTRODUCTION

Human life without technology is like birds without feathers. We are surrounded by technology at all times and use it to solve a variety of difficulties. It is the result of added knowledge and its use in all processes, skills, techniques, and methods used in manufacturing products and technical research (Sha-

DOI: 10.4018/978-1-6684-5250-9.ch021

pira et al., 2013). The advancement in the technological lives raises the need of more secure information systems to avoid the leak of information. As now-a-days, the real power lies in the information only. The internet is used by approximately 4.9 billion people across the world as of 2022.

The epidemic of the Corona virus has also demonstrated the relevance of technology in our daily lives. We can utilise technology to remain in touch, work, communicate, and, well, survive. When grocery shops and marketplaces were closed, technology aided us in meeting our food needs. Those who have managed to keep their jobs amid the epidemic have done so because to technological advancements.

Technology has progressed steadily from the stone era to roughly 100 years ago, and it has now developed and updated on a massive and widespread scale in a very short period of time. AI is a ground-breaking technology that has been growing rapidly and has the potential to change the world (Sinha et al., 2022; Lodha et al., 2022; Mohammad et al., 2022). Nobody can argue that technology has become so vital in our lives that it's almost impossible to picture life without it (Goyal, 2022; Panwar et al., 2022.; Kumar et al., 2022; Sobhani et al., 2022). Almost every industry has been impacted by technology and it is used in almost everything be it transactions, creating job profiles, education, business, healthcare, news, awareness, communication and even security purposes such as spy-cams, doorbells, etc. In today's world, life without technology is like living alone on an isolated island (Goyal, 2022.a; Goyal, 2022.b; Goyal, 2022.c). Artificial Intelligence (AI), Machine Learning (ML) and IOT are inseparable parts of our lives.

Every coin has two sides, so with the conveniences and boons of technology also come the harms and threats to individuals and organisations. With the data being online unwanted and mischievous people can access it through some loopholes and use it for fraudulent and malicious acts. As we are aware technology today is evolving at a very rapid pace and so are the loopholes in it. It is impossible to find all the vulnerabilities in the system beforehand. It is a huge challenge for us to make the systems secure as we need to catch all the loopholes to make sure the system is secure but if the hacker catches hold of even one vulnerability it can immensely damage and compromise a system and information.

The IT security systems are not too capable of protecting users and organisations from the unauthorised access of information by hackers. People can be easily hacked exposing them and their personal data high-risk attack subjects (Shu & Yao, 2012) Often it is too simple to trick people into clicking on harmful links and or downloading and installing malicious apps. and or backdoor's resulting in infecting their corporate networks and electronic devices. In terms of local cyberattacks, worldwide India has ranked at 11th and has already had 2,299,682 occurrences in the first quarter of 2020.

MALWARES

It is a software that is designed with the purpose of disrupting, damaging, stealing or performing nearly any function that could be desired by an attacker. Malwares are often delivered over networks. There are various types of malwares available today and hence, there are numerous ways to infect and disrupt devices. They damage the security and privacy of users and organisations with the help of technical loopholes and vulnerabilities and human greed and fear.

The following are some common malwares:

1. **Trojan Horse:** Trojan as the name suggests is inspired by the ancient Greek story of the misleading and deceptive Trojan horse that led to the fall of Troy. This virus is installed in the system like a legitimate looking program deceiving users of its true intentions (Mathew et al. 2010). Once

Figure 1. Top Cyber security Challenges

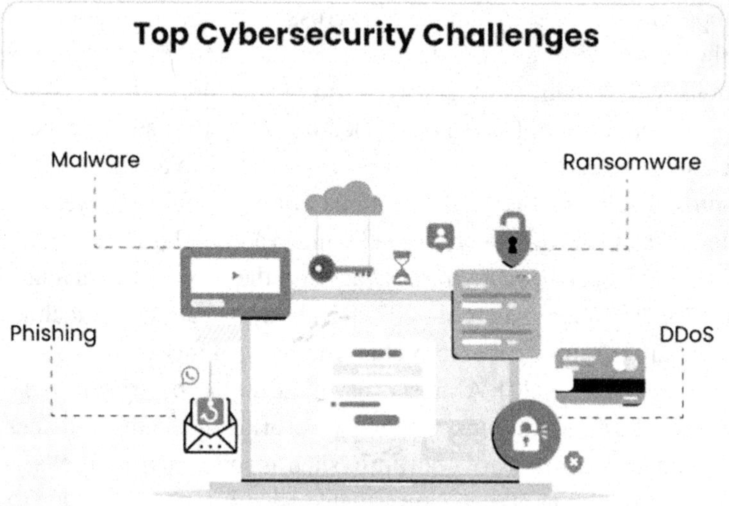

installed this can be used for all sorts of activities like spying on the user to copying, deleting or modifying data, disrupting the performance of the device, etc.

2. **Virus**: A virus is downloaded with non-suspicious looking files and can replicate themselves to other files and transfer to different devices with them. Virus needs the help of an active host to be triggered and replicate. A virus can also be used to harm the gadget by slowing its speed, altering data, stealing information, spoofing, using keyloggers, etc.
3. **Worms:** Like computer viruses worms also get downloaded as attachments and spam emails. Once installed, they are capable of self-replication and they spread without the help of a host once installed through the system. A worm can also cause the same harms as that of a computer virus, but its lack of requirement for an active host once installed makes it all the more dangerous.

Despite the fact that the worm was introduced on July 13, 2001, the biggest number of affected machines was discovered on July 19, 2001. The total number of infected hosts reached 359,000 on this day. In the summer of 2001, a worm known as CodeRed caused potentially billions of dollars in damage.

4. **Botnets:** When an attacker remotely takes control of a network of computers and other internet connected devices infected with the bot malware without the knowledge of the owner (Krebs, 2014). These devices are then infected and controlled with a common malware type. This network of bots is used to send spam and start DDoS attack or may also be rented out to other cyber-criminals.
5. **Ransomware:** It is a type of attack which prevents users from accessing either the entire system or a particular file or application till a ransom amount is paid to the attacker.
6. **Adware:** Adware is the display of advertisements on the system in the form of pop-ups when a certain program or file is running. Such type of malwares usually come with "free" versions of software and applications.

7. **Rootkit:** It is an ill-natured program which is used to take control of the victim's device without the knowledge of the user. Rootkits are extremely hard to spot and therefore they are very hard to remove. These can enter a system when users open spam emails and pop-ups or unwittingly download malicious software.
8. **Spyware:** It is an ill-natured software which tends to get installed covertly on your device and then violate your privacy and send stolen data and other sensitive information to a third party. This third party could be advertising firms, an opponent company, any other external user, etc. Spywares use ways like keylogging and spoofing to spy on the user.

SPYWARES

Spyware is a word used to describe a type of software that is intended to rip-off personal or organisational data. This task is carried out by performing a sequence of operations without the required user privileges, sometimes even in secret. Without your knowledge, a sophisticated spyware tool designed by experienced cyber warfare professionals may be hiding within your Android. It collects login credentials, snoops on sensitive data and monitors internet activity after it is installed. Spyware's main goal is to steal passwords, credit card data and bank account numbers.

The most common types of spywares include monitoring, system monitors, adware, including online tracking, and Trojans; other recognised varieties consist of keyloggers, web beacons, rootkits, and digital rights management capabilities that "phone home".

The following are some frequent methods for your device to become infected with spyware:

- Accepting a prompt or pop-up message without first reading it.
- Obtaining software from an untrustworthy source.
- Email attachments from unknown senders should be opened with caution.
- Pirating material such as movies, music, and video games is illegal.
- Clicking on a malicious link

Two of the most recent and dangerous spywares are the Pegasus and Chrysaor spywares. We have discussed below in detail what makes them so different and threatening from the other common spywares.

While the primary Pegasus form is meant to infect iPhones, a second variant, called Chrysaor by Google, is targeted to infiltrate Android smartphones. Both spywares employ the same vectors and provide the same outcomes, but the initial installation differs. Once the malicious website is opened on the iPhone, a chain of zero-day vulnerabilities is supplied to the phone.

iPhones are notorious for their tight security, and this hack, according to experts, was the first of its sort. The chain was called 'Trident' since it targeted three vulnerabilities in 2016. Trident, if successful, breaches the iPhone's security by jail breaking it and installing Pegasus without the user's consent or knowledge. Apple eventually issued a security patch to address the three particular flaws, but there may be more.

PEGASUS: A SPYWARE

An Israeli cyber-security outfit NSO group was responsible for the development of Pegasus. Pegasus is a spyware that can be covertly installed on almost all devices including phones operating on most Android and iOS versions up to 14.6. This software can collect valuable data, track calls, read messages, trace locations, plant info., gain access to the microphone and camera, etc.

In 2011, NSO Group released the first version of Pegasus spyware. It provides "approved governments with technology that aids in the fight against terrorism and crime" according to the firm. NSO Group has made contract terms public requiring it's clients to use this software solely for nation-wide safety and illicit investigations, and it claims to have the industry's best human rights policy.

Pegasus has been referred to as "the most sophisticated smartphone attack ever". What is it that makes the Pegasus Spyware so contagious that it has infected not only a large number of people in a single nation, but also a large number of people in other countries?

For the device to be infected through malwares there must be some contact between the user and the malicious programme. However, this isn't the case with Pegasus. Pegasus employs a series of 'network injections,' allowing the attacker to install the spyware and infect the device without requiring the target's interaction. The spyware maybe uses a zero-click exploit, meaning the installation needs no human interaction and can even be installed in a device through a missed call.

CHRYSAOR (PEGASUS FOR ANDROID):

Chrysaor is a fully built Android spy tool that allows attackers to track their targets' every move. Chrysaor has put in place sophisticated components to listen in on conversations, take screenshots, monitor the device's surroundings, steal important data, and read SMS messages (Mathew et al. 2010). This virus offers a once-in-a-lifetime opportunity to learn about the whole range of behaviours that may transform your phone into an ideal spying instrument.

NSO Group Technologies, which specialises in the production and selling of software and infrastructure for targeted assaults, is thought to have generated Chrysaor malware. Chrysaor is thought to be linked to the Pegasus malware, which was initially discovered on iOS and investigated by Citizen Lab and Lookout.

Exploitation And Infection

According to Google, the attackers infect individuals with the virus and provide it the required rights using intricate social engineering techniques. However, such a sophisticated attack is likely to have used zero-day weaknesses that have yet to be discovered. Chrysaor attempts to root a device once it has been installed in order to get complete control over it. The virus employed an ordinary exploit kit named "Frameproof" in the samples found so far, which is also used by low-level malware in the wild. This is a big change from the iOS version of the virus, which operated via specific zero-day exploits. This is another example of the close link between mobile malware generated by threat actors from various backgrounds. The most sophisticated attacks need to watched out by individuals and organisations.

How Can Chrysaor Record Live Audio Without the User Being Aware?

One of the most intriguing aspects of Chrysaor's functioning is the live audio recording, which necessitates the attackers overcoming significant obstacles. The inquiry was advanced by Check Point researchers, who discovered an extra layer of the malware's audio recording activity. let's understand how Chrysaor operates, employing several strategies to harvest user data, from Mountain View. SMS, phone logs, internet history, calendar, emails, or messages from Twitter, Facebook, WhatsApp, Skype, or Viber, among other things, can all be collected by the infection. Chrysaor also takes screenshots of the device and does 'keylogging,' which records what is typed on that terminal. Other virus spying tactics include Roomtap, which uses the phone's microphone to listen in on conversations. When the malware's audio surveillance preconditions are satisfied, it tells its command-and-control server, which then makes a call to the device. After that, the virus intercepts the call and verifies that the incoming number meets the required settings. If true, the call is hidden behind an overlay window, and it is then answered via the headset or the iTelephony API. The discourse is then muted, and Chrysaor disables the media. It then mutes the chat and disables the media button, ensuring that the user is ignorant of the James Bond operation taking place under the surface.

The virus's incredible ingenuity and attention to detail illustrate the complexities and problems that mobile malware poses to defenders. The virus's creators went to great lengths to keep the malware concealed from the user's view and to avoid drawing attention to it, all while abusing his device to the fullest extent possible. We have little doubt that, as with past malware, these intricate approaches will be duplicated by common malware in the wild. This is another example of why consumers and companies should take mobile threats seriously and utilise advanced security methods to identify and prevent zero-day vulnerabilities and top-tier malware.

HOW TO PREVENT THESE ADVANCED PERSISTENT THREAT (APT) ATTACKS

While eradicating a Pegasus or Chrysaor infection without data loss is impossible, a user can take steps to prevent or at least mitigate the effects of a malware or spyware attack. Here's a rundown:

- If you possess an iPhone, don't try to circumvent limitations by jail breaking it yourself.
- Install software updates and patches on a regular basis.
- Don't open unknown attachments, download strange files, click on suspicious links provided from an unfamiliar source.
- Back up your files to a physical storage device on a regular basis.
- Approve permission requests for apps cautiously.
- When not in use, turn off Wi-Fi, Bluetooth, and location services.
- In your device's settings, turn off push SMS messaging.
- Encrypt any personal information on your phone.

If your phone has been compromised, Citizen Lab recommends delinking your cloud accounts, replacing your device, changing all of your passwords, and improving your internet security on the new device.

WHAT ARE DATA BREACHES AND WHY ARE THEY HARMFUL?

Data breach is the extraction of sensitive information such as business secrets, employee and customer information, etc. without the knowledge or authorization of the owner Krebs, B. (2014). The breach can affect any organisation irrespective of its size and may occur as a cyber-attacks by a stranger, a former company employee or even unintentional loss of data, etc.

Why Do Data Breaches Occur?

For criminals, cybercrime is a profitable and ever-expanding business today. Hackers are on the lookout for info. they may exploit to extort money, compromise people profiles, or data to sell on the black market. These attacks can occur for a variety of causes such as mishaps, human error, and malicious intent, but targeted assaults usually take place for:

1. **Insider Leaks:** This can be caused by former employees and disgruntled workers who still have access to company systems, crucial info. and business partner profiles. Monetary profits, vengeance or profitable data is generally their cause of motivation.
2. **Theft or loss:** Sensitive information is stored in laptops, mobile phones, drives, PCs and servers. An attacker might physically seize any of these devices, or staff could mistakenly lose them, resulting in a breach.
3. **Payment fraud:** Unauthorized and unlawful monetary transactions are called payment frauds.

Unintentional public exposure: Many data breaches are triggered through unintended disclosure of sensitive information rather than by an assault. Employees, for example, may access sensitive information and store it to a non-secure place, or IT workers may inadvertently expose a critical internal server to the Internet.

HOW THEY TAKE PLACE USUALLY

Case Studies

1. **Yahoo:** Almost 3 billion user accounts had been affected in August 2013 on Yahoo. Information like contact numbers, names, DoBs and passwords were disclosed as per Yahoo in this breach.

As per Verizon, yahoo's parent company, three billion user accounts were compromised leading to making it the biggest data breach in October 2017.

2. **Marriott Hotels:** The personal data of 500 million customers had been hacked from the luxury hotel chain, Marriott. The hotel had recognised the breach ongoing since 2014 resulting after the purchase of the Starwood hotel groups in 2016. Personal Information such as names, addresses and passport numbers were compromised.

The Marriott breach was the focus of a concerted endeavour by Chinese intelligence-gathering agents, according to the New York Times in December 2018.

3. **Friend Finder Network:** In October 2016 above 412 million user accounts listed across the FriendFinder Network umbrella were compromised. Personal data such as email iDs, IP addresses, and passwords were revealed. The Network used the weak SHA-1 algorithm or plaintext to store user passwords, implying 99 percent of all passwords were hackable.
4. **MySpace:** The Russian hacker who was also alleged to be the brain behind the attacks on other social websites like Tumblr and LinkedIn was accountable for one of the all time biggest data breach. MySpace was brought by Time Inc. in February 2016 and just 3 months later the old users were notified that their info could be made available for sale online. The information (usernames and passwords) even though it was as old as to June 2013 it could be re-used to gain hold of info. on additional websites. The data breach affected 360 million people.
5. **Twitter:** Twitter had settled an argument over the accusation that "serious lapses" in the security of data had lead to access to personal user information by hackers on a couple of occasions with the U.S. Federal Trade Commission in 2010.

   In May 2018, over 300 million users were urged to modify their passwords upon finding a glitch that had caused some passwords to be stored in readable text on its internal system. Even though no such evidence of a data breach had been found during the internal investigation, it was suggested by the company to 330 million users to change their passwords and enable the two-factor authentication facility as an extra layer of security.
6. **Deep Root Analytics:** In 2017, Deep Root Analytics disclosed that its data was stored in documents that can be accessed publicly, it is a marketing firm that collects data for political advertisements. This leak included not only names, contact numbers, addresses, DoBs, but also some research on sentimental analysis targeted at political issues like weapon ownership and abortions of approximately 198 million American citizens which is roughly around 61% of the United States population and the data size was 1.1 TB.

There were lawsuits filed against the company as it left United States citizens loose to identify theft stating it failed to "safe and protect the public's privately identifiable data".

7. **MyFitnessPal:** In 2018, March, Under Armour revealed a hundred and fifty million consumers of one of its apps "MyFitnessPal" which included details like usernames and email addresses outed. Luckily the details like social security numbers and payment details were saved in this data breach.

In 2016, before Friend Finder Network's hack, it was found out the same weak SHA-1 algorithm was being used by the company.

8. **eBay:** Cyber-attackers managed to circumvent eBay security and acquired the data of 145 million users in the year 2014. Hackers managed to access the credentials of three of eBay's employees and accessed their database, and got the passwords and usernames of millions of users.

Initially, eBay thought no data was breached, but eventually, they accepted it when they realised the extent of the breach was clear and made a public announcement.

9. **Heartland Payment Systems:** It was revealed by Heartland Payment Systems that the debit and credit card transactions passing through their systems had been compromised affecting more than a hundred and thirty million users. Even though no cardholder information or merchant data was breached, counterfeit cards could be manufactured using the jeopardised data as the stolen data comprised the digital info. encoded onto the magnetic strips built onto the back of the debit and credit cards.

After the conviction of Albert Gonzalez, who was found guilty and sentenced for twenty years for his illicit acts towards Heartland data breach and attacks on TJX, noble, office max, etc. It was revealed 130 million credit numbers were pilfered.

10. **LinkedIn:** In 2012, the professional social network LinkedIn was hacked, affecting roughly 117 million users. Initially, the firm estimated that approximately six and a half million credentials had been extracted, But in the mid of 2016 it was announced that over a hundred million accounts had been compromised. Hackers were selling the stolen information on the dark web.

The company then encouraged its consumers to modify their passwords and use the two-factor authentication process for added safety.

Observations and How to Stop these Data Breaches

We've observed over 2000 verified examples of data breaches through internet reports, and we'd want to share some of our major takeaways with businesses to assist them safeguard their point of sale, networks, and more. Data breaches can happen to any business, not just companies that are rich.

We discovered that outsiders were responsible for 73% of the assaults. Members of organised criminal groups perpetrated half of the breaches in the report, while nation-state or state-affiliated actors perpetrated 12%. Even scarier, 28% of the attacks were carried out by insiders, or those who have lawful access to your system, such as employees or contractors (Harris et al., 2014).

Phishing campaigns are essentially futile as only 4% people tend to click on good news like that. 4% is still a huge number and can add up to become a serious concern.

Ransom ware is simple to set up and use, and it may be incredibly successful for criminals since they don't have to take your data; all they have to do is prevent you from using it. According to the research, ransom ware first appeared as a problem for organisations to be concerned about in 2013. Ransom ware was the most common type of malware in the 2018 study, appearing in 39 per-cent of cases where malware was discovered.

It boils down to two things, "defence and response". We all know that no defence is 100% effective. You should design defences that are powerful enough to push hackers in the direction of an easier target and if an enemy manages to get through, you must be ready to react fast and efficiently.

It's all about being proactive and planning ahead of time; develop and update a thorough security programme and incident response plan on a regular basis (Shu et al., 2017). Following are some ways to try and keep yourself safe from a breach:

- **Segment your network:** Install firewalls and isolate your network's data. Then, only give access to personnel who have a genuine need for it. The fewer people who have access to the information, the better.
- **Comply with PCI requirements:** Merchants who accept credit card payments must adhere to the Payment Card Industry Data Security Standards. Not only may businesses face fines, but they could also face a data breach if PCI compliance isn't completed.
- **Keep up with the latest updates:** Vulnerabilities that have been identified may be fixed simply by ensuring that your updates are installed on a regular basis.
- **Data should not be kept:** Business can gather a lot of data, which can clog up systems year after year and may not be required to maintain collecting. Businesses can potentially lose track of data, putting them at danger of allowing criminal hackers access to the database. Data retention should be limited and sensitive authentication data should be removed.
- **Protect data with tokens:** Tokenization substitutes the credit card's actual data with a token that, even if stolen, is worthless to hackers. Customer information is kept safe if a POS system never retained the original data in the first place.
- **Secure payment card applications**: Ensure that any apps fulfil high security criteria, as flaws allow hackers to get access to critical data and compromise systems and access sensitive data.
- **Archive important things:** Create a second server to store information that you still need but doesn't need to be online. It's possible that just one or two persons will require access to this server. At the same time, you'll be securing your equipment and optimising your network.
- **Put someone in charge:** While every employee should be on the lookout for anything that doesn't seem quite right, having one person in charge of this all of the time may be critical for firms. This individual can ensure that your data security plan is constantly up to date.

HOW DO THESE ATTACKS OCCUR?

It is a cyber-attack when an organisation or independent individual(s) purposefully attempts at stealing, altering, exposing, destructing or disabling the info. system of any other individual or organisation. Many recent assaults have shown unwanted data annihilation as their aim as side from the already existing economic gains as the incentive for these attacks.

Frequent Types of Cyber-Attacks:

- **Malware:**
  - Malware is a comprehensive term that surrounds a variety of threats including viruses, spyware and worms. They can exploit the weakness to break into a network when unsafe links or attachments which may be used to install harmful software are opened by a user.
  - Such malicious files when running inside a system, they can:
    § Refuse access to the essential components of the network system.
    § Disrupt the system, if not completely disable it.
    § Retrieve data from the hard disc to obtain info.
  - The most common types of malware attacks are Trojans, worms, Ransomware, Spyware and Viruses.

- **Phishing:**
  - Phishing attacks are the sending of legitimate looking bogus emails to unaware individuals. Such emails are quite frequently sent and carry links to nasty files or scripts which permit evil attackers to obtain entry to gadgets of people so as to control them or collect and extract important info. such as user data, install malicious scripts or files, gather financial information, and more.
  - Phishing assaults come in a variety of forms, including whaling, spear phishing and pharming (KNOW 2012).
- **DoS (Denial-of-Service) Attack:**
  - A DoS attack seeks to put an halt on a network or a system, preventing it from being accessed by the intended and the legitimate users. In a DoS attack it makes the target system or device to crash by swarming it with continuous and non-stop rapid online requests causing an overload and keeping the network busy or by transmitting information which can cause the system to crash down.
- **Password Attack:**
  - A password attack is any of the tactics used to gain unauthorised access to password-secured accounts. Such attacks are often aided and sped up with the help of good password guessing and cracking software applications.
- **MitM (Man-in-the-Middle) Attack:**
  - An MitM attack is a sort of cyber-attack in which an attacker listens in on the discussions of two targets. An attacker could try to "listen in" on a conversation between two systems, two people, or a human and a machine.
- **XXS (Cross-site Scripting) Attack:**
  - XXS is a security threat most commonly obtained in sites and applications which accept inputs from users. The insertion of unwelcome and spiteful scripts inside the code for a reliable application or website by an attacker is known as Cross-Site scripting. Such an attack is generally begun supplying the users with tempting and harmful link which they may find appealing to click on.
- **SQL Injections:**
  - In a SQL injection attack, a programme interprets data provided by a cyber criminal as a command and responds with sensitive information. An SQL injection may cause a variety of problems, putting your company's security at risk.

Other Types of Cyber-Attacks

- **Salami Attack:** A salami assault is a collection of minor strikes that combine to form a larger attack. Slicing fractions of cents from each transaction, for example, would not show up in calculations due to rounding up figures, but after billions of transactions, you may take a significant amount. Hackers frequently attempt to grab little "slices" from a variety of bank accounts and since these "slices" are very small amounts, it is extremely difficult for users to notice when this attack takes place and even when they notice a miscalculation of these amounts, the amounts are small enough for most users to ignore them rather than bother to raise a complaint.
- **Replay Attack:** When a cybercriminal eavesdrops on a secure network connection, intercepts it, and then fraudulently delays or resends it to misdirect the receiver into doing what the hacker

wants, this is known as a replay attack. For example when an attacker replays a money withdrawal request and takes another payment for the same item from the middle.

- **Dictionary Attack:** A dictionary attack is a way of getting into a password-protected computer, network, or other IT resource by inputting every word in a dictionary as a password in a methodical manner. A dictionary attack may also be used to try to figure out what key is needed to decode a communication or document that has been encrypted. It is used to run a dictionary (list) of all possible or common passwords through a system. If a password matches the attacker gains access to that system or file. This guessing of passwords would normally take a lot of time if done manually but with the help of the tools available in the market these days this attack can be carried out within minutes.
- **Brute Force Attack:** Brute force attack is like the dictionary attack and used to try and guess the password to hack its way into a user system or file. A brute force attack is a method of cracking passwords, login credentials, and encryption keys that relies on trial and error. It's a simple but effective method for getting illegal access to individual accounts as well as systems and networks of businesses. The difference between a dictionary attack and a brute force attack is that in a brute force assault, a huge number of possible key permutations are examined, but in a dictionary attack, just the words with the best chances of success are checked, which takes less time.
- **Bit-Flipping Attack:** A bit-flipping attack is a cryptographic cypher attack in which the attacker may modify the cipher-text in such a manner that the plaintext changes predictably, despite the attacker's inability to acquire the plaintext itself. For example let's say Harvey is sending a message to Claire asking for a hundred dollars, then the attacker Gale cannot read the cipher text message but flips some bits in them such that the message is now Harvey asking for $900 dollars instead which is sent to Claire. When the money is sent Gale will intercept the amount of $800 dollars in the middle.
- **Frame Injection Attack:** This attack can come from any already open tab or window. In this attack a frame is injected by the hacker into the open webpage.

How I Can Protect My Personal Data in These Attacks:

It's critical to take actions to take measures to protect and prevent ourselves and our personal info. from undesirable acts in order to protect our identities. These steps can include the following:

- **Use strong and secure passwords:** It is vital to ensure the safety of our data that we create complicated and distinctive passwords.
- **Review your credit report on a regular basis** to ensure whether a theft has been carried out to issue a new account or credit card under your name. Once a year, you have the legal right to a free credit report from each of the three main credit reporting agencies.
- **Observe your bank and other monetary accounts:** Check your accounts for unusual activity on a day-to-day basis. Make sure to file a report as soon as you see anything fishy.
- **Secure your phone:** Give your phone a password if it does not already have one. Even though inputting a password whenever you use your phone can be a little troublesome, it does help prevent and safeguard a future mishap in case your device or account were to be stolen or lost. Consider how much information a thief may have access to if your phone isn't password protected.
- **Always provide back-up to your files** to make sure of their security.

- **Application of a good-quality safety software:** Make sure to install and utilise an up-to-date and trusted virus and malware protection software application.
- **Clean your hard drive:** If you are giving away an old gadget for recycling, kindly ensure that the hard disc is empty before throwing it away.
- **Use only secure URLs:** https:// is the start of a trustworthy website. It is extremely critical to ensure the alphabet "s" in the "https://" is present especially when entering any confidential or personal details. The "s" here stands for secure.
- **Use the credit card monitoring or an identity theft protection service:** Provided the current frequency of breaches of data, it is important to consider such security services.
- It might take months, if not years, to clean up the wreckage left by a stolen identity.
- **Do not over-share on social platforms**: Never publish anything containing personal info., and keep your profiles private by adjusting your settings. While you're at it, don't post any vacation photos on social media until you've returned home. That signals to everyone that your home may be vacant, making it an easy target for burglars.
- **Take action as quickly as you can:** If you find anything unusual, notify the banking association right away. Notify them if your personal information was taken as a result of a data breach.

WHY DO MOST CYBER-ATTACKS OCCUR

One in three Americans are affected by cyber-attacks, which happen every 39 seconds. Only 38% of global corporations claim to be equipped to deal with a sophisticated cyber-attack. Seven out of 10 associations said their overall security risk rose in 2017. 54% of businesses reported one or more successful attacks that affected data and IT infrastructure. No files were utilised in 77% of these attacks. Cyber-security breaches are becoming more prevalent globally, especially in India. It is evident that we need to start working in this subject immediately away given how serious the threats to our cyber security are.

We have observed that most companies don't understand the importance of security and find it too expensive unless attacked. These companies therefore use vulnerable and cheaper algorithms like SHA-1 in their companies until a loss of data occurs. People and Organisations need to take security more seriously and also invest in good security equipment (Feng et al., 2018).

For attackers, cybercrime is a lucrative business that is continually expanding. Hackers are always on the lookout for vulnerable and personally identifiable information for the sake of stealing funds, compromising of identities, or selling data on the dark web. These breaches can happen for a variety of causes but most aimed attacks generally happen by one of these four forms:

- **Drive-by downloads:** This attack usually takes advantage of an out-dated operating system or application with a security vulnerability. Upon accessing a pirated or hacked website there is a risk that you may unknowingly download a malware or a malicious virus which in turn will harm and compromise the system (Giffin et al., 2004)
- **Exploiting system vulnerabilities:** Out-dated software can allow malwares to enter into the machine and raid precious data and thus, create security breaches (Necula et al., 2002).
- **Weak Passwords:** Experts advise us to use complicated and unique passwords in place of simple and basic ones as weak passwords are unsafe and tend to be easily guessed by hackers.

- **Targeted malware attacks:** Phishing and spam emails are employed by attackers to dupe the users into giving passwords, downloading malware files, or visiting vulnerable websites (Tan et al., 2002). Malware commonly enters your computer through email. Any links or attachments in an email from an unknown sender should be avoided (Gorman, 2009). As a result, your computer may become infected with malware. Also, keep in mind that an email might be designed to appear to originate from a reliable source even if it does not (Zheng & Litvinov, 2006).
- **Lack of well skilled employees:** A recent CSIS survey of IT decision-makers found that 80% of businesses noted a lack of cybersecurity skills and that 71% of businesses reported actual, quantitative impact. According to CyberSeek, a National Initiative for Cybersecurity Education (NICE)-funded project, as of January 2019, the US experienced a shortfall of close to 314000 cybersecurity employees. For context, there are currently 716,000 cybersecurity specialists employed nationwide. Since then, the number of available cybersecurity roles has increased by more than 50%, according to data gathered from job advertisements. By 2022, there will likely be more than 1.8 million unfilled positions due to a global shortage of cybersecurity professionals (Crumpler & Lewis 2019).

Figure 2. Top 10 Data Breach

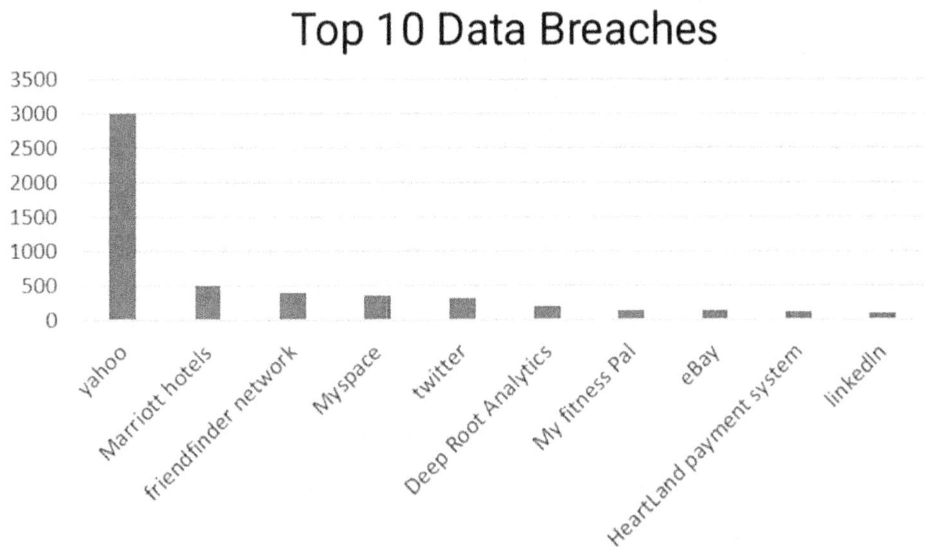

CONCLUSIONS

As we know technology is vital in today's world and we cannot make do without it. Technology is needed in almost every aspect of our day to day lives. But with technology and the data being online also come various threats to privacy and security. People with malicious intentions and skills take access of sensitive information for their profits and entertainments making people and organisations suffer enormous losses at times.

We have seen the most common kinds of attacks, how they are caused, what harms they can do, case studies for some of the most malicious data breaches and spyware attacks, how to try to prevent ourselves against them, why these attacks happen and how cybersecurity is flourishing day by day to provide necessary solutions. I believe we need to pay more attention to the security with the increasing dependency on ever-growing technology and the introduction of Virtual Reality, IOT and metaverse while taking precautions.

REFERENCES

Crumpler, W., & Lewis, J. A. (2019). The cybersecurity workforce gap. Washington, DC: Center for Strategic and International Studies (CSIS).

Feng, H. H., Giffin, J. T., Huang, Y., Jha, S., Lee, W., & Miller, B. P. (2004, May). Formalizing sensitivity in static analysis for intrusion detection. *IEEE Symposium on Security and Privacy, 2004 Proceedings*, 194–208.

Giffin, J. T., Jha, S., & Miller, B. P. (2004, February). Efficient Context-Sensitive Intrusion Detection. NDSS.

Gorman, S. (2009). Electricity grid in US penetrated by spies. *The Wall Street Journal, 8.*

Goyal, S. (2022c). Static code metrics-based deep learning architecture for software fault prediction. *Soft Computing*, 1–33. doi:10.100700500-022-07365-5

Goyal, S. (2022a). IoT-Based Smart Air Quality Control System: Prevention to COVID-19. In *IoT and Cloud Computing for Societal Good* (pp. 15–23). Springer.

Goyal, S. (2022b). Industry 4.0 in Healthcare IoT for Inventory and Supply Chain Management. *Cyber-Physical Systems: Foundations and Techniques*, 209-227.

Harris, E., Perlroth, N., & Popper, N. (2014). Neiman Marcus data breach worse than first said. *The New York Times, 23.*

KNOW. (2012). *W. Y. N. T. Global Trends in the Payment Card Industry*. Acquirers.

Krebs, B. (2014). Email attack on vendor set up breach at target. *Krebs on Security, 12.*

Kumar, A., Gupta, R., Sharma, N., & Goyal, S. (2022). Smart Quiz for Brain Stormers. In *Advances in Micro-Electronics, Embedded Systems and IoT* (pp. 399–406). Springer. doi:10.1007/978-981-16-8550-7_38

Lodha, C., Dhingra, K., Mondal, R., & Goyal, S. (2022). Smart Healthcare with Fitness Application. *Smart Intelligent Computer Applications*, *2*, 403–409.

Mathew, S., Petropoulos, M., Ngo, H. Q., & Upadhyaya, S. (2010, September). A data-centric approach to insider attack detection in database systems. In *International Workshop on Recent Advances in Intrusion Detection* (pp. 382-401). Springer. 10.1007/978-3-642-15512-3_20

Mohammed, K., Singh, H., Joshi, V., & Goyal, S. (2022). Smart Irrigation System for Agriculture 4.0. *Smart Intelligent Computer Applications*, *2*, 411–418.

Necula, G. C., McPeak, S., & Weimer, W. (2002, January). CCured: Type-safe retrofitting of legacy code. In *Proceedings of the 29th ACM SIGPLAN-SIGACT symposium on Principles of programming languages* (pp. 128-139). 10.1145/503272.503286

Panwar, A., Bafna, S., Raghav, A., & Goyal, S. (2022). Intelligent Traffic Management System Using Industry 4.0. In *Advances in Micro-Electronics, Embedded Systems and IoT* (pp. 357–364). Springer. doi:10.1007/978-981-16-8550-7_34

Shapira, Y., Shapira, B., & Shabtai, A. (2013). Content-based data leakage detection using extended fingerprinting. arXiv preprint arXiv:1302.2028

Shu, X., Tian, K., Ciambrone, A., & Yao, D. (2017). *Breaking the target: An analysis of target data breach and lessons learned.* arXiv preprint arXiv:1701.04940.

Shu, X., & Yao, D. D. (2012, September). Data leak detection as a service. In *International Conference on Security and Privacy in Communication Systems* (pp. 222-240). Springer.

Sinha, M., Chaurasiya, R., Pandey, A., Singh, Y., & Goyal, S. (2022). Securing Smart Homes Using Face Recognition. In *Advances in Micro-Electronics, Embedded Systems and IoT* (pp. 391–398). Springer. doi:10.1007/978-981-16-8550-7_37

Sobhani, S., Shirsale, S. B., Saxena, S., Paharia, V., & Goyal, S. (2022). Emergency Bot in Healthcare Using Industry 4.0. In *Advances in Micro-Electronics, Embedded Systems and IoT* (pp. 347–355). Springer. doi:10.1007/978-981-16-8550-7_33

Tan, K., Killourhy, K. S., & Maxion, R. A. (2002, October). Undermining an anomaly-based intrusion detection system using common exploits. In *International Workshop on Recent Advances in Intrusion Detection* (pp. 54-73). Springer. 10.1007/3-540-36084-0_4

Zheng, T., & Litvinov, E. (2006). Ex post pricing in the co-optimized energy and reserve market. *IEEE Transactions on Power Systems*, *21*(4), 1528–1538. doi:10.1109/TPWRS.2006.882457

Compilation of References

Jiang, T., Wang, Z., & Liu, G. (2016). Qos-Aware Throughput Maximization In Wireless Powered Underground Sensor Networks. *IEEE Transactions on Communications, 64*(11), 4776–4789. doi:10.1109/TCOMM.2016.2602863

Yue, Li, Fan, & Qin. (2016). Optimization-Based Artificial Bee Colony Algorithm for Data Collection in Large-Scale Mobile Wireless Sensor Networks. *Journal of Sensors,* 1-12.

Ge, Y., Cao, B., Feng, G., Tan, H. P., Kim, C. W., & Li, Y. (2013). An Experimental Study for Inter-User Interference Mitigation in Wireless Body Sensor Networks. *IEEE Sensors Journal, 13*(10), 3585–3595. doi:10.1109/JSEN.2013.2267053

Sun, Z., Liu, G., & Jiang, T. (2018). Joint Time and Energy Allocation for QoS-Aware Throughput Maximization in MIMO-Based Wireless Powered Underground Sensor Networks. *IEEE Transactions on Communications, 67*(2), 1400–1412.

Zuhairy, R., & Al Zamil, M. (2018). Energy-efficient load balancing in wireless sensor network: An application of multinomial regression analysis. *International Journal of Distributed Sensor Networks, 14*(3), 1-13.

Nair, M. M., Tyagi, A. K., & Sreenath, N. (2021). The Future with Industry 4.0 at the Core of Society 5.0: Open Issues, Future Opportunities and Challenges. *2021 International Conference on Computer Communication and Informatics (ICCCI)*, 1-7. 10.1109/ICCCI50826.2021.9402498

Madhav, A. V. S., & Tyagi, A. K. (2022). The World with Future Technologies (Post-COVID-19): Open Issues, Challenges, and the Road Ahead. In A. K. Tyagi, A. Abraham, & A. Kaklauskas (Eds.), Intelligent Interactive Multimedia Systems for e-Healthcare Applications. Springer. https://doi.org/10.1007/978-981-16-6542-4_22.

Mishra, S., & Tyagi, A. K. (2022). The Role of Machine Learning Techniques in Internet of Things-Based Cloud Applications. In S. Pal, D. De, & R. Buyya (Eds.), Artificial Intelligence-based Internet of Things Systems. Internet of Things (Technology, Communications and Computing). Springer. https://doi.org/10.1007/978-3-030-87059-1_4.

Nair, M. M., & Tyagi, A. K. (2021). Privacy: History, Statistics, Policy, Laws, Preservation and Threat Analysis. Journal of Information Assurance & Security, 16(1), 24-34.

Tyagi, A. K., Nair, M. M., Niladhuri, S., & Abraham, A. (2020). Security, Privacy Research issues in Various Computing Platforms: A Survey and the Road Ahead. Journal of Information Assurance & Security, 15(1), 1-16.

Mahajan, Pandey, & Hegde. (2018). Joint Localization And Data Gathering Over Small World WSN With Optimal Data Mule Allocation. *IEEE Transaction on Vehicular Technology, 67*(7), 6518-6532.

Al-Aubidy, K., Mutairi, A.W., & Derbas, A. (2017). Real-time healthcare monitoring system using wireless sensor network. *International Journal of Digital Signals and Smart Systems, 1*(1), 26-42.

Alagoz, Ozger, & Akan. (2018). Clustering In Multi-Channel Cognitive Radio Ad Hoc And Sensor Networks. *IEEE Communications Magazine, 56*(4), 156-162.

Han, Tang, He, Jiang, & Ansere. (2019). District Partition-Based Data Collection Algorithm with Event Dynamic Competition in Underwater Acoustic Sensor Networks. *IEEE Transactions on Industrial Informatics, 15*(10), 5755-5764.

Li, Pirbhulal, Wu, & Sangaiah. (2019). Medical Information Security For Wearable Body Sensor Networks In Smart Healthcare. *IEEE Consumer Electronics Magazine, 8*(5), 37-41.

Lombardo, Camarero, Valverde, Portilla, de la Torre, & Riesgo. (2012). Power management techniques in an FPGA-based WSN node for high performance applications. *7th International Workshop onReconfigurable Communication-centric Systems-on-Chip (ReCoSoC)*, 1-8. 10.1109/ReCoSoC.2012.6322888

Karsmakers, P., Mercuri, M., Vanrumste, B., Leroux, P., & Schreurs, D. (2016). Biomedical Wireless Radar Sensor Network For Indoor Emergency Situations Detection And Vital Signs Monitoring. *IEEE Topical Conference on Biomedical Wireless Technologies, Networks, and Sensing Systems (BioWireleSS), 32-35.*

Sarkar, S., & Misra, S. (2016). The Evolution of Wireless Sensor-Based Health Care. *IEEE Pulse, 7*(1), 21–25. doi:10.1109/MPUL.2015.2498498 PMID:26799723

Abdulsalam, Y. S., & Hedabou, M. (2021). Security and Privacy in Cloud Computing: Technical Review. *Future Internet, 14*(1), 11. doi:10.3390/fi14010011

Abiodun, M., Awotunde, J., Ogundokun, R., Adeniyi, E., & Arowolo, M. (2021). Security and Information Assurance for IoT-Based Big Data. In *Artificial Intelligence for Cyber Security: Methods, Issues and Possible Horizons or Opportunities* (Vol. 972). Springer. doi:10.1007/978-3-030-72236-4_8

Adams, C., & Gilchrist, J. (1999). The CAST-256 Encryption Algorithm. *Entrust Technologies*, 1–20. https://tools.ietf.org/html/rfc2612

Adams, J., Woodard, D., Dozier, G., Miller, P., Bryant, K., & Glenn, G. (2010). Geneticbased type ii feature extraction for periocular biometric recognition: Less is more. *International Conference on Pattern Recognition*, 205–208.

Adee, R., & Mouratidis, H. (2022). A Dynamic Four-Step Data Security Model for Data in Cloud Computing Based on Cryptography and Steganography. *Sensors (Basel), 22*(3), 1109. doi:10.339022031109 PMID:35161853

Aggarwal, C. C., & Yu, P. S. (2008). A general survey of privacy-preserving data mining models and algorithms. *Privacy-Preserving Data Mining*, 11-52. doi:10.1007/978-0-387-70992-5_2

Aginako, N., Castrillón-Santana, M., Lorenzo-Navarro, J., Martínez-Otzeta, J. M., & Sierra, B. (2017). Periocular and iris local descriptors for identity verification in mobile applications. *Pattern Recognition Letters, 91*, 52–59.

Agrawal, R., Chatterjee, J. M., Kumar, A., & Rathore, P. S. (Eds.). (2020). *Blockchain technology and the internet of things: Challenges and applications in bitcoin and security*. doi:10.1201/9781003022688

Ahamad, T., & Narayana, A. (2015). Girl education: A lifeline to rural transformation in India. *International Journal of Applied Research, 1*(6), 84–87. https://www.researchgate.net/publication/290691308_Girl_education_A_lifeline_to_rural_transformation_in_India

Ahmed, N., Michelin, R. A., Xue, W., Ruj, S., Malaney, R., Kanhere, S. S., Seneviratne, A., Hu, W., Janicke, H., & Jha, S. K. (2020). A survey of covid-19 contact tracing apps. *IEEE Access: Practical Innovations, Open Solutions, 8*, 134577–134601. doi:10.1109/ACCESS.2020.3010226

Ahonen, A. H. T., & Pietikainen, M. (2006). Face Description with Local Binary Patterns: Application to Face Recognition. *IEEE Transactions on Pattern Analysis and Machine Intelligence, 28*, 2037–2041.

Ahuja, K., Islam, R., Barbhuiya, F. A., & Dey, K. (2016). A preliminary study of CNNs for iris and periocular verification in the visible spectrum. *2016 23rd International Conference on Pattern Recognition (ICPR),* 181-6.

Ahuja, K., Islam, R., Barbhuiya, F. A., & Dey, K. (2017). Convolutional neural networks for ocular smartphone-based biometrics. *Pattern Recognition Letters*, *91*, 17–26.

AI. (2022). *The fourth industrial revolution.* Presented at the American Psychological Association in Minneapolis.

Akhbarifar, S., Javadi, H. H., Rahmani, A. M., & Hosseinzadeh, M. (2020). A secure remote health monitoring model for early disease diagnosis in cloud-based IoT environment. *Personal and Ubiquitous Computing*, *16*, 1–17. doi:10.100700779-020-01475-3 PMID:33223984

Akiyama, M., Kawamoto, T., Shimamura, M., Yokoyama, T., Kadobayashi, Y., & Yamaguchi, S. (2007, January). A proposal of metrics for botnet detection based on its cooperative behavior. In *2007 International Symposium on Applications and the Internet Workshops* (pp. 82-82). IEEE.

Akyildiz, I. F., Su, W., Sankarasubramaniam, Y., & Cayirci, E. (2002). A survey on sensor networks. *IEEE Communications Magazine*, *40*(8), 102–114. doi:10.1109/MCOM.2002.1024422

Al Riyami, A., Afifi, M., & Mabry, R. M. (2004). Women's Autonomy, Education and Employment in Oman and Their Influence on Contraceptive Use. *Reproductive Health Matters*, *12*(23), 144–154. doi:10.1016/S0968-8080(04)23113-5 PMID:15242223

Al-Azzawi. (2014). Detection of P2P Botnets Based on SVN. *Journal of Engineering & Technology*, *32*(A).

Aledhari, M., Razzak, R., Parizi, R. M., & Saeed, F. (2020). federated learning: A survey on enabling technologies, protocols, and applications. *IEEE Access: Practical Innovations, Open Solutions*, *8*, 140699–140725. doi:10.1109/ACCESS.2020.3013541 PMID:32999795

Al-Hamdani, W. A. (2014). *Secure E-Learning and Cryptography.* doi:10.4018/978-1-4666-4486-1.ch012

Al-Hammadi, Y. A. A. (2010). Behavioural correlation for malicious bot detection. *Doctor.* Retrieved March 22, 2019, from http://etheses.nottingham.ac.uk/1359/

Alhasan, A., Audah, L., Ibrahim, I., Al-Sharaa, A., Al-Ogaili, A. S., & Mohammed, M. J. (2020). A case-study to examine doctors' intentions to use IoT healthcare devices in Iraq during COVID-19 pandemic. *International Journal of Pervasive Computing and Communications.* Advance online publication. doi:10.1108/IJPCC-10-2020-0175

Ali, I., Hassan, A., & Li, F. (2019). Authentication and privacy schemes for vehicular ad hoc networks (vanets): A survey. *Vehicular Communications*, *16*, 45–61. doi:10.1016/j.vehcom.2019.02.002

Ali, M. (2015). Effect of Gender Inequality on Economic Growth (Case of Pakistan). *Journal of Economics and Sustainable Development*, *6*(9), 125–133. https://www.iiste.org/Journals/index.php/JEDS/article/view/22620/23290

Al-Issa, Y., Ottom, M. A., & Tamrawi, A. (2019). eHealth Cloud Security Challenges: A Survey. *Journal of Healthcare Engineering*, *2019*, 1–15. doi:10.1155/2019/7516035 PMID:31565209

Almuhammadi, S., & Al-Shaaby, A. (2017). *A Survey on Recent Approaches Combining Cryptography and Steganography.* doi:10.5121/csit.2017.70306

Alonso-Fernandez, F., & Bigun, J. (2014). Eye detection by complex filtering for periocular recognition. *IWBF 2014–2nd International Workshop on Biometrics and Forensics 2014.*

Alonso-Fernandez, F., & Bigun, J. (2015). Near-infrared and visible-light periocular recognition with gabor features using frequency-adaptive automatic eye detection. *IET Biometrics*, *4*, 74–89.

Alonso-Fernandez, F., & Bigun, J. (2016). A survey on periocular biometrics research. *Pattern Recognition Letters, 82*, 92–105.

Alraja, M. N., Farooque, M. M. J., & Khashab, B. (2019). The Effect of Security, Privacy, Familiarity, and Trust on Users' Attitudes Toward the Use of the IoT-Based Healthcare: The Mediation Role of Risk Perception. *IEEE Access: Practical Innovations, Open Solutions, 7*, 111341–111354. doi:10.1109/ACCESS.2019.2904006

Alshalali, T., Mbale, K., & Josyula, D. (2018). Security and privacy of electronic health records sharing using hyperledger fabric. *Proceedings - 2018 International Conference on Computational Science and Computational Intelligence, CSCI 2018*, 760–763. 10.1109/CSCI46756.2018.00152

Alsunaidi, S. J., Almuhaideb, A. M., Ibrahim, N. M., Shaikh, F. S., Alqudaihi, K. S., Alhaidari, F. A., Khan, I. U., Aslam, N., & Alshahrani, M. S. (2021). Applications of big data analytics to control covid-19 pandemic. *Sensors (Basel), 21*(7), 2282. Advance online publication. doi:10.339021072282 PMID:33805218

Al-Zobbi, M., Shahrestani, S., & Ruan, C. (2017). Implementing a framework for big data anonymity and analytics access control. *2017 IEEE Trustcom/BigDataSE/ICESS*. doi:10.1109/Trustcom/BigDataSE/ICESS.2017.325

Al-Zobbi, M., Shahrestani, S., & Ruan, C. (2017). Improving MapReduce privacy by implementing multi-dimensional sensitivity-based anonymization. *Journal of Big Data, 4*(1), 45. Advance online publication. doi:10.118640537-017-0104-5

Ambika, N. (2019). Energy-Perceptive Authentication in Virtual Private Networks Using GPS Data. In Security, Privacy and Trust in the IoT Environment (pp. 25-38). Springer. doi:10.1007/978-3-030-18075-1_2

Ambika, D., Radhika, K., & Seshachalam, D. (2016). Periocular authentication based on FEM using Laplace–Beltrami eigenvalues. *Pattern Recognition, 50*, 178–194.

Ambika, N. (2020). Encryption of Data in Cloud-Based Industrial IoT Devices. In S. Pal & V. G. Díaz (Eds*IoT: Security and Privacy Paradigm* (pp. 111–129). CRC press, Taylor & Francis Group.

AMFG. (2019). *Industry 4.0: 7 Real-World Examples*. AMFG.

Analytics Vidhya. (2021). *12 Data Plot Types for Visualization from Concept to code*. https://www.analyticsvidhya.com/blog/2021/12/12-data-plot-types-for-visualization/

Angel, S., & Setty, S. T. (2016). Unobservable communication over fully un- trusted infrastructure. OSDI, 551–569.

Angrishi, K. (2017). *Turning Internet of Things(IoT) into Internet of Vulnerabilities (IoV) : IoT Botnets*. Retrieved April 22, 2019, from http://arxiv.org/abs/1702.03681

An, J., Li, W., Le Gall, F., Kovac, E., Kim, J., Taleb, T., & Song, J. (2019). EiF: Toward an elastic IoT fog framework for AI services. *IEEE Communications Magazine, 57*(5), 28–33. doi:10.1109/MCOM.2019.1800215

Appari, A., & Johnson, M. E. (2010). Information security and privacy in healthcare: Current state of research. *International Journal of Internet and Enterprise Management, 6*(4), 279. doi:10.1504/IJIEM.2010.035624

Arcot, R. V. (2021). *Cyber-Physical Systems: The Core of Industry 4.0*. Academic Press.

Ardebili, Naserbakht, Bernstein, Alazmani-Noodeh, & Hakimi. (2021). Healthcare providers experience of working during the COVID-19 pandemic: A qualitative study. *American Journal of Infection Control, 49*, 547–554. chrome-extension://dagcmkpagjlhakfdhnbomgmjdpkdklff/enhanced-reader.html?pdf=https%3A%2F%2Fbrxt.mendeley.com%2Fdocument%2Fcontent%2Ffde9dc97-e038-3a64-999b-8fdf1699a4b0%0Amoz-extension://49275573-6aab-4b60-a5da-2b3c5083f8bb/enhanced-reader.html?openApp&pd

Arora, S., Murnane, J., Bhattacharjee, D., McConnel, S., & Panda, A. (2020). *US freight after COVID-19: A bumpy road to the next normal.* McKinsey & Company. Retrieved December 31, 2021 from https://www.mckinsey.com/industries/travel-logistics-and-infrastructure/our-insights/us-freight-after-covid-19-a-bumpy-road-to-the-next-normal

Arowolo, M., Ogundokun, R., Misra, S., Agboola, B. D., & Gupta, B. (2022). Machine learning-based IoT system for COVID-19 epidemics. *Computing*, 1–17. doi:10.100700607-022-01057-6

Asassfeh, M. R., Qatawneh, M., & Al Azzeh, F. M. (2018). Performance evaluation of blowfish algorithm on supercomputer IMAN1. *International Journal of Computer Networks and Communications*, *10*(2), 43–53. doi:10.5121/ijcnc.2018.10205

Atobishi, T., Gábor, S. Z., & Podruzsik, S. (2018). *Cloud computing and big data in the context of industry 4.0: opportunities and challenges*. Academic Press.

Aultman, J. M., & Dean, E. (2014). Beyond privacy: Benefits and burdens of e-health technologies in primary care. *The Journal of Clinical Ethics*, *25*(1), 50–64. PMID:24779319

Avram, M. G. (2014). Advantages and Challenges of Adopting Cloud Computing from an Enterprise Perspective. *Procedia Technology*, *12*, 529–534. doi:10.1016/j.protcy.2013.12.525

Awan, S., Javaid, N., Ullah, S., Khan, A. U., Qamar, A. M., & Choi, J. G. (2022). Blockchain Based Secure Routing and Trust Management in Wireless Sensor Networks. *Sensors (Basel)*, *22*(2), 411. doi:10.339022020411 PMID:35062371

Ayuya. (2020). *Industry 4.0 and Cybersecurity*. Academic Press.

Back, A., M¨oller, U., & Stiglic, A. (2001). Traffic analysis attacks and trade- offs in anonymity providing systems. In *International Workshop on Information Hiding*. Springer. 10.1007/3-540-45496-9_18

Badawy, S. M., & Radovic, A. (2020). Digital approaches to remote pediatric health care delivery during the COVID-19 pandemic: Existing evidence and a call for further research. *JMIR Pediatrics and Parenting*, *3*(1), e20049. doi:10.2196/20049 PMID:32540841

Bae, K., Moon, S., Choi, D., Choi, Y., Kim, H. D., & Ha, J. (2012). A practical analysis of fault attack countermeasure on AES using data masking. *Proceedings - 2012 7th International Conference on Computing and Convergence Technology (ICCIT, ICEI and ICACT), ICCCT 2012*, 508–513.

Bain, K. K. (2015). Customer Segmentation of SMEs Using K-Means Clustering Method and modelling. In *LRFM International Conference on Vocational Education and Electrical Engineering*. Universitas Negeri Surabaya.

Bain, K. K., Firli, I., & Tri, S. (2016). Genetic Algorithm For Optimized Initial Centers K-Means Clustering In SMEs. *Journal of Theoretical and Applied Information Technology*, *90*, 23.

Bakshi, S., Sa, P. K., & Majhi, B. (2015). A novel phase-intensive localpattern for periocular recognition under visible spectrum. *Biocybernetics and Biomedical Engineering*, *35*, 30–44.

Balakrishnan, B., & Balachandran, S. (2017). FLECH: Fuzzy logic based energy efficient clustering hierarchy for non-uniform wireless sensor networks. *Wireless Communications and Mobile Computing*, *2017*. doi:10.1155/2017/1214720

Balandina, E., Balandin, S., Koucheryavy, Y., & Mouromtsev, D. (2015). IoT use cases in healthcare and tourism. *IEEE 17th Conference on Business Informatics*, *2*, 37-44.

Balatchandirane, G. (2007). *Gender Discrimination in Education and Economic Development: A Study of Asia*. Retrieved from https://www.ide.go.jp/library/English/Publish/Download/Vrf/pdf/426.pdf

Baltrusaitis, T., Robinson, P., & Morency, L. P. (2016). OpenFace: an open source facial behavior analysis toolkit. *2016 IEEE Winter Conference on Applications of Computer Vision (WACV)*.

Banfield, J., & Raftery, A. (1993). Model-based gaussian and non-Gaussian Clustering. Biometrics, 49, 803-821.

Banisar, D. (2019). *National comprehensive data protection/privacy laws and bills 2019*. Privacy Laws and Bills.

Barla, P. (2010). Greenhouse gas issues in the North American trucking industry. *Energy Efficiency*, *3*(2), 123–131. doi:10.100712053-009-9066-6

Basha, E. A., Ravela, S., & Rus, D. (2008, November). Model-based monitoring for early warning flood detection. In *Proceedings of the 6th ACM conference on Embedded network sensor systems* (pp. 295-308). 10.1145/1460412.1460442

Bass, L., Clements, P., & Kazman, R. (2003). *Software Architecture in Practice* (2nd ed.). Addison Wesley.

Basumatary, R. (2012). School Dropout across Indian States and UTs: An Econometric Study. *International Research Journal of Social Sciences, 1*(4), 28-35. Retrieved from www.isca.in/IJSS/Archive/v1/i4/5.ISCA-IRJSS-2012-061.pdf

Baydilli, Y. Y., & Atila, Ü. (2020). Classification of white blood cells using capsule networks. *Computerized Medical Imaging and Graphics*.

Behera, M. R., & Otter, R. (2021). Federated Learning using Peer-to-peer Network for Decentralized Orchestration of Model Weights. doi:10.36227/techrxiv.14267468

Bellavista, P., & Zanni, A. (2016). Towards better scalability for IoT-cloud interactions via combined exploitation of MQTT and CoAP. In *2nd International Forum on Research and Technologies for Society and Industry Leveraging a better tomorrow (RTSI)* (pp. 1-6). Bologna, Italy: IEEE.

Benavot, A. (1989). Education, Gender, and Economic Development: A Cross-National Study. *Sociology of Education*, *62*(1), 14–32. doi:10.2307/2112821

Bera, B., Das, A.K., Obaidat, M., Vijayakumar, P., Hsiao, K.F., & Park, Y. (2020). AI-Enabled Blockchain-Based Access Control for Malicious Attacks Detection and Mitigation in IoE. *IEEE Consum. Electron. Mag.*

Berger, L. T., & Iniewski, K. (Eds.). (2012). *Smart Grid - Applications, Communications and Security*. John Wiley and Sons.

Berman, J. (2021). Pitt-Ohio rolls out new warehouse and distribution service for in Mid-Atlantic and Midwest regions. *Supply Chain Management Review*. Retrieved December 31, 2021 from https://www.scmr.com/article/pitt_ohio_rolls_out_new_warehouse_and_distribution_service_for_in_mid_atlan/news

Bethencourt, J., Sahai, A., & Waters, B. (2007). Ciphertext-policy attribute- based encryption. In *Security and Privacy, 2007. SP'07. IEEE Symposium on*. IEEE.

Bhaduri, A. (2003). *User controlled privacy protection in location-based services*. Academic Press.

Bhattacharjee, K. (2015). *Women's Education in Rural Bihar: Issues and Challenges*. Retrieved from https://www.researchgate.net/profile/Kishore_Bhattacharjee/publication /318080118_Women%27s_Education_in_Rural_Bihar_Issues_and_Challenges/links/5958d5d4aca272c78abf033b/Womens-Education-in-Rural-Bihar-Issues-and-Challenges.pdf

Bhowmik, M. K., De, B. K., Bhattacharjee, D., Basu, D. K., & Nasipuri, M. (2012). Multisensor fusion of visual and thermal images for human face identification using different SVM kernels. *Systems, Applications and Technology Conference (LISAT), 2012 IEEE Long Island*, 1-7.

Bhurjee, A. K., Kumar, P., & Padhan, S. K. (2018). Solid transportation problem with budget constraints under interval uncertain environments. *International Journal of Process Management and Benchmarking*, *7*(2), 172–182. doi:10.1504/IJPMB.2017.083104

Bidnur. (2020). A Study on Industry4.0 Concept. *International Journal of Engineering Research & Technology*, 613-618.

Binkley, J. R., & Singh, S. (2006). An Algorithm for Anomaly-based Botnet Detection. *Proceedings of the 2nd Conference on Steps to Reducing Unwanted Traffic on the Internet SRUTI'06*, 7. Retrieved from http://dl.acm.org/citation.cfm?id=1251303

Bloustein, E. J. (1964). Privacy as an aspect of human dignity: An answer to dean prosser. *NYUL Rev.*, *39*, 962.

Bongomin, O., Nganyi, E. O., Abswaidi, M. R., Hitiyise, E., & Tumusiime, G. (2020). Sustainable and dynamic competitiveness towards technological leadership of industry 4.0: Implications for East african community. *Journal of Engineering*.

Bonnard, R., Vieira, K. M. M., Arantes, S., Lorbieski, R., Nunes, C., & Mattei, A. P. (2019). A big data/analytics platform for industry 4.0 implementation in SMEs. *Cigi Qualita*.

Bortolameotti, R. (2014). *C&C Botnet Detection over SSL*. Retrieved from https://pdfs.semanticscholar.org/5a2e/8739648c9a8a1b57c090845df28a8ffac2b6.pdf

Botha, J., Grobler, M., Hahn, J., & Eloff, M. (2017). A high-level comparison between the south african protection of personal information act and inter- national data protection laws. *ICMLG2017 5th International Conference on Management Leadership and Governance*.

Bouabida, K., Malas, K., Talbot, A., Desrosiers, M.-È., Lavoie, F., Lebouché, B., Taghizadeh, N., Normandin, L., Vialaron, C., Fortin, O., Lessard, D., & Pomey, M.-P. (2022). Healthcare Professional Perspectives on the Use of Remote Patient-Monitoring Platforms during the COVID-19 Pandemic: A Cross-Sectional Study. *Journal of Personalized Medicine*, *12*(4), 529. doi:10.3390/jpm12040529 PMID:35455645

Bradley, P. S., & Fayyad, U. M. (1998). Refining Initial Points for K-Means Clustering. In *Proceedings of the 15th International Conference on Machine Learning (ICML98)* (pp. 91-99). Morgan Kaufmann.

Bratianu, C. (2020). Toward understanding the complexity of the COVID-19 crisis: A grounded theory approach. *Management and Marketing*, *15*(s1), 410–423. doi:10.2478/mmcks-2020-0024

Bulaghi, Z. A., Navin, A. H., Hosseinzadeh, M., & Rezaee, A. (2020). SENET: A novel architecture for IoT-based body sensor networks. *Informatics in Medicine Unlocked*, *20*, 1–9.

Burghouwt, P. (2015). *Detection of Botnet Command and Control Traffic in Enterprise Networks*. Academic Press.

Buriya, S., Patel, A. K., Yadav, S. S., Buriya, S., Patel, A. K., & Yadav, S. S. (2015). Botnet behavior analysis using Naïve Bayes classification algorithm without deep packet. *International Journal of Computer Engineering & Applications*, *9*(8), 45–54.

Burrell, D. N. (2020). Understanding the Talent Management Intricacies of Remote Cybersecurity Teams in Covid-19 Induced Telework Organizational Ecosystems. *Land Forces Academy Review*, *25*(3), 232–244. doi:10.2478/raft-2020-0028

Calo, S. B., Touna, M., Verma, D. C., & Cullen, A. (2017). Edge computing architecture for applying AI to IoT.In *IEEE International Conference on Big Data (Big Data)* (pp. 3012-3016). Boston, MA: IEEE. 10.1109/BigData.2017.8258272

Camara, C., Peris-Lopez, P., & Tapiador, J. E. (2015). Security and privacy issues in implantable medical devices: A comprehensive survey. *Journal of Biomedical Informatics*, *55*, 272–289. doi:10.1016/j.jbi.2015.04.007 PMID:25917056

Caminiti, S. (2021). Lack of workers is further fueling supply chain woes. *CNBC*. Retrieved October 18, 2021 from https://www.cnbc.com/2021/09/28/companies-need-more-workers-to-help-resolve-supply-chain-problems.html

Campanile, L., Iacono, M., Levis, A. H., Marulli, F., & Mastroianni, M. (2020). Privacy regulations, smart roads, blockchain, and liability insurance: Putting technologies to work. *IEEE Security and Privacy*, *19*(1), 34–43. doi:10.1109/MSEC.2020.3012059

Camp, J., Henry, R., Kohno, T., Mare, S., Myers, S., Patel, S., & Streiff, J. (2020). Toward a secure internet of things: Directions for research. *IEEE Security and Privacy*, *18*(4), 28–37. doi:10.1109/MSEC.2020.2970155

Cao, H., Deng, H.-W., & Wang, Y.-P. (2012). Segmentation of M-FISH images for improved classification of chromosomes with an adaptive Fuzzy C-Means Clustering Algorithm. *IEEE Transactions on Fuzzy Systems*, *20*, 1–8.

Carbon War Room. (2012). *Road Transport: Unlocking Fuel-Saving Technologies in Trucking and Fleets, November 2012* [Report]. Retrieved December 31, 2021 from https://rmi.org/wp-content/uploads/2017/04/Unlocking-Fuel-Saving-Technologies-in-Trucking-and-Fleets-Carbon-War-Room_0.pdf

Carbon, C.-C. (2020). Wearing face masks strongly confuses counterparts in reading emotions. *Frontiers in Psychology*, *11*, 2526.

Carvalho, H., Azevedo, S., & Cruz-Machado, V. (2012). Agile and resilient approaches to supply chain management: Influence on performance and competitiveness. *Logistics Research*, *4*(1-2), 49–62. doi:10.100712159-012-0064-2

Cassidey, W. B. (2020). US truck driver shortfall steeper than expected. *Journal of Commerce*. Retrieved December 31, 2021 from https://www.joc.com/trucking-logistics/labor/us-truck-driver-shortfall-steeper-expected_20201125.html#:~:text=A%20growing%20deficit&text=That's%20an%20improvement%20from%20the,all%20of%202019%20and%202018

Castrillón-Santana, & Lorenzo-Navarro, & Ramón-Balmaseda. (2016). On using periocular biometric for gender classification in the wild. *Pattern Recognition Letters*, *82*, 181-189.

Cavoukian, A. (2009). Privacy by design. Take the challenge. Information and privacy commissioner of Ontario, Canada.

CDC. (2020). *Cases in the U.S.* https://www.cdc.gov/coronavirus/2019-ncov/casesupdates/ cases-in-us.html

Census data: Government of India. (n.d.). Retrieved September 7, 2022, from https://censusindia.gov.in/census.website/data/

Chan, T. H., Ho, S.-W., & Yamamoto, H. (2015). Private information retrieval for coded storage. In *Information Theory (ISIT), 2015 IEEE International Symposium on*. IEEE. 10.1109/ISIT.2015.7282975

Chandra & Bedi. (2018). Survey on SVM and their application in image classification. *International Journal of Information Technology*.

Charm, T., Coggins, B., Robinson, K., & Wilkie, J. (2020). *The great consumer shift: Ten charts that show us how US shopping behavior is changing*. McKinsey & Company. Retrieved December 31, 2021 from https://www.mckinsey.com/business-functions/marketing-and-sales/our-insights/the-great-consumer-shift-ten-charts-that-show-how-us-shopping-behavior-is-changing

Cha, S., & Kim, H. (2017). *Detecting Encrypted Traffic: A Machine Learning Approach*. Springer. doi:10.1007/978-3-319-56549-1_5

Chaturvedi, S., & Chakrabarti, D. (2018). Operational efficiency in manufacturing process using design of experiments. *International Journal of Process Management and Benchmarking*, *7*(2), 249–261. doi:10.1504/IJPMB.2017.083111

Chaudhari, P. S., Pahade, M., Bhat, S., Sawant, T., & Jadhav, C. (2017). *A Survey on Methods of Cryptography and Data Encryption*. Academic Press.

Chaudhry, I. S. (2007). Gender Inequality in Education and Economic Growth: Case Study of Pakistan. *Pakistan Horizon*, *60*(4), 81-91. Retrieved from https://www.jstor.org/stable/41500094

Chauhan, A., & Kumar, S. (2022). A Study on Problems and Challenges Faced by Girl Students in Higher Education. *Philosophical Readings*, *13*(4), 130–135. doi:10.5281/zenodo.5833619

Chaum, D. (1983). Blind signatures for untraceable payments. In *Advances in cryptology* (pp. 199–203). Springer. doi:10.1007/978-1-4757-0602-4_18

Chaum, D. (1988). The dining cryptographers problem: Unconditional sender and recipient untraceability. *Journal of Cryptology, 1*(1), 65–75. doi:10.1007/BF00206326

Chaum, D. L. (1981). Untraceable electronic mail, return addresses, and digital pseudonyms. *Communications of the ACM, 24*(2), 84–90. doi:10.1145/358549.358563

Chaum, D., & Van Heyst, E. (1991). Group signatures. In *Workshop on the Theory and Application of of Cryptographic Techniques*. Springer.

Chen, C., Wang, Y., Hu, W., & Zheng, Z. (2020). Robust multi-view k-means clustering with outlier removal. *Knowledge-Based Systems, 210*.

Chen, J., Xu, Y., Ping, W., & Tan, B. C. Y. (2009). Am i afraid of my peers? understanding the antecedents of information privacy concerns in the online social context. *ICIS 2009 Proceedings - Thirtieth International Conference on Information Systems*.

Chen, L., Jordan, S., Liu, Y., Moody, D., Peralta, R., Perlner, R., & Smith-Tone, D. (2016). *NISTIR 8105 Report on Post-Quantum Cryptography*. Retrieved from https://nvlpubs.nist.gov/nistpubs/ir/2016/NIST.IR.8105.pdf

Chen. (2020). A practical approach to determining critical macroeconomic factors in air-traffic volume based on K-means clustering and decision-tree classification. *Journal of Air Transport Management, 82*, 101743.

Chen, C., Dantcheva, A., & Ross, A. (2013). Automatic Facial Makeup Detection with Application in Face Recognition. *International Conference on Biometrics*.

Chen, C., Wang, X., Wang, Y., Yang, D., Yao, F., Zhang, W., & Hu, D. (2020). Additive manufacturing of piezoelectric materials. *Advanced Functional Materials, 30*(52), 2005141. doi:10.1002/adfm.202005141

Chen, M., Li, W., Fortino, G., Hao, Y., Hu, L., & Humar, I. (2019). A dynamic service migration mechanism in edge cognitive computing. *ACM Transactions on Internet Technology, 19*(2), 1–15. doi:10.1145/3239565

Chenthara, S., Ahmed, K., Wang, H., Whittaker, F., & Chen, Z. (2020). Healthchain: A novel framework on privacy preservation of electronic health records using blockchain technology. In PLoS ONE (Vol. 15, Issue 12 December). doi:10.1371/journal.pone.0243043

Chen, Y., Qin, X., Wang, J., Yu, C., & Gao, W. (2020). Fed Health: A federated transfer learning framework for wearable healthcare. *IEEE Intelligent Systems, 35*(4), 83–93. doi:10.1109/MIS.2020.2988604

Cheung, K. S., Leung, W. K., & Seto, W. K. (2019). Application of Big Data analysis in gastrointestinal research. *World Journal of Gastroenterology, 25*(24), 2990–3008. doi:10.3748/wjg.v25.i24.2990 PMID:31293336

Chor, B., Goldreich, O., Kushilevitz, E., & Sudan, M. (1995). Private information retrieval. In *Foundations of Computer Science, 1995. Proceedings., 36th Annual Symposium on*. IEEE. 10.1109/SFCS.1995.492461

Chottani, A., Hastings, G., Murnane, J., & Neuhaus, F. (2018). *Distraction or Disruption? Autonomous trucks gain ground in US logistics*. McKinsey & Company. Retrieved December 31, 2021 from https://www.mckinsey.com/industries/travel-logistics-and-infrastructure/our-insights/distraction-or-disruption-autonomous-trucks-gain-ground-in-us-logistics

Chun, C.-N., & Chung, R. (2004). Iris recognition for palm-top application. In D. Zhang & A. K. Jain (Eds.), Biometric Authentication (pp. 426–433). Springer.

Chung, K., Chen, C., Tsai, H., & Chuang, Y. (2021). Social media privacy management strategies: A SEM analysis of user privacy behaviors. *Computer Communications*, *174*, 122–130. doi:10.1016/j.comcom.2021.04.012

Chung, W., & Hershey, L. (2012). Enhancing Information Privacy and Data Sharing in a Healthcare IT Firm: The Case of Ricerro Communications. *Journal of Information Privacy and Security*, *8*(4), 56–78. doi:10.1080/15536548.2012.10845666

Çınar, A., & Tuncer, S. A. (2021). Classification of lymphocytes, monocytes, eosinophils, and neutrophils on white blood cells using hybrid Alexnet-GoogleNet-SVM. *SN Appl. Sci.*, *3*, 503.

Cisco Security. (n.d.). https://www.cisco.com

Cleophas, C., Cottrill, C., Ehmke, J. F., & Tierney, K. (2019). Collaborative urban transportation: Recent advances in theory and practice. *European Journal of Operational Research*, *273*(3), 801–816.

Cole, D. (2014). We kill people based on metadata. *The New York Review of Books*, *10*, 2014.

Company structure and facts. (2021). Retrieved October 22, 2021 from https://www.fedex.com/en-us/about/company-structure.html

Conerly, B. (2021). The labor shortage is why supple chains are disrupted. *Forbes*. Retrieved on October 19, 2021 from https://www.forbes.com/sites/billconerly/2021/07/07/the-labor-shortage-is-why-supply-chains-are-disrupted/?sh=45a33476301d

Cormen, T., Leiserson, C., Rivest, R., & Stein, C. (2009). *Introduction to Algorithms* (3rd ed.). The MIT Press.

Cosmin, M. P., Marian, C. M., & Mihai, M. (2014). An Optimized Version of the K-Means Clustering Algorithm *Proceedings of the 2014 Federated Conference on Computer Science and Information Systems (ACSIS)*, *2*, 695.

Costello, B., & Karickhoff, A. (2019). *Truck driver shortage analysis*. American Trucking Association. Retrieved December 31, 2021 from https://www.trucking.org/sites/default/files/2020-01/ATAs%20Driver%20Shortage%20Report%202019%20with%20cover.pdf

Council of the European Union. (2020). *Council Resolution on Encryption – Security through encryption and security despite encryption*. White Paper, 13084/1/20 REV 1.

Cresswell, K., Williams, R., & Sheikh, A. (2021). Using cloud technology in health care during the COVID-19 pandemic. In The Lancet Digital Health (Vol. 3, Issue 1, pp. e4–e5). doi:10.1016/S2589-7500(20)30291-0

Crumpler, W., & Lewis, J. A. (2019). The cybersecurity workforce gap. Washington, DC: Center for Strategic and International Studies (CSIS).

Cybator, C. (2017). *Pitt-Ohio to be first trucking company with two LEED Gold Certified terminals*. Pittsburgh Green Story. Retrieved December 31, 2021 from https://pittsburghgreenstory.com/pitt-ohio-first-trucking-company-two-leed-gold-certified-terminals/

D'Arcy, J., Adjerid, I., & Angst, C.M. (2020). Too Good to Be True: Firm Social Performance and the Risk of Data Breach. *Information Systems Research, 31*, 1200–1223.

Dagher, G. G., Mohler, J., Milojkovic, M., & Marella, P. B. (2018). Ancile: Privacy-preserving framework for access control and interoperability of electronic health records using blockchain technology. *Sustainable Cities and Society, 39*(December), 283–297. doi:10.1016/j.scs.2018.02.014

Danezis, G. (2003). Statistical disclosure attacks. In *IFIP International Information Security Conference*. Springer.

Dantcheva, A., Cunjian, C., & Ross, A. (2012). Can Facial Cosmetics Affect the Matching Accuracy of Face Recognition Systems? *International Conference on Biometrics: Theory, Applications and Systems*, 391–398.

Davenport, T. H., & Dyché, J. (2013). Big data in big companies. *International Institute for Analytics*, *3*, 1–31.

De Cristofaro, E. (2021). A critical overview of privacy in machine learning. *IEEE Security and Privacy*, *19*(4), 19–27. doi:10.1109/MSEC.2021.3076443

De Sanctis, M., Muccini, H., & Vaidhyanathan, K. (2020). Data-driven adaptation in microservice-based iot architectures. *IEEE International Conference on Software Architecture Companion (ICSA-C)* (pp. 59-62). Salvador, Brazil: IEEE. 10.1109/ICSA-C50368.2020.00019

De Witte, N. A. J., Carlbring, P., Etzelmueller, A., Nordgreen, T., Karekla, M., Haddouk, L., Belmont, A., Øverland, S., Abi-Habib, R., Bernaerts, S., Brugnera, A., Compare, A., Duque, A., Ebert, D. D., Eimontas, J., Kassianos, A. P., Salgado, J., Schwerdtfeger, A., Tohme, P., ... Van Daele, T. (2021). Online consultations in mental healthcare during the COVID-19 outbreak: An international survey study on professionals' motivations and perceived barriers. *Internet Interventions: the Application of Information Technology in Mental and Behavioural Health*, *25*(May), 100405. Advance online publication. doi:10.1016/j.invent.2021.100405 PMID:34401365

Debauche, O., Mahmoudi, S., Mahmoudi, S. A., Manneback, P., & Lebeau, F. (2020). A new edge architecture for ai-iot services deployment. In *The 17th International Conference on Mobile Systems and Pervasive Computing (MobiSPC)* (pp. 10-19). Leuven, Belgium: Elsevier.

Debauche, O., Mahmoudi, S., & Guttadauria, A. (2022). A New Edge Computing Architecture for IoT and Multimedia Data Management. *Information (Basel)*, *13*(2), 89. doi:10.3390/info13020089

Decor, K. (n.d.). Available online: https://kitchendecor.club/files/now-beckham-hairstyle-david.html

Deedler, W. (1996). *Just what is Indian summer and did Indians really have anything to do with it?* National Weather Service. Retrieved from https://web.archive.org/web/20141009005228/http://www.crh.noaa.gov/dtx/stories/i-summer.php

Dehling, T., & Sunyaev, A. (2014). Information security and privacy of patient-centered health IT services: What needs to be done? *Proceedings of the Annual Hawaii International Conference on System Sciences*, 2984–2993. 10.1109/HICSS.2014.371

Delhi Iris Database, I. I. T. (Version 1.0). (n.d.). http://www4.comp.polyu.edu.hk/csajaykr/IITD/Database_Iris.htm

Deniz, M. (2021). *Fear of missing out (FoMo) mediate relations between social self-efficacy and life satisfaction*. Springer Open. doi:10.118641155-021-00193-w

Denzin, N. K., & Lincoln, Y. S. (Eds.). (2005). *The Sage handbook of qualitative research* (3rd ed.). Sage Publications Ltd.

Desai, D. (2017). SSL/TLS-based botnet attacks. *Zscaler*. Retrieved June 18, 2018, from https://www.zscaler.com/blogs/research/ssltls-based-malware-attacks

Dhamija, A., & Dhaka, V. (2015). A novel cryptographic and steganographic approach for secure cloud data migration. In *Green Computing and Internet of Things (ICGCIoT), 2015 International Conference on*. IEEE. 10.1109/ICGCIoT.2015.7380486

Dian, F. J., Vahidnia, R., & Rahmati, A. (2020). Wearables and the Internet of Things (IoT), applications, opportunities, and challenges: A Survey. *IEEE Access: Practical Innovations, Open Solutions*, *8*, 69200–69211. doi:10.1109/ACCESS.2020.2986329

Diaz, C. (2006). Anonymity metrics revisited. In *Dagstuhl Seminar Proceedings*. Schloss Dagstuhl-Leibniz-Zentrum fu¨r Informatik.

DiCorrado, E., Kelly, K., & Wright, M. (2015). *The Relationship between Mathematical Performance and GDP per Capita*. Retrieved from https://smartech.gatech.edu/bitstream/handle/1853/54222/the_relationship_between_mathematical_performance_and_gdp_per_capita_1.bk-2.pdf

Dilmaghani, S., Brust, M. R., Danoy, G., Cassagnes, N., Pecero, J., & Bouvry, P. (2019). Privacy and security of big data in AI systems: A research and standards perspective. *2019 IEEE International Conference on Big Data (Big Data)*. 10.1109/BigData47090.2019.9006283

Dimberg, U., Thunberg, M., & Elmehed, K. (2000). Unconscious facial reactions to emotional facial expressions. *Psychological Science*, *11*(1), 86–89.

Dingledine, R., Freedman, M. J., & Molnar, D. (2001). The free haven project: Distributed anonymous storage service. In *Designing Privacy Enhancing Technologies* (pp. 67–95). Springer. doi:10.1007/3-540-44702-4_5

Dingledine, R., Mathewson, N., & Syverson, P. (2004). *Tor: The second- generation onion router. Technical report.* Naval Research Lab Washington DC. doi:10.21236/ADA465464

Divya Priya, D., Shirisha, B., & Pravallika, B. (2018). Blowfish Encryption on Cloud Data Storage. *IACSIT International Journal of Engineering and Technology*, *7*(4), 4250–4252. doi:10.14419/ijet.v7i4.15597

Dopelt, K., Bashkin, O., Davidovitch, N., & Asna, N. (2021). Facing the unknown: Healthcare workers' concerns, experiences, and burnout during the covid-19 pandemic— a mixed-methods study in an israeli hospital. *Sustainability (Switzerland)*, *13*(16), 9021. Advance online publication. doi:10.3390u13169021

Drake, F. (2011). The search for extra-terrestrial intelligence. Philosophical Transactions of the Royal Society A: Mathematical, Physical and Engineering Sciences, 369(1936), 633-643. doi:10.1098/rsta.2010.0282

Duda, R. O., Hart, P. E., & Stork, D. G. (2001). Pattern classification (2nd ed.). Wiley.

Dun & Bradstreet. (2021). *Trucking industry insights from D&B Hoovers*. Retrieved December 31, 2021 from https://www.dnb.com/business-directory/industry-analysis.general_freight_trucking.html

Dwork, C., & Roth, A. (2014). The algorithmic foundations of differential privacy. *Foundations and Trends in Theoretical Computer Science*, *9*(3–4), 211–407.

Dwork, C. (2011). Differential privacy. In *Encyclopedia of Cryptography and Security* (pp. 338–340). Springer. doi:10.1007/978-1-4419-5906-5_752

Earp, J. B., & Payton, F. C. (2006). Information privacy in the service sector: An exploratory study of health care and banking professionals. *Journal of Organizational Computing and Electronic Commerce*, *16*(2), 105–122. doi:10.120715327744joce1602_2

Eberhart, R. C., & Shi, Y. (2011). *Computational intelligence: concepts to implementations*. Elsevier.

Ebrahim, M., Khan, S., & Khalid, U. Bin. (2014). *Symmetric Algorithm Survey: A Comparative Analysis*. https://arxiv.org/abs/1405.0398

Eckhoff, D., & Wagner, I. (2017). Privacy in the smart city–applications, technologies, challenges and solutions. *IEEE Communications Surveys and Tutorials*.

Eftekhar Ardebili, M., Naserbakht, M., Bernstein, C., Alazmani-Noodeh, F., Hakimi, H., & Ranjbar, H. (2021). Healthcare providers experience of working during the COVID-19 pandemic: A qualitative study. *American Journal of Infection Control, 49*(5), 547–554. doi:10.1016/j.ajic.2020.10.001 PMID:33031864

Eilers, P. H. C., & Goeman, J. J. (2004, March). Enhancing scatterplots with smoothed densities. *Bioinformatics, 20*(5), 623–628.

Ekman, P. (1993). Facial expression and emotion. *The American Psychologist, 48*(4), 384.

Elfenbein, H. A., & Ambady, N. (2002). Predicting workplace outcomes from the ability to eavesdrop on feelings. *The Journal of Applied Psychology, 87*(5), 963.

Elmansouri, O., Almhroog, A., & Badi, I. (2020). Urban transportation in Libya: An overview. *Transportation Research Interdisciplinary Perspectives, 8.*

El-Sherif, D. M., Abouzid, M., Elzarif, M. T., Ahmed, A. A., Albakri, A., & Alshehri, M. M. (2022). Telehealth and Artificial Intelligence Insights into Healthcare during the COVID-19 Pandemic. *Healthcare (Switzerland), 10*(2), 1–15. doi:10.3390/healthcare10020385 PMID:35206998

Ericson. (2019). *How to Choose Algorithms for Azure Machine Learning Studio.* Retrieved March 22, 2019, from https://docs.microsoft.com/en-us/azure/machine-learning/studio/algorithm-choice

Ermakova, T., Fabian, B., Kelkel, S., Wolff, T., & Zarnekow, R. (2015). Antecedents of health information privacy concerns. *Procedia Computer Science, 63*(Icth), 376–383. doi:10.1016/j.procs.2015.08.356

Ermakova, T., Fabian, B., & Zarnekow, R. (2013). Security and privacy system requirements for adopting cloud computing in healthcare data sharing scenarios. *19th Americas Conference on Information Systems, AMCIS 2013 - Hyperconnected World: Anything, Anywhere, Anytime, 4*, 2937–2945.

Ervural, B. C., & Ervural, B. (2018). Overview of cyber security in the industry 4.0 era. In *Industry 4.0: managing the digital transformation* (pp. 267–284). Springer. doi:10.1007/978-3-319-57870-5_16

Europol. (2017). *Banking Trojan* Retrieved March 25, 2019, from https://www.europol.europa.eu/.../banking_trojans_from_stone_age_to_space_era.pdf

Evans, M., Maglaras, L. A., He, Y., & Janicke, H. (2016). Human behaviour as an aspect of cybersecurity assurance. *Security and Communication Networks, 9*(17), 4667–4679. doi:10.1002ec.1657

Falk, G., Romero, P. D., Nicchitta, I. A., & Nyhof, E. C. (2021). *Unemployment rates during the COVID-19 pandemic - fas.* Retrieved October 23, 2021, from https://sgp.fas.org/crs/misc/R46554.pdf

Farivar, F., Haghighi, M. S., Jolfaei, A., & Alazab, M. (2019). Artificial Intelligence for Detection, Estimation, and Compensation of Malicious Attacks in Nonlinear Cyber-Physical Systems and Industrial IoT. *IEEE Transactions on Industrial Informatics, 16*(4), 2716–2725. doi:10.1109/TII.2019.2956474

Fathi, M., Khakifirooz, M., & Pardalos, P. M. (Eds.). (2019). *Optimization in large scale problems: Industry 4.0 and Society 5.0 Applications* (Vol. 152). Springer. doi:10.1007/978-3-030-28565-4

Fauzdar, C., Gupta, N., Goswami, M., & Kumar, R. (2022). MICMAC Analysis of Industry 4.0 in Indian Automobile Industry. *Journal of Scientific and Industrial Research, 81*(08), 873–881.

Federal Motor Carrier Safety Administration. (2020). *Summary of hours of service regulations.* Retrieved December 31, 2021 from https://www.fmcsa.dot.gov/regulations/hours-service/summary-hours-service-regulations

Feily, M., Shahrestani, A., & Ramadass, S. (2009). A survey of botnet and botnet detection. *Proceedings - 2009 3rd International Conference on Emerging Security Information, Systems and Technologies, SECURWARE 2009*, 268–273. https://doi.org/10.1109/SECURWARE.2009.48

Feng, H. H., Giffin, J. T., Huang, Y., Jha, S., Lee, W., & Miller, B. P. (2004, May). Formalizing sensitivity in static analysis for intrusion detection. *IEEE Symposium on Security and Privacy, 2004 Proceedings*, 194–208.

Fernandes, E., Jung, J., & Prakash, A. (2016). *Security Analysis of Emerging Smart Home Applications*. Retrieved from https://cdn2.vox-cdn.com/uploads/chorus_asset/file/6410049/Paper27_SP16_CameraReady_SmartThings_Revised_1_.0.pdf

Ferrández-Pastor, F., García-Chamizo, J., Nieto-Hidalgo, M., & Mora-Martínez, J. (2018). Precision Agriculture Design Method Using a Distributed Computing Architecture on Internet of Things Context. *Sensors (Basel)*, *18*(6), 1731. doi:10.339018061731 PMID:29843386

Fiat, A., & Naor, M. (1993). Broadcast encryption. In *Annual International Cryptology Conference*. Springer.

Figueiredo, D. R., Nain, P., & Towsley, D. (2004). On the analysis of the predecessor attack on anonymity systems. Computer Science Technical Report.

Finn, R. L., Wright, D., & Friedewald, M. (2013). Seven types of privacy. In *European data protection: coming of age* (pp. 3–32). Springer. doi:10.1007/978-94-007-5170-5_1

Flamand, E., Rossi, D., Conti, F., Loi, I., Pullini, A., Rotenberg, F., & Benini, L. (2018). GAP-8: A RISC-V SoC for AI at the Edge of the IoT. In *29th International Conference on Application-specific Systems, Architectures and Processors (ASAP)* (pp. 1-4). Milan, Italy: IEEE. 10.1109/ASAP.2018.8445101

Flynn, B., Cantor, D., Pagell, M., Dooley, K., & Azadegan, A. (2021). From the Editors: Introduction to managing supply chains beyond COVID-19-Preparing for the next global mega-disruption. Journal of Supply Chain Management, 57(1), 3-6.

Fox, G., & James, T. L. (2021). Toward an Understanding of the Antecedents to Health Information Privacy Concern: A Mixed Methods Study. *Information Systems Frontiers*, *23*(6), 1537–1562. doi:10.100710796-020-10053-0

Fragouli, C., & Soljanin, E. (2007). Network coding fundamentals. *Foundations and Trends in Networking*, *2*(1), 1–133. doi:10.1561/1300000003

Franca, R. B., Jones, E. C., Richards, C. N., & Carlson, J. P. (2010). Multi-objective stochastic supply chain modeling to evaluate tradeoffs between profit and quality. *International Journal of Production Economics*, *127*(2), 292–299. doi:10.1016/j.ijpe.2009.09.005

Franklin, R. G., & Zebrowitz, L. A. (2013). Older adults' trait impressions of faces are sensitive to subtle resemblance to emotions. *Journal of Nonverbal Behavior*, *37*(3), 139–151.

Fränti, P. (2018). Efficiency of random swap clustering. *Journal of Big Data*, *5*(13), 1–29.

Fränti, P., & Sieranoja, S. (2018). K-means properties on six clustering benchmark datasets. *Applied Intelligence*, *48*, 4743–4759. https://doi.org/10.1007/s10489-018-1238-7

Freedman, M. J., & Morris, R. (2002). Tarzan: A peer-to-peer anonymizing network layer. In *Proceedings of the 9th ACM conference on Computer and communications security*. ACM. 10.1145/586110.586137

Freij-Hollanti, R., Gnilke, O. W., Hollanti, C., & Karpuk, D. A. (2017). Private information retrieval from coded databases with colluding servers. *SIAM Journal on Applied Algebra and Geometry*, *1*(1), 647–664. doi:10.1137/16M1102562

Fung, B., Wang, K., & Yu, P. (n.d.). Top-down specialization for information and privacy preservation. *21st International Conference on Data Engineering (ICDE'05)*. 10.1109/ICDE.2005.143

Fusco, A., Dicuonzo, G., Dell'atti, V., & Tatullo, M. (2020). Blockchain in healthcare: Insights on COVID-19. *International Journal of Environmental Research and Public Health*, *17*(19), 1–12. doi:10.3390/ijerph17197167 PMID:33007951

Fu, X., Zhu, Y., Graham, B., Bettati, R., & Zhao, W. (2007). On flow marking attacks in wireless anonymous communication networks. *Journal of Ubiquitous Computing and Intelligence*, *1*(1), 42–53. doi:10.1166/juci.2007.005

Gaikwad. (2019). *Artificial Intelligence And It's Impacts On Industry 4.0.* Academic Press.

Gao, H., Zhuang, L., Van Der Maaten, L., & Weinberger, K. Q. (2017). Densely connected convolutional networks. *2017 IEEE Conference on Computer Vision and Pattern Recognition (CVPR)*, 2261-9.

Gardner, Keating, Williamson, & Elliott. (n.d.). Deep Learning Algorithms for classing subtypes of blood. *British Journal of Opthalmology.*

Garland, M. (2021). FedEx Diverts packages as labor shortage bits into service levels. *Supply Chain Dive*. Retrieved October 18, 2021 from https://www.supplychaindive.com/news/fedex-earnings-labor-shortage-peak-season-capacity/606988/

Gaudenzi, B., & Borghesi, A. (2006). Managing risks in the supply chain using the AHP method. *International Journal of Logistics Management*, *17*(1), 114–136. doi:10.1108/09574090610663464

Gaur, S., Moh, M., & Balakrishnan, M. (2013). Hiding behind the Clouds: Efficient, Privacy-Preserving Queries via Cloud Proxies. *Proc. of International Workshop on Cloud Computing Systems, Networks, and Applications.*

Gelinas, U. J. Jr, Sutton, S. G., & Fedorowicz, J. (2004). *Business processes and information technology*. South Western/ Thomson Learning.

Genovese, D. (2021). FedEx rerouting more than 600k packages a day because of labor shortages. *Fox Business*. Retrieved on October 19, 2021 from https://www.foxbusiness.com/lifestyle/fedex-rerouting-packages-daily-labor-shortage

Gentry, C. (2009). *A fully homomorphic encryption scheme*. Stanford University.

Georgios, L., Kerstin, S., & Theofylaktos, A. (2019). *Internet of things in the context of industry 4.0: An overview.* Academic Press.

Gerke, S., Shachar, C., Chai, P. R., & Cohen, I. G. (2020). Regulatory, safety, and privacy concerns of home monitoring technologies during COVID-19. *Nature Medicine*, *26*(8), 1176–1182. doi:10.103841591-020-0994-1 PMID:32770164

Giannakis, M., & Papadopoulos, T. (2016). Supply chain sustainability: A risk management approach. *International Journal of Production Economics*, *171*, 455–470. doi:10.1016/j.ijpe.2015.06.032

Giffin, J. T., Jha, S., & Miller, B. P. (2004, February). Efficient Context-Sensitive Intrusion Detection. NDSS.

Giraddi, Pujari, & Seeri. (2015). Identifying Abnormalities in the Blood cell Images using SVM Classifiers. *International Journal of Computers and Applications*, *111*(6).

Girish, R. (2019). *Augmented reality used to maintain equipment.* Academic Press.

GIRL Center (2022). *Gendered Effects of Covid-19 School Closures: India Case Study*. popcouncil.org

Gittleman, M., & Monaco, K. (2020). Truck-driving jobs: Are they headed for rapid elimination? *Industrial & Labor Relations Review*, *73*(1), 3–24. doi:10.1177/0019793919858079

Global cases of covid 19. (n.d.). https://www.google.com/search?q=global+cases+of+covid+19&rlz=1C1CHBF_enUS779US779&oq=global+cases+&aqs=chrome.0.0j69i57j0l6.2899j0j7&sourceid=chrome&ie=UTF-8

Gode & Ganar. (2014). Image retrieval by using colour, texture and shape features. *International Journal of Advanced Research in Electrical, Electronics and Instrumentation Engineering, 3.*

Goebel, J., & Holz, T. (2007). Rishi: identify bot contaminated hosts by IRC nickname evaluation. *HotBots'07 Proceedings of the First Conference on First Workshop on Hot Topics in Understanding Botnets*, 8. https://doi.org/10.1.1.177.8170

Goel, A., & Irnich, S. (2016). An exact method for vehicle routing and truck driver scheduling problems. *Transportation Science*, *51*(2), 737–754. doi:10.1287/trsc.2016.0678

Goh, M., Lim, J. Y. S., & Meng, F. (2007). A stochastic model for risk management in global supply chain networks. *European Journal of Operational Research*, *182*(1), 164–173. doi:10.1016/j.ejor.2006.08.028

GOI. (2012). *Gender Statistics of Punjab.* Retrieved from: http://www.pbplanning.gov.in/pdf/Gender%20Statistics%20 %202012%20final.pdf

GOI. (2017). *Statistical Abstract of Punjab.* Retrieved from Economic & Statistic Organisation of Punjab website: https:// www.esopb.gov.in/

Goldschlag, D., Reed, M., & Syverson, P. (1999). Onion routing. *Communications of the ACM*, *42*(2), 39–41. doi:10.1145/293411.293443

Gooley, D. (2017). The rise in ssl-based threats. *Zscaler.* Retrieved June 16, 2018, from https://www.zscaler.com/blogs/ research/rise-ssl-based-threats

Gorman, S. (2009). Electricity grid in US penetrated by spies. *The Wall Street Journal, 8.*

Gothwal, S., & Raj, T. (2018). Prioritising the performance measures of FMS using multi-criteria decision making approaches. *International Journal of Process Management and Benchmarking*, *8*(1), 59–78. doi:10.1504/IJPMB.2018.088657

Gouda, S. K., & Saranga, H. (2018). Sustainable supply chains for supply chain sustainability: Impact of sustainability efforts on supply chain risk. *International Journal of Production Research*, *56*(17), 5820–5835. doi:10.1080/0020754 3.2018.1456695

Govindan, K., & Chaudhuri, A. (2016). Interrelationships of risks faced by third party logistics service providers: A DEMATEL based approach. *Transportation Research Part E, Logistics and Transportation Review*, *90*, 177–195. doi:10.1016/j.tre.2015.11.010

Goyal, D., & Tyagi, A. (2020). *A Look at Top 35 Problems in the Computer Science Field for the Next Decade.* . doi:10.1201/9781003052098-40

Goyal, S. (2022b). Industry 4.0 in Healthcare IoT for Inventory and Supply Chain Management. *Cyber-Physical Systems: Foundations and Techniques*, 209-227.

Goyal. (2018). *What are Augmented Reality toys? How are they useful for children?* Academic Press.

Goyal, S. (2022a). IoT-Based Smart Air Quality Control System: Prevention to COVID-19. In *IoT and Cloud Computing for Societal Good* (pp. 15–23). Springer.

Goyal, S. (2022c). Static code metrics-based deep learning architecture for software fault prediction. *Soft Computing*, 1–33. doi:10.100700500-022-07365-5

Granqvist, K., Ahlstrom, L., Karlsson, J., Lytsy, B., & Andersson, A. E. (2021). Learning to interact with new technology: Health care workers' experiences of using a monitoring system for assessing hand hygiene – a grounded theory study. *American Journal of Infection Control*, *000*, 1–6. doi:10.1016/j.ajic.2021.09.023 PMID:34610392

Greco, L., Percannella, G., Ritrovato, P., Tortorella, F., & Vento, M. (2020). Trends in IoT based solutions for health care: Moving AI to the edge. *Pattern Recognition Letters, 135*, 346–353. doi:10.1016/j.patrec.2020.05.016 PMID:32406416

Gu, G., Porras, P., Yegneswaran, V., Fong, M., Lee, W., & Park, M. (n.d.). *BotHunter : Detecting Malware Infection Through IDS-Driven Dialog Correlation.* College of Computing, Georgia Institute of Technology.

Gu, G., Zhang, J., & Lee, W. (2008). BotSniffer : Detecting Botnet Command and Control Channels in Network Traffic. *Proceedings of the 15th Annual Network and Distributed System Security Symposium., 53*(1), 1–13. https://doi.org/10.1.1.110.8092

Guarda, P., & Zannone, N. (2009). Towards the development of privacy-aware systems. *Information and Software Technology, 51*(2), 337–350. doi:10.1016/j.infsof.2008.04.004

Gu, G., Perdisci, R., Zhang, J., & Lee, W. (2008). BotMiner: clustering analysis of network traffic for protocol-and structure-independent botnet detection. In *Proceedings of the 17th Conference on Security Symposium*. USENIX Association.

Guntuku, S., Narang, P., & Hota, C. (2013). *Real-time Peer-to-Peer Botnet Detection Framework based on Bayesian Regularized Neural Network.* http://arxiv.org/abs/1307.7464

Guo, K., Lu, Y., Gao, H., & Cao, R. (2018). Artificial Intelligence-Based Semantic Internet of Things in a User-Centric Smart City. *Sensors (Basel), 18*(5), 1341. doi:10.339018051341 PMID:29701679

Guo, K., Soornack, Y., & Settle, R. (2019). Expression-dependent susceptibility to face distortions in processing of facial expressions of emotion. *Vision Research, 157*, 112–122.

Gupta, B. B., Tewari, A., Cvitić, I., Peraković, D., & Chang, X. (2022). Artificial intelligence empowered emails classifier for Internet of Things based systems in industry 4.0. *Wireless Networks, 28*(1), 493–503. doi:10.100711276-021-02619-w

Gupta, S., Xu, H., & Zhang, X. (2011). Balancing privacy concerns in the adoption of Location-Based Services: An empirical analysis. *International Journal of Electronic Business, 9*(1/2), 118. doi:10.1504/IJEB.2011.040358

Habibzadeh, Krzyżak, & Fevens. (2014). *Comparative Study of Feature Selection for White Blood Cell Differential Counts in Low Resolution Images*. Springer Science and Business Media LLC.

Hagino, T. (2021). *Practical Node-RED Programming: Learn powerful visual programming techniques and best practices for the web and IoT.* Packt Publishing.

Hall, J. L., & Mcgraw, D. (2014). For telehealth to succeed, privacy and security risks must be identified and addressed. *Health Affairs, 33*(2), 216–221. doi:10.1377/hlthaff.2013.0997 PMID:24493763

Haltas, F., Uzun, E., Siseci, N., Posul, A., & Emre, B. (2014). An automated bot detection system through honeypots for large-scale. *International Conference on Cyber Conflict, CYCON*, 255–270. https://doi.org/10.1109/CYCON.2014.6916407

Hameed, N., & Shukri, A. M. (2014). *The Concept of 'Gender' According to Different Approaches.* Retrieved from: https://www.researchgate.net/publication/332289875_The_Concept_of_%27Gender%27_According_to_Different_Approaches

Hamerly, G., & Elkan, C. (2002). Alternatives to the K-means algorithm that find better clusterings. *Proceedings of the 11th International Conference on Information and Knowledge Management (CIKM 02)*, 600–607.

Hamurcu, M., & Eren, T. (2020). Strategic Planning Based on Sustainability for Urban Transportation: An Application to Decision-Making. *Sustainability, 12*(9), 3589.

Han, J., & Kamber, M. (2007). *Data mining Concepts and techniques* (2nd ed.). Morgan Kaufmann Publishers.

Hanushek, E. A. (2013). *Economic Growth in Developing Countries: The Role of Human Capital.* Retrieved from https://hanushek.stanford.edu/sites/default/files/publications/Education%20and%20Economic%20Growth.pdf

Hao, T., Huang, Y., Wen, X., Gao, W., Zhang, F., Zheng, C., ... Zhan, J. (2018). Edge AIBench: towards comprehensive end-to-end edge computing benchmarking. In *International Symposium on Benchmarking, Measuring and Optimization* (pp. 23-30). Beijing, China: Springer.

Hao, Y., Miao, Y., Tian, Y., Hu, L., Hossain, M. S., Muhammad, G., & Amin, S. U. (2019, March/April). Smart-Edge-CoCaCo: AI-Enabled Smart Edge with Joint Computation, Caching, and Communication in Heterogeneous IoT. *IEEE Network, 33*(2), 58–64. doi:10.1109/MNET.2019.1800235

Hareli, S., David, S., & Hess, U. (2013). Competent and Warm but Unemotional: The Influence of Occupational Stereotypes on the Attribution of Emotions. *Journal of Nonverbal Behavior, 37*, 307–317.

Harman, L. B., Flite, C. A., & Bond, K. (2012). State of the Art and Science Electronic Health Records: Privacy, Confidentiality, and Security. *American Medical Association Journal of Ethics, 14*(9), 712–719.

Harris, E., Perlroth, N., & Popper, N. (2014). Neiman Marcus data breach worse than first said. *The New York Times, 23.*

Hashizume, K., Rosado, D. G., Fernández-Medina, E., & Fernandez, E. B. (2013). An analysis of security issues for cloud computing. *Journal of Internet Services and Applications, 4*(1), 5. doi:10.1186/1869-0238-4-5

Hassanalieragh, M., Page, A., Soyata, T., Sharma, G., Aktas, M., Mateos, G., Kantarci, B., & Andreescu, S. (2015). Health monitoring and management using internet-of-things (iot) sensing with cloud-based processing: Opportunities and challenges. In *2015 IEEE International Conference on Services Computing*. IEEE. 10.1109/SCC.2015.47

Hassan, W. H. (2019). Current research on Internet of Things (IoT) security: A survey. *Computer Networks, 148*, 283–294. doi:10.1016/j.comnet.2018.11.025

Haverinen, J., Keränen, N., Falkenbach, P., Maijala, A., Kolehmainen, T., & Reponen, J. (2019). Digi-HTA: Health technology assessment framework for digital healthcare services. *Finnish Journal of EHealth and EWelfare, 11*(4), 326–341. doi:10.23996/fjhw.82538

Haynes, T. (2018). *Dopamine, Smartphones & You: A battle for your time.* https://sitn.hms.harvard.edu/flash/2018/dopamine-smartphones-battle-time/

Heavy and tractor-trailer truck drivers. (2020). *Occupational Outlook Handbook.* Retrieved March 8, 2022 from https://www.bls.gov/ooh/transportation-and-material-moving/heavy-and-tractor-trailer-truck-drivers.htm

He, K., Zhang, X., Ren, S., & Sun, J. (2016). Deep residual learning for image recognition. *29th IEEE Conference on Computer Vision and Pattern Recognition, CVPR 2016*, 770-778.

Hellemans, A. (2016). *Europe Bets €1 Billion on Quantum Tech.* IEEE Spectrum. doi:10.1109/GLOCOMW.2013.6825035

Hellinger & Seeger. (2011). *Cyber-Physical Systems-Driving force for innovation in mobility, health, energy and production.* Acatech Position Paper.

Hernandez-Ramos, J. L., Martinez, J. A., Savarino, V., Angelini, M., Napolitano, V., Skarmeta, A. F., & Baldini, G. (2020). Security and privacy in internet of things-enabled smart cities: Challenges and future directions. *IEEE Security and Privacy, 19*(1), 12–23. doi:10.1109/MSEC.2020.3012353

Hess, U., & Fischer, A. (2013). Emotional mimicry as social regulation. *Personality and Social Psychology Review, 17*(2), 142–157.

History of Pitt-Ohio. (2021). Retrieved December 31, 2021 from https://pittohio.com/myPittOhio/corporate/about/history-of-pitt-ohio

Hoffman, S., & Podgurski, A. (2012). Balancing Privacy, Autonomy, and Scientific Needs In Electronic Health Records Research. *SMU Law Review, 65*(1), 85–144.

Hoffman, D. A. (2020). Increasing access to care: Telehealth during COVID-19. *Journal of Law and the Biosciences, 7*(1), 1–15. doi:10.1093/jlb/lsaa043 PMID:32843985

Holz, T., Gorecki, C., Rieck, K., & Freiling, F. C. (2008). Detection and mitigation of fast-flux service networks. In *Proceedings of the 15th Annual Network and Distributed System Security Symposium (NDSS'08)*. Homeland Security Digital Library. https://www.hsdl.org

Horváth, D., & Szabó, R. Z. (2019). Driving forces and barriers of Industry 4.0: Do multinational and small and medium-sized companies have equal opportunities? *Technological Forecasting and Social Change, 146*, 119–132. doi:10.1016/j.techfore.2019.05.021

Hossain, M. S., & Hossain, M. M. (2018). Application of interactive fuzzy goal programming for multi-objective integrated production and distribution planning. *International Journal of Process Management and Benchmarking, 8*(1), 35–58. doi:10.1504/IJPMB.2018.088656

Hossain, M. S., Muhammad, G., & Guizani, N. (2020). Explainable AI and mass surveillance system based healthcare framework to combat COVID-I9 like pandemics. *IEEE Network, 34*(4), 126–132. doi:10.1109/MNET.011.2000458

Hosseini Nejad, R., Haddad Pajouh, H., Dehghantanha, A., & Parizi, R. M. (2019). A cyber kill chain based analysis of remote access trojans. In D. A., & C. K. (Eds.), Handbook of big data and iot security (pp. 273-299). Cham: Springer.

Hou, Y., Xiong, D., Jiang, T., Song, L. & Wang, Q. (2019). Social media addiction: Its impact, mediation, and intervention. *Journal of Psychosocial Research on Cyberspace.*

How much does a truck driver make in Pennsylvania? (2021). https://www.indeed.com/career/truck-driver/salaries/PA

Howard, A. G., Menglong, Z., Bo, C., Kalenichenko, D., Weijun, W., & Weyand, T. (2017). MobileNets: Efficient Convolutional Neural Networks for Mobile Vision Applications. Academic Press.

Hu & Gharavi. (2014). Smart Grid Mesh Network Security Using Dynamic Key Distribution With Merkle Tree 4-Way Handshaking. *IEEE Transactions on Smart Grid, 5*. . doi:10.1109/TSG.2013.2277963

Huang, L., & Liu, D. (2019). Patient clustering improves efficiency of federated machine learning to predict mortality and hospital stay time using distributed electronic medical records. arXiv preprint arXiv:1903.09296.

Huang, C., Wang, Y., & Li, X. (2020). Clinical features of patients infected with 2019 novel coronavirus in Wuhan, China. *Lancet, 395*(10223), 497–506.

Huang, X., Zhang, L., Wang, B., Li, F., & Zhang, Z. (2018). Feature clustering based support vector machine recursive feature elimination for gene selection. *Applied Intelligence, 48*, 594–607.

Hupfer & Louks. (2018). *Succeeding in the age of digital transformation*. Deloitte.

Hurley, D. J., Nixon, M. S., & Carter, J. N. (2005). Force field feature extraction for ear biometrics. *Computer Vision and Image Understanding, 98*, 491–512.

Hussain, A. (2019). Industrial revolution 4.0: Implication to libraries and librarians. *Library Hi Tech News, 37*(1), 1–5. doi:10.1108/LHTN-05-2019-0033

Hussein, M. R., Apu, E. H., Shahabuddin, S., Shams, A. B., & Kabir, R. (2020). *Overview of digital health surveillance system during COVID-19 pandemic: public health issues and misapprehensions*. https://arxiv.org/abs/2007.13633

Hyslip, T., & Pittman, J. (2015). A Survey of Botnet Detection Techniques by Command and Control Infrastructure. *Journal of Digital Forensics, Security, and Law, 10*(1), 7–26. doi:10.1145/1090191.1080118

IBM Cloud. (2021a). *Getting started with IBM Cloudant*. https://cloud.ibm.com/docs/Cloudant?topic=Cloudant-getting-started-with-cloudant

IBM Cloud. (2021b). *IBM Cloudant docs*. https://cloud.ibm.com/docs/Cloudant

IEEE 802.11s. (2011). *Part11: Wireless LAN medium access control (MAC) (PHY) speciðcations amendment 10: Mesh networking*. IEEE Press.

IEEE-USA Board of Directors (2010). *Building a Stronger and Smarter Electrical Energy Infrastructure*. IEEE.

Iris DatabaseC. A. S. I. A. V4. (n.d.). http://biometrics.idealtest.org/dbDetailForUser.do?id=14

Iris Image Database VersionC. A. S. I. A. 1.0. (n.d.). http://biometrics.idealtest.org/dbDetailForUser.do?id=1

Iris Image DatasetC. U. H. K. (n.d.). http://www.mae.cuhk.edu.hk/~cvl/main_database.htm

Iyengar, V. S. (2002). Transforming data to satisfy privacy constraints. *Proceedings of the eighth ACM SIGKDD international conference on Knowledge discovery and data mining - KDD '02*. 10.1145/775047.775089

Iyer, A. (2018). Moving from Industry 2.0 to Industry 4.0: A case study from India on leapfrogging in smart manufacturing. *Procedia Manufacturing, 21*, 663–670. doi:10.1016/j.promfg.2018.02.169

Jääskelä, J., Haverinen, J., Kaksonen, R., Reponen, J., Halunen, K., & Tokola, T. (n.d.). *Digi-HTA, assessment framework for digital healthcare services: Information security and data protection in health technology – initial experiences*. Academic Press.

Jacobsen, J. P. (2011). Gender Inequality A Key Global Challenge: Reducing Losses due to Gender Inequality. Assessment Paper, Copenhagen Consensus on Human Challenges, Wesleyan University.

Jacobs, J. A. (1996). Gender Inequality and Higher Education. *Annual Review of Sociology, 22*(1), 153–185. doi:10.1146/annurev.soc.22.1.153

Jaggi, S., Langberg, M., Katti, S., Ho, T., Katabi, D., & M'edard, M. (2007). Resilient network coding in the presence of byzantine adversaries. In *IN- FOCOM 2007. 26th IEEE International Conference on Computer Communications*. IEEE. 10.1109/INFCOM.2007.78

Jain, A. K., Murty, M. N., & Flynn, P. J. (1999, September). Data clustering: A review. *ACM Computing Surveys, 31*(3), 264–323.

Jain, N., & D'lima, C. (2018). Organisational culture preference for gen Y's prospective job aspirants: A personality-culture fit perspective. *International Journal of Process Management and Benchmarking, 7*(2), 262–275. doi:10.1504/IJPMB.2017.083122

Jain, P., Agarwal, R., Billaiya, R., & Devi, J. (2016). Women education in rural India. *International Journal of Advanced Education and Research, 1*(12), 27–29. http://www.alleducationjournal.com/archives/2016/vol1/issue12/1-12-19

Jakalan, A., Barazi, J., & Xiaowei, W. (2014). *Botnet Detection Techniques*. Retrieved from http://www.researchgate.net/publication/281374083

Jamison, S. G. (2019). Creating a national data privacy law for the united states. *Cybaris Intell. Prop. L. Rev., 10*, 1.

Javaid, M., & Haleem, A. (2019). Industry 4.0 applications in medical field: A brief review. *Current Medicine Research and Practice*, *9*(3), 102–109. doi:10.1016/j.cmrp.2019.04.001

Jia, M., Liang, W., Xu, Z., & Huang, M. (2016). *Cloudlet load balancing in wireless metropolitan area networks*. IEEE.

Jiang, R., Lu, R., & Choo, K. R. (2018). Achieving high performance and privacy-preserving query over encrypted multidimensional big metering data. *Future Generation Computer Systems*, *78*, 392–401. doi:10.1016/j.future.2016.05.005

Jianxiong, D., Suen, C. Y., & Krzyzak, A. (2008). Effective shrinkage of large multi-class linear SVM models for text categorization. *19th International Conference on Pattern Recognition, ICPR 2008*.

Jillela, R., Ross, A. A., Boddeti, V. N., Kumar, B. V., Hu, X., & Plemmons, R. (2013). Iris segmentation for challenging periocular images. In Handbook of Iris Recognition. Springer.

Jillela, R., & Ross, A. (2012). Mitigating Effects of Plastic Surgery: Fusing Face and Ocular Biometrics. *International Conference on Biometrics: Theory, Applications and Systems*, 402–411.

Joseph, D. L., & Newman, D. A. (2010). Emotional intelligence: An integrative meta-analysis and cascading model. *The Journal of Applied Psychology*, *95*(1), 54.

Juefei-Xu, F., & Savvides, M. (2012). Unconstrained periocular biometric acquisition and recognition using COTS PTZ camera for uncooperative and non-cooperative subjects. *Applications of Computer Vision (WACV), 2012 IEEE Workshop on*, 201-208.

Kacprzyk, J., & Pedrycz, W. (Eds.). (2015). *Springer handbook of computational intelligence*. Springer. doi:10.1007/978-3-662-43505-2

Kailash, Saha, R. K., & Goyal, S. (2018). Systematic literature review of classification and categorisation of benchmarking in supply chain management. *International Journal of Process Management and Benchmarking, 7*(2), 183-205.

Kaiser, F. K., Wiens, M., & Schultmann, F. (2021). Use of digital healthcare solutions for care delivery during a pandemic-chances and (cyber) risks referring to the example of the COVID-19 pandemic. *Health and Technology*, *11*(5), 1125–1137. doi:10.100712553-021-00541-x PMID:33875933

Kaku, M. (2008). *Physics of the Impossible*. Anchor Books.

Kalla, A., Hewa, T., Mishra, R. A., Ylianttila, M., & Liyanage, M. (2020). The Role of Blockchain to Fight against COVID-19. *IEEE Engineering Management Review*, *48*(3), 85–96. doi:10.1109/EMR.2020.3014052

Kamat, P., Zhang, Y., Trappe, W., & Ozturk, C. (2005). Enhancing source- location privacy in sensor network routing. In *Distributed Computing Systems, 2005. ICDCS 2005. Proceedings. 25th IEEE International Conference on*. IEEE.

Kammara, T., & Moh, M. (2019). Identifying IoT-based Botnets. In *Botnets: Architectures, Countermeasures, and Challenges*. CRC Press.

Kandasamy M. (2020). Perspectives for the use of therapeutic Botulinum toxin as a multifaceted candidate drug to attenuate COVID-19. *Med Drug Discov*.

Kang, H. S., Lee, J. Y., Choi, S., Kim, H., Park, J. H., Son, J. Y., ... Noh, S. D. (2016). Smart manufacturing: Past research, present findings, and future directions. *International Journal of Precision Engineering and Manufacturing-Green Technology, 3*(1), 111-128.

Kannan, C., Dakshinamoorthy, M., Ramachandran, M., Patan, R., Kalyanaraman, H., & Kumar, A. (2021). Cryptography-based deep artificial structure for secure communication using IoT-enabled cyber-physical system. *IET Communications*, *15*(6), 771–779. doi:10.1049/cmu2.12119

Kaplan, B. (2016). How Should Health Data Be Used? Privacy, Secondary Use, and Big Data Sales. *Cambridge Quarterly of Healthcare Ethics*, *25*(2), 312–329. doi:10.1017/S0963180115000614 PMID:26957456

Kapoor & Moh. (2015). Implementation and evaluation of the DFF protocol for Advanced Metering Infrastructure (AMI) networks. *Proceedings of 11th IEEE International Conference on Design of Reliable Communication Networks.*

Kapoor, A., Guha, S., Kanti Das, M., Goswami, K. C., & Yadav, R. (2020). Digital healthcare: The only solution for better healthcare during COVID-19 pandemic? *Indian Heart Journal*, *72*(2), 61–64. doi:10.1016/j.ihj.2020.04.001 PMID:32534691

Karahan, Ş., Karaöz, A., Özdemir, Ö. F., Gü, A. G., & Uludag, U. (2014). On identification from periocular region utilizing sift and surf. *Signal Processing Conference (EUSIPCO), 2014 Proceedings of the 22nd European*, 1392-1396.

Karim, A., Salleh, R. B., Shiraz, M., Shah, S. A. A., Awan, I., & Anuar, N. B. (2014). Botnet detection techniques: review, future trends, and issues. *Journal of Zhejiang University SCIENCE C, 15*(11), 943–983. https://doi.org/ doi:10.1631/jzus.C1300242

Karkra & Patel. (2015). Atlas based medical segmentation techniques-A review. *Geinternational Journal of Engineering Research, 3*(5).

Kartit, Z., Azougaghe, A., Kamal Idrissi, H., El Marraki, M., Hedabou, M., Belkasmi, M., & Kartit, A. (2016). *Applying Encryption Algorithm for Data Security in Cloud Storage.* doi:10.1007/978-981-287-990-5_12

Katabi, S. K. J. C. D. (2007). *Information slicing: Anonymity using unreliable overlays.* Academic Press.

Kaur, H., Alam, M. A., Jameel, R., Mourya, A. K., & Chang, V. (2018). A Proposed Solution and Future Direction for Blockchain-Based Heterogeneous Medicare Data in Cloud Environment. *Journal of Medical Systems*, *42*(8), 156. Advance online publication. doi:10.100710916-018-1007-5 PMID:29987560

Kefa, R. (2005). Elliptic Curve ElGamal Encryption and Signature Schemes. *Information Technology Journal*, *4*(3), 299–306. doi:10.3923/itj.2005.299.306

Kelly, D., Raines, R., Baldwin, R., Grimaila, M., & Mullins, B. (2012). Exploring extant and emerging issues in anonymous networks: A taxonomy and survey of protocols and metrics. *IEEE Communications Surveys and Tutorials*, *14*(2), 579–606. doi:10.1109/SURV.2011.042011.00080

Kerner, S. M. (2020, June 23). *IBM advances its Cloudant cloud database as DBaaS grows.* https://www.techtarget.com/searchdatamanagement/news/252485085/IBM-advances-its-Cloudant-cloud-database-as-DBaaS-grows

Keshta, I., & Odeh, A. (2021). Security and privacy of electronic health records: Concerns and challenges. *Egyptian Informatics Journal*, *22*(2), 177–183. doi:10.1016/j.eij.2020.07.003

Kevin, M., Ana, F., & Alexey, K. (2019). Smart information systems in cybersecurity. *The ORBIT Journal*, *2*(2), 1–26. doi:10.29297/orbit.v2i2.105

Khan, N. A., Brohi, S. N., & Zaman, N. (2020). Ten Deadly Cyber Security Threats Amid COVID-19 Pandemic. TechRxiv *Powered by IEEE,* 1–6. https://www.techrxiv.org/articles/Ten_Deadly_Cyber_Security_Threats_Amid_COVID-19_Pandemic/12278792

Khan, N. A., Brohi, S. N., & Zaman, N. (2020). Ten deadly cyber security threats amid COVID-19 pandemic. *AIMS Electronics and Electrical Engineering*, *5*(2), 146–157.

Khattak, S., Ramay, N. R., Khan, K. R., Syed, A. A., & Khayam, S. A. (2014). *A Taxonomy of Botnet Behavior.* Academic Press.

Khaund, K. (2015). Cybersecurity in Smart Buildings. *Frost & Sullivan Collaborative Industry Perspective*, 21. Retrieved from http://23873b0b5ea986687186-fddd749ce937721293aa13aa786d4227.r31.cf1.rackcdn.com/Documentation/Cybersecurity%20in%20Smart%20Buildings_White%20Paper.pdf

Kiciński, J., & Chaja, P. (2021). Industry 4.0—The Fourth Industrial Revolution. In *Climate Change, Human Impact and Green Energy Transformation* (pp. 115–140). Springer. doi:10.1007/978-3-030-69933-8_10

Kim, D. W., Choi, J. Y., & Han, K. H. (2020). Risk management-based security evaluation model for telemedicine systems. *BMC Med Inform Decis, 20*(1), 1–14. doi:10.118612911-020-01145-7 PMID:32522216

Kim, J. H., Youn, S., & Roh, J. J. (2011). Green Supply Chain Management orientation and firm performance: Evidence from South Korea. *International Journal of Services and Operations Management, 8*(3), 283–304. doi:10.1504/IJSOM.2011.038973

Kim, J., Kim, D., Lim, K.-W., Ko, Y.-B., & Lee, S.-Y. (2012, December). Improving the Reliability of IEEE 802.11s Based Wireless Mesh Networks for Smart Grid Systems. *Journal of Communications and Networks (Seoul), 14*(6), 629–639. doi:10.1109/JCN.2012.00029

Kimura, K., & Lipeles, A. (1996). *Fuzzy controller component.* U.S. Patent 14,860,040.

Kim, W., Lee, H., & Chung, Y. D. (2020). Safe contact tracing for COVID-19: A method without privacy breach using functional encryption techniques based-on spatio-temporal trajectory data. *PLoS One, 15*(12), e0242758. doi:10.1371/journal.pone.0242758 PMID:33306698

Kim, Y., & Davis, G. (2016). Challenges for global supply chain sustainability: Evidence from conflict materials reports. *Academy of Management Journal, 59*(6), 1896–1916. doi:10.5465/amj.2015.0770

King, E. M., & Winthrop, R. (2015). *Today's Challenges for Girls' Education.* Retrieved from https://www.brookings.edu/wp-content/.../Todays-Challenges-Girls-Educationv6.pdf

Kite-Powell, J. (2020). Using machine learning to reduce carbon emissions in the trucking industry. *Forbes.* Retrieved December 31, 2021 from https://www.forbes.com/sites/jenniferhicks/2020/09/29/using-machine-learning-to-reduce-carbon-emissions-in-the-trucking-industry/?sh=3145bfc1a9e6

Klasen, S. (2002). Low Schooling for Girls, Slower Growth for All? Cross-Country Evidence on the Effect of Gender Inequality in Education on Economic Development. *The World Bank Economic Review, 16*(3), 345–373. doi:10.1093/wber/lhf004

Klasen, S., & Lamanna, F. (2009). The Impact of Gender Inequality in Education and Employment on Economic Growth: New Evidence for a Panel of Countries. *Feminist Economics, 15*(3), 91–132. doi:10.1080/13545700902893106

K-means clustering. (n.d.). In *Wikipedia*. Retrieved from https://en.wikipedia.org/wiki/K-means_clustering

KNOW. (2012). *W. Y. N. T. Global Trends in the Payment Card Industry.* Acquirers.

Kolias, C., Kambourakis, G., Stavrou, A., & Voas, J. (2017). DDoS in the IoT: Mirai and other botnets. *Computer, 50*(7), 80–84. doi:10.1109/MC.2017.201

Konečný, J., McMahan, H. B., Ramage, D., & Richtárik, P. (2016). Federated Optimization: Distributed Machine Learning for On-Device Intelligence. https://arxiv.org/abs/1610.02527

Kordafshari, M. S., & Movaghar, A. (2019). Multicast Routing in Wireless Sensor Networks: A Distributed Reinforcement Learning Approach. *Journal of New Researches in Mathematics, 5*(20), 91–104.

Kotsiantis, S., Zaharakis, I., & Pintelas, P. (2007). Supervised machine learning: A review of classification techniques. *Frontiers in Artificial Intelligence and Applications*, *160*, 3.

Kovacs, K. (2016). *Spymel Trojan Uses Stolen Certificates to Evade Detection*. Retrieved from https://www.securityweek.com/spymel-trojan-uses-stolen-certificates-evade-detection

Kovács-Ondrejkovic. (2019). Decoding Global Trends in Upskilling and Reskilling. Academic Press.

Kowalenko. (2010). *The Smart Grid: A Primer.* IEEE.

Kozen, D. (1997). *Automata and Computability*. Springer. doi:10.1007/978-1-4612-1844-9

Kozleski, E. B. (2017). The Uses of Qualitative Research: Powerful Methods to Inform Evidence-Based Practice in Education. *Research and Practice for Persons with Severe Disabilities*, *42*(1), 19–32. doi:10.1177/1540796916683710

Krebs, B. (2014). Email attack on vendor set up breach at target. *Krebs on Security, 12*.

Kroes, J. R., & Ghosh, S. (2010). Outsourcing congruence with competitive priorities: Impact on supply chain and firm performance. *Journal of Operations Management*, *28*(1), 124–143. doi:10.1016/j.jom.2009.09.004

Kumar Dadsena, K., Sarmah, S. P., & Naikan, V. N. A. (2019). Risk evaluation and mitigation of sustainable road freight transport operation: A case of trucking industry. *International Journal of Production Research*, *57*(19), 6223–6245. doi:10.1080/00207543.2019.1578429

Kumar, A., Sinha, R., Bhattacherjee, V., Verma, D. S., & Singh, S. (2012). Modeling using K-means clustering algorithm. *2012 1st International Conference on Recent Advances in Information Technology (RAIT)*, 554-558.

Kumar, J., & Sangeeta. (2013). Status of Women Education in India. *Educationia Confab, 2*(4), 162-176. Retrieved from https://slidex.tips/download/status-of-women-education-in-india

Kumar, Khan, Kumar, Zakria, Golilarz, Zhang, Ting, Zheng, & Wang. (2021). *Blockchain-Federated-Learning and Deep Learning Models for COVID-19 Detection Using CT Imaging*. Academic Press.

Kumar, A., Gupta, R., Sharma, N., & Goyal, S. (2022). Smart Quiz for Brain Stormers. In *Advances in Micro-Electronics, Embedded Systems and IoT* (pp. 399–406). Springer. doi:10.1007/978-981-16-8550-7_38

Kumar, A., & Passi, A. (2010). Comparison and combination of iris matchers for reliable personal authentication. *Pattern Recognition*, *43*(3), 1016–1026.

Kumari, P., & Seeja, K.R. (2019). Periocular biometrics: A survey. *Journal of King Saud University-Computer and Information Sciences*.

Kumari, C. U., Jeevan Prasad, S., & Mounika, G. (2019). Leaf Disease Detection: Feature Extraction with K-means clustering and Classification with ANN. *3rd International Conference on Computing Methodologies and Communication (ICCMC)*.

Kumar, M. A., & Gopal, M. (2010). An Investigation on Linear SVM and its Variants for Text Categorization. *2nd International Conference on Machine Learning and Computing (ICMLC 2010)*, 27-31.

Kumar, S., Lim, W. M., Sivarajah, U., & Kaur, J. (2022). Artificial Intelligence and Blockchain Integration in Business: Trends from a Bibliometric-Content Analysis. *Information Systems Frontiers*. Advance online publication. doi:10.100710796-022-10279-0 PMID:35431617

Kutlu, H., Avci, E., & Özyurt, F. (2020). White blood cells detection and classification based on regional convolutional neural networks. *Medical Hypotheses*.

Lachure, D., & Lachure, G., & Jadhav. (2015). White blood cell study and detection using Machine Learning. *IEEE International Advance Computing Conference (IACC).*

Langin, C., Zhou, H., & Rahimi, S. (2009). *A Self-Organizing Map and its Modeling for Discovering Malignant Network Traffic*. https://doi.org/ doi:10.1109/CI-CYBS.2009.4925099

Laroche, M., Bergeron, J., & Barbaro-Forleo, G. (2001). Targeting consumers who are willing to pay more for environmentally friendly products. *Journal of Consumer Marketing, 18*(6), 503–520. doi:10.1108/EUM0000000006155

Lasi, H., Fettke, P., Kemper, H. G., Feld, T., & Hoffmann, M. (2014). Industry 4.0. *Business & Information Systems Engineering, 6*(4), 239–242. doi:10.100712599-014-0334-4

Lauer, S. A., Grantz, K. H., & Bi, Q. (2020). The Incubation Period of Coronavirus Disease 2019 (COVID-19)From Publicly Reported Confirmed Cases: Estimation and Application. *Annals of Internal Medicine, 172*(9), 577–582.

Le, T. H. N., Prabhu, U., & Savvides, M. (2014). A novel eyebrow segmentation and eyebrow shape-based identification. *Biometrics (IJCB), 2014 IEEE International Joint Conference on*, 1-8.

Lea, R. (2016, July 17). *Lecture 7- Dashboards and UI techniques for Node-RED.* http://noderedguide.com/lecture-7-dashboards-and-ui-techniques-for-node-red/

Learner, J. S. (2014). *Emotions and Decision making.* https://scholar.harvard.edu/files/jenniferlerner/files/annual_review_manuscript_june_16_final.final_.pdf

Lee, C., & Lim, C. (2021). From technological development to social advance: A review of Industry 4.0 through machine learning. *Technological Forecasting and Social Change, 167*, 120653. doi:10.1016/j.techfore.2021.120653

LeFevre, K., DeWitt, D. J., & Ramakrishnan, R. (2005). Incognito. *Proceedings of the 2005 ACM SIGMOD international conference on Management of data - SIGMOD '05.* 10.1145/1066157.1066164

LeFevre, K., DeWitt, D., & Ramakrishnan, R. (2006). Mondrian multidimensional K-anonymity. *22nd International Conference on Data Engineering (ICDE'06).* 10.1109/ICDE.2006.101

Lenert, L., & McSwain, B. Y. (2020). Balancing health privacy, health information exchange, and research in the context of the COVID-19 pandemic. *Journal of the American Medical Informatics Association: JAMIA, 27*(6), 963–966. doi:10.1093/jamia/ocaa039 PMID:32232432

Levannon, G., Crofoot, E., Steemers, F., & Erickson, R. (2021). *Labor shortages - the Conference Board.* Retrieved October 23, 2021, from https://www.conference-board.org/topics/labor-shortages

Levine, B. N., & Shields, C. (2002). Hordes: A multicast based protocol for anonymity. *Journal of Computer Security, 10*(3), 213–240. doi:10.3233/JCS-2002-10302

Li, N., Li, T., & Venkatasubramanian, S. (2007). t-closeness: Privacy beyond k-anonymity and l-diversity. In *Data Engineering, 2007. ICDE 2007. IEEE 23rd International Conference on.* IEEE.

Li, Q. (2020). A Survey on federated learning Systems: vision, hype and reality for data privacy and protection. arXiv preprintarXiv:1907.0969.

Li, T. (2020). Privacy in Pandemic: Law, Technology, and Public Health in the COVID-19 Crisis. SSRN *Electronic Journal, 52*(3). doi:10.2139/ssrn.3690004

Li, W., Milletarì, F., Xu, D., Rieke, N., Hancox, J., Zhu, W., Baust, M., Cheng, Y., Ourselin, S., Cardoso, M. J., & Feng, A. (2019). Privacy-Preserving Federated Brain Tumour Segmentation. Lecture Notes in Computer Science, 11861, 133–141. doi:10.1007/978-3-030-32692-0_16

Li, X., & Furht, B. (2019). Design and implementation of digital libraries. Handbook of Internet Computing, 415–150. doi:10.1201/9781420049121.ch18

Liang, X., Zhao, J., Shetty, S., & Li, D. (2017). *Towards data assurance and resilience in iot using blockchain. In MILCOM 2017-2017 IEEE Military Communications Conference (MILCOM)*. IEEE.

Liao, W. H., & Chang, C. C. (2010, August). Peer to peer botnet detection using data mining scheme. In *2010 International Conference on Internet Technology and Applications* (pp. 1-4). IEEE.

Li, H., Lu, R., Zhou, L., Yang, B., & Shen, X. (2013). An Efficient Merkle-Tree-Based Authentication Scheme for Smart Grid. *IEEE Systems Journal*, *8*(2), 655–663. doi:10.1109/JSYST.2013.2271537

Lim, Lee, & Hsu. (2014). Transformed Representations for Convolutional Neural Networks in Blood subtypes detection. *Modern Artificial Intelligence for Health Analytic Papers from the AAAI.*

Lin, J., Yu, W., Zhang, N., Yang, X., Zhang, H., & Zhao, W. (2017). A survey on internet of things: Architecture, enabling technologies, security and privacy, and applications. *IEEE Internet of Things Journal*, *4*(5), 1125–1142. doi:10.1109/JIOT.2017.2683200

Li, S. (2017). IoT Node Authentication. In *Securing the Internet of Things* (pp. 69–95). Elsevier. doi:10.1016/B978-0-12-804458-2.00004-4

Li, T., Sahu, A. K., Talwalkar, A., & Smith, V. (2020). Federated learning: Challenges, methods, and future directions. *IEEE Signal Processing Magazine*, *37*(3), 50–60. doi:10.1109/MSP.2020.2975749

Liu, D., Li, Y., Hu, Y., & Liang, Z. (2010, October). A P2P-Botnet detection model and algorithms based on network streams analysis. In *2010 International Conference on Future Information Technology and Management Engineering* (*Vol. 1*, pp. 55-58). IEEE.

Liu, G., Lee, K. Y., & Jordan, H. F. (1997, June). TDM and TWDM de Bruijn networks and shufflenets for optical communications. *IEEE Transactions on Computers*, *46*(6), 695–701. doi:10.1109/12.600827

Liu, Q., Luo, D., Haase, J. E., Guo, Q., Wang, X. Q., Liu, S., Xia, L., Liu, Z., Yang, J., & Yang, B. X. (2020). The experiences of health-care providers during the COVID-19 crisis in China: A qualitative study. *The Lancet. Global Health*, *8*(6), e790–e798. doi:10.1016/S2214-109X(20)30204-7 PMID:32573443

Liu, Y., Han, J., & Wang, J. (2011). Rumor riding: Anonymizing unstructured peer-to-peer systems. *IEEE Transactions on Parallel and Distributed Systems*, *22*(3), 464–475. doi:10.1109/TPDS.2010.98

Lobo, F. (2020). *Industry 4.0–manufacturing and the future of medical things*. Academic Press.

Lodha, C., Dhingra, K., Mondal, R., & Goyal, S. (2022). Smart Healthcare with Fitness Application. *Smart Intelligent Computer Applications*, *2*, 403–409.

Lorenzen-Huber, L., Boutain, M., Camp, L. J., Shankar, K., & Connelly, K. H. (2011). Privacy, Technology, and Aging: A Proposed Framework. *Ageing International*, *36*(2), 232–252. doi:10.100712126-010-9083-y

Lo, S. K., Lu, Q., Wang, C., Paik, H. Y., & Zhu, L. (2021). A Systematic Literature Review on Federated Machine Learning: From a Sofware Engineering Perspective. *ACM Computing Surveys*, *54*(5), 1–39. Advance online publication. doi:10.1145/3450288

Luenendonk, M. (2019). *Industry 4.0 definition,Design,Principles,Challenges, and the Future of employment*. Cleverism.

Luz, E., Moreira, G., Zanlorensi, L. A. Jr, & Menotti, D. (2017). Deep periocular representation aiming video surveillance. *Pattern Recognition Letters*.

Mabrouk, M., Rajan, S., Bolic, M., Forouzanfar, M., Dajani, H. R., & Batkin, I. (2016). Human Breathing Rate Estimation from Radar Returns Using Harmonically Related Filters. *Journal of Sensors*, *2016*, 1–7. Advance online publication. doi:10.1155/2016/9891852

Macawile, Quinones, Ballado, Cruz, & Caya. (2018). White blood cell classification and counting using convolutional neural network. *2018 3rd International Conference on Control and Robotics Engineering (ICCRE).*

Machanavajjhala, A., Gehrke, J., Kifer, D., & Venkitasubramaniam, M. (2006). l-diversity: Privacy beyond k-anonymity. In *Data Engineering, 2006. ICDE'06. Proceedings of the 22nd International Conference on.* IEEE.

Machanavajjhala, A., Gehrke, J., Kifer, D., & Venkitasubramaniam, M. (2006). L-diversity: Privacy beyond K-anonymity. *22nd International Conference on Data Engineering (ICDE'06).* 10.1109/ICDE.2006.1

Madhav, A. V. S., & Tyagi, A. K. (2022). The World with Future Technologies (Post-COVID-19): Open Issues, Challenges, and the Road Ahead. In A. K. Tyagi, A. Abraham, & A. Kaklauskas (Eds.), *Intelligent Interactive Multimedia Systems for e-Healthcare Applications.* Springer. doi:10.1007/978-981-16-6542-4_22

Madlen, H., Drewitz, K. P., Piel, J., Hrudey, I., Rohr, M., Brunnthaler, V., Hasenpusch, C., Ulrich, A., Otto, N., Brandstetter, S., & Apfelbacher, C. (2022). *Intensive Care Units Healthcare Professionals ' Experiences and Negotiations at the Beginning of the COVID-19 Pandemic in Germany : A Grounded Theory Study.* doi:10.1177/00469580221081059

Mahalingam, G., & Ricanek, K. (2013). Article. *EURASIP Journal on Image and Video Processing*, *36*. Advance online publication. doi:10.1186/1687-5281-2013-36

Mahalingam, G., Ricanek, K., & Albert, A. M. (2014). Investigating the periocular-based face recognition across gender transformation. *IEEE Transactions on Information Forensics and Security*, *9*, 2180–2192.

Mahoney, M. F. (2020). Telehealth, telemedicine, and related technologic platforms: Current practice and response to the Covid-19 pandemic. *Journal of Wound, Ostomy, and Continence Nursing*, *47*(5), 439–444. doi:10.1097/WON.0000000000000694 PMID:32970029

Maiden, T. (2021). Transportation, warehouse capacity lacking, costs soar in November: Logistics Managers' Index shows supply chain tightens further. *FreightWaves*. Retrieved March 8, 2022 from https://www.freightwaves.com/news/transportation-warehouse-capacity-lacking-costs-soar-in-november

Mainieri, T., Barnett, E., Valdero, T. R., Unipan, J. B., & Oskamp, S. (1997). Green buying: The influence of environmental concern on consumer behaviour. *The Journal of Social Psychology*, *137*(6), 189–204. doi:10.1080/00224549709595430

Malik, B. K. (2013). Child Schooling and Child Work in India: Does Poverty Matter? *International Journal of Child Care and Education Policy*, *7*(1), 80–101. doi:10.1007/2288-6729-7-1-80

Markus, H. R., & Kitayama, S. (1991). Culture and the self: Implications for cognition, emotion, and motivation. *Psychological Review*, *98*, 224–253.

Martin, F. R. (2018). *Integrating AI Into Blockchain Can Help The Economy In More Ways Than You.* https://analyticsindiamag.com/

Martin, E. A. (2009). *A dictionary of law.* OUP Oxford.

Martin, P. Y., & Turner, B. A. (1986). Grounded Theory and Organizational Research. *The Journal of Applied Behavioral Science*, *22*(2), 141–157. doi:10.1177/002188638602200207

Martynov, V. V., Shavaleeva, D. N., & Zaytseva, A. A. (2019, September). Information technology as the basis for transformation into a digital society and industry 5.0. In *2019 International Conference Quality Management, Transport and Information Security, Information Technologies (IT&QM&IS)* (pp. 539-543). IEEE.

Marwaha, S. (2016). A compositional analysis of life events leading to apprehension of School Dropout in Mohali. *Australian Journal of Science and Technology*, *2*(1), 40–45. www.aujst.com/vol-2-1/06_AJST.pdf

Maslow, A. H. (1950). *Self-actualizing people: a study of psychological health.* Personality.

Mason, P., & Williams, B. (2020). Does IRS Monitoring Deter Managers From Committing Accounting Fraud? *Journal of Accounting, Auditing & Finance*. Advance online publication. doi:10.1177/0148558X20939720

Masood, T., & Egger, J. (2019). Augmented reality in support of Industry 4.0—Implementation challenges and success factors. *Robotics and Computer-integrated Manufacturing*, *58*, 181–195. doi:10.1016/j.rcim.2019.02.003

Mastaneh, Z., & Mouseli, A. (2020). Technology and its Solutions in the Era of COVID-19 Crisis: A Review of Literature. Evidence Based Health Policy. *Management and Economics*, *4*, 138–149.

Mathew, S., Petropoulos, M., Ngo, H. Q., & Upadhyaya, S. (2010, September). A data-centric approach to insider attack detection in database systems. In *International Workshop on Recent Advances in Intrusion Detection* (pp. 382-401). Springer. 10.1007/978-3-642-15512-3_20

Maxwell, J. A. (2012). The Importance of Qualitative Research for Causal Explanation in Education. *Qualitative Inquiry*, *18*(8), 655–661. doi:10.1177/1077800412452856

Mazurek, G., & Małagocka, K. (2019). Perception of privacy and data protection in the context of the development of artificial intelligence. *Journal of Management Analytics*, *6*(4), 344–364. doi:10.1080/23270012.2019.1671243

McArthur, L. Z., & Baron, R. M. (1983). Toward an ecological theory of social perception. *Psychological Review*, *90*(3), 215.

McCarthy, J. (2007). *What is artificial intelligence?* Academic Press.

McMahan, H. B., Moore, E., Ramage, D., Hampson, S., & Arcas, B. A. y. (2016). *Communication-Efficient Learning of Deep Networks from Decentralized Data.* https://arxiv.org/abs/1602.05629

McNally, S. (2020). *ATA freight forecast projects continued long-term growth in volumes*. American Trucking Associations. Retrieved December 31, 2021 from https://www.trucking.org/news-insights/ata-freight-forecast-projects-continued-long-term-growth-volumes

Meenakshi, Anitha Ruth, Kanagavalli, & Uma. (2022). Automatic classification of white blood cells using deep features based convolutional neural network. *Multimedia Tools and Applications*, •••, 101.

Meera, K. P., & Jumana, M. K. (2015). Empowering Women through Education. *International Journal of Humanities and Social Science Invention*, *4*(10), 58–61. http://www.ijhssi.org/papers/v4(10)/Version-3/H04103058061.pdf

Meghisan-Toma, G. M., & Nicula, V. C. (2020) ICT Security Measures for the Companies within European Union Member States–Perspectives in COVID-19 Context. *Proceedings of the International Conference on Business Excellence, 14*, 362–370. 10.2478/picbe-2020-0035

Meindl, B., Ayala, N. F., Mendonça, J., & Frank, A. G. (2021). The four smarts of Industry 4.0: Evolution of ten years of research and future perspectives. *Technological Forecasting and Social Change*, *168*, 120784. doi:10.1016/j.techfore.2021.120784

Meingast, M., Roosta, T., & Sastry, S. (2006). Security and privacy issues with health care information technology. *Annual International Conference of the IEEE Engineering in Medicine and Biology - Proceedings*, 5453–5458. 10.1109/IEMBS.2006.260060

Melanson, T. (2018). *What Industry 4.0 means for manufacturers.* Available online: https://aethon. com/mobilerobots-and-industry4-0/

Mendelson, D., & Wolf, G. (2017). Health privacy and confidentiality. *Tensions and Traumas in Health Law.*

Merkle, R. (1979). *Secrecy Authentication and Public Key Systems.* Information Systems Laboratory, Stanford Electronics Laboratories. Retrieved from https://www.merkle.com/papers/Thesis1979.pdf

Meyerson, A., & Williams, R. (2004). On the complexity of optimal K-anonymity. *Proceedings of the twenty-third ACM SIGMOD-SIGACT-SIGART symposium on Principles of database systems - PODS '04.* 10.1145/1055558.1055591

Miller, J. D. (2019, March). *Hands-On Machine Learning with IBM Watson.* Packt Publishing. https://nodered.org/docs/creating-nodes/

Miller, A. R., & Tucker, C. (2009). Privacy protection and technology diffusion: The case of electronic medical records. *Management Science*, *55*(7), 1077–1093. doi:10.1287/mnsc.1090.1014

Miller, J. W., Saldanha, J. P., Rungtusanatham, M., & Knemeyer, M. (2017). How does driver turnover affect motor carrier safety performance and what can managers do about it? *Journal of Business Logistics*, *38*(3), 197–216. doi:10.1111/jbl.12158

Miller, P., Rawls, A., Pundlik, S., & Woodard, D. (2010). Personal Identification Using Periocular Skin Texture. *ACM Symposium on Applied Computing*, 1496–1500.

Mishra, S., & Tyagi, A. K. (2022). The Role of Machine Learning Techniques in Internet of Things-Based Cloud Applications. In S. Pal, D. De, & R. Buyya (Eds.), *Artificial Intelligence-based Internet of Things Systems. Internet of Things (Technology, Communications and Computing).* Springer. doi:10.1007/978-3-030-87059-1_4

Misra, L., Misra, S. N., & Mishra, S. (2017). A survey on women's education and their economic condition in Odisha. *The Clarion (Guwahati)*, *6*(2), 113–121. doi:10.5958/2277-937X.2017.00038.7

Mitchell, R. (2017). *Mirai: The Program that Make IoT Botnet Zombies.* Retrieved from https://www.allaboutcircuits.com/news/mirai-the-program-that-makes-iot-Botnet-zombies/

Mitra, S., Mishra, S. K., & Abhay, R. K. (2022). Out-of-school girls in India: A study of socioeconomic-spatial disparities. *GeoJournal.* Advance online publication. doi:10.100710708-022-10579-7 PMID:35261431

Mobinius. (2020). *Industrial Revolution 4.0: Top 9 Technologies in Detail.* Academic Press.

Mohamed, N., & Ahmad, I. H. (2012). Information privacy concerns, antecedents and privacy measure use in social networking sites: Evidence from Malaysia. *Computers in Human Behavior*, *28*(6), 2366–2375. doi:10.1016/j.chb.2012.07.008

Mohammed, K., Singh, H., Joshi, V., & Goyal, S. (2022). Smart Irrigation System for Agriculture 4.0. *Smart Intelligent Computer Applications*, *2*, 411–418.

Molnar, C. (2020). *Interpretable machine learning.* Lulu. com.

Monroe, C., & Kim, J. (2013, March). Scaling the Ion Trap Quantum Processor. *Science*, *339*(6124), 1164–1169. doi:10.1126cience.1231298 PMID:23471398

Moon, J. G., Jang, J. J., & Jung, I. Y. (2015). Bot detection via IoT environment. *Proceedings - 2015 IEEE 17th International Conference on High Performance Computing and Communications, 2015 IEEE 7th International Symposium on Cyberspace Safety and Security and 2015 IEEE 12th International Conference on Embedded Software and Systems, HPCC-CSS-ICESS 2015*, 1691–1692. https://doi.org/10.1109/HPCC-CSS-ICESS.2015.116

Moore, S. Y., Grunberg, L., & Krause, A. J. (2014,). The relationship between work and home: Examination of white and blue-collar generational differences in a large U.S. organization. *Psychology*. Retrieved October 23, 2021, from https://www.scirp.org/html/7-6901275_50892.htm

Moraes, E. C., & Lepikson, H. A. (2017, October). Industry 4.0 and its impacts on society. In Proc. Int. Conf. Ind. Eng. *Open Management*, *2017*, 729–735.

Mora, H., Signes-Pont, M. T., Gil, D., & Johnsson, M. (2018). Collaborative working architecture for IoT-based applications. *Sensors (Basel)*, *18*(6), 1676. doi:10.339018061676 PMID:29882868

Moreham, N. (2008). *Why is privacy important? privacy, dignity and development of the New Zealand breach of privacy tort*. Academic Press.

Morrar, R., Arman, H., & Mousa, S. (2017). The fourth industrial revolution (Industry 4.0): A social innovation perspective. *Technology Innovation Management Review*, *7*(11), 12–20. doi:10.22215/timreview/1117

Mulay, A., Gaspard, B., Naidu, R., Gonzalez-Toral, S., Semwal, T., & Manish Agrawal, A. (2021). FedPerf: A Practitioners' Guide to Performance of Federated Learning Algorithms. *Proceedings.Mlr.Press*, *148*(NeurIPS), 302–324. http://proceedings.mlr.press/v148/mulay21a.html

Muñoz, M., Moh, M., & Moh, T.-S. (2014). Improving Smart Grid Authentication using Merkle Trees. *Proc. IEEE International Conference on Parallel and Distributed Systems.*

Muñoz, M., Moh, M., & Moh, T.-S. (2014). Improving Smart Grid Security using Merkle Trees. *IEEE Conference on Communications and Network Security*, 522-523. 10.1109/CNS.2014.6997535

Münz, G., Li, S., & Carle, G. (2007). *Traffic Anomaly Detection Using K-Means Clustering*. Academic Press.

Murphy, N. (2020). Santa's got shipping issues: Why retailers are worried about gifts stuck just beyond the last mile. *Forbes*. Retrieved December 31, 2021 from https://www.forbes.com/sites/niallmurphy/2020/12/08/santas-got-shipping-issues-why-retailers-are-worried-about-gifts-stuck-just-beyond-the-last-mile/?sh=18c5dd406a9c

Murray, D., & Glidewell, S. (2019). *An Analysis of the Operational Costs of Trucking: 2019 Update*. American Transportation Research Institute. Retrieved March 8, 2022 from https://truckingresearch.org/wp-content/uploads/2019/11/ATRI-Operational-Costs-of-Trucking-2019-1.pdf

Nadian-Ghomsheh, A., Farahani, B., & Kavian, M. (2021). A hierarchical privacy-preserving IoT architecture for vision-based hand rehabilitation assessment. *Multimedia Tools and Applications*, *80*(20), 1–24. doi:10.100711042-021-10563-2 PMID:33613083

Nagaraj, A. (2021). Introduction to Sensors in IoT and Cloud Computing Applications. Bentham Science Publishers. doi:10.2174/97898114793591210101

Nageshwaran, G., Harris, R. C., & El Guerche-Seblain, C. (2021). Review of the role of big data and digital technologies in controlling COVID-19 in Asia: Public health interest vs. privacy. *Digital Health*, *7*, 1–12. doi:10.1177/20552076211002953 PMID:33815815

Naidoo, R. (2020). A multi-level influence model of COVID-19 themed cybercrime. *European Journal of Information Systems*, *29*(3), 306–321. doi:10.1080/0960085X.2020.1771222

Nair & Tyagi. (n.d.). Privacy: History, Statistics, Policy, Laws, Preservation and Threat Analysis. *Journal of Information Assurance &Security*, *16*(1), 24-34.

Nair, M. M., & Tyagi, A. K. (2021). Privacy: History, Statistics, Policy, Laws, Preservation and Threat Analysis. Journal of Information Assurance & Security, 16(1), 24-34.

Nair, N. (2010). Women's education in India: A situational analysis. *Indore Management Journal, 1*(4), 100-114. Retrieved from www.iimidr.ac.in/wp-content/.../Womens-Education-in-India-A-Situational-Analysis.pdf

Nair, M. M., & Tyagi, A. K. (2021). Privacy: History, Statistics, Policy, Laws, Preservation and Threat Analysis. *Journal of Information Assurance & Security*, *16*(1), 24–34.

Nair, M. M., & Tyagi, A. K. (2021). Privacy: History, statistics, policy, laws, preservation and threat analysis. *Journal of Information Assurance & Security*, *16*(1).

Narang, P., Khurana, V., & Hota, C. (2014). Machine-learning approaches for P2P botnet detection using signal-processing techniques. *Proceedings of the 8th ACM International Conference on Distributed Event-Based Systems - DEBS '14*, 338–341. https://doi.org/10.1145/2611286.2611318

Naresh, V. S., Reddi, S., Murthy, N. V. E. S., & Guessoum, Z. (2020). Secure Lightweight IoT Integrated RFID Mobile Healthcare System. *Wireless Communications and Mobile Computing*, *2020*, 1–13. Advance online publication. doi:10.1155/2020/1468281

Narvaez Rojas, C., Alomia Peñafiel, G. A., Loaiza Buitrago, D. F., & Tavera Romero, C. A. (2021). Society 5.0: A Japanese concept for a superintelligent society. *Sustainability*, *13*(12), 6567. doi:10.3390u13126567

Na, S., Xumin, L., & Yong, G. (2010). Research on k-means Clustering Algorithm: An Improved k-means Clustering Algorithm. *2010 Third International Symposium on Intelligent Information Technology and Security Informatics*, 63-67. 10.1109/IITSI.2010.74

Nayaki, D., Rubeena, & Denny. (2020). Cloud based Acute Lymphoblastic Leukemia Detection Using Deep Convolutional Neural Networks. *2020 Second International Conference on Inventive Research in Computing Applications (ICIRCA).*

Necula, G. C., McPeak, S., & Weimer, W. (2002, January). CCured: Type-safe retrofitting of legacy code. In *Proceedings of the 29th ACM SIGPLAN-SIGACT symposium on Principles of programming languages* (pp. 128-139). 10.1145/503272.503286

Newman, L. H. (2016). *The Botnet That Broke the Internet Isn't Going Away*. Retrieved from https://www.digitalshadows.com/about-us/news-and-press/wired-the-Botnet-that-broke-the-internet-isnt-going-away/

Nguyen, D. C., Ding, M., Pathirana, P. N., & Seneviratne, A. (2021). Blockchain and AI-Based Solutions to Combat Coronavirus (COVID-19)-Like Epidemics: A Survey. *IEEE Access: Practical Innovations, Open Solutions*, *9*, 95730–95753. doi:10.1109/ACCESS.2021.3093633 PMID:34812398

Nguyen, D. C., Pham, Q.-V., Pathirana, P. N., Ding, M., Seneviratne, A., Lin, Z., Dobre, O., & Hwang, W.-J. (2023). Federated Learning for Smart Healthcare: A Survey. *ACM Computing Surveys*, *55*(3), 1–37. doi:10.1145/3501296

Nicholson, P. (2015). *What lies beneath: advanced attacks that hide in ssl traffic*. Retrieved June 16, 2018, from https://www.a10networks.com/resources/articles/what-lies-beneath-advanced-attacks-hide-ssl-traffic

Nishio, T., & Yonetani, R. (2019). Client Selection for Federated Learning with Heterogeneous Resources in Mobile Edge. *IEEE International Conference on Communications.* 10.1109/ICC.2019.8761315

NIST 7628 Revision 1. (2014). *Guidelines for Smart Grid Cyber Security.* Retrieved from https://nvlpubs.nist.gov/nistpubs/ir/2014/NIST.IR.7628r1.pdf

NIST 7628. (2010). *Guidelines for Smart Grid Cyber Security*. Retrieved from https://www.nist.gov/smartgrid/upload/nistir-7628_total.pdf

NIST IR 8413. (2022). *Status Report on the Third Round of the NIST Post-Quantum Cryptography Standardization Process*. Retrieved from https://nvlpubs.nist.gov/nistpubs/ir/2022/NIST.IR.8413.pdf

NIST. (2008). *Multiple Biometric Grand Challenge (MBGC) dataset.* https://face.nist.gov/mbgc/

NIST. (2016). *Framework 3.0 a Beginner's guide.* Retrieved from https://www.nist.gov/el/smartgrid/framework-30-beginners-guide

NIST. (2019). *Smart Grid Advisory Committee 2019 Report.* Retrieved from https://protect-us.mimecast.com/s/n8sWC0RXxZu2wmlXFwUuGr?domain=nist.gov

Nithiya, C., & Sridevi, R. (2016). ECC algorithm & security in cloud. *International Journal of Advanced Research in Computer Science & Technology, 4*(1), 24–27.

Noto, G., & Bianchi, C. (2015). Dealing with Multi-Level Governance and Wicked Problems in Urban Transportation Systems: The Case of Palermo Municipality. *Systems, 3*(3), 62–80.

Nour, B., Sharif, K., Li, F., & Wang, Y. (2019). Security and privacy challenges in information-centric wireless internet of things networks. *IEEE Security and Privacy, 18*(2), 35–45. doi:10.1109/MSEC.2019.2925337

Oey, E., & Nofrimurti, M. (2018). Lean implementation in traditional distributor warehouse - a case study in an FMCG company in Indonesia. *International Journal of Process Management and Benchmarking, 8*(1), 1–15. doi:10.1504/IJPMB.2018.088654

Oh, K., Oh, B.-S., Toh, K.-A., Yau, W.-Y., & Eng, H.-L. (2014). Combining sclera and periocular features for multi-modal identity verification. *Neurocomputing, 128*, 185–198.

Ojala, T., Pietik¨ainen, M., & M¨aenp¨a¨a, T. (2000). Gray scale and rotation invariant texture classification with local binary patterns. *Proceedings of the European Conference on Computer Vision*, 404–420.

Ojansivu, V., & Heikkilä, J. (2008). Blur insensitive texture classification using local phase quantization. *International conference on image and signal processing*, 236-243.

Open J. S. Foundation. (n.d.a). *Node-RED, Developing Flows.* https://nodered.org/docs/developing-flows/

Open J. S. Foundation. (n.d.b). *Node-RED, First Flow Tutorial.* https://nodered.org/docs/tutorials/first-flow

Open J. S. Foundation. (n.d.c). *Node-RED, node-red-contrib-graphs, Version 0.3.5.* https://flows.nodered.org/node/node-red-contrib-graphs

Open J. S. Foundation. (n.d.d). *Node-RED, node-red-dashboard, Version 3.1.6.* https://flows.nodered.org/node/node-red-dashboard

Open J. S. Foundation. (n.d.e). *Node-RED, node-red-node-sentiment Version 0.1.6.* https://flows.nodered.org/node/node-red-node-sentiment

Orlikowski, W. J. (1993). CASE tools as organizational change: Investigating incremental and radical changes in systems development. *MIS Quarterly: Management Information Systems, 17*(3), 309–340. doi:10.2307/249774

Osifchin, N., & Vau, G. (1997). Power considerations for the modernization of telecommunications in Central and Eastern European and former Soviet Union (CCE/FSU) countries. *Second International Telecommunication Energy Special Conference Special Conference*, 9-16. 10.1109/TELESC.1997.655690

Ozturk, C., Zhang, Y., & Trappe, W. (2004). Source-location privacy in energy-constrained sensor network routing. In *Proceedings of the 2nd ACM workshop on Security of ad hoc and sensor networks*. ACM. 10.1145/1029102.1029117

Pacheco, J., & Hariri, S. (2016). IoT security framework for smart cyber infrastructures. *Proceedings - IEEE 1st International Workshops on Foundations and Applications of Self-Systems. FAS-W, 2016*, 242–247. doi:10.1109/FAS-W.2016.58

Padalkar, N. R., Sheikh-Zadeh, A., & Song, J. (2020). *Business Value of Smart Contract: Case of Inventory Information Discrepancies*. Academic Press.

Padole, C. N., & Proenca, H. (2012). Periocular recognition: Analysis ofperformance degradation factors. *Biometrics (ICB), 2012 5th IAPR International Conference on*, 439-445.

Padole, C., & Proenca, H. (2012). Periocular Recognition: Analysis of Performance Degradation Factors. *International Conference on Biometrics*, 439–445.

Palmer, C. (2021). Quantum Computing Quickly Scores Second Claim of Supremacy. *Engineering*, *7*(9), 1199–1200. doi:10.1016/j.eng.2021.07.006

Panwar, A., Bafna, S., Raghav, A., & Goyal, S. (2022). Intelligent Traffic Management System Using Industry 4.0. In *Advances in Micro-Electronics, Embedded Systems and IoT* (pp. 357–364). Springer. doi:10.1007/978-981-16-8550-7_34

Park, Y. J., & Shin, D. (2020). Contextualizing privacy on health-related use of information technology. *Computers in Human Behavior, 105*(October), 106204. doi:10.1016/j.chb.2019.106204

Parks, R., Chu, C. H., Xu, H., & Adams, L. (2011). Understanding the drivers and outcomes of healthcare organizational privacy responses. *International Conference on Information Systems 2011, ICIS 2011, 1*(2), 245–264.

Park, U., Jillela, R., Ross, A., & Jain, A. (2011, March). Periocular biometrics in the visible spectrum. *IEEE Transactions on Information Forensics and Security*, *6*(1), 96–106.

Park, U., Ross, A., & Jain, A. K. (2009). Periocular biometrics in the visible spectrum: A feasibility study. *Proceedings of the IEEE International Conference on Biometrics: Theory, Applications, and Systems*, 1–6.

Partala, J., Keräneny, N., & Särestöniemi, M. (2013) Security threats against the transmission chain of a medical health monitoring system. *2013 IEEE 15th International Conference on eHealth Networking, Applications and Services (Healthcom 2013),* 243–248. 10.1109/HealthCom.2013.6720675

Pastas Pastaz, J. S., & Pujos Tualombo, J. F. (2022). *Estado del arte utilizando mapeo sistemático de la seguridad del internet de las cosas para infraestructuras en hogares inteligentes* (Bachelor's thesis).

Pegkas, P. (2014). The Link between Educational Levels and Economic Growth: A Neoclassical Approach for the Case of Greece. *International Journal of Applied Economics*, *11*(2), 38–54. https://www2.southeastern.edu/orgs/ijae/index_files/IJAE%20SEPT%202014%20PEGKAS%207-30-2014%20RV.pdf

Pekkarinen, T. (2012). Gender differences in education. *Nordic Economic Policy Review*, 1. Retrieved from ftp.iza.org/dp6390.pdf

Perera, C., Zaslavsky, A., Christen, P., & Georgakopoulos, D. (2014). Context aware computing for the internet of things: A survey. *IEEE Communications Surveys and Tutorials*, *16*(1), 414–454. doi:10.1109/SURV.2013.042313.00197

Pérez-Lara, M., Saucedo-Martínez, J. A., Marmolejo-Saucedo, J. A., Salais-Fierro, T. E., & Vasant, P. (2020). Vertical and horizontal integration systems in Industry 4.0. *Wireless Networks*, *26*(7), 4767–4775. doi:10.100711276-018-1873-2

Pfitzmann, A., & Hansen, M. (2008). *Anonymity, unlinkability, undetectability, unobservability, pseudonymity, and identity management-a consolidated proposal for terminology.* Version v0.

Pfitzmann, A., & Hansen, M. (2010). *A terminology for talking about privacy by data, minimization: Anonymity, unlinkability, undetectability, unobservability, pseudonymity, and identity management.* Academic Press.

Pfitzmann, A., & Waidner, M. (1987). Networks without user observability. *Computers & Security*, *6*(2), 158–166. doi:10.1016/0167-4048(87)90087-3

Pham, D. T., Dimov, S. S., & Nguyen, C. D. (2003). Incremental K-means algorithm. *Proc. Instn Mech. Engrs. Part C. Journal of Mechanical Engineering Science*, *218*(7), 783–795. doi:10.1243/0954406041319509

Phillips, P. J., Bowyer, K. W., & Flynn, P. J. (2007, October). Comments on the casia version 1.0 iris data set. *IEEE Transactions on Pattern Analysis and Machine Intelligence*, *29*, 1869–1870.

Phillips, P., Flynn, P., Scruggs, T., Bowyer, K., Chang, J., Hoffman, K., Marques, J., Min, J., & Worek, W. (2005). Overview of the face recognition grand challenge. *IEEE International Conference on Computer Vision and Pattern Recognition*, 1, 947–954.

Plohmann, D., Gerhards-Padilla, E., & Leder, F. (2011, March). Botnets: measurement, detection, disinfection and defence. ENISA workshop on.

Pokharel, S. (2008). Gender Discrimination: Women Perspectives. *Nepalese Journal of Development and Rural Studies*, *5*(2), 80–87.

Polat, L., & Erkollar, A. (2020, September). Industry 4.0 vs. Society 5.0. In *The International Symposium for Production Research* (pp. 333-345). Springer.

Poller, J. (2019). *Hybrid Multi-cloud Artificial Intelligence (AI): IBM Watson Studio and Watson Machine Learning.* https://www.esg-global.com/hubfs/ibm/4761/index.html

Porambage, P., Ylianttila, M., Schmitt, C., Kumar, P., Gurtov, A., & Vasilakos, A. V. (2016). The Quest for Privacy in the Internet of Things. *IEEE Cloud Computing*, *3*(2), 36–45. doi:10.1109/MCC.2016.28

Prabhakar &Rajaguru. (2017). PCA and K-Means Clustering for Classification of Epilepsy Risk Levels from EEG Signals – A Comparative Study Between Them. *The 16th International Conference on Biomedical Engineering,* 80-87.

Primeau, N., Falcon, R., Abielmona, R., & Petriu, E. M. (2018). A Review of Computational Intelligence Techniques in Wireless Sensor and ActuatorNetworks. *IEEE Communications Surveys and Tutorials*, *20*(4), 2822–2854. doi:10.1109/COMST.2018.2850220

Prinsloo, J., Sinha, S., & von Solms, B. (2019). A review of industry 4.0 manufacturing process security risks. *Applied Sciences (Basel, Switzerland)*, *9*(23), 5105. doi:10.3390/app9235105

Priya & Aruna. (2012). SVM and Neural Network based Diagnosis of blood cell types. *International Journal of Computers and Applications*, *41*(1).

Proença, H. (2014). Ocular biometrics by score-level fusion of disparate experts. *IEEE Transactions on Image Processing*, *23*, 5082–5093.

Proença, H., & Briceño, J. C. (2014). Periocular biometrics: Constraining the elastic graph matching algorithm to biologically plausible distortions. *IET Biometrics*, *3*, 167–175.

Proenca, H., & Neves, J. C. (2018). Deep-PRWIS: Periocular Recognition Without the Iris and Sclera Using Deep Learning Frameworks. *IEEE Transactions on Information Forensics and Security*, *13*, 888–896.

Psaki, S., Haberland, N., Mensch, B., Woyczynski, L., & Chuang, E. (2022). Policies and Interventions to remove Gender-related Barriers to Girls' School Participation and Learning in Low- and Middle-income Countries: A Systematic Review of the Evidence. *Campbell Systematic Reviews*, *12*(1), e1207. doi:10.1002/cl2.1207

Quilala, T. F. G., Sison, A. M., & Medina, R. P. (2018). Modified Blowfish Algorithm. *Indonesian Journal of Electrical Engineering and Computer Science*, *12*(1), 38. doi:10.11591/ijeecs.v12.i1.pp38-45

Qureshi, M. B., Qureshi, M. S., Tahir, S., Anwar, A., Hussain, S., Uddin, M., & Chen, C.-L. (2022). Encryption Techniques for Smart Systems Data Security Offloaded to the Cloud. *Symmetry*, *14*(4), 695. doi:10.3390ym14040695

Qu, Y., Pokhrel, S. R., Garg, S., Gao, L., & Xiang, Y. (2021, April). A block chained federated learning framework for cognitive computing in industry 4.0 networks. *IEEE Transactions on Industrial Informatics*, *17*(4), 2964–2973. Advance online publication. doi:10.1109/TII.2020.3007817

Rabin, M. O. (1989). Efficient dispersal of information for security, load balancing, and fault tolerance. *Journal of the Association for Computing Machinery*, *36*(2), 335–348. doi:10.1145/62044.62050

Radanliev, P., De Roure, D., & Walton, R. (2020). COVID-19 what have we learned? The rise of social machines and connected devices in pandemic management following the concepts of predictive, preventive and personalized medicine. *The EPMA Journal*, *30*, 1–22. PMID:32839666

Rahim, F. A., Ismail, Z., & Samy, G. N. (2017). Healthcare employees' perception on information privacy concerns. *International Conference on Research and Innovation in Information Systems, ICRIIS, November 2013*, 3–8. 10.1109/ICRIIS.2017.8002498

Raju, R., & Moh, M. (2019). Using Machine Learning for Protecting the Security and Privacy of Internet-of-Things (IoT) Systems. In Fog and Edge Computing: Principles and Paradigms. Wiley.

Rasoo. (2018). *What is Augmented Reality in Smartphones?* Academic Press.

Rattani, A., Derakhshani, R., Saripalle, S. K., & Gottemukkula, V. (2016). ICIP 2016 competition on mobile ocular biometric recognition. *2016 IEEE International Conference on Image Processing (ICIP)*, 320-4.

Ravikumar, S. (2015). Image segmentation and classification of white blood cells with the extreme learning machine and the fast relevance vector machine. *Artificial Cells, Nanomedicine, and Biotechnology.*

Raymond, J.-F. (2001). Traffic analysis: Protocols, attacks, design issues, and open problems. In *Designing Privacy Enhancing Technologies* (pp. 10–29). Springer. doi:10.1007/3-540-44702-4_2

Ray, P., & Wimalasiri, J. (2006). The need for technical solutions for maintaining the privacy of EHR. *Annual International Conference of the IEEE Engineering in Medicine and Biology - Proceedings*, 4686–4689. 10.1109/IEMBS.2006.260862

Reed, M. G., Syverson, P. F., & Goldschlag, D. M. (1998). Anonymous connections and onion routing. *IEEE Journal on Selected Areas in Communications*, *16*(4), 482–494. doi:10.1109/49.668972

Reegu, F. A., Daud, S. M., Alam, S., & Shuaib, M. (2021). Blockchain-based Electronic Health Record System for efficient Covid-19 Pandemic Management. April, 1–5. doi:10.20944/preprints202104.0771.v1

Rego, A., Canovas, A., Jiménez, J. M., & Lloret, J. (2018). An intelligent system for video surveillance in IoT environments. *IEEE Access: Practical Innovations, Open Solutions*, *6*, 31580–31598. doi:10.1109/ACCESS.2018.2842034

Rego, S., Kumar, N., & Mukherjee, P. N. (2018). Impact of policy implementation on telecommunication diffusion in India. *International Journal of Process Management and Benchmarking*, *8*(1), 16–34. doi:10.1504/IJPMB.2018.088655

Regulation, P. (2018). General data protection regulation. *InTouch*.

Reiter, M. K., & Rubin, A. D. (1998). Crowds: Anonymity for web transactions. *ACM Transactions on Information and System Security*, *1*(1), 66–92. doi:10.1145/290163.290168

Rena, R. (2004). Gender Disparity in Education - An Eritrean Perspective. *USA: The Global Child Journal, 2*(1), 43-49. Retrieved from https://mpra.ub.uni-muenchen.de/10315/1/MPRA_paper_10315.pdf

Rezaei, M., & Fränti, P. (2016). Set-matching methods for external cluster validity. *IEEE Transactions on Knowledge and Data Engineering*, *28*(8), 2173–2186.

Riazi, M. S., Rouani, B. D., & Koushanfar, F. (2019). Deep learning on private data. *IEEE Security and Privacy*, *17*(6), 54–63. doi:10.1109/MSEC.2019.2935666

Rieffel, E., & Polak, W. (2011). *Quantum Computing, A Gentle Introduction*. The MIT Press.

Rieke, N., Hancox, J., Li, W., Milletarì, F., Roth, H. R., Albarqouni, S., Bakas, S., Galtier, M. N., Landman, B. A., Maier-Hein, K., Ourselin, S., Sheller, M., Summers, R. M., Trask, A., Xu, D., Baust, M., & Cardoso, M. J. (2020). The future of digital health with federated learning. *NPJ Digital Medicine*, *3*(1), 1–7. doi:10.103841746-020-00323-1 PMID:33015372

Rindfleisch, T. (1997). Privacy, Information Technology, and Health Care. *Communications of the ACM, 40*(8), 92-100. http://delivery.acm.org.sheffield.idm.oclc.org/10.1145/260000/257896/p92-rindfleisch.pdf?ip=154.59.124.32&id=257896&acc=ACTIVE SERVICE&key=BF07A2EE685417C5.33526737E11CAFEF.4D4702B0C3E38B35.4D4702B0C3E38B35&__acm__=1558621514_ee4cff6b52d7ab91993c4

Ritu & Kaushal R. (2015). Machine Learning Approach for Botnets Detection. In *3rd Security and Privacy Symposium*. IIIT – Delhi.

Rivest, R. L., Shamir, A., & Tauman, Y. (2001). How to leak a secret. In *International Conference on the Theory and Application of Cryptology and Information Security*. Springer.

Rohr, J. R., Raffel, T. R., Romansic, J. M., McCallum, H., & Hud-son, P. J. (n.d.). Evaluating the links between climate, disease spread, and amphibian declines. *Proceedings of the National Academy of Sciences of the United States of America*, 105(45).

Rojko, A. (2017). Industry 4.0 concept: Background and overview. *International Journal of Interactive Mobile Technologies, 11*(5).

Roman, R., Najera, P., & Lopez, J. (2011). Securing the internet of things. *Computer*, *44*(9), 51–58. doi:10.1109/MC.2011.291

Roman, R., Zhou, J., & Lopez, J. (2013). On the features and challenges of security and privacy in distributed internet of things. *Computer Networks*, *57*(10), 2266–2279. doi:10.1016/j.comnet.2012.12.018

Rosenbaum, B. P. (2014). Radio frequency identification (RFID) in health care: Privacy and security concerns limiting adoption. *Journal of Medical Systems*, *38*(3), 1–6. doi:10.100710916-014-0019-z PMID:24578170

Rosenblatt, L. (2021). No driver needed: Self-driving trucks are starting to move cargo on the nation's highways. *Pittsburgh Post-Gazette*. Retrieved December 31, 2021 from https://www.post-gazette.com/business/tech-news/2020/03/30/self-driving-trucks-autonomous-cars-Locomation-Wilson-Logistics-Maven-Machines-Idelic/stories/202003290032

Rosen, K. (1995). *Discrete Mathematics And Its Applications* (3rd ed.). McGraw-Hill, Inc.

Ross, A., Nandakumar, K., & Jain, A. (2006). Handbook of Multibiometrics. Academic Press.

Rouse, M. (2009, March). *Conficker*. Retrieved January 27, 2019, from http://whatis.techtarget.com/definition/Conficker

Roychowdhury, S., Koozekanani, D. D., & Keshab, K. P. (2014). Blood subtypes detection Using Machine Learning. *IEEE Journal of Biomedical and Health Informatics, 18*(5).

RTS Financial and RTS Carrier Services. (2020). *Best practices for hiring and retaining drivers*. Retrieved December 31, 2021 from https://www.rtsinc.com/articles/best-practices-hiring-and-retaining-drivers

Rubí, J. N., & Gondim, P. R. (2020). Interoperable internet of medical things platform for e-health applications. *Int J Distrib Sens, 16*(1), 1550147719889591. doi:10.1177/1550147719889591

Rubner, Y., & Tomasi, C. (2001). The earth mover's distance. *Perceptual Metrics for Image Database Navigation,* 13-28. doi:10.1007/978-1-4757-3343-3_2

Ruffman, T., Henry, J. D., Livingstone, V., & Phillips, L. H. (2008). A meta-analytic review of emotion recognition and aging: Implications for neuropsychological models of aging. *Neuroscience and Biobehavioral Reviews, 32*(4), 863–881.

Saad, S., Traore, I., Ghorbani, A., Sayed, B., Zhao, D., Lu, W., . . . Hakimian, P. (2011). Detecting P2P botnets through network behavior analysis and machine learning. *2011 Ninth Annual International Conference on Privacy Security and Trust*, 174–180. https://doi.org/10.1109/PST.2011.5971980

Sahagun, L. (2019, June 14). One in 4 Californians live in a 'high risk' wildfire area. Is the state ready for another fire season? *LA Times*.

Sahai, A., & Waters, B. (2005). Fuzzy identity-based encryption. In *Annual International Conference on the Theory and Applications of Cryptographic Techniques*. Springer.

Sahama, T., Simpson, L., & Lane, B. (2013). Security and Privacy in eHealth: Is it possible? *2013 IEEE 15th International Conference on E-Health Networking, Applications and Services, Healthcom 2013, Healthcom*, 249–253. 10.1109/HealthCom.2013.6720676

Saha, S., & Ahmad, T. (2021). Federated transfer learning: Concept and applications. *IntelligenzaArtificiale, 15*(1), 35–44. doi:10.3233/IA-200075

Sahlol, A. T., Kollmannsberger, P., & Ewees, A. A. (2020). Efficient Classification of White Blood Cell Leukemia with Improved Swarm Optimization of Deep Features. *Scientific Reports, 10*(1), 2536. doi:10.103841598-020-59215-9 PMID:32054876

Sahu, A. K., Datta, S., & Mahapatra, S. S. (2014). Green supply chain performance benchmarking using integrated IVFN-TOPSIS methodology. *International Journal of Process Management and Benchmarking, 3*(4), 511–551. doi:10.1504/IJPMB.2013.058272

Salam, M. A., & Bajaba, S. (2021). The role of transformative healthcare technology on quality of life during the COVID-19 pandemic. *Journal of Enabling Technologies, 15*(2), 87–107. doi:10.1108/JET-12-2020-0054

Salatin, P., & Shaaeri, H. (2015). Impact of Gender Inequality on Economic Growth. *China-USA Business Review, 14*(12), 584–591. doi:10.17265/1537-1514/2015.12.002

Samarati, P., & Sweeney, L. (1998). Generalizing data to provide anonymity when disclosing information (abstract). *Proceedings of the seventeenth ACM SIGACT-SIGMOD-SIGART symposium on Principles of database systems - PODS '98*. 10.1145/275487.275508

Samarati, P. (2001). Protecting respondents identities in microdata release. *IEEE Transactions on Knowledge and Data Engineering*, *13*(6), 1010–1027. doi:10.1109/69.971193

Sampath, G. (2016, December 11). Why children drop out from primary school. *The Hindu*. Retrieved from: https://www.thehindu.com/news/national/Why-children-drop-out-from-primary-school/article16792949.ece

Samudra, A. (2014). Trends and Factors affecting Female Literacy-An inter-district study of Maharashtra. [Retrieved from http://ijgws.com/journals/ijgws/Vol_2_No_2_June_2014/17.pdf]. *International Journal of Gender and Women's Studies*, *2*(2), 283–296.

Sanatinia, A., & Noubir, G. (2015). OnionBots: Subverting Privacy Infrastructure for Cyber Attacks. *Proceedings of the International Conference on Dependable Systems and Networks,* 69–80. https://doi.org/10.1109/DSN.2015.40

Sandelowski, M. (1995). Sample size in qualitative research. *Research in Nursing & Health, 18*(2), 179–183.

Santhanam, L., Xie, B., & Agrawal, D. (2008). Secure and Efficient Authentication in Wireless Mesh Networks using Merkle Trees. *33rd IEEE Conference on Local Computer Networks.* 10.1109/LCN.2008.4664310

Sardi, A., Rizzi, A., Sorano, E., & Guerrieri, A. (2020). Cyber Risk in Health Facilities: A Systematic Literature Review. *Sustainability*, *12*(17), 7002. doi:10.3390u12177002

Sarfraz, Z., Sarfraz, A., Iftikar, H. M., & Akhund, R. (2021). Is COVID-19 pushing us to the fifth industrial revolution (society 5.0)? *Pakistan Journal of Medical Sciences*, *37*(2), 591. doi:10.12669/pjms.37.2.3387 PMID:33679956

Satpathy, S., & Patnaik, S. (2021). Role of artificial intelligence in social media and human behaviour. *International Journal of Engineering and Advanced Technology*, *11*(1), 207–210. doi:10.35940/ijeat.A1926.1011121

Schneier, B. (1996). *Applied Cryptography* (2nd ed.). Wiley & Sons Inc.

Schneier, B. (2018). *Click here to kill everybody: security and survival in a hyper-connected world* (1st ed.). W.W. Norton & Company.

Schwartz, B. (1968). The social psychology of privacy. *American Journal of Sociology*, *73*(6), 741–752. doi:10.1086/224567 PMID:5695022

Sciara, G.-C. (2017). Metropolitan Transportation Planning: Lessons From the Past, Institutions for the Future. *Journal of the American Planning Association*, *83*(3), 262–276.

Sectoral e-Business Watch. (2009). *Case study: Smart grid journey at Austin Energy, Texas, USA*. In ICT and e-business impact in the energy supply industry, Bonn, Germany.

Self, S., & Grabowski, R. (2004). Does education at all levels cause growth? India, a case study. *Economics of Education Review*, *23*, 47–55. https://www.csus.edu/indiv/l/langd/self_grabowski.pdf

Selmic, R. R., Phoha, V. V., & Serwadda, A. (2016). *Wireless Sensor Networks*. Springer International Publishing AG. doi:10.1007/978-3-319-46769-6

Sethi, P., & Sarangi, S. R. (2017). Internet of Things: Architectures, Protocols, and Applications. *Journal of Electrical and Computer Engineering*, *2017*, 1–25. doi:10.1155/2017/9324035

Shaandri, B., Madara, S.R., & Maheswari, P. (2020). *IoT-Based Smart Tree Management Solution for Green Cities*. doi:10.1007/978-981-15-0663-5_9

Shahzad, M. A. (2020). NVIVO Based Text Mining on COVID-19 Studies: Precision Technologies and Smart Surveillance May Help to Discover, and Coup COVID-19 Transmogrify. SSRN *Electronic Journal*. doi:10.2139/ssrn.3623499

Shamir, A. (1979). How to share a secret. *Communications of the ACM, 22*(11), 612–613. doi:10.1145/359168.359176

Shamir, A. (1984). Identity-based cryptosystems and signature schemes. In *Workshop on the theory and application of cryptographic techniques*. Springer.

Shapira, Y., Shapira, B., & Shabtai, A. (2013). Content-based data leakage detection using extended fingerprinting. arXiv preprint arXiv:1302.2028

Sharma, A., & Mishra, A. (2021). *Cryptographic Algorithm For Enhancing Data Security : A Theoretical Approach.* Academic Press.

Sharma, S., Gupta, S., Gupta, D., Juneja, S., Gupta, P., Dhiman, G., & Kautish, S. (2022). Deep Learning Model for the Automatic Classification of White Blood Cells. Computational Intelligence and Neuroscience. doi:10.1155/2022/7384131

Sharma, U., & Ng, O. (2014). *What has worked for Bringing Out-of-school Children with Disabilities into Regular Schools? A Literature Review*. doi:10.5463/dcid.v25i2.355

Sharma, Y., & Balamurugan, B. (2020). Preserving the Privacy of Electronic Health Records using Blockchain. *Procedia Computer Science, 173*(2019), 171–180. doi:10.1016/j.procs.2020.06.021

Sharma, A., & Joshi, S. (2018). Green consumerism: Overview and further research directions. *International Journal of Process Management and Benchmarking*, *7*(2), 206–223. doi:10.1504/IJPMB.2017.083106

Sharma, T., Dyer, H. A., & Bashir, M. (2021). Enabling User-centered Privacy Controls for Mobile Applications: COVID-19 Perspective. *ACM Transactions on Internet Technology*, *21*(1), 1–24. Advance online publication. doi:10.1145/3434777

Sharmila, N., & Dhas, A. C. (2010). *Development of Women Education in India*. Retrieved from https://mpra.ub.uni-muenchen.de/20680/

Sherry, J., Lan, C., Popa, R. A., & Ratnasamy, S. (2015). BlindBox: Deep Packet Inspection over Encrypted Traffic. *Proceedings of the 2015 ACM Conference on Special Interest Group on Data Communication - SIGCOMM '15*, 213–226. https://doi.org/10.1145/2785956.2787502

Shinde, R., Patil, S., Kotecha, K., & Ruikar, K. (2021). Blockchain for Securing AI Applications and Open Innovations. *Journal of Open Innovation*, *7*(3), 189. Advance online publication. doi:10.3390/joitmc7030189

Shiota, M. N., Campos, B., & Keltner, D. (2003). The faces of positive emotion: Prototype displays of awe, amusement, and pride. *Annals of the New York Academy of Sciences*, *1000*(1), 296–299.

Shi, S., He, D., Li, L., Kumar, N., Khan, M. K., & Choo, K. K. R. (2020). Applications of blockchain in ensuring the security and privacy of electronic health record systems: A survey. *Computers & Security*, *97*, 101966. Advance online publication. doi:10.1016/j.cose.2020.101966 PMID:32834254

Shor, P. (1997, October). Polynomial-Time Algorithms for Prime Factorization and Discrete Logarithms on a Quantum Computer. *SIAM Journal on Computing*, *26*(5), 1484–1509. doi:10.1137/S0097539795293172

Shu, X., Tian, K., Ciambrone, A., & Yao, D. (2017). *Breaking the target: An analysis of target data breach and lessons learned.* arXiv preprint arXiv:1701.04940.

Shu, X., & Yao, D. D. (2012, September). Data leak detection as a service. In *International Conference on Security and Privacy in Communication Systems* (pp. 222-240). Springer.

Siddiqui, M. S., & Huong, C. S. (2007). Security Issues in Wireless Mesh Networks. *International Conference on Multimedia and Ubiquitous Engineering (MUE)*, 717-722.

Sieranoja, S., & Fränti, P. (2018). Random projection for k-means clustering. *Int. Conf. artificial intelligence and soft computing (ICAISC).*

Silva, S. S. C., Silva, R. M. P., Pinto, R. C. G., & Salles, R. M. (2013). Botnets: A survey. *Computer Networks, 57*(2), 378–403. doi:10.1016/j.comnet.2012.07.021

Singh, A.K., & Rabindranath, M. (2020). Gender Divide In Education In India: A Critical Study Based On Functionalist Theory Of Education. *Journal of Critical Reviews*. Doi:10.31838/jcr.07.02.105

Singh, K. (2016). Importance of Education in Empowerment of Women in India. *Motherhood International Journal of Multidisciplinary Research & Development, 1*(1), 39-48. Retrieved from https://motherhooduniversity.edu.in/images/papers/Khushboo%20Singh .pdf

Singh, S. K., Rathore, S., & Park, J. H. (2020). Blockiotintelligence: A blockchain-enabled intelligent IoT architecture with artificial intelligence. *Future Generation Computer Systems, 110*, 721–743. doi:10.1016/j.future.2019.09.002

Sinha, M., Chaurasiya, R., Pandey, A., Singh, Y., & Goyal, S. (2022). Securing Smart Homes Using Face Recognition. In *Advances in Micro-Electronics, Embedded Systems and IoT* (pp. 391–398). Springer. doi:10.1007/978-981-16-8550-7_37

Siriwardhana, Y., Gür, G., Ylianttila, M., & Liyanage, M. (2021). The role of 5G for digital healthcare against COVID-19 pandemic: Opportunities and challenges. *ICT Express, 7*(2), 244–252. doi:10.1016/j.icte.2020.10.002

Smeraldi, F., & Bigun, J. (2002). Retinal vision applied to facial features detection and face authentication. *Pattern Recognition Letters, 23*, 463–475.

Smereka & Kumar. (2013). What is a 'good' periocular region for recognition? *IEEE Comput. Soc. Conf. Comput. Vis. Pattern Recognit. Work.,* 117–124. doi:10.1109/CVPRW.2013.25

Smith, A. D. (2020a). Online vehicle purchase behavior and analytics among supply chain professionals: An exploratory study. *World Review of Intermodal Transportation Research, 9*(3), 264–296. doi:10.1504/WRITR.2020.108229

Smith, A. D. (2020b). Being green and social responsibility: Basic concepts and case studies in business excellence. *International Journal of Sustainable Entrepreneurship and Corporate Social Responsibility, 5*(2), 34–54. doi:10.4018/IJSECSR.2020070103

Smith, A. D. (2021a). Vendor managed inventory and strategy: Case study of global supply chains. *International Journal of Sustainable Economies Management, 3*(1), 1–20.

Smith, A. D. (2021b). Updating an empirical investigating risk perceptions associated with national ID cards in the wake of the global Covid-19 pandemic. *Health Marketing Quarterly, 38*(2-3), 70–90. doi:10.1080/07359683.2021.1980841 PMID:34554045

Smith, A. D. (2022). Exploring opioid addictions and responsibilities: Almost lost in the midst of the Covid-19 pandemic. *International Journal of Human Rights in Healthcare, 15*(1), 41–74. doi:10.1108/IJHRH-03-2021-0067

Snell, R. (2020). How Is COVID-19 Impacting Compliance Professionals across the Country? *Journal of Health Care Compliance*, 33–38.

Sobhani, S., Shirsale, S. B., Saxena, S., Paharia, V., & Goyal, S. (2022). Emergency Bot in Healthcare Using Industry 4.0. In *Advances in Micro-Electronics, Embedded Systems and IoT* (pp. 347–355). Springer. doi:10.1007/978-981-16-8550-7_33

Sodhro, A. H., Pirbhulal, S., & De Albuquerque, V. H. (2019). Artificial intelligence-driven mechanism for edge computing-based industrial applications. *IEEE Transactions on Industrial Informatics*, *15*(7), 4235–4243. doi:10.1109/TII.2019.2902878

Solihin, M. I., & Zanil, M. F. (2016, November). Performance comparison of Cuckoo search and differential evolution algorithm for constrained optimization. *IOP Conference Series. Materials Science and Engineering*, *160*(1), 012108. doi:10.1088/1757-899X/160/1/012108

Solimini, R., Busardò, F. P., Gibelli, F., Sirignano, A., & Ricci, G. (2021). Ethical and legal challenges of telemedicine in the era of the covid-19 pandemic. *Medicina*, *57*(12), 1–10. doi:10.3390/medicina57121314

Solove, D. J. (2005). A taxonomy of privacy. *U. Pa. L. Rev.*, *154*(3), 477. doi:10.2307/40041279

Solove, D. J. (2007). *The future of reputation: Gossip, rumor, and privacy on the Internet*. Yale University Press.

Son, J. Y., & Kim, S. S. (2008). Internet users' information privacy-protective responses: A Taxonomy and a nomological model. *MIS Quarterly: Management Information Systems*, *32*(3), 503–529. doi:10.2307/25148854

Sony, M. (2020). Pros and cons of implementing Industry 4.0 for the organizations: A review and synthesis of evidence. *Production & Manufacturing Research*, *8*(1), 244–272. doi:10.1080/21693277.2020.1781705

Sozzi, B. (2021). Fedex just painted a disturbing picture of the job market. *Yahoo News*. Retrieved October 19, 2021 from https://news.yahoo.com/fed-ex-just-painted-a-disturbing-picture-of-the-job-market-160422695.html

Sporrer, A. (2020). 5 trucking sustainability trends for 2021. *FreightWaves*. Retrieved March 8, 2022 from https://www.freightwaves.com/news/5-trucking-sustainability-trends-for-2021

Stahl, B. C., & Wright, D. (2018). Ethics and privacy in AI and big data: Implementing responsible research and innovation. *IEEE Security and Privacy*, *16*(3), 26–33. doi:10.1109/MSP.2018.2701164

Stajic, J. (2013, March). The Future of Quantum Information Processing. *Science*, 1163.

Stallings, W. (1999). *Cryptography and Network Security* (2nd ed.). Prentice Hall.

Stamp, M. (2011). *Information Security Principles and Practices* (2nd ed.). Wiley & Sons Inc.

Steer, D. (2021, Dec. 9). Visualizing Data. *Forbes*. https://www.forbes.com/sites/forbestechcouncil/2021/12/09/visualizing-data/?sh=1b0fc0a5519f

Strategies for Girls' Education. (n.d.). UNICEF. Retrieved from https://www.unicef.org/sowc06/pdfs/sge_English_Version_B.pdf

Strayer, W. T., Lapsely, D., Walsh, R., & Livadas, C. (2008). Botnet Detection Based on Network Behavior. *Botnet Detection*, *36*(August), 1–24. doi:10.1007/978-0-387-68768-1_1

Subandi, A., Meiyanti, R., Mestika Sandy, C. L., & Sembiring, R. W. (2017). Three-pass protocol implementation in vigenere cipher classic cryptography algorithm with keystream generator modification. *Advances in Science. Technology and Engineering Systems*, *2*(5), 1–5. doi:10.25046/aj020501

Subhedar, M. S., & Mankar, V. H. (2014). Current status and key issues in image steganography: A survey. *Computer Science Review*, *13*, 95–113. doi:10.1016/j.cosrev.2014.09.001

Su, G., & Moh, M. (2018). Improving Energy Efficiency and Scalability for IoT Communications in 5G Networks. *Proc. of the 12th ACM International Conference on Ubiquitous Information Management and Communication (IMCOM)*.

Sundaram, M. S., Sekar, M., & Subburaj, A. (2014). Women Empowerment: Role of Education. *International Journal of Management and Social Sciences*, *2*(12), 76–85. http://www.indianjournals.com/ijor.aspx?target=ijor:ijmss&volume

Sun, W., Liu, J., & Yue, Y. (2019). AI-enhanced offloading in edge computing: When machine learning meets industrial IoT. *IEEE Network*, *33*(5), 68–74. doi:10.1109/MNET.001.1800510

Sustainability – Green fleet & LEED certified buildings. (2021). *Pitt-Ohio*. Retrieved December 31, 2021 from https://pittohio.com/myPittOhio/corporate/about/sustainability/planet/green_fleet_and_LEED_certified_buildings

Sweeney, L. (2002). Achieving K-anonymity privacy protection using generalization and suppression. *International Journal of Uncertainty, Fuzziness and Knowledge-based Systems*, *10*(05), 571–588. doi:10.1142/S021848850200165X

Sweeney, L. (2002). K-anonymity: A model for protecting privacy. *International Journal of Uncertainty, Fuzziness and Knowledge-based Systems*, *10*(05), 557–570. doi:10.1142/S0218488502001648

Syakur, M. A., Khotimah, B. K., Rochman, E. M. S., & Satoto, B. D. (2018). Integration K-Means Clustering Method and Elbow Method For Identification of The Best Customer Profile Cluster. *IOP Conf. Ser.: Mater. Sci. Eng., 336*.

Syarif, M. A., Ong, T. S., Teoh, A. B. J., & Tee, C. (2014). Improved Biohashing Method Based on Most Intensive Histogram Block Location. In Neural Information Processing. ICONIP 2014. Lecture Notes in Computer Science (vol. 8836). doi:10.1007/978-3-319-12643-2_78

Taddicken, M. (2014). The 'privacy paradox' in the social web: The impact of privacy concerns, individual characteristics, and the perceived social relevance on different forms of self-disclosure. *Journal of Computer-Mediated Communication*, *19*(2), 248–273. doi:10.1111/jcc4.12052

Talal, M., Zaidan, A. A., Zaidan, B. B., Albahri, A. S., Alamoodi, A. H., Albahri, O. S., Alsalem, M. A., Lim, C. K., Tan, K. L., Shir, W. L., & Mohammed, K. I. (2019). Smart Home-based IoT for Real-time and Secure Remote Health Monitoring of Triage and Priority System using Body Sensors: Multi-driven Systematic Review. *Journal of Medical Systems*, *43*(3), 42. Advance online publication. doi:10.100710916-019-1158-z PMID:30648217

Tanenbaum, A. (1990). *Structured Computer Organization* (3rd ed.). Prentice Hall.

Tan, K., Killourhy, K. S., & Maxion, R. A. (2002, October). Undermining an anomaly-based intrusion detection system using common exploits. In *International Workshop on Recent Advances in Intrusion Detection* (pp. 54-73). Springer. 10.1007/3-540-36084-0_4

Tao, F., Fei, X., Ye, L., & Li, F. J. (2015). Secure network coding-based named data network mutual anonymity communication protocol. *Proceedings of International Conference on Electrical, Computer Engineering and Electronics (ICECEE)*, 1107–1114.

Tawalbeh, L. A., & Saldamli, G. (2021). Reconsidering big data security and privacy in cloud and mobile cloud systems. *Journal of King Saud University - Computer and Information Sciences, 33*(7), 810-819. doi:10.1016/j.jksuci.2019.05.007

Thabit, F., Alhomdy, S., & Jagtap, S. (2021). A new data security algorithm for the cloud computing based on genetics techniques and logical-mathematical functions. *International Journal of Intelligent Networks*, *2*, 18–33. doi:10.1016/j.ijin.2021.03.001

Thangamani, Prabha, & Prasad, Kumari, Raghavender, & Abidin. (2020). IoT Defense Machine Learning: Emerging Solutions and Future Problems. *Microprocessors and Microsystems*.

Thapa, C., & Camtepe, S. (2021). Precision health data: Requirements, challenges and existing techniques for data security and privacy. *Computers in Biology and Medicine, 129*(October), 104130. doi:10.1016/j.compbiomed.2020.104130

The Korea Times. (n.d.). Available online: https://www.koreatimes.co.kr/www/nation/2019/01/371_262460.html

The Wall Street Journal. (2016). *China's Latest Leap Forward Isn't Just Great—It's Quantum. Beijing launches the world's first quantum-communications satellite into orbit.* Retrieved 8/17/2016 from: https://www.wsj.com/articles/chinas-latest-leap-forward-isnt-just-greatits-quantum-1471269555

Theodoridis & Koutroumbas. (2009). *Pattern Recognition* (4th ed.). Academic Press Publications.

Tibshirani, R., Walther, G., & Hastie, T. (2000). *Estimating the number of clusters in a dataset via the gap statistic.* Technical Report 208, Department of Statistics, Stanford University.

Tikkinen-Piri, C., Rohunen, A., & Markkula, J. (2018). Eu general data protection regulation: Changes and implications for personal data collecting companies. *Computer Law & Security Review, 34*(1), 134–153. doi:10.1016/j.clsr.2017.05.015

Titone. (2020). *Brock augmented reality marketing*. Academic Press.

Tohidi, H., & Vakili, V. T. (2018). Lightweight authentication scheme for smart grid using Merkle hash tree and lossless compression hybrid method. *IET Communications, 12*(19). Advance online publication. doi:10.1049/iet-com.2018.5698

Tomb, J-F., White, O., Kerlavage, A. R., Clayton, R. A., Sutton, G. G., Fleischmann, R. D., & Ketchum, K. A. (1997). Enhanced Reader. Nature, 388, 539–547.

Tom, E., Keane, P. A., Blazes, M., Pasquale, L. R., Chiang, M. F., Lee, A. Y., & Lee, C. S. (2020). Protecting data privacy in the age of AI-enabled ophthalmology. *Translational Vision Science & Technology, 9*(2), 36. doi:10.1167/tvst.9.2.36 PMID:32855840

Topaloglu, M. Y., Morrell, E. M., Rajendran, S., & Topaloglu, U. (2021). In the Pursuit of Privacy: The Promises and Predicaments of Federated Learning in Healthcare. *Frontiers in Artificial Intelligence, 4*(October), 1–10. doi:10.3389/frai.2021.746497 PMID:34693280

Torgrimson, B. N., & Minson, C. T. (2005). Sex and gender: What is the difference? *Journal of Applied Physiology (Bethesda, Md.), 99*(3), 785–787. doi:10.1152/japplphysiol.00376.2005 PMID:16103514

Torky, M., & Hassanien, A. E. (2020). *COVID-19 Blockchain Framework: Innovative Approach.* https://arxiv.org/abs/2004.06081

Townsend, A. M., & Bennett, J. T. (2003). Privacy, technology, and conflict: Emerging issues and action in workplace privacy. *Journal of Labor Research, 24*(2), 195–205. doi:10.1007/BF02701789

Trakadas, P., Simoens, P., Gkonis, P., Sarakis, L., Angelopoulos, A., Ramallo-González, A., ... Chintamani, K. (2020). An artificial intelligence-based collaboration approach in industrial iot manufacturing: Key concepts, architectural extensions and potential applications. *Sensors (Basel), 20*(19), 5480. doi:10.339020195480 PMID:32987911

Treat Metrix. https://www.threatmetrix.com

Trinity Logistics. (2020). *Assessing Covid-19's impact on trucking companies.* Retrieved December 31, 2021 from https://trinitylogistics.com/assessing-covid-19s-impact-on-trucking-companies/

Triwijoyo, Budiharto, & Abdurachman. (2017). The Classification of Hypertensive Retinopathy using Convolutional Neural Network. *Procedia Computer Science.* doi:10.1109/ICIRCA48905.2020.9183249

Trokielewicz, M., & Szadkowski, M. (2017). Can we recognize horses by their ocular biometric traits using deep convolutional neural networks? Photonics Applications in Astronomy, Communications, Industry, and High Energy Physics Experiments 2017.

Tsai, J. Y., Cranor, L., Egelman, S., & Acquisti, A. (2007). The effect of online privacy information on purchasing behavior: An experimental study. *ICIS 2007 Proceedings - Twenty Eighth International Conference on Information Systems, 22*(2), 254–268.

Tsai, C., & Moh, M. (2017). Load Balancing in 5G Cloud Radio Access Networks Supporting IoT Communications for Smart Communities. *Proc. of 2017 IEEE International Symposium on Signal Processing and Information Technology (ISSPIT).*

Tsou, M. (2015). Research challenges and opportunities in mapping social media and big data. *Cartography and Geographic Information Science, 42*(supl), 70-74. doi:10.1080/15230406.2015.1059251

Tyagi, A. K., Nair, M. M., Niladhuri, S., & Abraham, A. (2020). Security, Privacy Research issues in Various Computing Platforms: A Survey and the Road Ahead. Journal of Information Assurance & Security, 15(1), 1-16.

Tyagi, A. K., Fernandez, T. F., Mishra, S., & Kumari, S. (2021). Intelligent Automation Systems at the Core of Industry 4.0. In A. Abraham, V. Piuri, N. Gandhi, P. Siarry, A. Kaklauskas, & A. Madureira (Eds.), *Intelligent Systems Design and Applications*. Springer. doi:10.1007/978-3-030-71187-0_1

Tyagi, A. K., Nair, M. M., Niladhuri, S., & Abraham, A. (2020). Security, privacy research issues in various computing platforms: A survey and the road ahead. *Journal of Information Assurance & Security, 15*(1).

Tyagi, A. K., Nair, M. M., Niladhuri, S., & Abraham, A. (2020). Security, privacy re-search issues in various computing platforms: A survey and the road ahead. *Journal of Information Assurance & Security, 15*(1).

Tyagi, A. K., Nair, M. M., Niladhuri, S., & Abraham, A. (2021). Security, Privacy Research issues in Various Computing Platforms: A Survey and the Road Ahead. *Journal of Information Assurance &Security, 15*(1), 1–16.

U.S.-Canada Power System Outage Task Force. (2004). *Final Report on the August 14, 2003 Blackout in the United States and Canada: Causes and Recommendations*. Retrieved from: http://energy.gov/sites/prod/files/oeprod/DocumentsandMedia/BlackoutFinal-Web.pdf

Ul Haq, M. N., & Kumar, N. (2021). A novel data classification-based scheme for cloud data security using various cryptographic algorithms. *International Review of Applied Sciences and Engineering*. doi:10.1556/1848.2021.00317

Ullah, I., & Youn, H. Y. (2020). Task Classification and Scheduling Based on K-Means Clustering for Edge Computing. *Wireless Personal Communications, 113*, 2611–2624. https://doi.org/10.1007/s11277-020-07343-w

UNESCO. (1993). The Education of Girls: The Ouagadougou Declaration and Framework for Action. *Pan-African Conference on the Education of Girls*. Retrieved from http://www.unesco.org/education/pdf /OUAGAD_E.PDF

UNICEF. (2005). *Barriers to Girls' Education, Strategies and Interventions- A UNICEF Report*. UNICEF. Retrieved from https://www.unicef.org/teachers/girls_ed/BarrierstoGE.pdf

UNICEF. (2020). *COVID-19 and Girls' Education in East Asia and Pacific*. unicef.org

Uriarte, A. G., Ng, A. H., & Moris, M. U. (2018). Supporting the lean journey with simulation and optimization in the context of Industry 4.0. *Procedia Manufacturing, 25*, 586–593. doi:10.1016/j.promfg.2018.06.097

Uzair, M., Mahmood, A., Mian, A., & McDonald, C. (2015). Periocular region-based person identification in the visible, infrared and hyperspectral imagery. *Neurocomputing, 149*, 854–867.

Vaidya, S., Ambad, P., & Bhosle, S. (2018). Industry 4.0–a glimpse. *Procedia Manufacturing, 20*, 233–238. doi:10.1016/j.promfg.2018.02.034

Vakil, B. (2021). The latest supply chain disruption: Plastics. *Harvard Business Review*. Retrieved October 22, 2021, from https://hbr.org/2021/03/the-latest-supply-chain-disruption-plastics

Valentino, L. A., Skinner, M. W., & Pipe, S. W. (2020). The role of telemedicine in the delivery of health care in the COVID-19 pandemic. *Haemophilia*, *26*(5), e230–e231. doi:10.1111/hae.14044 PMID:32397000

Valmik, M. N., & Kshirsagar, P. V. K. (2014). Blowfish Algorithm. *IOSR Journal of Computer Engineering*, *16*(2), 80–83. doi:10.9790/0661-162108083

Van Laerhoven, K. (2001). Combining the Self-Organizing Map and K-Means Clustering for On-Line Classification of Sensor Data. In G. Dorffner, H. Bischof, & K. Hornik (Eds.), Lecture Notes in Computer Science: Vol. 2130. *Artificial Neural Networks — ICANN 2001. ICANN 2001*. Springer. doi:10.1007/3-540-44668-0_65

van Steen, M., & Tanenbaum, A. S. (2016). A brief introduction to distributed systems. *Computing*, *98*(10), 967–1009. doi:10.100700607-016-0508-7

Van Weele, A., & van Raaij, E. (2005). The future of purchasing and supply management research: About relevance and rigor. *The Journal of Supply Chain Management*, *50*(1), 56–72. doi:10.1111/jscm.12042

Vargo, D., Zhu, L., Benwell, B., & Yan, Z. (2021). Digital technology use during COVID-19 pandemic: A rapid review. *Human Behavior and Emerging Technologies*, *3*(1), 13–24. doi:10.1002/hbe2.242

Vayena, E., Haeusermann, T., Adjekum, A., & Blasimme, A. (2018). Digital health: Meeting the ethical and policy challenges. *Swiss Medical Weekly*, *148*(34), w14571. doi:10.4414mw.2018.14571 PMID:29376547

Velásquez, N., Estévez, E. C., & Pesado, P. M. (2018). Cloud computing, big data and the industry 4.0 reference architectures. *Journal of Computer Science and Technology*, *18*(03), 18. doi:10.24215/16666038.18.e29

Vennila, S., & Priyadarshini, J. (2015). Scalable privacy preservation in big data a survey. *Procedia Computer Science*, *50*, 369–373. doi:10.1016/j.procs.2015.04.033

Ventrella, E. (2020). Privacy in emergency circumstances: data protection and the COVID-19 pandemic. *ERA Forum*, *21*(3), 379–393. 10.100712027-020-00629-3

Verma, D., White, G., & de Mel, G. (2019), Federated AI for the enterprise: a web services based implementation. *2019 IEEE International Conference on Web Services*, 20-27.

Verma, P., Dumka, A., Bhardwaj, A., Kaur, N., Ashok, A., Bisht, A. K., & Gangwar, R. P. S. (2022). *Security Issues for Wireless Sensor Networks*. CRC Press. doi:10.1201/9781003257608

Verma, P., Sharma, R. R. K., & Kumar, V. (2018). The sustainability issues of diversified firms in emerging economies context: A theoretical model and propositions. *International Journal of Process Management and Benchmarking*, *7*(2), 224–248. doi:10.1504/IJPMB.2017.083107

Verton, D. (2002). The Hacker Diaries. McGraw-Hill, Inc. doi:10.1036/0072223642

Viaene, S., & Dedene, G. (2004). Insurance Fraud: Issues and Challenges. *The Geneva Papers on Risk and Insurance. Issues and Practice*, *29*(2), 313–333. doi:10.1111/j.1468-0440.2004.00290.x

Vijay Singh, A. K. (2017). Detection of plant leaf disease using image segmentation and soft computing techniques. *Information Processing in Agriculture*, *4*, 4149.

Vikhram, Agarwal, Uprety, & Prasanth. (2018). Automatic Weed Detection and Smart Herbicide Sprayer Robot. *IACSIT International Journal of Engineering and Technology*.

Viola, P., & Jones, M. J. (2004). Robust real-time face detection. *International Journal of Computer Vision*, *57*, 137–154.

Vuksanović, D., Vešić, J., & Korčok, D. (2016). *Industry 4.0: The Future Concepts and New Visions of Factory of the Future Development*. . doi:10.15308.Sinteza-2016-293-298

Waddill, C. (2020). *The importance of OEE in ROI analysis for manufacturers*. Evocon. Retrieved October 23, 2021, from https://evocon.com/kb/why-oee-roi-provide-value-to-management/

Walid, H. (2020). *Efficient Masked Face Recognition Method during the COVID-19 Pandemic*. . doi:10.21203/rs.3.rs-39289/v1

Wang, Yin, Cao, Wei, Zheng, & Yang. (n.d.). *Detection of blood cells*. School of Computer Science and Technology, Shandong University.

Wang, F., Wang, Z., & Zhu, Y. (2019). Adaptive RSA Encryption Algorithm for Smart Grid. *Journal of Physics: Conference Series*, *1302*(2), 022097. doi:10.1088/1742-6596/1302/2/022097

Wang, K., Xu, P., Chen, C. M., Kumari, S., Shojafar, M., & Alazab, M. (2020). Neural architecture search for robust networks in 6G-enabled massive IoT domain. *IEEE Internet of Things Journal*, *8*(7), 5332–5339. doi:10.1109/JIOT.2020.3040281

Wang, K., Yu, P., & Chakraborty, S. (n.d.). Bottom-up generalization: A data mining solution to privacy protection. *Fourth IEEE International Conference on Data Mining (ICDM'04)*. 10.1109/ICDM.2004.10110

Wang, L., & Alexander, C. A. (2021). Cyber security during the COVID-19 pandemic. *AIMS Electronics and Electrical Engineering*, *5*(2), 146–157. doi:10.3934/electreng.2021008

Wang, Q., Su, M., Zhang, M., & Li, R. (2021). Integrating digital technologies and public health to fight covid-19 pandemic: Key technologies, applications, challenges and outlook of digital healthcare. *International Journal of Environmental Research and Public Health*, *18*(11), 6053. Advance online publication. doi:10.3390/ijerph18116053 PMID:34199831

Wang, T., & Yu, S. Z. (2009, August). Centralized Botnet detection by traffic aggregation. In *2009 IEEE International Symposium on Parallel and Distributed Processing with Applications* (pp. 86-93). IEEE.

Wang, X., & Yi, P. (2011, December). Security Framework for Wireless Communications in Smart Distribution Grid. *IEEE Transactions on Smart Grid*, *2*(4), 809–818.

Washburn, C., Murray, S., & Kueny, C. (2021). Electronic Logging Device System: Early outcomes of use in the trucking industry. *Professional Safety*, *66*(11), 26–30.

Weaver, M. (2009, July 8). *South Korea Cyber Attack*. Retrieved from https://www.theguardian.com/world/2009/jul/08/south-korea-cyber-attack

Welcome to BIT Mesra. (n.d.). Retrieved September 7, 2022, from https://www.bitmesra.ac.in/

Westin, A. F. (1968). Privacy and freedom. *Washington and Lee Law Review*, *25*(1), 166.

White, G., Ruther, M., Kahn, J. R., & Dong, D. (2016). *Gender inequality amid educational expansion in India: An analysis of gender differences in the attainment of reading and mathematics skills*. Academic Press.

Wijayanto, H., & Prabowo, I. A. (2020). Cybersecurity Vulnerability Behavior Scale in College During the Covid-19 Pandemic. *Jurnal Sisfokom*, *9*(3), 395–399. doi:10.32736isfokom.v9i3.1021

Wilkowska, W., & Ziefle, M. (2011). Perception of privacy and security for acceptance of E-health technologies: Exploratory analysis for diverse user groups. *2011 5th International Conference on Pervasive Computing Technologies for Healthcare and Workshops, PervasiveHealth 2011*, 593–600. 10.4108/icst.pervasivehealth.2011.246027

Williams, S. (2021). Plastics shortage hits plastic parts supply chain. *Industrial Specialties Mfg.* Retrieved March 9, 2022, from https://www.industrialspec.com/about-us/blog/detail/plastic-raw-material-shortages-rising-prices-delivery-delays-early-2021/

Williams, E., Das, V., & Fisher, A. (2020). Assessing the sustainability implications of autonomous vehicles: Recommendations for research community practice. *Sustainability, 12*(5), 1902. doi:10.3390u12051902

Wilson, P. (2016). Secure Systems. In *Design Recipes for FPGAs* (pp. 135–165). Elsevier. doi:10.1016/B978-0-08-097129-2.00010-6

Winder, R. J., Morrow, P. J., McRitchie, I. N., Bailie, J. R., & Hart, P. M. (2009). Algorithms for digital image processing in white blood cells. *Computerized Medical Imaging and Graphics, 33*(8), 608–622. doi:10.1016/j.compmedimag.2009.06.003 PMID:19616920

Winston, T. G., Paul, S., & Iyer, L. (2016). A study of privacy and security concerns on doctors' and nurses' behavioral intentions to use RFID in hospitals. *Proceedings of the Annual Hawaii International Conference on System Sciences,* 3115–3123. 10.1109/HICSS.2016.392

Wiseman, P. (2021). From paints to plastics, a chemical shortage ignites prices. *AP News.* Retrieved October 22, 2021, from https://apnews.com/article/coronavirus-pandemic-technology-business-health-hurricanes-46bce9cc36d-ab2b330309dae0354cf53

Wolford, B. (2019). What is gdpr, the eu's new data protection law. *GDPR. eu*, 13.

Wong, R., Moh, T.-S., & Moh, M. (2012). Efficient Semi-Supervised Learning BitTorrent Traffic Detection: An Extended Summary. In *Proc. of 13th Int. Conf on Distributed Computing and Networking – ICDCN 2012.* Springer.

Woodard, D., Pundlik, S., Lyle, J., & Miller, P. (2010). Periocular region appearance cues for biometric identification. *IEEE International Conference on Computer Vision and Pattern Recognition Workshops*, 162–169.

World Bank. (2019). *Belt and Road Initiative.* Retrieved from https://protect-us.mimecast.com/s/K-qTCgJQ3oTlZGn1SonuSv?domain=worldbank.org

World Economic Forum. (2021). *Global Gender Gap Report.* Retrieved from: https://www.weforum.org/reports/

World Health Organization. (2020). *Covid-19 situation reports-102.* https://www.who.int/docs/default-source/coronaviruse/situation-reports/20200501-covid-19-sitrep.pdf?sfvrsn=742f4a18_4

Wu, Y. (2020). Cloud-Edge Orchestration for the Internet-of-Things:Architecture and AI-Powered Data Processing. *Internet of Things Journal*, 1-15.

Wu, C., & Buyya, R. (2015). Cloud Computing. In *Cloud Data Centers and Cost Modeling* (pp. 3–41). Elsevier. doi:10.1016/B978-0-12-801413-4.00001-5

Wu, H., & Tsai, C. (2018). Toward Blockchains for Health-Care Systems. *IEEE Consumer Electronics Magazine, 7*(july), 65–71. doi:10.1109/MCE.2018.2816306

Xiao, X., & Tao, Y. (2006). Personalized privacy preservation. *Proceedings of the 2006 ACM SIGMOD international conference on Management of data - SIGMOD '06.* 10.1145/1142473.1142500

Xiao, X., & Tao, Y. (2007). M-invariance: towards privacy preserving re- publication of dynamic datasets. In *Proceedings of the 2007 ACM SIGMOD international conference on Management of data.* ACM. 10.1145/1247480.1247556

Xie, S., Hu, Z., & Wang, J. (2020). Two-stage robust optimization for expansion planning of active distribution systems coupled with urban transportation networks. *Applied Energy, 261.*

Xing, Y., Li, Y., & Wang, F. K. (2021). How privacy concerns and cultural differences affect public opinion during the COVID-19 pandemic: A case study. *Aslib Journal of Information Management*, *73*(4), 517–542. doi:10.1108/AJIM-07-2020-0216

Xiuming, J., & Jing, W. (2011). Research of remote sensing classification about land survey based on SVM. *2011 2nd International Conference on Artificial Intelligence, Management Science and Electronic Commerce (AIMSEC 2011),* 3230-3.

Xu & Wang (2013). Wireless Mesh Network in Smart Grid: Modeling and Analysis for Time Critical Communications. *IEEE Transactions on Wireless Communications, 12*(7), 3360 – 3371.

Xu, J., Cha, M., Heyman, J. L., Venugopalan, S., Abiantun, R., & Savvides, M. (2010). Robust local binary pattern feature sets for periocular biometric identification. *Biometrics: Theory Applications and Systems (BTAS), 2010 Fourth IEEE International Conference on*, 1-8.

Xu, J., Glicksberg, B. S., Su, C., Walker, P., Bian, J., & Wang, F. (2021). Federated Learning for Healthcare Informatics. *Journal of Healthcare Informatics Research*, *5*(1), 1–19. doi:10.100741666-020-00082-4 PMID:33204939

Xu, J., Xue, K., Li, S., Tian, H., Hong, J., Hong, P., & Yu, N. (2019). Healthchain: A Blockchain-Based Privacy Preserving Scheme for Large-Scale Health Data. *IEEE Internet of Things Journal*, *6*(5), 8770–8781. doi:10.1109/JIOT.2019.2923525

Xu, Y., Tiwari, A., Chen, H. C., & Turner, C. J. (2018). Development of a validation and qualification process for the manufacturing of medical devices: A case study based on cross-sector benchmarking. *International Journal of Process Management and Benchmarking*, *8*(1), 79–102. doi:10.1504/IJPMB.2018.088658

Yadav, S. B., Vadera, B., Mangal, A. D., Patel, N. A., & Shah, H. D. (2011). A Study on Status of Empowerment of Women in Jamnagar District. *National Journal of Community Medicine*, 2(3), 423–428. http://njcmindia.org/uploads/2-3_423-428.pdf

Yallop, A. C., & Aliasghar, O. (2020). No business as usual: A case for data ethics and data governance in the age of coronavirus. *Online Information Review*, *44*(6), 1217–1221. doi:10.1108/OIR-06-2020-0257

Yang, F., & Gu, S. (2021). Industry 4.0, a revolution that requires technology and national strategies. *Complex & Intelligent Systems*, *7*(3), 1311–1325. doi:10.100740747-020-00267-9

Yang, L., & Moh, M. (2011). Dual Trust Secure Protocol for Cluster-Based Wireless Sensor Networks. *Proc. IEEE 45th Asilomar Conference on Signals, Systems and Computers*, 1645-1649. doi: 10.1109/ACSSC.2011.6190298

Yang, X. S. (2020). Nature-inspired optimization algorithms: Challenges and open problems. *Journal of Computational Science*, *46*, 101104. doi:10.1016/j.jocs.2020.101104

Yan, L., Chang, Y., & Zhang, S. (2017). A lightweight authentication and key agreement scheme for smart grid. *International Journal of Distributed Sensor Networks*, *13*(2). Advance online publication. doi:10.1177/1550147717694173

Yan, Q., Zheng, Y., Jiang, T., Lou, W., & Hou, Y. T. (2015). PeerClean: Unveiling peer-to-peer botnets through dynamic group behavior analysis. *Proceedings - IEEE INFOCOM*, *26*, 316–324. doi:10.1109/INFOCOM.2015.7218396

Yan, Y., Qian, Y., Sharif, H., & Tipper, D. (2012, January). A Survey on Cyber Security for Smart Grid Communications. *Communication Surveys and Tutorials, IEEE*, *14*(4), 998–1010. doi:10.1109/SURV.2012.010912.00035

Yao, F. (2021). Hybrid Encryption Scheme for Hospital Financial Data Based on Noekeon Algorithm. *Security and Communication Networks*, *2021*, 1–10. doi:10.1155/2021/7578752

Yazdi, A. K., & Esfeden, G. A. (2018). Designing robust model of Six Sigma implementation based on critical successful factors and MACBETH. *International Journal of Process Management and Benchmarking*, *7*(2), 158–171. doi:10.1504/IJPMB.2017.083103

Yildirim, M., & Çinar, A. (2019). Classification of white blood cells by deep learning methods for diagnosing disease. *Revue d'Intelligence Artificielle*, *33*(5), 335–340. doi:10.18280/ria.330502

Yin, R. K. (2011). *Qualitative Research from Start to Finish.* The Guilford Press.

Young, J. (2021). Pandemic causes ecommerce to surge north of 32% in Q4. *Digital Commerce 360.* Retrieved December 31, 2021 from https://www.digitalcommerce360.com/article/quarterly-online-sales/

Yu, W., Chang, J., Yang, C., Zhang, L., Shen, H., Xia, Y., & Sha, J. (2017). Automatic classification of leukocytes using deep neural network. *2017 IEEE 12th International Conference on ASIC (ASICON),* 1041-1044.

Yu, W., Chang, J., Yang, C., Zhang, L., Shen, H., Xia, Y., & Sha, J. (2017). Automatic classification of leukocytes using deep neural network. *2017 IEEE 12th International Conference on ASIC (ASICON).* 10.1109/ASICON.2017.8252657

Yuan, C., & Yang, H. (2019). *Research on K-Value Selection Method of K-Means Clustering Algorithm.* doi:10.3390/j2020016

Yu, W., Liu, T., Valdez, R., Gwinn, M., & Khoury, M. J. (2010, March 22). Application of support vector machine modeling for prediction of common diseases: The case of diabetes and pre-diabetes. *BMC Medical Informatics and Decision Making*, *10*, 16.

Zaidan, A. S. A. (2020). Role of biological Data Mining and MachineLearningTechniques in Detecting and Diagnosing the Novel Coronavirus (COVID-19): A Systematic Review. *Journal of Medical Systems.*

Zalte, Patil, & Tone. (2022). Edge Computing Technology: An Overview. *AJOMC*, 96-99.

Zalte, S. S., Kamat, R. K., & Ghorpade, V. R. (2020). Mitigation of DDoS Attack in MANET. *IJEAT, 9*, 410-413.

Zalte, S. S., Patil, P. N., Deshmukh, S. N., & Kamat, R. K. (2021). Data Packet Security in MANET and VANET. *BBRC, 13*(15), 271-274.

Zech, J. R., Badgeley, M. A., Liu, M., Costa, A. B., Titano, J. J., & Oermann, E. K. (2018). Variable generalization performance of a deep learning model to detect pneumonia in chest radiographs: A cross-sectional study. *PLoS Medicine*, *15*(11), 1–17. doi:10.1371/journal.pmed.1002683 PMID:30399157

Zeidanloo, H. R., Shooshtari, M. J., Amoli, P. V., & Safari, M., & Zamani, M. (2010). A taxonomy of botnet detection techniques. *3rd IEEE International Conference on Computer Science and Information Technology (ICCSIT)*, 2, 158–162.

Zervoudi, E. K. (2020). *Fourth industrial revolution: opportunities, challenges, and proposed policies.* Industrial Robotics-New Paradigms.

Zhang, H. (1997). *Delay-insensitive networks* [M.S. thesis]. University of Waterloo, Waterloo, Canada.

Zhang, B. (2020). Classification of Encrypted Text Based on Artificial Intelligence. *IOP Conference Series. Materials Science and Engineering*, *740*(1), 012133. doi:10.1088/1757-899X/740/1/012133

Zhang, L., Yu, S., Wu, D., & Watters, P. (2011). A survey on latest botnet attack and defense. *Proc. 10th IEEE Int. Conf. on Trust, Security and Privacy in Computing and Communications, TrustCom 2011, 8th IEEE Int. Conf. on Embedded Software and Systems, ICESS 2011, 6th Int. Conf. on FCST 2011*, 53–60. https://doi.org/10.1109/TrustCom.2011.11

Zhang, W., Lu, Q., Yu, Q., Li, Z., Liu, Y., Lo, S. K., Chen, S., Xu, X., & Zhu, L. (2021, April 1). Block chain-based federated learning for device failure detection in industrial IoT. *IEEE Internet of Things Journal*, *8*(7), 5926–5937. Advance online publication. doi:10.1109/JIOT.2020.3032544

Zhang, X., Yang, C., Nepal, S., Liu, C., Dou, W., & Chen, J. (2013). A MapReduce based approach of scalable multidimensional Anonymization for big data privacy preservation on cloud. *2013 International Conference on Cloud and Green Computing*. 10.1109/CGC.2013.24

Zhang, X., Yang, L. T., Liu, C., & Chen, J. (2014). A scalable two-phase top-down specialization approach for data Anonymization using MapReduce on cloud. *IEEE Transactions on Parallel and Distributed Systems*, *25*(2), 363–373. doi:10.1109/TPDS.2013.48

Zhang, Y., Sun, W., Wang, L., Wang, H., Green, R. II, & Alam, M. (2011). A multi-level communication architecture of smart grid based on congestion aware wireless mesh network. *43rd North American Power Symposium (NAPS).*

Zhao & Kumar. (2018). *Improving Periocular Recognition by Explicit Attention to Critical Regions in Deep Neural Network.* Academic Press.

Zhao, Z., & Kumar, A. (2017). Accurate Periocular Recognition under Less Constrained Environment Using Semantics-Assisted Convolutional Neural Network. *IEEE Transactions on Information Forensics and Security*, *12*, 1017–1030.

Zheng, T., & Litvinov, E. (2006). Ex post pricing in the co-optimized energy and reserve market. *IEEE Transactions on Power Systems*, *21*(4), 1528–1538. doi:10.1109/TPWRS.2006.882457

Zhu, Zhang, & Jin. (n.d.). From federated learning to federated neural architecture search: a survey. *Complex & Intelligent Systems.* . doi:10.1007/s40747-020-00247-z

Zhu, Q., Cao, S., Chen, F., Chen, M. C., Chen, X., Chung, T. H., ... Pan, J. W. (2022). Quantum computational advantage via 60-qubit 24-cycle random circuit sampling. *Science Bulletin*, *67*(3), 240–245.

ZigBee Alliance. (2008). *ZigBee Specifications 053474r17.* Retrieved from https://www.zigbee.org/

Ziobro, P. (2021). FedEx earnings reflect labor shortage, supply-chain woes. *Wall Street Journal.* Retrieved October 19,2021, from wsj.com/articles/fedex-lowers-forecast-as-labor-shortage-supply-chain-woes-sap-results-11632256848

About the Contributors

Amit Kumar Tyagi is Assistant Professor (Senior Grade), and Senior Researcher at Vellore Institute of Technology (VIT), Chennai Campus, Chennai, Tamilandu, India. He received his Ph.D. Degree (Full-Time) in 2018 from Pondicherry Central University, India. He joined the Lord Krishna College of Engineering, Ghaziabad (LKCE) for the periods of 2009-2010, and 2012-2013. He was an Assistant Professor and Head- Research, Lingaya's Vidyapeeth (formerly known as Lingaya's University), Faridabad, Haryana, India in 2018-2019. His supervision experience includes more than 10 Masters' dissertations and one PhD thesis. He has contributed to several projects such as "AARIN" and "P3- Block" to address some of the open issues related to the privacy breaches in Vehicular Applications (such as Parking) and Medical Cyber Physical Systems (MCPS). He has published over 50 papers in refereed high impact journals, conferences and books, and some of his articles awarded best paper awards. Also, he has filed more than 20 patents (Nationally and Internationally) in the area of Deep Learning, Internet of Things, Cyber Physical Systems and Computer Vision. He has edited more than 15 books for IET, Elsevier, Springer, CRC Press, etc. Also, he has authored 3 Books on Internet of Things, Intelligent Transportation Systems, Vehicular Ad-hoc Network with BPB Publication, Springer and IET publisher. He is a Winner of Faculty Research Award for the Year of 2019, and 2020 (consecutive years) given by Vellore Institute of Technology, Chennai, India. Recently, he has been awarded best paper award for paper titled "A Novel Feature Extractor Based on the Modified Approach of Histogram of oriented Gradient", ICCSA 2020, Italy (Europe). His current research focuses on Next Generation Machine Based Communications, Blockchain Technology, Smart and Secure Computing and Privacy. He is a regular member of the ACM, IEEE, MIRLabs, Ramanujan Mathematical Society, Cryptology Research Society, and Universal Scientific Education and Research Network, CSI and ISTE.

* * *

Moses Kazeem Abiodun is a Computer Science Lecturer at Landmark University, Omu-Aran, Kwara State, Nigeria. He is an astute researcher and educator. His areas of specialization are in cloud computing, security, and machine learning. He is the author of several journal and book chapters in reputable journal outlets. He is also a reviewer for journals like Elsevier, Journal of Big Data, Multimedia and Tools Applications, and others.

Nehemiah Adebayo is a methodical data analyst and IT professional, broad software skills, and focus on continuous improvement. Experienced in Data Analysis, Web development, and various security. Setting up a worldwide strategic long-term aim of working in research roles that make use of BIG DATA to make a difference while also assuring the entire satisfaction of all stakeholders. Interests lay in the areas of business, social development, and scientific challenges that may sustainably assure our life and a safe world for generations to come.

Micheal Olaolu Arowolo is a Research Scholar at the Department of Electrical Engineering and Computer Science, University of Missouri, Columbia. He obtained his Ph.D. Degree in 2021, as a Faculty at Landmark University, Omu-Aran, Nigeria. His research interest encompasses Bioinformatics, Machine Learning, and Artificial Intelligence. He has published in several reputable journals, book chapters and conferences. He is a member of IEEE, European Alliance for Innovation, International Society for Computational Biology, and a Certified Oracle Expert.

Leila Azouz Saidane is a Professor at the National School of Computer Science (ENSI), at The University of Manouba, in Tunisia and the Chairperson of the PhD Commission at ENSI. She was the Director of this school and the supervisor of the Master's degree program in Networks and Multimedia Systems. She is the codirector of RAMSIS pole of CRISTAL Research Laboratory (Center of Research in Network and System Architecture, Multimedia, and Image Processing) at ENSI. She collaborated on several international projects. She is author and coauthor of several papers in refereed journals, magazines, and international conferences.

Shirisha Bansal is currently a third-year student at Manipal University Jaipur pursuing her major in computer Science Engineering. She is working in the field of Cyber Security. She currently lives in Jaipur, Rajasthan, India with her family and is highly interested in puzzles, art, and writing.

Ajeet Bhartee is working as an Assistant Professor in the department of CSE, Galgotia's College of Engineering and Technology, Greater Noida, India. He is pursuing Ph.D. degree from NIT. He has completed M-Tech and BE from reputed intuitions. He has published various papers in peer reviewed international/national journals and conferences.

N. P. G. Bhavani is currently working in the Dept of ECE at Saveetha Institute of Medical and Technical Sciences, Saveetha School of Engineering, Chennai. she has published research articles in various journals and conferences.

Karan Bhowmick is currently pursuing a Bachelor's degree in Information Technology at VIT, Vellore. His research interests lie in the field of Data Science with a special emphasis on predictive analytics as well as the application of machine learning for real-world issues.

Rihab Boussada has obtained a PhD degree in computer science from the National School of Computer Science (ENSI), at the University of Manouba, in Tunisia, in April 2019. She received her bachelor's degree in network administration and Services from the High Computer Science Institute of El Manar (ISI), Tunisia in 2012. She received her computer science engineering degree in Information Technology also from High Computer Science Institute of El Manar (ISI), Tunisia in 2015. In September 2015, she joined the High Computer Science Institute of El Manar (ISI) to teach several courses in the field of networking. In October 2017, she held the position of assistant in the Higher Institute of Information and Communication Technologies (ISTIC). Since 2019, she has been an Assistant Professor at Sesame

University. Her research interests include Internet of Things (IoT), security, privacy preserving, Internet of the future, blockchain technology.

Divya Budhia Gupta is pursuing Ph.D. (Lovely Professional University), UGC-NET qualified, has done M.A. Economics (D.A.V. College, Jalandhar), and B.Sc. Economics (PCM S.D. College for Women, Jalandhar). She is working as Assistant Professor and Head, Department of Economics, PCM S.D. College for Women, Jalandhar, Punjab (India). Her area of research is Education. She has experience of 13 years. She has presented papers in various international and national conferences/seminars. She has also got various research papers published in refereed national and international journals and has contributed chapters in edited books. She has authored one book on Business Statistics. She has also guided many post graduate students for their research projects and is actively involved in various activities at the institutional level.

Su-Qun Cao is currently working in the Faculty of Electronic Information Engineering, Huaiyin Institute of Technology, China. He has published research articles in various journals and conferences.

Sheela Chandrashekar is currently working as Asst. Professor at Jain University Dept of BCA with progressive teaching experience of 15 years in Computer Science. She holds a mater's degree in computer science from Kuvempu state University She is awarded with M.Phil degree from PRIST University, Tanjavur. Currently she is pursuing Doctoral degree from Jain University with research area in face recognition She has research output in one SCI journal and one conference and also she has co-authored few computer science books.

Aswani Kumar Cherukuri is a Professor of the School of Information Technology and Engineering at Vellore Institute of Technology, India. He has close to 20 years of academic and research experience. His research interests cover the fields of Machine Learning and Information Security. He published more than 150 research papers in various journals & conferences. He executed major research projects funded by Govt. of India. He is a senior member of ACM and life member of CSI, ISTE.

Kirubakaran D. is currently working in the Dept of EEE at St. Joseph's Institute of TEchnology. He has published research articles in various journals and conferences.

Mohamed Elhoucine Elhdhili earned his engineering and master's degrees in computer science at the National School of Computer Science, University of Manouba, Tunisia. Then, he received his PhD degree from the same school. Since 2018, he holds the position of assistant professor at the National School of Computer Science. Previously, he worked as an assistant professor at the Higher Institute of Informatics, Ariana, Tunisia. His research focuses on issues related to computer networks: Security, Trust, Privacy, Key Management, Blockchain, and quality of service (QoS).

Udochukwu Iheanacho Erondu is currently on his Master's degree program at the Department of Computer Science, Landmark University. His area of specialization includes Security, Machine Learning, Big Data Analytics, Data Science, and Artificial Intelligence.

Somya Goyal has done her Bachelor of Engineering (Gold Medalist) and Masters from Maharishi Dayanand University, Rohtak. Her Research interest includes Machine Learning, Software Engineering, IoT, Data Analytics.

Ayush Gupta is currently a third-year student at Manipal University Jaipur pursuing his major in computer and commination Engineering. He is a tech geek and worked in the field of technical project management. He currently lives in Jaipur, Rajasthan, India with his family and is highly interested in soccer, skateboarding and music.

Balkis Hamdane has obtained a PhD degree in ICT from the Higher School of Communication of Tunis (Sup'Com) in November 2016. She obtained an engineer and a master diploma in Telecommunications from Sup'Com in 2009, and 2010 respectively. Dr. Hamdane joined the Higher Institute of Computer Science of El Manar (ISI) then the National Engineering School of Tunis (ENIT) to teach several courses in the field of networking and security. Since 2018, she has been an Assistant Professor at Higher Institute of Technological Studies in Communications of Tunis (Iset'Com). Dr Hamdane's actual research interests include network security, information centric networking, trust management, etc. She has published several papers in international conferences.

Carol Hargreaves is Director of the Data Analytics Consulting Centre at the National University of Singapore (NUS) and holds a joint position as an Associate Professor in the Department of Statistics & Data Science and the Department of Mathematics. Her research area includes Artificial Intelligence & Machine Learning Applications in the Maritime, Healthcare, and the Financial Industry. She has published book chapters and numerous research articles in international journals. Associate Professor Carol Hargreaves has extensive experience in leading teams of analysts to solve multidisciplinary real-world data science problems. She developed and took charge of multiple innovative projects in the Pharmaceutical, Healthcare, Maritime, Telecommunications, and Fast-Moving Consumer Goods (FMCG) Industry.

Aman Jantan is an Associate Professor and Senior Lecturer at the School of Computer Science, Universiti Sains Malaysia, Malaysia. He specialises in Digital Forensics, Malware, IDS, Computer & network security, E-Commerce, Web Intelligence and Compiler Design & Development Techniques. Dr. Aman has won several grants and awards in difference hemispheres within his field and beyond. However, he has over 70 publications in highly indexed journals with hundreds of citations.

Firuz Kamalov received the B.A. degree in mathematics from Macalester College, USA, in 2004, and the Ph.D. degree in mathematics from the University of Nebraska-Lincoln, USA, in 2011. He is currently an Associate Professor at Canadian University Dubai, United Arab Emirates. He is the lead author of several high impact journal articles in fields of feature selection, imbalanced data, time series forecasting, and cross product C*-algebras. His research interests include machine learning and functional analysis. During his studies, he was a recipient of the DeWitt Wallace Scholarship as well as the Othmer Fellowship. He was also a recipient of multiple research grants, including CRPG 2019 (USD 2.04mil). He currently serves as a Chief Editor of GJOM.

R. K. Kamat is Dean of Computer Science and Technology, Shivaji University, Kolhapur, India. He received his both B.Sc. and M.Sc. in Electronics with distinction in 1991 and 1993 respectively. Further he completed Mphil and PhD in electronics at Goa university. Presently, he is working with Department of Electronics and Department of Computer Science in Shivaji University, Kolhapur. He has published more than 150+ research papers in reputed international journals including IEEE and authored 12 books with Springer, CRC Press and IGI global USA.

Inderpreet Kaur is BTech, MTech in CSE. She has completed her PhD From Mewar University. Currentely working as a Professor in the department of CSE, Galgotia's College of Engineering and Technology, Greater Noida, India. She has more than 17 Years of Teaching and Research Experience. Her areas of interest and research includes Computer Networks Security, Blockchain Technology, Cyber security. She has published various papers in peer reviewed international/national journals and conferences. She has also published number of book chapters in reputed publications like Springer.

Tushinder Preet Kaur is currently Professor at Mittal School of Business (ACBSP USA, Accredited), Lovely Professional University, Phagwara, Punjab (India). In academic career spanning over 15 years, she has served at Khalsa College of Women, Amritsar and departmental research scholar at Punjab School of Economics, GNDU, Amritsar. She has presented papers in various national and international conferences. She has to her credit various research papers published in refereed, national and international journals of repute. She has authored many chapters in referred books and has also authored one book. She has chaired the session and acted as a Resource person for various national seminars/conferences. She has also conducted one day Faculty Development Programme entitled, "How to teach Managerial Economics" to various faculty members in LPU. She has taken one day session entitled Gender Inequality: A Serious Threat to our country. Currently, she is assisting Mittal School of Business as a Coordinator of Research. She is also a member of Doctoral Board for Economics and evaluated many research scholars at various platforms. She has guided and supervised one Doctorate Research Scholar. Apart from Teaching, she has counselled many students for better carrier opportunities. She has also developed Curriculum as well as Pedagogy for the effective teaching. She has guided two M. Phil. scholars and 8 Post Graduation students for research and also coordinated with the other faculties for various research activities. She has been a Steering Committee member and organized Conferences, Workshops and Business Summit in LPU. Last but not the least, she has been a part of Panel for the various entry level exams of the University.

Sujatha Kesavan is presently working as Professor in EEE, Department at Dr. M.G.R Educational and Research Institute, Chennai, Tamil Nadu, India. She has 20 years of teaching experience in various Engineering colleges. She completed her BE in the year 1999 from Bharathiyar University, ME in 2004 and Ph. D in 2011 from Anna University. She has presented/published papers in National/International conferences/journals and also published many books with Elsevier and Springer publisher. She is also a reviewer for journals published by Springer and Elsevier publishers. Presently doing her research in the area of Image Processing for Process Control. She is awarded the Best Researcher award for the academic year 2011–2012 and 2014 by IET. Also obtained travel grant from DST in 2014 for attending the conference. She is also awarded the young researcher award at the international conference at China in year 2015. She has also published 4 patents including one international patent with the Chinese University at Huaiyin Institute of Technology, China and also initiated international cooperation research between Huaiyin Institute of Technology, China and Dr.MGR Educational and Research Institute.

Ishita Kumar is currently pursuing her undergrad degree at Vellore Institute of Technology, India. Her research interests are in visualization, data science, and machine learning. Her current research is associated with the optimization of the Round Robin CPU scheduling algorithm.

Saraf Pavan Kumar is an Associate Professor in the School of Management at National Institute of Technology Karnataka (NITK), Surathkal. He has received Doctorate in Management from the Indian Institute of Technology Kharagpur (IIT Kharagpur) in the year 2011. He has more than 20 plus years of academic and industry experience. He is also on the advisory board of a few start-up companies and educational institutions. His research interest includes human resource analytics, organizational development ,business application of information systems and contemporary issues in management.

Sree Krishna M. was born in India on 12th December 1989. Currently working as Assistant Professor and also pursuing her PhD degree at Sathyabama Institute of Science and Technology, Chennai, India. She has 8 years of experience in the field of teaching, published nearly 10 papers in International Journals.

Renu Mishra is working as an Associate Professor in the Department of CSE, Galgotia's College of Engineering and Technology, Greater Noida, India. She has received her Ph.D. degree from Rajiv Gandhi Proudyogiki Vishwavidyalaya (RGPV), Bhopal, INDIA. She has completed M-Tech degree in Information Technology from the RGPV, Bhopal. She has received B.Tech degree in Information Technology from U.P.T.U. Lucknow. She has more than 14 Years of Teaching and Research Experience. Her areas of interest and research includes Computer Networks Security, Blockchain Technology, Cyber security. She has published various papers in peer reviewed international/national journals and conferences. She has also published number of book chapters in reputed publications like Springer. She has delivered many invited/key notes talks at International & National Conferences/ Workshops/Seminars in India & abroad. She is an active member of advisory/technical program committee of reputed International/ National conferences & reviewer of number of reputed Journals.

Melody Moh obtained her MS and Ph.D., both in computer science, from Univ. of California - Davis. She joined San Jose State University in 1993, and has been a Professor since Aug 2003, and has been the Chair of the Department of Computer Science since 2019. Her research interests include cloud computing, mobile, wireless networking, security/privacy, and machine-learning applications. She has received over 1,500K dollars of research and education grants from both NSF and industry, has published over 170 refereed papers in international journals, conferences and as book chapters, and has consulted for various companies.

Melesio Muñoz holds a master's degree in computer science from San José State University, as well as two bachelor's degrees from the University of California at Santa Cruz, in computer and information sciences and in history. He has worked as a research assistant for the SETI Institute as well as the California and Carnegie Extrasolar Planet Search and is a co-discover of the extrasolar planet HD88133b. Melesio is currently in the second decade of his career in the electrical construction industry, and occasionally teaches courses at local San Francisco Bay Area colleges.

Ambika N. is a MCA, MPhil, Ph.D. in computer science. She completed her Ph.D. from Bharathiar university in the year 2015. She has 16 years of teaching experience and presently working for St. Francis

College, Bangalore. She has guided BCA, MCA and M.Tech students in their projects. Her expertise includes wireless sensor network, Internet of things, cybersecurity. She gives guest lectures in her expertise. She is a reviewer of books, conferences (national/international), encyclopaedia and journals. She is advisory committee member of some conferences. She has many publications in National & international conferences, international books, national and international journals and encyclopaedias. She has some patent publications (National) in computer science division.

Janaki N. is currently working in the Dept of EEE at VISTAS. She has published research articles in various journals and conferences.

Suchithra Nair is currently working as Associate Professor and Head of MS (IT) Department, Jain, Deemed to be University She holds degree from Manonmaniam Sundaaranar University, Tirunevali. She has completed MCA degree from Manonmaniam Sundaaranar University, Tirunevali. She is into Progressive teaching and Research experience of 16 years in Computer Science & Information Technology Department She has Research output in Journals and Conferences Excellent Academic administration experience.

Devang Pathak is in senior year of his undergraduate degree from Vellore Institute of Technology, India. He has been immensely interested in new technology and has projects in web development and machine learning. His primary research interest is in machine learning. His current research is concerned with machine learning algorithms to detect brain tumor.

Maheswari R. is working as Associate Professor, School of Computer Science and Engineering, VIT Chennai. She obtained her B.E (CSE) from the Government College of Engineering and M.E (Embedded System & Technologies) from the College of Engineering, Anna University, PhD (CSE) from VIT. She has published SIX patents in her research domain and has received many awards like Outstanding FOSSEE Contributor Award from IIT Bombay & MHRD, Govt. of India, Best Faculty Award, Best achiever award, Best researcher award, Best Alumni Chapter Award, Best paper and Excellent paper awards, Best Club Coordinator award. She has published more than 50 research works in various Books, Book Chapters and International Journals in her domain of expertise like IoT, Data Analytics, and High-Performance System.

Parvathi R. is a Professor of School of Computing Science and Engineering at VIT University, Chennai since 2011. She received the Doctoral degree in the field of spatial data mining in the same year. Her teaching experience in the area of computer science includes more than two decades and her research interests include data mining, big data, and computational biology.

Dhriti Rajani is a student at VIT Chennai pursuing Integrated M.Tech(CSE with specialization in Software Engineering). She is also working on EPICS in IEEE project which is a project funded by IEEE.

Gopika S. is working as an Assistant Professor, Computer Science and Engineering, Sathyabama Institute of Science & Technology, Chennai. Research Interest in the field of Medical Imaging, Data Analytics, Machine Learning, Deep Learning etc., Published nearly 10+ articles and 2 patents in the field of my research area.

Rajasree S. is working as Assistant Professor in New Horizon College of Engineering. Her area of research includes Machine Learning and Data Science. She has published papers in various journals and conferences. She has around 10 years in the field of teaching.

Poonam Sahoo is a Doctoral Research Scholar in the School of Management at National Institute of Technology Karnataka, Surathkal (NITK), Surathkal, India.Her research interests include organizational behavior, business analytics, Information systems, and human resource management. She has presented papers in international doctoral management conferences.

Vishnu Sharma is working as Prof and head in CSE, GCET. Dr Sharma has Doctor of Philosophy - PhD in CSE from Madhav Institute of Technology and Science, Gwalior in the field of Mobile Ad-hoc Networks. areas of interest and research includes Computer Networks, Blockchain Technology, AI, ML, Cyber security. He has published various papers in peer reviewed international/national journals and conferences. He has also published number of book chapters in reputed publications like Springer. He has delivered many invited/key notes talks at International & National Conferences/ Workshops/Seminars in India & abroad. He is an active member of advisory/technical program committee of reputed International/National conferences & reviewer of number of reputed Journals.

Alan D. Smith is presently University Professor of Marketing in the Department of Marketing at Robert Morris University, Pittsburgh, PA. Previously he was Chair of the Department of Quantitative and Natural Sciences and Coordinator of Engineering Programs at the same institution, as well as Associate Professor of Business Administration and Director of Coal Mining Administration at Eastern Kentucky University. He holds concurrent PhDs in Engineering Systems/Education from The University of Akron and Business Administration (OM and MIS), respectively, and a MS in Business Analytics (2019) from Kent State University, as well as author of numerous articles and book chapters.

Hepi Suthar is currently working as a PhD Research Scholar in the School of Information Technology, AI & Cyber Security Department at Rashtriya Raksha University, Gujarat. She received her Diploma & B.E. degree in Computer Science and Engineering from Government Engineering College, Gujarat and M. Tech. in Cyber Security & Incident Response from Gujarat Forensic Science University, Gujarat. She worked in GTU affiliated college, for nearly five years, worked at different dynamic Universities like Marwadi University Rajkot, Gujarat, Vishwakarma University, Pune. Her current research interests are cyber security, digital forensic, malware analysis & reverse engineering, dark & deep web also in threat management and data privacy compliances. She published paper on comparative analysis on study on SSD, HDD & SSHD (2019), one book Chapter on an approach of data recovery from SSD: Cyber Forensic. She published book on Computer Forensic (2022).

Kavitha T. is currently working in the Dept of Civil at Dr.MGR Educational and Research Institute. she has published research articles in various journals and conferences.

Carlos Andrés Tavera Romero, Post-Doctorate, is currently working as Professor at Santiago de Cali University. Published various articles in reputed journals with indexing like SCOPUS, SCI and Web of Science. Research Area is Image processing, Networks, Data Mining, etc.

Chee Ling Thong is an Assistant Professor at Institute of Computer Science and Digital Innovation, UCSI University. Her research interests include Digital Innovation and Information Management. She has received three research grants from UCSI University Malaysia as Principal Investigator for projects entitled 'Android-based Time Tracker for Shuttle Bus ', 'iOS Time and Location Tracker for Shuttle Bus' and 'Mobile Car App for Travel Agency'. The first two projects were completed and fully implemented at UCSI University. The last project was completed and its implementation in the travel agency is at the initial stage. The first and last projects were fully copyrighted by Intellectual Property Corporation of Malaysia (MyIPO). As part of the outcome of these research projects, two mobile applications were successfully commercialised. Also, Chee Ling was the award winner for "Best Product Innovation and Commercialization Awards 2021". The award was conferred by UCSI University, Malaysia. Being an active researcher, she involved in journal publications and international research conferences annually.

Rashmi Uchil is an Assistant Professor at School of Management, National Institute of Technology Karnataka (NITK). She has nearly 3.6 years of service in the corporate sector as well more than 18 years of experience in academics. She is presently working as an Assistant professor at National Institute of Technology Karnataka (NITK). Her areas of interest are acquisitions, international finance, organizational behavior, and cross border acquisitions.

Pattabiraman Venkatasubbu, Professor, School of Computer Science and Engineering, Vellore Institute of Technology (VIT) – Chennai Campus, Chennai – 600127, Tamil Nadu, India has 20 years of professional experience, out of which he spent as much as 18 years in teaching and research and the remaining 2 years in industry. He has published more than 50 papers in various national and international peer-reviewed journals in the last five years. He has also presented several papers in international conferences. His research expertise covers a wide range of subject areas, including Knowledge Discovery and Data Mining, Big Data Analytics, Machine Learning, Deep Learning, Database technologies, etc.

Mohd Najwadi Yusoff has served for several years in industrial with leading players in Cyber Security and ECommerce. He also has long history of working in different areas of computer security as a Security Researcher, Malware Analyzer, Penetration Tester, Security Consultant, Professional Trainer as well as University Lecturer. Dr. Mohd Najwadi is imminently qualified in the field of cyber security; he holds PhD in Security in Computing and several professional qualifications namely Professional Technologist (MBOT), CISSP, CISM, CEH, CHFI, CCFP, HCNA and he is a Huawei Certified Academy Instructor (HCAI). As a cyber security expert, Dr. Mohd Najwadi has worked in variety of project as Forensic Investigator, Malware Analyzer, Penetration Tester and Expert Witness. He has strong collaboration with Fintech companies, telecommunication companies and governmental bodies.

Index

A

B

C

D

E

F

G

H

I

J

K

L

M

N

O

P

Q

R

S

T

U

V

W

Z

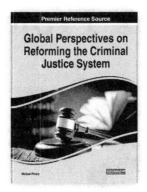

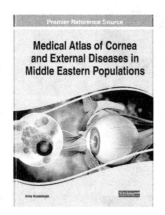

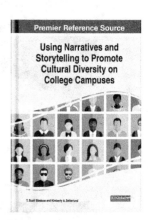

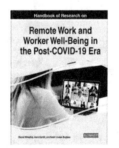

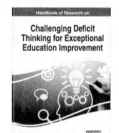

Printed in the United States
by Baker & Taylor Publisher Services